THE
Great Operas
OF MOZART

COMPLETE LIBRETTOS IN THE ORIGINAL LANGUAGE

ENGLISH VERSIONS

by W. H. Auden and Chester Kallman

Ruth and Thomas Martin

John Bloch

Essays on W. A. Mozart and each opera

by Nathan Broder

The Norton Library

W · W · NORTON & COMPANY · INC ·

NEW YORK

W. W. Norton & Company, Inc. is the publisher of current
or forthcoming books on music by William Austin, Milton Babbitt,
John Backus, Anthony Baines, Sol Berkowitz, Friedrich Blume, How-
ard Boatwright, Nadia Boulanger, Paul Brainard, Nathan Broder,
Manfred Bukofzer, John Castellini, John Clough, Edward T. Cone,
Doda Conrad, Aaron Copland, Hans David, Paul Des Marais, Otto
Erich Deutsch, Frederick Dorian, Alfred Einstein, Gabriel Fontrier,
Walter Gerboth, Harold Gleason, Richard Franko Goldman, Noah
Greenberg, Donald Jay Grout, James Haar, F. Ll. Harrison, Daniel
Heartz, Richard Hoppin, A. J. B. Hutchings, Charles Ives, Roger
Kamien, Hermann Keller, Leo Kraft, Stanley Krebs, Paul Henry
Lang, Jan LaRue, Maurice Lieberman, Irving Lowens, Joseph
Machlis, Carol McClintock, Alfred Mann, W. T. Marrocco, Arthur
Mendel, William J. Mitchell, Douglas Moore, Joel Newman, John
F. Ohl, Carl Parrish, Vincent Persichetti, Marc Pincherle, Walter
Piston, Gustave Reese, Alexander Ringer, Curt Sachs, Arnold Schoen-
berg, Denis Stevens, Robert Stevenson, Oliver Strunk, J. A. Westrup,
Emanuel Winternitz, Walter Wiora, and Percy M. Young.

CONTENTS

MOZART AND THE OPERA

Opera, born about 1600, is one of the youngest of the major art-forms, younger even than the novel. Yet today, while some of the earliest novels — *Don Quixote,* for example — are still very much alive and read with pleasure, there is no opera in the standard repertory that dates from the first half of the lifetime of the lyric stage. Occasionally a work by one of the masters of that early period — Monteverdi, Handel, Rameau — is revived, but as far as the general music-loving public is concerned, opera begins with Gluck and Mozart.

Why Gluck and Mozart? A proper answer to the question would require a detailed study of the swift development and the drastic changes that opera has undergone in the three and a half centuries of its existence. But perhaps enough of a summary can be given here to serve our purpose. The cultural and social and economic conditions that governed the production of opera determined its subjects, its forms, and its musical content. Throughout its first century and a half, serious opera was subsidized or supported chiefly by the courts or the nobility, and the tastes of the upper classes and of the times dictated a choice of subjects from mythology and ancient and medieval history and legend. The rise of the virtuoso singer resulted in emphasis on the aria, often to the detriment, or even the exclusion, of dramatic considerations. The chorus, an important element of the earliest operas, was dropped where funds were not available — most of the 17th-century Venetian operas, which were not subsidized, did without it.

The protagonists of these works were gods and demigods, rulers and generals, and heroes of legendary romance. In the more affluent theaters and in operas written for special state occasions, spectacle was emphasized, enhanced by elaborate stage machinery. With rare exceptions, librettists and composers aimed to present the reactions of the characters to the machinations of fate, to events that often took place offstage or were assumed to be known by the audience. The composers' main dramatic concern was the representation of moods and passions, for which the sometimes complicated plots served as framework. And these moods and passions were expressed in terms of music that gave the principal singers opportunity to display their virtuosity.

Alongside the serious opera in its main national manifestations—the Italian *opera seria,* the French *tragédie lyrique* — there grew up the comic opera. From humble beginnings in partly improvised farce it developed quickly, branched out into different national types, absorbing along the way some forms and procedures from serious opera. Here there was no dealing with gods and goddesses, with the high and mighty, except for purposes of parody or satire. The characters were from the middle and lower classes, the plots and settings from everyday contemporary life. To the arias and duets of serious opera were gradually added numbers for three, four, and more singers. Instead of the static scenes of the *opera seria*, comic opera developed fluidity by joining solo and ensemble numbers into extended finales. By the end of the 18th century this type of work, again in various manifestations — the Italian *opera buffa* or *dramma giocoso*, the French *opéra comique*, the German *Singspiel* — had driven the serious opera off the European stage.

Except for Gluck. That master's *Orpheus and Eurydice* — to name only the most frequently performed of his great works — has traits of the old *opera seria* and *tragédie lyrique*. With the former it shares a succession of rather static scenes; with the latter, a number of stately dances; and with both, a favorite mythological subject. But unlike many of its predecessors, it is more than a mere succession of arias and duets strung together on a thread of recitative. The arias are all germane to the plot and not simply opportunities for the exercise of vocal acrobatics. There are fine choruses, a rich orchestra, and above all the kind of noble serenity and harmony of proportion that is always associated in our minds with the idea of classicism. Perhaps it is these qualities that account for Gluck's survival in the operatic repertory.

With Mozart the situation is different. He was one of many gifted composers practicing the lively and popular art of comic opera in the last quarter of the 18th century. Many of these composers were far more celebrated and successful than he. But, except for an occasional revival, none of their works has survived, while all five of the operas in this book have been frequently performed ever since they were written. The most obvious reason for this is the sheer abundance of great music in Mozart's operas. There is fine music in many of the operas of his contemporaries, but none of these works is so richly stocked as *Figaro, Don Giovanni,* or *The Magic Flute.* And this outpouring of the highest type of musical invention is accompanied by an element that is rare in opera before Mozart. It is the element of characterization, of the musical delineation of individuals. Susanna is much more than a soubrette, Leporello much more than the comic servant, and there were no precedents in opera for such musical portraits as those of the Countess and Don Giovanni. And this differentiation of personality is often maintained even in ensemble numbers, an uncommon achievement in pre-19th-century opera.

During the 19th century the fortunes of Mozart's operas vacillated in various countries at various times. For a time his last opera, *La Clemenza di Tito,* now neglected—it is an old-fashioned *opera seria,* though with some fine numbers in it — was more frequently performed in England and other places than his other stage works. The Italian public never did accept Mozart's operas wholeheartedly; to early-19th-century Italian audiences his works were too complicated harmonically and placed too much emphasis on the orchestra. In Central Europe, on the other hand, there was never any wavering. Indeed, the success of *The Magic Flute* placed a firm foundation under the hitherto rickety structure of German opera, and there is a direct line from that work through Beethoven's *Fidelio* to Weber's *Der Freischütz.* The *opera buffa* style and pattern fell out of fashion in the course of the century. Important new forms and ideas came into existence. Yet despite the onslaughts of the Romantic opera, grand opera, the Wagnerian music drama, and *verismo,* Mozart remained a pillar of the repertory, as he still is today, even in Italy.

Mozart wrote his first opera in 1768, when he was twelve years old, and finished his last one three months before his death in 1791. In the twenty-three years between he completed sixteen additional works for the stage and began several others. There were consequently few periods in his brief and crowded life when he was not either writing an opera or dreaming of writing one. The theater, then as now, was a principal road to fame and fortune for a composer. But this was by no means the only reason for Mozart's absorbing interest in the lyric stage. Throughout his career musical drama exerted an extraordinary fascination upon him. Whenever he found a suitable libretto his vivid imagination caught fire; and the craftsman in him rose eagerly to the challenge of shaping the music to the capacities of the singers who were to perform the work. He even wrote a considerable amount of music to be interpolated in other composers' operas: singers who were dissatisfied with the music allotted to them there, came to him for new arias to replace the ones they did not like — a customary procedure in those days.

Mozart's earliest composition for the stage, aside from some arias, was *Apollo et Hyacinthus,* a Latin comedy performed by students at the university in Salzburg in 1767. His next was a full-length Italian comic opera, *La finta semplice,* written at Vienna in 1768. It was the Emperor himself who had suggested that the little prodigy compose an opera and conduct it himself, but despite this encouragement from on high and despite herculean efforts, Wolfgang's father, Leopold, was unable to defeat court intrigue, and the work was not produced in Vienna but in Salzburg a year later. It is smoothly and professionally written, and there are a few numbers in it that give faint hints of the future master. Shortly after *La finta semplice* was completed Mozart composed *Bastien und Bastienne,* a German opera, for performance in the little private theater of his father's friend Dr. Anton Mesmer, who later became widely known as a hypnotist (he is parodied by Despina in a famous scene of *Così fan tutte*) . This one-act piece for only three characters, with a simple plot and simple music, has a childlike charm that has kept it alive in the repertory of opera workshops and school groups.

The next work, *Mitridate, rè di Ponto,* a full-length *opera seria,* was commissioned for Milan while the Mozarts were on a tour in Italy. It was performed in that city with considerable success in 1770. This was followed in 1771, again in Milan, by a "theatrical serenade," *Ascanio in Alba,* commissioned by the Empress Maria Theresa for the festivities celebrating the wedding of Archduke Ferdinand with an Italian princess, Maria Ricciarda Beatrice of Modena. Upon Mozart's return to Salzburg from this trip he wrote another "serenade," *Il Sogno di Scipione,* as part of the celebrations attending the installation of a new archbishop, Hieronymus von Colloredo, who was to prove a difficult employer. The two "serenades" are short works of a type common in the 18th century — allegorical pieces paying homage to the personages for whom they were written. They are ceremonial in character, feature pomp and spectacle — there is a good deal of ballet in *Ascanio* — and contain a minimum of drama. The last opera Mozart wrote for Italy was a "drama for music," *Lucio Silla,* produced at Milan in 1772. It had a run of more than twenty performances. In *Mitridate* the fourteen-year-old composer faithfully followed the outer patterns of Italian models; he was still too young to exploit the possibilities of drama offered by the libretto. In *Lucio Silla,* however, there are signs of deeper understanding and growing power.

In 1775, when Mozart was eighteen, he wrote an *opera buffa, La finta giardiniera,* for performance in Munich. This work, a curious mixture of the comic and the serious, shows its composer already a master of every operatic type of musical gesture. Though the material itself is not yet as consistently engrossing as it was to become in his later works, some of the arias are as fine as any that were being written at the time. From the same year dates another opera of the "serenade" type, *Il Rè pastore,* composed for the festivities greeting a visit to Salzburg by Archduke Maximilian. An aria from this work, *L'Amerò, sarò costante,* with obbligato violin, is still favored by sopranos. Salzburg offered little incentive to compose operas, and Mozart's unhappiness with his native city in general and its autocratic ruler in particular led him to take a long leave to hunt for a better post elsewhere. During a stay in Mannheim and later in Paris he yearned to write an opera, to show what he could do. But the opportunity never arose. The disconsolate composer returned to Salzburg in January 1779, after an absence of sixteen months, having failed in his quest for a position. His next work for the stage was incidental music for a play, *König Thamos* (1779), consisting of some noble choruses and vivid orchestral entr'actes. In the same year he wrote a good part of a *Singspiel* on a Turkish subject, which was published after his death under the title *Zaïde.* He never completed it.

The first definite opera commission in five years came towards the end of 1780, from Munich. For performance during the carnival season there Mozart wrote *Idomeneo,* an *opera seria* on a subject selected by the Munich authorities. It seems certain that Mozart would not have chosen an *opera seria* if the choice had been his. The form was moribund by this time; to an eager young composer its stately procession of scenes and arias must have seemed stale and lifeless. But Mozart was in no position — and no mood — to complain. He poured into the old patterns a wealth of fine music. *Idomeneo* has never gained a firm foothold in the repertory, despite many attempts to revive it. The operagoer is thus deprived of some remarkable music, notably several powerful and moving choruses, at least two arias of exquisite beauty, a great quartet, and extraordinarily trenchant and expressive accompanied recitatives.

A year after the successful première of *The Abduction from the Seraglio* at Vienna in 1782, Mozart sketched two Italian *opere buffe, L'Oca del Cairo* and *Lo Sposo deluso,* but they remained fragments. For an imperial party at the palace in Schönbrunn he wrote the music for a little entertainment called *The Impresario,* consisting of an overture, two arias, and two concerted numbers. This was in February 1786. Shortly afterwards came *The Marriage of Figaro,* to be succeeded by *Don Giovanni* in 1787, *Così fan tutte* in 1790, and *The Magic Flute* in 1791. A few weeks before the completion of *The Magic Flute* the composer, already suffering from what was to be a fatal illness, was ordered to prepare an *opera seria* for the coronation of Emperor Leopold II as king of Bohemia in Prague. He set to work feverishly, and, entrusting the recitatives to an assistant, finished and rehearsed *La Clemenza di Tito* in eighteen days. Such a work, written under such conditions, could not evoke Mozart's best efforts. (There is no question of exhaustion of his miraculous inventive powers; when the sick man returned from Prague he resumed work on the great Requiem.) After a flurry of popularity following Mozart's death, the opera disappeared from the boards, although some of its arias are still occasionally sung.

The Abduction
from the Seraglio

(*1782*)

OPERA IN THREE ACTS

Libretto by C. F. BRETZNER

Adapted by G. STEPHANIE THE YOUNGER

English Version by JOHN BLOCH

THIS ENGLISH VERSION WAS FIRST PERFORMED BY THE
NEW YORK CITY OPERA COMPANY ON OCTOBER 30, 1957.

INTRODUCTION

In 1782 the following announcement was published in Leipzig:

"A certain person by the name of Mozart, in Vienna, has had the audacity to misuse my drama *Belmonte and Constanza* for an opera libretto. I hereby protest most solemnly against this infringement of my rights and reserve the right to take further measures.

Christoph Friedrich Bretzner,
Author of *Das Räuschchen* [*A Little Tipsiness*]"

The "certain person" had arrived in Vienna on March 16, 1781. He had been summoned there by his employer, the Archbishop of Salzburg, who was visiting the Imperial capital. A few weeks after Mozart arrived, he wrote to his father about a libretto to be given him by Gottlieb Stephanie, stage-manager of the recently established German Opera in Vienna (Stephanie was called "junior," to distinguish him from his older brother, an actor). This was the stormiest period in the young composer's life. For several years he had felt increasingly chafed and hemmed in by the provinciality of Salzburg and the galling restrictions placed upon his activities by the stern Archbishop. In Vienna during this spring of 1781 the situation exploded. After bitter quarreling with his patron Mozart wrote to his worried and unhappy father on May 9: "My patience has been so long tried that at last it has given out. I am no longer so unfortunate as to be in Salzburg service. Today is a happy day for me."*

Having taken the fateful step of breaking his ties with the Salzburg court — his official dismissal was sealed physically on June 8 with a kick from Count Arco, director of the Archbishop's kitchens — Mozart embarked upon a life of feverish activity. Always optimistic, he was convinced that he would soon obtain a lucrative and dignified post. To earn his livelihood, he gave concerts, took pupils, and composed furiously. This crowded schedule was further complicated by his falling in love with Constanze Weber; the intrigues by her mother and her guardian eventually resulted in Mozart's marriage to Constanze, under less than blissful circumstances, on August 4, 1782. Meanwhile, however, from the spring of 1781 to the following May he completed the Serenade in B-flat for twelve winds and double bass, K. 361, and wrote, among other works, the Wind Serenade in E-flat, K. 375; two sets of variations for violin and piano, K. 359, 360; one for piano alone, K. 352; three violin sonatas, K. 376, 377, 380; the Sonata for two pianos in D, K. 448; a new finale (K. 382) for the Clavier Concerto in D, K. 175; two arias for soprano and orchestra, K. 119, 383; the Fantasy and Fugue in C for piano, K. 394; three marches for orchestra, K. 408; a minuet for a symphony, K. 409 — and *The Abduction from the Seraglio.*

* The quotations from Mozart's letters are from Emily Anderson, *The Letters of Mozart and His Family.* Reprinted by permission of Miss Anderson and Macmillan & Co., Ltd., London.

*   *
*

On June 16, 1781, Mozart wrote to his father:

I think I mentioned the other day that before his departure Count Rosenberg
[general director of the Court Theater] commissioned Schröder [a famous Viennese
actor] to hunt up a libretto for me. It has now been found, and Stephanie junior,
who is manager of the opera, has got it. Bergopzoomer, a really good friend of
Schröder's and mine, gave me the hint at once. So off I went to Stephanie, *en
forme de visite.* For we thought it possible that his partiality for Umlauf [a
popular composer of light operas] might make him play me false. This suspicion
proved, however, quite unfounded . . . The opera is in four acts; and he tells me
that the first act is exceedingly fine, but that the rest is on a much lower level.
If Schröder allows us to alter it as we think advisable, a good libretto can be
made out of it. He does not want to give it to the management in its present
state, that is, until he has discussed it with Schröder, as he knows in advance
that it would be rejected. So the two of them can settle the matter between
them. After what Stephanie told me, I did not express any desire to read it. For,
if I do not like it, I must say so plainly, or I should be the victim. Besides, I
do not want to lose the favor of Schröder, who has the greatest respect for me.
Therefore I can always make the excuse that I have not read it.

Well, I must now explain why we were suspicious of Stephanie. I regret to
say that the fellow has the worst reputation in Vienna, for he is said to be rude,
false, and slanderous and to treat people most unjustly. But I pay no attention to
these reports. There may be some truth in them, for everyone abuses him. On
the other hand, he is in great favor with the Emperor. He was most friendly to
me the very first time we met, and said: "We are old friends already and I
shall be delighted if it be in my power to render you any service." I believe
and hope too that he himself may write an opera libretto for me. Whether he
has written his plays alone or with the help of others, whether he has plagiarized
or created, he still understands the stage, and his plays are invariably popular.
I have only seen two new pieces of his, and these are certainly excellent . . .

Stephanie handed the libretto over to Mozart on July 30. Two days later
the composer reported to his father: "The libretto is quite good. The subject is
Turkish and the title is: *Belmonte and Constanza,* or *The Abduction from the
Seraglio.* I intend to write the overture, the chorus in Act I, and the final chorus
in the style of Turkish music." He then named the singers who were to par-
ticipate in the first performance — always an important point with Mozart, who
carefully tailored his music to the capacities of the artists who were to perform it.

I am so delighted at having to compose this opera [he continued] that I have
already finished Cavalieri's first aria, Adamberger's, and the trio which closes
Act I. The time is short, it is true, for it is to be performed in the middle of
September; but the circumstances connected with the date of performance and,
in general, all my other prospects stimulate me to such a degree that I rush to
my desk with the greatest eagerness and remain seated there with the greatest
delight. The Grand Duke of Russia is coming here, and that is why Stephanie
entreated me, if possible, to compose the opera in this short space of time. For
the Emperor and Count Rosenberg are to return soon and their first question will

be whether anything new is being prepared? Stephanie will then have the satisfaction of being able to say that Umlauf's opera, on which he has been engaged for a long time, will soon be ready and that I am composing one for the occasion. And he will certainly count it a merit on my part to have undertaken to compose it for this purpose in so short a time. No one but Adamberger and Fischer knows anything about it yet, for Stephanie begged us to say nothing, as Count Rosenberg is still absent and any disclosure may easily lead to all kinds of gossip. Stephanie does not even wish to be regarded as too good a friend of mine; but he wants it to be thought that he is doing all this because Count Rosenberg desires it; and indeed the Count on his departure did actually order him to look around for a libretto, but no more.

By August 22 Mozart had finished the first act. A week later he reported that the Russian Grand Duke was not coming until November — good news, because it would give him more time to work on the opera. Theater rehearsals began in September, but soon came to a halt, because it had been decided to produce Gluck's *Iphigenia in Tauros* and *Alceste* for the Grand Duke Paul instead. The delay stretched for months, while Stephanie made changes in the text — many of them requested by Mozart. By the end of May 1782 the work was finished. Rehearsals began again on June 3 and the first performance took place at the Burgtheater on July 16, with the following cast:

Constanze	Caterina Cavalieri
Blonde	Therese Teiber
Belmonte	Johann Valentin Adamberger
Pedrillo	Johann Ernst Dauer
Osmin	Ludwig Karl Fischer
Bassa Selim	Dominik Jautz

Cavalieri and Teiber had been members of the German Opera in the Burgtheater since it was established in 1778. The former, an Austrian by birth, sang frequently in the concerts Mozart gave in Vienna; she participated in the première of *Der Schauspieldirektor* (1786) and was the Donna Elvira in the first Vienna performance of *Don Giovanni* (1788). It was for her that Mozart wrote the recitative and aria *In quali eccessi . . . Mi tradì* to be interpolated in *Don Giovanni*. Adamberger was a well-known tenor, who also sang in the first performance of *Der Schauspieldirektor*. For him Mozart composed the tenor arias *Per pietà, non ricercate*, K. 420, and *Misero! o sogno! . . . Aura, che intorno*, K. 431. Dauer had the reputation of a good tenor and an excellent actor. Fischer was regarded as one of the finest basses in Germany. Mozart wrote two recitatives and arias for his use in concerts: *Così dunque tradisci . . . Aspri rimorsi atroci*, K. 432, and *Alcandro, lo confesso . . . Non so, d'onde viene*, K. 512. Just why the Pasha was left a speaking role is not clear, but the facts that Osmin would be sung by a strong bass and that Jautz, a first-rate actor, was available to speak the Pasha's lines may have had something to do with it.

There was nothing new in most of the opera's plot. Turkish subjects had long been employed in English, Italian, French, and German comic plays and operas. The noble Sultan or Pasha was a familiar character in such works, as was his villainous underling, often called Osmin. The reuniting of parted lovers and escapes and elopements were recurring elements in the plots of these and other pieces. Mozart himself had worked on an opera of this type in 1779, but left it unfinished. (It became known in the 19th century as *Zaide.*) Bretzner's play, *Belmonte and Constanza,* had been set to music before it reached Mozart (and at least twice afterwards), and this setting, by Johann André, first performed at Berlin in May 1781, quickly achieved considerable popularity.

Mozart and Stephanie made some drastic changes in Bretzner's play. They built up Osmin's role from an insignificant one to one of prime importance. "As we have given the part of Osmin to Herr Fischer," wrote Mozart to his father September 26, 1781,

> who certainly has an excellent bass voice (in spite of the fact that the Archbishop told me that he sang too low for a bass and that I assured him that he would sing higher next time), we must take advantage of it, particularly as he has the whole Viennese public on his side. But in the original libretto Osmin has only this short song and nothing else to sing, except in the trio and the finale; so he has been given an aria in Act I, and he is to have another in Act II. I have explained to Stephanie the words I require for this aria — indeed, I had finished composing most of the music for it before Stephanie knew anything whatever about it. I am enclosing only the beginning and the end, which is bound to have a good effect. Osmin's rage is rendered comical by the accompaniment of the Turkish music. In working out the aria I have given full scope now and then to Fischer's beautiful deep notes . . . The passage "Drum beim Barte des Propheten" is indeed in the same tempo, but with quick notes; but as Osmin's rage gradually increases, there comes (just when the aria seems to be at an end) the allegro assai, which is in a totally different measure and in a different key; this is bound to be very effective. For just as a man in such a towering rage oversteps all the bounds of order, moderation, and propriety and completely forgets himself, so must the music too forget itself. But as passions, whether violent or not, must never be expressed in such a way as to excite disgust, and as music, even in the most terrible situations, must never offend the ear, but must please the hearer, or in other words must never cease to be *music*, I have gone from F (the key in which the aria is written), not into a remote key, but into a related one, not, however, into its nearest relative D minor, but into the more remote A minor.

Mozart and Stephanie also shifted numbers about for greater effectiveness, and they changed the ending — in Bretzner's play Belmonte is revealed as the Pasha's long-lost son.

The letter from which we have just quoted throws light on other parts of the work too:

> Let me return to Belmonte's aria in A major, "O wie ängstlich, o wie feurig." Would you like to know how I have expressed it — and even indicated his throbbing heart? By the two violins playing octaves. This is the favorite aria of all

those who have heard it, and it is mine also. I wrote it expressly to suit Adamberger's voice. You feel the trembling — the faltering — you see how his throbbing breast begins to swell; this I have expressed by a crescendo. You hear the whispering and the sighing — which I have indicated by the first violins with mutes and a flute playing in unison.

The Janissary chorus is, as such, all that can be desired, that is, short, lively, and written to please the Viennese. I have sacrificed Constanza's aria a little to the flexible throat of Mlle. Cavalieri, "Trennung war mein banges Los und nun schwimmt mein Aug' in Tränen." I have tried to express her feelings, as far as an Italian bravura aria will allow it. I have changed the "Hui" to "schnell," so it now runs thus — "Doch wie schnell schwand meine Freude." I really don't know what our German poets are thinking of. Even if they do not understand the theater, or at all events operas, yet they should not make their characters talk as if they were addressing a herd of swine. Hui, sow!

Now for the trio at the close of Act I. Pedrillo has passed off his master as an architect — to give him an opportunity of meeting his Constanza in the garden. Pasha Selim has taken him into his service. Osmin, the steward, knows nothing of this, and being a rude churl and a sworn foe to all strangers, is impertinent and refuses to let them into the garden. It opens quite abruptly — and because the words lend themselves to it, I have made it a fairly respectable piece of real three-part writing. Then the major key begins at once pianissimo — it must go very quickly — and wind up with a great deal of noise, which is always appropriate at the end of an act. The more noise the better, so that the audience may not have time to cool down with their applause.

I have sent you only fourteen bars of the overture, which is very short with alternate fortes and pianos, the Turkish music always coming in at the fortes. The overture modulates through different keys and I doubt whether anyone, even if his previous night had been a sleepless one, could go to sleep over it . . . But I cannot compose any more, because the whole story is being altered — and, to tell the truth, at my own request. At the beginning of Act III is a charming quintet or rather finale, but I should prefer to have it at the end of Act II. In order to make this practicable, great changes must be made, in fact an entirely new plot must be introduced — and Stephanie is up to the eyes in other work. So we must have a little patience. Everyone abuses Stephanie. It may be that in my case he is only very friendly to my face. But after all he is arranging the libretto for me — and, what is more, as I want it — exactly — and, by Heaven, I do not ask anything more of him.

Three weeks later, evidently in answer to his father's criticism of Stephanie's text, Mozart wrote the following brilliantly revealing paragraph:

Now as to the libretto of the opera. You are quite right so far as Stephanie's work is concerned. Still, the poetry is perfectly in keeping with the character of stupid, surly, malicious Osmin. I am well aware that the verse is not of the best, but it fitted in and it agreed so well with the musical ideas which already were buzzing in my head, that it could not fail to please me; and I would like to wager that when it is performed, no deficiencies will be found. As for the poetry which was there originally, I really have nothing to say against it. Belmonte's aria "O wie ängstlich" could hardly be better written for the music. Except for "Hui" and "Kummer ruht in meinem Schoos," . . . the aria too is not bad, particularly the first part. Besides, I should say that in an opera the poetry must be altogether the obedient daughter of the music. Why do Italian comic operas please everywhere —

in spite of their miserable libretti — even in Paris, where I myself witnessed their success? Just because there the music reigns supreme and when one listens to it all else is forgotten. Why, an opera is sure of success when the plot is well worked out, the words written solely for the music and not shoved in here and there to suit some miserable rhyme (which, God knows, never enhances the value of any theatrical performance, be it what it may, but rather detracts from it) — I mean, words or even entire verses which ruin the composer's whole idea. Verses are indeed the most indispensable element for music — but rhymes — solely for the sake of rhyming — the most detrimental. Those high and mighty people who set to work in this pedantic fashion will always come to grief, both they and their music. The best thing of all is when a good composer, who understands the stage and is talented enough to make sound suggestions, meets an able poet, that true phoenix; in that case no fears need be entertained as to the applause even of the ignorant. Poets almost remind me of trumpeters with their professional tricks! If we composers were always to stick faithfully to our rules (which were very good at a time when no one knew better), we should be concocting music as unpalatable as their libretti.

* *

*

The opera was an immediate success. Mozart's report on the première is unfortunately lost, but on July 20 he wrote his father:

I hope that you received safely my last letter informing you of the good reception of my opera. It was given yesterday for the second time. Can you really believe it, but yesterday there was an even stronger cabal against it than on the first evening! The whole first act was accompanied by hissing. But indeed they could not prevent the loud shouts of "bravo" during the arias. I was relying on the closing trio [of Act I], but, as ill-luck would have it, Fischer went wrong, which made Dauer (Pedrillo) go wrong too; and Adamberger alone could not sustain the trio, with the result that the whole effect was lost and that this time it was not repeated. I was in such a rage (and so was Adamberger) that I was simply beside myself and said at once that I would not let the opera be given again without having a short rehearsal for the singers. In the second act both duets were repeated as on the first night, and in addition Belmonte's rondo "Wenn der Freude Tränen fliessen." The theater was almost more crowded than on the first night and on the preceding day no reserved seats were to be had, either in the stalls or in the third circle, and not a single box. My opera has brought in 1200 gulden in the two days.

The Emperor's comment and Mozart's answer have frequently been quoted: "Too beautiful for our ears, and far too many notes, my dear Mozart," Joseph II is supposed to have said, to which the young composer is said to have replied, "Exactly as many as are needed, Your Majesty." Contemporary reviewers all praised the music highly, although some of them, like Leopold Mozart, had misgivings about the libretto. One complaint, for example, was that the new ending was less "natural" than Bretzner's. But the music swept everything before it. *The Seraglio* was by far the most popular of Mozart's stage works during his lifetime. It was performed forty-two times in Vienna from 1782 to 1788. The performance on August 6, 1782, was given at the request of Gluck, who congratulated the young composer and invited him to dinner. On October 8 Mozart conducted himself, in honor of the Grand Duke Paul and his duchess, who were visiting Vienna again. Before Mozart's death in 1791 the opera had been produced in at least twenty-eight other German theaters, as well as in Prague, Warsaw, and Amsterdam. (From all of these performances Mozart received nothing, in those days of no copyright. The only payment to him recorded for this work is the standard commissioning fee for a new opera, one hundred ducats. The celebrated Paisiello was given three hundred ducats by the same management for his *Il Rè Teodoro in Venezia*.) Goethe wrote in 1787 that all his efforts to achieve simplicity and modest proportions in his first libretto for a *Singspiel* went for nothing when Mozart appeared. *"The Seraglio* ruined everything . . ." Even the once aggrieved Bretzner came to recognize the genius of that "certain person." After the composer's death Bretzner translated *Così fan tutte* into German; in his foreword he spoke of "the delightful and distinguished music of this masterpiece by the immortal Mozart." Perhaps the most penetrating words about *The Seraglio* were written by Carl Maria von Weber:

> I venture to express the belief that in Mozart's *Seraglio* experience in artistic creation reached its maturity, after which only experience in life added to his creative powers. The world was justified in expecting from him more operas like *Figaro* and *Don Giovanni*. Another *Seraglio* he could not write, with the best will in the world. I think I see in it what his happy years of youth mean to every man, the blossoming of which he can never recapture in the same way, for in the process of eliminating flaws irretrievable charms vanish too.

CAST OF CHARACTERS

PASHA SELIM . . . . *Speaking role*

CONSTANZA, beloved of Belmonte . . . . *Soprano*

BLONDA, maid of Constanza . . . . *Soprano*

BELMONTE, a Spanish nobleman . . . . *Tenor*

PEDRILLO, servant of Belmonte . . . . *Tenor*

OSMIN, overseer of the country palace of the Pasha . . . . *Bass*

KLAAS, a boatsman . . . . *Speaking role*

A Mute, Janissaries, Slaves, Guards.

PLACE: The country palace of the Pasha.

TIME: Middle of the 16th century.

THE PLOT

ACT. I

Belmonte, a young Spanish nobleman, stands in the courtyard of the Pasha Selim's palace, wondering how he may gain access to his beloved Constanza, who has been captured by pirates and is now held prisoner by the Turkish monarch, together with her maid Blonda and Belmonte's servant Pedrillo. When the villainous overseer Osmin arrives to pick figs in the garden, Belmonte asks the whereabouts of his former valet, now court gardener; but Osmin, detesting Pedrillo as a schemer and rival for Blonda, furiously drives the stranger away. Pedrillo enters to further antagonize the departing Osmin. Belmonte reappears and is joyfully reunited with his servant. Reassured that Constanza still loves him, Belmonte says he has a ship waiting in the harbor. Pedrillo urges patience and begins to lay plans for escape. Alone, Belmonte gives vent to his longing for Constanza.

When Pedrillo returns with word that the Pasha approaches, both men hide. Hailed by a chorus of Janissaries, the Pasha leads on Constanza with whom he pleads his love. The distraught girl confesses that she loves another, whereupon the angry monarch gives her one more day to change her mind. Constanza leaves. Pedrillo brings on Belmonte, introducing him as an architect to the Pasha, who engages the young man. Belmonte and Pedrillo then enter the palace, despite the protestations of Osmin.

ACT II.

In the palace garden, Blonda discourages the surly advances of Osmin and sends the overseer packing. She is joined by Constanza, lamenting her separation from Belmonte. Blonda urges her to have courage and withdraws as the Pasha makes his entrance. In reply to his renewed demands Constanza declares that even tortures can not force her to love him. When the Pasha leaves, Blonda returns, wondering if Constanza has reached an accord with the Pasha. As she muses on her own feminine weakness, Pedrillo brings news of Belmonte's arrival and the plan for the abduction from the seraglio. After Pedrillo leaves to await Belmonte, Blonda rejoices in her coming freedom and then rushes to tell Constanza the joyful tidings. Pedrillo comes back, trying to build up his courage for the escapade. He is met by Osmin whom he engages in a drinking bout; both sing the praises of wine. The inebriated overseer is led away by Pedrillo, who returns to witness the reunion of Belmonte and Constanza. The four lovers reaffirm their faith in one another.

ACT III.

At midnight, Pedrillo brings a ladder to rescue the girls from the palace. When Belmonte arrives, Pedrillo urges him to sing, so as not to arouse the suspicions of the guards, accustomed to the valet's nightly serenadings; Belmonte utters love's praises. When he has finished, Pedrillo takes up a mandolin and signals the escape with a beautiful romanza. Constanza appears at the upper window and is carried off by Belmonte. Pedrillo climbs to Blonda's room. Suddenly Osmin enters, awakened by a mute who has heard noises. Spying the ladder, the overseer takes up watch. When Blonda and Pedrillo attempt to flee, they are apprehended. Guards then bring on Belmonte and Constanza. Osmin joyfully anticipates his revenge. The Pasha arrives and is informed of the attempted abduction. Constanza begs in vain for her lover's life. When the young man steps forward to declare his noble birth, the Pasha recognizes in him the son of his old enemy who once forced his exile from Spain. The Pasha leaves with Osmin.

As the lovers prepare themselves for death, the Pasha abruptly returns magnanimously declaring that he is above petty revenge. The lovers' joy is temporarily interrupted by a final outburst of rage from Osmin, who rushes off entirely defeated. The couples happily sail away as the court sings the Pasha's praises.

DIE ENTFÜHRUNG AUS DEM SERAIL

ERSTER AUFZUG

(*Platz vor dem Palast des Bassa am Ufer des Meeres.*)

ERSTER AUFTRITT

BELMONTE (*allein*)

1. Arie

BELMONTE

Hier soll ich dich denn sehen,
Constanze, dich mein Glück!
O Himmel, hör' mein Flehen:
Gib mir die Ruh' zurück!
Ich duldete der Leiden,
O Liebe, allzuviel.
Gib mir dafür nun Freuden,
Und bringe mich an's Ziel.

Dialog

Aber wie soll ich in den Palast
    kommen?
Wie sie sehen?
Wie sprechen?

ZWEITER AUFTRITT

(*Osmin erscheint mit einer Leiter. Er lehnt sie an einen Feigenbaum vor dem Palast, steigt hinauf und nimmt Feigen ab.*)

2. Arie und Duett

OSMIN

Wer ein Liebchen hat gefunden,
Die es treu und redlich meint,
Lohn' es ihr durch tausend Küsse,
Mach' ihr all' das Leben süsse,
Sei ihr Tröster,
Sei ihr Freund.
Tralla-le-ra, tralla-le-ra.
Doch sie treu zu erhalten,
Schliess' er Liebchen sorglich ein;
Denn die losen Dinger haschen
Jeden Schmetterling und naschen
Gar zu gern von fremdem Wein.
Tralla-le-ra, tralla-le-ra.

Dialog

BELMONTE

He, Alter, he! hört Ihr nicht? Ist hier
des Bassa Selim Palast?
(*Osmin sieht ihn an, dreht sich herum und singt wie zuvor.*)

OSMIN

Sonderlich beim Mondenscheine,
Freunde, nehmt sie wohl in Acht:
Oft lauscht da ein junges Herrchen,
Kirrt und lockt das kleine Närrchen,
Und dann Treue gute Nacht!
Tralla-le-ra, tralla-le-ra.

BELMONTE

Verwünscht seist du samt deinem
    Liede!
Ich bin dein Singen nun schon müde,
So hör' doch nur ein einzig' Wort!

OSMIN

Was Henker, lasst Ihr Euch gelüsten,
Euch zu ereifern, Euch zu brüsten!
Was wollt Ihr? was wollt Ihr? was
    wollt Ihr?
Hurtig, ich muss fort!

BELMONTE

Ist das des Bassa Selim Haus?

OSMIN

Das ist des Bassa Selim Haus.

BELMONTE

So wartet doch! Ein Wort!

OSMIN

Ich kann nicht weilen, geschwind, denn
ich muss eilen.

BELMONTE

Seid Ihr in seinen Diensten, Freund?

OSMIN

Eh?

BELMONTE

Seid Ihr in seinen Diensten, Freund?

THE ABDUCTION FROM THE SERAGLIO

ACT ONE

A square in front of the Pasha's palace on the shore of the sea.

SCENE 1

No. 1. Aria

BELMONTE *(alone)*

Now I at last shall see you,
Constanza, O my treasure.
If all my prayers are answered
You'll soon be in my arms.
I've longed for you in sadness, Beloved.
How I've longed for you.
Now let our hearts be joyful,
For freedom is at hand.

Dialogue

But how can I get into the palace?
How can I see her, speak to her?

SCENE 2

No. 2. Song and Duet

(Osmin appears with a ladder. He leans it against a fig tree in front of the palace, climbs up and begins to pick figs.)

OSMIN *(singing to himself)*

If you ever find a sweetheart
Who'll be faithful to the end,
You should kiss her very often,
Her resistance try to soften.
Be her comfort. Be her friend.
Tra la le ra, tra la le ra.

Dialogue

BELMONTE

Maybe I can find out something from
this old man. Hey, friend! Isn't this
the house of Pasha Selim?

OSMIN

(sings, as before, during work)
But if you would keep her faithful,
You must safely lock her in.
For she soon will start believing
That your company's fatiguing,
And she'll drink a stranger's wine.
Tra la le ra, tra la le ra.

Dialogue

BELMONTE

Hey, old man, hey! Don't you hear me?
Is this the Pasha Selim's palace?

OSMIN

(looks at him, turns around and sings as before)

When the silvery moon is shining,
You must keep her well in sight,
For a dandy may be lurking
To decoy her with his smirking,
And then — faithful love goodnight.
Tra la le ra, tra la le ra.

BELMONTE

A plague on you and on your singing
That in my ears is ever ringing.
Just let me speak a word or two.

OSMIN

Why put yourself in such a passion,
And talk to me in such a fashion?
What is it? What is it? What is it?
Hurry, I must go.

BELMONTE

Is this the Pasha Selim's house?

OSMIN

Eh?

BELMONTE

Is this the Pasha Selim's house?

OSMIN *(wants to leave)*

This is the Pasha Selim's house.

BELMONTE

But wait awhile!

OSMIN

I cannot stay here.

BELMONTE

A word!

OSMIN

Be quick, I can't delay here!

BELMONTE

Are you the Pasha's servant, friend?

OSMIN

Eh?

OSMIN

Ich bin in seinen Diensten, Freund!

BELMONTE

Wie kann ich den Pedrill wohl
sprechen,
Der hier in seinen Diensten steht?

OSMIN

Den Schurken, der den Hals soll
brechen!
Seht selber zu,
Wenn's anders geht!
Seht selber zu, wenn's anders geht!

BELMONTE (*für sich*)

Was für ein alter grober Bengel!

OSMIN (*für sich*)

Das ist just so ein Galgenschwengel.

BELMONTE

Ihr irrt, Ihr irrt, Ihr irrt, es ist ein
braver Mann.

OSMIN

So brav, so brav, so brav,
Dass man ihn spiessen kann.

BELMONTE

Ihr müsst ihn wahrlich nicht recht
kennen.

OSMIN

Recht gut, ich liess ihn heut'
verbrennen.
Auf einen Pfahl gehört sein Kopf!
(*Will fort.*)

BELMONTE

So bleibet doch!

OSMIN

Was wollt Ihr noch?

BELMONTE

Ich möchte gerne—

OSMIN (*spöttisch*)

So hübsch von ferne
Um's Haus 'rum schleichen, und
Mädchen stehlen?
Fort, Eures Gleichen braucht man hier
nicht!

BELMONTE

Ihr seid besessen,
Sprecht voller Galle
Mir so vermessen
In's Angesicht?

OSMIN

Nur nicht in Eifer—

BELMONTE

Schont Euren Geifer.

OSMIN

Ich kenn' Euch schon!

BELMONTE

Lasst Euer Droh'n!

OSMIN

Marsch, geht zum Teufel!
Ihr kriegt, ich schwöre,
Sonst ohne Gnade
Die Bastonade;
Noch habt Ihr Zeit!

BELMONTE

Es ist kein Zweifel,
Ihr seid von Sinnen,
Welch' ein Betragen
Auf meine Fragen!
Gebt doch Bescheid!

DRITTER AUFTRITT

Dialog

OSMIN

Könnt ich mir doch so einen Schurken
auf die Nase setzen, wie den Pedrillo;
so einen Gaudieb, der Tag und Nacht
nichts tut, als nach meinen Weibern
herumzuschleichen und zu schnobern,
ob's nichts für seinen Schnabel setzt.
Aber ich laure ihm sicher auf den
Dienst, und wohl bekomm dir die
Prügelsuppe, wenn ich dich einmal
beim Kanthaken kriege! Hätt er sich
nur beim Bassa nicht so einge-
schmeichelt, er sollte den Strick
längst um den Hals haben.

(PEDRILLO *kommt herein*)

PEDRILLO

Nun, wie steht's, Osmin? Ist der Bassa
noch nicht zurück?

OSMIN

Sieh darnach, wenn du's wissen willst.

BELMONTE

Are you the Pasha's servant, friend?

OSMIN

I am the Pasha's servant, friend.

BELMONTE

Then tell me where to find Pedrillo.
He must be working hereabouts.

OSMIN

That scoundrel, whose neck I'd like to
    break!
Find out yourself. I will not tell.

BELMONTE (*to himself*)

Just hear him puffing like a bellows.

OSMIN (*to himself*)

One of those good-for-nothing fellows!

BELMONTE (*to Osmin*)

You're wrong, you're wrong, you're
    wrong.
He is a nice young man.

OSMIN

So nice, so nice, so nice!
I'll kill him if I can.

BELMONTE

You surely never can have known him.

OSMIN

Oh, yes indeed. I'd like to roast him.

BELMONTE

I cannot fathom your dislike.

OSMIN

His head belongs upon a pike.
(*starts to leave*)

BELMONTE

Pray, stay a while.

OSMIN

What is it now?
What is it?

BELMONTE

I'd only like to —

OSMIN (*mockingly*)

Oh, so you'd like to —
Go in there sneaking
To steal our women?
Off! We don't want you prowling
    around!
Off! Off! Off!

BELMONTE

Your temper's awful,
Your conduct frightful,
Your insults bawling before my face!

OSMIN

You think you're clever!

BELMONTE

No more than ever.

OSMIN

But we shall see!

BELMONTE

Don't threaten me!

OSMIN

Go to the devil!
You'll get, I swear it,
For your bravado the bastinado!
You must be gone!

BELMONTE

There is no doubt, sir,
You are a madman.
Why do you flout, sir,
All of my questions?
You show no sense.

OSMIN

You must get out!

(*forces Belmonte out*)

SCENE 3

Dialogue

OSMIN

As if I needed another scoundrel like
    that Pedrillo! A rascal who does
    nothing night and day except sneak
    around my harem looking for a new
    delight to satisfy his appetite. But I'm
    watching him and, Allah help him
    if I ever catch him. If he hadn't
    wormed his way into the good graces
    of the Pasha he'd have had a rope
    around his neck a long time ago.

(*Pedrillo enters.*)

PEDRILLO

What's going on, Osmin? Has the
    Pasha come back?

OSMIN

Look for yourself, if you want to know

PEDRILLO

Schon wieder Sturm im Kalender? Hast du das Gericht Feigen für mich gepflückt?

OSMIN

Gift für dich, verwünschter Schmarotzer!

PEDRILLO

Was in aller Welt ich dir nur getan haben muss, dass du beständig mit mir zankst. Lass uns doch einmal Friede machen.

OSMIN

Friede mit dir? Mit so einem schleichenden, spitzbübischen Passauf, der nur spioniert, wie er mir eins versetzen kann? Erdrosseln möcht ich dich!

PEDRILLO

Aber sag nur, warum, warum?

OSMIN

Warum? Weil ich dich nicht leiden kann.

3. Arie

OSMIN

Solche hergelauf'ne Laffen,
Die nur nach den Weibern gaffen,
Mag ich für Teufel nicht;
Denn ihr ganzes Tun und Lassen ist,
Uns auf den Dienst zu passen,
Doch mich trügt kein solch' Gesicht.
Eure Tücken, eure Ränke,
Euren Finten, eure Schwänke
Sind mir ganz bekannt.
Mich zu hintergehen,
Müsst ihr früh aufstehen:
Ich hab' auch Verstand, ich!
Ich hab' auch Verstand.
Drum beim Barte des Propheten!
Ich studiere Tag und Nacht,
Dich so mit Manier zu töten,
Nimm dich wie du willst in Acht!

(Geht ab)

VIERTER AUFTRITT

Dialog

PEDRILLO

Geh nur, verwünschter Aufpasser; es ist noch nicht aller Tage Abend. Wer weiss, wer den andern überlistet; und dir misstrauischem, gehässigem Menschenfeinde eine Grube zu graben, sollte ein wahres Fest für mich sein.

(*Belmonte kommt herein*)

BELMONTE

Pedrillo, guter Pedrillo!

PEDRILLO

Ach mein bester Herr! Ist's möglich? Sind Sie's wirklich? Bravo, Madame Fortuna, bravo, das heisst doch Wort gehalten! Schon verzweifelte ich, ob einer meiner Briefe Sie getroffen hätte.

BELMONTE

Sag, guter Pedrillo, lebt meine Constanze noch?

PEDRILLO

Lebt, und noch, hoff ich, für Sie. Seit dem schrecklichen Tage, an welchem das Glück uns einen so hässlichen Streich spielte und unser Schiff von den Seeräubern erobern liess, haben wir mancherlei Drangsal erfahren. Glücklicherweise traf sich's noch, dass der Bassa Selim uns alle drei kaufte: Ihre Constanze nämlich, meine Blonde und mich. Er liess uns sogleich hier auf sein Landhaus bringen. Donna Constanze ward seine auserwählte Geliebte.

BELMONTE

Ah! Was sagst du?

PEDRILLO

Nun, nur nicht so hitzig! Sie ist noch nicht in die schlimmsten Hände gefallen. Der Bassa ist ein Renegat und hat noch so viel Delikatesse, keine seiner Weiber zu seiner Liebe zu zwingen; und so viel ich weiss, spielt er noch immer den unerhörten Liebhaber.

BELMONTE

Wär es möglich? Wär Constanze noch treu?

PEDRILLO

Stormy weather again? Did you pick those figs for me?

OSMIN

Poison for you, you parasite!

PEDRILLO

What in the world have I done to you that you always fight with me? Let's make peace for once.

OSMIN

Peace with you, with such a slippery sneak who is always spying on me and figuring out how to torment me? I'd like to throttle you!

PEDRILLO

But tell me, why, why?

OSMIN

Why? Because I can't stand you.

No 3. Aria

OSMIN (singing)

Wait, you good-for-nothing donkey,
Lazy, woman-chasing monkey.
I detest you like the plague,
For your one and only purpose is
Sneaking inside the harem.
But I shall not be deceived.
Your conniving, your pretenses,
Your intriguing, your offenses,
I have found them out.
You won't find me sleeping
While you're slyly creeping.
I am no one's fool.
No, I am no one's fool.
By the Prophet's beard,
I swear it,
I shall labor night and day
Till I see you on the gallows
Take whatever care you may.
Just as sure as I'm Osmin,
Watch out for me!

Dialogue

PEDRILLO

What a ferocious fellow you are! And I've never done anything to you!

OSMIN

You have the face of a gallows' bird, and that's enough!
(sings)
You'll be hung, then beheaded,
Then you're drowned and then you're shredded.
Next you broil and you're toasted.
On a spit you will be roasted.
(storms into the palace)

SCENE 4

Dialogue

PEDRILLO

Go on, you blasted watchdog. We're not done yet. Who knows who'll outwit the other? And to lay a trap for you, you suspicious, ill-tempered misanthrope, would really make me happy.

BELMONTE (entering)

Pedrillo, good Pedrillo!

PEDRILLO

Ah, my dear master! Is it possible? Is it really you? Bravo, Dame Fortune, bravo! That's what I call keeping my word. I had given up hope that one of my letters would reach you.

BELMONTE

Tell me, good Pedrillo, is my Constanza still alive?

PEDRILLO

Alive, and still, I hope, for you. Since that day luck played a trick on us and let our ship be captured by pirates many terrible things have happened. Luckily the Pasha Selim bought all three of us, your Constanza, my Blonda and me. He brought us right here to his country place. Donna Constanza has become his chosen one.

BELMONTE

Ah! What are you saying?

PEDRILLO

Not so fast! She hasn't fallen into the worst possible hands. The Pasha may be a renegade, but he has enough delicacy not to force his women to love him; and, as far as I know, he's still playing the unrequited lover.

BELMONTE

Is it possible? Is Constanza still true to me?

PEDRILLO

Sicher noch, lieber Herr! Aber wie's mit meinem Blondchen steht, weiss der Himmel! Das arme Ding schmachtet bei einem alten hässlichen Kerl, dem sie der Bassa geschenkt hat; und vielleicht—ach, ich darf gar nicht dran denken!

BELMONTE

Doch nicht der alte Kerl, der soeben ins Haus ging?

PEDRILLO

Eben der.

BELMONTE

Und dies ist der Liebling des Bassa?

PEDRILLO

Liebling, Spion und Ausbund aller Spitzbuben, der mich mit den Augen vergiften möchte, wenn's möglich wäre.

BELMONTE

O guter Pedrillo, was sagst du?

PEDRILLO

Nur nicht gleich verzagt! Unter uns gesagt: ich hab auch einem Stein im Brett beim Bassa. Durch mein bisschen Geschick in der Gärtnerei hab ich seine Gunst weggekriegt, und dadurch hab ich so ziemlich Freiheit, die tausend andere nicht haben würden. Da sonst jede Mannsperson sich entfernen muss, wenn eine seiner Weiber in den Garten kommt, kann ich bleiben; sie reden sogar mit mir, und er sagt nichts darüber. Freilich mault der alte Osmin, besonders, wenn mein Blondchen ihrer Gebieterin folgen muss.

BELMONTE

Ist's möglich? Du hast sie gesprochen? O sag, sag! Liebt sie mich noch?

PEDRILLO

Hm! Dass Sie daran zweifeln! Ich dächte, Sie kennten die gute Constanze mehr als zu gut, hätten Proben genug ihrer Liebe. Doch damit dürfen wir uns gar nicht aufhalten. Hier ist bloss die Frage, wie's anzufangen ist, hier wegzukommen?

BELMONTE

O da hab ich für alles gesorgt! Ich hab hier ein Schiff in einiger Entfernung vom Hafen, das uns auf den ersten Wink einnimmt, und—

PEDRILLO

Ah, sachte, sachte! Erst müssen wir die Mädels haben, ehe wir zu Schiffe gehen, und das geht nicht so husch, husch wie Sie meinen!

BELMONTE

O lieber, guter Pedrillo, mach nur, dass ich sie sehen, dass ich sie sprechen kann! Das Herz schlägt mir vor Angst und Freude!

PEDRILLO

Pfiffig müssen wir das Ding anfangen, und rasch müssen wir's ausführen, damit wir den alten Aufpasser übertölpeln. Bleiben Sie hier in der Nähe. Jetzt wird der Bassa bald von einer Lustfahrt auf dem Wasser zurückkommen. Ich will Sie ihm als einen geschickten Baumeister vorstellen, denn Bauen und Gärtnerei sind seine Steckenpferde. Aber lieber, goldner Herr, halten Sie sich in Schranken; Constanze ist bei ihm—

BELMONTE

Constanze bei ihm? Was sagst du? Ich soll sie sehen?

PEDRILLO

Gemach, gemach ums Himmels willen, lieber Herr, sonst stolpern wir! Ah, ich glaube, dort seh ich sie schon angefahren kommen. Gehn Sie nur auf die Seite, wenn er kommt; ich will ihm entgegen gehen. (*Geht ab*)

FÜNFTER AUFTRITT

4. Arie

BELMONTE

Constanze! Constanze! dich wiederzusehen, dich!
O wie ängstlich, o wie feurig
Klopft mein liebevolles Herz!
Und des Wiedersehens Zähre
Lohnt der Trennung bangen Schmerz.
Schon zittr' ich und wanke,
Schon zag' ich und schwanke,
Es hebt sich die schwellende Brust.
Ist das ihr Lispeln?
Es wird mir so bange.
War das ihr Seufzen?
Es glüht mir die Wange.
Täuscht mich die Liebe?
War es ein Traum?

PEDRILLO

I'm sure of it, dear master. But as for my Blonda — Heaven knows. The poor thing is pining away with an ugly old man to whom the Pasha gave her, and maybe — but I can't let myself think about that.

BELMONTE

Not the old man who just went into the house?

PEDRILLO

The same.

BELMONTE

And he's the Pasha's favorite?

PEDRILLO

Favorite, spy and worst rascal. He'd kill me with just a look if he could.

BELMONTE

Good Pedrillo, what are you saying?

PEDRILLO

Don't give up so quickly. Just between us, I carry a little weight with the Pasha, too. Through my little bit of skill with gardening I won some favor with him, and through that a good deal of freedom, more than a thousand others have. Even though other men have to leave when one of his wives comes into the garden, I can stay. They even talk to me and he says nothing. Naturally, old Osmin grumbles when my Blonda has to follow her mistress.

BELMONTE

Is it possible? You have spoken to her? Tell me, tell me, does she still love me?

PEDRILLO

Hm! That you can doubt it! I thought you knew her well enough that you didn't need proof. But we can't waste time on that. There is only one question. How do we get away from here?

BELMONTE

Oh, I have taken care of everything. I have a ship near the harbor that is ready to take us at a moment's notice —

PEDRILLO

Easy, easy. First we have to have the girls and then we can get on the ship. But that doesn't happen as fast as you think.

BELMONTE

Dear, good Pedrillo. Just arrange for me to see her, to speak to her. My heart is full of anxiety and joy.

PEDRILLO

We must be crafty and carry out the plan quickly if we want to outwit the old watchdog. Stay close to here. The Pasha will return soon from an excursion on the water. I'll introduce you as a talented architect, because buildings and gardens are his hobby. But, dear Master, stay close. Constanza is with him.

BELMONTE

Constanza is with him? What are you saying? I'm going to see her?

PEDRILLO

Easy, easy, dear Master, for heaven's sake, or else we'll stumble. Oh, I think I see them coming. Go over there when he comes. I'll go to meet him. (*Exit.*)

SCENE 5
No. 4. Aria

BELMONTE

Constanza, Constanza!
When shall I behold you? When?
Oh how anxious, oh how fiery
Beats my eager, loving heart.
In the pleasure of our meeting
We will vow to never part,
Never more to be apart.
I shiver, I tremble.
I shudder and quiver.
My heart fills with longing and joy.
Is that her whisper?
Oh, such a lovely melody!
Was that her sighing
Or just a haunting memory?
Does love deceive me?
Was it a dream?
Is that her whisper?
Was that her sighing?
Oh melody so lovely
That now returns to haunt me,
Returns now to haunt me.
Oh how anxious, oh how fiery
Beats my eager, loving heart.

(Pedrillo kommt hurtig gelaufen)

Dialog

PEDRILLO

Geschwind, geschwind auf die Seite und versteckt! Der Bassa kommt.

(Belmonte versteckt sich)

5. Chor der Janitscharen

CHOR

Singt dem grossen Bassa Lieder,
Dem grossen Bassa Lieder,
Töne feuriger Gesang,
Und vom Ufer halle wieder,
Vom Ufer halle wieder
Unsrer Lieder Jubelklang.
Weht ihm entgegen,
Kühlende Winde.
Ebne dich sanfter,
Wallende Flut.
Singt ihm entgegen,
Fliegende Chöre,
Singt ihm der Liebe Freuden ins Herz.

(Chor und Pedrillo gehen ab. Bassa Selim und Constanze sind allein.)

SIEBENTER AUFTRITT

Dialog

BASSA SELIM

Immer noch traurig, geliebte Constanze? Immer in Tränen? Sieh, dieser schöne Abend, diese reizende Gegend, diese bezaubernde Musik, meine zärtliche Liebe für dich. Sag, kann nichts von allem dich endlich beruhigen, endlich dein Herz rühren? Sieh, ich könnte befehlen, könnte grausam mit dir verfahren, dich zwingen.

(Constanze seufzt)

Aber nein, Constanze, dir selbst will ich dein Herz zu danken haben, dir selbst!

CONSTANZE

Grossmütiger Mann! O dass ich es könnte, dass ich's erwidern könnte —aber—

BASSA SELIM

Sag, Constanze, sag, was hält dich zurück?

CONSTANZE

Du wirst mich hassen.

BASSA SELIM

Nein, ich schwöre dir's. Du weisst, wie sehr ich dich liebe, wieviel Freiheit ich dir vor allen meinen Weibern gestatte, dich wie meine einzige schätze.

CONSTANZE

O so verzeih!

6. Arie

Ach ich liebte, war so glücklich,
Kannte nicht der Liebe Schmerz,
Schwur ihm Treue, dem Geliebten,
Gab dahin mein ganzes Herz.
Doch wie schnell schwand meine Freude!
Trennung war mein banges Los,
Und nun schwimmt mein Aug' in Tränen!
Kummer ruht in meinem Schoss.

Dialog

Ach, ich sagt es wohl, du würdest mich hassen. Aber verzeih, verzeih dem liebekranken Mädchen! Du bist ja so grossmütig, so gut. Ich will dir dienen, deine Sklavin sein bis ans Ende meines Lebens, nur verlange nicht ein Herz von mir, das auf ewig versagt ist.

BASSA SELIM

Ha, Undankbare! Was wagst du zu bitten?

CONSTANZE

Töte mich, Selim, töte mich, nur zwinge mich nicht, meineidig zu werden! Noch zuletzt, wie mich der Seeräuber aus den Armen meines Geliebten riss, schwur ich aufs feierlichste—

BASSA SELIM

Halt ein, nicht ein Wort! Reize meinen Zorn nicht noch mehr. Bedenke, dass du in meiner Gewalt bist!

CONSTANZE

Ich bin es, aber du wirst dich ihrer nicht bedienen, ich kenne dein gutes, dein mitleidsvolles Herz. Hätte ich's sonst wagen können, dir das meinige zu entdecken?

BASSA SELIM

Wag es nicht, meine Güte zu missbrauchen!

CONSTANZE

Nur Aufschub gönne mir, Herr, nur Zeit, meinen Schmerz zu vergessen!

Dialogue

PEDRILLO (*hurrying in*)

Hurry over to the side and hide. The Pasha is coming!

(*Belmonte hides.*)

SCENE 6

No. 5. Chorus

(*The chorus of Janissaries enters, followed by the Pasha and Constanza.*)

CHORUS

Praise the mighty Pasha Selim,
Lift your voices in acclaim
As we proudly wait to hail him.
Let our joyous song resound.
Bear him before you,
Soft cooling breezes.
Carry him onward,
Swift flowing stream.
Soothe him with singing,
Heavenly chorus.
Tell him how love brings
Joy to the heart.
Sing the praises of great Selim,
The mighty Pasha Selim.
Lift your voices in acclaim
As we proudly wait to hail him.
Let our joyous song resound.

(*Exeunt.*)

SCENE 7

Dialogue

SELIM

Still sad, dear Constanza? Still in tears? See this lovely evening, this charming place, this enchanted music, my tender love for you? Tell me, can't any of this bring you peace, move your heart? I could command you, treat you badly, force you. (*Constanza sighs.*) But no, Constanza. I want you to give me your heart, only you.

CONSTANZA

Generous man! If I only could, if I could return your love, but —

SELIM

Tell me, Constanza, tell me what holds you back?

CONSTANZA

You will hate me.

SELIM

No, I swear to you. You know I love you, and how much more freedom I give you than my other wives, as if you were my only love.

CONSTANZA

Forgive me.

No. 6. Aria

Ah, I loved him.
I was happy,
Never dreamed that we must part.
And I promised my beloved
That forever he'd have my heart.
Yet how soon my joy has vanished.
Parting was our bitter lot.
And my eyes are red with weeping,
They burn with weeping.
Only sorrow fills my heart.

Dialogue

CONSTANZA

I told you you would hate me. But forgive, forgive a lovesick girl. You are so generous, so good. I will serve you, be your slave to the end of my life, but don't ask for my heart. That is promised forever.

SELIM

Ungrateful! What do you dare to ask?

CONSTANZA

Kill me, Selim, kill me, but don't force me to be untrue to my word. When the pirates tore me from the arms of my beloved I swore —

SELIM

Enough. Not another word! Don't make me more angry. Remember, you are in my power.

CONSTANZA

I know it, but you wouldn't use your power. I know your good, your merciful heart. Otherwise would I have told you my secret?

SELIM

Don't misuse my goodness!

CONSTANZA

Just give me time to forget my sorrow.

BASSA SELIM

Wie oft schon gewährt ich dir diese Bitte.

CONSTANZE

Nur noch diesmal!

BASSA SELIM

Es sei, zum letzten Male! Geh, Constanze, geh! Besinne dich eines Bessern, und morgen—

CONSTANZE (*im Abgehn*)

Unglückliches Mädchen! O Belmonte, Belmonte!

ACHTER AUFTRITT

BASSA SELIM

Ihr Schmerz, ihre Tränen, ihre Standhaftigkeit bezaubern mein Herz immer mehr, machen mir ihre Liebe nur noch wünschenswerter. Ha, wer wollte gegen ein solches Herz Gewalt brauchen? Nein, Constanze, nein, auch Selim hat ein Herz, auch Selim kennt Liebe!

(*Pedrillo kommt mit Belmonte herein*)

PEDRILLO

Herr, verzeih, dass ich es wage, dich in deinen Betrachtungen zu stören!

BASSA SELIM

Was willst du, Pedrillo?

PEDRILLO

Dieser junge Mann, der sich in Italien mit vielem Fleiss auf die Baukunst gelegt, hat von deiner Macht, von deinem Reichtum gehört und kommt her, dir als Baumeister seine Dienste anzubieten.

BELMONTE

Herr, könnte ich so glücklich sein, durch meine geringen Fähigkeiten deinen Beifall zu verdienen!

BASSA SELIM

Hm! Du gefällst mir. Ich will sehen, was du kannst. (*zu Pedrillo*) Sorge für seinen Unterhalt. Morgen werde ich dich wieder rufen lassen. (*Geht ab*)

NEUNTER AUFTRITT

PEDRILLO

Ha! Triumph, Triumph, Herr! Der erste Schritt war getan.

BELMONTE

Ach, lass mich zu mir selbst kommen! Ich habe sie gesehen, hab' das gute, treue, beste Mädchen gesehen! O Constanze! Was könnt ich für dich tun, was für dich wagen?

PEDRILLO

Ha! Gemach, gemach, bester Herr! Stimmen Sie den Ton ein bisschen herab; Verstellung wird uns weit bessere Dienste leisten. Wir sind nicht in unserm Vaterlande. Hier fragen sie den Henker darnach, ob's einen Kopf mehr oder weniger in der Welt gibt. Bastonade und Strick um den Hals sind hier wie ein Morgenbrot.

BELMONTE

Ach, Pedrillo, wenn du die Liebe kenntest!

PEDRILLO

Hm! Als wenn's mit unser einem gar nichts wäre. Ich habe so gut meine zärtlichen Stunden als andere Leute. Und denken Sie denn, dass mir's nicht auch im Bauche grimmt, wenn ich mein Blondchen von so einem alten Spitzbuben, wie der Osmin ist, bewacht sehen muss?

BELMONTE

O wenn es möglich wäre, sie zu sprechen—

PEDRILLO

Wir wollen sehen, was zu tun ist. Kommen Sie nur mit mir in den Garten, aber um alles in der Welt vorsichtig und fein. Denn hier ist alles Aug und Ohr. (*Sie wollen in den Palast, Osmin kommt ihnen in der Tür entgegen und hält sie zurück.*)

ZEHNTER AUFTRITT

OSMIN

Wohin?

PEDRILLO

Hinein!

OSMIN (*zu Belmonte*)

Was will das Gesicht? Zurück mit dir, zurück!

PEDRILLO

Ha, gemach, Meister Grobian, gemach! Er ist in des Bassa Diensten.

OSMIN

In des Henkers Diensten mag er sein! Er soll nicht herein!

PEDRILLO

Er soll aber herein!

OSMIN

Kommt mir nur einen Schritt über die Schwelle—

SELIM

How often I've granted you that wish already.

CONSTANZA

Just one more time.

SELIM

So be it, for the last time. Go, Constanza, go! Choose the better, and tomorrow —

CONSTANZA (*leaving*)

Unlucky girl! O Belmonte, Belmonte!

SCENE 8

SELIM

Her pain, her tears, her constancy enchant my heart more and more, make her love more desirable. Who can use power against such a heart? No, Constanza, no. Selim, too, has a heart, and Selim knows love.

PEDRILLO

Lord, forgive me for daring to intrude into your meditations.

SELIM

What do you want, Pedrillo?

PEDRILLO

This young man, an architect, who has been working diligently at his profession in Italy, has heard of your power and your wealth and has come to offer you his services.

BELMONTE

Lord, if I could be so lucky as to offer you my small talents.

SELIM

Hm. You please me. I will see what you can do. (*to Pedrillo*) Take care of his needs. Tomorrow I will call you. (*Exit.*)

SCENE 9

PEDRILLO

Oh, triumph, triumph, Master. The first step has been taken.

BELMONTE

Oh, let me awaken. I have seen her, have seen the good, true, fine girl. O, Constanza, Constanza! What can't I do for you, dare for you?

PEDRILLO

Easy, easy, dear Master. Calm down a little. A little pretending will stand us in good stead here. We aren't at home. Here they ask the hangman whether one head more or less in the world makes any difference. The bastinado and a rope around the neck are as common here as breakfast.

BELMONTE

O, Pedrillo, if you knew love!

PEDRILLO

Hm! As if that weren't anything to people like me! I have my tender hours just like other people. And don't you think that it irritates me, too, when I see my Blonda with that old rascal Osmin?

BELMONTE

If it were only possible to speak to her —

PEDRILLO

We will see what there is to do. Come with me into the garden. But be careful, for here everything is eyes and ears. (*They start to go into the palace but Osmin stops them.*)

SCENE 10

OSMIN

Where are you going?

PEDRILLO

Inside!

OSMIN (*to Belmonte*)

Who is that? Back with you, back!

PEDRILLO

Easy, grouchy, easy. He is in the Master's service.

OSMIN

I don't care if he's in the hangman's service. He won't come in.

PEDRILLO

He will come in.

OSMIN

Just come one step over the threshold —

BELMONTE
Unverschämter! Hast du nicht mehr
Achtung für einen Mann meines
Standes?

OSMIN
Ei, Ihr mögt mir vom Stande sein!
Fort, fort, oder ich will euch Beine
machen.

PEDRILLO
Alter Dummkopf! Es ist ja der Baumeister, den der Bassa angenommen
hat.

OSMIN
Meinethalben sei er Stockmeister, nur
komm er mir nicht zu nahe. Ich
müsste nicht sehen, dass es so ein
Kumpan deines Gelichters ist, und
dass das so eine abgeredete Karte ist,
uns zu überlisten. Der Bassa ist weich
wie Butter, mit dem könnt ihr
machen was ihr wollt, aber ich habe
eine feine Nase. Gaunerei ist's um
den ganzen Kram,.mit euch fremden
Gesindel; und ihr abgefeimten Be-
trüger habt lange ein Plänchen angelegt, eure Pfiffe auszuführen; aber
wart ein bisschen! Osmin schläft
nicht. Wär ich Bassa, ihr wär't
längst gespiesst. Ja, schneid't nur Gesichter, lacht nur höhnisch in den
Bart hinein!

PEDRILLO
Ereifere dich nicht so, Alter, es hilft
dir doch nichts. Sieh, soeben werden
wir hinein spazieren.

OSMIN
Ha, das will ich sehen!
(*Stellt sich vor die Tür*)

PEDRILLO
Mach keine Umstände.

BELMONTE
Weg, Niederträchtiger!

7. TERZETT

OSMIN
Marsch! marsch! marsch! trollt euch
fort,
Sonst soll die Bastonade
Euch gleich zu Diensten steh'n.

BELMONTE
Ei, ei, ei, das wär ja Schade,
Mit uns so umzugeh'n.

OSMIN
Kommt nur nicht näher.

PEDRILLO und BELMONTE
Weg von der Türe.

OSMIN
Sonst schlag' ich drein!

PEDRILLO und BELMONTE
Wir geh'n hinein!

OSMIN
Marsch! fort, marsch! fort, marsch!
fort!

PEDRILLO und BELMONTE
Platz! fort! Platz! fort! Platz! fort!
Wir geh'n hinein!

OSMIN
Sonst schlag' ich drein!

PEDRILLO und BELMONTE
Platz! fort, fort, fort, fort, fort!

OSMIN
Marsch! fort, fort, fort, fort, fort!

PEDRILLO und BELMONTE
Wir geh'n hinein!

OSMIN
Marsch, marsch!
(*Stossen Osmin fort und gehen hinein.*)

ZWEITER AUFZUG
(*Garten am Palast des Bassa Selim; an
der Seite Osmin's Wohnung.*)

ERSTER AUFTRITT
Dialog

BLONDE
O des Zankens, Befehlens und Murrens
wird auch kein Ende! Einmal für
allemal: das steht mir nicht an!
Denkst du alter Murrkopf etwa eine
türkische Sklavin vor dir zu haben,
die bei deinen Befehlen zittert! O da
irrst du dich sehr! Mit europäischen
Mädchen springt man nicht so herum; denen begegnet man ganz anders.

8. Arie
Durch Zärtlichkeit und Schmeicheln,
Gefälligkeit und Scherzen
Erobert man die Herzen
Der guten Mädchen leicht.
Doch mürrisches Befehlen,
Und Poltern, Zanken, Plagen
Macht, dass in wenig Tagen
So Lieb' als Treu' entweicht.

Dialog

OSMIN
Ei seht doch mal, was das Mädchen
vorschreiben kann! Zärtlichkeit?
Schmeicheln? Es ist mir wie pure
Zärtlichkeit! Wer Teufel hat dir das
Zeug in den Kopf gesetzt? Hier sind
wir in der Türkei, und da geht's aus
einem andern Tone. Ich dein Herr,
du meine Sklavin; ich befehle, du
musst gehorchen!

BELMONTE

Shameless! Don't you have any respect for a man of my station?

OSMIN

I don't care about your station. Go on or I'll give you wings.

PEDRILLO

Stupid old man. He is the architect the Pasha has just hired.

OSMIN

I don't care what he is, but don't let him come too close. I see that he came out of the same mold as you and that you'll make trouble. The Pasha is soft as butter and you can do what you want with him, but I'm more careful. You're a swindler, you and your foreign friend, and you have a plan to cheat us, but wait a while. Osmin isn't asleep. If I were the Pasha I would have got rid of you long ago. Sure, you can make faces and sneer.

PEDRILLO

Don't get so excited, old man, it doesn't help. See, we just want to go in.

OSMIN

We'll see about that. (*stands in front of the door*)

PEDRILLO

Step aside!

BELMONTE

Out of the way, scoundrel!

No. 7. Trio

OSMIN (*singing*)

March, march, march!
Now get out or soon you will be feeling
The lashing of my whip.

BELMONTE AND PEDRILLO

Ay! Ay! Ay!
'Twould be a pity
If we should feel your whip.

OSMIN

Do not come near me.

BELMONTE AND PEDRILLO

Then leave the doorway.

OSMIN

Do not come near me
Or I'll let fly.

BELMONTE AND PEDRILLO

We're going in.

OSMIN

March off, march off, march off!

BELMONTE AND PEDRILLO

Move on, move on, move on!
We're going in.
(*They push Osmin aside and enter the palace.*)

ACT TWO

SCENE I

The garden of the palace of Pasha Selim. On one side, Osmin's house.

SCENE 1

Dialogue

BLONDA

There isn't any end to the quarrels, orders and grumbling. Once and for all, it doesn't please me. Do you think, old Grouch, that you have a Turkish slave here who trembles at your command? You're very wrong. With European girls you don't act that way. One treats them quite differently.

No. 8. Aria

With tenderness and coaxing,
Devoted love and rapture,
A man will surely capture
A gentle maiden's heart.
But selfish spite and rudeness,
Abusive, vulgar crudeness
Without doubt will make you suffer
And drive true love away.
With tenderness and coaxing,
Devoted love and rapture,
A man will surely capture
A gentle maiden's heart.

Dialogue

OSMIN

Just listen to what the girl suggests. Tenderness. Coaxing. I'm tender enough. What devil put this rubbish in your head? Here in Turkey we sing another tune. I am the master, you the slave. I command, you obey.

BLONDE

Deine Sklavin? Ich deine Sklavin? Ha, ein Mädchen eine Sklavin! Noch einmal sag mir das, noch einmal!

OSMIN (*für sich*)

Ich möchte toll werden, was das Mädchen für ein starrköpfiges Ding ist. (*laut*) Du hast doch wohl nicht vergessen, dass dich der Bassa mir zur Sklavin geschenkt hat?

BLONDE

Bassa hin, Bassa her! Mädchen sind keine Ware zum verschenken! Ich bin eine Engländerin, zur Freiheit geboren und trotz jedem, der mich zu etwas zwingen will!

OSMIN (*beiseite*)

Gift und Dolch über das Mädchen! Beim Mahomet, sie macht mich rasend. Und doch lieb ich die Spitzbübin, trotz ihres tollen Kopfes! (*laut*) Ich befehle dir, augenblicklich mich zu lieben!

BLONDE

Ha ha ha! Komm mir nur ein wenig näher, ich will dir fühlbare Beweise davon geben.

OSMIN

Tolles Ding! Weisst du, dass du mein bist und ich dich dafür züchtigen kann?

BLONDE

Wag's nicht, mich anzurühren, wenn dir deine Augen lieb sind.

OSMIN

Wie? Du unterstehst dich—

BLONDE

Da ist was zu unterstehen! Du bist der Unverschämte, der sich zuviel Freiheit herausnimmt. So ein altes hässliches Gesicht untersteht sich, einem Mädchen wie ich, jung, schön, zur Freude geboren, wie einer Magd zu befehlen! Wahrhaftig, das stünde mir an! Uns gehört das Regiment; ihr seid unsere Sklaven und glücklich, wenn ihr Verstand genug habt, euch die Ketten zu erleichtern.

OSMIN

Bei meinem Bart, sie ist toll! Hier in der Türkei?

BLONDE

Türkei hin, Türkei her! Weib ist Weib, sie sei wo sie wolle! Sind eure Weiber solche Närrinnen, sich von euch unterjochen zu lassen, desto schlimmer für sie; in Europa verstehen sie das Ding besser. Lass mich nur einmal Fuss hier gefasst haben, sie sollen bald anders werden.

OSMIN

Beim Allah, die wär imstande, uns allen die Weiber rebellisch zu machen!

BLONDE

Aufs Bitten müsst ihr euch legen, wenn ihr etwas von uns erhalten wollt; besonders Liebhaber deines Gelichters.

OSMIN

Freilich, wenn ich Pedrillo wär, so ein Drahtpüppchen wie er, da wär ich vermutlich willkommen, denn euer Mienenspiel hab ich lange weg.

BLONDE

Erraten, guter Alter, erraten! Das kannst du dir wohl einbilden, dass mir der niedliche Pedrillo lieber ist, wie dein Blasebalggesicht. Also wenn du klug wärst—

OSMIN

Sollt ich dir die Freiheit geben, zu tun und zu machen, was du wolltest, he?

BLONDE

Besser würdest du immer dabei fahren: denn so wirst du sicher betrogen.

OSMIN

Gift und Dolch! Nun reisst mir die Geduld! Den Augenblick hinein ins Haus! Und wenn du's wagst——

BLONDE

Mach mich nicht lachen.

OSMIN

Ins Haus, sag ich!

BLONDE

Nicht von der Stelle!

OSMIN

Mach nicht, dass ich Gewalt brauche.

BLONDE

Gewalt werd ich mit Gewalt vertreiben. Meine Gebieterin hat mich hier in den Garten bestellt; sie ist die Geliebte des Bassa, sein Augapfel, sein alles; und es kostet mich ein Wort, so hast du fünfzig auf die Fussohlen. Also geh!

OSMIN (*für sich*)

Das ist ein Satan! Ich muss nachgeben, so wahr ich ein Muselmann bin; sonst könnte ihre Drohung eintreffen.

BLONDA

Your slave? *Me,* your slave? A girl a slave? Tell me again, just tell me once more.

OSMIN (*to himself*)

Her stubborness will drive me crazy. (*aloud*) You haven't forgotten that the Pasha gave you to me as a slave.

BLONDA

Pasha this, Pasha that! Girls aren't wares to be peddled. I am an Englishwoman, born to freedom, and despite everything no one can force me to do anything.

OSMIN (*aside*)

Poison and daggers for the girl! By Mohammed, she drives me wild. But I love the rascal, despite her stubbornness. (*aloud*) I command you to fall in love with me this instant.

BLONDA

Ha! Come a little closer and I'll give you proof of my love.

OSMIN

Crazy thing! Do you know that you are mine and I can punish you?

BLONDA

Don't try it, don't get me angry if you value your eyes.

OSMIN

What? You dare to —

BLONDA

What is there to dare? You're shameless and take too much freedom. Does an ugly old face like you dare to order me — young, beautiful, born free — around like a servant? Wouldn't that be nice? We are in command, you are our slaves, and you're lucky if you have enough sense to make your chains lighter.

OSMIN

By my beard, she's insane. Here, here in Turkey—

BLONDA

Turkey here, Turkey there. A woman is a woman anywhere. If your wives are stupid enough to let themselves live under a yoke, so much the worse for them. In Europe we understand

this thing better. Just let me get started here and things will soon be different.

OSMIN

By Allah, she's capable of making all our women rebellious. But —

BLONDA

If you want something you have to come begging. Especially lovers like you.

OSMIN

Truly, if I were a puppet like Pedrillo, I would be welcome. I've watched you two for a long time.

BLONDA

True, old man, true. You can be sure that handsome Pedrillo is dearer to me than an old bellows-face like you. And if you're smart —

OSMIN

I should give your freedom to do what you want?

BLONDA

You'd do better by it, because you're surely going to be deceived.

OSMIN

Poison and daggers! Now my patience is over. Get into the house this minute. And if you dare —

BLONDA

Don't make me laugh.

OSMIN

Into the house, I say.

BLONDA

I won't move from this spot.

OSMIN

Don't make me force you.

BLONDA

I'll meet force with force. My Mistress ordered me here to the garden. She is the Pasha's beloved, the apple of his eye, his everything. One word from me will bring you fifty lashes on the soles of your feet. Now go!

OSMIN (*to himself*)

She's a devil. I must give in, as I'm a Moslem, or she can make her threats come true.

9. Duett

Ich gehe, doch rate ich dir,
Den Schurken Pedrillo zu meiden,
Den Schurken Pedrillo zu meiden.

BLONDE

Fort, pack' dich, befiehl nicht mit mir,
Du weisst ja, ich kann es nicht leiden,
Du weisst ja, ich kann es nicht leiden.

OSMIN

Versprich mir!

BLONDE

Was fällt dir da ein!
Fort, lass mich allein!

OSMIN

Zum Henker!
Beim Allah! ich werde nicht gehen,
Bis du zu gehorchen mir schwörst.

BLONDE

Nicht so viel, das sollst du bald sehen,
Und wenn du der Grossmogul wärst.

OSMIN

O Engländer! seid ihr nicht Toren,
Ihr lasst euern Weibern den Willen!

BLONDE

Ein Mädchen zur Freiheit geboren,
Lässt nie sich als Sklavin befehlen:
Und ist auch die Freiheit verloren,
Doch bleibt sie noch Fürstin der Welt.

OSMIN

Wie ist man geplagt und geschoren,
Wenn man so ein Früchtchen erhält!

BLONDE

Nun troll' dich.

OSMIN

So sprichst du mit mir?

BLONDE

Nicht anders!

OSMIN

Nun, bleib' ich erst hier.

BLONDE

Ein andermal, jetzt musst du gehen!

OSMIN

Wer hat solche Frechheit gesehen!

BLONDE

Es ist um die Augen geschehen
Wofern du noch länger verweilst.

OSMIN

Nur ruhig, ich will ja gern gehen,
Bevor du gar Schläge erteilst.
(*Osmin geht ab. Constanze kommt
langsam heran.*)

ZWEITER AUFTRITT

Dialog

BLONDE

Wie traurig das gute Mädchen daher
kommt! Freilich tut's weh, den Geliebten zu verlieren und Sklavin zu
sein. Es geht mir wohl auch nicht viel
besser; aber ich habe doch noch das
Vergnügen, meinen Pedrillo manchmal zu sehen, ob's gleich auch mager
und verstohlen genug geschehen
muss; doch wer kann wider den
Strom schwimmen!

10. Rezitativ und Arie

CONSTANZE

Welcher Kummer herrscht in meiner
Seele
Seit dem Tag, da ich mein Glück
verloren!
O Belmont! hin sind die Freuden,
Die ich ach! an deiner Seite kannte;
Banger Sehnsucht Leiden,
Wohnen nun dafür
In der beklemmten Brust.
Traurigkeit ward mir zum Lose,
Weil ich dir entrissen bin.
Gleich der wurmzernagten Rose
Gleich dem Gras im Wintermoose
Welkt mein banges Leben hin.
Selbst der Luft darf ich nicht sagen
Meiner Seele bittern Schmerz.
Denn unwillig ihn zu tragen,
Haucht sie alle meine Klagen
Wieder in mein armes Herz.

Dialog

BLONDE

Ach mein bestes Fräulein, noch immer
so traurig?

CONSTANZE

Kannst du fragen, die du meinen Kummer weisst? Wieder ein Abend, und
noch keine Nachricht, noch keine
Hoffnung! Und morgen — ach Gott,
ich darf nicht daran denken!

BLONDE

Heitern Sie sich wenigstens ein bisschen
auf. Sehn Sie, wie schön der **Abend**
ist, wie blühend uns alles entgegen-

No. 9. Duet

OSMIN (*singing*)
I'm going, but listen to me.
Stay away from that rascal Pedrillo.

BLONDA
I will not obey your command.
You know that I cannot abide you.
Your mind's gone astray.
Go leave me, I say.

OSMIN
You promised. O hang it!
By Allah, I swear I won't go now,
Not until you swear to obey.

BLONDA
I swear it, I swear it, I swear it!
I swear that I'll never obey you,
Not if you were Allah himself.

OSMIN
Oh, Englishmen, you are misguided
In granting your women such station.

BLONDA
A girl who by freedom is guided
Will never submit to dictation.
However my fate be decided,
Still I am proud, proud and unbowed.

OSMIN
And how you are duped and derided
When such disrespect is allowed.

BLONDA
Be off now.

OSMIN
You say that to me?

BLONDA
You heard me.

OSMIN
I'll stay where I am.

BLONDA (*pushes him*)
I tell you again you must leave me.

OSMIN
Her freshness and impudence peeve
me.

BLONDA

(*pretends to attack him*)

I'll scratch out your eyes if you stay
here.
I warn you, it's time to depart.

OSMIN (*timidly retiring*)
Excuse me, I think I'll be going
Before you get off to a start.

(*hurries out*)

SCENE 2

Dialogue

BLONDA
How sad the good maiden looks as she
comes. Indeed it's hard to lose your
lover and to become a slave. And
it doesn't fare much better for me.
But, at least, I have the pleasure
once in a while of seeing my Pedrillo,
even if it doesn't happen often and
the moments have to be stolen. But
who can swim against the tide?

No. 10. Recitative and Aria

CONSTANZA (*singing*)
Ah, what sorrow fills my soul and spirit
Since the day that he and I were
parted.
O, Belmonte, gone are the pleasures
And the joy I knew
When you were with me.
Only grief and sadness
Take the place of love
In my unhappy heart.
Loneliness fills me with longing
While afar from you I stay.
Like a wilted, withered flower,
Like the grass in wintry hour,
Fades my lonely life away.
Yet the breezes keep denying
All my sorrow's bitter pain,
And the breezes with their sighing
Just return my bitter crying
To my aching heart again.

Dialogue

BLONDA
O, my dear lady. Still so sad?

CONSTANZA
Can you ask, you who know my sorrow? Another evening, and still no
news, no hope. And in the morning
— Oh God, I don't dare think about
that.

BLONDA
At least be a little more cheerful. See
what a beautiful evening it is, how
everything in bloom smiles, how the

lacht, wie freudig uns die Vögel zu ihrem Gesang einladen! Verbannen Sie die Grillen, und fassen Sie Mut!

CONSTANZE

Wie glücklich bist du, Mädchen, bei deinem Schicksal so gelassen zu sein! O dass ich es auch könnte!

BLONDE

Das steht nur bei Ihnen, hoffen Sie—

CONSTANZE

Wo nicht der mindeste Schein von Hoffnung mehr zu erblicken ist?

BLONDE

Hören Sie nur: ich verzage mein Lebtag nicht, es mag auch eine Sache noch so schlimm aussehen. Denn wer sich immer das Schlimmste vorstellt, ist auch wahrhaftig am schlimmsten dran.

CONSTANZE

Und wer sich immer mit Hoffnung schmeichelt und zuletzt betrogen sieht, hat alsdann nichts mehr übrig als die Verzweiflung.

BLONDE

Jedes nach seiner Weise. Ich glaube bei der meinigen am besten zu fahren. Wie bald kann Ihr Belmonte mit Lösegeld erscheinen oder uns listiger Weise entführen? Wären wir die ersten Frauenzimmer, die den türkischen Vielfrassen entkämen? Dort seh ich den Bassa.

CONSTANZE

Lass uns ihm aus den Augen gehn.

BLONDE

Zu spät. Er hat Sie schon gesehen. Ich darf aber getrost aus dem Wege trollen, er schaffte mich ohnehin fort. (*im Weggehen*) Courage, wir kommen gewiss noch in unsre Heimat! (*Bassa Selim kommt herein.*)

BASSA SELIM

Nun, Constanze, denkst du meinem Begehren nach? Der Tag ist bald verstrichen. Morgen musst du mich lieben, oder—

CONSTANZE

Muss? Welch albernes Begehren! Als ob man die Liebe anbefehlen könnte wie eine Tracht Schläge! Aber freilich, wie ihr Türken zu Werke geht, lässt sich's auch allenfalls befehlen. Aber ihr seid wirkich zu beklagen. Ihr kerkert die Gegenstände eurer Begierden ein und seid zufrieden, eure Lüste zu büssen.

BASSA SELIM

Und glaubst du etwa, unsere Weiber wären weniger glücklich als in euren Ländern?

CONSTANZE

Die nichts besseres kennen!

BASSA SELIM

Auf diese Art wäre wohl keine Hoffnung, dass du je anders denken wirst.

CONSTANZE

Herr! Ich muss dir frei gestehen, denn was soll ich dich länger hinhalten, mich mit leerer Hoffnung schmeicheln, dass du dich durch mein Bitten erweichen liessest, ich werde stets so denken wie jetzt: dich verehren, aber—lieben? Nie!

BASSA SELIM

Und du zitterst nicht vor der Gewalt, die ich über dich habe?

CONSTANZE

Nicht im geringsten. Sterben ist alles, was ich zu erwarten habe, und je eher dies geschieht, je lieber wird es mir sein.

BASSA SELIM

Elende! Nein! Nicht sterben, aber Martern von allen Arten—

CONSTANZE

Auch die will ich ertragen: du schreckst mich nicht, ich erwarte alles.

11. Arie

Martern aller Arten, aller Arten
Mögen meiner warten,
Ich verlache Qual und Pein.
Nichts, nichts
Soll mich erschüttern,
Nur dann, würd' ich zittern,
Wenn ich untreu,
Untreu könnte sein.
Lass dich bewegen,
Verschone mich,
Des Himmels Segen
Belohne dich!
Doch dich rührt kein Flehen,
Standhaft, sollst du sehen,
Duld' ich jede Qual und Not.
Ordne nur, gebiete,
Drohe, strafe, wüte,
Zuletzt befreit mich doch der Tod.

(*Entfernt sich.*)

birds invite us with their joyous song. Throw away your cares and take courage.

CONSTANZA

How lucky you are, girl, to take your fate so calmly. If I only could.

BLONDA

That remains up to you. If you hope —

CONSTANZA

Where there isn't even a ray of hope?

BLONDA

Listen to me. I never give up hope, no matter how slim it seems. Who always sees things in the worst light is the worst off.

CONSTANZA

And who deceives himself with hope and is at last betrayed by it has nothing but despair in the end.

BLONDA

Everyone to his taste. I believe my way is best. How soon can Belmonte appear with ransom money, or free us by some ruse? Are we the first women to escape from a Turkish harem? I see the Pasha.

CONSTANZA

Let's escape his notice.

BLONDA

Too late. He has seen us. I'd better go, he'll only send me away anyhow. (while leaving) Courage, we'll soon be home again.

SCENE 3

SELIM

Now, Constanza, have you thought it over? The day is almost gone. Tomorrow you must love me, or —

CONSTANZA

Must? How stupid. As if you could order love the way you order a beating. But maybe the way you Turks work you can do that. But you are really to be pitied. You pen up your sweethearts and are just satisfied to fulfill your desires.

SELIM

And do you think our women are less lucky than those in other lands?

CONSTANZA

They don't know any better.

SELIM

In this way there is no hope that you'll ever think differently.

CONSTANZA

Lord, I must tell you, and why should I hold it back anymore, I can't flatter myself that you'll weaken through my pleas. I will always think as I do. I will honor you, but love you — never.

SELIM

You don't tremble before the power I hold over you?

CONSTANZA

Not in the least. Death is the only thing I have to wait for, and the sooner it comes the better.

SELIM

Death? Never. But tortures past endurance.

CONSTANZA

I will bear them, too. You don't frighten me. I await anything.

No. 11. Aria

CONSTANZA (singing)

Tortures past endurance
I will brave with assurance.
I defy them, I defy them.
I defy the pangs of pain.
No, no, no. Nothing shakes my purpose.
But then, ah then,
Would I tremble if I failed him,
If I were untrue.
Then I would tremble.
Oh, grant your mercy,
Great is my need.
May heaven's blessing
Reward your deed.
If you will not spare me
Willing, clear of vision,
I await no grace from you.
Order me. Command me.
Torture. Threaten. Thunder.
At last in death I shall be free.

(Exit.)

VIERTER AUFTRITT

BASSA SELIM

Ist das ein Traum? Wo hat sie auf einmal den Mut her, sich so gegen mich zu betragen? Hat sie vielleicht Hoffnung, mir zu entkommen? Ha, das will ich verwehren! (*will fort*) Doch das ist's nicht, dann würde sie sich eher verstellen, mich einzuschläfern suchen. Ja, es ist Verzweiflung! Mit Härte richt ich nichts aus, mit Bitten auch nicht, also, was Drohen und Bitten nicht vermögen, soll die List zuwege bringen. (*Bassa Selim geht ab.*)

FÜNFTER AUFTRITT

BLONDE

Kein Bassa, keine Constanze mehr da? Sind sie miteinander eins worden? Schwerlich, das gute Kind hängt zu sehr an ihrem Belmonte! Ich bedaure sie von Grund meines Herzens. Sie ist zu empfindsam für ihre Lage. Freilich, hätt ich meinen Pedrillo nicht an der Seite, wer weiss, wie mir's ginge! Doch würd ich nicht so zärteln wie sie. Die Männer verdienen wahrlich nicht, dass man ihrethalben sich zu Tode grämt. Vielleicht würd ich muselmännisch denken.

SECHSTER AUFTRITT

PEDRILLO

Pst, pst! Blondchen! Ist der Weg rein?

BLONDE

Komm nur, komm! Der Bassa ist wieder zurück. Und meinem Alten habe ich eben den Kopf ein bisschen gewaschen. Was hast du denn?

PEDRILLO

O Neuigkeiten, Neuigkeiten, die dich entzücken werden.

BLONDE

Nun? Hurtig heraus damit!

PEDRILLO

Erst, liebes Herzens-Blondchen, lass dir vor allen Dingen einen recht herzlichen Kuss geben; du weisst ja, wie gestohlnes Gut schmeckt.

BLONDE

Pfui, pfui! Wenn das deine Neuigkeiten alle sind.

PEDRILLO

Närrchen, mach darum keinen Lärm, der alte spitzbübische Osmin lauert uns sicher auf den Dienst.

BLONDE

Nun? Und die Neuigkeiten?

PEDRILLO

Sind, dass das Ende unserer Sklaverei vor der Tür ist. (*Er sieht sich vorsichtig um*) Belmonte, Constanzes Geliebter, ist angekommen, und ich hab ihn unter dem Namen eines Baumeisters hier im Palast eingeführt.

BLONDE

Ah, was sagst du? Belmonte da?

PEDRILLO

Mit Leib und Seele!

BLONDE

Ha, das muss Constanze wissen! (*Will fort*)

PEDRILLO

Hör nur, Blondchen, hör nur erst: Er hat ein Schiff hier in der Nähe in Bereitschaft, und wir haben beschlossen, euch diese Nacht zu entführen.

BLONDE

O allerliebst, allerliebst! Herzens-Pedrillo, das verdient einen Kuss! Geschwind, geschwind zu Constanze! (*Will fort*)

PEDRILLO

Halt nur, halt, und lass erst mit dir reden. Um Mitternacht kommt Belmonte mit einer Leiter zu Constanzes Fenster, und ich zu dem deinigen, und dann geht's heidi davon!

BLONDE

O vortrefflich! Aber Osmin?

PEDRILLO

Hier ist ein Schlaftrunk für den alten Schlaukopf, den misch ihm fein manierlich ins Getränk, verstehst du? Ich habe dort auch schon ein Fläschchen angefüllt. Geht's hier nicht, wird's dort wohl gehen.

BLONDE

Sorg nicht für mich! Aber kann Constanze ihren Geliebten nicht sprechen?

PEDRILLO

Sobald es vollends finster ist, kommt er hier in den Garten. Nun geh und bereite Constanze vor; ich will hier Belmonte erwarten. Leb wohl, Herzchen, leb wohl!

BLONDE

Leb wohl, guter Pedrillo! Ach, was werd ich für Freude anrichten! (*Pedrillo geht ab.*)

12. Arie

Welche Wonne, welche Lust
Regt sich nun in meiner Brust!

SCENE 4

Dialogue

SELIM

Is this a dream? Where does she suddenly get the courage to oppose me? Does she perhaps have hopes of escaping? I'll forestall that. (*starts to leave*) No, that can't be, she'd rather pretend to lull me. Yes, it's desperation. With harshness I won't gain anything, or with pleas. So what threats and pleas can't accomplish I'll gain by ruse. (*Exit.*)

SCENE 5

BLONDA (*entering*)

No Pasha and no Constanza? Have they finally agreed? Hardly. She is too devoted to Belmonte. I sympathize with her from the bottom of my heart. She is too sensitive for her situation. If I didn't have my Pedrillo near me who knows what I'd do. I am not as soft as she is. Men don't deserve that we pine away on their account. Perhaps I'm beginning to think like a Moslem.

SCENE 6

PEDRILLO (*entering*)

Pst, Pst, Blonda. Is the way clear?

BLONDA

Come on, come on. The Pasha has gone again. And I scared the old man. What do you have?

PEDRILLO

News. News that will delight you.

BLONDA

What? Tell me quickly.

PEDRILLO

First, dear heart, ahead of everything else, give me a kiss. You know how stolen sweets are.

BLONDA

If that's all the news you have for me —

PEDRILLO

Ninny, don't make any noise. Osmin is probably watching.

BLONDA

What about the news?

PEDRILLO

The end to our slavery is at the door. (*looks around*) Belmonte, Constanza's lover, has come and I brought him to the palace in the disguise of an architect.

BLONDA

What are you saying? Belmonte here?

PEDRILLO

Body and soul.

BLONDA

Constanza should know. (*starts to leave*)

PEDRILLO

Listen to me, Blonda. Hear me first. He has a ship ready nearby and we have decided this is the night to escape.

BLONDA

Wonderful, wonderful. Dear Pedrillo, that deserves a kiss. Hurry, hurry to Constanza. (*starts to leave*)

PEDRILLO

Wait, wait and let me talk to you. At midnight Belmonte will come with a ladder to Constanza's window and I to yours, and then we're off.

BLONDA

Wonderful. But what about Osmin?

PEDRILLO

Here is a sleeping potion for the old dog. Mix it carefully in his drink, do you understand? I also have a flask. If we can't do it one place we'll do it another.

BLONDA

Don't worry about me. But can't Constanza speak to her lover?

PEDRILLO

As soon as it's really dark come here to the garden. Now go and tell Constanza. I'll wait here for Belmonte. Goodbye, dearest, goodbye.

BLONDA

Goodbye, dear Pedrillo. (*He leaves.*) What pleasure I'm going to bring.

No. 12. Aria

(*singing*)

What a pleasure, what relief.
No more mis'ry, no more grief.

Voller Freuden will ich springen,
Ihr die frohe Nachricht bringen,
Und mit Lachen
Und mit Scherzen
Ihrem schwachen, kranken Herzen
Trost und Rettung prophezeih'n.
(*Sie eilt ab.*)

SIEBENTER AUFTRITT
Dialog
PEDRILLO

Ah, dass es schon vorbei wäre! Dass
wir schon auf offner See wären, unsre
Mädels im Arm und dies verwünschte Land im Rücken hätten! Doch
sei's gewagt; entweder jetzt oder
niemals! Wer zagt, verliert!

13. Arie

Frisch zum Kampfe! frisch zum
    Streite!
Nur ein feiger Tropf verzagt.
Sollt' ich zittern?
Sollt' ich zagen?
Nicht mein Leben mutig wagen?
Nein, ach nein, es sei gewagt!
(*Osmin kommt herein.*)

ACHTER AUFTRITT
Dialog
OSMIN

Ha! Gehr's hier so lustig zu? Es muss
dir verteufelt wohl gehen.

PEDRILLO

Ei, wer wird so ein Kopfhänger sein;
es kommt beim Henker dabei nichts
heraus! Das haben die Pedrillos von
jeher in ihrer Familie gehabt. Fröh-
lichkeit und Wein versüsst die här-
teste Sklaverei. Freilich könnt ihr
armen Schlucker das nicht begreifen,
dass es so ein herrlich Ding um ein
Gläschen guten alten Lustigmacher
ist. Wahrhaftig, da hat euer Vater
Mahomet einen verzweifelten Bock
geschossen, dass er euch den Wein
verboten hat. Wenn das verwünschte
Gesetz nicht wäre, du müsstest ein
Gläschen mit mir trinken, du möch-
test wollen oder nicht. (*für sich*)
Vielleicht beisst er an: er trinkt ihn
gar zu gern.

OSMIN

Wein mit dir? Ja, Gift—

PEDRILLO

Immer Gift und Dolch, und Dolch und
Gift! Lass doch den alten Groll einmal fahren und sei vernünftig. Sieh

einmal, ein paar Flaschen **Cyper-
wein**! Ah! Die sollen mir vortrefflich
schmecken!

OSMIN (*für sich*)

Wenn ich trauen dürfte?

PEDRILLO

Das ist ein Wein, das ist ein Wein!
(*Er setzt sich nach türkischer Art auf
die Erde und trinkt aus der kleinen
Flasche.*)

OSMIN

Kost einmal die grosse Flasche auch.

PEDRILLO

Denkst wohl gar, ich habe Gift hinein
getan? Ha, lass dir keine grauen
Haare wachsen! Es verlohnte sich der
Mühe, dass ich deinetwegen zum
Teufel führe. Da sieh, ob ich trinke.
(*Er trinkt aus der grossen Flasche ein
wenig.*) Nun, hast du noch Beden-
ken? Traust mir noch nicht? Pfui,
Osmin, sollst dich schämen! Da
nimm!
(*Er gibt ihm die grosse Flasche.*)
Oder willst du die kleine?

OSMIN

Nein, lass nur, lass nur! Aber wenn du
mich verrätst— (*Sieht sich sorgfäl-
tig um.*)

PEDRILLO

Als wenn wir einander nicht weiter
brauchten. Immer frisch! Mahomet
liegt längst auf'm Ohr und hat nö-
tiger zu tun, als sich um deine
Flasche Wein zu bekümmern.

14. Duett

Vivat Bacchus! Bacchus lebe!
Bacchus war ein braver Mann.

OSMIN

Ob ich's wage? ob ich trinke?
Ob's wohl Allah schen kann?

PEDRILLO

Was hilft das Zaudern?
Hinunter! hinunter!
Nicht lange, nicht lange gefragt!
(OSMIN *trinkt.*)

OSMIN

Nun wär's geschehen!
Nun wär's geschehen!
Dass heiss ich, das heiss ich gewagt.

PEDRILLO und OSMIN

Es leben die Mädchen,
Die Blonden, die Braunen!
Sie leben, sie leben, sie leben hoch!

I could sing it, I could shout it.
I could tell the world about it.
Soon by laughter and by teasing
I will see her burden easing.
We will say goodbye to all our sorrow
When I tell her this great news.
There's no more grief.

(*She leaves and Pedrillo enters.*)

SCENE 7

Dialogue

PEDRILLO

If it were only over. If we were already
on the open sea, our girls in our
arms and this cursed land behind us.
But be brave. Now or never. He
who hesitates is lost.

No. 13. Aria

(*singing*)

Let us go then. Let us show them.
Only cowards are afraid.
Should I tremble?
Should I waver?
Should I risk my neck to save her?
No, ah, no I must be brave.
Let us go then. Let us show them.
Only cowards are afraid.

SCENE 8

Dialogue

OSMIN (*entering*)

Having a good time? You must be
devilishly happy.

PEDRILLO

Who wants to be sad? Happiness and
wine sweeten the hardest slavery. But
you poor people can't understand
what a wonderful thing a glass of
wine is. Truly the Prophet Mohammed was on the wrong track when
he forbade wine. If that silly law
didn't exist you could have a little
glass with me. (*to himself*) Maybe
he'll bite. He'd like a drink.

OSMIN

Wine with you? Yes, poison —

PEDRILLO

Always poison and daggers, daggers
and poison! Forget about your
grudge for once and be sensible.

Look, here are a couple of flasks of
wine from Cyprus. Ah! (*He shows
him two flasks, one larger than the
other.*) These will taste marvelous to
me.

OSMIN (*to himself*)

If I only dared to!

PEDRILLO

What a wine! What a wine! (*sits on
the ground Turkish fashion, and begins to drink from the small flask*)

OSMIN

Drink out of the big one, too.

PEDRILLO

Do you think I've put poison in it?
Don't get any gray hair over it. You
wouldn't be worth going to the devil
over. See how I drink? (*drinks a
little*) Now are you still worried?
Don't you trust me? You should be
ashamed! Here, take it. (*gives him
the large flask*) Or do you want the
small one?

OSMIN

No, no. But if you've tricked me —
(*looks cautiously around*)

PEDRILLO

As if we won't need each other later.
Mohammed has been asleep a long
time and has bigger things to worry
about than a bottle of wine.

No. 14. Duet

PEDRILLO (*singing*)

Viva Bacchus! Long life, Bacchus!
Bacchus was a worthy man.

OSMIN

Should I dare it?
Should I drink it?
What if Allah sees me now?

PEDRILLO

What use delaying?
Now drink it, now drink it,
No longer delaying.

OSMIN (*drinks*)

Now I have done it.
How daring am I!

PEDRILLO AND OSMIN

Long life to the maidens,
The dark ones, the fair ones.
Long life to all.

PEDRILLO

Das schmeckt trefflich!

OSMIN

Das schmeckt herrlich!

PEDRILLO und OSMIN

Ach! das heiss' ich Göttertrank!
Vivat Bacchus, Bacchus lebe,
Bacchus, der den Wein erfand!
Vivat Bacchus, Bacchus lebe,
Es leben die Mädchen,
Die Blonden, die Braunen,
Sie leben hoch!

Dialog

PEDRILLO

Wahrhaftig, das muss ich gestehen, es
geht doch nichts über den Wein!
Wein ist mir lieber, als Geld und
Mädchen. Bin ich verdriesslich, mür-
risch, launisch: hurtig nehm ich
meine Zuflucht zur Flasche, und
kaum seh ich den ersten Boden:
weg ist all mein Verdruss! Meine
Flasche macht mir kein schiefes
Gesicht, wie mein Mädchen, wenn
ihr der Kopf nicht auf dem rechten
Fleck steht. Und schwatzt mir von
Süssigkeiten der Liebe und des Ehe-
standes, was Ihr wollt: Wein auf der
Zunge geht über alles!

OSMIN

(*fängt bereits an, die Wirkung des
Weins und des Schlaftrunks zu
spüren, und wird bis zum Ende des
Auftritts immer schläfriger und
träger, doch darf's der Schauspieler
nicht übertreiben und muss nur immer halb träumend und schlaftrunken bleiben*).
Das ist wahr—Wein—Wein—ist ein
schönes Getränk; und unser grosser
Prophet mag mir's nicht übelnehmen-
Gift und Dolch, es ist doch eine
hübsche Sache um den Wein! Nicht-
Bruder Pedrillo?

PEDRILLO

Richtig, Bruder Osmin, richtig!

OSMIN

Man wird gleich so munter (*er nickt
zuweilen*)—so vergnügt—so aufge-
räumt. Hast du nichts mehr, Bruder?
(*Er langt auf eine lächerliche Art nach
einer zweiten Flasche, die Pedrillo
ihm reicht.*)

PEDRILLO

Hör du, Alter, trink mir nicht zu viel,
es kommt einem in den Kopf.

OSMIN

Trag doch keine—Sorge, ich bin so—

so—nüchtern wie möglich. Aber das
ist wahr (*Er fängt an, auf der Erde
hin und her zu wanken.*) es schmekt
—vortrefflich!

PEDRILLO (*für sich*)

Es wirkt, Alter, es wirkt!

OSMIN

Aber verraten musst du mich nicht,
Brüderchen — verraten — denn —
wenn's Mahomet nein, nein—der
Bassa wüsste—denn siehst du liebes
Blondchen—ja oder nein!

PEDRILLO (*für sich*)

Nun wird's Zeit, ihn fortzuschaffen!
(*laut*) Nun komm, Alter, komm, wir
wollen schlafen gehn!
(*Er hebt ihn auf.*)

OSMIN

Schlafen? Schämst du dich nicht? Gift
und Dolch! Wer wird denn so
schläfrig sein—es ist ja kaum Morgen!

PEDRILLO

Ho, ho, die Sonne ist schon hinunter!
Komm, komm, dass uns der Bassa
nicht überrascht!

OSMIN (*im Abführen.*)

Ja, ja—eine Flasche, guter Bassa, geht
über alles! Gute Nacht, Brüderchen,
gute Nacht.
(*Pedrillo führt ihn hinein, kommt aber
gleich wieder zurück.*)

PEDRILLO (*macht's Osmin nach*)

Gute Nacht, Brüderchen, gute Nacht!
Hahahaha, alter Eisenfresser, erwischt man dich so? Gift und Dolch!
Du hast deine Ladung! Nur fürcht
ich, ist's noch zu zeitig am Tage; bis
Mitternacht sind noch drei Stunden,
und da könnt er leicht wieder aus-
geschlafen haben. Ach, kommen Sie,
kommen Sie, liebster Herr! Unser
Argus ist blind, ich hab ihn tüchtig
zugedeckt.
(*Belmonte kommt herein.*)

BELMONTE

O dass wir glücklich wären! Aber sag:
ist Constanze noch nicht hier?

PEDRILLO

Eben kommt sie da den Gang herauf.
Reden Sie alles mit ihr ab, aber fassen Sie sich kurz, denn der Verräter
schläft nicht immer.
(*Während der Unterredung des Belmonte mit Constanze unterhält sich
Pedrillo mit Blonde, der er durch
Pantomime den ganzen Auftritt mit
dem Osmin vormacht und jenem*)

PEDRILLO

What a flavor!

OSMIN

How delicious!

PEDRILLO AND OSMIN

Ah, this is a god-like wine.
Viva Bacchus! Long life, Bacchus!
For he first discovered wine.

Dialogue

PEDRILLO

I have to say truly there is nothing
better than wine. I love wine more
than money or women. If I'm annoyed, grouchy, bad tempered, I take
refuge in the bottle and all my
troubles are gone. Wine doesn't make
faces at me like a woman does if
something goes wrong. And talk to
me all you want about love and
faithfulness, wine on the tongue is
better than anything else.

OSMIN

(*He begins to feel the effects of the
wine and the sleeping potion. Until
the end of the act he gets sleepier
and sadder.*)

That's true. Wine — wine is a beautiful drink. And, may the Great
Prophet not take it amiss, wine is a
great thing, isn't it, Brother Pedrillo?

PEDRILLO

Right, Brother Osmin, right.

OSMIN

One becomes so lively, (*begins to nod*)
so merry. Do you have more,
Brother? (*reaches ridiculously toward the second bottle, which Pedrillo gives to him.*)

PEDRILLO

Listen, old man, don't drink too much.
It goes to your head.

OSMIN

Don't worry. I'm as sober as I ever
was. But it's true. (*begins to rock
back and forth on the ground*) It
tastes wonderful.

PEDRILLO (*to himself*)

It's working, old man, it's working.

OSMIN

But don't betray me, Little Brother,
for if Mohammed — no, no, — if the
Pasha knew — that you see Blonda,
yes or no —

PEDRILLO (*to himself*)

Now to finish it. (*aloud*) Come, old
man, we should go to sleep. (*lifts
him up*)

OSMIN

Sleep? Aren't you ashamed? Poison and
daggers! Who can be so sleepy —
it isn't even morning —

PEDRILLO

The sun has set already. Come, come,
so the Pasha doesn't catch us.

OSMIN

(*while being taken away*)

Yes, yes — a bottle — good Pasha — is
better — than anything. Good night,
Little Brother. Good night. (*Pedrillo
takes him off but comes right back.*)

SCENE 9

PEDRILLO (*imitating Osmin*)

Good night, Little Brother, good night.
Is that the way one catches you?
Poison and daggers! You're loaded.
But I'm afraid it's too early. It's still
three hours to midnight and maybe
he'll sleep it off. Come, come, dear
Master. Our Argus is blind. I tucked
him in.

BELMONTE (*enters*)

How lucky we are! But tell me, isn't
Constanza here yet?

PEDRILLO

She's coming down the pathway. Tell
her everything, but make it short,
the old man won't sleep forever.
(*During the scene between Belmonte
and Constanza Pedrillo talks to
Blonda and through pantomime tells
her the whole story of Osmin, ending with the fact that at midnight
he will bring a ladder to her window
to carry her off.*)

CONSTANZA

(*rushes to his arms*)

O my Belmonte!

*nachahmt; zuletzt unterrichtet er sie
ebenfalls, dass er um Mitternacht
mit einer Leiter unter ihr Fenster
kommen wolle, um sie zu entführen.)*

CONSTANZE

O mein Belmonte!

BELMONTE

O Constanze!
(Einander im Arm.)

CONSTANZE

Ist's möglich? Nach so viel Tagen der
Angst, nach so viel ausgestandenen
Leiden, dich wieder in meinen Ar-
men.

BELMONTE

O dieser Augenblick versüsst allen
Kummer, macht mich all meinen
Schmerz vergessen.

CONSTANZE

Hier will ich an deinem Busen liegen
und weinen! Ach, jetzt fühl ich's, die
Freude hat auch ihre Tränen.

15. Arie

BELMONTE

Wenn der Freude Tränen fliessen,
Lächelt Liebe dem Geliebten hold;
Von den Wangen sie zu küssen,
Ist der Liebe, schönster, grösster Sold.
Ach Constanze! dich zu sehen,
Dich voll Wonne, voll Entzücken
An dies treue Herz zu drücken,
Lohnet mir nicht Kron' und Pracht.
Ha! dieses sel'ge Wiederfinden,
Lässt innig erst mich ganz empfinden
Welchen Schmerz die Trennung macht.

16. Quartett

CONSTANZE

Ach Belmonte! ach mein Leben!

BELMONTE

Ach Constanze, ach mein Leben!

CONSTANZE

Ist es möglich? welch Entzücken!
Dich an meine Brust zu drücken,
Nach so vieler Tage Leid!

BELMONTE

Welche Wonne, dich zu finden!
Nun muss aller Kummer schwinden,
O wie ist mein Herz erfreut!

CONSTANZE

Sich' die Freudentränen fliessen!

BELMONTE

Holde, lass hinweg sie küssen!

CONSTANZE

Dass es doch die letzte sei.

BELMONTE

Ja, noch heute wirst du frei!

PEDRILLO

Also, Blondchen, hast's verstanden?
Alles ist zur Flucht vorhanden,
Um Schlag zwölfe sind wir da.

BLONDE

Unbesorgt, es wird nichts fehlen,
Die Minuten werd' ich zählen,
Wär der Augenblick schon da!

ALLE

Endlich scheint die Hoffnungssonne
Hell durch's trübe Firmament.
Voll Entzücken,
Freud', und Wonne
Seh'n wir unsrer Leiden End'!

BELMONTE

Doch ach! bei aller Lust
Empfindet meine Brust
Noch manch' geheime Sorgen.

CONSTANZE

Was ist es? Liebster, sprich:
Geschwind, erkläre dich,
O halt' mir nichts verborgen!

BELMONTE

Man sagt du sei'st—

CONSTANZE

Nun weiter!
*(Belmonte and Constanze sehen einan-
der stillschweigend und furchtsam
an.)*

PEDRILLO

Doch Blondchen, ach! die Leiter!
Bist du wohl so viel wert?
*(zeigt, dass er wage gehenkt zu
werden.)*

BLONDE

Hans Narr! schnappt's bei dir über?
Ei, hättest du nur lieber
Die Frage umgekehrt!

PEDRILO

Doch Herr Osmin—

BLONDE

Lass hören!

CONSTANZE *(zu Belmonte)*

Willst du dich nicht erklären?

BELMONTE

O Constanza!

CONSTANZA

Is it possible after so many days of anguish, after so much suffering, to have you in my arms again?

BELMONTE

This moment sweetens any grief, makes me forget my pain.

CONSTANZA

Let me lie here and weep on your bosom. Now I feel it. Joy has its tears, too.

No. 15. Aria

When the tears of bliss are flowing
Love rejoices at the tender sight.
For a kiss through sadness glowing
Is a pleasure born of love's delight.
Ah, Constanza, but to see you
And with rapture to caress you,
To my faithful heart to press you,
Is a prize no gold can buy.
Until the time we find each other
Love has ordained that we discover
All the pain that parting brings.

No. 16. Quartet

CONSTANZA

Ah, ah, Belmonte my dearest.

BELMONTE

Ah, ah, Constanza my dearest.

CONSTANZA

You, my lover! What enchantment!
Once again I can embrace you
After all those days of grief.

BELMONTE

Ah, Constanza, at last I've found you.
Broken are the chains that bound you.
How it throbs, my joyous heart.

CONSTANZA

Now I weep, but weep for gladness.

BELMONTE

Let me kiss away your sadness.

CONSTANZA

Gone is grief forevermore.

BELMONTE

Now we're free to leave this shore.

PEDRILLO

Now, my Blonda, we have done it,
Fought a battle and have won it,
And escaped our friend Osmin.

BLONDA

I was sure from the beginning,
Had no doubt about our winning
From that silly fool, Osmin.

CONSTANZA, BLONDA, BELMONTE
AND PEDRILLO

Rays of hope in fullest measure
Shine through Sorrow's cloudy sky.
Filled with rapture,
Joy and gladness,
We bid all our grief goodbye.

BELMONTE

But yet, I cannot rest.
There burns within my breast
An anguish past believing.

CONSTANZA

What is it, loved one, say?
Confide in me I pray.
Reveal to me your grieving.

BELMONTE

They say — you are —
(*Belmonte and Constanza look at each other quietly and anxiously.*)

CONSTANZA

Pray tell me.

PEDRILLO

But Blonda, ah —
I ask you.
You're sure that you've been true?

BLONDA

What's that? Have you been drinking?
Your question I've been thinking
Applies much more to you.

PEDRILLO

But this Osmin —

BLONDA

What of him?

CONSTANZA

Won't you confide your sorrow?

BELMONTE

They say —you are . . .

CONSTANZA

Continue. Won't you confide your sorrow?

BELMONTE (*zu Constanze*)

Ich will, doch zürne nicht,
Wenn ich nach dem Gerücht,
Das ich gehört,
Es wage, dich zitternd, bebend frage,
Ob du den Bassa liebst?

CONSTANZE

O wie du mich betrübst!

PEDRILLO (*zu Blonde*)

Hat nicht Osmin etwan,
Wie man fast glauben kann,
Sein Recht als Herr probiret
Und bei dir exerciret?
Dann wär's ein schlechter Kauf!

BLONDE (*gibt ihm eine Ohrfeige*)

Da nimm die Antwort drauf!

PEDRILLO

Nun bin ich aufgeklärt!

BELMONTE

Constanze, ach vergib!

BLONDE (*zu Pedrillo*)

Du bist mich gar nicht wert!

CONSTANZE (*zu Belmonte*)

Ob ich dir treu verblieb?

BLONDE (*zu Constanze*)

Der Schlingel fragt gar an,
Ob ich ihm treu geblieben?

CONSTANZE (*zu Blonde*)

Dem Belmont sagte man,
Ich soll den Bassa lieben!

PEDRILLO

Dass Blonde ehrlich sei,
Schwör' ich bei allen Teufeln!

BELMONTE

Constanze ist mir treu,
Daran ist nicht zu zweifeln.

CONSTANZE und BLONDE

Wenn unsrer Ehre wegen
Die Männer Argwohn hegen,
Verdächtig auf uns seh'n,
Das ist nicht auszusteh'n.

BELMONTE und PEDRILLO

Sobald sich Weiber kränken,
Dass wir sie untreu denken,
Dann sind sie wahrhaft treu,
Von allem Vorwurf frei.

PEDRILLO

Liebstes Blondchen! ach verzeihe,
Sieh', ich bau' auf deine Treue
Mehr jetzt als auf meinen Kopf.

BLONDE

Nein! das kann ich dir nicht schenken,
Mich mit so was zu verdenken,
Mit dem alten dummen Tropf!

BELMONTE

Ach Constanze! ach mein Leben!
Könntest du mir doch vergeben,
Dass ich diese Frage tat.

CONSTANZE

Belmont! wie, du konntest glauben,
Dass man dir dies Herz kann rauben,
Das nur dir geschlagen hat?

PEDRILLO

Liebstes Blondchen! ach verzeihe!

BELMONTE

Ach verzeihe!

PEDRILLO

Ach verzeihe!

BELMONTE

Ich bereue!

PEDRILLO

Ich bereue!

CONSTANZE

Ich verzeihe deiner Reue.

BLONDE

Ich verzeihe deiner Reue.

BELMONTE

I will. You must forgive,
If after all the things that I have
    heard,
I ask you, with doubt and fear,
I ask you if you have been untrue.

CONSTANZA

Ah, how this wounds my heart!

PEDRILLO

Did not Osmin receive,
As one might well believe,
The key, the key to your affection,
Escaping my detection?
Then you and I are through,
Then you and I are really through.

BLONDA

(hits him on the ear)

That's how I answer you.

PEDRILLO (holds his cheek)

Now I have seen the light.

BELMONTE (kneeling)

I fall on bended knee.

BLONDA (angrily)

Yes, and it serves you right.

CONSTANZA (sighing)

You have no faith in me.

BLONDA (to Constanza)

This rascal wants to know
If I have ever failed him.

CONSTANZA (to Blonda)

They've even tried to show
That I love Pasha Selim.

PEDRILLO (to Belmonte)

My Blonda has been true,
By all the gods I swear it.

BELMONTE (to Pedrillo)

Constanza has been true,
I hasten to declare it.

CONSTANZA, BLONDA, BELMONTE
AND PEDRILLO (simultaneously)

CONSTANZA

They've even tried to show
That I love Pasha Selim.

BLONDA

The rascal wants to know
If I have ever failed him.

BELMONTE

Constanza has been true.
I hasten to declare it.

PEDRILLO

My Blonda has been true.
By all the gods I swear it.

CONSTANZA, BLONDA,
BELMONTE AND PEDRILLO

All: When $\begin{cases}\text{we}\\\text{men}\end{cases}$ begin to doubt $\begin{cases}\text{them}\\\text{us}\end{cases}$
And whisper things about $\begin{cases}\text{them,}\\\text{us,}\end{cases}$
With jealousy $\begin{cases}\text{we're}\\\text{they're}\end{cases}$ torn,
Provoking only scorn.

PEDRILLO

Dearest Blonda, be forgiving,
In your faith I am believing,
More indeed than in my soul.

BLONDA

No, I never can forgive you, no.
For I heard you loudly swearing
That I loved that stupid drone.

BELMONTE

Ah, Constanza, hear my pleading.
If you only were not heeding
All my cruel, unfeeling wrongs.

CONSTANZA

Belmonte, how could you be saying
That I'd ever been betraying
What to you alone belongs.

BELMONTE

Ah, forgive me!
Ah, Constanza, ah, my dearest.

PEDRILLO

Ah, forgive me!

BELMONTE

I implore you.

PEDRILLO

Be forgiving.
Dearest Blonda, be forgiving.

CONSTANZA

I forgive you on repentance.

BLONDA

I forgive you.

ALLE

Wohl, es sei nun abgetan,
Es lebe die Liebe,
Nur sie sei uns teuer!
Nichts fache das Feuer der Eifersucht
an,
Nichts, nichts, nichts,
Nichts fache das Feuer der Eifersucht
an!

DRITTER AUFZUG

*Platz vor dem Palast des Bassa Selim;
auf einer Seite der Palast des Bassa,
gegenüber die Wohnung des Osmin,
hinten Aussicht aufs Meer. Es ist
Mitternacht.*

ERSTER AUFTRITT

*Pedrillo und Klaas, der eine Leiter
bringt, kommen herein.*

Dialog

PEDRILLO

Hier, lieber Klaas, hier leg sie indes nur
nieder und hole die zweite vom
Schiff. Aber nur hübsch leise, dass
nicht viel Lärm gemacht wird, es
geht hier auf Tod und Leben.

KLAAS

Lass mich nur machen, ich versteh das
Ding auch ein bisschen; wenn wir
sie nur erst an Bord haben.

PEDRILLO

Ach, lieber Klaas, wenn wir mit unsrer
Beute glücklich nach Spanien kommen, ich glaube Don Belmonte
lässt dich in Gold einfassen.

KLAAS

Das möchte wohl ein bisschen zu warm
aufs Fell gehn; doch das wird sich
schon geben. Ich hole die Leiter.
(*Geht ab.*)

PEDRILLO

Ach, wenn ich sagen sollte, dass mir's
Herz nicht klopfte, so sagt ich eine
schreckliche Lüge. Die verzweifelten
Türken verstehn nicht den mindesten
Spass; und ob der Bassa gleich ein
Renegat ist, so ist er, wenn's aufs
Kopfab ankommt, doch ein völliger
Türke.

(*Klaas bringt die zweite Leiter.*)

So, guter Klaas, und nun lichte die
Anker und spanne alle Segel auf,
denn eh' eine halbe Stunde vergeht,
hast du deine völlige Ladung.

KLAAS

Bring sie nur hurtig, und dann lass
mich sorgen. (*Geht ab.*)

ZWEITER AUFTRITT

PEDRILLO

Ach, ich muss Atem holen! Es zieht
mir's Herz so eng zusammen, als
wenn ich's grösste Schelmstück vor-
hätte! Ach, wo mein Herr auch
bleibt!

BELMONTE (*ruft leise*)

Pedrillo! Pedrillo!

PEDRILLO

Wie gerufen!

BELMONTE

Ist alles fertig gemacht?

PEDRILLO

Alles! Jetzt will ich ein wenig um den
Palast herum spionieren, wie's aus-
sieht. Singen Sie indessen eins. Ich
habe das so alle Abende getan; und
wenn Sie da auch jemand gewahr
wird, oder Ihnen begegnet, denn alle
Stunden macht hier eine Janitscha-
renwache die Runde, so hat's nichts
zu bedeuten, sie sind das von mir
schon gewohnt; es ist fast besser, als
wenn man Sie so still hier fände.

BELMONTE

Lass mich nur machen, und komm bald
wieder. (*Pedrillo geht ab.*)

DRITTER AUFTRITT

O Constanze, Constanze, wie schlägt
mir das Herz' Je näher der Augenblick kommt, desto ängstlicher zagt
meine Seele; ich fürchte und
wünsche, bebe und hoffe. O Liebe,
sei du meine Leiterin!

No. 17. Arie

Ich baue ganz auf Deine Stärke
Vertrau' o Liebe Deiner Macht.
Denn ach! was wurden nicht für Werke
Schon oft durch Dich zu Stand'
gebracht!
Was all'r Welt unmöglich scheint,
Wird durch die Liebe doch vereint.
(*Pedrillo kommt herein.*)

VIERTER AUFTRITT

Dialog

PEDRILLO

Alles liegt auf dem Ohr; es ist alles so
ruhig, so stille als den Tag nach der
Sündflut.

CONSTANZA, BLONDA,
BELMONTE AND PEDRILLO

Now let all our doubts be gone.
Our love shall be lasting.
Our hearts ever faithful.
No longer the flame of suspicion will
burn.

(*Exeunt.*)

ACT III

*The square in front of the palace of
Pasha Selim. On one side, the palace
of the Pasha, opposite the house of
Osmin; in the background, a view
of the sea. It is midnight.*

SCENE 1

(*Enter Pedrillo and Klaas, carrying a
ladder.*)

Dialogue

PEDRILLO

Here, my dear Klaas, put this ladder
down and get the other one from
the ship. But be very quiet, don't
make any noise. It's a matter of life
and death.

KLAAS

Let me do it. I understand the situation a little, too. If we can just get
them on board.

PEDRILLO

Ah, dear Klaas, if we get to Spain
safely, I think Don Belmonte will
cast you in gold.

KLAAS

That might be too warm for comfort.
But that will take care of itself.
I'll get the ladder. (*Exit.*)

PEDRILLO

If I said my heart wasn't pounding
I'd tell a terrible lie. These Turks
don't understand even a small joke.
And though the Pasha is a renegade,
he's a full-blooded Turk when it
comes to cutting off heads. (*Klaas
returns with a second ladder.*) So,
good Klaas, lift your anchor, and
spread all your sails, because in half
an hour you will have a full cargo.

(*Klaas leaves.*)

SCENE 2

PEDRILLO

I have to catch my breath. My heart
is going as wildly as if I were going
to commit a terrible crime. But where
is my Master?

BELMONTE (*calls softly*)
Pedrillo, Pedrillo.

PEDRILLO

Just in time.

BELMONTE

Is everything ready?

PEDRILLO

Everything. Now I'll spy around the
palace and see how things look. In
the meantime sing something. I used
to do that every evening. And if anyone meets you or notices you — the
Janissaries make the rounds every
hour —they won't think anything of
it. They're used to my singing. And
it would be better than just standing here.

BELMONTE

I'll take care of that. Hurry back. (*Pedrillo leaves.*)

SCENE 3

BELMONTE

O, Constanza, Constanza. How my
heart is pounding. The nearer the
moment comes, the more anxious is
my soul. I fear and wish, I tremble
and hope. O Love, guide me.

No. 17. Aria

BELMONTE (*singing*)

I place my faith in pure devotion,
On love's sweet power I rely,
For, ah, the force of deep emotion
Will bring me strength in all I try.
Though pain and sorrow may befall,
I know that true love conquers all.

SCENE 4

Dialogue

PEDRILLO (*entering*)
Everyone is asleep. It's as quiet as on
the day after the great flood.

BELMONTE

Nun, so lass uns sie befreien. Wo ist die Leiter?

PEDRILLO

Nicht so hitzig. Ich muss erst das Signal geben.

BELMONTE

Was hindert dich denn, es nicht zu tun? Mach fort.

PEDRILLO (*Sieht nach der Uhr*)

Eben recht, Schlag zwölf. Gehen Sie dort an die Ecke, und geben Sie wohl acht, dass wir nicht überrascht werden.

BELMONTE

Zaudre nur nicht! (*Geht ab.*)

PEDRILLO

(*indem er seine Mandoline hervorholt*) Es ist doch um die Herzhaftigkeit eine erzläppische Sache. Wer keine hat, schafft sich mit aller Mühe keine an! Was mein Herz schlägt! Mein Papa muss ein Erzpoltron gewesen sein. (*fängt an zu spielen*) Nun, so sei es denn gewagt!

18. Arie

Im Mohrenland gefangen war
Ein Mädchen hübsch und fein,
Sah rot und weiss, war schwarz von
        Haar,
Seufzt' Tag und Nacht und weinte gar,
Wollt' gern erlöset sein.
Da kam aus fremdem Land' daher
Ein junger Rittersmann
Den jammerte das Mädchen sehr,
Juchhe! rief er: "wag ich Kopf und
        Ehr',
Wenn ich sie retten kann." (*für sich*)
Noch geht alles gut, es rührt sich noch
        nichts.
(*Belmonte kommt hervor.*)

Dialog

BELMONTE

Mach ein Ende, Pedrillo.

PEDRILLO

An mir liegt es nicht, das sie sich noch nicht zeigen. Entweder schlafen sie fester als jemals, oder der Bassa ist bei der Hand. Wir wollen's weiter versuchen. Bleiben Sie nur auf Ihrem Posten.

(*Belmonte geht wieder fort.*)

Arie

"Ich komm' zu dir in finst'rer Nacht,
Lass, Liebchen, husch mich ein;
Ich fürchte weder Schloss noch Wacht,
Holla, horch auf! um Mitternacht
Sollst du erlöset sein."
Gesagt, getan!
Glock zwölfe stand
Der tapf're Ritter da,
Sanft reicht sie ihm die weiche Hand,
Früh man die lere Zelle fand
Fort war sie hopsasa!
(*Belmonte kommt wieder herein.*)

Dialog

Sie macht auf, Herr, sie macht auf!

BELMONTE

Ich komme, ich komme!

CONSTANZE (*oben am Fenster*)

Belmonte!

BELMONTE

Constanze, hier bin ich; hurtig die Leiter!
(*Pedrillo stellt die Leiter an Constanzes Fenster, Belmonte steigt hinein; Pedrillo hält die Leiter.*)

PEDRILLO

Was das für einen abscheulichen Spektakel macht. (*Hält die Hand aufs Herz*) Es wird immer ärger, weil es nun Ernst wird. Wenn sie mich hier erwischten, wie schön würden sie mit mir abtrollen, zum Kopfabschlagen, zum Spiessen oder zum Hängen. Je nu, der Anfang ist einmal gemacht, jetzt ist's nicht mehr aufzuhalten, es geht nun schon einmal aufs Leben oder auf den Tod los!

BELMONTE

(*kommt mit Constanze unten zur Tür heraus*)

Nun, holder Engel, nun hab ich dich wieder, ganz wieder! Nichts soll uns mehr trennen.

CONSTANZE

Wie ängstlich schlägt mein Herz, kaum bin ich imstande, mich aufrecht zu halten; wenn wir nur glücklich entkommen!

PEDRILLO

Nur fort, nicht geplaudert, sonst könnt es freilich schief gehen, wenn wir da lange Rat halten und seufzen!
(*Stösst Belmonte und Constanze fort.*)

BELMONTE

Now let's set them free. Where's the ladder?

PEDRILLO

Don't be in such a hurry. I must give the signal first.

BELMONTE

What's stopping you? Hurry.

PEDRILLO

(*looks at his watch*)

Just right. The stroke of twelve. Go over there toward the corner and .make sure we won't be surprised.

BELMONTE

Don't waste any time. (*Exit.*)

PEDRILLO

(*while he picks up his mandolin*)

Courage is a strange thing. If you don't have it, you can't find it. How my heart is pounding! My father must have been a real coward. (*begins to play*) Might as well risk it.

No. 18. Aria

PEDRILLO

(*sings and accompanies himself*)

In Moorish land a lovely maid
Was bound by lock and key.
White was her skin
And black her hair,
Long did she weep in deep despair.
Would no one set her free?
Then from a foreign land there came
A young and daring knight.
And when he heard the maiden's plea
I'll risk my head and heart," quothe he,
"To help you in your plight."
(*Everything is working out according to plan. No one stirs.*)

Dialogue

BELMONTE (*coming out*)

Hurry, end it, Pedrillo!

PEDRILLO

It isn't my fault that they haven't appeared yet. Either they are sleeping more soundly than ever or the Pasha is nearby. We'll try again. Stay at **your post**. (*Belmonte leaves again.*)

PEDRILLO

(*continues singing*)

"I will be there at dead of night,
Then, loved one, we shall flee.
I do not fear the castle's might.
Holla, my love, if all goes right
Tonight I'll set you free."
Just as he vowed at midnight hour
The gallant knight was there,
Lowered his lady from the tower.
Later they found the cell was bare,
No trace of the maiden fair.

Dialogue

PEDRILLO

She's opening the window, Master, she's opening.

BELMONTE

I'm coming, I'm coming.

CONSTANZA

(*opening the window*)

Belmonte.

BELMONTE

Constanza, I am here. Hurry with the ladder. (*Pedrillo leans the ladder against Constanza's window. Belmonte climbs up. Pedrillo holds the ladder.*)

PEDRILLO

What a horrible racket it makes. (*puts his hand over his heart*) And it gets worse because it's becoming more serious. If they find me they will take me to behead me, to roast me or to hang me. Well, we can't stop once we've started it. From here on it's life or death.

BELMONTE

(*comes out of the door with Constanza*)

Now, sweet angel, we're together again. Nothing will separate us again.

CONSTANZA

My heart is beating so wildly I'm almost weak. If we only escape safely.

PEDRILLO

Let's not chatter. Let's go. Everything can go wrong if we hold a council. (*pushes Belmonte and Constanza out*) Now quickly to the shore. I'll be right there. (*They leave.*)

Nur frisch nach dem Strande zu! Ich komme gleich nach.

(*Belmonte und Constanze ab.*)

Nun, Kupido, du mächtiger Herzensdieb, halte mir die Leiter und hülle mich samt meiner Gerätschaft in einen dicken Nebel ein!

(*Er hat unter der Zeit die Leiter an Blondes Fenster gelegt und ist hinaufgestiegen.*)

Blondchen, Blondchen, mach auf, um Himmels willen, zaudre nicht, es ist um Hals und Kragen zu tun!

(*Es wird das Fenster geöffnet, er steigt hinein.*)

FÜNFTER AUFTRITT

Osmin und ein schwarzer Stummer öffnen die Tür von Osmin's Haus wo Pedrillo hineingestiegen ist. Osmin, noch halb schlaftrunken, hat eine Laterne. Der Stumme gibt Osmin durch Zeichen zu verstehen, dass es nicht richtig sei; dess er Leute gehört habe usw.)

OSMIN

Lärmen hörtest du? Was kann's denn geben? Vielleicht Schwärmer? Geh, spioniere, bringe mir Antwort.

(*Der Stumme lauscht ein wenig herum; endlich wird er die Leiter an Osmin's Fenster gewahr, erschrickt und zeigt sie Osmin, der wie im Taumel, mit der Laterne in der Hand an seine Haustür gelehnt, steht und nickt.*)

Gift und Dolch! Was ist das? Wer kann ins Haus steigen? Das sind Diebe oder Mörder. (*Er tummelt sich herum weil er aber noch halb schlaftrunken ist, stösst er sich hier und da.*) Hurtig, hole die Wache! Ich will unterdessen lauern.

(*Der Stumme ab; Osmin setzt sich auf die Leiter mit der Laterne in der Hand und nickt ein. Pedrillo kommt rückwärts wieder zum Fenster herausgestiegen und will die Leiter wieder herunter.*)

BLONDE

(*oben am Fenster, wird Osmin gewahr und ruft Pedrillo zu.*)

O Himmel, Pedrillo wir sind verloren!

PEDRILLO

(*sieht sich um, und sowie er Osmin gewahr wird, stutzt er, besieht ihn und steigt wieder zum Fenster hinein*)

Ach, welcher Teufel hat sich wider uns verschworen!

OSMIN

(*auf der Leiter dem Pedrillo nach, ruft*)

Blondchen, Blondchen!

PEDRILLO

(*im Hineinsteigen zu Blonde*)

Zurück, nur zurück!

OSMIN (*steigt wieder zurück*)

Wart, Spitzbube, du sollst mir nicht entkommen. Hilfe! Hilfe! Wache! Hurtig, hier gibt's Räuber, herbei, herbei!

(*Pedrillo kommt mit Blonde unten zur Haustür heraus, sieht schüchtern nach der Leiter und schleicht sich dann mit Blonde darunter weg.*)

BLONDE und PEDRILLO (*im Abgehen*)

O Himmel steh uns bei sonst sind wir verloren!

OSMIN

Zu Hilfe, zu Hilfe! Geschwind! (*Er will nach*)

(*Wache, mit Fackeln, kommt herein und hält Osmin auf.*)

WACHE

Halt, halt! Wohin?

OSMIN

Dorthin, dorthin.

WACHE

Wer bist du?

OSMIN

Nur nicht lange gefragt, sonst enkommen die Spitzbuben. Seht ihr denn nicht? Hier ist noch die Leiter.

WACHE

Das sehn wir; kannst nicht du sie angelegt haben?

OSMIN

Gift und Dolch! Kennt ihr mich denn nicht? Ich bin Oberaufseher der Gärten beim Bassa. Wenn ihr noch lange fragt, so hilft euer Kommen nichts.

(*Ein Teil der Wache bringt Pedrillo und Blonde zurück.*)

Ah, endlich! Gift und Dolch! Seh ich recht! Ihr beide? Warte, spitzbübischer Pedrillo, dein Kopf soll am längsten festgestanden sein.

PEDRILLO

Brüderchen, Brüderchen, wirst doch Spass verstehn? Ich wollt dir dein Weibchen nur ein wenig spazieren führen, weil du heute dazu nicht aufgelegt bist. Du weisst schon (*heimlich zu Osmin*) wegen des Cyperweins.

PEDRILLO

Now, Cupid, you mighty heart-stealer, hold the ladder for me and wrap me in a thick cloud. (*He has leaned the ladder at Blonda's window and climbed it.*) Blonda, Blonda, open up, for the love of Heaven. Don't hesitate. The rope is already around my neck. (*The window is opened and he steps inside.*)

SCENE 5

(*Osmin and a Mute open the door of Osmin's house where Pedrillo has entered. Osmin, half-asleep, has a lantern. The Mute makes Osmin understand through pantomime that something is wrong, that he has heard people moving about, etc.*)

OSMIN

You heard noise? What can that be? Revelers? Go, Spy, bring me an answer. (*The Mute snoops around and finds the ladder at Osmin's window. He is startled and shows it to Osmin, who half-drunk, leans against his door and nods.*) Poison and daggers! What is it? Who can be in the house? It's either thieves or murderers. (*He staggers around and, because he is still half-drunk, keeps hitting himself.*) Hurry. Bring the watch. I'll keep an eye out here. (*The Mute exits. Osmin sits on the ladder with the lantern in his hand and nods. Pedrillo comes out the window backwards and starts down the ladder.*)

BLONDA

(*at the window. She spots Osmin and calls Pedrillo.*)

O heavens, Pedrillo, we are lost.

PEDRILLO

(*looks around and as soon as he sees Osmin, climbs in the window again*)

Oh, what devil has conspired against us?

OSMIN

(*on the ladder, after Pedrillo calls*)

Blonda! Blonda!

PEDRILLO

(*going in*)

Back. Back.

OSMIN

(*climbing down again*)

Wait, rascal, you won't get away. Help! Help! Guard. Hurry, robbers, here, here. (*Pedrillo comes out the door with Blonda, looks at the ladder, and they start to sneak away.*)

PEDRILLO AND BLONDA

(*leaving*)

Heaven stay with us or we are lost.

OSMIN

Help. Help. Hurry. (*starts to follow them*)

GUARD

(*with a torch, holding Osmin back*)

Wait, wait. Which way?

OSMIN

There. There.

GUARD

Who are you?

OSMIN

Don't ask so much or the rascal will get away. See, here is the ladder.

GUARD

We see that. But couldn't you have put it there yourself?

OSMIN

Poison and daggers! Don't you know me? I am head overseer of the Pasha's garden. If you delay much longer your coming won't have helped a bit. (*A unit of the guard bring Pedrillo and Blonda back*) At last. Poison and daggers! Do I see right? Both of you? Wait, rascal Pedrillo, your head will roll.

PEDRILLO

Little Brother, little Brother, don't you understand a little fun? I just wanted to take your little wife for a walk, because you aren't up to it today. You know (*to Osmin alone*) because of the Cyprian wine.

OSMIN

Scoundrel. Are you trying to make a fool of me? I don't understand fun of that sort. Your head must fall, for I'm a true Moslem.

OSMIN

Schurke, glaubst du mich zu betäuben? Hier verstehe ich keinen Spass; dein Kopf muss herunter, so wahr ich ein Muselmann bin.

PEDRILLO

Und hast du einen Nutzen dabei? Wenn ich meinen Kopf verliere, sitzt deiner um so viel fester? (*Ein anderer Teil der Wache, auch mit Fackeln, bringt Belmonte und Constanze.*)

BELMONTE (*widersetzt sich noch*)

Schändliche, lasst mich los!

WACHE

Sachte, junger Herr, sachte! Uns entkommt man nicht so geschwinde.

OSMIN

Sieh da, die Gesellschaft wird immer stärker! Hat der Herr Baumeister auch wollen spazieren· gehen! O ihr Spitzbuben! Hatte ich heute nicht recht, (*zu Belmonte*) dass ich dich nicht ins Haus lassen wollte? Nun wird der Bassa sehen, was für sauberes Gelichter er um sich hat.

BELMONTE

Das beiseite! Lass hören, ob mit euch ein vernünftig Wort zu sprechen ist? Hier ist ein Beutel mit Zechinen, er is euer, und noch zweimal so viel; lasst mich los.

CONSTANZE

Lasst euch bewegen!

OSMIN

Ich glaube, ihr seid besessen? Euer Geld brauchen wir nicht, das bekommen wir ohnehin; eure Köpfe wollen wir. (*zur Wache*) Schleppt sie fort zum Bassa!

CONSTANZE *und* BELMONTE

Habt doch Erbarmen, lasst euch bewegen!

OSMIN

Um nichts in der Welt! Ich habe mir längst so einen Augenblick gewünscht. Fort, fort! (*Die Wache führt Belmonte und Constanze fort, samt Pedrillo und Blonde.*)

19. Arie

O! wie will ich triumphieren,
Wenn sie euch zum Richtplatz führen,
Und die Hälse schnüren zu.
Schnüren zu!
Hüpfen will ich, lachen, springen,
Und ein Freudenliedchen singen,
Denn nun hab' ich vor euch Ruh.
Schleicht nur säuberlich und leise,

Ihr verdammten Harems-Mäuse,
Unser Ohr entdeckt euch schon:
Und eh' ihr uns könnt entspringen,
Seht ihr euch in unsern Schlingen,
Und erhaschet euren Lohn.
(*Osmin geht ab.*)
Verwandlung—Zimmer des Bassa.

SECHSTER AUFTRITT
Dialog

BASSA SELIM (*zu einem Offizier*)

Geht, unterrichtet euch, was der Lärm im Palast bedeutet; er hat uns im Schlaf aufgeschreckt, und lasst mir Osmin kommen.

(*Der Offizier will abgehen, indem kommt Osmin, zwar hastig, doch noch ein wenig schläfrig.*)

OSMIN

Herr, verzeih, dass ich es so früh wage, deine Ruhe zu stören!

BASSA SELIM

Was gibt's, Osmin, was gibt's? Was bedeutet der Aufruhr?

OSMIN

Herr, es ist die schändlichste Verräterei in deinem Palast—

BASSA SELIM

Verräterei?

OSMIN

Die niederträchtigen Christensklaven entführen uns die Wieber. Der grosse Baumeister, den du gestern auf Zureden des Verräters Pedrillo aufnahmst, hat deine schöne Constanze entführt.

BASSA SELIM

Constanze? Entführt? Ah, setzt ihnen nach!

OSMIN

O, s'ist schon dafür gesorgt! Meiner Wachsamkeit hast du es zu danken, dass ich sie wieder beim Schopf gekriegt habe. Auch mir selbst hatte der spitzbübische Pedrillo eine gleiche Ehre zugedacht, und er hatte mein Blondchen schon beim Kopf, um mit ihr in alle Welt zu reisen. Aber Gift und Dolch, er soll mir's entgelten! Sieh, da bringen sie sie!

(*Belmonte und Constanze werden von der Wache hereingeführt.*)

PEDRILLO

What use would it be to you? If I lose my head will your own rest more easily? (*Another unit of the guard brings in Belmonte and Constanza. They are carrying torches.*)

BELMONTE

(*still resisting*)

Wretches, let me go.

GUARD

Easy, young man, easy. One doesn't escape easily from us.

OSMIN

See that? The party gets larger. Did the architect want to go for a walk, too? O, you rascals. Wasn't I right today? (*to Belmonte*) When I didn't want to let you into the house? Now the Pasha will see what kind of people he has around him.

BELMONTE

Forget about that. Let me see if you can talk sensibly. Here is a purse containing gold. If you let me free you will have twice as much.

CONSTANZA

Please help us.

OSMIN

You're insane. We don't need your gold. We'll get that anyway. We want your heads. (*to the guard*) Take them to the Pasha.

BELMONTE AND CONSTANZA

Have pity. Help us.

OSMIN

For nothing in the world. I've waited a long time for this. Take them away. (*The guard takes them out.*)

No. 19. Aria

Ha, with triumph I am singing
For I know that you'll be swinging
When the hangman strings you up,
Strings you up.
I'll be dancing, laughing, springing
And with joy I shall be singing
For at last you will be gone.
Sneaking nightly round the harem,
Chasing women, trying to snare 'em.
But your plan went wrong I fear.
Since before you had succeeded

We took all precautions needed
And your doom is very near.
Oh, with triumph I am singing,
For I know that you'll be swinging
When the hangman strings you up,
Strings you up.

(*Exit.*)

SCENE II

A room of the Pasha.

SCENE 6

Dialogue

SELIM (*to an officer*)

Go see what this noise in the palace means. It startled us in our sleep. And bring Osmin here. (*The officer starts to leave as Osmin hurries in sleepily.*)

OSMIN

Lord, forgive me, that I dare disturb your rest so early.

SELIM

What is the matter, Osmin? What is it? What is all this noise?

OSMIN

Lord, there is terrible treachery in your palace.

SELIM

Treachery?

OSMIN

The wretched Christian slaves are stealing our wives from us. The great architect that you hired at the suggestion of Pedrillo has stolen your beautiful Constanza.

SELIM

Constanza? Stolen? Follow them.

OSMIN

Oh, we've taken care of that. Thanks to me. I caught them. And that Pedrillo tried to do me a similar honor. He had stolen my Blonda and was headed to the four corners of the world. But, poison and daggers, he'll pay for this! See, they're bringing them in. (*Belmonte and Constanza are brought in by the guard.*)

BASSA SELIM

Ah, Verräter! Ist's möglich? Ha, du
heuchlerische Sirene! War das der
Aufschub, den du begehrtest? Miss-
brauchtest du so die Nachsicht, die
ich dir gab, um mich zu hintergehen?

CONSTANZE

Ich bin strafbar in deinen Augen, Herr,
es ist wahr; aber es ist mein Geliebter, mein einziger Geliebter, dem
lang schon dieses Herz gehört. O
nur für ihn, nur um seinetwillen fleh
ich um Aufschub. O lass mich sterben! Gern, gern will ich den Tod
erdulden; aber schone nur sein
Leben—

BASSA SELIM

Und du wagst's, Unverschämte, für ihn
zu bitten?

CONSTANZE

Noch mehr: für ihn zu sterben!

BELMONTE

Ha, Bassa! Noch nie erniedrigte ich
mich zu bitten, noch nie hat dieses
Knie sich vor einem Menschen ge-
beugt; aber sieh, hier lieg ich zu
deinen Füssen und flehe dein Mitleid
an. Ich bin von einer grossen span-
ischen Familie, man wird alles für
mich zahlen. Lass dich bewegen,
bestimme ein Lösegeld für mich und
Constanze so hoch. du willst. Mein
Name ist Lostados.

BASSA SELIM (*staunend*)

Was hör ich! Der Kommandant von
Oran, ist er dir bekannt?

BELMONTE

Das ist mein Vater.

BASSA SELIM

Dein Vater? Welcher glückliche Tag,
den Sohn meines ärgsten Feindes in
meiner Macht zu haben! Kann was
angenehmeres sein? Wisse, Elender,
dein Vater, dieser Barbar, ist schuld,
dass ich mein Vaterland verlassen
musste. Sein unbiegsamer Geiz entriss
mir eine Geliebte, die ich höher als
mein Leben schätzte. Er brachte
mich um Ehrenstellen, Vermögen,
um alles. Kurz, er zernichtete mein
ganzes Glück. Und dieses Mannes
einzigen Sohn habe ich nun in
meiner Gewalt! Sage, er an meiner
Stelle, was würde er tun?

BELMONTE (*ganz niedergedrückt*)

Mein Schicksal würde zu beklagen sein.

BASSA SELIM

Das soll es auch sein. Wie er mit mir
verfahren ist, will ich mit dir verfahren. Folge mir, Osmin, ich will dir
Befehle zu ihren Martern geben. (*zu
der Wache*) Bewacht sie hier.

20. *Recitative und Duett*

BELMONTE

Welch' ein Geschick! O Qual der
Seele!
Hat sich denn alles wider mich ver-
schworen!
Ach! Constanze! durch mich bist du
verloren,
Welch' eine Pein!

CONSTANZE

Lass, ach Geliebter, lass dich das nicht
quälen!
Was ist der Tod?
Ein Uebergang zu Ruh',
Und dann, an deiner Seite,
Ist er Vorgeschmack der Seligkeit.

BELMONTE

Engelsseele! Welch' holde Güte!
Du flössest Trost in mein erschüttert
Herz!
Du linderst mir den Todesschmerz,
Und ach! ich reisse dich in's Grab!
Ha! du solltest für mich sterben,
Ach Constanze! kann ich's wagen,
Noch die Augen aufzuschlagen?
Ich bereite dir den Tod.

CONSTANZE

Ach! für mich gibst du dein Leben;
Ich nur zog dich in's Verderben,
Und ich soll nicht mit dir sterben?
Wonne ist mir dies Gebot.

CONSTANZE und BELMONTE

Ach Geliebter! dir zu leben,
War mein Wunsch und all' mein
Streben!
Ohne dich ist's mir nur Pein,
Länger auf der Welt zu sein.

BELMONTE

Ich will alles gerne leiden.
Weil ich dir zur Seite bin.

SELIM

Traitors! Is it possible? You deceitful siren. Is this the delay you needed? Did you abuse my trust to deceive me?

CONSTANZA

I am guilty in your eyes, Lord, it is true; but this is my beloved, my own beloved, who has long had my heart. Only for him, only on his behalf did I beg for a delay. Oh, let me die, gladly, gladly will I meet death, only spare his life.

SELIM

You dare, shameless woman, to beg for him?

CONSTANZA

More than that — to die for him.

BELMONTE

Pasha! I have never lowered myself to begging before. My knee has never bent before any man. But I lie at your feet and beg you. I am of an old Spanish family. They will pay any ransom for me. Set as high a ransom on myself and Constanza as you wish. My name is Lostados.

SELIM (stunned)

What do I hear? Do you know the commandant of Oran?

BELMONTE

He is my father.

SELIM

Your father? What a lucky day to get the son of my archenemy in my power. Could anything be more pleasant? Know, wretch, that your father, this barbarian, forced me to leave my native land. His greed tore me from my beloved who meant more to me than anything in the world. He made me lose honors, in- heritance, everything. In short, he destroyed my happiness. And this man's only son is now in my power. Tell me, if you were in my place, what would you do?

BELMONTE
(completely shattered)

My destiny would be pitiful.

SELIM

And so shall it be. As he did to me I shall do to you. Follow me, Osmin. I will give you orders for their tor- ture. (to the guard) Watch them here.

SCENE 7

No. 20. Recitative and Duet

BELMONTE (singing)

Ah, cruel fate.
Our hope has vanished.
Have all the stars conspired
To seal our destiny?
Ah, Constanza,
Because of me you perish.
Oh, cruel fate.

CONSTANZA

No, my beloved.
Leave this grief and torment.
For what is death?
The path to final freedom.
And when we die together
We shall find eternal happiness.

BELMONTE

My Constanza,
You calm my sorrow,
You give me peace
And ease my troubled heart.
You lend me strength to meet my fate.
And I, I only give you death.
I have failed you,
You must perish.
O, Constanza,
Must you perish
Through the deed of one you cherish
When I lead you to the grave?

CONSTANZA

Belmonte,
You bring only gladness.
It was I who caused this sadness.
When we die, we'll die together.
In death we'll be together.
Gladly will I share your fate.

CONSTANZA AND BELMONTE

O, Beloved, your devotion
Fills my heart with strong emotion.
Without you life would be vain.
Without you there's only pain.

BELMONTE

I have drawn you to the tomb.
Ah, Constanza, I brought sadness.

CONSTANZE

Mutig sterb ich, und mit Freuden,
Weil ich dir zur Seite bin.

CONSTANZE und BELMONTE

Um dich, Geliebter,
Geb' ich gern mein Leben hin.
O welche Seligkeit!
Mit dem Geliebten sterben,
Ist seliges Entzücken,
Mit wonnevollen Blicken
Verlässt man da die Welt!

ACHTER AUFTRITT

*(Pedrillo und Blonde werden von
einem andern Teil der Wache hereingeführt.)*

Dialog

PEDRILLO

Ach, Herr, wir sind hin! An Rettung
ist nicht mehr zu denken. Man macht
schon alle Zubereitungen, um uns
aus der Welt zu schaffen. Es ist er-
schrecklich, was sie mit uns anfangen
wollen! Ich, wie ich im Vorbeigehen
gehört habe, soll in Oel gesotten und
dann gespiesst werden. Das ist ein
sauber Traktament! Ach, Blondchen,
Blondchen, was werden sie wohl mit
dir anfangen?

BLONDE

Das gilt mir nun ganz gleich. Da es
einmal gestorben sein muss, ist mir
alles recht.

PEDRILLO

Welche Standhaftigkeit! Ich bin doch
von gutem altchristlichen Geschlecht
aus Spanien, aber so gleichgültig
kann ich beim Tode nicht sein! Weiss
der Teufel—Gott sei bei mir, wie
kann mir auch jetzt der Teufel auf
die Zunge kommen?

NEUNTER AUFTRITT

BASSA SELIM

Nun, Sklave! Elender Sklave! Zitterst
du?
Erwartest du dein Urteil?

BELMONTE

Ja, Bassa, mit so vieler Kaltblütigkeit,
als Hitze du es aussprechen kannst.
Kühle deine Rache an mir, tilge das
Unrecht, so mein Vater dir angetan;
ich erwarte alles und tadle dich
nicht.

BASSA SELIM

Es muss also wohl deinem Geschlechte
ganz eigen sein, Ungerechtigkeiten zu
begehen, weil du das für so ausge-
macht annimmst? Du betrügst dich.
Ich habe deinen Vater viel zu sehr
verabscheut, als dass ich je in seine
Fusstapfen treten könnte. Nimm
deine Freiheit, nimm Constanze,
segle in dein Vaterland, sage deinem
Vater, dass du in meiner Gewalt
warst, dass ich dich freigelassen, um
ihm sagen zu können, es wäre ein
weit grösser Vergnügen, eine erlittene
Ungerechtigkeit durch Wohltaten zu
vergelten, als Laster mit Lastern
tilgen.

BELMONTE

Herr! Du setzest mich in Erstaunen—

BASSA SELIM

(ihn verächtlich ansehend).

Das glaub ich. Zieh damit hin, und
werde du wenigstens menschlicher als
dein Vater, so ist meine Handlung
belohnt.

CONSTANZE

Herr, vergib! Ich schätzte bisher deine
edle Seele, aber nun bewundere ich—

BASSA SELIM

Still! Ich wünsche für die Falschheit,
so Sie an mir begangen, dass Sie es
nie bereuen möchten, mein Herz aus-
geschlagen zu haben. *(Im Begriff
abzugehen).*

PEDRILLO

*(Tritt ihm in den Weg und
fällt ihm zu Füssen)*

Herr, dürfen wir beide Unglückliche
es auch wagen, um Gnade zu flehen?
Ich war von Jugend auf ein treuer
Diener meines Herrn.

OSMIN

Herr, beim Allah, lass dich ja nicht
von dem verwünschten Schmarotzer
hintergehn! Keine Gnade! Er hat
schon hundertmal den Tod verdient.

BASSA SELIM

Er mag ihn also in seinem Vaterlande
suchen. *(zur Wache)* Man begleite
alle vier an das Schiff. *(gibt Belmonte ein Papier)* Hier ist euer Passport.

OSMIN

Wie, meine Blonde soll er auch mitneh-
men?

CONSTANZA

No, Beloved, only gladness.
I will meet the end with joy
For you, Beloved.

CONSTANZA AND BELMONTE

Death is not an hour to fear.
Oh, what true happiness
When you are here beside me.
I know our love will guide me
When we must say farewell,
When we must say to this world
Farewell.

SCENE 8

Dialogue

PEDRILLO

(*Pedrillo and Blonda are brought in by
another group of the Guard.*)

O, Master, we are here. We can't
even think of rescue. They are making all arrangements to send us out
of this world. It's frightening what
they're planning to do with us. I
heard, as I passed by, that I was to
be cooked in oil and then put on a
spit. What treatment! And Blonda,
Blonda, what are they going to do
with you?

BLONDA

It doesn't matter to me. Since I must
die anything is all right.

PEDRILLO

What courage! I come from a good
Christian house in Spain, but I
can't be this calm toward death. The
Devil knows — God help me, how
can I speak of the Devil now?

SCENE 9

SELIM

Now, slaves, miserable slaves, are you
trembling? Are you awaiting your
sentence?

BELMONTE

Yes, Pasha. As calmly as you speak
heatedly. Cool your wrath on me,
sentence me as my father did you. I
await anything and don't blame you.

SELIM

Your people must indulge in injus-
tices because you seem to take them
so much for granted. But you're deceiving yourself. I dislike your father
too much to follow in his footsteps.
Take your freedom. Take Constanza,
sail to your home. Tell your father
that you were in my power and that
I set you free. Tell him it gave me
far greater pleasure to reward an
injustice with justice than to keep on
repaying evil with evil.

BELMONTE

Lord, you astound me.

SELIM

(*looking at him with contempt*)

I believe that. Remember this. And if
you are more merciful than your
father my action will be rewarded.

CONSTANZA

Lord, forgive me. Before I esteemed
your noble soul, and now I admire —

SELIM

Enough. You have been false to me,
but I hope you never have cause to
regret rejecting my heart. (*starts to
leave*)

PEDRILLO

(*steps in front of him and
falls before him*)

Lord, can we two unfortunate ones
also ask for mercy? Since my childhood I have been a faithful servant
to my Master.

OSMIN

My Lord, by Allah, don't let this cursed
parasite betray you. No mercy. He
has earned his death a hundred
times.

SELIM

Then he can earn death also in his
native land. (*to the Guard*) Take all
four of them to the ship. (*gives
Belmonte a paper.*) And here is your
passport.

OSMIN

What, shall he take my Blonda, too?

BASSA SELIM (*scherzhaft*).

Alter, sind dir deine Augen nicht lieb?
Ich sorge besser für dich als du
denkst.

OSMIN

Gift und Dolch! Ich möchte bersten.

BASSA SELIM

Beruhige dich. Wen man durch Wohl-
tun nicht für sich gewinnen kann,
den muss man sich vom Halse
schaffen.

BELMONTE

Nie werd ich deine Huld verkennen,
Mein Dank bleibt ewig dir geweiht.
An jedem Ort, zu jeder Zeit
Werd' ich Dich gross und edel nennen.
Wer so viel Huld vergessen kann,
Den seh' man mit Verachtung an.

ALLE

Wer so viel Huld vergessen kann,
Den seh' man mit Verachtung an.

CONSTANZE

Nie werd' ich, selbst im Schoss der
Liebe,
Vergessen was der Dank gebeut.
Mein Herz, der Liebe nun geweiht,
Hegt auch dem Dank geweihte Triebe.
Wer so viel Huld vergessen kann,
Den seh' man mit Verachtung an.

ALLE

Wer so viel Huld vergessen kann,
Den seh' man mit Verachtung an.

PEDRILLO

Wenn ich es je vergessen könnte,
Wie nah' ich am Erdrosseln war,
Und all' der anderen Gefahr,
Ich lief', als ob der Kopf mir brennte.
Wer so viel Huld vergessen kann,
Den seh' man mit Verachtung an.

ALLE

Wer so viel Huld vergessen kann,
Den seh' man mit Verachtung an.

BLONDE

Nehmt meinen Dank mit tausend
Freuden.

Herr Bassa! lebt gesund und froh!
Osmin! das Schicksal will es so,
Ich muss von dir auf ewig scheiden;
(*auf Osmin zeigend*)
Wer so wie du nur zanken kann,
Den sieht man mit Verachtung an.

OSMIN

Verbrennen sollte man die Hunde,
Die uns so schändlich hintergeh'n;
Es ist nicht länger anzuseh'n,
Mir starrt die Zunge fast im Munde,
Um ihren Lohn zu ordnen an.
Erst geköpft, dann gehangen,
Dann gespiesst auf heisse Stangen,
Dann verbrannt, dann gebunden
Und getaucht, zuletzt geschunden!
(*Osmin läuft voll Wut ab.*)

CONSTANZE, BLONDE, BELMONTE,
PEDRILLO

Den edlen
Mann entstellt die Rache,
Grossmütig, menschlich, gütig sein,
Und ohne Eigennutz verzeih'n,
Ist nur der grossen Seelen Sache.

CONSTANZE

Wer dieses nicht erkennen kann,
Den seh' man mit Verachtung an.

CONSTANZE, BLONDE, BELMONTE,
PEDRILLO

Wer dieses nicht erkennen kann,
Den seh' man mit Verachtung an.

CHOR

Bassa Selim lebe lange,
Bassa Selim glücklich lebe!
Ehre sei sein Eigentum!
Seine holde Stirn umschwebe
Jubel, Freude, Glück und Ruhm!

SELIM (*teasing*)

Old Man, aren't your eyes dear to you? I am looking out for you better than you think.

OSMIN

Poison and daggers! I'm going to burst.

SELIM

Be calm. If you can't win something through kindness it is better not to have it.

No. 21 Finale

BELMONTE (*singing*)

You saved my life in princely fashion.
This debt I never can repay.
On every hour of every day
I'll praise your name and your compassion.
The mercy, Lord, you gave to me
Will never more forgotten be.

CONSTANZA

Now I am filled with joy and pleasure
For all the bounty you have shown.
My heart that lived for love alone
Has learned a lesson it will treasure.
The mercy, Lord, you gave to me
Will nevermore forgotten be.

PEDRILLO

I hope you'll never need remind me
About the tortures Osmin planned,
The boiling oil he kept at hand,
And how the hangman marched behind me.
The mercy, Lord, you gave to me
Will nevermore forgotten be.

ALL

The mercy, Lord, you gave to me
Will nevermore forgotten be.

BLONDA

I'd like a word, dear Pasha Selim,
About the things that I've been through.
No disrespect, of course, to you,
But that Osmin, I'd like to whale him.

(*pointing to Osmin*)

For you deserve just what you got.
Don't think I'm sorry. I am not.

OSMIN

Your torment made my life so hectic.
You are a nasty, scheming lot.
So I deserve just what I got?
I'm feeling ill.
I'm apoplectic!
I should have sentenced you to rot.
You'd be hung, then beheaded.
Then be drowned and then be shredded.
How you'd broil when they toast you.
On a spit I'd let them roast you.

(*runs away furiously*)

ALL

The wisest man
Believes in mercy.
Unselfish, gentle, kind is he
Who with such wisdom set us free.
We call him noble,
The noble Selim Pasha.

CONSTANZA

The moral, Lord, you taught to me
Will nevermore forgotten be.

ALL

The moral, Lord, you taught to me
Will nevermore forgotten be.

CHORUS OF JANISSARIES

Pasha Selim, may we praise him.
Honor to his mighty name.
May his virtue ever bring him
Triumph, gladness, luck and fame.
And his crown will be resplendent,
Shining with his mighty name.

The Marriage of Figaro

(1786)

OPERA IN FOUR ACTS

Libretto by LORENZO DA PONTE

English Version by RUTH AND THOMAS MARTIN

THIS ENGLISH VERSION WAS FIRST PERFORMED BY THE NEW YORK CITY OPERA COMPANY ON OCTOBER 14, 1948.

INTRODUCTION

One evening in the spring of 1783 Mozart visited his admirer and former landlord, Baron Raimund Wetzlar von Plankenstein, at the baron's home in Vienna. There he met an Italian writer, concerning whom he wrote to his father:

> Our poet here is now a certain Abbate da Ponte. He has an enormous amount to do in revising pieces for the theater and he has to write *per obbligo* an entirely new libretto for Salieri, which will take him two months. He has promised after that to write a new libretto for me. But who knows whether he will be able to keep his word — or will want to? For, as you are aware, these Italian gentlemen are very civil to your face. Enough, we know them! If he is in league with Salieri, I shall never get anything out of him. But indeed I should dearly love to show what I can do in an Italian opera! [1]

Since this meeting was to result in one of the most important collaborations in the history of opera, and in the creation of three masterpieces — *Le Nozze di Figaro, Don Giovanni,* and *Così fan tutte* — , it may be well to sketch here the career of the less well known partner.

His real name was Emanuele Conegliano and he was born March 10, 1749, at Ceneda, a small town in northeastern Italy. His father, a Jew, was left a widower, and when Emanuele was fourteen had himself and his three sons baptized so that he could marry a young Catholic girl. In accordance with a custom of the time, the eldest son took the name of the sponsor, Monsignor Lorenzo da Ponte, bishop of Ceneda. Young Lorenzo studied in the seminary of the town and later at Portogruaro. By the time he was twenty-two he was giving instruction in rhetoric and the Italian language and had taken minor orders for the priesthood. From Portogruaro he went to Venice, where he eked out a precarious living by teaching and writing poetry and by less legitimate activities, plunging zestfully into the dissolute life of the Venetian Republic. He got into, and out of, one scrape after another until, in 1779, the patience of even the lenient authorities of Venice was overtaxed, and they banished da Ponte from all Venetian territories. He made his way to Vienna, armed with a letter of introduction to Antonio Salieri, court composer to Joseph II. There Salieri helped to get him appointed theater poet and da Ponte enjoyed some years of success, writing many librettos (including the three for Mozart) as well as poems for special occasions. After the death of Joseph II (1790) da Ponte left Vienna. Most of the next thirteen years (1792-1805) were spent in London, where he was for part of the time poet of the King's Theatre. In 1805 da Ponte, as a result of one of his frequent financial crises, came to the United States. He tried the grocery business, first in New York and then in Elizabethtown, N. J., returned to New York to teach Italian, attempted for eight years to establish himself as a business man in Sunbury, Pa., and for a year in Philadelphia, but came back in 1819 to New York. Here he taught

---

[1] Emily Anderson, *Letters of Mozart and His Family,* London, 1938, III, 1263 f. It was to Vienna that Mozart wanted to display his ability in the field of Italian opera. His last previous work of this sort, *Idomeneo* (1780-81), was written for Munich.

Italian again and in 1825 was appointed professor of Italian Literature at Columbia College (a post that gave him prestige but no salary). In the same year Manuel Garcia and his daughter Maria Malibran came to New York and da Ponte persuaded them to produce *Don Giovanni* (for the first time in America) at the Park Theater. In the 1820s da Ponte wrote his memoirs, which still make lively reading today, even though the author understandably glossed over or omitted the less savory episodes in his life, and his memory of events that took place thirty or forty years before he wrote about them is not reliable. He died in New York on August 17, 1838, at the age of eighty-nine.

It was not two months but more than two years after Mozart reported his conversation with da Ponte to his father before the opportunity arose for them to work together. In 1785 Mozart was at the height of his creative powers and in greater demand as a composer than at any time before or after in his brief life. In that one year were published two symphonies (K. 385 and 319), the six quartets dedicated to Haydn, three piano concertos (K. 413-415), and the Fantasy and Sonata in C minor for piano (K. 475 and 457), among other things. Leopold Mozart reported in a letter to his daughter dated November 3-4 that a journalist in Salzburg had remarked to him: "It is really astonishing to see what a number of compositions your son is publishing. In all the announcements of musical works I see nothing but Mozart. The Berlin announcements, when quoting the quartets, only add the following words: 'It is quite unnecessary to recommend these quartets to the public. Suffice it to say that they are the work of Herr Mozart.' "[2] But beneath all this activity was Mozart's burning desire to "show what I can do in an Italian opera" — a desire that had gnawed at him ever since he had come to Vienna in 1781 and that had led him to seek a suitable libretto even before he had met da Ponte. The latter finally kept his promise. Here is his own account. The time is the late summer or early fall of 1785.

> . . . I began quietly thinking about the plays I was to write for my two dear friends Mozart and Martín [Vicente Martín y Soler]. As to the former, I readily perceived that the greatness of his genius demanded a subject which should be ample, elevated, and abounding in character and incident. When we were talking about it one day, he asked me if I could easily adapt Beaumarchais' comedy, *The Marriage of Figaro*. The proposal pleased me very well, and I promised to do as he wished. But there was a great difficulty to be overcome. Only a few days before, the Emperor had forbidden the company at the German theater to act this same comedy, as it was, he said, too outspoken for a polite audience. How could one suggest it to him for an opera? Baron Wetzlar very generously offered to give me a very fair sum for the words and to have the opera produced in London or in France if it could not be done at Vienna. But I declined his offers and proposed that words and music should be written secretly and that we should await a favorable opportunity to show it to the theatrical managers or to the Emperor, which I boldly undertook to do. Martín was the only one to whom I told our great secret, and out of his regard for Mozart he very readily agreed to my postponing writing for him until I had finished *Figaro*.

---

[2] Anderson, III, 1331.

So I set to work, and as I wrote the words he composed the music for them. In six weeks all was ready. As Mozart's good luck would have it, they were in need of a new work at the theater. So I seized the opportunity and without saying anything to anybody, I went to the Emperor himself and offered him *Figaro*.

"What!" he said, "Don't you know that Mozart, though excellent at instrumental music, has only written one opera, and that nothing very great?"

"Without Your Majesty's favor," I said humbly, "I too should have written only one play in Vienna."

"That is true," he replied, "but I've forbidden this *Marriage of Figaro* to the German company."

"Yes," I said, "but as I was writing a play to be set to music and not a comedy, I have had to leave out a good many scenes and shorten a great many more, and I've left out and shortened whatever might offend the refinement and decorum of an entertainment at which Your Majesty presides. And as for the music, as far as I can judge it is extraordinarily fine."

"Very well," he answered, "if that is so, I'll trust your taste as to the music, and your discretion as to the morals. Have the score sent to the copyist."

I hastened at once to Mozart and had not finished telling him the good news when one of the Emperor's lackeys came with a note requesting him to go to the palace at once with the score. He obeyed the royal command and had various pieces performed before the Emperor, who liked them wonderfully well and was, without exaggeration, amazed by them.[3]

Some explanation and correction of this account is in order. That da Ponte, in 1785, "perceived the greatness" of Mozart's genius is by no means certain. We must remember that he was writing forty years after the event, when Mozart's fame had spread to America, where da Ponte was seeking to bolster his own reputation. The secrecy that da Ponte attaches to the composition of the work is a figment of his lively imagination. Even the Salzburg journalist mentioned by Leopold in the letter quoted above "said something about a new opera," when Wolfgang had just begun to write it. In another letter, dated November 11, Leopold reported that Wolfgang, "in order to keep the morning free for composing, . . . is now taking all his pupils in the afternoon, etc." All was not ready in six weeks. Mozart began composing the opera at the end of October 1785 and finished it six months later — on April 29, 1786. The earlier Mozart opera mentioned by the Emperor is probably *The Abduction from the Seraglio,* which is of course not the only one he had written up to that time. Da Ponte's line of attack was based on either knowledge or sound instinct, for the Emperor, in his memorandum (dated January 31, 1785, and not, therefore, "only a few days before") forbidding a Viennese production of Beaumarchais' play, had added that the censor could permit it to be performed if the offending sections were altered.

Additional information is supplied by another contemporary, Michael Kelly, an Irish tenor living in Vienna, the creator of the roles of Basilio and Don Curzio:

[3] *Memoirs of Lorenzo da Ponte,* transl. and ed. by L. A. Sheppard, London: Routledge & Kegan Paul Ltd., 1929, p. 129 ff.

There were three operas on the tapis, one by Regini [Vincenzo Righini], another by Salieri *(The Grotto of Trophonius),* and one by Mozart, by special command of the Emperor . . . These three pieces were nearly ready for representation at the same time, and each composer claimed the right of producing his opera for the first. The contest raised much discord, and parties were formed. The characters of the three men were all very different. Mozart was as touchy as gunpowder, and swore he would put the score of his opera into the fire if it was not produced first; his claim was backed by a strong party: on the contrary, Regini was working like a mole in the dark to get precedence.

The third candidate was Maestro di Cappella to the court, a clever shrewd man, possessed of what Bacon called, crooked wisdom, and his claims were backed by three of the principal performers, who formed a cabal not easily put down. Every one of the opera company took part in the contest. I alone was a stickler for Mozart, and naturally enough, for he had a claim on my warmest wishes, from my adoration of his powerful genius, and the debt of gratitude I owed him, for many personal favors.

The mighty contest was put an end to by His Majesty issuing a mandate for Mozart's *Nozze di Figaro,* to be instantly put into rehearsal; and none more than Michael O'Kelly, enjoyed the little great man's triumph over his rivals.

. . . I remember at the first rehearsal of the full band, Mozart was on the stage with his crimson pelisse and gold-laced cocked hat, giving the time of the music to the orchestra. Figaro's song, *Non più andrai, farfallone amoroso,* Bennuci [Francesco Benucci] gave, with the greatest animation, and power of voice.

I was standing close to Mozart, who, *sotto voce,* was repeating, Bravo! Bravo! Bennuci; and when Bennuci came to the fine passage, *Cherubino, alla vittoria, alla gloria militar,* which he gave out with Stentorian lungs, the effect was electricity itself, for the whole of the performers on the stage, and those in the orchestra, as if animated by one feeling of delight, vociferated Bravo! Bravo! Maestro. Viva, viva, grande Mozart. Those in the orchestra I thought would never have ceased applauding, by beating the bows of their violins against the music desks. The little man acknowledged, by repeated obeisances, his thanks for the distinguished mark of enthusiastic applause bestowed upon him. [4]

La folle Journée, ou Le Mariage de Figaro is the second of a group of three plays about the same principal characters by Pierre-Augustin Caron de Beaumarchais (1732-99), the first being *Le Barbier de Séville, ou La Précaution inutile* (1775), and the third, *L'autre Tartuffe, ou La Mère coupable* (1792). Beaumarchais, a bold and brilliant man with many irons in the fire (among other things he was instrumental in securing French help for the American colonists in their revolt against England), completed *Le Mariage de Figaro* in 1778. When Louis XVI read the manuscript he exclaimed: "This is detestable, it will never be played!" Apparently the King felt that the very foundations of the social structure in Europe were threatened by the impudent Figaro. Beaumarchais was not a man to take royal censorship meekly, and he enlisted the aid of powerful members of the aristocracy, including several who were close to Queen Marie Antoinette. The affair became a celebrated one

[4] *Reminiscences of Michael Kelly,* London, 1826, I, 257 ff.

in Paris. Private performances were given in the homes of the nobility; eventually the King yielded and the first public performance took place in Paris on April 27, 1784. The play was a resounding success and ran for 68 performances. Two German translations were printed immediately. It was only nine months after the play opened in Paris that Joseph II, as we have seen, felt obliged to place obstacles in the way of its production in German at Vienna.

There was justification for Louis XVI's nervousness. Under the cloak of a gay and witty comedy of intrigue, Beaumarchais poked fun at the dissoluteness of the upper classes and at the legal procedures of the time (with which he had had many unfortunate experiences himself), emphasized the enslavement of the lower orders, and bitterly attacked the power placed in the hands of undeserving men merely because they were born into a certain class of society. The fact that the scene of the play was placed in· Spain deceived no one. It was no less an authority than Napoleon who later said that Beaumarchais' play was "the Revolution already in action."

But it was not the political aspect of *Le Mariage de Figaro* that appealed to Mozart. He had never had much interest in politics and his letters are almost bare of references to such matters. Neither the American Revolution nor the French is mentioned once in his correspondence. What attracted him, we must suppose, was the clever and comical convolutions of the complicated plot, in which the victory in the seemingly unequal struggle between the Count and his valet is always about to be won by one or the other antagonist only to be torn out of his grasp by some new crisis. And what must have pleased him above all were the wonderful opportunities for music in this comedy (Beaumarchais had already provided for some songs and dances) and especially for the musical delineation of the fairly numerous and sharply differentiated characters, who, although outgrowths of stock figures of the old Italian *commedia dell'arte,* had achieved in Beaumarchais' hands a freshness and humanity rare in opera librettos of the time.

In making a libretto out of the play, da Ponte did a masterly job. He cut Beaumarchais' cast of sixteen characters down to eleven, telescoped the five acts of the original into four, tightened the more discursive portions of the play, changed the order of some scenes and combined others to make for swifter action and especially to give opportunities for set musical numbers as well as for the great second-act finale. Wherever possible he kept original scenes and, frequently, lines. All the political and many of the satirical social references were deleted. The main lines of Beaumarchais' plot were retained and in some respects the plot was even improved, from the dramaturgical standpoint. Thus, for example, in the play the Countess makes a first, insignificant, appearance towards the end of Act I, but da Ponte keeps her off the stage until she can appear alone at the beginning of Act II. The character of some of the personages is changed. Figaro is still an impertinent rogue, but there is no bitterness in him. The Countess becomes a more sympathetic person and the trace of amorousness in her relation to Cherubino disappears. And so with the other important characters. Through da Ponte's skill and above all through the magic of Mozart's marvelous music all of the characters gain an added dimension of warmth and humanity.

The first performance of the opera took place at the Imperial Court Theater in Vienna on May 1, 1786, with the following cast:

Count Almaviva	Stefano Mandini
Countess Almaviva	Luisa Laschi
Susanna	Anna Storace
Figaro	Francesco Benucci
Cherubino	Mme. Bussani
Marcellina	Mme. Mandini
Basilio } Don Curzio }	Michael Kelly
Bartolo } Antonio }	Francesco Bussani
Barbarina	Nannina Gottlieb

"At the end of the opera," says Kelly, "I thought the audience would never have done applauding and calling for Mozart, almost every piece was encored, which prolonged it nearly to the length of two operas, and induced the Emperor to issue an order on the second representation, that no piece of music should be encored. Never was anything more complete, than the triumph of Mozart and his *Nozze di Figaro*."[5] It was a short-lived triumph, at least in Vienna. After eight more performances that season it was dropped from the repertory; the success of a new hit — Martín's *Una Cosa rara* — eclipsed the memory of Mozart's opera and it was not given again in Vienna until three years later.

Meanwhile, however, *Figaro* was performed in Prague in December 1786, "with such success," Leopold reported to his daughter January 12, 1787, "that the orchestra and a company of distinguished connoisseurs and lovers of music sent [Wolfgang] letters inviting him to Prague and also a poem which was composed in his honor." From Prague Mozart wrote to a friend two days later that at a ball he attended "I looked on . . . with the greatest pleasure while all these people flew about in sheer delight to the music of my *Figaro,* arranged for quadrilles and waltzes. For here they talk about nothing but *Figaro.* No opera is drawing like *Figaro.* Nothing, nothing but *Figaro.* Certainly a great honor for me!"[6] Because of this great success, the manager of the Prague Italian opera company commissioned Mozart to write another opera, a commission that resulted in *Don Giovanni*.

Figaro was soon (1787) produced in Germany and quickly became popular there. It was performed in Italy (at Monza) in 1787; in Paris, 1793; London, 1812; New York, 1824; St. Petersburg, 1836; Rio de Janeiro, 1848. Today

---

[5] Kelly, p. 261. A rugged individualist by the name of Count Karl von Zinzendorf attended the first performance and made a careful note of it in his diary. Here is his comment, in its entirety: "The opera bored me."
[6] Anderson, III, 1343, 1344.

there is probably no city in which opera is performed that has not seen *Figaro*. It has been given in many languages; Einstein's edition of the Köchel catalogue of Mozart's works lists 14 different translations into German alone.

No better brief outline of the plot of the opera can be given than in the words of the author of the play. Here is a first draft, by Beaumarchais himself, of the story of *Le Mariage de Figaro*. It corresponds in almost every detail with da Ponte's libretto and is in fact a better summary of Mozart's opera than of the final version of Beaumarchais' play.

Program of *Le Mariage de Figaro*

Figaro, steward at the castle of Aguas Frescas, has borrowed ten thousand francs from Marceline, housekeeper of the same castle, and has given her a note promising to repay the money at a certain time or to marry her if he should default. Meanwhile, very much in love with Suzanne, Countess Almaviva's young chambermaid, he prepares to marry her; for the Count, himself enamored of young Suzanne, has favored this marriage in the hope that a dowry he has promised to give her would enable him to obtain from her in secret her yielding to the *droit du seigneur*, a right that he had renounced for the benefit of his servants when he was married. This little domestic intrigue is conducted on behalf of the Count by the rather unscrupulous Basile, music-master of the castle. But the young and virtuous Suzanne believes herself obliged to apprise her mistress and her betrothed of the Count's gallant intentions, and the Countess, Suzanne, and Figaro band together to foil the plans of the lord of the manor. A small page, beloved by everyone at the castle but mischievous and overheated, like all precocious lads of thirteen or fourteen, slips saucily away from his master and by his liveliness and perpetual thoughtlessness more than once involuntarily places obstacles in the way of the Count's progress, at the same time getting himself into hot water, which leads to some very effective incidents in the piece . . . The Count, finally perceiving that he is being made the victim, but unable to imagine how it is being done, resolves upon vengeance by favoring Marceline's claims. Thus, desperate because he cannot make the young woman his mistress, he tries to marry the old one to Figaro, who is disgusted by all this. But at the moment when Almaviva believes himself avenged, when, as first magistrate of Andalusia, he condemns Figaro to marry Marceline that day or pay the ten thousand francs — which Figaro cannot possibly do —, it is revealed that Marceline is Figaro's unknown mother. This ruins all of the Count's plans and he cannot flatter himself that he is either fortunate or avenged. During this time, the Countess, who has not given up the hope of winning back her unfaithful spouse by catching him at fault, has arranged with Suzanne that the latter pretend to grant the Count a rendezvous at last in the garden, and that the wife appear there in place of the mistress. But an unforeseen incident apprises Figaro of the rendezvous granted by his fiancée. Furious because he believes himself deceived, he hides at the appointed spot, in order to surprise the Count with Suzanne. While he is still raging, he is himself pleasantly surprised to discover that the whole affair is only a game between the Countess and her chambermaid for the purpose of fooling the Count; he finally joins in the game good-humoredly; Almaviva, convinced of unfaithfulness by his wife, throws himself at her feet, begs her forgiveness, which she laughingly grants him, and Figaro marries Suzanne. [7]

[7] Eugène Lintilhac, *Histoire générale du théâtre en France*, Paris, n.d., IV, 414-16.

CAST OF CHARACTERS

COUNT ALMAVIVA . . . . *Baritone*

COUNTESS ALMAVIVA . . . . *Soprano*

SUSANNA, her chambermaid, affianced to Figaro . . . . *Soprano*

FIGARO, valet to the Count . . . . *Bass*

CHERUBINO, the Count's page . . . . *Soprano*

MARCELLINA . . . . *Mezzo Soprano*

BASILIO, music master . . . . *Tenor*

DON CURZIO, a judge . . . . *Tenor*

BARTOLO, a doctor from Seville . . . . *Bass*

ANTONIO, the Count's gardener and Susanna's uncle . . . . *Bass*

BARBARINA, his daughter . . . . *Soprano*

Country men and women, Court attendants, Hunters, and Servants.

PLACE: Castle of Count Almaviva, about three leagues from Seville.

THE PLOT

ACT I.

Figaro, valet to Count Almaviva, is to marry Susanna, the Countess' maid. Susanna tells Figaro that the Count has been making love to her. Bartolo and Marcellina enter. Figaro once promised to marry the elderly Marcellina, and these two now plan how they will force him to keep his word. Cherubino, the page, appears and tells Susanna of his troubled love life. Having been caught alone with Barbarina, the gardener's daughter, he is to be sent away and begs Susanna to intercede. A knock is heard, Cherubino hides behind a large chair, the Count enters and asks that Susanna meet him in the garden. As another knock is heard the Count makes for Cherubino's hiding place, while the page jumps into the chair, where Susanna covers him with a cloth. Basilio enters. He speaks of Cherubino's attentions to the Countess and the Count reveals himself. Cherubino's presence is then revealed and the Count sends him away to join his regiment in battle.

ACT II.

Susanna and the Countess are in despair over the Count's infidelity. Figaro suggests a plan to make the Count jealous and goes to find Cherubino, who is to be disguised as Susanna. A knock is heard at the door. It is the Count, and Cherubino runs into the other room. The Count demands to know who is there. He decides to break the door down, and goes out, taking the Countess with him, to get the tools. While they are gone, Susanna takes Cherubino's place in the other room; the page exits through the window. The Count is surprised on opening the door to find Susanna. He is about to repent when the gardener arrives to tell of a man jumping through the window. Figaro asserts that he was the man. The gardener produces a paper dropped by Cherubino, but the Count takes it before Figaro can get it. Figaro, coached by the ladies, saves the situation by saying the paper is Cherubino's commission and he had it for sealing. At that moment Bartolo enters with Marcellina. They acquaint the Count with the old promise of Figaro to Marcellina.

ACT III.

Susanna and the Countess decide that the latter will impersonate Susanna at the garden rendezvous. When the Countess retires, the Count accosts Susanna who finally promises to meet him in the garden. Figaro is brought to trial in the Count's court and turns out to be the long-lost son of Bartolo and Marcellina, which means, of course, that he cannot marry her. The peasant girls come in and Cherubino, disguised, is with them. He is discovered, and the Count, angrier than ever, becomes confused when Barbarina asks to marry the page.

The scene changes to the wedding hall. As the Count places the bridal veil on her head, Susanna slips him the invitation to meet her in the garden.

ACT IV.

The scene is the garden at night. Figaro, learning a part of the plan between the Countess and Susanna, becomes angry and jealous. He conceals himself as the two enter, disguised in each other's clothes. The Count arrives to find Cherubino trying to kiss the Countess, whom they both believe to be Susanna. Then the Count makes love to the supposed Susanna. Figaro comes upon Susanna disguised as the Countess and tells her where the Count and Susanna are. He suddenly realizes who it is, but decides to keep silent to pay her back for her trick. He pretends to make passionate love to the Countess until Susanna jealously reveals herself. They put on an act for the Count, who arrives at this moment, and he seizes Figaro and calls his servants. Everyone then appears except the Countess and they all take Susanna to be their mistress. She implores forgiveness but the Count is adamant until the real Countess appears. All is forgiven and the opera ends with the Count much subdued.

LE NOZZE DI FIGARO

ATTO PRIMO

Camera quasi smobiliata con un
seggiolone nel mezzo.

No. 1 — Duettino

FIGARO

Cinque—dieci—venti—trenta—
Trentasei—quarantatre—

SUSANNA

Ora sì ch' io son contenta,
Sembra fatto inver per me.

FIGARO

Cinque—dieci—*etc.*

SUSANNA

Guarda un pò, mio caro Figaro,
Guarda adesso il mio cappello.

FIGARO

Sì, mio core or è più bello,
Sembra fatto in ver per te.

a 2.

Ah! il mattino alle nozze vicino,

Qanto è dolce al $\begin{cases} \text{mio} \\ \text{tuo} \end{cases}$ tenero sposo

Questo bel cappellino vezzoso,

Che Susanna ella stessa si fè!

SUSANNA (*recitativo*)

Cosa stai misurando,
Caro il mio Figaretto?

FIGARO

Io guardo se quel letto.
Che ci destina il Conte,
Farà buona figura in questo loco,

SUSANNA

In questa stanza?

FIGARO

Certo! a noi la cede
Generoso il padrone.

SUSANNA

Io per me te la dono.

FIGARO

E la ragione?

SUSANNA

La ragione l'ho qui.

FIGARO

Perchè non puoi far, che passi un pò
qui!

THE MARRIAGE OF FIGARO

ACT ONE

(Scene: *An incompletely furnished room, with an armchair in the middle. Figaro has a ruler in his hand; Susanna is seated at a mirror, trying on a small, flowered hat.*)

No. 1 Duettino

FIGARO (*measuring*)
Seven . . . fourteen . . . twenty . . .
Thirty . . . thirty-seven . . . and forty-three . . .

SUSANNA
(*looking at herself in the mirror*)
I must say, it's to my liking,
Just the very thing for me.
Won't you look, my darling Figaro.
Turn around, turn around.
Isn't this a lovely bonnet?

FIGARO
Seven . . . fourteen . . . twenty . . .
thirty . . . *etc.*

SUSANNA
(*continuing to look in the mirror*)
Tell me frankly, my dear Figaro,
Do you like me in this bonnet?
Don't you love the trimming on it?

FIGARO
Yes, my sweet, the way you've done it,
It's a pretty sight to see,
And it suits you to a T.

SUSANNA
Just look at it!

FIGARO
Yes, my sweetheart. It's very charming!

SUSANNA
I must say, it's to my liking,
Very smart and very striking,
Just the very thing for me.

FIGARO
Very smart and very striking,
And it suits you to a T.

BOTH
I (you) have made it myself (yourself) for the wedding,
As your (my) bride I am (you are) planning to wear it.
I'm so happy, I hardly can bear it!
What a wonderful day that will be!

FIGARO
Susanna, my Susanna!

SUSANNA
My darling, my beloved!

BOTH
What a wonderful day that will be!

RECITATIVE

SUSANNA
Will you tell me, my precious, what on earth you are doing?

FIGARO
I was just making sure that the space I have been measuring is sufficient for the bed the Count will give us.

SUSANNA
You mean we'll sleep here?

FIGARO
Surely! The Count was kind enough to make this our bedroom.

SUSANNA
You can have it, for my part!

FIGARO
Why, don't you like it?

SUSANNA
I should say that I don't.

FIGARO
Then why not speak out and say **what is wrong?**

SUSANNA

Perchè non voglio; sei tu mio servo,
o no?

FIGARO

Ma non capisco,
Perchè tanto ti spiace
La più comoda stanza del palazzo.

SUSANNA

Perch' io son la Susanna, e tu sei
pazzo.

FIGARO

Grazie!—non tanti elogi! Guarda un
poco
Se potriasi star meglio in altro loco.

No. 2 Duettino

FIGARO

Se a caso Madama
La notte ti chiama:
Din—din—in due passi
Da quella puoi gir.
Vien poi l' occasione,
Che vuolmi il padrone:
Don—don—in tre salti
Lo vado a servir.
Così se il mattino
Il caro contino
Din—din—din e ti manda
Tre miglia lontan,
Don—don—a mia porta
Il diavol lo porta,
Ed ecco in tre salti . . .

FIGARO

Susanna, pian pian!

SUSANNA

Ascolta—

FIGARO

Fa presto!

a 2.

SUSANNA

Se udir brami il resto,
Discaccia i sospetti
Che torto mi fan.

FIGARO

Udir bramo il resto,
I dubbi, i sospetti
Gelare mi fan.

Recitativo

SUSANNA

Or bene, ascolta, e taci.

FIGARO

Parla, che c' è di nuovo?

SUSANNA

Il signor conte,
Stanco d' andar cacciando
Le straniere bellezze forestiere,
Vuole ancor nel castello
Ritentar la sua sorte;
Nè già di sua consorte, bada bene,
Appetito gli viene.

FIGARO

E di chi dunque?

SUSANNA

Della tua Susannetta.

FIGARO

Di te?

SUSANNA

Di me medesma, ed ha speranza ch'al
nobil suo progetto utilissima sia tal
vicinanza.

FIGARO

Bravo! Tiriamo avanti!

SUSANNA

Queste le grazie son; questa la cura
ch' egli prende di te, della tua sposa.

FIGARO

O guarda un po', che carita pelosa!

SUSANNA

Chetati, or viene il meglio; Don Basilio,
mia maestro di canto, e suo factotum,
nel darmi la lezione, mi ripete ogni di
questa canzone.

FIGARO

Chi! Basilio! oh, birbante!

SUSANNA

E tu credevi,
Che fosse la mia dote
Merto del tuo bel muso?

SUSANNA

I just don't want to. Must you know all I'm thinking?

FIGARO

But I can't fathom why you find it so distasteful that we're getting the best room in the castle.

SUSANNA

Because I am Susanna, and you are stupid.

FIGARO

Thank you, I like your frankness. Look around, then, and perhaps you can find us better quarters.

No. 2 Duettino

FIGARO

Some night if your mistress should ring for assistance,
Ding dong ding dong —
In a wink you could answer the call.
Suppose I am needed to wait on my master,
Dong dong dong dong—
I could be there in no time at all.

SUSANNA

Suppose your dear master
Should send you on an errand,
Our dearest, our generous master,
Ding dong ding dong —
On an errand some three miles away,
Ding ding, dong dong—
In no time he would stand in my doorway.
Before I could stop him . . .

FIGARO

Susanna, hold on, Susanna, no more.

SUSANNA

While you are on an errand . . .

FIGARO

No more.

SUSANNA

And further . . .

FIGARO

Let's hear it.

SUSANNA

I'll tell you the story, the whole of the story,
But cast all suspicions and doubts from your mind.

FIGARO

I must hear the story, the whole of the story,
For doubts and suspicions still torture my mind.

RECITATIVE

SUSANNA

All right, then, but listen calmly.

FIGARO (worriedly)

Tell me, what is your story?

SUSANNA

Our noble master, tired of pursuing foreign beauties as partners for romances, has decided his castle will provide better chances. It's not his own dear wife, though, I can tell you, who has captured his fancy.

FIGARO

Well then, who is it?

SUSANNA

I give you three guesses!

FIGARO (surprised)

Not you?

SUSANNA

You're right the first time, and he is hoping that having us so near him will go far to advance his little project.

FIGARO

Perfect! We're making headway.

SUSANNA

That's why he seems so kind, therefore so thoughtful in respect to the bridal couple's comfort.

FIGARO

Just think of that! Such overwhelming kindness!

SUSANNA

But listen, now comes the best part: Don Basilio, who teaches me singing, acts as his mouthpiece, and during ev'ry lesson he keeps harping forever on the subject.

FIGARO

Who, Basilio? How revolting!

SUSANNA

Did you imagine the Count promised me a dowry on the strength of your good looks?

FIGARO

Me n' lusingato!

SUSANNA

Ei la destina per ottener da me certe
mezz'ore ... che il diritto feudale ...

FIGARO

Come! nè feudi suoi non l'ha il conte
abolito?

SUSANNA

Ebben, ora è pentito e par che tenti
riscattarlo da me.

FIGARO

Bravo! mi piace! che caro signor
Conte!
Ci vogliam divertir; trovato avete . . . .
Chi suona?—la Contessa.

SUSANNA

Addio, Fi-Fi-Figaro bello.

FIGARO

Coraggio, mio tesoro.

SUSANNA

E tu cervello!

FIGARO

Bravo, signor padrone! Ora incomincio
A capire il mistero, e a veder schietto
Tutto il vostro progetto; A Londra,
   è vero?
Voi ministro, io corriero; e la Susanna,
Secreta ambasciatrice!—
Non sarà—non sarà, Figaro il dice!

No. 3 CAVATINA

FIGARO

Se vuol ballare, signor Contino,
Il chitarrino le suonerò.
Se vuol venire nella mia scuola,
La capriola le insegnerò.
Saprò, ma piano—meglio ogni arcano
Dissimulando scoprir potrò.
L' arte schermendo, l' arte adoprando,

Di quà pungendo, di là scherzando,
Tutte le machine rovescierò.

RECITATIVO

BARTOLO

Ed aspettaste il giorno
Fissato per le nozze
A parlarmi di questo?

MARCELLINA

Io non mi perdo,
Dottor mio, di coraggio.
Per romper de' sponsali
Più avanzati di questo
Bastò spesso un pretesto; Ed egli ha
   meco,
Oltre questo contratto,
Certi impegni ... so io ... basta ...
   conviene
La Susanna atterrir, convien con arte
Impuntigliarla a rifiutare il conte.
Egli, per vendicarsi,
Prenderà il mio partito,
E Figaro così fia mia marito.

BARTOLO

Bene, io tutto farò: senza riserva
Tutto a me palesate. (Avrei pur gusto
Di dare in moglie la mia serva antica
A chi mi fece un di rapir l' amica.)

No. 4 ARIA

BARTOLO

La vendetta—oh! la vendetta
È un piacer serbato ai saggi
L' obbliar l' onte, gli oltraggi
È bassezza, è ognor viltà
Coll'astuzia, coll'arguzia,
Col giudizio, col criterio
Si potrebbe—il fatto è serio!

FIGARO

I was inclined to think so!

SUSANNA

He wants to bribe me to grant him his feudal right as lord and master on the night of our wedding.

FIGARO

What? Did he not abolish that right when he got married?

SUSANNA

He did, but now he's sorry and he would like to restore it for me.

FIGARO

Would he? Who wouldn't? A truly noble gesture. How amusing, indeed! But I will show him. (*A bell is heard.*) Who's ringing? It's the Countess.

SUSANNA

I'll have to answer.
Fi-Fi-Figaro, darling!

FIGARO

Goodbye, my love, be cheerful!

SUSANNA

And you, be careful. (*Exit Susanna.*)

FIGARO

(*striding forcefully up and down the room, and rubbing his hands*)

Splendid, my dearest master! Now I'm beginning to unscramble this puzzle and see your purpose in its proper dimensions. We're off to London. You as envoy, I as courier, and my Susanna . . . ambassadress in secret! That shall never be so . . . Figaro has spoken!

No. 3 CAVATINA

FIGARO

Should my dear master want some diversion,
I'll play the music on my guitar,
Should he, for instance, wish to go dancing,
He'll face the music, I'll lead the band.
And then I'll take my cue, without ado,
And slyly, very, very, very, very, very slyly,
Using discretion, I shall uncover his secret plan.

Subtly outwitting, innocent seeming,
Cleverly hitting, planning and scheming,
I'll get the best of the hypocrite yet,
I'll beat him yet!
Subtly outwitting, innocent seeming
Cleverly hitting, planning and scheming,
Teach him a lesson he'll never forget.
This time I shall upset his plan.
Should my dear master, *etc.*

RECITATIVE

(*Enter Bartolo and Marcellina.*)

BARTOLO

Why did you have to wait till the morning of their wedding to appoint me as your lawyer?

MARCELLINA

(*holding a contract in her hand*)

I am well able, even at the last moment, to separate a couple engaged to be married. All I need is a pretext. And as for Figaro, he has made me commitments for some money I lent him. Therefore, our strategy is only too clear. If we succeed in making Susanna reject the Count's advances, then, for the sake of vengeance, he will favor our project and Figaro will thus become my husband.

BARTOLO

(*He takes the contract from Marcellina.*) Splendid! I'll do all I can, sparing no efforts to accomplish your object. (*to himself*) How I would love to arrange a match for my old servant Marcellina with the rogue who foiled my marriage to Rosina.

(*Exit Marcellina.*)

No. 4 ARIA

BARTOLO

Taking vengeance, yes, taking vengeance!
That's the peak of exultation
For a man of rank and station.
Bearing shame without opposition,
Taking insults with submission,
That's behaving in basest form,
That's behaving just like a worm,
A frightened worm.

Ma credete si farà.
Se tutto il codice dovessi volgere,
Se tutto l' indice dovessi leggere,
Con un equivoco, con un sinonimo
Qualche garbuglio si troverà.
Tutta Siviglia conosce Bartolo,
Il birbo Figaro vinto sarà.

RECITATIVO

MARCELLINA

Tutto ancor non ho perso,
Mi resta la speranza;
Ma Susanna s' avanza—io vo' pro-
  varmi—. . .
Fingiam di non vederla.
E quella buona perla
La vorrebbe sposar.

SUSANNA

(Di me favella.)

MARCELLINA

Ma da Figaro, alfine,
Non può meglio sperarsi; l' argent fait
  tout!

SUSANNA

Che lingua! manco male
Ch' ognun sa quanto vale!

MARCELLINA

Brava! questo è giudizio!
Con quegli occhi modesti,
Con quell' aria pietosa!
E poi . . .

SUSANNA

Meglio è partir.

MARCELLINA

Che cara sposa!

No. 5 DUETTINO

MARCELLINA

Via resti servita, madama brillante.

SUSANNA

Non sono sì ardita, madama piccante.

MARCELLINA

No, prima a lei tocca.

SUSANNA

No, no, tocca a lei

a 2.

Io so i dover miei, non fo inciviltà.

MARCELLINA

La sposa novella!

SUSANNA

La dama d'onore!

MARCELLINA

Del Conte la bella!

SUSANNA

Di Spagna l'amore!

MARCELLINA

I meriti!

SUSANNA

L'abito!

Do it my way, take the sly way,
Spread confusion, and distraction.
Give them action, give them action!
I will show you how to function,
Using strategy and unction,
Show no pity, no compunction,
And before they know what hit them
You will outwit them!
Take my word, it can be done,
And the case can still be won.
Always proceeding with utmost legality
I shall discover a fine technicality,
I shall equivocate, argue and litigate
Until a loophole I can produce.
I have ability, mental agility,
Legal facility and versatility,
With my experience and infallibility
Any opponent surely will lose.
Oh, what confusion I shall produce!
All of the city knows Doctor Bartolo—
As for that Figaro,
I'll cook his goose. (*Exit*)

RECITATIVE

(*Marcellina enters; then Susanna, with
a night-cap, a ribbon and a dressing-
gown.*)

MARCELLINA

With such expert assistance I'm con-
fident of winning. If it isn't Susanna!
(*to herself*) I shall pretend that I
don't even see her. (*aloud*) And
that's the little gem he has chosen
for a wife!

SUSANNA

(*aside, remaining in the background*)
She speaks of me.

MARCELLINA

After all, from a Figaro, one can't
really expect much, but, "money
talks."

SUSANNA (*to herself*)

Old spinster! It's too bad that she
could not find a husband.

MARCELLINA

Really! I can't imagine what he sees in
this female. She's all skin and bones.
I wish I . . . (*Both are about to leave
but meet at the door.*)

SUSANNA

How do you.do?

MARCELLINA

How nice to see you!

No. 5 DUETTINO

MARCELLINA (*curtsying*)
To greet you, my lady, I'm honoured
supremely.

SUSANNA (*curtsying*)
By your recognition I'm flattered extremely.

MARCELLINA (*curtsying*)
Please enter before me!

SUSANNA (*curtsying*)
No, no, you go first!

MARCELLINA (*curtsying*)
I beg you, ignore me!

SUSANNA (*curtsying*)
No, no, you go first.

MARCELLINA (*curtsying*)
I know my position,
Bow to tradition,
Fine and patrician,
With all due respect.

SUSANNA (*curtsying*)
Your noble position,
Fine and patrician,
Inspires respect.

MARCELLINA (*curtsying*)
I know my position,
Bow to tradition,
And my ambition is being correct.
The bride of the hour!

SUSANNA (*curtsying*)
A lady of station!

MARCELLINA (*curtsying*)
The Count's little flower!

SUSANNA (*curtsying*)
The pride of the nation!

MARCELLINA (*to herself*)
Her attitude! Her poses!

SUSANNA
Dignified! Mature!

MARCELLINA (*infuriated*)
I swear I shall fly at her
In one, in one minute more.

SUSANNA (*mockingly*)
Decrepit old battle-axe, I'll settle **your**
score.

MARCELLINA

Il posto!

SUSANNA

L'età!

MARCELLINA

Per Bacco! precipito,
Se ancor resto quà!

SUSANNA

Sibilla decrepita
Da rider mi fa!

RECITATIVO

SUSANNA

Va là, vecchia pedante, dottoressa ar-
rogante, perchè hai letti due libri, e
seccata madama in gioventù.

CHERUBINO

Susannetta, sei tu?

SUSANNA

Son io, cosa volete?

CHERUBINO

Ah! cor cio, che accidente!

SUSANNA

Cor vostro? cosa avvenne?

CHERUBINO

Il Conte ieri,
Perchè trovommi sol con Barbarina
Il congedo mi diede:
E se la Contessina,
La mia bella comare,
Grazia non m' intercede, io vado via,
Io non ti vedo più, Susanna mia.

SUSANNA

Non vedete più me? Bravo!
Ma dunque
Non più per la Contessa
Segretamente il vostro cor sospira?

CHERUBINO

Ah, che troppo rispetto ella m'inspira!
Felice te, che puoi vederla quando
   vuoi, che la vesti il mattino, che la
   sera la spogli, che le metti gli spilloni,
   i merletti . . . ah! se in tuo loco . . .
Cos' hai li? dimmi un poco.

SUSANNA

Ah! il vago nastro, e la notturna cuffia
Di comare sì bella!

CHERUBINO

Deh dammelo, sorella—
Dammelo per pietà.

SUSANNA

Presto quel nastro.

CHERUBINO

O caro, o bello, o fortunato nastro!
Io non te'l renderò che colla vita!

SUSANNA

Cos' è quest' insolenza?

CHERUBINO

Eh via, sta cheta.
In ricompensa poi
Questa mìa canzonetta io ti vò dare.

SUSANNA

E che ne debbo fare?

CHERUBINO

Leggila alla padrona,
Leggila tu medesma,
Leggila a Barbarina, a Marcellina,
Leggila ad ogni donna del palazzo.

SUSANNA

Povero Cherubin, siete voi pazzo?

MARCELLINA (*curtsying*)
I praise your deportment without reservation!

SUSANNA (*curtsying*)
And I, your experience and broad reputation.

MARCELLINA (*curtsying*)
So young and so pretty!

SUSANNA (*curtsying*)
The belle of the city!

MARCELLINA (*curtsying*)
What distance between us!

SUSANNA (*curtsying*)
The true Spanish Venus!

MARCELLINA
So innocent! So simple!

SUSANNA (*infuriated*)
Durable! So old!

MARCELLINA
How dare she make fun of me,
It is a disgrace!

SUSANNA (*mockingly*)
So old, so old, so old!
Decrepit old battle-axe,
I'll laugh right in her face!

(*Exit Marcellina angrily.*)

RECITATIVE

SUSANNA
Conceited old spinster! Do you think you can snub me just because, in the old days, you taught my mistress her ABC's?

CHERUBINO (*entering in haste*)
Ah, Susanna, it's you!

SUSANNA
Come here, what's the matter?

CHERUBINO
Ah, he caught me! What misfortune!

SUSANNA
He caught you? Who has caught you?

CHERUBINO
Yesterday the Count found me visiting alone with Barbarina, and for that he dismissed me. And if my dearest Countess, my kind benefactress, cannot obtain my pardon, (*anxiously*) I have to leave and won't see you again, my dear Susanna.

SUSANNA
You won't see me again? How dreadful! But I always thought it was the Countess who was the object of your secret affection.

CHERUBINO
Ah, my lady is much too high above me! Oh, lucky you! You may always see her when you want to; you dress her each morning, you undress her each evening, you may fasten all her pins, tie her ribbons . . . (*with a sigh*) Were I in your place . . . What is that? Let me see it.

SUSANNA (*imitating Cherubino*)
Ah, that is one of her favourite ribbons and belongs to her night-cap.

CHERUBINO
(*snatching the ribbon from her*)
Oh give it to me, Susanna, please, you must let me see.

SUSANNA (*trying to get it back*)
What are you doing?

CHERUBINO (*circling the chair*)
O sweetest, O loveliest, O most divine of ribbons! (*covering the ribbon with kisses*) Not for the whole wide world will I return it.

SUSANNA
(*following him, but then stopping, as though exhausted*)
How dare you take that ribbon?

CHERUBINO
Don't get excited! I'll give you my new love-song in exchange. That will make the bargain even.

SUSANNA
What shall I do with love-songs?

CHERUBINO
Sing it to the Countess, sing it to yourself, sing it to Barbarina, to Marcellina, (*in an ecstasy of joy*) sing it to all the ladies in the castle!

SUSANNA
You must have lost your mind, poor Cherubino!

No. 6 ARIA

CHERUBINO

Non so più cosa son, cosa faccio,
Or di fuoco, ora sono di ghiaccio;
Ogni donna cangiar di colore,
Ogni donna mi fa palpitar.
Solo ai nomi di' amor, di diletto,
Mi si turba, mi s' altera il petto,
E a parlare mi sforza d' amore
Un desio ch'io non posso spiegar.
Parlo d'amor vegliando,
Parlo d' amor sognando,
All' acqua, all ombra, ai monti,
Ai fiori, all' erbe, ai fonti,
All' eco, all' aria, ai venti,
Che il suon de' vani accenti
Portano via con se.
E se non ho chi m' oda,
Parlo d'amor con me.

RECITATIVO

CHERUBINO

Ah, son perduto!

SUSANNA

Che timor!

SUSANNA

Il Conte! Misera me!

IL CONTE

Susanna, tu mi sembri
Agitata e confusa.

SUSANNA

Signor—io chiedo scusa,
Ma se mai qui sorpresa
Per carità, partite!

IL CONTE

Un momento e ti lascio:
Odi.

SUSANNA

Non odo nulla.

IL CONTE

Due parole: tu sai,
Che ambasciatore a Londra
Il Re mi dichiarò; di condur meco
Figaro destinai.

SUSANNA

Signor—se osassi—

IL CONTE

Parla parla, mia cara; e con quel
    dritto,
Ch' oggi prendi su me, fin chè tu vivi,
Chiedi, imponi, prescrivi—

SUSANNA

Lasciatemi, signor, dritti non prendo,
    non ne vò, non ne intendo.
Oh, me infelice!

IL CONTE

Ah no, Susanna, io ti vò far felice! Tu
    ben sai quanto io t'amo; a te Basilio
    tutto già disse. Or senti, se per
    pochi momenti meco in giardin sull'
    imbrunir del giorno, ah per questo
    favore io pagherei.

BASILIO

E uscito poco fa.

IL CONTE

Chi parla?

SUSANNA

O dei!

IL CONTE

Esci, ed alcun non entri.

SUSANNA

Ch' io vi lasci quì solo?

BASILIO

Da madama sarà; vado a cercarlo.

IL CONTE

Quì dietro mi porrò.

No. 6 Aria

CHERUBINO

I can't give you a good explanation
For this new and confusing sensation.
Ev'ry lady I see makes me tremble,
Makes me tremble with pleasure and
    pain.
When of love there is merely a mention,
I am spellbound and rapt with atten-
    tion.
I weave romances and daydreams
    together,
Filled with longing I cannot explain.
If I knew what it is I'd confess it,
But I am at a loss to express it,
Yet I know that it always excites me,
That it thrills me again and again.
Love is my inspiration,
Only consideration.
In rivers, woods and flowers,
I feel its magic streaming,
Awake, asleep and dreaming.
In gentle winds and showers,
I hear its mellow tone.
Love is my conversation,
Theme without variation,
I tell my love-song
To glens and mountains,
To rivers and fountains,
To moon and stars in heaven.
The gentle breezes echo my ev'ry word
    and tone.
And if no one will listen . . .
Then I will talk alone of love,
Talk to myself alone.

Recitative

(*As Cherubino is leaving, he sees the
Count in the distance, turns around
in fright, and hides himself behind
the arm-chair.*)

CHERUBINO

Wait, I hear footsteps.

SUSANNA
(*trying to screen Cherubino*)

It's the Count!
Hide quickly or you are lost!

COUNT (*entering*)

Susanna, you seem nervous, so confused
and excited.

SUSANNA

My lord, you must excuse me, but if
someone should come in now . . . I
beg of you, don't stay here.

COUNT
(*seats himself in the arm-chair and
takes Susanna's hand*)

It will take but a minute. Listen.

SUSANNA (*pulling her hand back*)

I will not listen.

COUNT

Just two words. You know the king has
appointed me ambassador to London, and I arranged for Figaro to go
with me.

SUSANNA (*timidly*)

If I dared ask you—

COUNT (*rising*)

Ask me, ask me, my darling, and with
that right you exert over me, (*tenderly, and trying to take her hand
again*) now and always, ask me,
compel me, command me.

SUSANNA (*angrily*)

I do not wish that right, I ask no
privilege, I don't want to exert it.
I'm so unhappy.

COUNT

No, no, Susanna, I want you to be
happy. You must know how much I
love you. I'm sure Basilio told you
already! Now listen, if you only consent to meet me tonight in the garden
of the castle, I will amply repay you
for this favor.

BASILIO (*offstage*)

He left not long ago.

COUNT

Basilio!

SUSANNA

Good heavens!

COUNT

Hurry, don't let him enter.

SUSANNA (*very agitated*)

I should leave you alone here?

BASILIO (*offstage*)

He can't be very far, perhaps with the
Countess.

COUNT (*pointing to the chair*)

I'll step behind this chair.

SUSANNA

Non vi celate.

IL CONTE

Taci, e cerca ch' ei parta.

SUSANNA

Ohimè! che fate!

BASILIO

Susanna, il ciel vi salvi; avreste a caso
Veduto il Conte?

SUSANNA

E cosa
Deve far meco il Conte? Animo, uscite.

BASILIO

Aspettate, sentite
Figaro di lui cerca.

SUSANNA

(O cielo!) ei cerca
Chi, dopo voi, più l' odia.

IL CONTE

(Vediam come mi serve.)

BASILIO

Io non ho mai
Nella moral sentito,
Ch' uno ch' ama la moglie odi il
marito, per dir che il Conte v'ama.

SUSANNA

Sortite, vil ministro dell'altrui sfrena-
tezza; io non ho d'uopo della vostra
morale, del Conte, del suo amor.

BASILIO

Non c'è alcun male. Ha ciascun i suoi
gusti,
Io mi credea che preferir doveste per
amante, come fan tutte quante, un
signor liberal, prudente, e saggio, a
un giovinastro, a un paggio.

SUSANNA

A Cherubino?

BASILIO

A Cherubino, Cherubin d'amore,
ch'oggi sul far del giorno passegiava
qui intorno per entrar.

SUSANNA

Uom maligno, un' impostura è questa.

BASILIO

È un maligno con voi, chi ha gli occhi
in testa?
E quella canzonetta
Ditemi in confidenza, io sono amico,
Ad altrui nulla dico,
E per voi? per madama?

SUSANNA

(Chi diavol gliel' ha detto?)

BASILIO

A proposito, figlia,
Instruitelo meglio.
Egli la guarda a tavola sì spesso,
E con tale immodestia,
Che s' il Conte s' accorge, e sul tal
punto,
Sapete, egli è una bestia.

SUSANNA

Scellerato! e perchè andate voi
Tai menzogne spargendo?

BASILIO

Io! che ingiustizia!
Quel che compro io vendo;
A quel che tutti dicono
Io no ci aggiungo un pelo.

IL CONTE

Come! che dicon tutti?

BASILIO

(O bello!)

SUSANNA

(O cielo!)

No. 7 Terzetto

IL CONTE

Cosa sento? tosto andate
E scacciate il seduttor.

BASILIO

In mal punto son quì giunto!
Perdonate, o mio signor.

SUSANNA

Che ruina! me meschina!
Sono oppressa dal dolor!

SUSANNA

No, that's too risky.

COUNT

Quiet, get rid of him quickly.

SUSANNA

Oh, Lord, how awful!

(*The Count tries to hide behind the arm-chair; Susanna stands between him and Cherubino; the Count draws her gently away. Meanwhile the page passes in front of the chair, and crouches in it. Susanna covers him with the dressing-gown.*)

BASILIO (*enters*)

Susanna, heaven bless you! Do you by chance know where the Count is?

SUSANNA

And what on earth should the Count do here? Go now, I'm busy.

BASILIO

Just a minute, it seems that Figaro wants to see him.

SUSANNA

The Count, the one man who hates him more than you do?

COUNT (*aside*)

Let's see how he will serve me.

BASILIO

That is not so. There is no such conclusion, that if one loves the wife, one must hate the husband. In fact, my master loves you.

SUSANNA

Get out of here this minute with your hints and suggestions. (*resentfully*) I have no interest in your lectures on morals, in your master, in his love.

BASILIO

Don't take it that way, I don't mean to offend you. I was just thinking that you would prefer the type of lover which most women admire, a lord who is liberal and prudent, to a young pipsqueak, a pageboy.

SUSANNA (*anxiously*)

Not Cherubino?

BASILIO

Yes, Cherubino, Cherubin the Cupid, who earlier this morning was prowling near your door, trying to enter.

SUSANNA (*forcefully*)

You're a villain, who tells malicious falsehoods!

BASILIO

To have eyes in one's head, is that malicious? For instance, this love-song . . . tell me, just between us, I can be trusted, and will breathe it to no one . . . is it for you or the Countess?

SUSANNA (*in consternation, to herself*)

Who the devil could have told him?

BASILIO

Apropos, my dear girl, you should train him much better. When he serves at table, he gazes at the Countess with such obvious longing that if the Count should take notice you can imagine, in that case, what's bound to happen.

SUSANNA

Oh, you liar! Have you nothing more to do than to spread vicious gossip?

BASILIO

I? You're mistaken. I just sell what I purchase, I echo what they all say, not adding in the slightest.

COUNT (*steps forward*)

Really! What are they saying?

BASILIO (*to himself*)

Delightful!

SUSANNA

Ah, heavens!

No. 7 TRIO

COUNT (*to Basilio*)

That's the limit!
Go this minute,
Find the culprit and throw him out.

BASILIO

How ill-chosen was my story,
Just a rumor, without a doubt.

SUSANNA

We'll be ruined by the scandal
If this gossip gets about!

IL CONTE, BASILIO
Ah! già svien la poverina!
Come, oh Dio! le batte il cor!

BASILIO
Pian pianin su questo seggio . . .

SUSANNA
Dove sono? Cosa veggio?
Che insolenza! andate fuor!

IL CONTE, BASILIO
Siamo qui per aiutarvi,
È sicuro il vostro onor.

BASILIO
Ah! del paggio quel che ho detto,
Era solo un mio sospetto.

SUSANNA
È un' insidia, una perfidia.
Non credete all' impostor.

IL CONTE
Parta, parta il damerino.

SUSANNA, BASILIO
Poverino! poverino!

IL CONTE
Poverino! poverino!
Ma da me sopreso ancor.

SUSANNA
Come?

BASILIO
Che?

IL CONTE
Da tua cugina
L' uscio ier trovai rinchiuso
Picchio; m' apre Barbarina

Paurosa fuor dell' uso,
Io dal muso insospettito
Guardo, cerco in ogni sito.
Ed alzando pian pianino
Il tappeto al tavolino,
Vedo il paggio—
Ah! cosa veggio?

SUSANNA
Ah, crude stelle!

BASILIO
Ah, meglio ancora!

a 3

IL CONTE
Onestissima signora!
Or capisco come va!

SUSANNA
Accader non può di peggio!
Giusti Dei! che mai sarà!

BASILIO
Così fan tutte le belle,
Non c'è alcuna novità.

RECITATIVO

IL CONTE
Basilio, in traccia tosto
Di Figaro volate; io vo' che veda.

SUSANNA
Ed io che senta; andate.

IL CONTE
Restate: che baldanza! E quale scusa
Se la colpa è evidente?

COUNT

Don't delay any longer,
Go and throw the scoundrel out.

SUSANNA

This is awful! What will happen?
Heaven help us! (*half fainting*) I am
feeling very faint.

COUNT AND BASILIO

(*Both support her.*) Ah, poor girl her
strength is failing!
We must help her, revive her fast,
Or, good Lord, she might not last.

BASILIO

(*approaching the arm-chair to sit down
in it*)
Let us put her in this arm-chair.

SUSANNA

Ah, where am I?
Am I dreaming? (*recovering*) You in-
sult me, (*repulsing them both*)
Go away, leave me alone.

BASILIO AND COUNT

We are only here to help you,
I assure you, we meant no harm.

BASILIO (*to the Count*)

What I told you
Was a rumor, mere suspicion,
With no foundation.

SUSANNA

He is vicious and malicious;
It's a lie, it is not true.

COUNT

Order him to leave the city.

BASILIO AND SUSANNA

What a pity!

COUNT (*ironically*)

What a pity!
I have caught him once before!

SUSANNA

Caught him?

BASILIO

How?

SUSANNA

How?

BASILIO

Did you?

SUSANNA AND BASILIO

Really? Where?

COUNT

At Barbarina's.
Yesterday I went to see Antonio.
I knocked, Barbarina opened and
looked extremely nervous. I began to
grow suspicious and examined every
corner.
When I gently drew the cover
From the table, I found beneath it . . .
(*showing how he found the page, he
lifts the dressing-gown from the chair
and discovers Cherubino; astonished*)
Cherubino!
Ha! What does this mean?

SUSANNA (*agitated*)

Ah, this is awful!

BASILIO (*laughing sardonically*)

Ah! this is priceless!

COUNT

Now at last my eyes are open!

SUSANNA

Nothing worse than this could happen!

COUNT

Now I see how matters stand!

SUSANNA

This affair is out of hand. How will
this end?
No one knows how this will end.

BASILIO

That's the way all women do it,
They will never show their hand.

COUNT

Now at last my eyes are open,
Now I see how matters stand.

RECITATIVE

COUNT

Basilio, go right away and tell Figaro
I want him. (*pointing to Cherubino,
who does not move from the spot*)
He has to see this.

SUSANNA (*animatedly*)

Yes, and hear this. Hurry.

COUNT

No, wait. Are you brazen? How dare
you face him, if your guilt is so
obvious?

SUSANNA

Non ha d' uopo di scusa un' innocente.

IL CONTE

Ma costui quando venne?

SUSANNA

Egli era meco, quando voi quì giun-
geste e mi chiedea d'impegnar la
padrona a intercedergli grazia. Il
vostro arrivo in scompiglio lo pose,
ed allor in quel loco si nascose.

IL CONTE

Ma s'io stesso m'assisi, quando in
camera entrai!

CHERUBINO

Ed allora di dietro io mi celai.

IL CONTE

E quando io là mi posi?

CHERUBINO

Allor io pian mi volsi, e quì m'ascosi.

IL CONTE

O cielo! dunque ha sentito
Quello ch'io ti dicea!

CHERUBINO

Feci per non sentir, quanto potea.

IL CONTE

O perfidia!

BASILIO

Frenatevi, vien gente.

IL CONTE

E voi restate qui, picciol serpente!

No. 8 Coro

CORO

Giovani liete, fiori spargete
Davanti il nobile nostro Signor;
Il suo gran core vi serba intatto
D'un più bel fiore l'almo candor.

RECITATIVO

IL CONTE

Cos'è questa commedia?

FIGARO

(Eccoci in danza: secondami, cor mio.)

SUSANNA

(Non ci ho speranza.)

FIGARO

Signor, non isdegnate questo del nostro affetto meritato tributo; or che
aboliste un diritto sì ingrato a chi
ben ama.

IL CONTE

Quel dritto or non v'è più, cosa si
brama?

FIGARO

Della vostra saggezza il primo frutto
oggi noi coglierem: le nostre nozze
si son già stabilite, or a voi tocca
costei che un vostro dono illibata
serbò, coprir di questo simbolo
d'onestà, candida vesta.

IL CONTE

(Diabolica astuzia! ma fingere convien.) Son grato, amici, ad un senso
si onesto! ma non merto per questo,
nè tributi, nè lodi, è un dritto ingiusto ne' miei feudi abolendo, a natura,
al dover lor dritti io rendo.

TUTTI

Evviva! evviva! evviva!

SUSANNA

Che virtù!

FIGARO

Che giustizia!

IL CONTE

A voi prometto compier la cerimonia,
chiedo sol breve indugio; io voglio
in faccia de miei più fidi, e con più

SUSANNA

I have nothing to hide, for I am blameless.

COUNT

What about Cherubino?

SUSANNA

He was with me when we heard you approaching. He came to beg me to plead for my lady's gracious intercession. And your arrival completely upset him, so he hid in that chair in desperation.

COUNT

But I sat in that arm-chair when I entered the room.

CHERUBINO (timidly)

At that time I was hiding behind it.

COUNT

But when I stepped behind it?

CHERUBINO

Then I slipped into the seat, under this cover.

COUNT (to Susanna)

Confound it! Then he has heard the whole of our conversation.

CHERUBINO

I tried my very best not to listen.

COUNT

Oh, you rascal!

BASILIO

Someone's coming, be careful!

COUNT

(pulling Cherubino out of the armchair)

And you stand up at once, you little serpent.

No. 8 CHORUS

(Enter Figaro, carrying a white veil in his hand, and peasants, dressed in white, who strew flowers from small baskets before the Count.)

Strew in his praises
Roses and daisies,
Let us all honor him,
Master and lord.
He has respected,
Nobly protected
Maidenly honor,
Virtue's reward.

He is sagacious,
Friendly and gracious
In his benevolence,
Loved and adored,
Our noble lord.

RECITATIVE AND CHORUS

COUNT (surprised, to Figaro)

What's the meaning of this nonsense?

FIGARO (aside to Susanna)

The fun is beginning! You bear me out, Susanna.

SUSANNA (aside)

I am discouraged.

FIGARO

My lord, we beg your pardon, do not reject this token of our loyal affection. You abolished a custom, so repulsive to all who love sincerely.

COUNT

That custom has been annulled, why do you worry?

FIGARO

We are the first ones to reap the fruits of the new decree. We have already set the time for our wedding, and call upon you to place this symbol of virtue on the head of my bride, chaste and spotless, thanks to your noble deed, your gen'rous action.

COUNT (aside)

What devilish cunning! But I will play along. (aloud) I'm truly grateful for your keen understanding; but I merit no credit, neither tribute nor praises for changing laws which were unjust and immoral. I am bound to uphold the rights of nature.

ALL

Three cheers for our generous master!

SUSANNA (sarcastically)

He is great!

FIGARO

He is noble!

COUNT (to Figaro and Susanna)

You have my promise to celebrate this marriage. Give me a little time, though. I need it to gather my faithful subjects; then, with fitting pomp

ricca pompa rendervi appien felici.
(Marcellina si trovi.) Andate amici.

CORO

Giovani, liete, fiori spargete, etc.

RECITATIVO

FIGARO

Evviva!

SUSANNA

Evviva!

BASILIO

Evviva!

FIGARO

E voi non applaudite?

SUSANNA

È afflitto poveretto,
Perchè il padron lo scaccia dal castello.

FIGARO

Ah! in un giorno sì bello!

SUSANNA

In un giorno di nozze.

FIGARO

Quando ognuno v'amira!

CHERUBINO

Perdono, mio signor!

IL CONTE

Nol meritate.

SUSANNA

Egli è ancora fanciullo.

IL CONTE

Men di quel che tu credi.

CHERUBINO

È ver mancai; ma dal mio labbro
alfine.

IL CONTE

Ben, ben, io vi perdono;
Anzi farò di più; vacante è un posto
D'uffizial nel reggimento mio;
Io sceglo voi; partite tosto, addio.

SUSANNA E FIGARO

Ah! fin domani sol.

IL CONTE

No, parta tosto.

CHERUBINO

A ubbidirvi, signor, son già disposto.

IL CONTE

Via per l'ultima volta
La Susanna abbracciate.
(Inaspettato è il colpo.)

FIGARO

Ehi, capitano,
A me pure la mano. (Io vuò parlarti,
　　pria che tu parta;) addio, picciolo
　　Cherubino;
Come cangia in un punto il tuo destino!

No. 9 ARIA

FIGARO

Non più andrai, farfallone amoroso,
Notte e giorno d'intorno girando,
Delle belle turbando il riposo,
Narcisetto, Adoncino d'amor.
Non più avrai, questi bei pennacchini,
Quel cappello leggiero e galante,
Quella chioma, quell'aria brillante,
Quel vermiglio donnesco color.
Fra guerrieri, poffar Bacco!
Gran mustacchi, stretto sacco,
Schioppo in spalla, sciabla al fianco,
Collo dritto, muso franco;
Un gran casco, o un gran turbante,
Molto onor, poco contante.
Ed invece del fandango
Una marcia per il fango.
Per montagne e per valloni
Colle nevi, e i sollioni,
Al concerto di tromboni
Di bombarde, e di cannoni,
Che le palle in tutti i tuoni

and circumstance I shall unite you.
(*aside*) I will send for Marcellina.
(*aloud*) Farewell, till later.

CHORUS
(*The peasants strew the rest of the flowers.*) Strew in his praises, *etc.*

(*Exeunt*)

RECITATIVE

FIGARO
Let's cheer him!

SUSANNA
Let's cheer him!

BASILIO
Let's cheer him!

FIGARO (*to Cherubino*)
Why don't you join the cheering?

SUSANNA
Poor fellow, he's dejected because the Count has banned him from the castle.

FIGARO
What? On this festive occasion?

SUSANNA
When the whole world admires you?

FIGARO
On the day of our wedding?

CHERUBINO (*kneeling*)
Forgive me, noble lord.

COUNT
You don't deserve it.

SUSANNA
He is only a child.

COUNT
Don't belittle his talents.

CHERUBINO
I may be little, but I hear like a grown-up.

COUNT
(*raising Cherubino from his knees*)
Enough. I will forgive you. And I will do even more. I need a captain in my regiment stationed at Seville. The post is yours, depart at once. (*The Count prepares to leave; Susanna and Figaro detain him.*)
Good-bye.

SUSANNA AND FIGARO
Please let him stay today.

COUNT
No, you have heard me.

CHERUBINO
(*sighing with great feeling*)
I'm prepared to obey your lordship's order.

COUNT
For the very last time, kiss Susanna good-bye. (*Cherubino embraces Susanna who is still confused.*) (*aside*)
That was a stroke of genius!

FIGARO
Well, mister captain, (*Exeunt the Count and Basilio*) best of luck on your journey. (*softly, to Cherubino*) Despite his order, stay till tomorrow. (*with feigned joy*) Good-bye, now, dear little Cherubino! What a glorious future lies before you!

No. 9 ARIA

FIGARO (*to Cherubino*)
From now on, my adventurous lover,
No romantic philand'ring excursions.
Such diversions are done with and over,
Cherubino, my young cavalier.
You had better forget all your fin'ry,
Feathered caps which you wore to perfection,
Powdered ringlets and creamlike complexion
In the army will soon disappear.
From now on *etc.*
Off with soldiers coarsely swearing,
Long mustaches proudly wearing!
With a rifle and a saber
In the army you will labor,
Trumpets clashing
And helmets flashing,
Lots of fame, but not much money,
And instead of minuetting,
Through the mud you'll stagger sweating.
Up the stony mountains wheezing,
Sometimes broiling, sometimes freezing,
To the tune of trumpets wailing,
While the cannon-balls are hailing
And the rifle bullets sailing,
Whistling by your pretty ear.
You had best forget your fin'ry *etc.*

All'orecchio fan fischiar.
Cherubino, alla vittoria,
Alla gloria militar.

ATTO SECONDO

*Magnifica Camera con alcova da letto
in fondo. Allato all'alcova, alla sinistra degli attori porta practicabile di
un gabinetto; dalla parte opposto
finestra practicabile. A sinistra, all
quinta damezzo, porta di entrata; dal
lato apposto, all'ultima quinta, porta
di un gabinetto.*

No. 10 CAVATINA

LA CONTESSA

Porgi, amor, qualche ristoro
Al mia duolo, a' miei sospir:
O mi rendi il mio tesoro,
O mi lascia, almen morir!

RECITATIVO

LA CONTESSA

Vieni, cara Susanna,
Finiscimi l'istoria.

SUSANNA

È già finita.

LA CONTESSA

Dunque volle sedurti?

SUSANNA

Oh il signor Conte non fa tai compli-
menti colle donne mie pari; egli
venne a contratto di danari.

LA CONTESSA

Ah! il crudel più non m'ama.

SUSANNA

E come poi è geloso di voi?

LA CONTESSA

Come lo sono i moderni mariti, per
sistema infedeli, per genio capricci-
osi, e per orgoglio poi tutti gelosi. Ma
se Figaro t'ama, ei sol potria.

FIGARO

La lalalalalalala.

SUSANNA

Eccolo, vieni, amico, madama impazi-
ente.

FIGARO

A voi non tocca stare in pena per
questo.
Alfin di che si tratta? Al signor Conte
piace la sposa mia; indi secreta-
mente ricuperar vorria il diritto
feudale; possibile è la cosa e
naturale.

LA CONTESSA

Possibil?

SUSANNA

Natural?

FIGARO

Naturalissima, e se Susanna vuol,
possibilissima.

SUSANNA

Finiscila una volta.

FIGARO

Ho già finito, quindi prese il partito,
di sceglier me corriero, e la Susanna
consiglera segreta d'ambasciata; a
perch'ella ostinata ognor rifiuta il
diploma d'onor, ch'ei le destina, minaccia di protegger Marcellina, questo e tutto l'affare.

SUSANNA

Ed hai coraggio di trattar scherzando
un negozio si serio?

FIGARO

Non vi basta
Che scherzando io ci pensi? Ecco il
progetto:
Per Basilio un biglietto
Io gli fo capitar che l'avvertisca
Di certo appuntamento,
Che per l'ora del ballo
A un amante voi deste.

LA CONTESSA

O ciel! che sento?
Ad un uom si geloso?

FIGARO

Ancora meglio; cosi potrem più presto
imbarazzarlo, confonderlo, imbro-
gliarlo, rovesciargli i progetti, empier-
lo di sospetti, e porgli in testa, che
la moderna festa ch'ei di fare a me
tenta, altri a lui faccia, onde quà

From now on, my adventurous lover
etc.
Cherubino on to glory,
On to glory and to fame!

(*Exeunt in military style.*)

ACT TWO

(Scene: *A luxurious room, with an alcove and three doors.*)

No. 10. CAVATINA

COUNTESS

Pour, O love,
Sweet consolation
On my lonely, my broken heart.
Give me back his lost affection,
Or, I beg you, let me die.
Bring me comfort in my suff'ring,
Hear my broken-hearted sigh.
Give me back my lord and husband,
Or, I beg you, let me die.

RECITATIVE

COUNTESS

Come, Susanna, sit down here and finish the story.

SUSANNA (*entering*)

That's all there is to it.

COUNTESS

And you say that he loves you?

SUSANNA

Oh, no, my master doesn't pay such a compliment to a girl of my station; he thinks he can buy me with money.

COUNTESS

So he loves me no longer?

SUSANNA

How is it, then, that he's jealous of you?

COUNTESS

It is the same way with all modern husbands, by nature unfaithful, by character capricious, and conceited enough to be jealous. But if Figaro loves you, he might be able . . .

FIGARO
(*enters singing*)

La, la, la, *etc.*

SUSANNA

There he is! (*to Figaro*) Come, my darling, my lady is waiting.

FIGARO (*with casual gaiety*)

No need to worry, there's no reason whatever. The matter's very simple: my noble lord takes a fancy to my Susanna, so he decides in secret that he'll restore a custom he has lately abolished. The thing is very possible and very natural.

COUNTESS

Very possible?

SUSANNA

Very natural?

FIGARO

It is most natural, and, if Susanna wants it, is most possible.

SUSANNA

When will you ever finish?

FIGARO

I have already. That is why he decided he needs me as his courier and that Susanna should become his ambassadress in secret; and because she has stubbornly refused to accept the assignment, he's offended and threatens to take sides with Marcellina. That's the gist of the story.

SUSANNA

How can you treat such a serious business as a matter of joking?

FIGARO

Aren't you happy that I don't take it seriously? Here is my project: through Basilio I'll send a little note to the Count to inform him about an appointment (*to the Countess*) that the Countess supposedly made with a lover.

COUNTESS

Good Lord! How risky! With a husband so jealous!

FIGARO

So much the better. Because we can more readily attack him, baffle him, disconcert him, get him wholly bewildered, inflame him with suspicion, and make him grasp that what

perda il tempo, ivi la traccia, così
quasi ex abrupto, e senza ch'abbia
fatto per frastonarci alcun disegno
vien l'ora delle nozze, in faccia a lei
non fia, ch'osi d'opporsi ai voti miei.

SUSANNA
È ver, ma in di lui vece, s'opporrà
Marcellina.

FIGARO
Aspetta al Conte!
Farai subito dir, che verso sera
Attendati in giardino;
Il picciol Cherubino,
Per mio consiglio, non ancor partito,
Da femmina vestito
Faremo che in sua vece ivi sen vada;
Questa è l'unica strada
Onde monsù sorpreso de madama
Sia costretto a far poi quel che si
    brama.

LA CONTESSA
Che ti par?

SUSANNA
Non c'è mal.

LA CONTESSA
Nel nostro caso . . .

SUSANNA
Quand'egli è persuaso . . .

SUSANNA
E dove è il tempo?

FIGARO
Ito è il Conte alla caccia, e per
    qualch'ora
Non sarà di ritorno. Io vado, e tosto
Cherubino vi mando. Lascio a voi
La cura di vestirlo.

LA CONTESSA
E poi?

FIGARO
E poi
Se vuol ballare,
Signor Contino,
Il chitarrino
Le suonerò.

RECITATIVO

LA CONTESSA
Quanto duolmi, Susanna,
Che questo giovinotto abbia del Conte

Le stravaganze udito!—ah! tu non sai
Ma per qual causa mai
Da me stessa ei non venne?
Dov'è la canzonetta?

SUSANNA
Eccola. Appunto
Facciam che ce la canti.
Zitto! vien gente, è desso.
    Avanti, avanti,
Signor uffiziale!

CHERUBINO
Ah! non chiamarmi
Con nome sì fatale; ei mi rammenta
Che abbandonar deggio comare tanto
    buona!

SUSANNA
E tanto bella!

CHERUBINO
Ah! si, certo.

SUSANNA
Ah! si, certo!

SUSANNA
Ah! si certo! Ipocritone!
Via presto la canzone,
Che stamane a me deste,
A madama cantate.

LA CONTESSA
Chi n'è l'autor?

SUSANNA
Guardate, egli ha due braci
Di rossor sulla faccia.

LA CONTESSA
Prendi la mia chitarra, e l'accompagna.

CHERUBINO
Io sono sì tremante,
Ma se madama vuole . . .

SUSANNA
Lo vuole, si, lo vuol, manco parole.

No. 11 ARIETTA

CHERUBINO
Voi che sapete
    che cosa è amor,
Donne vedete
    s'io l'ho nel cor.

he does to others they will do unto him, and even with int'rest! While he is losing time as well as his bearings, our wedding hour will come before he ever finds an opportunity to hinder us from getting married, (*indicating the Countess*) or has a chance to make any effective opposition.

SUSANNA

That's true, but in his stead Marcellina will oppose us.

FIGARO

I know it, so therefore, you give the Count a hint that late this evening you'll meet him in the garden, and little Cherubino (on my advice he has not yet departed) dressed up as a woman, will keep the rendezvous in place of Susanna. That's the only solution whereby his lordship, surprised by my lady, can be forced to accede to all her dictates.

COUNTESS

How is that?

SUSANNA

Good enough.

COUNTESS

All things considered . . .

SUSANNA

If he thinks it will work . . . But is there time left?

FIGARO

The Count has gone hunting and won't come back here for at least sev'ral hours. I'll go now and (*about to go*) send you Cherubino immediately. You have ample time to get him ready.

COUNTESS

And then?

FIGARO

And then?
Should my dear master want some diversion,
I'll play the music on my guitar. (*Exit Figaro.*)

RECITATIVE

COUNTESS

How it grieves me, Susanna, to think that Cherubino heard all the nonsense my wayward husband told you. Ah, you don't know yet . . . but for what earthly reason didn't he see me in person? Where did you put his love-song?

SUSANNA

Here it is. As soon as he comes we'll have him sing it. Listen, who is it? Our hero! (*enter Cherubino.*) Come in, come in, most worthy major gen'ral!

CHERUBINO

Please do not call me by such a fatal title, for it reminds me that soon I must leave her, my dearest kindest lady . . .

SUSANNA

Who is so pretty!

CHERUBINO (*sighing*)

So sweet! So lovely!

SUSANNA (*mocking him*)

So sweet! So lovely! You little hypocrite! Now quickly sing that lovesong which you gave me this morning so the Countess may hear it.

COUNTESS

Who wrote the song?

SUSANNA (*pointing to Cherubino*)

Who wrote it? Look at his face and see him blush like a school-girl.

COUNTESS

Take my guitar, Susanna, and accompany.

CHERUBINO

Today I'm not in voice, but if madame desires . . .

SUSANNA

She surely does. Come on, no more preambles.

No. 11 ARIETTA

(*Susanna plays on the guitar.*)

CHERUBINO

You know the answer, you hold the key.
Love's tender secret, share it with me,
Ladies, I beg you, share it with me.

Quello ch'io provo
  vi vidisò dirò,
È per me nuovo
  capir nol so.
Sento un affetto
  pien di desir
Ch'ora è diletto
  ch'ora è martir.
Gelo, e poi sento
  l'alma avvampar,
E in un momento
  torno a gelar.
Ricerco un bene
  fuori di me,
Non so ch'il tiene
  non so cos'è.
Sospiro, e gemo
  senza voler.
Palpito e tremo
  senza saper.
Non trovo pace
  notte nè di;
Eppur mi piace
  languir così.

RECITATIVO

LA CONTESSA

Bravo! che bella voce! Io non sapea
Che cantaste si bene.

SUSANNA

Oh! in verità
Egli fa tutto ben quello che fa.
Presto, a noi, bel soldato;
Figaro v'informò . . .

CHERUBINO

Tutto mi disse.

SUSANNA

Lasciatemi veder—andrà benissimo;
Siam d'uguale statura. Giù quel manto.

LA CONTESSA

Che fai?

SUSANNA

Niente paura.

LA CONTESSA

E se qualcuno entrasse?

SUSANNA

Entri, che mal facciamo?
La porta chiuderò; ma come poi
Acconciargli i cappelli?

LA CONTESSA

Una mia cuffia prendi nel gabinetto,
Presto—che carta è quella?

CHERUBINO

La patente.

LA CONTESSA

Che sollecita gente!

CHERUBINO

L'ebbi or or da Basilio.

LA CONTESSA

Dalla fretta obbliato hanno il sigillo.

SUSANNA

Il sigillo di che?

LA CONTESSA

Della patente.

SUSANNA

Cospetto, che premura!
Ecco la cuffia.

LA CONTESSA

Spicciati: va bene;
Miserabili noi, se il Conte viene!

No. 12 ARIA

SUSANNA

Venite, inginocchiatevi,
Restate fermo lì.
Pian piano or via giratevi;
Bravo! va ben così,
La faccia ora volgetemi,
Olà! quegli occhi a me.
Dritissimo, guardatemi,
Madama quì non è.
Restate fermo
Or via giratevi
Guardatemi, bravo
Più alto quel colletto;
Quel ciglio un po' più **basso**,

This new sensation I undergo,
It is so diff'rent from all I know.
Filled with excitement, walking on air,
First I am happy, soon I despair.
Now I am chilly, next time aflame,
Not for a moment am I the same.
I am pursuing some sunny ray,
But it eludes me, try as I may.
I can't stop sighing, hard as I try,
And then I tremble, not knowing why.
From this dilemma I find no peace,
And yet I want it never to cease.
You know the answer, *etc.*

RECITATIVE

COUNTESS

Bravo, your voice is lovely. I did not know you were such an expert singer.

SUSANNA

To tell the truth, all he does he always does well. Now come here, handsome soldier. Figaro told you all?

CHERUBINO

Every detail.

SUSANNA

Then let me see your height. (*measuring herself with Cherubino*) It will go splendidly . . . you are just about my size. Take your coat off. (*takes off his cloak*)

COUNTESS

Be careful!

SUSANNA

No need to worry.

COUNTESS

If somebody should enter?

SUSANNA

Let him, what harm are we doing? (*locking the door*) But I must lock the door. What shall we do so his hair will not show?

COUNTESS

Get him a bonnet out of my wardrobe dresser, hurry! (*Susanna goes into the small room to get a bonnet. Cherubino approaches the Countess and shows her the commission, which he carries in his pocket. She takes it, opens it and notices that the seal is missing*) What have you got there?

CHERUBINO

My commission.

COUNTESS

They didn't waste a moment.

CHERUBINO

I got it from Basilio.

COUNTESS

(*returns the commission to him*) In their hurry they even forgot the seal.

SUSANNA

(*returning with a cap in her hand*) The seal on what?

COUNTESS

On his commission.

SUSANNA

How could they be so careless? Here is the bonnet.

COUNTESS

There you are. That's perfect! How disastrous for us if the Count came home now!

No. 12 ARIA

SUSANNA

Come here and kneel in front of me,
(*She takes Cherubino and makes him kneel a slight distance from the Countess, who has seated herself.*)
And let me try my skill.
Don't wiggle, don't wiggle!
For Heaven's sake, stand still,
Be patient and stand still.
(*She combs his hair, first from one side, then takes him by the chin and turns him as she combs the other side.*)
Now slowly turn your head around.
Bravo, that's very nice.
(*While Susanna is dressing his hair, Cherubino regards the Countess tenderly.*)
Now turn your face the other way,
And look me in the eye!
(*Continues to dress his hair; she places the bonnet on him.*)
Hold still and let me try.
Look straight at me, not ev'rywhere.
The Countess is not sitting there,
So wait till by and by.
If you would keep your mind on this
We'd get it over soon.
The more you play, the more delay.
At this rate we'll take all afternoon.

Le mani sotto il petto,
Vedremo poscia il passo
Quando sarete in piè.
Mirate il bricconcello,
Mirate quanto è bello!
Che furba guardatura!
Che vezzo, che figura!
Se l'amano le femmine
Han certo il lor perchè.

RECITATIVO

LA CONTESSA

SUSANNA
Quante buffonerie!

SUSANNA
Ma se ne sono io medesma gelosa!
Ehi, serpentello, volete tralasciar
d'esser sì bello?

LA CONTESSA
Finiam le ragazzate; or quelle maniche
oltre il gomito gli alza, onde più
agiatamente l'abito gli si adatti.

SUSANNA
Ecco!

LA CONTESSA
Più indietro, cosi. Che nastro è quello?

SUSANNA
E quel ch'esso involommi.

LA CONTESSA
E questo sangue?

CHERUBINO
Quel sangue . . . io non so come, poco
pria sdrucciolando . . . in un sasso
. . . la pelle io mi sgraffiai . . . e la
piaga col nastro io mi fasciai.

SUSANNA
Mostrate: non è mal; cospetto! ha il

braccio più candido del mio!
qualche ragazza . . .

LA CONTESSA
E segui a far la pazza? Va nel mio gabinetto, e prendi un poco d'inglese
taffetà, ch'è sullo scrigno. In quanto
al nastro . . . per il colore mi spiacea
di privarmene.

SUSANNA
Tenete, e da legargli il braccio?

LA CONTESSA
Un altro nastro prendi insiem col mio
vestito.

CHERUBINO
Ah, più presto m'avria quello guarito!

LA CONTESSA
Perchè? questo è migliore . . .

CHERUBINO
Allor che un nastro . . . legò la chioma
. . . ovver toccò la pelle . . .
d'ogetto . . .

LA CONTESSA
Forestiero, è buon per le ferite, non è
vero? Guardate qualità ch'io non
sapea!

CHERUBINO
Madama scherza, ed io frattanto
parto!

LA CONTESSA
Poverin! Che sventura!

CHERUBINO
Oh me infelice!

LA CONTESSA
Or piange . . .

Can't you be quiet?
Don't be so fidgety!
Behave yourself! That's it!
The motions slightly slower,
The skirt a little lower,
The glance a trifle shyer,
The motions slightly slower,
Now you must walk around.
We'll give you some suggestions
While you are passing by.
(*aside to the Countess*)
Just see our prima donna!
He plays his part with honor.
The clever little shammer
Is full of charm and glamour.
No powder or cosmetic would better
  his complexion.
His glance is so poetic, his figure is
  perfection!
If women fall in love with him, they
  know the reason why,
Oh, certainly, they know the reason
  why.
Yes, yes, I see it clearly,
The reason why *etc.*

RECITATIVE

COUNTESS

My, you are worse than children!

SUSANNA

He looks so sweet I could almost be
jealous! (*takes Cherubino by the
chin*) You little rascal, where do you
get the right to look so pretty?

COUNTESS

I wish you'd stop this nonsense. I think
you'd better roll up his sleeves past
his elbows. Then, when we put his
dress on, it will not fit so tightly.

SUSANNA (*doing so*)
This way.

COUNTESS

Up farther, like this. (*discovers a ribbon wrapped about his arm*) What
is that ribbon?

SUSANNA

The one he stole this morning.

COUNTESS

Why is it bloodstained?

CHERUBINO

Oh, really, I can't imagine. Just before,
when I stumbled on the gravel, I
guess I scraped my elbow, and I
bandaged the wound with this ribbon.

SUSANNA

Let's see it. That's not bad! Good
gracious! His arm is much whiter
than my own, just like a woman's!

COUNTESS

You still keep up this nonsense? Go
and look in my closet, and get a piece
of adhesive plaster. Quick, it's in the
dresser. As for that ribbon, you know,
I like the color, I would hate to part
with it.
(*Susanna dashes off; the Countess con-
templates her ribbon; Cherubino,
kneeling, observes her attentively.*)

SUSANNA

(*gives the plaster and the scissors to the
Countess*)
I found it, but don't we need a ban-
dage?

COUNTESS

Another ribbon! Bring it along when
you come back. (*Susanna leaves
through the door at the back, taking
with her Cherubino's cloak.*)

CHERUBINO

Ah, the old one would have healed it
much quicker!

COUNTESS

And why? This one is better.

CHERUBINO

But any ribbon which touched the skin,
or bound the hair of someone, somebody . . .

COUNTESS (*interrupting him*)
Who's a stranger will heal your cuts
and bruises, don't you think so? It
seems to have some pow'rs I never
heard of.

CHERUBINO

My lady's joking, and I must go away.

COUNTESS

My poor boy! What misfortune!

CHERUBINO

How I am suff'ring!

COUNTESS (*much moved*)
You're crying!

CHERUBINO
Oh ciel! Perchè morir non lice! Forse
vicino all'ultimo momento . . . questa
bocca oseria!

LA CONTESSA
Siate saggio, cos'è questa follia?
Chi picchia alla mia porta?

IL CONTE
Perchè chiusa?

LA CONTESSA
Il mio sposo!
O Dei! son morta!
Voi quì senza mantello!
In questo stato—un ricevuto foglio,
La sua gran gelosia!

IL CONTE
Cosa indugiate?

LA CONTESSA
Son sola—ah si, son sola.

IL CONTE
E a chi parlate?

LA CONTESSA
A voi . . . certo a voi stesso.

CHERUBINO
Dopo quel ch' è successo,
Il suo furore . . . non trovo altro con-
siglio.

LA CONTESSA
Ah! mi difenda il cielo in tal periglio!

IL CONTE
Che novità? Non fu mai vostra
usanza
Di rinchiudervi in stanza.

LA CONTESSA
È ver, ma io . . .
Io stava quì mettendo . . .

IL CONTE
Via mettendo . . .

LA CONTESSA
Certe robe, era meco la Susanna.
Che in sua camera è andata.

IL CONTE
Ad ogni modo
Voi non siete tranquilla.
Guardate questo foglio.

LA CONTESSA
(Numi! è il foglio,
Che Figaro gli scrisse.)

IL CONTE
Cos' è codesto strepito?
In gabinetto
Qualche cosa è caduta.

LA CONTESSA
Io non intesi niente.

IL CONTE
Convien che abbiate gran pensieri in
mente.

LA CONTESSA
Di che?

IL CONTE
Là v' è qualcuno.

LA CONTESSA
Chi volete che sia?

IL CONTE
Lo chiedo a voi;
Io vengo in questo punto.

LA CONTESSA
Ah! sì . . . Susanna . . . appunto . . .

IL CONTE
Che passò, mi diceste· alla sua stanza?

LA CONTESSA
Alla sua stanza, o quì, non vidi bene.

IL CONTE
Susanna, e d'onde viene,
Che siete sì turbata?

LA CONTESSA
Per la mia cameriera?

IL CONTE
Io non so nulla;
Ma turbata senz' altro.

LA CONTESSA
Ah questa serva
Più che non turba me, turba voi stesso

IL CONTE
E vero, è vero, e lo vedrete adesso.

CHERUBINO

O Lord, why don't you let me die now? Close to my death, I might get up the courage to confess how I really . . .

COUNTESS

(drying his eyes with her handkerchief) Cherubino, you are a little baby. (A knock is heard at the door) Who's knocking at my door?

COUNT (outside)

Why locked in?

COUNTESS

It's my husband! Good Heavens! I'm ruined . . . with you here without your jacket . . . in this condition . . . he has received a letter . . . he's so terribly jealous!

COUNT (more loudly)

Why this delay?

COUNTESS (confused)

I'm alone. Yes, yes, I'm coming . . .

COUNT

To whom were you speaking?

COUNTESS

To you . . . surely to you only.

CHERUBINO

After all that has happened, his awful temper, I cannot let him find me! (runs into the small room and shuts the door)

COUNTESS

May God above protect me in this danger! (takes the key and runs to admit the Count)

COUNT

(enters, in a hunting costume) This is something new! It was never your custom to lock yourself in.

COUNTESS

That's true, but this time, I only was arranging . . .

COUNT

Arranging . . .

COUNTESS

Some of my dresses, and Susanna was with me; she has gone into her own room . . .

COUNT

At any rate, it seems that something upset you. Can you explain this letter?

COUNTESS (aside)

Heavens! The letter that Figaro has written! (Cherubino, in the small room, noisely knocks over a small table and chair.)

COUNT

What was that awful noise in there? A piece of furniture fell down in your boudoir.

COUNTESS

Strange, I did not hear it.

COUNT

In that event, you must be hard of hearing.

COUNTESS

Who, I?

COUNT

Somebody's in there!

COUNTESS

Who could possibly be there?

COUNT

I'm asking you that. I only just came in here.

COUNTESS

Of course, Susanna. How could I . . .

COUNT

Just before, you were saying she went to her room.

COUNTESS

Maybe to her room or that one, I was not watching.

COUNT

Then tell me, how does it happen you are so embarrassed?

COUNTESS (with a forced laugh)

For what possible reason?

COUNT

I can't explain it, but you do seem embarrassed.

COUNTESS

Is it not you, rather, who should be embarrassed about Susanna?

COUNT

That's not the issue! If it's Susanna, then I must see her.

No. 13 Terzetto

IL CONTE
Susanna, or via sortite,
Sortite, così vo'!

LA CONTESSA
Fermatevi! sentite!
Sortire ella non può.

SUSANNA
(Cos' è codesta lite—
Il paggio dove andò?)

IL CONTE
E chi vietarlo or osa? Chi?

LA CONTESSA
Lo vieta l' onestà.
Un abito di sposa
Provando ella si stà.

a 3.

IL CONTE
(Chiarissima è la cosa,
L' amante qui sarà!)

LA CONTESSA
(Bruttissima è la cosa,
Chi sa cosa sarà!)

SUSANNA
(Capisco qualche cosa,
Veggiamo come va!)

IL CONTE
Susanna,

LA CONTESSA
Fermatevi!

IL CONTE
Or via sentite.

LA CONTESSA
Sentite.

IL CONTE
Sortite,

LA CONTESSA
Fermatevi,

IL CONTE
Io così vo'!

LA CONTESSA
Sortire ella non può.

IL CONTE
Dunque parlate almeno,
Susanna se quì siete!

LA CONTESSA
Nemmen, nemmen, nemmeno,
Io v'ordino, tacete,

a 3

IL CONTE, LA CONTESSA
Consorte mia, giudizio!
Un scandalo, un disordine,
Schiviam per carità!

SUSANNA
O cieló, un precipizio,
Un scandolo, un disordine,
Quì certo nascerà.

Recitativo

IL CONTE
Dunque, voi non aprite?

LA CONTESSA
E perchè deggio
Le mie camere aprir?

IL CONTE
Ebben, lasciate,
L' aprirem senza chiave. Ehi, gente!

LA CONTESSA
Come?
Porreste a repentaglio
D'una dama l' onore?

IL CONTE
È vero, io sbaglio, posso senza rumore,
senza scandalo alcun di nostra gente,
andar io stesso a prender l'occor-
rente. Attendete pur quì . . . ma
perchè in tutto sia il mio dubbio
distrutto, anco le porte io primo
chiuderò.

LA CONTESSA
(Che imprudenza!)

IL CONTE
Voi la condiscendenza
Di venir meco avrete;
Madama, eccovi il braccio; andiamo!

No. 13 Trio

(Susanna enters through the door she used on leaving, and halts on seeing the Count at the door of the small room.)

COUNT
Susanna, what's the matter?
Come out now, do you hear?

COUNTESS
Impossible, she cannot,
Right now she can't appear.

SUSANNA
What's all this angry chatter?
The page no longer here?

COUNT
What reason can prevent her? Speak!

COUNTESS
She's modest, she's modest!
That is why.
A wedding dress was sent her,
She has to try it on.

COUNT
I grasp the situation,
Her lover hides inside.

COUNTESS
Your shameful accusation
Severely wounds my pride.
Your impudent accusation
Is baseless and unwise.

SUSANNA
A ticklish situation,
It cannot be denied.
A ticklish situation,
He took us by surprise.

COUNT
Disgraceful situation!
I took them by surprise.
Susanna, what is the matter?
Come out now! Haven't you heard?

COUNTESS
Impossible! She cannot!
Right now she can't appear.

COUNT
Well, if I may not see you,
Susanna, let me hear you,

COUNTESS
You will not hear her talking.
Expressly, I forbid it!
(Susanna hides in the alcove.)

COUNT
My lady, please consider,
Be careful, I warn you.

SUSANNA
Oh Heavens! This is dreadful!
A scandal, a catastrophe
Will surely come to pass.

COUNTESS
Your lordship, think it over.
No scandal or catastrophe
Must ever come to pass.

SUSANNA
Good Lord, what a disaster,
A scandal, a catastrophe
Will surely come to pass.

COUNT, COUNTESS AND SUSANNA
Your lordship, (my lady) think it over,
A scandal, a catastrophe
Will surely come to pass.

RECITATIVE

COUNT
Are you going to open?

COUNTESS
And for what reason should I open my room?

COUNT
All right, don't open. I'll get in just the same. Ho, servants!

COUNTESS
How dare you! Can it be your intention to disgrace me in public?

COUNT
Of course not, why should I? Without noise or disturbance, nor arousing a scandal before our servants, I'll go myself, then, to get all that is needed. You will wait for me here. But before leaving, so that all doubts are excluded, I shall make sure and lock all the doors. *(locks the door to Susanna's room)*

COUNTESS *(aside)*
This is worse yet.

COUNT
No, on second thought, be kind enough to come with me. *(with feigned gaiety)* My lady, may I escort you? Here is my arm.

LA CONTESSA
Andiamo!

IL CONTE
Susanna starà quì finchè torniamo.

No. 14. DUETTINO

SUSANNA
Aprite, presto aprite,
Aprite, è la Susanna
Sortite via, sortite,
Andate via di quà.

CHERUBINO
Ahimè! che scena orribile!
Che gran fatalità!

SUSANNA
Le porte son serrate;

CHERUBINO
Che mai sarà?

CHERUBINO
Qui perdersi non giova.

SUSANNA
V' uccide se vi trova.

CHERUBINO
Veggiamo un po' qui fuori,
Dà proprio nel giardino.

SUSANNA
Fermate, Cherubino.
Fermate, per pietà.

CHERUBINO
Qui perdersi non giova
M'uccide se mi trova.

SUSANNA
Tropp' alto per un salto,
Fermate per pietà!

CHERUBINO
Lasciami, pria di nuocerle,
Nel foco volerei.
Abbraccio te per lei;
Addio così si fa.

SUSANNA
Ei va aperire, o Dei!
Fermate per pietà!

RECITATIVO

SUSANNA
Oh! guarda il demonietto, come fugge!
E già un miglio lontano
Ma non perdiamci invano;
Entriam in gabinetto;
Venga poi lo smargiasso,
Io quì l'aspetto.

IL CONTE
Tutto è come il lasciai, volete dunque
Aprir voi stessa, o deggio?

LA CONTESSA
Ahimè! fermate,
E ascoltatemi un poco;
Mi credete capace
Di mancare al dover?

IL CONTE
Come vi piace,
Entro quel gabinetto;
Chi v'è chiuso vedrò.

LA CONTESSA
Si, lo vedrete,
Ma uditemi tranquillo.

IL CONTE
Non è dunque Susanna?

COUNTESS (*shuddering*)
So be it.

COUNT (*indicating the small room*)
Susanna won't mind waiting till we are
back here. (*Exeunt*)

No. 14 DUETTINO

(*Susanna runs out of the alcove.*)

SUSANNA
(*at the door of the small room*)
Unlock the door and hurry!
It's I, it is Susanna!
Come out now, and quickly,
Come out this very minute,
You must get out of here!

CHERUBINO
(*coming out of the small room, confused and breathless*)
O Lord, what a calamity,
How can I get away?

SUSANNA
You can't, I fear.

CHERUBINO
I've got to get away!

SUSANNA
He locked the door from outside.
In Heaven's name, what can we do?

CHERUBINO
To stay is out of question.

SUSANNA
Then make a good suggestion.

CHERUBINO
(*going towards the window which looks
out on the garden, as though he
were going to jump out*)
Let's see about the window,
It is above the garden.

SUSANNA (*holding him back*)
Don't do it, Cherubino,
Don't do it, don't jump, it is too high!

CHERUBINO
(*trying to free himself from her*)
It's suicide, I know it!

SUSANNA
Don't do it, Cherubino.

CHERUBINO
It really does not matter!

SUSANNA
It's much too high for jumping,
You never will get by.

CHERUBINO
No other day is left for me.
(*releasing himself from her*)
I would never cause my lady any
shame.
Embrace her in my name!
Good-bye now, and here I go.

SUSANNA
He really means to do it!
For Heaven's sake, stay here,
Don't do it, don't do it!
(*Cherubino jumps out. Susanna
screams, sits down for a moment,
and then goes to the balcony.*)

RECITATIVE

SUSANNA
Look at the little devil! How he can
run! He's already a mile away. But
it is up to me now to deal with our
lord and master. Come ahead, Mister
Tyrant, I shall be ready.

(*She enters the small room and locks
the door behind her.*)
(*The Countess and the Count enter.
The Count brings a hammer and a
crow-bar. After entering, he examines
all the doors.*)

COUNT
Ev'rything's as we left it. Will you
yourself unlock the door now, or
shall I? (*preparing to force open
the door*)

COUNTESS
Just wait one moment. I entreat you to
listen. (*The Count tosses the hammer
and crow-bar onto a chair.*) Do you
think I could fail you in my duty
as your wife?

COUNT
That is the question. Meanwhile I am
proceeding to find out who is there.

COUNTESS
(*timidly and trembling*)
Yes, there is someone, but listen to me
calmly.

COUNT (*incensed*)
So it's not Susanna?

LA CONTESSA

No, ma invece è un oggetto, che
ragion di sospetto, non vi deve lasciar; per questa sera, una burla innocente, di far si disponeva, ed io vi
giuro che l'onor, l'onestà . . .

IL CONTE

Chi è dunque? dite . . . l'ucciderò.

LA CONTESSA

Sentite, (ah non ho cor!)

IL CONTE

Parlate.

LA CONTESSA

E un fanciullo.

IL CONTE

Un fanciul?

LA CONTESSA

Si, Cherubino.

IL CONTE

E mi farà il destino
Ritrovar questo paggio in ogni loco?
Come? Non è partito?—Scellerati!
Ecco i dubbi spiegati; ecco l'imbroglio,
Ecco il raggiro, onde m'avverte il
foglio.

No. 15 FINALE

IL CONTE

Esci ormai, garzon malnato;
Sciagurato, non tardar!

LA CONTESSA

Ah! signore, quel furore,
Per lui fammi il cor tremar!

IL CONTE

E d'opporvi ancor osate?

LA CONTESSA

No, sentite!

IL CONTE

Via parlate.

LA CONTESSA

Giuro al ciel che ogni sospetto
E lo stato, in che il trovate,
Sciolto il collo, nudo il petto.

IL CONTE

Sciolto il collo, nudo il petto!
Seguitate!

LA CONTESSA

Per vestir femminee spoglie . . .

IL CONTE

Ah! comprendo, indegna moglie,
Mi vo' tosto vendicar.

LA CONTESSA

Mi fa torto quel trasporto,
M'oltraggiate a dubitar.

IL CONTE

Quà la chiave.

LA CONTESSA

Egli è innocente!
Voi sapete.

IL CONTE

Non so niente.
Va lontan dagli occhi miei!
Un'infida, un'empia sei,
E mi cerchi d'infamar.

LA CONTESSA

Vado, si, ma . . .

IL CONTE

Non ascolto.

LA CONTESSA

Non son rea!

COUNTESS

No, but somebody else who can give
you no reason for suspicion or doubt.
We were rehearsing, just a harmless
diversion, a frolic for this evening,
and I assure you that my honor, your
good faith . . .

COUNT

Who is it? Say it, (*with increasing
anger*) I'll strike him dead!

COUNTESS

Please listen? Ah! I'm afraid!

COUNT

Speak freely.

COUNTESS

It's just a child.

COUNT

Just a child?

COUNTESS

Yes, Cherubino.

COUNT (*aside*)

Why must I find that page-boy trailing
my footsteps like a shadow? (*aloud*)
What? Has he not left? He defied
me. Now I begin to see daylight in
this confusion. This is the cunning
plot of which the letter warned me.

No. 15 FINALE

COUNT

(*with violence, at the door of the
small room*)

Out you come. Don't waste a moment,
wretched, disobedient page!

COUNTESS (*pulling him back
from the small room*)

Dearest husband, what excitement!
I am frightened by your rage.

COUNT

And you still would dare oppose me?

COUNTESS

You must listen!

COUNT

I am waiting!

COUNTESS

Let me tell you.

COUNT

I am waiting. The answer, what is it?

COUNTESS

As a joke you have to take it,
No bad intention, (*trembling and
alarmed*)
And the costume, in which you find
him,
Open collar, shoulders naked . . .

COUNT

Open collar! Shoulders naked! Do continue!

COUNTESS

To disguise him as a woman . . .

COUNT

(*goes toward the small room, then
turns around*)

How indecent, how outrageous!
For his boldness he shall pay!

COUNTESS (*forcefully*)

You offend me most severely
By accusing me this way.

COUNT

Let me enter! (*turning back*)

COUNTESS

He is not guilty. (*gives him the key*)
You know better.

COUNT

I know nothing!
Go away at once and leave me,
You're unfaithful and deceived me.
You have covered me with shame.

COUNTESS

I leave you, yes . . . but . . .

COUNT

I won't listen.

COUNTESS

But . . .

COUNT

I won't listen.

COUNTESS

I am blameless.

COUNT

I don't believe you!
I shall kill him.

COUNTESS

Ah, his ear is deaf to reason,
Jealous rage has made him blind.

IL CONTE
Vel leggo in volto.

a 2.

Mora mora, e più non sia
Rea cagion del mio penar.

LA CONTESSA
Ah! la cieca gelosia
Qualche eccesso gli fa far.

LA CONTESSA, IL CONTE
Susanna!

SUSANNA
Signore!
Cos'è quel stupore?
Il brando prendete,
Il paggio uccidete,
Quel paggio malnato
Vedetelo quà.

a 3

LA CONTESSA
Che storia è mai questa!
Susanna v'è là!

IL CONTE
Che scola! la testa,
Girando mi va!

SUSANNA
Confusa han la testa,
Non san come va.

IL CONTE
Sei sola?

SUSANNA
Guardate!
Quì ascoso sarà.

IL CONTE
Guardiamo, guardiamo,
Quì ascoso sarà.

LA CONTESSA
Susanna, son morta,
Il fiato mi manca.

SUSANNA
Più lieta, più franca;
In salvo è di già.

IL CONTE
Che sbaglio mai presi!
Appena lo credo!
Se a torto v'offesi
Perdono vi chiedo,
Ma far burla simile
E poi crudeltà.

LA CONTESSA, SUSANNA
Le vostre follie
Non mertan pietà.

IL CONTE
Io v'amo.

LA CONTESSA
Nol dite!

IL CONTE
Vel giuro!

LA CONTESSA
Mentite!
Son l'empia, l'infida,
Che ognora v'inganna.

IL CONTE
Quell'ira, Susanna,
M'aita a calmar!

SUSANNA
Così si condanna
Chi può sospettar.

LA CONTESSA
Ah! dunque la fede
D'un'anima amante
Si fiera mercede
Doveva sperar!

SUSANNA
Signora!

IL CONTE
Rosina!

LA CONTESSA
Crudele!
Più quella non sono!
Ma il misero oggetto
Del vostro abbandono,
Che avete diletto
Di far disperar.

COUNT

He must die for his treason!
Nothing less can ease my mind!
Now I know you!

COUNTESS

What suspicion! What injustice!

COUNT

Unworthy woman,
I shall kill him, *etc.* . . . .
(*astonished*)
Susanna! (*opens the door; Susanna
gravely issues from the doorway and
remains there.*)

COUNTESS (*astonished*)

Susanna!

SUSANNA

Your lordship! You seem so bewildered!
(*ironically*) The wicked offender has
come to surrender.
Your treacherous rival is standing right
here.

COUNT (*aside*)

They fooled me!
This thing is confusing my brain!
However . . .

COUNTESS (*aside*)

I can't understand it.
Susanna, explain!

SUSANNA (*aside*)

How all this has happened
They cannot explain.
You mean, sir, he still might be there?
Why don't you go look, then,
He still might be there.

COUNT

All right, then, he still might be there.
(*The Count goes into the small room.*)

COUNTESS

Susanna, I'm weary, I'm breathless
with terror.

SUSANNA

(*quickly indicates to the Countess the
window from which Cherubino
leaped*)
Don't worry, be cheerful, the page is
not there.

COUNT

(*comes out of the small room in confusion*)
How badly mistaken,

Completely mistaken!
I scarcely believe it . . .
If I did offend you,
I beg your forgiveness.
I'm sure you will give it.
But such cruel escapades
Are quite out of place.

COUNTESS (*with her handkerchief at
her mouth to conceal her agitation*)
AND SUSANNA

Your foolish behavior
Can merit no grace.

COUNT

I love you!

COUNTESS

(*gradually recovering from her confusion*)
Don't say it!

COUNT

I swear it!

COUNTESS

You're lying!
(*forcefully and angrily*)
I'm wicked, unfaithful,
And always deceive you.

COUNT

Please help me, Susanna,
Her anger to calm.

SUSANNA

Your jealous suspicion has done all this
harm.

COUNTESS (*resentfully*)

My love, always faithful,
So true and unswerving,
Is surely deserving of better reward.

COUNT

Oh, help me, Susanna,
Her anger to calm.

SUSANNA

Your jealous suspicion has done all this
harm.
(*beseechingly*) My lady!

COUNT (*beseechingly*)

Rosina!

COUNTESS (*to the Count*)

You traitor!
Those days are forgotten!
I once was contented,
Adored by my lover,
But now I'm tormented
And scorned by my lord.

a 3

SUSANNA, IL CONTE

Confuso, pentito,
È (son) troppo punito;
Abbiate pietà!

LA CONTESSA

Soffrir si gran torto
Quest'alma non sa!

IL CONTE

Ma il paggio rinchiuso?

LA CONTESSA

Fu sol per provarvi.

IL CONTE

Ma i tremiti, i palpiti?

LA CONTESSA

Fu sol per burlarvi.

IL CONTE

Ma un foglio sì barbaro?

LA CONTESSA, SUSANNA

Di Figaro è il foglio,
E a voi, per Basilio.

IL CONTE

Ah! perfidi! io voglio . . .

LA CONTESSA, SUSANNA

Perdono non merta
Chi agli altri nol da.

IL CONTE

Ebben, se vi piace,
Commune è la pace,
Rosina inflessibile
Con me non sarà.

LA CONTESSA

Oh! quanto Susanna,
Son dolce di core!
Di donne al furore,
Chi più crederà!

SUSANNA

Cogli uomin, signora,
Girate, volgete,
Vedrete, che ognora
Si cade poi là.

IL CONTE

Guardatemi!

LA CONTESSA

Ingrato!

IL CONTE

Ho torto; e mi pento.

a 3

Da questo momento,
Quest'alma a conoscerla (mi, vi)
Apprender potrà.

FIGARO

Signore, di fuori
Son già i suonatori;
Le trombe sentite,
I pifferi udite;
Tra canti, tra balli
De' vostri vassalli
Corriamo, voliamo
Le nozze a compir.

IL CONTE

Pian Piano, men fretta.

FIGARO

La turba m'aspetta.

IL CONTE

Un dubbio toglietemi
In pria di partir.

LA CONTESSA, SUSANNA, FIGARO

La cosa è scabrosa,
Com' ha da finir?

IL CONTE

Con arte le carte
Convien quì scoprir.
Conoscete, signor Figaro,
Questo foglio chi vergò?

FIGARO

Nol conosco.

SUSANNA, IL CONTE

Nol conosci?

FIGARO

Nol conosco, no, no, no.

SUSANNA

E nol desti a Don Basilio?

LA CONTESSA

Per recarlo.

SUSANNA
Dejected, repentant,
He begs for your pardon.
Don't harbor resentment,
Be kind and forgive.

COUNT
Dejected, repentant,
I beg your forgiveness.
Ah, don't harbor resentment,
Have mercy, forgive.

COUNTESS
You traitor,
I'll never forgive you as long as I live.

COUNT
But what of the page, then?

COUNTESS
To test and provoke you.

COUNT
Your fright and embarrassment?

COUNTESS
Was just to mislead you.

COUNT
But what does the letter mean?

COUNTESS AND SUSANNA
By Figaro written and sent through
Basilio.

COUNT
What infamy, how dare they . . .

SUSANNA AND COUNTESS
If you want forgiveness,
You, too, must forgive.

COUNT (*tenderly*)
If all have consented,
The quarrel is ended.
Rosina, I beg of you,
This time to forgive.

COUNTESS
I feel it, Susanna, I weaken already.
Why is it that women can never be
firm?

SUSANNA
When men are in question,
However you treat them,
You never defeat them,
As hard as you scheme.

COUNT (*tenderly*)
You pardon me?

COUNTESS
I cannot.

COUNT
(*covering her hand with kisses*)
I treated you unjustly,
I am sorry.

SUSANNA, COUNTESS AND COUNT
He means it (I mean) sincerely,
He hopes (I hope) from now on his
(my) mistake to redeem.

FIGARO (*enters*)
Dear master, just listen,
The music is sounding,
The trumpets are blaring,
The fiddles are playing,
The echoes are ringing,
The people are singing, (*taking Sus-
anna by the arm and about to leave*)
The wedding procession is ready to
start.

COUNT (*detaining him*)
There's time, so don't hurry.

FIGARO
The crowd is impatient.

COUNT
There's time, so don't hurry, just one
explanation before we depart.

SUSANNA, COUNTESS AND FIGARO
A new complication with which to
contend.
A bad situation, but how will it end?

COUNT
I know that this ruse will accomplish
my end.
With this complication they cannot
contend.
Kindly tell me, mister Figaro, (*shows
him the letter*) did you ever see this
note?

FIGARO (*pretending to examine it*)
Never saw it, never saw it.

SUSANNA AND COUNTESS
Never saw it?

FIGARO
No.

SUSANNA
Didn't give it to Basilio?

COUNTESS
To deliver . . .

IL CONTE
Tu c'intendi?

FIGARO
Oibò! Oibò!

SUSANNA
E non sai del damerino?

LA CONTESSA
Che stasera nel giardino.

IL CONTE
Già caspisci?

FIGARO
Io non lo sò!

IL CONTE
Cerchi invan difesa e scusa,
Il tuo ceffo già t'accusa,
Vedo ben, che vuoi mentir.

FIGARO
Mente il ceffo, io già non mento.

LA CONTESSA, SUSANNA
Il talento aguzzi invano
Palesato abbiam l'arcano,
Non v'è nulla da ridir.

IL CONTE
Che rispondi?

FIGARO
Niente, niente.

IL CONTE
Dunque accordi?

FIGARO
Non accordo.

LA CONTESSA, SUSANNA
Eh! via chetati, balordo,
La burletta ha da finir.

FIGARO
Per finirla lietamente
E all'usanza teatrale,
Un'azion matrimoniale
Le faremo ora seguir.

a 3

LA CONTESSE, SUSANNA, IL CONTE
Deh! signor, nol contrastate,
Consolate i mei (lor) desir!

IL CONTE
Marcellina, Marcellina,
Quanto tardi a comparir!

ANTONIO
Ah! signor, signor!

IL CONTE
Cosa è stato?

ANTONIO
Che insolenza! ch'il fece? chi fu?

LA CONTESSA, IL CONTE, FIGARO,
SUSANNA
Cosa dici? cos' hai? cosa è nato?

ANTONIO
Ascoltate.

a 4

Via parla, dì su.

ANTONIO
Dal balcone che guarda in guardino,
Mille cose ogni dì gittar veggio,
E poc'anzi può darsi di peggio,
Vidi un uom, signor mio, gittar giù.

IL CONTE
Dal balcone?

ANTONIO
Vedete i garofani.

IL CONTE
In giardino?

LA CONTESSE, SUSANNA
Figaro all'erta.

IL CONTE
Cosa sento?

LA CONTESSA, SUSANNA, FIGARO
Costui ci sconcerta!
Quel briaco che viene a far quì?

COUNT
What about it?

FIGARO
Oh no, oh no!

SUSANNA
You don't know about a lover . . .

COUNTESS
Who this evening in the garden . . .

COUNT
You remember?

FIGARO
Why, not at all.

COUNT
Stop evading and denying,
I can see that you are lying.
It is written on your face.

FIGARO
Well, my face may lie but I don't.

SUSANNA AND COUNTESS
What's the use of all the ruses?
We can see through your excuses,
And the truth you can't deny.

COUNT
What's your answer?

FIGARO
Nothing, nothing.

COUNT
You admit it?

FIGARO
No, I will not.

SUSANNA AND COUNTESS
There's no point in telling stories,
You have carried things too far.

FIGARO
In theatrical tradition,
Let us have a happy ending, (*taking
Susanna by the arm*)
With a wedding celebration
When the final curtain falls.

SUSANNA, FIGARO AND COUNTESS
Won't you give us (them) your per-
mission,
Say the word we (they) long to hear?
Let us (the) two at last be married,
Say the word we (they) long to hear.

COUNT (*aside*)
Marcellina, Marcellina,
You are late in getting here.

ANTONIO
(*enters excitedly with a pot of geraniums*)
Ah, my lord, my lord!

COUNT (*anxiously*)
What has happened?

ANTONIO (*enraged*)
Who has dared, who has done this to
me?

THE OTHERS
What's the matter with you,
What has happened?

ANTONIO
I won't have it!

THE OTHERS
What have you to say?

ANTONIO
I won't have it.

THE OTHERS
What have you to say?

ANTONIO
From the window that looks on the
garden
Ev'ry day they throw down many ob-
jects.
But today, it is really the limit,
They have thrown a whole man to the
ground.

COUNT (*with vivacity*)
From the window?

ANTONIO (*showing the pot*)
Just look at the geraniums.

COUNT
Into the garden?

ANTONIO
Yes.

SUSANNA AND COUNTESS
(*softly to Figaro*)
Figaro, help us!

COUNT
Do you mean it?

FIGARO, SUSANNA AND COUNTESS
(*aside*)
Our plan will be ruined!
(*aloud*) Is this drunkard quite out of
his mind?

IL CONTE
Dunque un uom . . . ma dov'è gito?

ANTONIO
Ratto, ratto il birbone è fugito,
E ad un tratto di vista m'uscì.

SUSANNA
Sai che il paggio?

FIGARO
So tutto, lo vidi.
Ah! ah! ah! ah!

IL CONTE
Taci là!

ANTONIO
Cosa ridi?

FIGARO
Ah! ah! ah! ah!

IL · CONTE
Taci là.

FIGARO
Tu sei cotto dal sorger del dì.

IL CONTE
Or ripetimi; un uom dal balcone?

ANTONIO
Dal balcone.

IL CONTE
In giardino?

ANTONIO
In giardino.

LA CONTESSA, SUSANNA, FIGARO
Ma, signore, se in lui parla il vino!

IL CONTE
Segui pure: nè in volto il vedesti?

ANTONIO
No, nol vidi.

LA CONTESSA, SUSANNA
Olà, Figaro ascolta!

FIGARO
Via, piangone, sta zitto una volta,
Per tre soldi far tanto tumulto!
Giacchè il fatto non può stare occulto,
Sono io stesso saltato di lì.

IL CONTE, ANTONIO
Chi? voi stesso?

LA CONTESSA, SUSANNA
Che testa! che ingegno!

FIGARO
Che stupore!

IL CONTE
Già creder nol posso!

ANTONIO
Come mai diventasti sì grosso!
Dopo il salto non fosti così.

FIGARO
A chi salta succede così.

ANTONIO
Chi'l direbbe?

LA CONTESSA, SUSANNA
Ed insiste quel pazzo!

IL CONTE
Tu che dici?

ANTONIO
A me parve il ragazzo.

IL CONTE
Cherubin?

LA CONTESSA, SUSANNA
Maledetto!

FIGARO
Esso appunto
Da Siviglia a cavallo quì giunto
Da Siviglia, ov'ei forse sarà!

ANTONIIO
Questo no, questo no, che il cavallo
Io non vidi saltare di là.

COUNT (*to Antonio, fiercely*)
And this man, what became of him later?

ANTONIO
He went by like a shot from a cannon,
In a flash he had left me behind.

SUSANNA (*softly, to Figaro*)
Cherubino . . .

FIGARO (*softly, to Susanna*)
I know it, I saw him.
(*aloud*) Ha ha ha ha!

COUNT
Quiet there!

FIGARO
Ha, ha, ha, ha!

ANTONIO
What's so funny?

FIGARO
Ha, ha, ha, ha!

COUNT
Hold your tongue, all of you, hold your tongue!

FIGARO
Are you tipsy from morning till night?

COUNT
Now repeat what you just said to me!
He fell from the window?

ANTONIO
From the window.

COUNT
On the flowers?

ANTONIO
On the flowers.

SUSANNA, COUNTESS AND FIGARO
But, your lordship, he's drunk, can't you see?

COUNT
Just continue! Tell your story!
You saw what he looked like?

ANTONIO
No, I did not.

SUSANNA AND COUNTESS
(*softly, to Figaro*)
Look out, Figaro, help us, Figaro, help us!

FIGARO (*to Antonio*)
Will you ever be finished complaining?

Such a fuss over nothing whatever.
(*pointing contemptuously to the geraniums*)
If the truth can no longer be hidden,
I myself was the man whom you saw.

COUNT
You! And why?

FIGARO
What surprise!

SUSANNA AND COUNTESS
(*aside*)
How brilliant! How clever!

ANTONIO
You? And why?

COUNT
I cannot believe it!

ANTONIO
In that case you have grown very quickly.

COUNT
That sounds unlikely.

ANTONIO
After jumping you looked very small.

FIGARO
When one jumps one becomes very small.

ANTONIO
You don't say so!

SUSANNA AND COUNTESS
(*aside*)
Who believes all this nonsense?

COUNT (*to Antonio*)
Come, describe him.

ANTONIO
He looked like a youngster.

COUNT (*violently*)
Cherubin?

SUSANNA AND COUNTESS
(*aside*)
I can't bear it. I can't bear it.

FIGARO
Cherubino, Cherubino! (*ironically*)
Who returned from Seville on horseback,
For it's there he was sent by the Count.

ANTONIO (*with stupid simplicity*)
No, no, no! He was not on horseback,
He jumped out the window on foot.

IL CONTE
Che pazienza! Finiam questo ballo.

LA CONTESSA, SUSANNA
Come mai, giusto ciel, finirà!

IL CONTE
Dunque tu?

FIGARO
Saltai giù.

IL CONTE
Ma perchè?

FIGARO
Il timor

IL CONTE
Che timor?

FIGARO
Là rinchiuso;
Aspettando quel caro visetto
Tippe, tappe, un susurro fuor d'uso
Voi gridaste, lo scritto biglietto,
Saltai giù dal terrore confuso,
E stravolto m'ho un nervo del piè.

ANTONIO
Vostre dunque saran queste carte,
Che perdeste?

IL CONTE
Olà, porgile a me!

FIGARO
Sono in trappola!

LA CONTESSA, SUSANNA
Figaro all'erta!

IL CONTE
Dite un pò questo foglio cos'è?

FIGARO
Tosto, tosto, n'ho tante, aspettate.

ANTONIO
Sarà forse il sommario dei debiti.

FIGARO
No, la lista degli osti.

IL CONTE
Parlate!
E tu lascialo.

LA CONTESSA, SUSANNA, FIGARO
Lascialo, e parti.

ANTONIO
Parto sì, ma se torno a trovarti.

FIGARO
Vanne, vanne, non temo di te.

IL CONTE
Dunque?

LA CONTESSA
O ciel! la patente del paggio.

SUSANNA
Giusti Dei! la patente!

IL CONTE
Corragio!

FIGARO
Oh che testa! quest'è la patente
Che poc'anzi il fanciullo mi diè.

IL CONTE
Perchè fare?

FIGARO
Vi manca . . .

IL CONTE
Vi manca?

LA CONTESSA
Il suggello.

SUSANNA
Il suggello.

FIGARO
E l'usanza di porvi il suggello.

COUNT
Don't be foolish. Let's get to the point.

SUSANNA AND COUNTESS
(aside)
Heaven knows what will come out of
this.

COUNT (to Figaro, fiercely)
It was you?

FIGARO (innocently)
That is true.

COUNT
But what for?

FIGARO
I was scared.

COUNT
You were scared?

FIGARO (indicating the maid's room)
I had come here and was waiting to
see my Susanna,
When I heard angry voices from outside.
You were raging; I thought of my
letter;
Scared to death, I jumped down from
the window (pretends that his foot
hurts him)
And I twisted my foot when I fell.

ANTONIO
Then these papers (handing Figaro
some folded papers) I found in the
garden must be yours?

COUNT
Oho! (takes them from him) Give
them to me.

FIGARO
(softly, to the Countess and Susanna)
Now I'm in for it.

SUSANNA AND COUNTESS
(softly, to Figaro)
Figaro, help us, Figaro, help us!

COUNT
(opens the paper and immediately
folds it again)
Do you know what this paper may be?

FIGARO
(taking some papers out of his pocket)
Yes, I know it, I know it,
Just a moment..

ANTONIO
Well, perhaps it's a list of his creditors.

FIGARO
No, I don't buy on credit.

COUNT (to Figaro)
Speak up now. (to Antonio) And you,
let him be.

SUSANNA, COUNTESS AND FIGARO
Off with you, Antonio.

ANTONIO
I will go, but the next time I see
you . . . (exit)

FIGARO
Go away, I'm not frightened of you.

SUSANNA, COUNTESS AND FIGARO
Off with you, good riddance.

COUNT
(reopens the paper and folds it again
quickly) (to Figaro) Well now?

COUNTESS (to Susanna)
Good Heavens, the page's commission!

SUSANNA (to Figaro)
That is right, his commission!

COUNT (ironically, to Figaro)
Speak freely.

FIGARO (pretending to recollect)
O how stupid, now I know it.
That is the commission
Which the boy has entrusted to me.

COUNT
For what reason?

FIGARO (confused)
It needed . . .

COUNT
It needed . . .

(COUNTESS (to Susanna, softly)
Needed sealing.

SUSANNA (to Figaro, softly)
Needed sealing.

COUNT
I'm waiting . . .

FIGARO (pretending to ponder)
It's the custom . . .

COUNT
Well, what is the custom?

FIGARO
It's the custom to seal a commission.

a 4

IL CONTE

Questo birbo mi toglie il cervello!
Tutto, tutto è un mistero per me!

LA CONTESSA, SUSANNA

Se mi solvo da questa tempesta,
Più non havvi naufragio per me!

FIGARO

Sbuffa invano, e la terra calpesta,
Poverino! nè sa men di me.

MARCELLINA, BARTOLO, BASILIO

Voi, signor, che giusto siete,
Ci dovete or ascoltar.

a 4

IL CONTE

Son venuti a vendicarmi,
Io mi sento a consolar!

LA CONTESSA, SUSANNA, FIGARO

Son venuti a sconcertarmi,
Qual rimedio ritrovar!

FIGARO

Son tre stolidi, tre pazzi,
Cosa mai vengono a far?

IL CONTE

Pian pianin, senza schiamazzi
Dica ognun quel che gli par.

MARCELLINA

Un impegno nuziale
Ha costui con me contratto,
E pretendo che il contratto
Deva meco effettuar.

LA CONTESSA, SUSANNA, IL CONTE

Come? come?

IL CONTE

Olà! silenzio!
Io son quì per giudicar.

BARTOLO

Io da lei scelto avvocato
Vengo a far le sue difese,
Le legittime pretese
Io vi vengo a palesar.

BASILIO

Io com'uom al mondo cognito
Vengo qui per testimonio,
Del promesso matrimonio
Con prestanza di danar.

LA CONTESSA, SUSANNA, FIGARO

Son tre matti, son tre matti!

IL CONTE

Olà! silenzio, lo vedremo,
Il contratto leggeremo,
Tutto in ordin deve andar.

LA CONTESSA, SUSANNA, FIGARO

Son confusa(o) son stordita(o)
Disperata(o), sbalordita(o)!
Certo un diavol del inferno
Qui li ha fatti capitar!

IL CONTE, MARCELLINA, BARTOLO,
BASILIO

Che bel colpo! che bel caso!
E cresciuto a tutti il naso!
Qualche nume a noi propizio
Qui ci ha fatti capitar!

ATTO TERZO

*Gran Sala, ornata per una
Festa Nuziale.*

RECITATIVO

IL CONTE

Che imbarazzo è mai questo!
Un foglio anonimo,
La cameriera in gabinetto chiusa,
La padrona confusa—un uom che salta
Dal balcone in giardino,
Un altro appresso,
Che dice esser quel desso,

COUNT
(aside, notices that the seal is missing, tears up the paper and angrily throws it away)
Oh, that rascal is driving me crazy.
This affair is a myst'ry to me.

SUSANNA AND COUNTESS
(aside)
If I ever escape from this shipwreck,
Nevermore will I venture to sea.

FIGARO *(aside)*
Let him threaten as much as he pleases,
He will not get the better of me.
(Enter Marcellina, Basilio and Bartolo.)

MARCELLINA, BASILIO AND BARTOLO
Lord, our case demands a hearing.
That is why we came today.

COUNT *(aside)*
They have come here for retribution.
Things begin now to go my way.

FIGARO, SUSANNA AND COUNTESS
(aside)
They have come to give us trouble,
We must lead their plans astray.

FIGARO
Bent on asinine obstruction,
Those three fools are here today.

COUNT
Let's not make a rash deduction,
First each one must have his say.

MARCELLINA
This man gave his solemn promise
That in time we would be married;
I insist upon this bargain
Being promptly carried out.

SUSANNA, COUNTESS AND FIGARO
Bargain? Bargain?

COUNT
No more, let nobody dare interrupt me,
It is I who judge this case.

BARTOLO
With this lady's wish compliant
I am here as her attorney,
And I warrant that my client
Has a strictly legal case.

SUSANNA, COUNTESS AND FIGARO
He's a scoundrel, he's a scoundrel!

COUNT
Enough! Be silent! Let's hear Don Basilio.
It is I who judge this case.

BASILIO
I, as man of prime celebrity,
Give my word and testimonial
That their plans were matrimonial,
With a bonus in advance.

SUSANNA AND COUNTESS
Ev'ryone of them is crazy.

COUNT
Hold on! According to proper proceeding,
We must first give the contract a reading,
We must follow the legal course.

SUSANNA, COUNTESS AND FIGARO
What a course events have taken!

MARCELLINA, BARTOLO, COUNT
AND BASILIO
What a perfect case of trapping.

SUSANNA, COUNTESS AND FIGARO
We are beaten, badly shaken.

MARCELLINA, BARTOLO, COUNT
AND BASILIO
This time we have caught them napping.

SUSANNA, COUNTESS AND FIGARO
Surely some infernal power
Must have brought them here today.

MARCELLINA, BARTOLO, COUNT
AND BASILIO
Some propitious, kindly power
Must have brought us here today,
On this day!

ACT THREE

(A richly decorated hall prepared for a wedding festivity, with two thrones.)

RECITATIVE

COUNT *(walking up and down)*
What a hopeless confusion! An anonymous letter, the maid-in-waiting shut in her mistress' boudoir, her mistress embarrassed, one man who jumps out of the window to the garden, somebody else who claims that he has

Non sò cosa pensar!
Potrebbe forse qualcun de' miei vassalli
... a simil razza è commune l'ardir,
ma la Contessa — ah, che un dubbio
l'offende! Ella rispetta troppo se
stessa, e l'honor mio, l'onore ...
dove, diamin, l'ha posto umano er-
rore!

LA CONTESSA
Via! fatti core, digli che ti attenda in
giardino.

IL CONTE
Saprò se Cherubino era giunto a Sivi-
lia, a tale oggetto ho mandato Basilio.

SUSANNA
O cielo! e Figaro?

LA CONTESSA
A lui non dei dir nulla, invece tua,
voglio andarci io medesma.

IL CONTE
Avanti sera dovrebbe ritornar.

SUSANNA
O Dio! non oso!

LA CONTESSA
Pensa ch'è in tua mano il mio riposo.

IL CONTE
E Susanna? Chi sà, ch'ella tradite abbia il segreto mio, oh, se ha parlato,
gli fo sposar la vecchia.

SUSANNA
Marcellina!
Signor?

IL CONTE
Cosa bramate?

SUSANNA
Mi par che siate in collera.

IL CONTE
Volete qualche cosa?

SUSANNA
Signor, la vostra sposa
Ha i soliti vapori,
E vi chiede il vasetto degli odori.

IL CONTE
Prendete.

SUSANNA
Or vel riporto.

IL CONTE
Ah no, potete
Riternerlo per voi.

SUSANNA
Per me? Questi non son mali
Da donne triviali.

IL CONTE
Un'amante che perde il caro sposo,
Sul punto d'ottenerlo.

SUSANNA
Pagando Marcellina colla dote
Che voi mi prometteste.

IL CONTE
Ch'io vi promisi! Quando?

SUSANNA
Credea d'averlo inteso.

IL CONTE
Si, se voluto aveste
Intendermi voi stessa.

SUSANNA
È mio, dovere,
E quel di sua Eccellenza è il mio
volere.

No. 16 DUETTO

IL CONTE
Crudel! perchè finora
Farmi languir così?

SUSANNA
Signor, la donna ognora
Tempo ha di dir di si.

IL CONTE
Dunque, in giardin verrai?

SUSANNA
Se piace a voi, verrò.

IL CONTE
È non mi mancherai?

SUSANNA
No, non vi mancherò.

IL CONTE
Verrai?

SUSANNA
Si.

done it. I don't know what to think. It might have been even one of the domestics, they are the kind who would take such a chance. As for the Countess . . . any doubt would be insult; she has too much respect for herself and for my honor. My honor! What has human weakness done to my honor!

COUNTESS
(*entering with Susanna, and keeping in the background, unseen by the Count*)
Come, don't be downcast. Tell him he may meet you in the garden.

COUNT
I'll make sure that Cherubino arrived at Seville. I've sent Basilio expressly for that purpose.

SUSANNA
Good Heavens, and Figaro?

COUNTESS
He must not know about it. Instead of you, I'll await him myself.

COUNT
Before this evening he ought to be back.

SUSANNA
My lady, I'm frightened!

COUNTESS
Remember that my fate is in your hands now. (*She retires.*)

COUNT
And Susanna? Who knows, maybe she has already betrayed my secret. If she has done so, Figaro must marry Marcellina.

SUSANNA (*aside*)
Marcellina! (*aloud*) My lord!

COUNT (*gravely*)
What do you wish?

SUSANNA
You seem in bad humor.

COUNT
What is it that you want?

SUSANNA
My lord, just now the Countess is suff'ring from a headache and sent me to get your flask of smelling salts.

COUNT
Take it.

SUSANNA
I'll soon return it.

COUNT
No, no, don't bother, you may need it yourself.

SUSANNA
Myself? People of my kind do not suffer from headaches.

COUNT
But a bride about to lose her bridegroom on the day of her wedding?

SUSANNA
I'll pay off Marcellina with the dowry that you promised to give me.

COUNT
I made that promise? Did I?

SUSANNA
That's how I understood you.

COUNT
Yes, yes, if you had only wished to understand me.

SUSANNA
It is my duty, and what your lordship wishes is my desire.

No. 16 Duet

COUNT
But why, why make me suffer,
Longing for your reply?
But why, but why?
Will you not tell me why?

SUSANNA
In time we women grant you
What we at first deny.

COUNT
Then we shall meet this evening?

SUSANNA
If so you wish, my lord.

COUNT
You will not fail to be there?

SUSANNA
No, no, you have my word.

COUNT
You promise?

SUSANNA
Yes.

IL CONTE
Non mancherai?

SUSANNA
No.

IL CONTE
Dunque verrai?

SUSANNA
No.

IL CONTE
No?

SUSANNA
Si, se place a voi, verrò.

IL CONTE
Non mancherai?

SUSANNA
No.

IL CONTE
Dunque verrai?

SUSANNA
Si.

IL CONTE
Non mancherai?

SUSANNA
Si.

IL CONTE
Si?

SUSANNA
No, no, non vi mancherò.

IL CONTE
Mi sento dal contento
Pieno di gioja dal contento
Pieno di gioja il cor!

SUSANNA
Scusatemi se mento,
Voi che intendente amor.

RECITATIVO

IL CONTE
E perchè fosti meco stamattina sì
austera?

SUSANNA
Col paggio ch'ivi c'era.

IL CONTE
Ed a Basilio, che per me ti parlò?

SUSANNA
Ma qual bisogno abbiam noi che un
Basilio . . .

IL CONTE
È vero, è vero, e mi prometti poi . .
se tu manchi, o cor mio . . .
Ma la Contessa attenderà il vasetto.

SUSANNA
Eh, fu un pretesto,
Parlato io non avrei senza di questo.

IL CONTE
Carissima!

SUSANNA
Vien gente.

IL CONTE
È mia senz'altro!

SUSANNA
Forbitevi la bocca signor scaltro.

FIGARO
Ehi, Susanna, ove vai?

SUSANNA
Taci; senz'avvocato
Hai già vinta la causa.

FIGARO
Cos'è nato?

COUNT
Won't disappoint me?

SUSANNA
No.

COUNT
This very evening?

SUSANNA
You have my word,
I will not fail my word.

COUNT
The sweet promise you gave me
Raises my hope so high.

SUSANNA (aside)
All those who know what love is,
Forgive me for this lie.

COUNT
You'll meet me in the garden?

SUSANNA
If that's your wish, I might.

COUNT
You will not disappoint me?

SUSANNA
I shall be there tonight.

COUNT
You promise?

SUSANNA
Yes.

COUNT
Won't disappoint me?

SUSANNA
No.

COUNT
I have your promise?

SUSANNA
No.

COUNT
No?

SUSANNA
Yes, I shall be there tonight.

COUNT
Won't disappoint me?

SUSANNA
No.

COUNT
And you will be there?

SUSANNA
Yes.

COUNT
Won't disappoint me?

SUSANNA
Yes.

COUNT
Yes?

SUSANNA
No, I shall be there tonight.

COUNT
The sweet promise you gave me, etc.

RECITATIVE

COUNT
But why in the world were you so cross
to me this morning?

SUSANNA
I knew the page was listening.

COUNT
And to Basilio, who was speaking for
me?

SUSANNA
I do not see why we need a Basilio . . .

COUNT
Of course, dear, how clever! And I
may have your word you will not
disappoint me? But the Countess, she
is waiting for her smelling salts.

SUSANNA
She really isn't. I had to make some
pretext to address you.

COUNT (taking her hand)
Adorable!

SUSANNA (drawing it away)
They're coming!

COUNT (aside)
She has surrendered.

SUSANNA
Don't count your chickens before
they're hatched.

FIGARO
(enters; aside to Susanna)
Say, Susanna, what's up?

SUSANNA (aside, to Figaro)
Plenty! Without a lawyer we have won
the decision. (Exit)

FIGARO (follows her)
What has happened?

No. 17 Recitativo
ed Aria

IL CONTE

Hai già vinta la causa! Cosa sento?
In qual laccio cadea! Perfidi! Io voglio
In tal modo punirvi, a piacer mio
La sentenza sarà. Ma s'ei pagasse
La vecchia pretendente?
Pagarla? in qual maniera? E poi v'è
    Antonio,
Che all'incognito Figaro ricusa
Di dare una nipote in matrimonio.
Coltivando l'orgoglio
Di questo mentecatto,
Tutto giova a un raggiro:
Il colpo è fatto.
Vedrò, mentr'io sospiro,
Felice un servo mio?
E un ben che invan desio,
Ei posseder dovrà!
Vedrò per man d'amore
Unita a un vile oggetto
Chi in me destò un affetto,
Che per me poi non ha!
Ah no! lasciarti in pace
Non vo' questo contento:
Tu non nascesti, audace,
Per dare a me tormento,
E forse ancor per ridere
Di mia infelicità!
Già la speranza sola
Delle vendette mie
Quest'anima consola,
È giubilar mi fa!

Recitativo

DON CURZIO

È decisa la lite;
O pagarla, o sposarla.
Ora ammutite.

MARCELLINA

Io respiro.

FIGARO

Ed io moro.

MARCELLINA

Alfin sposa io sarò d'un uom che
adoro.

FIGARO

Eccellenza! m'appello . . .

IL CONTE

È giusta la sentenza;
O pagar, o sposar, bravo Don Curzio!

DON CURZIO

Bontà di sua Eccellenza.

BARTOLO

Che superba sentenza!

FIGARO

In che superba?

BARTOLO

Siam tutti vendicati.

FIGARO

Io non la sposerò.

BARTOLO

La sposerai.

DON CURZIO

O pagarla, o sposarla, lei t'ha prestati
due mille pezzi duri.

FIGARO

Son gentiluomo, e senza
L' assenso de' miei nobili parenti . . .

IL CONTE

Dove sono? chi sono?·

FIGARO

Lasciate ancor cercarli;
Dopo dieci anni io spero di trovarli.

BARTOLO

Qualche bambin trovato?

FIGARO

No, perduto, dottor, anzi rubato.

IL CONTE

Come?

MARCELLINA

Cosa?

No. 17 Recitative and Aria

COUNT

"You have won the decision?"
What the devil!
Are they trying to fool me?
Hypocrites!
I'll cure them.
I'll see that both the traitors are pun-
ished.
I'll base the verdict on my pleasure
alone.
If he succeeded in paying Marcellina!
How can he? He has no money!
Besides, Antonio won't permit his be-
loved niece Susanna,
To marry such a nobody as Figaro.
I will flatter the ego
Of that conceited drunkard.
It will further my purpose.
It can't go better!
Shall I look on desiring,
And see my servant happy?
Shall I see him acquiring
Favors for which I yearn?
Shall I, in helpless fashion,
Allow a hateful marriage,
While I restrain a passion
Which she does not return?
Shall I not lift a finger
To conquer her affection,
Look on without objection,
Aloof and unconcerned?
Ah, no! I won't!
Ah, no, I will not give you
So great a satisfaction.
You shall not dare to spite me,
Oppose me and torment me.
You'll have no chance to laugh at me,
While I am cast aside.
Only the thought of vengeance
Offers me consolation.
Triumphant vindication
Shall satisfy my pride,
My deeply wounded pride.

2ND TIME

Shall satisfy my pride,
And fill my heart with joy.

(*He prepares to leave, but meets Don
Curzio, who enters with Marcellina,
Figaro, and Bartolo.*)

RECITATIVE

CURZIO (*stammering*)
The ca-case has b-been d-decided. He

must marry her or pay her, th-that
is the v-verdict.

MARCELLINA
What a wedding!

FIGARO
What a funeral!

MARCELLINA (*aside*)
At last I'll be the wife of the man I
worship!

FIGARO
I appeal this, your lordship.

COUNT
The sentence is a just one, either marry
or pay. Good work, Don Curzio.

CURZIO
You f'-f'-flatter, your l-lordship.

BARTOLO
What a glorious sentence!

FIGARO
In what way glorious?

BARTOLO
Full justice has been rendered.

FIGARO
But I will not give in.

BARTOLO
Oh, yes, you will!

CURZIO
Either m-marry or p-pay her; Did she
not l-lend you two thousand silver
pieces?

FIGARO
I am a nobleman and cannot be married without my parents' consent.

COUNT
And these parents, where are they?

FIGARO
I still am on the look-out. In about ten
years I am sure I will have found
them.

BARTOLO
So you are a foundling?

FIGARO
No, a lostling. It seems that I was kidnaped.

COUNT
Kidnaped?

MARCELLINA
Kidnaped?

BARTOLO
La prova?

DON CURZIO
Il testimonio?

FIGARO
L' oro, le gemme, i ricamati panni,
Che ne' più teneri anni
Mi ritrovaro addosso i masnadieri,
Sono gl' indizi veri
Di mia nascità illustre: e soprattutto
Questo al mio braccio impresso gero-
  glifico.

MARCELLINA
Una spatola impressa al braccio destro.

FIGARO
E a voi ch'il disse?

MARCELLINA
O Dio! È desso.

FIGARO
È ver, son io.

DON CURZIO
Chi?

IL CONTE
Chi?

BARTOLO
Chi?

MARCELLINA
Rafaello!

BARTOLO
E i ladri ti rapir?

FIGARO
Presso un castello

BARTOLO
Ecco tua madre.

FIGARO
Balia?

BARTOLO
No, tua madre.

IL CONTE, DON CURZIO
(Sua madre!)

FIGARO
(Cosa sento?)

MARCELLINA
Ecco tuo padre.

No. 18 SESTETTO

MARCELLINA
Riconosci in questo amplesso
Una madre, amato figlio.

FIGARO
Padre mio, fate lo stesso,
Non mi fate più arrossir.

BARTOLO
Resistenza la coscienza
Far non lascia al tuo desir.

DON CURZIO
Ei suo padre? ella sua madre?

IL CONTE
(Son smarrito, son stordito!)

DON CURZIO
L' imeneo non può seguir.

MARCELLINA
Figlio amato!

BARTOLO
Figlio amato!

FIGARO
Parenti amati!

IL CONTE
(Meglio è assai di quà partir!)

SUSANNA
Alto alto, signor Conte,
Mille doppie son quì pronte,
A pagar vengo per Figaro,
Ed a porlo in libertà.

IL CONTE, DON CURZIO
Non sappiam com' è la cosa,
Osservate un poco là.

SUSANNA
Già d'accordo colla sposa!
Giusti Dei! che infedeltà!
Lascia, iniquo!

BARTOLO
Then prove it!

CURZIO
Where is your evidence?

FIGARO
That I can offer! The gold and precious jewels that my abductors found near me, the fine embroidered linen I was wearing are the confirmation of my noble extraction. Still more conclusive, there is a symbol branded on my arm.

MARCELLINA
A spatula printed on your right arm?

FIGARO
How did you know that?

MARCELLINA
Great heavens, it's he, then!

FIGARO
Of course, it's I, then.

CURZIO
Who?

COUNT
Who?

BARTOLO
Who?

MARCELLINA
Emanuel!

BARTOLO
You say that robbers stole you?

FIGARO
From near a castle.

BARTOLO
Here is your mother.

FIGARO
My wet nurse?

BARTOLO
No, your mother.

CURZIO AND COUNT
His mother?

FIGARO
You don't mean it?

MARCELLINA
And here's your father!

No. 18 Sextet

MARCELLINA (embracing Figaro)
Now at last I may embrace you,
For I am your loving mother.

FIGARO (to Bartolo)
Father dear, why not do likewise?
Do not make me blush with shame!

BARTOLO (embracing Figaro)
It's my duty to inform you
Of the justice of your claim.

CURZIO
He the father, and she his mother!
Then this match is null and void.

COUNT
Worse misfortune could not happen!
All my hopes have been destroyed.
(about to go)

MARCELLINA
I'm your mother!

BARTOLO
I'm your father!

FIGARO
Beloved parents!

MARCELLINA
He's your father!

BARBARINA
She's your mother!

FIGARO
Beloved parents!
(Enter Susanna with a purse in her hand.)

SUSANNA (detaining the Count)
Wait a minute, not so hasty!
I have brought along the money.
It's the ransom for my Figaro,
So that I can buy him free.

COUNT AND CURZIO
There has been a great sensation.
Take a look and you will see.

MARCELLINA AND BARTOLO
Come, embrace me!

FIGARO
I love you dearly!

SUSANNA
(turns and sees Figaro embracing Marcellina)
So he marries Marcellina!
Lord in Heav'n,
To be so false, so false to me!
Don't come near me! (about to go)

FIGARO

No, t'arresta
Senti, o cara—

SUSANNA

Senti questa.

a 6

(Fremo! smanio dal furore
Una vecchia me la fa!)

IL CONTE

(Fremo! smanio dal furore
Il destino me la fa!)

DON CURZIO

Freme, smania dal furore,
Il destino, gliela fa!

MARCELLINA, FIGARO, BARTOLO

È un effetto di buon core,
Tutto amore è quel che fa.

MARCELLINA

Lo sdegno calmate
Mia cara figliuola,
Sua madre abbracciate,
Che or vostra sarà.

a 4

Sua madre?

SUSANNA

Tua madre?

FIGARO

Mia madre,

E questo è mio padre,
Che a te lo dirà.

a 6

SUSANNA, MARCELLINA, FIGARO,
BARTOLO

Al dolce contento di questo momento
Quest'anima appena resister or sa.

IL CONTE, DON CURZIO

Al fiero tormento—di questo momento
Quest-anima appena resister or sa.

RECITATIVO

MARCELLINA

Eccovi, o caro amico, il dolce frutto
dell'antico amor nostro.

BARTOLO

Or non parliamo di fatti si rimoti, egli
è mio figlio, mia consorte voi siete,
e le nozze farem quando volete.

MARCELLINA

Oggi, e doppie saranno.
Prendi, questo è il biglietto
Del denar che a me devi, ed è tua dote.

SUSANNA

Prendi ancor questa borsa.

BARTOLO

E questa ancora.

FIGARO

Bravi! gittate pur, ch'io piglio ognora.

FIGARO (*detaining Susanna*)
Wait a moment!
You're mistaken!
Listen, my darling, listen, listen!

SUSANNA
(*tears herself away and boxes Figaro's ears*)
I am list'ning!

MARCELLINA AND BARTOLO
This peculiar fit of fury
Shows you truly how she loves you.
Women often act that way.

SUSANNA
I'm beside myself with fury,
Being tricked in such a way;
Tricked and cheated by a spinster
In a most dishonest fashion,
In a most distasteful way.

COUNT
I'm beside myself with fury,
Things have not turned out my way.

CURZIO
Anger and quarrels, jealous rages, fits of fury
Are the order of the day.

MARCELLINA
(*runs to embrace Susanna*)
No longer be angry, my dear little daughter,
From this moment onward
I'm mother to you.
For I am his mother
And mother to you.

SUSANNA (*to Bartolo*)
His mother?
BARTOLO
His mother!
SUSANNA (*to the Count*)
His mother?
COUNT
His mother!
SUSANNA (*to Don Curzio*)
His mother?
CURZIO
His mother!
SUSANNA (*to Marcellina*)
His mother?
MARCELLINA
His mother!
ALL
His mother!

SUSANNA (*to Figaro*)
Your mother?

FIGARO
And this is my father,
He says so himself.

SUSANNA
(*to Bartolo, the Count, Don Curzio and Marcellina*)
His father? etc.
(*All four rush to embrace each other.*)

SUSANNA, FIGARO, BARTOLO AND MARCELLINA
In one blessed moment
Our fears have been thwarted.
A happier future at last is in sight.

COUNT AND CURZIO
In one cursed moment
My (his) plans have been thwarted
It fills me (him) with envy
And bitter resentment
To see them all so happy with sudden delight.
In one cursed moment
My (his) plans have been thwarted.
Not even the hope of revenge is in sight.
(*Exeunt the Count and Don Curzio.*)

RECITATIVE

MARCELLINA
There he is, dearest doctor, the blooming flower of our one-time romance.

BARTOLO
Let's not warm up such overaged proceedings. He is my offspring, you indeed are his mother, so our marriage shall be whenever you want it.

MARCELLINA
To-day! It shall be a double wedding. Take this, (*gives the note to Figaro*) it is the note for the money you owe me. Take it as dowry.

SUSANNA
(*throws a purse to the ground*)
Take this purse in addition.

BARTOLO (*does the same*)
And also this one.

FIGARO
Thank you! Just keep right on, I'm getting wealthy.

SUSANNA

Voliamo ad informar di ogni avven-
tura Madama e nostro zio.
Chi al par di me contenta?

FIGARO

Io.

BARTOLO

Io.

MARCELLINA

Io.

a 4

E schiatti il signor Conte al gusto mio!

RECITATIVO

BARBARINA

Andiam, andiam, bel paggio; in casa
mia tutte ritroverai
Le più belle ragazze del castello.
Di tutte sarai tu certo il più bello.

CHERUBINO

Ah! se il Conte mi trova,
Misero me! Tu sai
Che partito ei mi crede per Siviglia.

BARBARINA

O ve' che maraviglia
E se ti trova, non sarà cosa nuova.
Odi: vogliamo vestirti come noi;
Tutte insiem andrem poi
A presentar de' fiori a Madamina;
Fidati, Cherubin, di Barbarina.

No. 19 RECITATIVO ED ARIA

LA CONTESSA

E Susanna non vien! Sono ansiosa
Di saper come il Conte
Accolse la proposta; alquanto ardito
Il progretto mi par, ad uno sposo
Sì vivace e geloso!
Ma che mal c'è? Cangiando i miei
vestiti
Con quelli di Susanna, e i suoi co'
miei
Al favor della notte . . . O cielo! a qual

Umil stato fatale io son ridotta
Da un consorte crudel, che dopo
avermi
Con un misto inaudito
D'infedeltà, di gelosia, di sdegno
Prima amata, indi offesa, e alfin
tradita,
Fammi or cercar da una mia serva
aita!
Dove sono i bei momenti
Di dolcezza e di piacer?
Dove andaro i giuramenti
Di quel labbro menzogner?
Perchè mai, se in pianti e in pene
Per me tutto si cangiò
La memoria del mio bene
Dal mio sen non trapassò!
Ah! se almen la mia costanza
Nel languire amando ognor.
Mi portasse una speranza
Di cangiar l'ingrato cor!

RECITATIVO

ANTONIO

Io vi dico, signor, che Cherubino
È ancora nel castello,
E vedete per prova il suo cappello.

IL CONTE

Ma come se a quest'ora
Esser giunto a Siviglia egli dovria?

ANTONIO

Scusate, oggi Siviglia è a casa mia.
Là vestissi da donna, e là lasciati
Ha gli altri abiti suoi.

IL CONTE

Perfidi!

ANTONIO

Andiam, e li vedrete voi.

LA CONTESSA

Cosa mi narri? E che ne disse il Conte?

SUSANNA

Gli si leggeva in fronte
Il dispetto e la rabbia.

SUSANNA

Now let us go and tell all that has happened to the Countess and Uncle Antonio. Who is as glad as I am? Who is as glad as I am?

FIGARO

I am!

BARTOLO

I am!

MARCELLINA

I am!

ALL

The Count is wild with fury, but we don't care a bit!

(*All exeunt, embracing.*)

RECITATIVE

(*Enter Barbarina, and Cherubino.*)

BARBARINA

Come on, come on, dear page, you will have fun were you to come along to my house. You will see all the pretty girls of the castle, but none of them is as beautiful as you are.

CHERUBINO

But, if the Count should find me, Heaven forbid! You know, he believes I have left for Seville.

BARBARINA

Since when does that disturb you? And if he found you, it would not be the first time. Listen, you must let us dress you like a girl. Then we all will present a nice bouquet of flowers to the Countess. Just leave it all to me, your Barbarina. (*Exeunt*)

No. 19 RECITATIVE AND ARIA

(*The* COUNTESS *enters.*)

COUNTESS

And Susanna is late . . .
I am anxious to find out
How his lordship accepted the proposal.
I must admit that our project is bold.
And with a husband so impulsive and so jealous!
But what's the harm?
I only want to meet him in a dress of Susanna's while she wears mine,
By the favour of darkness.
Ah, Heaven! To what shameful state of existence

Have I descended through the fault of my husband,
Who, after treating me with scorn unexampled
And with disdain,
With jealous rages betrayed me,
First beloved, then offended,
At last deserted,
Forced me to plead now for my maid's assistance!
Are they over, those cherished moments,
Hours together so sweetly shared?
Are they broken, those fervent pledges
His deceitful lips declared?
If a bitter fate inclined me
Such unhappiness to know,
Why do memories remind me
Of those joys of long ago?
Are they over, *etc.*
If at last my heart's devotion
Could achieve but one reward,
And revive the dead emotion
Of my false and heartless lord! (*Exit*)

RECITATIVE

(*Enter the Count, and Antonio, with a hat in his hand.*)

ANTONIO

There's no doubt, my lord, that Cherubino is still here in the castle, and I brought his hat with me to prove it.

COUNT

But how can that be? By this time he is due at Seville.

ANTONIO

Today, sir, if you'll excuse me, Seville is my house. There they dressed him in girl's clothes and there he also has left his new uniform.

COUNT

Reprobates!

ANTONIO

Please come, and I'll be glad to show you. (*Exeunt*)

(*Enter the Countess and Susanna.*)

COUNTESS

Isn't that marvelous? What was the Count's reaction?

SUSANNA

Oh, he was so furious that he hardly could bear it.

LA CONTESSA
Piano che meglio or lo porremo in
　gabbia!
Dov'è l'appuntamento
Che tu gli proponesti?

SUSANNA
In giardino.

LA CONTESSA
Fissiamigli un loco.
Scrivi.

SUSANNA
Ch'io scriva? ma signora. . . .

LA CONTESSA
Eh, scrivi dico, e tutto
Io prendo su me stessa.

LA CONTESSA
Canzonetta sull'aria.

No. 20 DUETTINO

SUSANNA
Sull'aria.

LA CONTESSA
Che soave zefiretto,

SUSANNA
Zefiretto . . .

LA CONTESSA
Questa sera spirerà,

SUSANNA
Questa sera spirerà . . .

LA CONTESSA
Sotto i pini del boschetto.

SUSANNA
Sotto i pini del boschetto . . .

LA CONTESSA
Ei già il resto capirà.

SUSANNA
Certo il resto capirà.

SUSANNA
Piegato è il foglio; or come si sigilla?

LA CONTESSA
Ecco, prendi una spilla,
Servirà di sigillo. Attendi, scrivi,
Sul riverso del foglio:
Rimandate il sigillo.

SUSANNA
È più bizzarro
Di quel della patente.

LA CONTESSA
Presto, nascondi, io sento venir gente.

No. 21. CORO

Ricevete, o padroncina,
Queste rose, e questi fior,
Che abbiam colti stammattina
Per mostrarvi il nostro amor.
Siamo tante contadine,
E siam tutte poverine,
Ma quel poco che rechiamo
Ve lo diamo di buon cuor.

RECITATIVO

BARBARINA
Queste sono, Madama,
Le ragazze del loco,
Che il poco ch'han vi vengono ad
　offrire,
E vi chiedon perdon del loro ardire.

LA CONTESSA
O brave! vi ringrazio,

SUSANNA
Come sono vezzose.

LA CONTESSA
E chi è, narratemi, quell'amabil fanciulla ch'ha l'aria si modesta?

COUNTESS

Was he! So much the better for our intentions. And where is the appointment which you proposed to give him?

SUSANNA

In the garden.

COUNTESS

Be more specific. Write to him.

SUSANNA

But is that not too daring?

COUNTESS

Do as I tell you. (*Susanna sits down and writes.*) Let all the blame fall on my shoulders. (*dictating*) Write a message "to Romeo."

No. 20 DUETTINO

SUSANNA (*writing*)

"To Romeo

COUNTESS (*dictating*)

"When the breeze is gently blowing,

SUSANNA

gently blowing . . .

COUNTESS

And the evening shadows fall,

SUSANNA

and the evening shadows fall . . .

COUNTESS

In the grove where pines are growing,

SUSANNA (*enquiringly*)

pines are growing! . . .

COUNTESS

In the grove where pines are growing."

SUSANNA (*writing*)

In the grove where pines are growing."

COUNTESS

And the rest he will recall.

SUSANNA

Yes, the rest he will recall.

SUSANNA AND COUNTESS

And the rest he will recall.

COUNTESS

Let us read it together. (*They read the letter together.*)

SUSANNA AND COUNTESS

"When the breeze is gently blowing," *etc.*

SUSANNA (*folds the letter*)

The note is ready, and how shall we seal it?

COUNTESS

(*draws a pin and gives it to her*)

This way. Let's take a pin. We will use that to seal it. And further, write on the back of the letter: "Return the pin, please."

SUSANNA

That's an idea. It makes it sound mysterious.

COUNTESS

Hurry and hide it! I hear somebody coming. (*Susanna puts the note in her bosom.*)

No. 21 CHORUS

(*Enter Cherubino, dressed as a country girl; and Barbarina, with several other country girls, dressed in the same way, carrying nosegays.*)

GIRLS

Mistress dear, accept these flowers,
Daisies, roses bright with dew,
Freshly cut in morning hours
Just to show our love for you.
Though we're poor and simple peasants,
Please accept these humble presents
As a token of affection
From our hearts so loyal and true.

RECITATIVE

BARBARINA

There they are, my lady, all the girls of the village who bring to you the best they have to offer, and they hope you'll forgive them their presumption.

COUNTESS

How lovely! I am grateful.

SUSANNA

They're so pretty and charming.

COUNTESS

And who is, I ask you, that delightful young girl there? She looks so shy and modest.

BARBARINA
Ell'è una mia cugina e per le nozze è
venuta jer sera.

LA CONTESSA
Onoriamo la bella forestiera, venite quì,
datemi i vostri fiori.
Come arrossì! Susanna, non ti pare
Che somigli ad alcuno?

SUSANNA
Al naturale!

ANTONIO
Eh! cospettaccio, è questi l'uffiziale.

LA CONTESSA
Oh stelle!

SUSANNA
Malandrinio!

IL CONTE
Ebben, madama?

LA CONTESSA
Io sono, o signor mio, irritata e sorpresa
al par di voi.

IL CONTE
Ma stamane?

LA CONTESSA
Stamane per l'odierna festa volevan
travestirlo al modo stesso, che l'han
vestito adesso.

IL CONTE
E perchè non partisti?

CHERUBINO
Signor.

IL CONTE
Saprò punire la tua disubbidienza.

BARBARINA
Eccellenza! Eccellenza! voi mi dite sì
spesso qual volta m'abbraciate, e mi
baciate: "Barbarina, se m'ami, ti
darò quel che brami."

IL CONTE
Io dissi questo?

BARBARINA
Voi, or datemi, padrone, in sposo
Cherubino, e v'amerò, com'amo il mio
gattino.

LA CONTESSA
Ebbene, or tocca a voi.

ANTONIO
Brava, figliuola! Hai buon maestro,
che ti fa la scola.

IL CONTE
Non sò, qual uom, qual demone, qual
Dio, rivolga tutto quanto a torto mio.)

FIGARO
Signor, se trattenete
Tutte queste ragazze,
Addio festa, addio danza.

IL CONTE
E che? vorresti
Ballar col piè stravolto?

FIGARO
Eh, non mi duol più molto.
Andiam, belle fanciulle.

LA CONTESSA
Come si caverà dall'imbarazzo?

SUSANNA
Lasciate fare a lui.

IL CONTE
Per buona sorte,
I vasi eran di creta.

FIGARO
Senza fallo!
Andiamo, dunque, andiamo.

ANTONIO
Ed intanto a cavallo
Di galoppo a Siviglia andava il paggio.

FIGARO
Di galoppo o di passo, buon viaggio.
Venite o belle giovani.

IL CONTE
E a te la sua patente era in tasca
rimasta.

BARBARINA

That one? She is my cousin. She came last night to be here for the wedding.

COUNTESS

Let us honour our guest on her arrival. Come here to me. (*takes Cherubino's flowers and kisses him on the forehead*) May I accept your flowers? Look at her blush! Susanna, do you not notice a resemblance to someone?

SUSANNA

Yes, it is striking.
(*Antonio enters stealthily, pulls off Cherubino's bonnet, and puts his officer's cap on him.*)

ANTONIO

What do you know! If that's not Cherubino!

COUNTESS

Good Heavens!

SUSANNA (*aside*)

What a devil!

COUNT

What now, my lady!

COUNTESS

This time, my dear husband, I'm annoyed and astonished as much as you are.

COUNT

But this morning?

COUNTESS

This morning we were getting ready for tonight's celebration and we dressed him exactly as you see him.

COUNT

And why have you not left?

CHERUBINO

(*tearing his cap off his head*)
My lord . . .

COUNT

I'll have you punished for insubordination.

BARBARINA

Dearest master, dearest master, ev'ry time when you kissed me, do you remember, you always told me: "Barbarina, if you love me, there's no wish I won't grant you."

COUNT

So, did I say that?

BARBARINA

Surely. Now, dearest master, let me marry Cherubino, and in return I'll love you like my kitten.

COUNTESS (*to the Count*)

My lord, it's up to you now.

ANTONIO

Well said, my daughter. One can see you had an expert teacher.

COUNT (*aside*)

I'd like to know what nemesis, what demon, converts each situation to my undoing?

(*Figaro enters.*)

FIGARO

My lord, if you detain these girls here very much longer, good-bye party, good-bye dancing!

COUNT

What's that? You're planning to dance with your twisted foot?

FIGARO

(*pretends to straighten his leg, then tries to dance. He calls all the girls, starts to go; the Count calls him back.*)
It doesn't hurt at all now. Come on, girls, let's be going.

COUNTESS (*to Susanna*)

Now how will he get out of this predicament?

SUSANNA (*to the Countess*)

Oh, don't be concerned about him.

COUNT

It's very lucky the flower bed was a soft one.

FIGARO

Very lucky. No more delaying, let's go now. (*starts to go*)

ANTONIO (*holds him back*)

And meanwhile, on horseback, Cherubino was galloping to Seville!

FIGARO

Maybe galloping, maybe trotting, what's the difference? You girls, we must be off now. (*starts to go*)

COUNT

(*conducts him back to the center of the stage*)
But you had his commission still in your pocket.

FIGARO

Certamente, che razza di domande.

ANTONIO

Via non gli far più moti, ei non t'intende. Ed ecco chi pretende che sia un bugiardo il mio signor nipote.

FIGARO

Cherubino!

ANTONIO

Or ci sei.

FIGARO

Che diamin canta?

IL CONTE

Non canta, no, ma dice, ch'egli saltò stamane in sui garofani.

FIGARO

Ei lo dice! Sarà . . . se ho saltato io, si può dare ch'anch'esso abbia fatto lo stesso.

IL CONTE

Anch'esso?

FIGARO

Perchè no? Io non impugno mai quel che non sò.

No. 22 FINALE

FIGARO

Ecco la marcia, andiamo!

Ai vostri posti, o belle;
Susanna, dammi il braccio!

SUSANNA

Eccolo.

IL CONTE

Temerari!

CONTESSA

Io son di ghiaccio!

IL CONTE

Contessa!

LA CONTESSA

Or non parliamo,
Ecco quì le due nozze,
Riceverle dobbiamo; alfin si tratta
D'una vostra protetta.
Seggiamo!

IL CONTE

Seggiamo; e meditiam vendetta!

DUE DONNE

Amanti costanti, seguaci d'onor,
Cantate, lodate, sì saggio signor.
A un dritto cedendo,
Che oltraggia, che offende,
Ei caste vi rende, ai vostri amator.

TUTTI

Cantiamo, lodiamo, sì saggio signor.

FIGARO

Why, of course, sir! (*aside*) He kills me with his questions!

ANTONIO

(*to Susanna, who is making signs to Figaro*)

Don't make him any signals, he cannot see them. (*He leads Cherubino forward and presents him to Figaro.*) Here's someone who maintains that my brilliant nephew is a champion liar.

FIGARO

Cherubino!

ANTONIO

That's the one.

FIGARO (*to the Count*)

What is his story?

COUNT

He told the truth. He said that he was the one who jumped on the geraniums.

FIGARO

Did he say so? Could be . . . just because I jumped, there's no possible reason why he could not do likewise.

COUNT

He also?

FIGARO

And why not? One sheep will blindly follow the other's lead. (*The Spanish march is heard in the distance.*)

No. 22 FINALE

FIGARO

There's the procession, let's join it.
Go to your places, dear ladies, take your places!
Susanna, be my partner! (*takes Susanna's arm*)

SUSANNA

Willingly! (*All exeunt except the Count and Countess. The march is heard more clearly.*)

COUNT

How dare they!

COUNTESS

Ah, were it over!

COUNT

My lady!

COUNTESS

Let's not discuss it!
Both the couples are coming,
We must receive them well.
At least in one bride
You have shown special interest.
Be seated.

COUNT

With pleasure; (*aside*) and plan a fitting vengeance.

(*The Count and Countess seat themselves on the thrones. Enter Figaro, Susanna, Marcellina, Barbarina, Bartolo, Antonio, hunters with guns, Court attendants and country people. Two girls bring the little bridal hat with white plumes, two others a white veil, two others gloves and a nosegay. They are followed by Figaro with Marcellina. Two other girls carry a similar hat for Susanna, etc. They are followed by Bartolo with Susanna. Bartolo leads Susanna to the Count, and she kneels to receive from him the hat, etc. Figaro leads Marcellina to the Countess for the same purpose.*)

2 GIRLS

O, come, faithful lovers, in happy accord,
And gratefully join us in praise of our lord.
The right of his forbears he kindly ignored,
Revoking a custom his subjects abhorred.
O, come, lift your voices in praise of our lord.
A practice he ended
Which shamed and offended,
And leaves chaste and spotless
The one you adored.
Come all, lift your voices in praise of our lord.

ALL

With hearts ever grateful
We sing to our lord,
And may Heaven's blessing
His wisdom reward.
(*Susanna, kneeling, plucks the Count's sleeve, shows him the note, then reaches to her head, and while the Count pretends to adjust her bonnet, she gives him the note. He quickly hides it, and she rises and curtsies.*)

IL CONTE

È già solita usanza;
Le donne ficcan gli aghi in ogni loco,
Ah! ah! capisco il gioco!

FIGARO

Un biglietto amoroso
Che gli diè nel passar qualche galante,
Ed era sigillato d'una spilla
Ond'ei si punse il dito;
Il Narcisso or lo cerca: oh, che
    stordito!

IL CONTE

Andate amici, e sia per questa sera
Disposto l'apparato nuziale,
Colla più ricca pompa; io vo' che sia
Magnifica la festa; e canti, e fuochi,
E gran cena, e gran ballo; e ognuno
    impari
Com'io tratto color che a me son cari.

CORO

Amanti costanti, *etc.*

ATTO QUARTO

*Gran Viale del Giardino, che conduce
al Castello.*

No. 23 Cavatina

BARBARINA

L'ho perduta, me meschina!
Ah! chi sà dove sarà?
E mia povera cugina,
E il padron cosa dirà?

Recitativo

FIGARO

Barbarina, cos'hai?

BARBARINA

L'ho perduta, cugino.

FIGARO

Cosa?

MARCELLINA

Cosa?

BARBARINA

La spilla,
Che a me diede il padrone
Per recar a Susanna.

FIGARO

A Susanna la spilla?
E così, tenerella, il mestiero già sai . . .
di far tutto si ben quel che tu fai?

BARBARINA

Cos'è? vai meco in collera?

FIGARO

E non vedi ch'io scherzo? osserva: questa
è la spilla che il Conte da recare ti
diede alla Susanna, e servia di sigillo
a un bigliettino; vedi s'io sono in-
strutto.

BARBARINA

E perchè il chiedi a me quando sai tutto?

FIGARO

Avea gusto d'udir come il padrone ti
diè la commissione.

BARBARINA

Che miracoli! "Tieni, fanciulla, reca
questa spilla a la bella Susanna, e
dille: questo è il sigillo de' pini!"

Figaro comes to receive Susanna and they dance. A little later Marcellina rises. Bartolo receives her from the Countess.)

COUNT
(takes out the note and pricks his finger with the pin as he opens it; he shakes his finger, squeezes it, sucks it, and throws the pin to the ground.)
I wonder why these careless females must fasten all they handle with pins and needles!
Ha, ha, I get the point now!

FIGARO
(sees it all and says to Susanna)
Just a note of affection
Which some lady has given him in passing.
She must have used a pin to seal the letter, see.
And now he stuck his finger. *(The Count reads the note, kisses it, looks for the pin, finds it and sticks it in his lapel.)*
Now he is trying to find it.
Oh, is he stupid!

COUNT
Dear friends and subjects,
I'll see you all this evening,
Tonight we'll celebrate the double wedding
With the greatest of splendor.
For this must be a magnificent occasion,
With music and fireworks,
And a banquet, also dancing,
So I may show you
How much love and good-will
I feel I owe you.

CHORUS
O, come, faithful lovers, in happy accord, *etc.*

ACT FOUR

(Scene: A small room. Enter Barbarina. She looks for something on the floor.)

No. 23 CAVATINA

BARBARINA
I have lost it,
Heaven help me,
I have lost the little pin.

How on earth could that have been?
I can't find it, I can't find it,
This is awful, simply awful!
Oh, what trouble I am in!
I keep looking, but cannot find it.
This is dreadful, I am desperate!
This is my unlucky day!
Cousin Susanna, and the Count . . .
What will they say, what will they say?

RECITATIVE

(Figaro enters with Marcellina.)

FIGARO
Barbarina, what is it?

BARBARINA
I have lost it, dear cousin.

FIGARO
Lost it?

MARCELLINA
Lost it?

BARBARINA
The pin that his lordship gave me to take back to Susanna.

FIGARO
To Susanna, a pin? *(angrily)* I am awfully happy that you show so much talent . . . *(recollecting himself)* in performing assignments you are given.

BARBARINA
What's wrong? Why do you growl at me?

FIGARO
Can't you see I am joking?
(searches the floor for a moment, then draws a pin from Marcellina's dress or bonnet, and gives it to Barbarina) Now listen: this is the pin the Count has given you to return to Susanna; it had served as a seal upon a letter. See, I know all about it.

BARBARINA
If you know more than I, why do you ask me?

FIGARO
I just wanted to hear how my dear master has worded his instructions.

BARBARINA
Oh, is that it? "Please, Barbarina, take this little pin here, bring it back to Susanna and tell her: 'Here is the seal to the pine-grove.' "

FIGARO

Ah! ah! de' pini.

BARBARINA

E ver ch'ei mi soggiunse; "guarda che
alcun non veda." Ma tu già tacerai.

FIGARO

Sicuramente.

BARBARINA

A te già niente preme.

FIGARO

Oh niente, niente.

BARBARINA

Addio, mio bel cugino; vo da Susanna,
e poi da Cherubino.

FIGARO

Madre!

MARCELLINA

Figlio!

FIGARO

Son morto.

MARCELLINA

Calmati, figlio mio!

FIGARO

Son morto, dico.

MARCELLINA

Flemma, flemma, e poi flemma:
il fatto è serio, e pensarci convien. Ma
guarda un poco, che ancor non sai
di chi si prenda gioco.

FIGARO

Ah quella spilla, o madre, è quella
stessa che poc'anzi ei raccolse.

MARCELLINA

È ver, ma questo al più ti porge un
dritto di stare in guardia e vivere in
sospetto; ma non sai se in effetto—

FIGARO

All'erta dunque! il loco del congresso
so dov'è stabilito.

MARCELLINA

Dove vai, figlio mio?

FIGARO

A vendicar tutt'i mariti, addio.

MARCELLINA

Presto avvertiam Susanna. Io la credo
innocente. Quella faccia! quell'aria di
modestia . . . è caso ancora ch'ella non
fosse . . . ah, quando il cor non ciurma
personale interesse, ogni donna è por-
tata a la difesa del suo povero sesso,
da quest'uomini ingrati a torto op-
presso.

No. 24 ARIA

MARCELLINA

Il capro e la capretta
Son sempre in amistà,
L'agnello all'agnelletta
La guerra mai non fa.
Le più feroci belve
Per selve e per campagne
Lascian le lor compagne
In pace e libertà.
Sol noi povere femmine,
Che tanto amiam quest'uomini,
Trattate siam dai perfidi
Ognor con crudeltà.

*Giardino. In fondo un Viale di Pini.
Dai lati due Padiglioni chiusi prati-
cabili.*

RECITATIVO

BARBARINA

Nel padiglione a manca, ei così disse,
è questo, è questo. E poi se non
venisse? Oh, ve, che brava gente! A
stento darmi un arancio, una pera,
e una ciambella, "Per chi madamigella?" "Oh per qualcun, signori."

FIGARO

Ah, ha, the pine-grove!

BARBARINA

It's true, though, that he added: "Don't let a soul observe you." But you don't really count.

FIGARO

Why, of course not.

BARBARINA

It's none of your business.

FIGARO

Indeed not, it isn't!

BARBARINA

It's high time that I hurried to see Susanna, and later, Cherubino. (*Dances off.*)

FIGARO

(*as if crushed*) Mother!

MARCELLINA

Yes, dear.

FIGARO

This kills me!

MARCELLINA

Don't get excited, son.

FIGARO

This is outrageous!

MARCELLINA

Not so hasty, think it over.
It is a problem; we must give it some thought. You must make sure that you're not the target of some new deception.

FIGARO

But, dearest mother, I tell you, that is the pin for which the Count was looking.

MARCELLINA

If so, that makes it all the more important to act with caution and foster your least suspicion. After all, you do not know yet.

FIGARO

But soon I will. I know the spot exactly they have set for their meeting.

MARCELLINA

My dear son, where are you going?

FIGARO

To take revenge for cheated husbands, so help me! (*He leaves, furious.*)

MARCELLINA

Quickly, I'll warn Susanna, I believe she is guiltless. She looks honest and surely true to Figaro . . . and if by chance I should be mistaken . . . now that I am her mother and no longer her rival, as a woman I am bound to become a defender of the whole female sex; for all men are ungrateful and should be punished.

No. 24 ARIA

MARCELLINA

The birds and beasts are able
To live in loving pairs.
The horses in ev'ry stable
Will never fight their mares.
A goose will find her gander
A friendly good companion,
Never will he philander
Or wander very far.
The rooster loves each feather
Of his beloved hen,
The lion and his chosen lioness
Are happy in their den.
The most ferocious creatures
Have some redeeming features.
But when it comes to mankind
That's something else again.
We members of the female sex
Are victims of the men we love.
For all his faults and shameless ways
The woman always pays.
We tolerate their jealousy,
We offer them fidelity,
We love with lavish generosity.
They pay us back with misery
And break our tender hearts.

RECITATIVE

(Scene: *A thickly grown garden with two parallel pavilions.*)

BARBARINA

(*alone, holding some fruit and cookies*) He said the left pavilion, it must be here.
I see it, yes, this one. I only hope he'll get here. Good lord, what stingy people!
The most I could make them give me was an apple and a tomato. "For whom are those provisions?" "Just for a certain person." "That's what I thought."
The misers! The Count can't stand him, but I, I love him dearly. A

"Già lo sappiam," ebbene! il padron
l'odia; ed io gli voglio bene, però
costommi un bacio, e cosa importa,
forse qualcun me'l renderà. Son morta!

FIGARO
È Barbarina! Chi va là?

BASILIO
Son quelli che invitasti a venir.

BARTOLO
Che brutto ceffo! sembri un cospirator?
Che diamin sono quegli infausti
apparati?

FIGARO
Lo vedrete tra poco. In questo stesso
loco celebrerem la festa della mia
sposa onesta e del feudal signor.

BASILIO
(Ah buono, capisco come egli è, accor-
dati si son senza di me.)

FIGARO
Voi da questi contorni non vi scostate,
intanto io vado a dar certi ordini, e
torno in pochi istanti, a un fischio
mio correte tutti quanti.

BASILIO
Hai diavoli nel corpo!

BARTOLO
Ma che guadagni?

BASILIO
Nulla; Susanna piace al Conte; ella
d'accordo gli diè un appuntamento
ch'a Figaro non piace.

BARTOLO
E che? dunque dovria soffrirlo in pace?
Quel che soffrono tanti ei soffrir non
potrebbe? E poi sentite che guadagno
può far? Nel mondo, amico, l'accoz-
zarla con grandi, fu pericolo ognora,
dan novanta per cento e han vinto
ancora.

No. 25 ARIA

BASILIO
In quegl'anni, in cui val poco
La mal pratica ragion,
Ebbi anch'io lo stesso foco,
Fui quel pazzo, ch'or non son,
Ma col tempo e coi perigli,
Donna Flemma capitò;
E i capricci ed i puntigli
Dalla testa mi cavò
Presso un picciolo abituro,
Seco lei mi trasse un giorno,
E togliendo giù dal muro
Del pacifico soggiorno
Una pelle di somaro.
Prendi, disse, o figlio caro,
Poi disparve, e mi lasciò,
Mentre ancor tacito guardo quel dono,
Il ciel s'annuvola
Rimbomba il tuono,
Mista alla grandine scroscia la piova.
Ecco le membra coprir mi giova
Col manto d'asino che mi donò.
Finisce il turbine, io fo due passi.
Che fiera orribile dianzi a me fassi;
Già, già mi tocca, l'ingorda bocca,
Già di difendermi speme non ho,
Ma il fiuto ignobile del mio vestito,
Tolse alla belva sì l'appetito,
Che disprezzandomi si rinselvò.
Cosi conoscere mi fè la sorte,
Ch'onte, pericoli, vergogna, e morte,
Col cuoio d'asino fuggir si può.

kiss is what it cost me . . . it does not matter. I'll get it back very soon. (*Frightened, she enters the pavilion on the left.*) Good gracious! (*Enter Figaro in a cloak, and carrying a lantern. Then Basilio, Bartolo, a group of workmen, etc.*)

FIGARO

It's Barbarina! Who is there?

BASILIO

Remember, you have asked us to come.

BARTOLO

You look so savage, ready to cut our throats.
What is the point of these infernal preparations?

FIGARO

Very soon you shall know it. You are about to witness the unannounced revival of an old Spanish custom by the Count and my bride.

BASILIO

(*aside*) Oh, charming, charming! I see the light of day.
They arranged this affair without my help.

FIGARO

Stand where no one can see you and watch what happens. I'll give a few last minute orders, but I'll return here shortly, and when I whistle, rush forward and surprise them. (*All exeunt except Bartolo and Basilio.*)

BASILIO

He's acting like a madman.

BARTOLO

Can you explain it?

BASILIO

Gladly. The Count loves Susanna; she is pleased to accord him an appointment, and Figaro is displeased.

BARTOLO

Well? And? Is he supposed to take it calmly?

BASILIO

Why should he be exempted from what so many have suffered? And then, I ask you, what on earth could he gain? One learns one's lesson. In this life, dearest doctor, one must be realistic. You can't eat your cake and also have it.

No. 25 ARIA

BASILIO

Youth is headstrong, overbearing,
Too impulsive, as a rule.
I myself was young and daring,
I was just as big a fool.
But the passing years have brought me
Sense enough to swallow pride;
And experience at last has taught me
Not to swim against the tide.
Once, while I was on a journey,
I met Father Time in person.
In his hand he held an object
Which he offered me as present.
'Twas the hide of a donkey.
"Son," he said, "take this and wear it,
You won't regret it."
Then he disappeared in air,
Left me speechless standing there.
While I was lost in amazement and wonder,
A dreadful storm arose.
Thunder was crashing,
And like a waterfall the rain was splashing,
And lightning flashing.
I had no shelter, coat or umbrella.
Only the donkey hide lay there nearby.
I slipped it over me,
It kept me dry.
The sun came out again and I proceeded.
A horrid animal came out of nowhere,
Its mouth wide open, about to eat me.
I stood there, petrified.
What could I do?
My life was doomed, that much I knew.
All of a sudden the beast turned and bolted,
Smelling the donkey hide, it was revolted.
I smelled so horrible, it lost its appetite
And ran away.
Take this advice, my friend,
And learn this lesson:
Malice and calumny, injustice, dishonor,
Will never penetrate a donkey's hide.
(*Basilio and Bartolo leave.*)

No. 26 Recitativo ed Aria

FIGARO

Tutto è disposto: l'ora
Dovrebbe esser vicina; io sento gente . . .
È dessa! non è alcun; buja è la notte,
Ed io comincio omai
A far il scimunito
Mestiere di marito!
Ingrata! nel momento
Della mia cerimonia
Ei godeva leggendo, e nel vederlo,
Io rideva di me senza saperlo!
O Susanna! Susanna!
Quanta pena mi costi!
Con quell'ingenua faccia,
Con quegli occhi innocenti,
Chi creduto l'avria!
Ah! che il fidarsi a donna è ognor
  follia!

Aprite un po' quelgi occhi,
Uomini incauti, e sciocchi,
Guardate queste femmine,
Guardate cosa son.

Queste chiamate Dee
Dagli ingannati sensi,
A cui tributa incensi
La debole ragion,
Son streghe, che incantano per farci
  penar;
Sirene che cantano per farci affogar;
Civette che allettano per trarci, le
  piume,
Comete che brillano per toglierci il
  lume;
Son rose spinose,
Son volpi vezzose!
Son orse benigne,
Colombe maligne:
Maestre d'inganni, amiche d'affanni,
Che fingono, mentono,
Amore non sentono,
Non senton pietà.
Il resto nol dico.
Già ognuno lo sa.

RECITATIVO

SUSANNA

Signora, ella mi disse,
Che Figaro verravvi.

MARCELLINA

Anzi è venuto,
Abbassa un pò la voce.

SUSANNA

Dunque un ci ascolta, e l'altro
Dee venir a cercarmi:
Incominciam.

MARCELLINA

Io voglio quì celarmi.

SUSANNA

Madama, voi tremate; avreste freddo?

LA CONTESSA

Parmi umida, la notte: io mi ritiro;

FIGARO

Eccoci de la crisi al grande istante!

SUSANNA

Io sotto queste piante, (se madama il
  permette), resto al prendere il fresco
  una mezz'ora.

FIGARO

Il fresco! il fresco!

LA CONTESSA

Restaci in buon'ora.

SUSANNA

Il birbo è in sentinella,
Divertiamci anche noi,
Diamogli la mercè de'dubbi suoi.

No. 27 Recitativo ed Aria

SUSANNA

Giunse alfin il momento,
Che godrò senza affanno
In braccio all'idol mio:
Timide cure, uscite dal mio petto,
A turbar non venite il mio diletto.
Oh! come par che all'amoroso foco
L'amenità del loco,
La terra, e il ciel risponda,
Come la notte i furti miei seconda!
Deh! vieni, non tardar, o gioja bella,
Vieni ove amore per goder t'appella;

No. 26 RECITATIVE AND ARIA

(Figaro enters.)

FIGARO

It won't be long now, they should
arrive at any moment.
Someone is coming . . . Susanna?
No, it's not, the darkness deceived me.
On the night of my wedding
I am already playing the role of
jealous husband. Imagine!
At the moment of the wedding
procession,
When the Count read her message,
I was laughing!
I was laughing at myself, and did not
know it!
O Susanna, Susanna, what despair you
have caused me!
Who could have thought you faithless,
You were always so honest,
So naive and so winning,
Ah, to put faith in woman, in woman!
Foolish beginning!
O, fellow man, be smarter!
Don't be a blinded martyr.
Wake up and look at women-folk
And see them as they are,
And see them as they really are.
Though you may call them angels,
And like a slave adore them,
Your love will merely bore them,
But you will bear the scar.
Like witches with sorcery, they charm
and decoy.
Their dealings are double,
Like sirens with treachery, they sing
and destroy.
They flatter their vanity and cater to
fashion,
They cause us unhappiness and show
no compassion.
Like roses with briars,
Like soft-spoken liars,
Appearing delightful,
Yet vicious and spiteful.
Their dealings are double,
They get us in trouble.
Deceitful and jealous,
To love they are callous,
Their heart is of stone,
Yes, made of stone!
The rest I need hardly to tell you,
All that is sufficiently known.
Why don't you men get smarter, *etc.*
(Retires.)

RECITATIVE

(Enter the Countess, Susanna, disguised, and Marcellina.)

SUSANNA

My lady, I heard from Marcellina that
Figaro will be here.

MARCELLINA

He's here already, so better speak more
softly.

SUSANNA

One man in ambush, the other should
be here any moment. The fun begins!

MARCELLINA

*(enters the pavilion where Barbarina
is; Figaro in the background.)* I
will leave you alone here.

SUSANNA

My lady, you are trembling. Are you
cold?

COUNTESS

The night is damp and chilly. I'll go
inside now.

FIGARO

(aside) We are arriving at the crucial
moment.

SUSANNA

I'll stay a little longer, if my lady will
permit me. It is early and the night
air is refreshing.

FIGARO

Refreshing! Refreshing!

COUNTESS

(hides herself) You have my permission.

(aside) I know the rogue is spying. It
will give me much pleasure to reimburse him in full for his suspicions.

No. 27 RECITATIVE AND ARIA

SUSANNA

This at last is the moment,
So divine and so cherished,
I longingly awaited.
Soon he will come here,
With loving arms enbrace me,   ,
And no worry or fear shall mar our
rapture.
Close to the heart of Nature's friendly
powers,
Delicate, fragrant flowers,
The pine trees, the sky surround us.

Finchè non splende in ciel notturna
face,
Finchè l'aria è ancor bruna, e il mondo
tace.
Quì mormora il ruscel,
quì scherza l'aura,
Che col dolce susurro il cor ristaura;
Quì ridono i fioretti, e l'erba è fresca
Ai piaceri d'amor quì tutto adesca.
Vieni, ben mio, tra queste piante ascose,
Ti vo' la fronte incoronar di rose.

RECITATIVO

FIGARO

Perfida! e in quella forma
Meco mentìa! non so s'io veglio o
dormo!

CHERUBINO

Là, là, là, là, là, là, là.

LA CONTESSA

Il picciol paggio.

CHERUBINO

Io sento gente, entriamo
Ove entrò Barbarìna.
Oh! vedo quì una donna.

LA CONTESSA

Ahime meschina!

CHERUBINO

M'inganno! a quel cappello,
Che nell'ombra vegg'io, parmi Susanna.

LA CONTESSA

E se il Conte ora vien, sorte tiranna!

No. 28 FINALE

CHERUBINO

Pian pianin le andrò più presso;
Tempo perso non sarà.

LA CONTESSA

Ah!. se il Conte arriva adesso.
Qualche imbroglio accaderà.

CHERUBINO

Susannetta?
Non risponde?
Colla mano il volto asconde
Or la burlo in verità.

LA CONTESSA

Arditello! sfacciatello,
Ite presto via di quà.

CHERUBINO

Smorfiosa, maliziosa,
Io già sò perchè sei quà.

IL CONTE

Ecco quì la mia Susanna!

SUSANNA, FIGARO

Ecco quì l'uccellatore!

CHERUBINO

Non far meco la tiranna!

SUSANNA, IL CONTE, FIGARO

Ah, nel sen mi batte il core!
Un altr'uom con lei si sta.

LA CONTESSA

Via, partite o chiamo gente!

CHERUBINO

Dammi un bacio, o non fai niente.

LA CONTESSA

Anche un bacio! che corragio!

SUSANNA, IL CONTE, FIGARO

Alla voce è quegli il paggio.
Temerario! Temerario!

CHERUBINO

E perchè far io non posso,
Quel che il Conte ognor farà?
Oh! ve' che smorfie!
Sai ch'io fui dietro il sofà.

Aiding the lovers,
Night casts her veil around us.
Beloved, don't delay, the night is
  falling.
Hasten where love's delight is sweetly
  calling.
Until the stars grow pale and night is
  waning,
While the world is still and calm is
  reigning.
The brooklet rustles on, the breeze is
  blowing,
And the timorous heart with hope is
  glowing,
The flowers all with shining dew are
  gleaming,
While the world is long asleep and
  dreaming.
Come, my beloved, the starry sky above
  you,
Come, my beloved, with all my heart I
  love you.

RECITATIVE

FIGARO

Shame on her! Behind my back she
  plans to deceive me!
It's like a dreadful nightmare!

CHERUBINO

(*enters*) La, la, la, la, la, la, la.

COUNTESS

It's Cherubino.

CHERUBINO

Here are the pavilions. Barbarina must
  be in the left one.
I recognized my lady.

COUNTESS

I can't avoid him!

CHERUBINO

But no. I was mistaken; by her dress
  I can tell it is Susanna.

COUNTESS

If my husband comes now, Heaven
  protect me!

No. 28 FINALE

CHERUBINO

On my tip-toes I'll go nearer,
Here's the chance to have some fun.

COUNTESS

Oh, good Lord, it's Cherubino,
Now the trouble has begun.

CHERUBINO

(*to the Countess*) Come, Susannna!
  Won't you answer?
She pretends she does not see me,
But I'll show her that I know her little
  game,
Posing as a noble dame. (*takes her
  hand and caresses it*)

COUNTESS

(*tries to free herself; disguising her
  voice*) Shameless meddler, don't
  come near me,
Take yourself away from here.

CHERUBINO

Susanna, stop pretending,
I know well why you are here.
You needn't be condescending . . .
You await your cavalier,
And you hope he'll soon be here!
That's the reason you are here.

COUNTESS

Who allowed you to molest me?
Go at once away from here!
Shameless meddler! Go at once away
  from here!
Who allowed you to molest me?
Go at once away from here!

COUNT

(*in the distance*) Here you are, my
  sweet Susanna!

SUSANNA AND FIGARO

(*in the distance*) Here's our roving
  Don Giovanni.

CHERUBINO

Don't act prudish and affected!

SUSANNA, COUNT AND FIGARO

Ah, this shock came unexpected!

COUNTESS

Go, or I must call assistance!

CHERUBINO

(*keeping her hand in his*) Let me kiss
  you, don't be so silly.

3 OTHERS

I am sure it's Cherubino.

COUNTESS

I should kiss you, what presumption!

CHERUBINO

Why am I not once permitted
What the Count does ev'ry day?

SUSANNA, LA CONTESSA, IL CONTE,
FIGARO

Se il ribaldo ancor sta saldo,
La facenda guasterà.

CHERUBINO

Prendi intanto!

LA CONTESSA

O cielo! il Conte!

CHERUBINO

O cielo! il Conte

FIGARO

Vo' veder cosa fan là.

IL CONTE

Perchè voi non ripetete,
Ricevete questo quà.

SUSANNA, LA CONTESSA, IL CONTE

Ah! Ci ha fatto un bel guadagno,
Colla sua curiosità.

FIGARO

Ah! Ci ho fatto un bel guadagno,
Colla mìa curiosità.

IL CONTE

Partito è alfin l'audace,
Accostati, ben mio!

LA CONTESSA

Giacchè così vi piace,
Eccomi quì, signor!

FIGARO

Che compiacente femmina!
Che sposa di buon cor!

IL CONTE

Porgimi la manina.

LA CONTESSA

Io ve la do.

IL CONTE

Carina!

FIGARO

Carina?

IL CONTE

Che dita tenerelle!
Che delicata pelle!
Mi pizzica, mi stuzzica,
M'empie d'"un nuovo ardor!

SUSANNA, LA CONTESSA, FIGARO

La cieca prevenzione
Delude la ragione,
Inganna i sensi ognor.

IL CONTE

Oltre la dote, o cara!
Ricevi anco un brillante
Che a te porge un'amante
In pegno del suo amor.

3 OTHERS
(*aside*) How offensive, how insulting!

CHERUBINO
Is it not time now to stop pretending?
This very morning, remember,
When I hid behind the chair?

SUSANNA
What effront'ry!

COUNTESS
What presumption!

COUNT AND FIGARO
His behaviour is outrageous!

ALL EXCEPT CHERUBINO
(*aside*) If this rascal keeps insisting,
he will lead our plans astray.

CHERUBINO
(*tries to kiss the Countess*)
To begin with . . .
(*The Count comes between the Countess and Cherubino, and receives the kiss.*)

COUNTESS
Good Lord, my husband!

CHERUBINO
(*joins Barbarina in the pavilion*) Good Lord, my master!

FIGARO
(*drawing near the Count*) I must see what's going on.

COUNT
(*intending to give a box on the ear to Cherubino, he gives it to Figaro*)
Just to cool youthful ardor, take this little gift from me!

FIGARO
This is pretty meager payment
For the int'rest I have shown!

SUSANNA
(*laughing*) He is getting the proper treatment,
He received the proper treatment
For the envy he has shown!

COUNT AND COUNTESS
(*laughing*) That is just the proper treatment
For the boldness he has shown.
He received the proper treatment
For the boldness he has shown.

SUSANNA
Serves him right for being curious,
Always spying on his own!
Maybe next time he'll know better,
And leave well enough alone.

COUNT AND COUNTESS
He has made me simply furious
Wih his high and mighty tone,
Maybe next time he'll know better
And leave well enough alone.

FIGARO
All I got for being curious,
Is a bruised and aching bone, ah,
The next time I shall know better
And leave well enough alone. (*Figaro retires.*)

COUNT
(*to the Countess*) At last no one disturbs us.
Come over here, my dearest.

COUNTESS
Your word is my commandment,
Here I am, my lord.

FIGARO
How willing and obedient!
She's always in accord.

COUNT
Give me your hand, my darling.

COUNTESS
Here is my hand.

COUNT
I love you!

FIGARO
He loves her!

COUNT
What soft and lovely fingers!
Their tender touch still lingers,
It moves my heart to ecstasy,
Rapture and joy combined.

SUSANNA, COUNTESS AND FIGARO
Such wild infatuation
Is mere hallucination,
It blinds the human mind, the feeble human mind.

COUNT
Darling, besides your dowry,
Accept this little present,
A diamond ring as token
Of my undying love. (*gives the Countess a ring*)

LA CONTESSA
Tutto Susanna piglia
Dal suo benefattor.

SUSANNA, IL CONTE, FIGARO
Va tutto a maraviglia,
Ma il meglio manca ancor.

LA CONTESSA
Signor, d'accese fiaccole,
Io veggio il balenar.

IL CONTE
Entriam, mia bella Venere,
Andiamoci a celar!

SUSANNA, FIGARO
Mariti scimuniti,
Venite ad imparar!

LA CONTESSA
Al buio signor mio?

IL CONTE
E quello che vogl'io,
Tu sai, che là per leggere,
Io non desio entrar.

FIGARO
La perfida lo seguita,
E vano il dubitar.

SUSANNA, LA CONTESSA
I furbi sono in trappola,
Comincia ben l'affar.

IL CONTE
Chi passa?

FIGARO
Passa gente.

LA CONTESSA
È Figaro! men vo!

IL CONTE
Andate, andate! io poi verrò.

FIGARO
Tutto è tranquillo e placido;
Entrò la bella Venere,
Col vago Marte prendere
Nuovo Vulcan del secolo
In rete la potrò.

SUSANNA
Ehi? Figaro, tacete!

FIGARO
Oh! questa è la Contessa.
A tempo quì giungete,
Vedrete la voi stessa
Il Conte, e la mia sposa;
Di propria man la cosa
Toccar io vi farò.

SUSANNA
Parlate un po' più basso:
Di quà non muovo il passo,
Ma vendicar mi vo'.

FIGARO
(Susanna!) Vendicarsi?

SUSANNA
Sì.

FIGARO
Come potria farsi?

SUSANNA
L'iniquo io vo' sorprendere,
Poi so quel che farò.

FIGARO
La volpe vuol sorprendermi,
E secondarla vo'.

FIGARO
Ah se madama il vuole!

SUSANNA
Su via, manco parole!

FIGARO
Ah, madama!

SUSANNA
Su via, manco parole.

FIGARO
Eccomi a' vostri piedi,
Ho pieno il cor di foco,
Esaminate il loco,
Pensate al traditor!

SUSANNA
(Come la man mi pizzica!)

FIGARO
(Come il polmon mi s'altera!)

SUSANNA
(Che smania! che furor!)

FIGARO
(Che smania! che calor.)

COUNTESS

Gladly Susanna welcomes
Her benefactor's gift.

SUSANNA, COUNT AND FIGARO

Our (My) plans is fast proceeding,
The best is yet to come.

COUNTESS

(*to the Count*) My lord, I see the
glow of flaming torches in the night.

COUNT

Well, then, let us avoid them all
And hurry out of sight.

SUSANNA AND FIGARO

Come on, you foolish husbands,
It's time you saw the light!

COUNTESS

You mean there in the dark?

COUNT

What else would suit us better?
I do not want to read to you in there,
Susanna dear.

COUNTESS AND SUSANNA

Our plan is working splendidly,
Now comes the best of all.

FIGARO

She follows very willingly.
There is no doubt at all. (*Figaro
crosses the stage.*)

COUNT

(*in a feigned voice*) Who goes there?

FIGARO

(*in a rage*) Lots of people!

COUNTESS

It's Figaro! I'll hide. (*goes into the
right pavilion*)

COUNT

You go ahead, then! I'll meet you
soon. (*disappears among the bushes*)

FIGARO

Now all is still and calm again.
The lovers meet in secrecy,
But I shall guide their destiny,
Biding my time judiciously,
To catch them both at once.

SUSANNA

(*in a feigned voice*) Ho, Figaro! Be
quiet!

FIGARO

(*aside*) Ah, that must be the Countess.
(*aloud*) Your coming here is timely.
Observe in what a manner
Your husband and my Susanna
Arranged a secret meeting.
Just wait and you will see.

SUSANNA

(*forgetting to change her voice*) Be
careful and speak softly.
I swear I will not leave here
Till I have had revenge!

FIGARO

(*aside*) Susanna! (*aloud*) You want
vengeance?

SUSANNA

Yes.

FIGARO

Vengeance? May I be at your service?

SUSANNA

(*aside*) The traitor thinks he's fooling
me,
But he is very wrong.

FIGARO

(*aside*) The vixen thinks she's fooling
me,
So I will play along.
(*slyly joining the game*) Countess, I
am delirious!

SUSANNA

(*aside*) What's this, can he be serious?

FIGARO

Ah, my lady!

SUSANNA

(*aside*) Indeed, he must be serious.

FIGARO

I'm on my knees before you,
You know that I adore you.
Remember what you told me,
You're here to take revenge!

SUSANNA

(*aside*) I hardly can restrain myself!

FIGARO

(*aside*) What a delightful comedy!

SUSANNA

(*aside*) My blood begins to boil!

FIGARO

(*aside*) Her blood begins to boil!

SUSANNA

E senz' alcun affetto?

FIGARO

Suppliscavi il rispetto!
Non perdiam tempo invano:
Datemi un po' la mano,
Datemi un po'—

SUSANNA

Servitevi, signor!

FIGARO

Che schiaffo!

SUSANNA

Che schiaffo! e questo,
E ancora questo, e questo,
E poi quest' altro,
E questo, signor scaltro,
E poi quest' altro ancor.

FIGARO

O schiaffi graziosissimi,
O mio felice amor.

SUSANNA

Impara, impara o perfido!
A fare il seduttor.

FIGARO

Pace, pace, mio dolce tesoro!
Io conobbi la voce che adoro,
E che impressa ognor serbo nel cor.

SUSANNA

La mia voce?

FIGARO

La voce che adoro.

a 2

Pace, pace, mio dolce tesoro,
Pace, pace, mio tenero amor.

IL CONTE

Non lo trovo, girai tutto il bosco.

SUSANNA, FIGARO

Questi è il Conte, alla voce il conosco.

IL CONTE

Ehi? Susanna? Sei sorda? Sei muta?

SUSANNA

Bella! bella! non l'ha conosciuta!

FIGARO

Chi?

SUSANNA

Madama.

FIGARO

Che dici! Madama?

SUSANNA, FIGARO

La commedia, idol mio, terminiamo,
Consoliamo il bizzarro amator.
Sì Madama, voi siete il ben mio.

IL CONTE

La mia sposa? Ah, senz'arme son io!

FIGARO

Un ristoro al mio cor concedete.

SUSANNA

Io son quì, faccio quel che volete.

IL CONTE

Ah! ribaldi!

SUSANNA, FIGARO

Ah! corriamo, mio bene,
E le pene compensi il piacer.

SUSANNA

(*aside*) I hardly can restrain my
temper.
Now he has gone too far!

FIGARO

(*aside*) She hardly can restrain her
temper,
And I fear I've gone too far!

SUSANNA

(*disguising her voice slightly*) Suppose
you are rejected?

FIGARO

That would be unexpected.
We can't lose time debating. (*rubbing
his hands*)
Grant me some sign of favor . . .
Give me your hand.

SUSANNA

(*resumes her natural voice, and boxes
his ears*) Right here where it
belongs!

FIGARO

You slapped me!

SUSANNA

Take this one, and this one, (*continues
to box his ears*)
And still another, and this one,
And still another!

FIGARO

Don't hit so hard, I beg you!

SUSANNA

And take this, you scheming traitor,
Take this one and still another one!

FIGARO

Oh, precious welcome punishment
From her beloved hand!

SUSANNA

I'll teach you to behave yourself,
And mind your own affairs!

FIGARO

I am a happy man!

SUSANNA

I warn you not to let it happen again.
You got what you deserve as punish-
ment,
You false and wicked man!

FIGARO

(*kneels*) My apology, darling, I owe
you.
From your voice it was easy to know you,
From your sweet little voice I adore.

SUSANNA (*surprised and laughing*)
From my voice?

FIGARO

How could I mistake it?

FIGARO AND SUSANNA

Darling, darling, I love and adore you,
Dearest love, let us quarrel no more.

COUNT (*enters*)
Where she is I cannot discover.

FIGARO AND SUSANNA

That's the voice of the frustrated lover.

COUNT

(*turns toward the pavilion in which
the Countess has hidden, and opens
it*) Ho, Susanna! Can't you hear
me? Where are you?

SUSANNA

Splendid, splendid, he still does not
know her.

FIGARO

Who?

SUSANNA

My lady.

FIGARO

The Countess?

SUSANNA

The Countess!

SUSANNA AND FIGARO

Now to bring the burlesque to an ending,
We must even the score with the Count.

FIGARO (*falls at Susanna's feet*)
Ah, my lady, I love you so madly!

COUNT

It's the Countess! Ah, and I have no
weapons!

FIGARO

Won't you favour my loving proposal?

SUSANNA

I am ready and at your disposal.

COUNT

Ah, betrayers, betrayers!

SUSANNA AND FIGARO

Let us hurry away and be happy,
Let us bury our troubles in joy.

(*Susanna enters the pavilion on the
left.*)

IL CONTE
Gente, gente! all'armi!

FIGARO
Il padrone!

IL CONTE
Gente, ajuto!

FIGARO
Son perduto!

BARTOLO, BASILIO, ANTONIO,
DON CURZIO
Cos'avvenne?

IL CONTE
Il scellerato
M'ha tradito, m'ha infamato,
E con chi, state a veder,

BARTOLO, BASILIO, ANTONIO,
DON CURZIO
Son stordito, sbalordito!
Non mi par che ciò si ver.

FIGARO
Son storditi sbalorditi!
Oh che scena! che piacer!

IL CONTE
Invan resistete; uscite Madama,
Il premio or avrete di vostra onestà.
Il paggio!

ANTONIO
Mia figlia!

FIGARO
Mia madre!

BASILIO, BARTOLO, ANTONIO,
DON CURZIO
Madama!

IL CONTE
Scoperta è la trama, la perfida è quà.

SUSANNA
Perdono! perdono!

IL CONTE
No, no, non sperarlo!

FIGARO
Perdono! Perdono!

IL CONTE
No, no! non vo' darlo!

a 6
Perdono!

IL CONTE
No, no, no, no, no!

LA CONTESSA
Almeno per loro perdono otterò.

a 5
O cielo! che veggio, delirio! vaneggio
Che creder non so!

IL CONTE
Contessa, perdono!

LA CONTESSA
Più docile io sono,
E dico di sì.

TUTTI
Ah! tutti contenti saremo così.
Questo giorno di tormenti,
Di capricci e di follia,
In contenti, e in allegria
Solo amor può terminar
Sposi, amici! al ballo, al gioco
Alle mine date foco,
Ed al suon di lieta marcia
Corriam tutti a festeggiar.

COUNT
Hurry, hurry, come with weapons!

FIGARO (*pretending great fear*)
That's my master.
(*Enter Bartolo, Basilio, Don Curzio, Antonio, and servants with torches.*)

COUNT
Guards and servants, come and help me!

FIGARO
I'm outnumbered!

BASILIO. CURZIO, ANTONIO AND BARTOLO
What has happened?

COUNT
This wretched scoundrel has betrayed me,
Acted basely, and with whom you soon shall see.

BASILIO, CURZIO, ANTONIO AND BARTOLO
I am speechless and bewildered!
Can it be that this is true?

FIGARO
They are speechless and bewildered.
They cannot believe it's true.

COUNT
There's no use resisting, insisting on hiding.
Come out now, my Countess, and get your reward!
(*The Count reaches into the left pavilion and pulls out a resisting Cherubino, then Barbarino, Marcellina and Susanna.*)
Cherubino!

ANTONIO
My daughter!

FIGARO
My mother!

BASILIO, CURZIO, ANTONIO AND BARTOLO
My lady!

COUNT
Your plot is discovered, most faithless of wives,
So false to her lord!

SUSANNA
(*kneels before the Count, holding her handkerchief before her face*)
Forgive me, forgive me!

COUNT
No, never, never!

FIGARO (*kneels*)
Forgive her, forgive her!

COUNT
There's no chance whatever!

ALL OTHERS (*kneeling*)
Forgive her!

COUNT
No, no, no, no, no, no!

ALL OTHERS
Forgive her!

COUNT (*more forceful*)
No, no, no, no, no, no!

COUNTESS
(*comes out of the other pavilion and is about to kneel when the Count prevents her*)
I know you'll forgive them,
For my sake at least!

BASILIO, CURZIO, COUNT AND ANTONIO
I cannot conceive it, I scarcely believe it,
I hardly can credit my eyes!
What's this I see?

COUNT (*supplicatingly*)
My lady, forgive me,
Beloved, forgive me!

COUNTESS
How could I refuse it,
My heart speaks for you.

ALL
We are all contented and happy again.
All day long we were tormented,
Angry, foolish, and excited,
But at last we are united
By the magic force of love.
Lovers and couples,
With laughter and singing,
Let the wedding bells chime in with joyous ringing!
And to joyous strains of music,
Sing and dance till break of day.
Let's make merry,
And to joyous strains of music,
Sing and dance till break of day!

Don Giovanni

(1787)

OPERA IN TWO ACTS

Libretto by Lorenzo da Ponte

After the Play by Tirso de Molina

English Version by W. H. Auden *and* Chester Kallman

THIS ENGLISH VERSION WAS FIRST PERFORMED BY THE NATIONAL BROADCASTING COMPANY OPERA THEATRE ON TELEVISION IN NEW YORK ON APRIL 10, 1960.

INTRODUCTION

The Marriage of Figaro was so triumphant a success when it was performed by the Italian company at Prague in the winter of 1786-1787 that Pasquale Bondini, the director of the troupe, commissioned Mozart to write a new work for the following season. The composer asked da Ponte for a libretto. The poet had also had requests for librettos from Antonio Salieri, who was shortly to become court *Kapellmeister,* and Vicente Martín y Soler, composer of *Una Cosa rara,* an opera very popular at that time (Mozart was to quote an air from it in *Don Giovanni*). "I loved and esteemed all three of them," wrote da Ponte in his Memoirs, "and hoped to find in each compensation for past failures and some increment to my glory in opera. I wondered whether it might not be possible to satisfy them all, and write three operas at one spurt." Salieri wanted an Italian adaptation of an opera he had composed for Paris. For Martín, da Ponte chose the *Arbore di Diana,* and for Mozart *Don Giovanni,* "a subject that pleased him mightily."

> The three subjects fixed on [continues da Ponte], I went to the Emperor, laid my idea before him, and explained that my intention was to write the three operas contemporaneously.
>
> "You will not succeed," he replied.
>
> "Perhaps not," said I, "but I am going to try. I shall write evenings for Mozart, imagining I am reading the *Inferno*; mornings I shall work for Martín and pretend I am studying Petrarch; my afternoons will be for Salieri. He is my Tasso!"

He set to work, he tells us, with a bottle of wine at his right, a box of snuff at his left, and an inkwell in the middle. There was also a bell, with which to summon the maid,

> a beautiful girl of sixteen — I should have preferred to love her only as a daughter, but alas! . . . To tell the truth the bell rang rather frequently, especially at moments when I felt my inspiration waning. She would bring me now a little cake, now a cup of coffee, now nothing but her pretty face, a face always gay, always smiling, just the thing to inspire poetical emotion and witty thoughts. I worked twelve hours a day, with a few interruptions, for two months on end . . . In sixty-three days the first two operas were entirely finished and about two thirds of the last. [1]

The subject of Don Juan had been a favorite one on the stage for more than a century when da Ponte and Mozart decided to use it. The fearless libertine and his punishment at the hands of the statue of one of his victims had supplied the plot for plays, ballets, and operas. Probably the first was the

[1] *The Memoirs of Lorenzo da Ponte,* transl. by Elisabeth Abbott, New York, 1959, p. 83 f.

Spanish comedy *El Burlador de Sevilla,* published in 1630 and attributed to Tirso de Molina, pseudonym for Gabriel Tellez. Here the main elements of the plot are already established, as are characters corresponding to Leporello ("Catalinon"), the Commendatore ("Don Gonzalo de Ulloa"), Donna Anna, Zerlina ("Aminta"), Masetto ("Patricio"), and Don Ottavio ("Marquis de la Mota"). This play already ends with Catalinon's description of his master's awful fate and a cheerful roundup of the other characters. Other dramatizations of the story soon appeared in Italy and France, the most important of these being Molière's *Dom Juan ou Le Festin de pierre,* first performed at Paris in 1665 and published in 1682. Molière's significant contribution is the creation of the ˙character of Donna Elvira, who is more prominent in his version than Donna Anna. Other treatments of the story include one by Thomas Shadwell, *The Libertine* (1676), for which Purcell wrote incidental music, and another by Carlo Goldoni (1736), which was probably known by da Ponte. Early in the 18th century French and Italian operas were based on the subject, and in 1761 the ballet *Don Juan,* with music by Gluck and a scenario, based on Molière, by the Imperial ballet-master Gasparo Angolini, was produced in Vienna. The subject was a particular favorite in Italy in the last quarter of the century, and of these Italian Don Juan operas the most popular was the one-act *Convitato di pietra (The Stone Guest),* with a libretto by Giuseppe Bertati and music by Giovanni Gazzaniga. It was performed at Venice early in 1787 and was quickly taken up by many other Italian theaters. Apparently its libretto and music reached Vienna very soon, for it was this opera that served as model for da Ponte and Mozart.

As he had done with Beaumarchais' *Figaro,* da Ponte kept a good deal of the model but made some important changes. He cut out two characters — Donna Ximena, another lady in love with the Don, and Lanterna, the Don's cook — and built up the part of Donna Anna, who leaves the stage early in Bertati's libretto. Most of Act I from the point where Elvira interrupts Don Giovanni's attempt to make love to Zerlina to the end of the great finale is da Ponte's invention. In the first two scenes of Act II da Ponte borrowed some incidents from Tirso da Molina and Molière and added some of his own. In addition to thus extending Bertati's version, da Ponte rewrote what he kept of it in wittier and more elegant language. Whether and to what extent Mozart influenced the construction of the libretto is unknown, but it seems likely that he had a hand in it: the idea of the three orchestras in the first finale, for example, might easily have stemmed from the composer.

Mozart worked on the opera through the spring and summer of 1787. This did not prevent him from turning out other masterpieces in the same period, such as the string quintets in C major, K. 515; G minor, K. 516; and C minor, K. 406 (a transcription of the Serenade for Winds, K. 388); the Sonata in C for piano, four hands, K. 521; the *Musical Joke,* K. 522; *Eine kleine Nachtmusik,* K. 525; and the Violin Sonata in A major, K. 526.

As usual, Mozart was familiar with the capacities of the singers who were to appear in *Don Giovanni,* having heard them when he was in Prague the previous December and January for performances of *Figaro.* At the beginning of October Mozart and his wife were back in Prague, where he finished the opera, working part of the time in a little country house called the Villa Bertramka, belonging to his friends the Duscheks. (Franz Duschek was an outstanding pianist, his wife, Josepha, a much admired singer.) Da Ponte came and worked for a week with the cast but then had to hurry back to Vienna. A piquant touch was lent to the proceedings by the presence of a living, though retired, Don Juan. A few days before the opening, Casanova, an old friend of da Ponte's, was in Prague. Mozart may have asked him, in da Ponte's absence, to make some changes in the libretto. Some twenty lines by Casanova, designed for the end of the sextet in Act II, survive; they were not used in the score.[2] As was Mozart's custom, he left the Overture for the last. The familiar tale about how he sat up all the night before the performance writing it, with Constanze encouraging him by plying him with punch and telling him stories, most likely refers not to the night before the première but to that before the dress rehearsal. As Abert points out, it would have been too dangerous to place uncorrected parts of this difficult piece before the orchestra on so important an occasion as the first public performance. Since much of the music in the Overture was taken from the opera, and since Mozart, as was his habit, had already composed it all in his head, it was simply a matter of writing it down.

The first performance took place, after some delays, on October 29, 1787, at the National Theater, with the following cast:

Don Giovanni	Luigi Bassi
Donna Anna	Teresa Saporiti
Don Ottavio	Antonio Baglioni
Commendatore ⎫ Masetto ⎬	Giuseppe Lolli
Donna Elvira	Caterina Micelli
Leporello	Felice Ponziani
Zerlina	Caterina Bondini

Bassi, who was then twenty-two, was in his fourth year as a member of Bondini's company. He is described in contemporary reports as handsome and a skilled actor in both tragic and comic roles. His voice was a somewhat light baritone but "always very flexible, full, and agreeable." Teresa Saporiti was much admired for her artistry and her beauty. She was then twenty-four, and lived to the age of a hundred and six. Baglioni is reported to have had a voice of good quality, pure and expressive, and to have been a finished and tasteful performer. Lolli also had considerable repute as a singer. Little is known about Caterina Micelli, but Ponziani, a bass buffo, was praised as a singer and

[2] See Paul Nettl, *Don Giovanni und Casanova,* in *Mozart-Jahrbuch 1957,* Salzburg, 1958, p. 108.

character actor. His clear enunciation and the evenness of his voice were especially admired. Caterina Bondini, wife of the company's director, was a favorite of the Prague public as both singer and actress.

From these descriptions, and from the music that Mozart wrote for these singers, it would appear that he was favored with a cast that was strong in every member. The opera aroused excited enthusiasm. Mozart wrote to a friend that it was received "with the greatest applause." Guardasoni, stage director of the company, wrote to da Ponte: "Long live da Ponte! Long live Mozart! All impresarios, all virtuosos should bless their names. So long as they live we shall never know what theatrical poverty means!" Under date of November 1, a Prague newspaper reported:

> On Monday the 29th the Italian opera company gave the eagerly awaited opera by Maestro Mozart, *Don Giovanni or the Stone Banquet*. Connoisseurs and musicans say that its like has never been performed in Prague. Herr Mozart himself conducted, and when he stepped into the orchestra he was cheered three times; the same thing happened when he walked out of it. The opera is extremely difficult to perform, and everyone marvels at the excellent production it nevertheless received, after so short a rehearsal period. Both singers and orchestra put forth their best efforts to show their gratitude to Mozart with good execution. Much expense was incurred for several choruses and the scenery, all of which Herr Guardasoni presented brilliantly. The extraordinarily large attendance guarantees a general success.

* *
*

Mozart returned to Vienna after a few happy weeks. On May 7, 1788, at the request of the Emperor, *Don Giovanni* was produced in Vienna. Composer and librettist had already received a fee from the Prague company — 100 ducats (about $200) and 50 ($100) respectively; under the circumstances, the payments they received from the Emperor — 225 florins (about $100) and 100 ($45) — were rather generous, for that time. For this performance Mozart reluctantly added three numbers, to please the singers. One was *Mi tradì quell' alma ingrata,* asked for by the Elvira, Caterina Cavalieri, who had created the role of Constanza in *The Abduction from the Seraglio.* Another was *Dalla sua pace,* for the tenor Francesco Morella, a recent addition to the Vienna company, who seems to have found *Il mio tesoro* too difficult. The third was a buffo duet, *Per queste tue manine,* for Leporello and Zerlina, which was inserted in place of *Il mio tesoro* as a concession to the Viennese taste for slapstick comedy. All three items are superfluous to the drama, and the duet is always omitted in modern performances, but the two arias have been retained.[3]

Don Giovanni was given fifteen times that year in Vienna, but then disap-

[3] The statement, frequently made, that Mozart omitted the final sextet in the Vienna performances has recently been shown to be apparently incorrect. See Christof Bitter, *Don Giovanni in Wien 1788,* in *Mozart-Jahrbuch 1959,* Salzburg, 1960, p. 146.

peared from the boards and did not return until after Mozart's death. Meanwhile it was produced in some fifteen German theaters outside Vienna while its composer was still alive. It reached Warsaw in 1789, Amsterdam in 1794, Budapest and St. Petersburg in 1797, Paris (in a much mutilated version) in 1805, Copenhagen in 1807, Bergamo and Rome in 1811, London in 1817 (in a public performance; amateur performances had been given there earlier). The first performance in America took place at the Park Theatre in New York in 1826. Manuel Garcia and his Italian company were appearing there, and put on *Don Giovanni* at the urging of the aging da Ponte, who had established himself in New York as a teacher of Italian.[4] Other first performances include: Buenos Aires, 1827; Dublin, 1828; Calcutta, 1833; Madrid and Bucharest, 1834; Helsinki, 1840; Melbourne, 1861; and Cairo, 1870.

In Vienna *Don Giovanni* was received with mixed feelings. The Emperor, who was away from the capital through most of 1788, received reports about it and wrote to Count Rosenberg that Mozart's music was too difficult to sing. After he heard it, in December, he said to da Ponte: "That opera is divine; I should even venture that it is more beautiful than *Figaro*. But such music is not meat for the teeth of my Viennese!" When da Ponte told Mozart of this, the composer said, "Give them time to chew on it." Except in Prague, the opera was not generally regarded as a success. A journalist in Mainz reported that while the music was indeed "grand and harmonious," it was "more heavy and artistic than pleasing and popular." When it was first produced in Frankfurt in 1789 a local critic predicted a short run for it: "The music is not popular enough to rouse a public sensation." The following year a Berlin reviewer granted that the music was beautiful but added that "here and there it is very complicated, difficult, and overburdened with instruments." According to Franz Niemtschek, one of Mozart's earliest biographers, after nine rehearsals in Florence the first act was declared to be unperformable. But there were some non-Bohemian listeners, even in those early days, who had a more penetrating view. In 1791 Bernhard Anselm Weber, a conductor and composer living in Berlin, wrote in a review of *Don Giovanni*:

> Add a deep knowledge of art to the happiest gift for inventing fascinating melodies and then combine both with the greatest possible originality, and you have the striking portrait of Mozart's musical genius. Never can one find in his works an idea that one has heard before; even his accompaniment is always new. Without interruption one is hurried along, as it were, restlessly from one idea to the next, so that one's wonder at the last swallows up one's admiration for all the preceding ideas, and even when straining all one's forces one can scarcely grasp all the beauties that are offered to the soul. If one should want to charge Mozart with a weakness, then surely this would be the only one: that this abundance of beauties almost exhausts the soul, and that the effect of the whole is sometimes veiled by it. But fortunate the artist whose only failing consists in *too great* perfection!

[4] Da Ponte had had an English translation printed of his libretto and placed it on sale in several shops before the performance. He was in one store one morning to collect what was due him — six dollars — when he noticed lottery tickets for sale, at six dollars each. He bought one — and won five hundred dollars.

And Goethe, who declared that Mozart would have been the composer to set *Faust* to music, wrote to Schiller in 1797: "You would have seen the desires that you had for opera fulfilled to a high degree recently in *Don Juan;* but this work stands in complete isolation, and because of Mozart's death any hope for something similar is shattered."[5]

*   *
*

As the work became better known, admiration for it grew and spread. Its smooth integration of forceful, even violent, drama with comedy, the skill with which it clothed universal types in flesh and blood, and above all the magnificent music that Mozart poured into it made a profound impression not only upon composers but also upon writers and philosophers other than Goethe. Beethoven grumbled at the licentiousness of the subject, but no one could have been more keenly aware of the mastery of its treatment; he copied out the Masked Trio, so that he could study it more carefully. When Rossini was asked which of his own operas was his favorite, he replied characteristically, *"Don Giovanni."* E. T. A. Hoffmann devoted to this opera one of his fantastic tales (published in 1814), which may still be read with profit, for embedded in the exuberant imaginativeness of the prose is a penetrating psychological study of the characters in the opera. The same masterwork inspired Sören Kierkegaard to write a long essay in which esthetics and analysis are mingled. Schopenhauer considered *Don Giovanni* a sublime expression of the supernatural, and coupled it with *Hamlet* and *Faust* as among "the most perfect masterpieces of the greatest masters."

In the second half of the 19th century, when the general tendency was to regard Mozart as a cherubic composer of simple, cheerful music, an exception had to be made for *Don Giovanni*. It was hard to reconcile that strange work — whose chief protagonist, as Bernard Shaw pointed out, "was the first Byronic hero in music" — with the serene and angelic plaster-figure conception of Mozart. Wolf-Ferrari was moved to ask, naïvely but seriously, "Mozart can be charming too when he has to; but if he is to be regarded as *only* charming . . . how is one to account for the Commendatore, for example, where joking is no longer possible?" Tchaikovsky wrote that "the scenes with Donna Anna, her heartrending grief, her thirst for vengeance, are rendered by Mozart with such compelling truth that they can be compared in depth of expression only with the best scenes in Shakespeare's tragedies."

In our own century *Don Giovanni* has continued to provoke discussion. It has even been subjected to psychoanalysis. Otto Rank, a pupil of Freud, published a study in 1924 in which he analyzed not only the hero of the opera

[5] Most of the quotations in the above paragraph are translated from Otto E. Deutsch, *Mozart: Die Dokumente seines Lebens,* Kassel, 1961. B. A. Weber's statement about the profusion of fine ideas in Mozart is very similar to one in Dittersdorf's *Autobiography,* published ten years later.

but also its composer, an analysis in which special stress is laid on the death of Leopold Mozart at a time when Wolfgang had begun to work on the opera. A small literature exists on the question of whether *Don Giovanni* is basically a comic or a serious opera. To this question the most convincing answer was supplied by Alfred Einstein: "the work presents no riddle: it is an *opera buffa* with *seria* roles — for instance, those of Donna Anna and Don Ottavio — and *buffa* roles. . . . Where material like this is concerned, in which, as in *Faust,* such dark, primeval, and demonic forces are inextricably combined, analysis can never be complete. The work is *sui generis,* incomparable and enigmatic from the evening of its first performance to the present day."

CAST OF CHARACTERS

DON GIOVANNI, a young nobleman . . . . *Baritone*

DON OTTAVIO . . . . *Tenor*

LEPORELLO, servant of Don Giovanni . . . . **Bass**

IL COMMENDATORE, Donna Anna's father . . . . **Bass**

MASETTO, a peasant . . . . *Baritone*

DONNA ANNA, betrothed to Don Ottavio . . . . *Soprano*

DONNA ELVIRA, a lady of Burgos . . . . *Soprano*

ZERLINA, betrothed to Masetto . . . . *Soprano*

Peasants, Musicians, Dancers, Demons.

PLACE: Sevilla.

TIME: Middle of the 17th century.

THE PLOT

ACT I.

In front of the Castilian palace of Don Pedro, Commandant of the Knights of Malta, Leporello bewails his fate as servant to the dissolute nobleman, Don Giovanni. From the palace emerges Donna Anna, daughter of the Commandant, frantically struggling from Don Giovanni's embrace. When her father rushes out in response to her cries, Giovanni kills the old man with his sword and escapes with his servant. Donna Anna, who had momentarily fled, now returns with her fiancé, Don Ottavio. He tries to console her, but she bids him leave.

Roaming the neighborhood in quest of other quarry, Giovanni withdraws as Donna Elvira, a former sweetheart of the Don, arrives in search of the man she loves. Leporello tries to discourage her by reciting his master's list of conquests. The peasants, Masetto and Zerlina, dance in with their friends, celebrating their approaching wedding. Giovanni, joining the merrymakers with Leporello, is attracted by Zerlina and, bidding his servant attend to Masetto, invites the bride to his house. Elvira overhears and interrupts their idyll, warning the girl against her new suitor. Meeting unexpectedly with Anna and Ottavio, Giovanni drags Elvira away lest she disclose his true identity to Donna Anna. But the orphaned daughter of the Commandant has already recognized Don Giovanni as her attacker, and calling on Ottavio for vengeance, she describes to him the events that preceded her father's death. Left alone, Ottavio dwells on his love for the grief-stricken Anna.

With Leporello in attendance, Don Giovanni grooms himself in preparation for a feast in honor of Zerlina.

As Masetto and his sweetheart approach the gate of Don Giovanni's mansion, she begs forgiveness for her apparent neglect of her rustic swain. When Giovanni has led the couple away Elvira, Anna and Ottavio, masked and robed in dominos, gather to the music of the minuet, vowing to punish the Don. Don Giovanni appears and invites the trio to the ball.

The peasants crowd Giovanni's ballroom, from which the host entices Zerlina to a neighboring chamber. When she cries for help, the avenging maskers burst open the door and denounce the Don, who barely makes his escape.

ACT II.

Giovanni and Leporello approach Elvira's house so that the servant may woo her in the Don's guise, thus enabling Giovanni to serenade her pretty maid. Masetto, leading a band of peasants to punish the wicked Giovanni, is disarmed by a ruse of the Don (dressed as Leporello) and badly beaten. Zerlina, attracted by her lover's lamentations, consoles him.

Elvira, still believing Leporello to be her beloved Giovanni, leads him near a cloister where Ottavio and Anna also gather. Zerlina and Masetto follow shortly; the group denounces Leporello, thinking him the Don. Frightened, the servant unmasks, pretends to vow vengeance on his master and then escapes. Ottavio, following the distraught Donna Anna, again seeks to console her with his love, leaving Elvira to lament the perfidies of the man she still loves in spite of all.

Giovanni and Leporello hide in a cemetery, where they find themselves in the shadow of the tomb of the Commandant. They impudently invite his statue to dinner, to which it bows its head and accepts.

In Donna Anna's mansion, Don Ottavio urges his suit, but she begs for a proper delay until her father's death is avenged.

Don Giovanni gives directions to Leporello for the banquet he plans for the Stone Guest. Elvira rushes in and implores him for the last time to reform, but the Don waves her aside. Rushing from the hall she screams in terror. Giovanni, going to investigate, meets the statue of the Commandant in the doorway and is summoned to hell, resisting to the end, while flames burst through the mansion. The principals examine the ruins and deliver the closing moral: sad is the fate that awaits a libertine.

DON GIOVANNI

ATTO I

SCENA I

Piazza. Da un lato il Palazzo del Commendatore; dall'altro una locanda.— S'appressa l'alba.

LEPORELLO
(indi Don Giovanni e Donna Anna.)

LEPORELLO
Notte e giorno faticar,
Per chi nulla sà gradir;
Piòva e vento sopportar,
Mangiar male e mal dormir.
Voglio far il gentiluomo,
E non voglio più servir;
Nò, nò, nò, non voglio più servir.

Oh che caro galantuomo:
Vuol star dentro colla bella,
Ed io far la sentinella!
Voglio far il gentiluomo,
E non voglio più servir,
Nò, nò, nò, non voglio più servir.
Ma mi par, che venga gente,
Non mi voglio far sentir, Ah!

(Entra Don Giovanni, e Donna Anna.)

ANNA
Non sperar, se non m'uccidi,
Ch'io ti lasci fuggir mai.

GIOVANNI
Donna folle, indarno gridi!
Chi son io tu non saprai.

LEPORELLO
(Che tumulto! oh, ciel, che gridi)
Il padron in nuovi guai!

GIOVANNI
(Taci, e trema al mio furore.)

ANNA
Scellerato!

GIOVANNI
Sconsigliata!

ANNA
Genti, servi! Al traditore!
Come furia disperata
Ti saprò perseguitar.

GIOVANNI
(Questa furia disperata
Mi vuol far precipitar.)

LEPORELLO
(Sta a veder ch'il malandrino
Mi farà precipitar.)
(Esce Donna Anna.)
Don Giovanni, il Commendatore,
Leporello.

166

DON GIOVANNI

ACT ONE

SCENE I

(A Garden. Night.)

Introduction

LEPORELLO

(wrapt in a dark mantle, impatiently pacing to and fro before the steps to the palace)

On the go from morn till night,
Running errands, never free,
Hardly time to snatch a bite;
This is not the life for me.
I would like to play the master,
Would no more a servant be,
No, no, no, no, no, no,
I would a master be.

(facing the palace)

What a difference between us!
Warm you lie in arms of beauty
While I freeze on sentry duty;
I would like to play the master,
Would no more your servant be,
No, no, no, no, no, no,
I would your master be.
What was that? We're in for trouble.
This is not the life for me,
No, no, no, no, no,
This is no life for me.

(hides himself)

(Enter Donna Anna, holding Don Giovanni firmly by the arm.)

DONNA ANNA

No, you won't, you shan't escape me!
I will never let you go!

DON GIOVANNI

(trying to conceal his features)

Do not scream! You'll wake the household.
Kiss me, dear, and let me go!

DONNA ANNA

No, you won't, you shan't escape me,
I shall never let you go.
Fire and murder! Save me! Seize him!
Fire and murder! *(freeing herself)*
 Try to stop me!
  (turning to the palace)
Help me! Save me!

DON GIOVANNI

Now! Now let me go.
(almost hissing; covering his mouth)
Stop that noise or I shall hurt you.
Stop, I tell you!
  (seizing her roughly)
Must I hurt you?

DONNA ANNA

From my unrelenting fury
You shall never get away.
From my unrelenting, my avenging fury
You shall never get away.
Fire and murder! Try to stop me!
Save me! Help me!
(During this action the Commendatore enters, hastily, a torch in his left hand, a sword in his right. Seeing the Commendatore approach, she runs into the house.)

DON GIOVANNI

From her unrelenting fury
I had better get away.
Stop, I tell you!
I shall hurt you.
How am I to get away?
(He haughtily confronts the Commendatore.)

LEPORELLO

Master cursing, the lady screaming,
How am I to get away?
Well, we're in a pretty pickle;
How am I to get away?
Yes, we're in a pickle this time,
Yes, a very pretty pickle,
And I cannot get away
From this pretty pickle this time,
And I think that I can say
For this pretty pickle this time
There will be the deuce to pay!

COMMENDATORE

Lasciala, indegno;
Battiti meco.

GIOVANNI

Va, non mi degno
Di pugnar teco.

COMMENDATORE

Così pretendi
Da me fuggir?

LEPORELLO

(Potessi almeno
Di quà partir.)

COMMENDATORE

Battiti!

GIOVANNI

Misero! Attendi,
Se vuoi morir.

(*Si battono—il Commendatore cade*)

COMMENDATORE

Ah soccorso! Son tradito.
L'assassino m'ha ferito,
E dal seno palpitante
Sento l'anima partir.

GIOVANNI

Ah, già cade il sciagurato,
Affannoso e agonizzante;
Già dal seno palpitante
Veggo l'anima partir.

LEPORELLO

(Qual misfatto! qual eccesso!
Entro il sen dallo spavento
Palpitar il cor mi sento—
Io non so che far, che dir!)

GIOVANNI (*Sotto voce*).

Leporello, ove sei?

LEPORELLO

Son quì per mia disgrazia, e voi—

GIOVANNI

Son quí.

LEPORELLO

Chi è morto—voi, o il vecchio?

GIOVANNI

Che domanda da bestia! Il vecchio!

LEPORELLO

Bravo! Due imprese leggiadre: sforzar
la figlia ed ammazzar il padre!

GIOVANNI

L'ha voluto suo danno.

LEPORELLO

Ma Donn'Anna cos'ha voluto?

GIOVANNI

Taci! Non mi seccar, vien meco—se
non vuoi qualche cosa ancor tu—

(*Minacciandolo*).

LEPORELLO

Non vo' nulla, Signor! Non parlo più.

(*Partono*).

*Donna Anna, Don Ottavio, e Servi con
fiaccole.*

ANNA

Ah, del padre in periglio in soccorso
voliam!

OTTAVIO

Tutto il mio sangue verserò, se bisogna.
Ma dov'è il scellerato?

RECITATIVE E DUETTO.

ANNA

In questo loco. (*Vedendo il corpo di
suo padre.*) Ma qual mai s'offre, oh
Dei, spettacolo funesto agli occhi
miei! Padre mio! Mio caro padre!

COMMENDATORE

Where is the villain? Draw, sir, and
fight me!

DON GIOVANNI

No! Pride forbids me to draw on grey-
beards.

COMMENDATORE

Faint-hearted coward! I challenge you.

DON GIOVANNI

Force me not!

COMMENDATORE

Draw, I say!

DON GIOVANNI

Force me not! (*draws his sword*)
Dotard, on guard, then!
Your death is near.

(*He strikes the torch out of the Commendatore's hand. The Commendatore attacks. They fight and the Commendatore falls mortally wounded.*)

LEPORELLO

If I could only get out of here!
(*The moon rises slowly; lights appear
in the palace windows; great excitement within; servants hasten with
torches behind the closed gates.*)

COMMENDATORE

Ah, I'm wounded! Ah, I'm dying!
God, protect my child from evil!
From this mortal scene of sorrow
My immortal soul must fly.

(*He dies.*)

DON GIOVANNI

Ah, he's fallen! Ah, he's dying!
Paying dearly for his folly.
On this world of love and beauty
He must close his aged eye.

(*Servants return with Don Ottavio and
hasten with him from the street into
the palace.*)

LEPORELLO

Who has fallen? Who is dying?
How I shiver, how I shudder!
Rooted to the spot by terror,
I can neither move nor cry.

Recitative

DON GIOVANNI (*softly*)

Are you there, Leporello?
(*He sheathes his sword and dons his
cloak.*)

LEPORELLO

I only wish I wasn't. Are *you* there?

DON GIOVANNI

Of course.

LEPORELLO

Are you a ghost? Is *he* one?

DON GIOVANNI

What an imbecile question! He's done
for.

LEPORELLO

Bravo! Pretty good for one evening. To
rape the daughter and then skewer
the father!

DON GIOVANNI

He compelled me; I had to.

LEPORELLO

And Donn'Anna . . . also compelled
you?

DON GIOVANNI

Silence! No more from you. Remember, (*threatening to strike him*) you
can join the old man if you wish.

LEPORELLO

From now on I'll be dumb as any fish.

(*Exeunt.*)

(*Donna Anna enters; she agitatedly
descends the steps with Don Ottavio
and servants bearing torches.*)

DONNA ANNA

Quick! His life is in danger. We must
come to his help.

DON OTTAVIO

(*raising his drawn sword*)

I will defend him. I will save him or
perish.
But I see and hear no one.

DONNA ANNA

I fear some evil.

Recitative and Duet

DONNA ANNA (*seeing the corpse*)

What, O God, do I see! What spectacle
of horror appears before me! (*sinks
down beside the body*) It can't be!
Not my father! (*throws herself upon
the corpse*) Speak to me, father!

OTTAVIO

Signore!

ANNA

Ah, l'assassino mel trucidò! Quel sangue, quella piaga—quel volto tinto e
coperto del color di morte! Ei non
respira più—fredde le membra! Padre mio! Caro padre! Padre amato!
Io manco—io moro!

OTTAVIO

Ah soccorrete, amici, il mio tesoro! Cer-
catemi, recatemi qualche odor, qualche spirito. Ah non tardate! Donn'-
Anna, sposa, amica! Il duolo estremo
la meschinella uccide.

ANNA

Ahi!

OTTAVIO

Già riviene! Datele nuovi aiuti.

ANNA

Padre mio!

OTTAVIO

Celate, allontanate agli occhi suoi quel-
l'oggetto d'orrore. Anima mia! Con-
solati, fa core!

DUETTO.

ANNA

Fuggi, crudele, fuggi!
Lascia che mora anch'io!
Ora ch'è morto, oh Dio!
Chi a me la vita diè!

OTTAVIO

Senti cor mio, deh senti!
Guardami un solo istante!
Ti parla il caro amante.
Che vive sol per te!

ANNA

Tu sei, perdon, mio bene!
L'affanno mio, le pene!
Ah, il padre mio dov'è?

OTTAVIO

Il padre lascia, o cara!
La rimembranza amara:
Hai sposo e padre in me!

ANNA

Ah, vendicar, s'il puoi,
Giura quel sangue ognor!

OTTAVIO

Lo giuro agli occhi tuoi.
Lo giuro al nostro amor!

A 2

Che giuramenti oh Dei!
Che barbaro momento!
Fra cento affanni e cento
Vammi ondeggiando il cor!

(*Partono*).

DON OTTAVIO

Who did this?

DONNA ANNA

Ah, the assassin has struck him down! He's wounded! Look, he's bleeding! So silent, so still and so unnaturally pallid! (*Don Ottavio offers to raise her; she refuses.*) So icy to the touch, breathing no longer! (*She rises.*) Tell me, father, that I'm dreaming! Answer me, father! (*She reels.*) Have mercy! Have pity!

(*Don Ottavio supports her, and leads her to the stone seat.*)

DON OTTAVIO (*to the servants*)

Help! Do not stand there gaping, but help your mistress! Bring smelling salts immediately. Go at once, get some brandy. Be quick, I tell you! Donn' Anna! Dearest! Beloved! O Grace of Heaven, let her not die of sorrow!

(*A maid hurries into the palace and returns immediately with a smelling-bottle which she offers to Donna Anna.*)

DONNA ANNA

Ah!

DON OTTAVIO

Look, she's stirring! Give her a sip of brandy!

DONNA ANNA (*with a deep sigh*)

Let me dream it.

DON OTTAVIO (*to servants*)

And quickly! Remove this blood-bespattered body! She musn't see it again. (*Serving-men raise the Commendatore, and bear him into the palace.*) Wake, Donna Anna! I love you! Be comforted!

DONNA ANNA (*springing up, and repulsing Don Ottavio as if insane*)

Heartless tormentor, leave me! Leave me to die beside him. Cold is he now and lifeless Who gave my life to me.

DON OTTAVIO

Hear me, dear heart, Donn' Anna, Turn to your faithful lover Whose heart is in your keeping, O turn your eyes to me!

DONNA ANNA

(*perceiving her error and giving Don Ottavio her hands*)

Let me once more embrace him. Once more! Once! Father! My father!

(*approaching the spot where the Commendatore fell*)

But where, O where is he?

DON OTTAVIO

Donn' Anna, weep no longer. Time will abate your sorrow. Your husband and father I'll be.

DONNA ANNA

Gone! Forever! O where, O where is he?

DON OTTAVIO

Weep no longer! Time will abate your sorrow. Both husband and father, Both husband and father I'll be.

(*Donna Anna stands with lofty demeanor opposite Don Ottavio.*)

DONNA ANNA

Ah! Will you swear to avenge him? Blood must for blood be poured.

DON OTTAVIO

(*raising his hand as for taking an oath*)

I swear it. I swear it. By the eyes I love, I swear it. I swear it on my sword.

DONNA ANNA

Though cunning as the serpent He fly from retribution, Our righteous wrath shall find him, Blood shall for blood be poured. Blood for blood is calling. Vengeance! No ocean deep shall hide him Nor subterranean cavern; Our righteous wrath shall find him, Death be his just reward, At last his just reward.

DON OTTAVIO

Though cunning as the serpent He fly from retribution, Our righteous wrath shall find him, Blood shall for blood be poured. I swear it! By love I swear it. I swear it on my sword. No ocean deep shall hide him Nor subterranean cavern, Our righteous wrath shall find him, Death be his just reward.

(*Exeunt slowly into palace. The curtain falls rapidly.*)

SCENA II

Strada.—Don Giovanni e Leporello.

GIOVANNI

Orsù spicciati presto—cosa vuoi?

LEPORELLO

L'affar di cui si tratta è importante.

GIOVANNI

Lo credo.

LEPORELLO

Importantissimo.

GIOVANNI

Meglio ancora. Finiscila.

LEPORELLO

Ma giurate di non andar in collera.

GIOVANNI

Lo giuro sul mio onore, purchè non
parli del Commendatore.

LEPORELLO

Siamo soli?

GIOVANNI

Lo vedo.

LEPORELLO

Nessun ci sente?

GIOVANNI

Via!

LEPORELLO

Vi posso dire tutto liberamente.

GIOVANNI

Tutto, sì.

LEPORELLO

Dunque quand'è così, caro signor padrone, la vita che menate è da briccone—

GIOVANNI

Temerario! In tal guisa!

LEPORELLO

E il giuramento.

GIOVANNI

Zitto! Non si parli di giuramento. Taci,
o ch'io—
          (*Minacciandolo*).

LEPORELLO

Non parlo più! Non fiato, padron mio.

GIOVANNI

Così saremo amici. Or odi un poco. Sai
tu perchè son qui?

LEPORELLO

Non ne so nulla. Ma essendo l'alba
chiara, non sarebbe qualche nuova
conquista? Io lo devo saper per porla
in lista.

GIOVANNI

Va là che sei 'l grand'uom! Sappi ch'io
sono innamorato d'una bella dama, e
son certo che m'ama. La vidi, le par-
lai: meco al Casino questa notte verrà. Zitto, mi pare senti rodor di femmina.

LEPORELLO (*a parte*).

Cospetto! Che odorato perfetto!

GIOVANNI

All'aria mi par bella.

LEPORELLO (*a parte*).

E che occhio, dico!

GIOVANNI

Ritiriamoci un poco, e scopriamo ter-
ren.

LEPORELLO

(Già prese foco.)

DONNA ELVIRA;

(*Don Giovanni, e Leporello,
in disparte.*)

ARIA.

ELVIRA

Ah! Chi mi dice mai
Quel barbaro dov'è?
Che per mio scorno amai,
Che mi mancò di fè.
Ah se ritrovo l'empio,
E a me non torna ancor,
Vò farne orrendo scempio,
Gli vò cavar il cor.

SCENE II

(*A street. Early morning.*)

Recitative

DON GIOVANNI

Come on, what is your message? Let me have it!

LEPORELLO

Listen with great attention! It's important.

DON GIOVANNI

I'm listening.

LEPORELLO

I mean it, seriously!

DON GIOVANNI

I shall listen with gravity.

LEPORELLO

You promise me that you will not get furious?

DON GIOVANNI

Yes, yes, but on condition it's not to do with the Commendatore.

LEPORELLO

No one's looking?

DON GIOVANNI

Of course not.

LEPORELLO

No one's in earshot?

DON GIOVANNI

No.

LEPORELLO

And I'm allowed to speak with absolute frankness?

DON GIOVANNI

Yes.

LEPORELLO

Very well, it is this: if you continue leading this kind of life much longer (*shouting in his ear*) You'll go to Hell, sir!

DON GIOVANNI

You damned scoundrel! But how dare you!

LEPORELLO

Now, now, you promised.

DON GIOVANNI

To hell with what I promised. Silence . . . or else . . .

LEPORELLO

I'll never speak. Not even in a whisper.

DON GIOVANNI

Be good and I'll forgive you. Let's change the subject. Why do you think I'm here?

LEPORELLO

I never think, sir. So early in the morning . . . could the reason . . . be some charming adventure? For the sake of our list you'll have to tell me.

DON GIOVANNI

That's better, that's more like my Leporello. It is another lovely little creature, and I know that she loves me. I've met her. We have spoken, and she has promised she will meet me tonight . . . Ah, how delicious! That scent is, surely, feminine.

LEPORELLO

For women you've a nose like a bloodhound!

DON GIOVANNI

From here I'd say she's pretty.

LEPORELLO

And an eagle's eyesight.

DON GIOVANNI

We had better take cover till we know if she is . . .

LEPORELLO

Partridge or plover.

(*Exeunt.*)

(*Donna Elvira enters. She is wearing a travelling dress.*)

Trio

DONNA ELVIRA

Let him beware who left me,
His vows of love denied,
Who gave a heart once candid
A self-reproach to hide—
Sorrow and shame to hide.

(*Don Giovanni and Leporello reappear.*)

No more shall they be hidden,
Now shamelessly I have sworn,
Directly I'll denounce him.
And make him bear the scorn
That I alone have borne.

GIOVANNI (*a* LEPORELLO).

Udisti? Qualche bella dal vago abban-
donata. Poverina! Poverina! Cerchi-
am di consolar il suo tormento.

LEPORELLO (*a parte*).

Così ne consolò mille e ottocento.

GIOVANNI

Signorina! Signorina!

ELVIRA

Chi è là!

GIOVANNI

Stelle! Che vedo?

LEPORELLO (*a parte*).

Oh bella! Donna Elvira!

ELVIRA

Don Giovanni! Sei quì? Mostro, fellon,
nido d'inganni!

LEPORELLO (*a parte*).

Che titoli cruscanti! Manco male che lo
conosce bene.

GIOVANNI

Via, cara Donna Elvira, calmate quella
collera! Sentite—lasciatemi parlar!

ELVIRA

Cosa puoi dire dopo azion sì nera? In
casa mia entra furtivamente, a forma
d'arte, di giuramenti e di lusinghe
arrivi a sedurre il cor mio! M'inna-
mori, o crudele! Mi dichiari tua sposa, e poi,—mancando della terra e del
Ciel al santo diritto,—con enorme
delitto, dopo tre dì da Burgos allon-
tani. M'abbandoni, mi fuggi—e lasci
in preda al rimorso ed al pianto per
pena forse che t'amai cotanto!

LEPORELLO (*a parte*).

Pare un libro stampato!

(Leporello busies himself with Don Giovanni's attire, helps him draw on his gloves, etc.)

DON GIOVANNI *(to Leporello)*

She's troubled. Could some bad man have left a girl so lovely?

DONNA ELVIRA

My rage, I swear, shall make him
Regret that he was born . . .

DON GIOVANNI *(with contemptuous pity)*

How she suffers! How she suffers!

DONNA ELVIRA

That he was ever born!
Ah! That he was ever born!

DON GIOVANNI

We ought to try to bring her consolation.

LEPORELLO *(aside)*

The girls you have consoled would make a nation.

(Leporello steals about Donna Elvira to catch sight of her face; unsuccessful, he informs Don Giovanni pantomimically of his failure.)

DONNA ELVIRA

Why did you lie and leave me?
Where, traitor, have you run?
Come back and I'll forgive you
The harm that you have done,
Whatever wrong you've done.
But if you still are faithless,
Still my affection scorn,
Though you were dead to feeling,
You'll bear what I have borne!

DON GIOVANNI

O poor darling! How pathetic!

DONNA ELVIRA

Should you repeat your scorn,
Ah! beware what I have sworn!

DON GIOVANNI

We really ought to bring her consolation.

LEPORELLO *(aside)*

Consoling girls, I think, is your vocation.

DONNA ELVIRA

You'll bear what I have borne,
What I have borne.

(Don Giovanni clears his throat several times, to attract Donna Elvira's notice; she does not hear him, but grows more and more excited. Finally, his patience gives way and he steps up to her boldly, but politely.)

DON GIOVANNI

Gracious lady, *(raising his hat)* may I help you . . . ?

Recitative

DONNA ELVIRA

Who's that?

DON GIOVANNI *(starting back)*

(Well, of all people!)

LEPORELLO *(aside)*

(How perfect! Donn' Elvira!)

DONNA ELVIRA

Don Giovanni! It's you, treacherous beast, poisonous serpent!

LEPORELLO *(aside)*

(A flattering description! One would think she knew him as well as I do.)

DON GIOVANNI

Now, dear, dear, Donn' Elvira, control yourself, be sensible and listen. Allow me to explain.

DONNA ELVIRA

Nothing you say can justify your actions. Did you not worm your way into my affections? Did you not court me . . . with sighs and vows of everlasting devotion? Till my pure heart believed you and, alas, came to love you. First you promised me marriage . . . and then denying . . . every tie, every law of earth and Heaven . . . with incredible baseness, after three days . . . you stole away from Burgos . . . You forsook me . . . You vanished . . . And I was left to remorse and vain repentance. Dear must I pay for loving you so dearly!

LEPORELLO *(aside)*

(She's been reading romances!)

GIOVANNI

Oh, in quanto a questo ebbi le mie ragioni.

(*a* LEPORELLO).

É vero?

LEPORELLO

É vero. (*Ironicamente.*) E che ragioni forti!

ELVIRA

E quali sono, se non la tua perfidia, la legerezza tua? Ma il giusto Cielo vuole ch'io ti trovassi per far le sue, le mie vendette.

GIOVANNI

Via, cara Donna Elvira, siate più ragionevole! (*A parte.*) Mi pone a cimento costei. (*Forte.*) Se non credete al labbro mio, credete a questo galantuomo.

LEPORELLO

Salvo il vero?

GIOVANNI (*forte*).

Via dille un poco.

LEPORELLO (*piano*).

E cosa devo dirle?

GIOVANNI (*forte, partendo*).

Si, si, dille pur tutto.

ELVIRA (*a* LEPORELLO).

Ebben, fa presto.

LEPORELLO (*esitando*).

Madama—veramente—in questo mondo concio—sia cosa—quando—fosse che—il quadro non è tondo—

ELVIRA

Sciagurato! Così del mio dolor gioco ti prendi? Ah voi—(*Verso Don Giovanni che non crede partito.*) Stelle! L'iniquo fuggì! Misera me! Dove? In qual parte?

LEPORELLO

Eh, lasciate che vada! Egli non merita ch'a lui voi più pensiate.

ELVIRA

Il scellerato m'ingannò, mi tradì!

LEPORELLO

Eh consolatevi! Non siete voi, non foste, e non sarete nè la prima, nè l'ultima. Guardate questo non piccolo libro: è tutto pieno dei nomi di sue belle. Ogni villa, ogni borgo—ogni paese, è testimone di sue donnesche imprese.

LEPORELLO

Madamina!
Il catalogo è questo,
Delle belle, che amò il padron mio:
Un catalogo egli è ch'ho fatto io:
Osservate, leggete con me!
In Italia seicento e quaranta,
In Alemagna duecento trent'una;
Cento in Francia, in Turchia novant'-
    una,
Ma, ma in Ispagna, son già mille e tre!
V'han fra queste contadine.
Cameriere, cittadine;
V'han contesse, baronesse,
Marchesine, principesse,
E v'han donne d'ogni grado,
D'ogni forma, d'ogni età.

DON GIOVANNI

For various reasons I was obliged to do
it.

(*to Leporello*) (As *you* know.)

LEPORELLO (*ironically*)

(As *I* know.)

DON GIOVANNI AND LEPORELLO

Very important reasons.

DONNA ELVIRA

Too well I know them. Your shameless
love of lying, your utter lack of feeling. The righteous hand of Heaven
has led me hither. And for your mis-
deeds you shall answer.

DON GIOVANNI

O come, now, come, you are talking
foolishly. (We're in for a difficult
scene.) Since you refuse to hear what
I say, this honest fellow shall speak
for me.

LEPORELLO

(Trust me, Lady!)

DON GIOVANNI (*to Leporello*)

You tell this lady.

LEPORELLO (*aside to Don Giovanni*)

(But what am I to tell her?)

DON GIOVANNI (*aloud*)

You tell her the whole story.

DONNA ELVIRA (*to Leporello*)

The truth! No lying!

(*Don Giovanni escapes.*)

LEPORELLO

Dear lady . . . to speak frankly . . . the
world we live in . . . is, as you know,
a vale of sorrow where . . . a square
is not a circle.

DONNA ELVIRA

O you coward! How dare you mock a
poor defenseless woman! (*turning to
Don Giovanni*) And you . . . vanished! The villain has fled, stolen
away! But where? Which direction?

LEPORELLO

Down! Be glad that he hasn't taken
you with him; and forget that you
know him.

DONNA ELVIRA

How can I do it, how forget his deceit?

(*Donna Elvira turns to the bench before the house, and seats herself
sadly.*)

LEPORELLO

Madam, console yourself: You're not
the first, believe me, to be his victim,
nor will you be the last of them. (*He
takes out a book.*) I pray you glance
at this lengthy volume containing all
of the names of those he's conquered,
their descriptions, with the dates and
hours and locations of his wide-
spread, intimate recreations.

Aria

LEPORELLO

At your pleasure, you may have a
perusal
Of the list that I keep for my master;
But perhaps you'll digest it much faster
If you skim through together with me:
I maintain it imma-cu-late-ly.

Down for Italy, six-hundred-forty;
Down for England, a hundred-eleven;
For San Marino a mere ninety-seven;
But prim and proper
Spain contributes a thousand-and-
three!
Can that be? Yes, it's three.

There are bar-maids, basket-weavers,
There are dairy-maids and divas,
Countless countesses, princesses,
In the ranks of his successes,
Every possible condition,
Occupation, form and age—
All arouse his gallant rage!

In Arabia, ten dozen were foolish;
In Dalmatia, a hundred were wanton;
Here's Helvetia—a gross in each
Canton;
But, but, but over-prudish
Spain contributes a thousand-and-
three!
You are one . . . of those three.

Yes, with jealously well-hid wives,
Weeping widows, mellow midwives,
And innumerable nurses
He has suffered no reverses;
Every possible condition,
Occupation, form and age—
All arouse his gallant rage!

Nella bionda, egli ha l'usanza
Di lodar la gentilezza,—
Nella bruna la costanza,
Nella bianca la dolcezza!
Vuol d'inverno la grassotta
Vuol d'estate la magrotta;
E la grande, maestosa;
La piccina, ognor vezzosa.
Delle vecchie fa conquista
Per piacer di porle in lista:
Sua passion predominante
E la giovin principiante
Non si picca, se sia ricca—
Se sia brutta, se sia bella!
Purchè porti la gonnella,
Voi sapete quel che fa!

(*Parte*).

ELVIRA

In questa forma dunque mi tradì il scellerato? È questo il premio che quel
barbaro rende all'amor mio? Ah vendicar vogl'io l'ingannato mio cor!
Pria ch'ei mi fugga, si ricorra—si vada; Io sento in petto sol vendetta
parlar, rabbia, e dispetto!

(*Parte*).

SCENA III

*Il Contado, con una veduta del
Palazzo di Don Giovanni.*

ZERLINA; MASETTO

Contadini e Contadine

ZERLINA

Giovinette, cha fate all'amore,
Non lasciate, che passi l'età:
Se nel seno vi bulica il core,
Il rimedio vedetelo quà!
La la la, la la la!
Che piacer che sarà.

CORO

Ah, che piacer che sarà,
La la la la lera, la la la lera.

MASETTO

Giovinetti leggieri di testa,
Non andate girando quà e là
Poco dura dei matti la festa,
Ma per me cominciata non ha!
Lera, lera la!
Che piacer, che piacer che sarà!
Lera la, lera la!

CORO

Che piacer! La, la, lera!

ZERLINA E MASETTO

Vieni, vieni, carina godiamo,
E cantiamo, e balliamo, e suoniamo!
Che piacer, che piacer che sarà!

CORO

Che piacer! La, la, lera!

Don Giovanni; Leporello; (e detti)

GIOVANNI

Manco male è partita! Oh guarda, guarda, che bella gioventù! Che belle
donne!

LEPORELLO

(Tra tante per mia fe, vi sarà qualche
cosa anche per me.)

GIOVANNI

Cari amici, buon giorno! Seguitate a
star allegramente; seguitate a suonar,
buona gente. C'è qualche sposalizio?

All the praises with which he courts
them
Follow orders whereby he sorts them:
Blondes are modest, dark ones gracious,
Red-heads candid, white sagacious.
Bulk attracts him during winter,
During summer, more the splinter.
He will woo them tall and florid,
Sporting clouds about the forehead;
  He will woo them
Teeny-tiny, teeny-tiny, teeny-tiny,
Teeny-tiny, of barely bean-size
And in all manner of in-between-size.
Ripe duennas he has contented
  That his list
Might be somewhat augmented;
But the most-of-all he savors
Uninitiated favors.
Ill or healthy,
Poor or wealthy,
Plain or pretty,
Dull or witty,
High-born, lowly,
Scraggy hags or beauties,
Be they female, they're his duties—
How he meets them, this can show,
How he greets them, this can show.
Be they female, they're his duties
In a service that you know,
This can show
That you know,
In a service that you know. (*Exit
hastily into the villa.*)

Recitative

DONNA ELVIRA

To think my love was yielded, not to
love or desire, but to obsession! That
is worse than I ever had imagined.
Vengeance alone he merits! And I'd
felt that my love gave me a power
sent by Heaven to save him, although
he left me. I shall love him no more;
never shall I weaken! (*Exit into the
house.*)

SCENE III

(*The open country. Zerlina, Masetto
and the villagers are singing and
dancing.*)

Duet and Chorus

ZERLINA (*to the maidens*)

Pretty maid with your graces adorning
the dew-spangled morning,

The red rose and the white fade away,
  Both wither away,
  All fade in a day.
Of your pride and unkindness relenting,
  to kisses consenting,
All the pains of your shepherd allay,
As the cuckoo flies over the may.

(*The maidens form a ring and dance
around Zerlina.*)

MASETTO (*to the lads*)

What is youthful desire but a feather that
veers with the weather,
But a fancy that wanders astray,
  This way, that way,
  This way, that way?
Then if one from the day of their meet-
ing
Stay true to his sweeting,
Let us crown them with laurel and bay:
  With a-ho and a-heigh,
As the cuckoo flies over the may.

(*The boys dance.*)

CHORUS

Ah! As the cuckoo flies over the may.
Fa la la la.

(*Zerlina and Masetto leave the group
and advance to center where the
chorus forms a ring around them.*)

ZERLINA AND MASETTO

Let us turn, let us twist with a motion,
Quick and lively as fish in the ocean,
The two halves of a single devotion,
As the cuckoo flies over the may.

(*Don Giovanni and Leporello come out
of the villa and stop to look on.*)

Recitative

DON GIOVANNI (*to Leporello*)

(There's no sign of that nuisance.)
What have we? Well, now! Some
honest rustic folk; and lots are lovely!

LEPORELLO (*aside*)

(So long as there are lots, he may leave
one or two behind for me.)

DON GIOVANNI

(*stepping between Zerlina and Masetto,
while Leporello turns to the maidens*)

To you all, a good-morning! Please
don't stop your revelries for my sake;
I adore these untutored country
pleasures! Is this all for a wedding?

ZERLINA

Sì, signore; e la sposa son io.

GIOVANNI

Me ne consolo. Lo sposo?

MASETTO

Io, per servirla.

GIOVANNI

Oh bravo! Per servirmi! Questo è vero
parlar da galantuomo.

LEPORELLO

Basta che sia marito.

ZERLINA

Oh, il mio Masetto è un uom d'ottimo
core!

GIOVANNI

Oh, anch'io, vedete: voglio che siamo
amici. Il vostro nome?

ZERLINA

Zerlina.

GIOVANNI

E il tuo?

MASETTO

Masetto.

GIOVANNI

Oh, caro il mio Masetto! Cara la mia
Zerlina, v'esibisco la mia protezione.
Leporello! Cosa fai là, birbone?

LEPORELLO

(Che fa all'amore con qualcuna delle
femmine.) Anch'io, caro padrone,
esibisco la mia protezione.

GIOVANNI

Presto va con costor, nel mio palazzo
conducili sul fatto. Ordina ch'abbia-
no cioccolatte, caffè, vini, prosciutti
—cerca divertir tutti. Mostra loro il
giardin, la galleria, le camere. In effetto fa che resti contento il mio Masetto. Hai capito?

LEPORELLO

Ho capito. Andiam.

MASETTO

Signore!

GIOVANNI

Cosa c'è?

MASETTO

La Zerlina senza me non può star.

LEPORELLO

In vostro loco ci starà sua eccellenza—
e saprà bene fare le vostre parti.

GIOVANNI

Oh, la Zerlina è in man d'un cavalier.
Va pur, fra poco ella meco verrà.

ZERLINA

Va, non temere: nelle mani son io d'un
cavaliere.

MASETTO

E per questo—

LEPORELLO

E per questo non c'è da dubitar.

MASETTO

Ed io, sospetto!

GIOVANNI

Olà! Finiam le dispute. Se subito, sen-
z'altro replicar, non te ne vai, Masetto, guarda ben, ti pentirai.

ARIA

MASETTO

"Ho capito, signor sì!
"Chino il capo, e me ne vò
"Giacchè piace a voi così
"Altre repliche non fò.
"Cavalier voi siete già,
"Dubitar non posso affè,
"Me lo dice la bontà,

ZERLINA (*curtseying*)

Yes, it is, sir; with myself as the bride, sir.

DON GIOVANNI

Fervent good wishes! The bridegroom?

MASETTO (*bows*)

Me . . . at your service.

DON GIOVANNI

I like that! At my service! Your simplicity is no less than noble!

LEPORELLO (*aside*)

(Noble enough to cuckold!)

ZERLINA

No one's more generous than my dear Masetto.

DON GIOVANNI

What could be better! Let us be friends forever! (*to Zerlina*) What is your name, dear?

ZERLINA

Zerlina.

DON GIOVANNI

And you are?

MASETTO

Masetto.

DON GIOVANNI

(*linking arms with Masetto, the other arm around Zerlina's waist*)

My excellent Masetto, my unexcelled Zerlina, I am pleased to offer you my protection! (*to Leporello, who is among the girls*) Leporello! What do you think you're doing?

LEPORELLO

I think that I was pleased, sir, to be offering these girls my protection.

DON GIOVANNI

You have no time for that. You'll go at once to the castle with my friends here. There you will order for all, refreshment — cold ham, sweet wine and pastries. See that all have amusement—show the maze in the garden, the music boxes, the gallery! (*with emphasis*) Above all, be sure the best is provided for Masetto! (*poking Leporello in the ribs*) Do you follow?

LEPORELLO

Like a shadow. (*to the villagers*) We're off . . .

MASETTO

My lordship . . .

DON GIOVANNI

You're still here?

(*While the rest enter the inn Don Giovanni detains Zerlina.*)

MASETTO

But I cannot leave Zerlina alone . . .

LEPORELLO (*to Masetto*)

Have you forgotten your most noble protector? Be sure he will protect her in your place nobly.

DON GIOVANNI

Precious Zerlina will be my special care. My word. I think that will more than suffice.

ZERLINA

Please! You must go now. In a nobleman's hands, what harm can touch me?

MASETTO

Must I tell you?

ZERLINA

And you might have more faith in me as well!

MASETTO (*tries to take her hand*)

I trust you *with* me.

DON GIOVANNI

(*stepping between them*)

Now, now . . . Let's not be quarrelsome. I would not wish to change for bad my early good impression: (*touching his sword*) Masetto, be discreet; or else—be sorry!

Aria

MASETTO

(*dumbfounded, staring at Don Giovanni*)

Yes, your lordship. See, I stand, cap in hand,
At your service to command.
When the master bids him go,
Shall the servant answer No?
O no, no, no, good gracious no.
Who am I that I should doubt
What his lordship is about?

"Che volete aver per me.
"Bricconaccia! malandrina!

(*a* ZERLINA).

"Fosti, ognor, la mia ruina!
(*a Lep.*) Vengo, vengo. (*a Zer.*) Resta!
resta!
"É una cosa molto onesta;
"Faccia il nostro cavaliere,
"Cavaliera ancora te."

(*Parte con Leporello, Masetto,
e' Paesani*).

Don GIOVANNI *e* ZERLINA

GIOVANNI

Alfin siam liberati, Zerlinetta gentile, da
quel scioccone. Che ne dite, mio ben,
so far pulito?

ZERLINA

Signore, è mio marito.

GIOVANNI

Chi! Colui? Vi par ch'un onest'uomo,
un nobil cavalier qual io mi vanto,
possa soffrir che quel visetto d'oro,
quel viso inzuccherato da un bifolcac-
cio vil sia strapazzato?

ZERLINA

Ma, signore, io gli diedi parola di spo-
sarlo.

GIOVANNI

Tal parola non vale un zero, voi non
siete fatta per esser paesana. Un'altra
sorte vi procuran quegli occhi bric-
concelli, quei labretti sì belli, quelle
dituccia candide e odorose, parmi
toccar giuncata, e fiutar rose.

ZERLINA

Ah, non vorrei—

GIOVANNI

Che non vorreste?

ZERLINA

Alfine ingannata restar. Io so che rado
colle donne voi altri cavalieri siete
onesti e sinceri.

GIOVANNI

É un'impostura della gente plebea: la
nobiltà ha dipinta negli occhi l'onestà. Orsù non perdiamo tempo. In
quest'istante io vi voglio sposar.

ZERLINA

Voi?

GIOVANNI

Certo io. Quel casinetto è mio: soli saremo. E là, gioiello mio, ci sposeremo.

GIOVANNI

Là ci darem la mano,
Là mi dirai di sì!
Vedi, non è lontano
Partiam, ben mio, da qui!

ZERLINA

Vorrei, e non vorrei;
Mi trema un poco il cor:
Felice, è ver sarei,
Ma può burlarmi ancor.

GIOVANNI

Vieni mio bel diletto!

ZERLINA

Mi fa pietà Masetto.

GIOVANNI

Io cangierò tua sorte.

ZERLINA

Presto, non son più forte.

GIOVANNI

Vieni! Vieni! Là ci darem la mano,
Là mi dirai di sì!

Gentlemen, as we have heard,
Pay their debts and keep their word.
(*aside to Zerlina*) Happy, aren't you?
I could kill you!
So you'll play the strumpet, will you!
(*to Leporello who wants to lead him
off*) Just a moment. (*to Zerlina*) For
the last time . . .
Do not make my love your pastime.
(*to Zerlina and Don Giovanni*) When
his Lordship woos a maiden
(*sarcastically to Zerlina*) She becomes
Milady too.
No, Zerlina . . . I won't let you.
How I wish I'd never met you!
(*to Leporello*) Let's be going. (*to
Zerlina*) So, I'll leave you.
Do not let this parting grieve you.
When his Lordship woos a maiden
She becomes Milady too,
If the fairy-tales are true.
When his Lordship woos a maiden
She becomes Milady too.
If the fairy-tales are true,
You'll become a lady too.
(*Exit with Leporello, who hurries him
into the tavern.*)

Recitative

DON GIOVANNI

And we're alone, Zerlina, for the first
time alone without that idiot . . .
(*tries to embrace her*) was it not very
neat, how I dispatched him?

ZERLINA (*drawing back*)
But, sir, we're getting married.

DON GIOVANNI

You! To *him*! What can he know of
beauty? And how can I, who live by
fine perceptions, seeing your grace
and sensing your refinement, how can
I see you wasted in servitude to that
unworthy bumpkin?!

ZERLINA

But, my lord, I can hardly go back on
my promise!

DON GIOVANNI

It would hardly be right to keep it! Is
a promise sacred that would enslave
a goddess? I dare not think so, when
a glance more vivacious than Aurora,
a Diana's complexion, lips that the
Queen of Love herself must envy,
are in themselves a promise of noble
fortune!

ZERLINA
But I'm afraid, sir . . .

DON GIOVANNI
Afraid of fortune?

ZERLINA
Not that, sir . . . I'm afraid of deceit.
I hear too often how you noblemen
treat us country maidens when your
promises win us.

DON GIOVANNI
Slanderous ravings of the envious low-
born! A man of birth has an honesty
native to his blood! Be not afraid, my
dearest; submit to fortune. We'll be
mated today!

ZERLINA
Sir!

DON GIOVANNI
Sir, no longer. (*pointing to his castle*)
Soon, in the book of Heaven, your
name and my name will always be
together—Donna Zerlina!

Duettino

DON GIOVANNI
Here with our hands entwining,
Let our designs agree:
Lingering here serves no one;
Why not walk on with me?

ZERLINA
My heart is more than willing;
I tremble to depart,
Yet fear you may deceive me
Should I obey my heart.

DON GIOVANNI
Come to your noble lover!

ZERLINA
Must poor Masetto suffer?

DON GIOVANNI
Peasant you'll be no longer!

ZERLINA
Faintly
I would that I were stronger.
(*Donna Elvira appears on the veran-
dah and watches what is going on.*)

DON GIOVANNI
Dearest, gently,
Here with our hands entwining.

ZERLINA

Vorrei e non vorrei;
Mi trema un poco il cor.

DUETTO

Andiam, andiam mio bene,
A ristorar le pene
D'un innocente amor.

Donna Elvira (e detti.)

ELVIRA

Fermati, scellerato! Il Ciel mi fece udir
le tue perfidie; io sono a tempo di
salvar questa misera innocente dal
tuo barbaro artiglio.

ZERLINA

Meschina! cosa sento!

GIOVANNI (*a parte*).

Amor, consiglio! (*A* ELVIRA.) Idol
mio, non vedete ch'io voglio divertir-
mi.

ELVIRA

Divertirti, è vero, divertirti? Io so, crudele, come tu ti diverti.

ZERLINA

Ma, signor cavaliere, è ver quel ch'ella
dice?

GIOVANNI (*a* ZERLINA.)

La povera infelice è di me innamorata,
e per pietà deggio fingere amore,
ch'io son per mia disgrazia uom di
buon core.

(*Don Giovanni parte*).

ELVIRA

Ah! fuggi il traditor!
Non lo lasciar più dir;
Il labbro è mentitor,
Fallace il ciglio!
Da miei tormenti impara
A creder a quel cor;
E nasca il tuo timor
Dal mio periglio,
Ah fuggi, fuggi!
Ah fuggi il traditor!

ZERLINA

I fear you may deceive me.

DON GIOVANNI

Why not walk on with me?

ZERLINA

I tremble to depart.

DON GIOVANNI

Let our designs agree.

ZERLINA

Should I obey my heart?

DON GIOVANNI

Come to your noble lover!

ZERLINA

Must poor Masetto suffer?

DON GIOVANNI

Peasant you'll be no longer.

ZERLINA
(*disengaging herself, and escaping to the other side*)
Dearly
I hope I can be stronger.

DON GIOVANNI (*insistingly*)
My love! Be mine!

ZERLINA
(*throwing herself into his arms*)
I will!

DON GIOVANNI AND ZERLINA

Together let us purely
Indulge a whim we surely
Are faultless to fulfill.
For nobleman and peasant,
While doing what is pleasant
Cannot be doing ill.
(*Donna Elvira descends the steps and posts herself at the back, stage center.*)

DON GIOVANNI
Consent!

ZERLINA
My love! Be true.

DON GIOVANNI
I will!

DON GIOVANNI AND ZERLINA

We'll go without delay,
And cheerfully at play
Love innocently still.

(*Exeunt, arm in arm.*)

Recitative

DONNA ELVIRA
(*desperately, intercepting Don Giovanni*)

Dare to go one step further! Thank God I have arrived in time to stop you, expose your baseness, and prevent one poor innocent becoming one more tearful repentant!

ZERLINA

What is the lady saying?

DON GIOVANNI (*aside*)
(That's all I needed!) (*softly to Donna Elvira*) Do be reasonable, dearest—I'm looking for amusement.

DONNA ELVIRA (*aloud*)

For amusement! Precisely! For amusement! Alas I know too well what you think amusement!

ZERLINA (*to Don Giovanni*)

Is she telling the truth, sir? This all is so confusing.

DON GIOVANNI (*softly, to Zerlina*)

She loves me to distraction, so I feigned that I loved her because I thought it might settle her reason; and thus I am repaid for acting in pity!

Aria

DONNA ELVIRA

Beware this wicked man,
Escape him while you can:
His words are all a lie
And false his beaming eye.

Too well, too long I listened,
Too well he played his part,
Too late I know him now:
Believe a broken heart.

O hear me, hear me,
O hear me, I implore!
Pay heed to him no more.
His words are all a lie
And false his beaming eye.
Ah! How false that beaming eye!

(*Exit leading off Zerlina.*)

Don GIOVANNI, *Don* OTTAVIO, *Donna* ANNA; *indi Donna* ELVIRA.

GIOVANNI

Mi par ch'oggi il demonio si diverta
d'opporsi ai miei piacevoli progressi,
vanno mal tutti quanti.

OTTAVIO

Ah! Ch'ora, idolo mio, son vani i pianti! Di vendetta si parli. Oh, Don Giovanni!

GIOVANNI (*a parte*).

Mancava questo intoppo!

ANNA

Amico! A tempo vi ritroviam! Avete core, avete anima generosa?

GIOVANNI (*a parte*).

Sta a vedere ch'il diavolo gli ha detto qualche cosa? (*Forte*). Che domanda! Perchè?

ANNA

Bisogno abbiamo della vostra amicizia.

GIOVANNI (*a parte*).

Respiro. (*Forte.*) Commandate, i congiunti, i parenti; questa man, questo ferro, i beni, il sangue spenderò per servirvi. Ma voi, bella Donn'Anna, perchè così piangete? Sì crudele chi fu, ch'osò la calma turbar del viver vostro?

(*Entra* ELVIRA).

Ah ti ritrovo ancor, perfido mostro.

QUARTETTO.
ELVIRA (*a* ANNA).

Non ti fidar, o misera!
Di quel ribaldo cor!
Me già tradì quel barbaro—
Ti vuol tradir ancor.

ANNA E OTTAVIO

Cieli! Che aspetto nobile!
Che dolce maestà!
Il suo dolor, le lagrime
M'empiono di pietà.

GIOVANNI

La povera ragazza
É pazza, amici miei:
Lasciatemi con lei!
Forse si calmerà.

ELVIRA

Ah, non credete al perfido!

GIOVANNI

É pazza; non badate.

ELVIRA

Restate, oh Dei restate!

ANNA E OTTAVIO

A chi si crederà?

ANNA, OTTAVIO E GIOVANNI

(Certo moto d'ignoto tormento
Dentro l'alma girare mi sento,
Che mi dice per quella infelice
Cento cose che intender non sa.)

Recitative

(*Enter Donna Anna and Don Ottavio, dressed in mourning.*)

DON GIOVANNI

To hell with this exasperating morning! The very devil seems to be against me! Nothing goes as I planned it.

DON OTTAVIO

I'm certain he will hélp. He has great influence. He is brave and resourceful. (*seeing Don Giovanni*) Come, let us ask him!

DON GIOVANNI (*aside*)

(And now the final straw!)

DONNA ANNA (*to Don Giovanni*)

God save you who sent you just at this time! I have been hearing about your generous kindly nature.

DON GIOVANNI (*aside*)

(I shall not be surprised to hear the devil has been talking!) (*to Donna Anna*) I am flattered. But why?

DONNA ANNA

Never did any have more need of your friendship!

DON GIOVANNI (*aside*)

(My luck is with me this time!) (*to Donna Anna*) I am honored! All my household, all my kindred, all my goods, my invention, my cunning, my life itself are all at your service. But what, gracious young lady, has caused that look of sorrow? It were better to die than dare to injure so pure, so fair a creature!

(*Donna Elvira enters.*)

DONNA ELVIRA

Ah, at your lies again! I shall expose you!

Quartet

DONNA ELVIRA (*to Donna Anna*)

Noble and kind he seems to be,
I once believed him true:
Know that this man was false to me,
And will be false to you.

DONNA ANNA AND DON OTTAVIO

Weeping? Seldom have I beheld
Such grace and majesty.
What makes her look so sorrowful,
What can her story be?

(*Don Giovanni tries to persuade Donna Elvira to step aside, but she refuses; finally he grasps her right hand, and draws her away toward his right.*)

DON GIOVANNI

(*whispers to Donna Elvira*)

She's mentally afflicted
And weeps when contradicted:
Stand back or you'll upset her.
I know these cases better.
Leave her alone with me.

DONNA ELVIRA

He lies: he is deceiving you!

DON GIOVANNI

Poor girl, you must excuse her!

DONNA ELVIRA

O God! You must believe me!

DONNA ANNA AND DON OTTAVIO (*aside*)

Whom ought we to believe?
Which one should we believe,
Whose word believe,
Whom ought we to believe?

DONNA ELVIRA

Believe me!
He lies, he is deceiving you, believe me!

DON GIOVANNI

She's crazy!

DONNA ANNA

Something tells me there's more to discover,
I begin to be filled with suspicion,
I believe this poor lady could tell us
Many things, (dreadful things), that we dare not suspect.

DON OTTAVIO

Something tells me there's more to discover,
I begin to be filled with suspicion,
I believe this poor lady could tell us
Many things that we dare not suspect.

ELVIRA

(Sdegno, rabbia, dispetto, spavento
Dentro l'alma girare mi sento,
Che mi dice di quel traditore
Cento cose che intender non sa.)

OTTAVIO

Io di quà non vado via,
Se non so com'è l'affar.

ANNA

Non ha l'aria di pazzia
Il suo tratto, il suo parlar.

GIOVANNI

(Se men vado, si potria
Qualche cosa sospettar.)

ELVIRA

Da quel ceffo si dovria
La ner'alma giudicar.

OTTAVIO (a GIOVANNI).

Dunque quella?

GIOVANNI

É pazzarella.

ANNA (a ELVIRA).

Dunque quegli?

ELVIRA

É un traditore.

GIOVANNI

Infelice!

ELVIRA

Mentitore!

ANNA E OTTAVIO

Incomincio a dubitar.

GIOVANNI

Zitto, zitto, che la gente
Si raduna a noi d'intorno:
Siate un poco più prudente—
Vi farete criticar.

ELVIRA

Non sperarlo, ah, scellerato!
Ho perduta la prudenza—
Le tue colpe ed il mio stato
Voglio a tutti palesar.

ANNA E OTTAVIO

Quegli accenti sì sommessi!
Quel cangiarsi di colore
Sono indizi troppo espressi
Che mi fan determinar.

(ELVIRA parte)

GIOVANNI

Povera sventurata! I passi suoi
Voglio seguir, non voglio
Che faccia un precipizio. Perdonate,
Bellissima Donn'Anna:
Se servirvi poss'io,
In mia casa v'aspetto. Amici, addio!

(Parte).

ANNA

Don Ottavio, son morta.

OTTAVIO

Cos'è stato?

ANNA

Per pietà soccorretemi!

OTTAVIO

Mio ben, fate coraggio.

ANNA

Oh, Dei! Quegli è il carnefice del padre
mio!

OTTAVIO

Che dite?

ANNA

Non dubitate più. Gli ultimi accenti
Che l'empio proferì, tutta la voce
Richiama nel cor mio di quell'indegno,
Che nel mio appartamento—

DON GIOVANNI

Will they guess that there's more to
    discover?
I can see they are filled with suspicion.
In her folly I fear she will tell them
What I hoped they would never
    suspect.

DONNA ELVIRA

Scorn and anger and hatred assist me!
Give me courage to make my decision!
Let him tremble! I'm going to tell them
All the things that they do not suspect.

DON OTTAVIO (*aside*)

I shall stay till I discover who is lying,
he or she.

DONNA ANNA (*aside*)

There is nothing mad about her words
or looks that I can see.

DON GIOVANNI

They suspect me. If I go now, they will
think that I'm afraid.

DONNA ELVIRA

(*to Don Giovanni, in exasperation*)

His the lying, his the cunning, mine the
innocence betrayed!

DON OTTAVIO (*to Don Giovanni*)

What do *you* say?

DON GIOVANNI

She's mad, I tell you.

DONNA ANNA (*to Donna Elvira*)

What do *you* say?

DONNA ELVIRA

That he betrayed me.

DON GIOVANNI

(*He tries to separate the women.*) Pure
delusion!

DONNA ELVIRA (*to Don Giovanni*)

You betrayed me! You betrayed me!

DONNA ANNA AND DON OTTAVIO

She has been betrayed, I fear.

DON GIOVANNI
(*softly, to Donna Elvira*)

Stop it, stop it, stop this moment,
Do not make a scene in public.
Do control yourself, I beg you.
Have you lost all sense of shame?

DONNA ELVIRA (*to Don Giovanni*)

Villain, you shall never stop me.
Neither fear nor shame can stop me.
But the wrong that you have done me,
To the world I shall proclaim.

DONNA ANNA AND DON OTTAVIO
(*aside, observing Don Giovanni*)

Mark his manner. How it changes.
How he frowns and how he whispers.
I begin to doubt his story.
Can it be that he's to blame?

(*Don Giovanni, mastering Donna Elvira by his gaze, leads her away, and
then returns.*)

Recitative

DON GIOVANNI

The poor afflicted creature! But she
ought not to be by herself. I fear for
her life in her condition. So if you
will both excuse me, I'll leave you.
If you ever should need me, you
know where you can find me. Until
then, good-morning!

(*Exit hastily.*)

Recitative

DONNA ANNA

Don Ottavio, support me!

DON OTTAVIO

Donna Anna!

DONNA ANNA
(*throwing herself into his arms*)

Revelation has come to me!

DON OTTAVIO

My dearest, what is the matter?

DONNA ANNA

I know now! I know now! (*pointing
after Don Giovanni*)
That was the murderer! He killed my
father!

DON OTTAVIO

You're certain?

DONNA ANNA

Certain beyond all doubt!
His every gesture, his words before he
left,
Each intonation, brought to mind all at
once
With startling clearness, the libertine
intruder . . .

OTTAVIO

Oh, Ciel! Possibile,
Che sotto il sacro manto d'amicizia
Ma come fu?—Narratemi
Lo strano avvenimento.

ANNA

Era già alquanto
Avanzata la notte,
Quando nelle mie stanze, ove soletta
Mi trovai per sventura, entrar io vidi
In un mantello avvolto
Un uom, ch'al primo istante
Avea preso per voi;
Ma riconobbi poi
Ch'un inganno era il mio.

OTTAVIO

Stelle! Seguite.

ANNA

Tacito a me s'appressa,
E mi vuol abbracciar; sciogliermi cerco,
Ei più mi stringe, io grido;
Non viene alcun; con una mano cerca
D'impedire la voce,
E coll'altra m'afferra
Stretta così, che già mi credo vinta.

OTTAVIO

Perfido! E alfin?

ANNA

Alfine il vuol, l'orrore
Dell'infame attentato accrebbe sì
La lena mia; che a forza
Di svincolarmi, torcermi, e piegarmi.
Da lui mi sciolsi.

OTTAVIO

Ohimè! Respiro!

ANNA

Allora
Rinforzo i stridi miei, chiamo soccor-
so—
Fugge il fellon, arditamente il seguo
Fin nella strada per fermarlo; e sono
Assalitrice d'assilita. Il padre
V'accorre, vuol conoscerlo, e l'indegno;
Che del povero vecchio era più forte.
Compiè il misfatto suo col dargli morte.

ARIA

Or sai chi l'onore rapir a me volse,
Chi fu il traditore, ch'il padre mi tolse.
Vendetta ti chieggo—la chiede il tuo
cor.
Rammenta la piaga del misero seno—
Rimira di sangue coperto il terreno,
Se 'l cor in te langue d'un giusto furor.

(*Parte*).

OTTAVIO

"Come mai creder deggio
"Di sì nero delitto
"Capace un cavaliere!
"Ah, di scoprire il vero
"Ogni mezzo si cerchi, io sento in petto
"E di sposo, e d'amico
"Il dover che mi parla,
"Disingannarla voglio, o vendicarla.

DON OTTAVIO

O no! I can't believe that he would dare
To offer his assistance . . . But tell me all . . . all that until today your grief had hidden.

DONNA ANNA

(repressing her emotions)

Midnight had sounded. All the city was quiet.
I dismissed my duenna; and
Near my bed, at my devotions was kneeling,
When there appeared a man, his cloak
About him—I thought him you a moment
And I gently reproached him; but then I saw
How dreadfully I was mistaken.

DON OTTAVIO

Quickly! Continue!

DONNA ANNA

Silently he approached me.
I was dragged to my feet, pulled to him roughly.
He tried to kiss me. I shouted, but
No one heard. With one hand I was stifled
To prevent me from screaming; with the other
He pressed me ever more close. I thought
That he must conquer!

DON OTTAVIO

Horrible! And then?

DONNA ANNA

And then my will, in shock reborn,
With terror inhuman, restored my dwindled
Forces doubly, and I could renew
My struggle, strike at him, and with fury tear
Myself from him!

DON OTTAVIO

Then God had heard you!

DONNA ANNA

When once I was free, I screamed more loudly.
"Help me!" I shouted. He fled in fear;
But I more quickly followed into

The street itself to stop him,
To see him, and the pursued became
The pursuer. My father came running.
I was desperate, and I left them
To arouse all the aid I might for my father,
There to defend my honor. Yet,
An old man defenseless, *(in an agony of grief, almost collapsing)* there he was murdered! *(collecting herself)*

Aria

You know who is guilty,
The lecher assassin
Who dared my dishonor
And struck down my father!
The shade of my father,
For vengeance it cries!

If but for a moment
You falter in purpose,
Invoke, then, his body,
His blood on the stones
    in the torchlight,
And, fresh in that vision,
Your fury will rise.
Your love and your honor
Must nourish your hatred
In one dedication
To strike down
    the killer,
Your life have one vision,
To see that he dies!

My father, I see him!
He wanders, unshriven,
Between earth and heaven,
For vengeance he cries.

Rearmed in that vision,
Your fury will rise,
To search out the killer,
To see that he dies!

The horrible scene
Is clear to my eyes:
The blood of my father,
For vengeance it cries!

(Exit.)

Recitative

DON OTTAVIO

Can it be that a person of such high birth is guilty of an atrocious murder? Loth am I still to think it. But my promise has bound me. And now the voices of affection and of duty speak in chorus together: "Prove that she was mistaken, or else avenge her!"

"Dalla sua pace la mia dipende—
"Quel ch'a lei piace vita mi rende;
"Quel che le incresce morte mi da;
"S'ella sospira, sospiro anch'io;
"É mia quell'ira, quel pianto è mio—
"E non ho bene se non l'ha."

(*Parte*).

LEPORELLO (*indi Don Giovanni.*)
LEPORELLO

Io deggio ad ogni patto
Per sempre abbandonar questo bel matto.
Eccolo qui: guardate
Con qual indifferenza se ne viene.

GIOVANNI

Leporellino mio, va tutto bene?

LEPORELLO

Don Giovannino mio, va tutto male.

GIOVANNI

Come? Va tutto male?

LEPORELLO

Vado a casa
Come voi m'ordinaste
Con tutta quella gente.

GIOVANNI

Bravo!

LEPORELLO

A forza di chiacchiere,—
Di vezzi, e di bugie,
Ch'ho imparato sì bene a star con voi,
Cerco d'intrattenerli.

GIOVANNI

Bravo!

LEPORELLO

Dico
Mille cose a Masetto per placarlo.
Per trargli dal pensier la gelosia,

GIOVANNI

Ma bravo, in fede mia!

LEPORELLO

Faccio che bevano e gli uomini e le
donne;
Son già mezzo ubbriachi:
Altri canta, altri scherza—
Altri seguita a ber; in sul più bello
Chi credete che capiti?

GIOVANNI

Zerlina.

LEPORELLO

Bravo!
E con lei chi venne?

GIOVANNI

Donna Elvira.

LEPORELLO

Bravo! E disse di voi.

GIOVANNI

Tutto quel mal ch'in bocca le venìa?

LEPORELLO

Ma bravo, in fede mia.

GIOVANNI

E tu cosa facesti?

LEPORELLO

Tacqui.

GIOVANNI

Ed ella—

LEPORELLO

Seguì a gridar.

GIOVANNI

E tu?

LEPORELLO

Quando mi parve,
Che già fosse sfogata, dolcemente
Fuor dell'orto la trassi, e con bell'arte
Chiusa la porta a chiave io me n'andai,
E sulla via soletta io la lasciai.

Aria

DON OTTAVIO

Shine, lights of heaven,
Guardians immortal,
Shine on my true love,
Waking or sleeping;
Sun, moon and starlight,
Comfort her woe.

O nimble breezes,
O stately waters,
Obey a lover,
Proclaim her beauty
And sing her praises
Where'er you go.

While grief beclouds her
I walk in shadow,
My thoughts are with her,
Waking or sleeping:
Sun, moon and starlight,
Comfort our woe.

(*Exit.*)

Recitative

(*Leporello enters from the tavern; after him, Don Giovanni from his villa.*)

LEPORELLO

I'm going, got to leave him . . . and soon, before I learn shocking bad habits. Ah, look at him now, the rascal . . . As gay as though he'd nothing on his conscience.

DON GIOVANNI (*gaily*)

Hail, uppermost of servants! Are they behaving?

LEPORELLO (*crossly*)

Hail, nethermost of masters! Behaving badly.

DON GIOVANNI

What do you mean by badly?

LEPORELLO

As you told me . . . I led on those peasants . . . got them here inside the castle . . .

DON GIOVANNI

Bravo!

LEPORELLO

And there, with much flattery, cajolery and lying—all the arts I have learned so well from you, sir—did what I could to amuse them.

DON GIOVANNI

Bravo!

LEPORELLO

At the start Masetto appeared extremely jealous . . . I managed, though, I think, to reassure him.

DON GIOVANNI

Bravo! Poor love-sick Masetto!

LEPORELLO

Wine was so plentiful that both the men and women were soon more than half tipsy. Some were singing, some guffawing, others oafishly drunk. Then, without warning . . . Can you guess who burst in on us?

DON GIOVANNI (*indifferently*)

Zerlina.

LEPORELLO

Bravo! But guess who was with her!

DON GIOVANNI

Donn' Elvira.

LEPORELLO (*astonished*)

Bravo! She talked about you.

DON GIOVANNI (*humorously*)

Not, I'm afraid, in terms of great affection.

LEPORELLO

Bravo! Poor love-sick Donn'Elvira!

DON GIOVANNI

And what, what did you answer?

LEPORELLO

Nothing.

DON GIOVANNI

And she, then . . .

LEPORELLO

Started screaming.

DON GIOVANNI

And you . . .

LEPORELLO

Waited awhile until her lungs were exhausted. Then I gently coaxed her out through the garden. We reached the gate and, while she was talking, I turned the key behind her and left her to her loving meditations.

GIOVANNI

Bravo! Bravo! Arcibravo!
L'affar non può andar meglio; inco-
minciasti,
Io saprò terminar. Troppo mi premono
Queste contadinotte:
Le voglio divertir finchè vien notte.

GIOVANNI

Finch'han dal vino
Calda la testa,
Una gran festa,
Fa preparar:
Se trovi in piazza,
Qualche ragazza,
Teco ancor quella
Cerca menar;
Senz'alcun ordine,
La danza sia,
Ch'il minuetto,
Chi la follia
Chi l'Alemana,
Farai ballar;
Ed io frattanto,
Dall'altro canto,
Con questa e quella,
Vo' amoreggiar.
Ah, la mia lista,
Doman mattina,
D'una decina deve aumentar.

SCENA IV

Campagna. Da un lato,
il Palazzo di Don
GIOVANNI (*dall'altro, un Padiglione.*)

ZERLINA E MASETTO
ZERLINA

Masetto, senti un pò! Masetto, dico!

MASETTO

Non mi toccar.

ZERLINA

Perchè?

MASETTO

Perfida! Il tatto sopportar dovrei
D'una mano infedele?

ZERLINA

Ah, no! Taci, crudele!
Io non merto da te tal trattamento.

MASETTO

Come! Ed hai l'ardimento di scusarti?
Star sola con un uom? Abbandonarmi
Il dì delle mie nozze—porre in fronte
A un villano d'onore
Questa marca d'infamia! Ah, se non
fosse
Se non fosse lo scandalo, vorrei—

ZERLINA

Ma se colpa io non ho—ma se da lui
Ingannata rimasi? E poi che temi
Tranquillati, mia vita!
Non mi toccò la punta delle dita.
Non me lo credi, ingrato?
Vien qui, sfogati, ammazzami—
Fa pur tutto di me quel che ti piace,
Ma poi, Masetto, poi, ma poi fa pace.

ZERLINA

Batti, batti, o bel Masetto,
La tua povera Zerlina;
Starò qui come agnellina,
Le tue botte ad aspettar.
Lascierò stracciarmi il crine;
Lascierò stracciarmi gli occhi;
E le care tue manine
Lieta poi saprò baciar.

DON GIOVANNI

Bravo, bravo! Neatly managed! You couldn't have done better. The work you've started shall be mine to complete. What a delight you are, nymphs of pasture and meadow! I love you one and all. Come to your shepherd!

Aria

DON GIOVANNI

All things are ready,
Dainties in plenty,
Wine on the table,
Candles aglow.
(to Leporello)
Off, Leporello,
Down to the village,
Bring me more girls back,
Willing or no.

While to the violin,
Dancers go flying,
Mad with excitement,
Pulses a-throbbing,
Swirling and twirling,
Light on the toe.
Noticed by no one,
I shall be busy
Playing that game where
Maidens cry O,
Fair maids cry O.
Ah, in the morning
Bring me my list and
Down a full dozen
More shall go.

Yes, in the morning
At least a dozen
More shall go.
Quick, Leporello,
Off to the village,
Bring me more girls back,
Willing or no.

(He signals to Leporello to fetch the peasants from the tavern; he then hastens into his villa, Leporello going to the tavern.)

SCENE IV

(A garden. Two closed doors in the wall. Two alcoves. The chorus of peasants, scattered here and there, are sitting or lying on banks of turf.)

Recitative

ZERLINA

(coming with Masetto from the tavern; tries to take his hand)
Masetto, what is wrong? Why won't you listen?

MASETTO

Keep well away.

ZERLINA

Away?

MASETTO

You know the reason . . . butterfly! You needn't try your tricks on this man; I don't care to be bothered.

ZERLINA

But why, why are you angry? I've done nothing at all to be ashamed of.

MASETTO

Hussy! If you're not ashamed of it, you should be! To stay there with that man, deserting me the very day of our wedding. I'm a very respectable fellow and I won't be dishonored. Oh if it wouldn't . . . if it wouldn't . . . be scandalous. I'd give you . . . (goes excitedly to the other side)

ZERLINA (interrupting)

It was not what you think! I was surprised at a nobleman's interest, I'd never met one. My wonder made me linger. He never touched the tip of one small finger! Don't you believe me? All right, then . . . I'm wrong. Punish me! Be horrible! I know and repent what I committed — a pure, pathetic folly — be that admitted.

Aria

ZERLINA

Do not spare me, dear Masetto,
Punish your Zerlina meetly;
Like a lambkin, humbly, sweetly,
I repentant shall submit.
Turn against me, it will be for me;
I am lost if you ignore me:
Strike and I shall benefit.

(Masetto crosses over.)

As you love your lamb, be hateful;
Strike her down in righteous fury:
She will then, so meekly grateful,
Kiss your strictly loving hand,
O I shall kiss your hand,
Yes, I shall kiss your hand.

Ah, lo vedo, non hai core!
Pace, pace, o vita mia!
In contento, ed allegria,
Notte e dì vogliam passar.

MASETTO

Guarda un pò, come seppe
Questa strega sedurmi!
Siamo pure i deboli di testa.

*I detti.—Don Giovanni,
(di dentro.) Servi.*

GIOVANNI

Sia preparato tutto a una gran festa.

ZERLINA

Ah, Masetto, Masetto! Odi la voce
Del monsù cavaliere!

MASETTO

Ebben, che c'è?

ZERLINA

Verrà.

MASETTO

Lascia che venga.

ZERLINA

Ah, se vi fosse
Un buco da fuggir—

MASETTO

Di cosa temi?
Perchè diventi pallida? Ah, capisco!
Capisco, bricconcella!
Hai timor, ch'io comprenda
Com'è tra voi passata la faccenda.

FINALE

MASETTO

Presto, presto, pria ch'ei venga
Por mi vò da qualche lato:
V'è una nicchia, qui celato
Cheto, cheto, mi vo' star

ZERLINA

Senti, senti! dove vai!
Non t'ascondar, o Masetto!
Se ti trova, poveretto,
Tu non sai quel che può far?

MASETTO

Faccia, dica quel che vuole.

ZERLINA

Ah, non giovan le parole!

MASETTO

Parla forte e qui t'arresta.

ZERLINA

Che capriccio ha nella testa?

MASETTO *(a parte)*.

Capirò se m'è fedele,
E in qual modo andò l'affar.

ZERLINA

Quell'ingrato, quel crudele
Oggi vuol precipitar.

(*Masetto goes away again, but not so crossly; he steals a few glances at Zerlina.*)

Do not spare me, dear Masetto,
Punish your Zerlina meetly;
Like a lambkin, humbly, sweetly,
I repentant shall submit.

(*She tries to take his hand but he always draws back.*)

O dear Masetto, do not spare me!
   I shall not weep a bit
As repentant I submit.
Will you strike me? Can you bear to?
Confess you love me! (*Zerlina seizes one of his hands.*) Do you dare to?
Why resist me?

Say that you are cross no longer!
Though your wrath be strong as you are,
You know well your love is stronger,
And you love me in your heart,
And forgive me from your heart.

When our lips and lives united
So completely then are happy,
That all heaven seems delighted,
Can you keep them still apart?

(*Masetto, persuaded, gazing joyfully at Zerlina.*)

No, no, no, no, no, no,
You cannot keep us apart.
No, no, no, no, no, no,
We cannot remain apart.

Recitative

MASETTO (*gaily*)

She's a bundle of witchcraft, and it's hopeless resisting! Is there really a man as strong as a woman?

DON GIOVANNI (*within*)

We shall need more refreshments! New guests are coming!

ZERLINA (*frightened*)

Oh! Masetto, Masetto, I hear his lordship! If he comes to the garden . . .

MASETTO (*suspiciously*)

What's wrong with that?

ZERLINA

He'll see . . .

MASETTO

You and your bridegroom.

ZERLINA

If only I knew a place where we could hide!

MASETTO

Why need we hide there? And why are you so terrified? Oh! I see now! How could I be so stupid! You're afraid I'll discover just how untouched you *have* been by your lover!

(*It gradually grows dark.*)

Finale

MASETTO

I'll be certain, I'll be foxy:
When he comes, I just won't be here.
(*pointing at the arbor*)
From that shadow I can see here
While they can't see me in there.

(*He goes. Zerlina detains him.*)

ZERLINA

Don't be silly, do not leave me,
Don't slip away in such a hurry.
Don't you realize how I worry
You'll take harm, or don't you care?
   How I worry
You'll take harm, and you don't care!

MASETTO

What have I to fear precisely?

ZERLINA (*aside*)

(How can I explain it nicely?)

MASETTO

Raise your voice for me to hear you!

ZERLINA

Lower yours or he may hear you!

MASETTO (*softly, aside*)

I am done with being lenient:
If she's faithless, I have to know!

(*He hides.*)

(*Enter Don Giovanni with four gaily dressed servants.*)

ZERLINA (*softly, aside*)

This is dreadful, inconvenient.
I'm afraid how things will go!

GIOVANNI (*ai Contadini*).

Su, svegliatevi da bravi!
Su, coraggio, o buona gente.
Vogliam star allegramente!
Vogliam ridere e scherzar.
Alla stanza della danza
Conducete tutti quanti;
Ed a tutti in abbondanza
Gran rinfreschi fate dar.

(*Partono i Contadini*).

CORO

Su, svegliati, etc.

ZERLINA

Tra questi alberi celata,
Si può dar che non mi veda.

GIOVANNI

Zerlinetta mia garbata!
Ti ho già vista—non scappar!

ZERLINA

Ah! Lasciatemi andar via!

GIOVANNI

No, no, resta gioia mia.

ZERLINA

Se pietade avete in core!

GIOVANNI

Si, ben mio, son tutto amore
Vieni un poco, in questo loco,
Fortunata io ti vò far

ZERLINA (*i parte*).

Ah! s'ei vede lo sposo mio,
So ben io quel che può far.

GIOVANNI

Masetto!

MASETTO

Si, Masetto!

GIOVANNI

E chiuso là perchè?
La bella tua Zerlina—
Non può la poverina
Più star senza di te.

MASETTO

Capisco, si signore.

GIOVANNI

Adesso fate core;
I suonatori udite!
Venite omai con me.

ZERLINA

Si, si facciamo core,
Ed a ballar cogli aitri
Andiamo tutti tre.

MASETTO

Si, Si facciamo core, etc.

(*Partono*).

Donna ANNA, *Donna* ELVIRA, *e Don*
OTTAVIO

ELVIRA

Bisogna aver coraggio,
O cari amici miei;
E i suoi misfatti rei
Scoprir potremo allor.

OTTAVIO

L'amica dice bene—
Coraggio aver conviene,

(*ad* ANNA).

Discaccia, o vita mia!
L'affanno ed il timor.

ANNA

Il passo e periglioso,
Può nascer qualche imbroglio;
Temo pel caro sposo—
E per noi temo ancor.

DON GIOVANNI (*to the peasants*)

Let your watchword be abandon!
Be of care and time forgetful;
Unforeboding, unregretful,
Take your wine and take your love!

(*to the servants*)

Take my guests at once and guide them
To the ballroom and the tables;
See refreshment is supplied them
Ever better than enough!

(*Don Giovanni, looking everywhere for
Zerlina, at last discovers her, and
gives Leporello a sign to take the
peasants and servants into the villa.*)

SERVANTS

Let your watchword be abandon!
Be of care and time forgetful!
Unforeboding, unregretful,
Take your love and take your wine!

(*Exeunt.*)

ZERLINA (*trying to hide*)

Kindly shadow, lend me haven
From my fear and my temptation.

DON GIOVANNI

Still, my love, so fondly craven . . .
(*detains her*) Must you, must you
From your fortune ever fly?

ZERLINA (*trying to escape*)

Let me go, sir, please, I dare not.

DON GIOVANNI

Can you see my pain and care not?

ZERLINA

May not noble pity move you?

DON GIOVANNI

Pity me, who can but love you.

(*indicating the arbor, which he approaches backward, drawing Zerlina
after him*)

Warmly in that shade delighting,
Ever let our sorrows die!

ZERLINA

If Masetto were to find us,
I could not do less than die!
  O why must you
So shake my heart, why O why?

(*Don Giovanni goes toward the arbor,
sees Masetto and stands petrified.*)

DON GIOVANNI

Masetto?

MASETTO

Yes, Masetto!

DON GIOVANNI (*confused*)

We're lucky, it appears . . .
(*recovering himself*)
Zerlina felt dejected
At being so neglected;
She came to me in tears
And begged my help in finding you.

MASETTO (*ironically*)

I'm sorry, sir . . . and grateful too.

DON GIOVANNI

It's I who should be very grateful,
  I am very . . .

(*steps between them, giving each an
arm*)

For now you both together
Can join the dance with me!

ZERLINA

Yes, let us go together . . .

ZERLINA AND MASETTO

And join in making merry . . .

ZERLINA, MASETTO AND DON GIOVANNI

To music and to dancing
We always can agree!

(*Enter Don Ottavio, Donna Anna, and
Donna Elvira, masked.*)

DONNA ELVIRA

Nor should we lack in daring;
For all his shameless courage,
In truth resides our power—
The truth, the truth need never wait!

DON OTTAVIO

Discretion paired with daring
Would be our truest courage;
Unscrupulous in power,
His power yet is great.

DONNA ANNA

We know he slew my father!
We want no more than justice!
Why more need we now consider
  What cannot alter —
We were, we are . . . his fate!
Though I may fear his power,
  Yet while I tremble
I steel my heart with hate!

Don GIOVANNI; LEPORELLO. *E detti.*
LEPORELLO (*dalla finestra*).

Signor, guardate un poco!
Che maschere galanti!

GIOVANNI

Falle passar avanti,
Dì che ci fanno onor.

A 3

ANNA, ELVIRA E OTTAVIO

Al volto, ed alla voce
Si scopre il traditore.

LEPORELLO

Ps! ps! Signore maschere!

ANNA E ELVIRA

Via, rispondete.

OTTAVIO

Cosa chiedete?

LEPORELLO

Al ballo, se vi piace,
V'invita il mio signor.

OTTAVIO

Grazie di tanto onore.
Andiam, compagne belle.

LEPORELLO (*a parte*).

L'amico anche su quelle
Prova farà d'amor.

A 3

ANNA E OTTAVIO

Protegga il giusto Cielo
Il zelo del mio cor!

ELVIRA

Vendichi il giusto Cielo
Il mio tradito amor!

(*Partono*).

SCENA V

*Sala da Ballo nel Palazzo di
Don Giovanni.*

(*Zerlina, Don Giovanni, Leporello,
Masetto, Contadini, Contadine;
Servi con rinfreschi; Suonatori*).

GIOVANNI

Riposate, vezzose ragazze.

LEPORELLO

Rinfrescatevi, bei giovinetti.

GIOVANNI E LEPORELLO

Tornerete a far presto le pazze,
Tornerete a scherzar e ballar!

GIOVANNI

Ehi, caffè!

LEPORELLO

Cioccolatte!

MASETTO (*a* ZERLINA).

Ah, Zerlina, giudizio!

GIOVANNI

Sorbetti!

LEPORELLO

Confetti!

MASETTO (*a* ZERLINA).

Ah, Zerlina, giudizio!

A 2

MASETTO E ZERLINA (*a parte*).

Troppo dolce comincia la scena;
In amaro potria terminar.

(Leporello opens the window from within. Music is heard.)

LEPORELLO

Sir, look who's just arrived here —
Some people masquerading!

DON GIOVANNI *(at the window)*

Good! Just what we were needing —
Ask them to join the ball.

DONNA ELVIRA, DONNA ANNA AND
DON OTTAVIO

(all three have seen Don Giovanni; aside)

(Regretless, unforeboding,
He dances to perdition!)

LEPORELLO *(to Don Ottavio)*

Psst! Pst! You there in domino!
Psst! Psst!

DONNA ELVIRA AND DONNA ANNA

You'd better answer.

LEPORELLO

Psst! Psst! You there in domino!

DON OTTAVIO

I beg your pardon . . .

LEPORELLO

To dancing and refreshment,
My master bids you all.

DON OTTAVIO

Tell him we should be honored.

(to Donna Anna and Donna Elvira)

Your arms, my gracious ladies . . .

LEPORELLO *(aside)*

(He'd better watch his ladies
Lest in the list they fall!)

(goes in and shuts the window)

(Donna Anna, Donna Elvira and Don Ottavio unmask, and advance to the front.)

DONNA ANNA

Immortal love, protect us,
Our hopes and wills unite.
Our zeal, O God of justice,
Regard, approve, requite!

DON OTTAVIO

Immortal love, protect us,
Our hopes and wills unite.
Our zeal, O God of justice,
Regard, approve, requite!

DONNA ELVIRA

Merciful God, inspire me
To know and want the right!
Rightly may vengeance solace
My love's disheartened plight!

(All resume their masks. Exeunt.)

SCENE V

(A brilliantly lighted ballroom. Don Giovanni is leading some young girls to seats; Leporello is among the men; a dance is just over.)

DON GIOVANNI

Would you girls like to sit for a minute?

LEPORELLO

Won't you men have a little refreshment?

DON GIOVANNI AND LEPORELLO

Your vertiginous joy you must lengthen
In the strengthening joy of repose,
Then be back on your toes!

DON GIOVANNI *(to the servants)*

Muscatel!

(Refreshments are served.)

LEPORELLO

Bring the chocolates!

MASETTO

(holding Zerlina by her gown)

Now Zerlina, be cautious!

DON GIOVANNI

The almonds!

LEPORELLO

The ices!

MASETTO

Now Zerlina, be cautious!

ZERLINA AND MASETTO

(aside, in confusion)

Though I fear such a lavish beginning
May portend some improvident end,
Yet
To resist might be thought to offend.

GIOVANNI

Sei pur vaga, brillante Zerlina.

ZERLINA

Sua bontà.

MASETTO (*a parte*).

La briccona fa festa!

LEPORELLO

Sei pur cara, Giannotta, Sandrina!

MASETTO (*a parte*).

Tocca pur, che ti cada la testa!

ZERLINA (*a parte*).

Quel Masetto mi par stralunato.
Brutto, brutto si fa quest'affar.

GIOVANNI E LEPORELLO (*a parte*).

Quel Masetto mi par stralunato.
Qui bisogna cervello adoprar.

MASETTO (*a parte*).

La briccona mi fa disperar!

Donna ANNA, *Donna* ELVIRA,
Don OTTAVIO.
I detti.

LEPORELLO

Venite pur avanti,
Vezzose mascherette.

GIOVANNI

È aperto a tutti quanti,
Viva la libertà.

ANNA, ELVIRA E OTTAVIO

Siam grati a tanti segni
Di generosità.

GIOVANNI (*a* LEPORELLO).

Ricominciate il suono!
Tu accoppia i ballerini,
Meco tu dei ballare,
Zerlina, vien pur quà.

LEPORELLO

Da bravi via! Ballate.

ELVIRA (*a parte*).

Quell'è la contadina.

ANNA (*a parte*).

Io moro!

OTTAVIO (*a parte*).

Simulate.

GIOVANNI E LEPORELLO (*a parte*).

Va bene in verità!

MASETTO (*a parte*).

Va bene in verità

GIOVANNI (*a* LEPORELLO).

A bada tien Masetto.

LEPORELLO

Non balla il poveretto.

GIOVANNI

Il tuo compagno io sono,
Zerlina, vien pur quà.

DON GIOVANNI

You, Zerlina, grow ever more winning.

ZERLINA (*smiling shyly*)

How you talk!

MASETTO (*aside, enraged*)

She has not learned her lesson.

LEPORELLO

(*among the girls, imitating his master*)

Ever winning, Giannotta, Sandrina!

MASETTO

When her holiday's over she'll catch it!

ZERLINA

(*aside, looking at Masetto*)

I don't like how Masetto is watching,
I'm afraid how Masetto will act.

DON GIOVANNI AND LEPORELLO
(*aside*)

I don't like how Masetto is watching,
This affair must be managed with tact.

ZERLINA

I don't like how Masetto is watching . .

MASETTO (*angrier*)

She will bear with some watching . . .

ZERLINA

I'm afraid how Masetto will act.

MASETTO

When her holiday's over she'll catch it.

ZERLINA

I don't like how Masetto is watching,
I'm afraid how Masetto will act—
When will he have tact?

DON GIOVANNI AND LEPORELLO

I don't like how Masetto is watching,
This affair must be managed with tact,
And that is a fact!

MASETTO

She will catch it! She bears watching
For the trouble she loves to attract!

(*Enter Don Ottavio, Donna Anna and
Donna Elvira, masked.*)

LEPORELLO (*to them*)

Permit me, for my master,
To welcome you with pleasure.

DON GIOVANNI (*saluting them*)

Your pleasure be as you will;
And what you will, be done.

DONNA ELVIRA, DONNA ANNA
AND DON OTTAVIO

(*They curtsey; he bows.*)

How noble is your kindness
To us and everyone!

DON GIOVANNI

All do as they will . . .

DONNA ELVIRA, DONNA ANNA AND
DON OTTAVIO

How noble . . .

DON GIOVANNI

That is the law here!

DONNA ELVIRA, DONNA ANNA AND
DON OTTAVIO

You show your kindness
To us and everyone!

DON GIOVANNI

Do what you will is our only law.
(*Servants place three chairs at left
front.*)

LEPORELLO AND DON GIOVANNI

All that you may desire,
May here be done!
Do as thou wilt, is here the law—
Thy will be done, thy will be done!

DON OTTAVIO, DONNA ANNA AND
DONNA ELVIRA

All that you may,
May here be done!
Do as thou wilt, is here our law!
Thy will be done, thy will be done!

DON GIOVANNI (*to the musicians*)

Music again for dancing!

(*to Leporello*)

Be sure that all have partners.

(*to Zerlina*)

You are the one I've chosen—
Zerlina, you'll be mine!

(*Don Giovanni dances with Zerlina.*)

LEPORELLO
Vien quà, Masetto caro,
Facciam quel ch'altri fa.

MASETTO
No, no, ballar non voglio,

LEPORELLO
Eh balla, amico mio.

MASETTO
No.

LEPORELLO
Si, caro Masetto.

MASETTO
Ballare no, non voglio.

LEPORELLO
Eh, balla, amico mio:
Facciam quel ch'altri fa.

ANNA (*a parte*).
Resister non poss'io.

OTTAVIO E ELVIRA (*a parte*).
Fingete per pietà!

GIOVANNI (*a* ZERLINA).
Vieni con me, mia vita!

MASETTO (*a* LEPORELLO).
Lasciami. Ah no! Zerlina!

GIOVANNI
Vieni, vieni.

ZERLINA
Oh, Numi! Son tradita!

LEPORELLO
Qui nasce una rovina.
(*Si nasconde*).

ANNA, ELVIRA E OTTAVIO (*a parte*).
L'iniquo da se stesso,
Nel laccio se ne va.

ZERLINA (*di dentro*).
Gente! Aiuto! Aiuto gente!

ANNA, ELVIRA E OTTAVIO
Soccorriamo l'innocente.

MASETTO
Ah, Zerlina!

ZERLINA (*di dentro*).
Scellerato!

ANNA E OTTAVIO
Ora grida da quel lato.

LEPORELLO (*to the peasants*)
It's time again for dancing!

DONNA ELVIRA (*to Donna Anna*)
The girl of whom I told you . . .

DONNA ANNA (*to Don Ottavio*)
He's with her!

DON OTTAVIO (*to Donna Anna*)
Hide your feelings!

DON GIOVANNI AND LEPORELLO
How smoothly things combine!

MASETTO (*ironically*)
How smoothly, how smoothly,
How smoothly things combine.

DON GIOVANNI (*to Leporello*)
Take care of our Masetto.

LEPORELLO
(*to Masetto, compassionately*)

Don't stand there stiff and frozen,
Don't be bashful . . . Come join
The others, dear Masetto,
It's too much fun to miss!

DON GIOVANNI (*to Zerlina*)
Zerlina, when I hold you,
          I tremble . . .
O grant me one small kiss!

(*He embraces her, and tries to kiss her;
Zerlina opposes him, escapes and
hides behind the dancers.*)

MASETTO (*opposing Leporello*)
No, no! I do not want to!

LEPORELLO
You know you really want to!

MASETTO
No!
          LEPORELLO (*turning him*)
Yes! You know you want to—don't
you?
          MASETTO
I know I will not!

DONNA ANNA
I can no more dissemble!

DONNA ELVIRA AND DON OTTAVIO
You must, a little while!

(*Zerlina, passing between the dancers,
has gradually approached the door
at right; here Don Giovanni reaches
her, puts his arm around her waist,
and draws her toward the door.*)
          LEPORELLO
Won't you?
          MASETTO
I won't! I tell you!

LEPORELLO
You force me to compel you
To dance a bit and smile!
(*forces Masetto to dance with him*)

DON GIOVANNI
Heart of my heart, I need you,
          Need you too much!
(*leads her off against her will.*)

MASETTO (*struggling*)
Let me by! You hear! Zerlina!

ZERLINA
O don't, sir! All these people . . .

LEPORELLO
The catalogue is growing.

DONNA ELVIRA, DONNA ANNA AND
DON OTTAVIO
Now soon the vile intriguer
Will be exposed as vile!

ZERLINA (*from within*)
Help me, everybody, help me!

(*Tumult.*)

DONNA ELVIRA, DONNA ANNA AND
DON OTTAVIO
(*All turn toward the door.*)
Quickly, quickly we must save her,
Quickly or it may be too late!

MASETTO
O Zerlina! O Zerlina!

ZERLINA
Let me go!

DONNA ELVIRA, DONNA ANNA AND
DON OTTAVIO
(*All hasten to the door.*)
Quickly, quickly to the door
Through which he took her!

ZERLINA (*di dentro*).
Scellerato!

ANNA E OTTAVIO
Ah gittiamo giù la porta!

ZERLINA (*tornando*).
Soccorretemi! Son morta!

GLI ALTRI
Siamo qui per tua difesa!

GIOVANNI
(*Tornando colla spada tratta e verso*

LEPORELLO).
Ecco il birbo che t'ha offesa;

(*Tenendolo*).

Ma da me la pena avrà
Mori iniquo!

LEPORELLO
Ah, cosa fate?

GIOVANNI
Mori, dico!

LEPORELLO
Ah, cosa fate?

OTTAVIO (*a* GIOVANNI).
Nol sperate, nol sperate

ANNA, OTTAVIO E ELVIRA
L'empio crede con tal frode
Di nasconder l'empietà.

(*Cavosi le maschere*).

GIOVANNI
Donna Elvira!

ELVIRA
Sì, malvagio!

GIOVANNI
Don Ottavio!

OTTAVIO
Sì, signore!

GIOVANNI
Ah, credete—

ANNA
Traditore!

ANNA, ELVIRA E OTTAVIO
Traditore! traditore!
Tutto, tutto già si sa!
Trema, trema! scellerato!

ZERLINA
Saprà tosto il mondo intero
Il misfatto orrendo e nero—
    La tua fiera crudeltà.

GIOVANNI E LEPORELLO
È confusa la mia testa:
Non so più quel ch'io mi faccia,
È un'orribile tempesta
Minacciando, oh Dio, mi va!
                    (*Si ode il tuono*).

ZERLINA

Let me go!

DONNA ELVIRA, DONNA ANNA AND
DON OTTAVIO

Quickly, quickly break the door down
If it's bolted!

ZERLINA

I can fight no more!
Can no one save me from this devil?
(*They try to force the door.*)

DONNA ANNA, DON OTTAVIO,
DONNA ELVIRA AND MASETTO

We are coming to your rescue!
A moment longer, O be courageous!

(*They break open the door. Don Giovanni comes out holding Leporello by the arm; he pretends as though he would stab him, but does not take his sword out of the scabbard.*)

DON GIOVANNI

How disgusting! How outrageous!
How you dared offend a bride!
Salacious brute! I shall kill you!

LEPORELLO (*kneeling*)

Why must you scare me?

DON GIOVANNI

Flout me, will you?

LEPORELLO

At least have mercy!

DON GIOVANNI

You deserve none!

LEPORELLO

O master, spare me!

DON OTTAVIO

(*taking out a pistol to Don Giovanni*)
You'll release him, Don Giovanni!
(*unmasking*)
No mere farce will unconvince us . . .

DONNA ELVIRA (*unmasking*)

No mere farce will unconvince us . . .
Unconvince us . . .

DON OTTAVIO

Unconvince us, unconvince us . . .
(*lets Leporello go*)

DONNA ANNA (*unmasking*)

No mere farce will unconvince us . . .

DON OTTAVIO, DONNA ELVIRA
AND DONNA ANNA

Of the guilt you cannot hide,
Cannot hide!

DON GIOVANNI

Donn'Elvira?

DONNA ELVIRA

One who knows you!

DON GIOVANNI

Don Ottavio?

DON OTTAVIO

Yes, your lordship.

DON GIOVANNI

Why this intrigue?

DONNA ANNA

See your judges . . .

DONNA ANNA, DONNA ELVIRA,
DON OTTAVIO, ZERLINA AND MASETTO

Here together to expose you!

ZERLINA

All is known and all shall know,
All mankind shall be your foe!
What you are, earn you hatred
Everywhere you dare to go!

DONNA ANNA AND DONNA ELVIRA

All is known and all shall know,
All mankind shall be your foe,
     That unholy
Thing you are, earn you hatred
Everywhere you dare to go!

DON OTTAVIO AND MASETTO

All is known and all shall know,
All mankind shall be your foe,
What you are shall earn you hate
Everywhere you dare to go —

ALL FIVE

Hatred! Hatred! Hatred!
(*All the men threateningly approach Don Giovanni, who calmly awaits them, leaning on his sword.*)
Tremble as your end approaches!
Now surrounded, shamed and thwarted,
Know that doom was all you courted,
Where your lust has ever led
All the life that you have led!
                    Justice!
Justice!

TUTTI (*eccetto Giovanni e Leporello*)

Odi il tuon della vendetta,
Che ti fischia intorno intorno,
Sul tuo capo in questo giorno
Il suo fulmine cadrà.

GIOVANNI E LEPORELLO

Ma non manca in me coraggio,

GIOVANNI

Non mi perdo, o mi confondo.

LEPORELLO

Non si perde, o si confonde;
Se cadesse ancora il mondo—

GIOVANNI E LEPORELLO

Nulla mai temer mi fa!

FINE DELL'ATTO PRIMO.

ATTO II

SCENA I

*Piazza, come nel prim'Atto. A lato la
casa de* ELVIRA, *con finestra, e porta
praticabile.*

DON GIOVANNI; LEPORELLO
DUETTO

GIOVANNI

Eh via, buffone,
Non mi seccar.

LEPORELLO

No no, padrone,
Non vò restar.

GIOVANNI

Sentimi, amico.

LEPORELLO

Vò andar, vi dico.

GIOVANNI

Ma che ti ho fatto,
Che vuoi lasciarmi?

DONNA ANNA AND ZERLINA

For your crimes revenge approaches!

DONNA ELVIRA, DON OTTAVIO AND
MASETTO

Justice, justice for the crimes,
    Of your life approaches!

DON GIOVANNI AND LEPORELLO

What a tempest! How like furies!
They delight in my (his) damnation!
What an awkward situation!
How I wish I were in bed!

ALL FIVE

Mark the voice of wrath eternal!
To our own, accord is given:
Mortal vengeance armed by Heaven
Soon must fall upon your head!
    Vengeance! Vengeance!

(*Don Giovanni, behind whom Leporello shelters himself, attempts to
clear a path for himself with his
sword, but is hindered by Don Ottavio.*)

DON GIOVANNI

Though you arm your rage with lightning . . .

LEPORELLO

Never will his courage fail him . . .

ALL FIVE

Mark the voice!

DON GIOVANNI

Cry your vengeance in the thunder . . .

LEPORELLO

Cry your vengeance in the thunder . . .

ALL FIVE

Mark the voice!

DON GIOVANNI AND LEPORELLO

Yet I (he) will not shrink in wonder,
I (he) will not shrink in wonder
    Nor be taught
Regret, remorse or dread!

DONNA ELVIRA, DONNA ANNA AND
ZERLINA

Mortal vengeance armed by Heaven
Soon will fall upon your head!

DON OTTAVIO AND MASETTO

Mortal vengeance is armed by Heaven
Soon to fall upon your head!

ALL FIVE

The revenge of man and God
Soon to fall upon your head!

(*Don Giovanni, seizing Leporello by the
collar, and pushing him on before,
makes his way through the peasants
pressing upon him, and exits.*)

END OF ACT ONE

ACT TWO

SCENE I

(*A street.*)

Duet

DON GIOVANNI

Talk if you must but talk to yourself,
then: listen I won't.

LEPORELLO

No, but you *shall* hear what I've been
saying: stay here I won't.

DON GIOVANNI

You want to leave me?

LEPORELLO

Leave you this moment.

DON GIOVANNI

All of a sudden? Now, what's the
matter?

LEPORELLO

Nothing important: you nearly killed
me.

DON GIOVANNI

That was a joke. I was only joking.
What a funny fellow you are.

LEPORELLO

Then let me tell you your funny little,
funny little joke went too far.

DON GIOVANNI

Come, you big booby, solemn expressions
do not become you.
You're being silly, you're being silly,
your being very, very, very silly!
Grumble away, then! Abuse me! Heed
you I don't.
And don't imagine that you'll impress
me,
Because you won't.

LEPORELLO

Oh niente affatto!
  Quasi ammazzarmi,
Ed io non burlo,
  Ma voglio andar.

GIOVANNI

Va, che sei matto.

LEPORELLO

Non vò restar.

GIOVANNI

Leporello!

LEPORELLO

Signore?

GIOVANNI

Vien qui, facciamo pace.
                    (*Da una borsa*).
Prendi.

LEPORELLO

Cosa?

GIOVANNI

Quattro doppie.

LEPORELLO

Oh sentite!
Per questa volta ancora
La cerimonia accetto;
Ma non vi ci avvezzate—non credete;
Di sedurre i miei pari
Come le donne, a forza di denari.

GIOVANNI

Non parliam più di ciò. Ti basta
  l'animo
Di far quel ch'io ti dico?

LEPORELLO

Purchè lasciam le donne.

GIOVANNI

Lasciar le donne! Pazzo!
Lasciar le donne! Sai ch'esse per me
Son necessarie più del pan che mangio
Più dell'aria che spiro.

LEPORELLO

E avete core
D'ingannarle poi tutte?

GIOVANNI

È tutto amore
Chi a una sola è fedele
Verso l'altra é crudele. Io, ch'in me
  serbo
Sì esteso sentimento,
Vò bene a tutte quante.
Le donne poi, che calcolar non sanno,
Il mio buon natural chiamano inganno.

LEPORELLO

Non ho veduto mai
Naturale più benigno!
Orsù cosa vorreste?

GIOVANNI

Odi! Vedesti tu la cameriera
Di Donna Elvira?

LEPORELLO

Io no.

GIOVANNI

Non hai veduto
Qualche cosa di bello!
Caro il mio Leporello: ora io con lei
Vò tentar la mia sorte; ed ho pensato,
Giacchè siam verso sera,
Per aguzzarle meglio l'appetito,
Di presentarmi a lei col tuo vestito.

LEPORELLO

E perchè non potreste
Presentarvi col vostro?

GIOVANNI

Han poco credito
Con gente di tal rango
Gli abiti signorili
Sbrigati, via!

LEPORELLO

Signor, per più ragioni—

GIOVANNI

Finiscila, non soffro opposizioni.
  Donna Elvira (*E detti.*)

TERZETTO
ELVIRA (*alla finestra*).

Ah taci, ingiusto core!
Non palpitarmi in seno!
È un empio, è un traditore
È colpa aver pietà.

LEPORELLO

I can see nothing, nothing to laugh at.
Joke! Joke! Joke! Joke!
No, no, no, no, no, no, no, no, no, no, no,
Like it I don't and stay here I won't.
It isn't funny, it isn't funny.
Stay here I won't.
And don't you imagine that you amuse me,
Because you don't.

(*Leporello tries to go. Don Giovanni detains him.*)

Recitative

DON GIOVANNI

Leporello!

LEPORELLO

I'm leaving.

DON GIOVANNI

Come back! (*gives him money*) A little something. Catch it!

LEPORELLO

How much?

DON GIOVANNI

Four gold pieces.

LEPORELLO (*counting it*)

Four? No joking? Well, just this once and for the sake of our friendship. But I must tell you frankly I'm a decent lad and not to be led astray like a woman by compliments and money.

DON GIOVANNI

I don't care what you are. I have some work for you. Are you prepared to do it?

LEPORELLO

If you give up the women.

DON GIOVANNI

Give up the women! Idiot! Give up the women! Why, they are the purpose of my life, I would as soon stop eating, I would sooner stop breathing!

LEPORELLO

You won't be happy until all have surrendered?

DON GIOVANNI

You know my *motto.* "Who is true to one only is untrue to all others." I could embrace an infinity of women and still have love left over. But the poor darlings have no head for figures, and cannot understand generous natures.

LEPORELLO

Till now I never heard of such a generous nature, such vast affection. And now, what are you after?

DON GIOVANNI

Ah, yes. (*confidentially*) Perhaps you know the maid in service with Donn' Elvira.

LEPORELLO

No. Why?

DON GIOVANNI

You haven't seen her? She is something so rare and ravishing, and unsullied, that I am burning to be better acquainted. It would amuse me on such a pleasant evening, if we exchanged our cloaks with one another, and I, disguised as you, will serenade her.

LEPORELLO

Why would that be amusing? What's the reason behind it?

DON GIOVANNI

In my experience, some girls in her position shy when they see the gentry. (*takes off his cloak*) Off with it! Take mine!

LEPORELLO

No, wait . . . I've a suspicion . . .

DON GIOVANNI (*angrily*)

Immediately! I brook no opposition.

(*They exchange cloaks and hats.*)
(*Donna Elvira is at the window. It gradually becomes dark.*)

Trio

DONNA ELVIRA

Can hopefulness yet move me?
Why is my heart insistent?
He did not, he does not love me,
Nor shall his love be mine.

LEPORELLO

Zitto! Di Donna Elvira,
Signor, la voce io sento.

GIOVANNI

Cogliere io vò il momento!
Tu fermati un po' là.
Elvira, idolo mio!

ELVIRA

Non è costui l'ingrato?

GIOVANNI

Si vita mia, son io,
E chieggo carità.

ELVIRA

Numi! Che strano affetto
Mi si risveglia in petto!

LEPORELLO (a parte).

State a veder la pazza!
Ch'ancor gli crederà.

GIOVANNI

Discendi, o gioia bella!
Vedrai che tu sei quella,
Che adora l'alma mia,
Pentito io sono già!

ELVIRA

No! Non ti credo, o barbaro.

GIOVANNI

Ah, credimi, o m'uccido!

LEPORELLO (a parte).

Se seguitate, io rido.

GIOVANNI

Idolo mio, vien quà!

A 3

ELVIRA

Dei! Che cimento è questo?
Non so s'io vado, o resto!
Ah proteggete voi
La mia credulità?

GIOVANNI (a parte).

Spero che cada presto—
Che bel colpetto è questo;
Più fertile talento
Del mio no, non si da!

LEPORELLO (a parte).

Già quel mendace labbro
Torna a sedur costei;
Deh proteggete, o Dei!
La sua credulità!

GIOVANNI

Amico, che ti par!

LEPORELLO

Mi par ch'abbiate
Un'anima di bronzo.

GIOVANNI

Va là, che sei il gran gonzo! Ascolta
   bene;
Quando costei qui viene,
Tu corri ad abbracciarla—
Falle quattro carezze—
Fingi la voce mia; poi con bell'arte
Cerca teco condurla in altra parte.

LEPORELLO

Ma, signor—

LEPORELLO
(*aside, to Don Giovanni*)

Master, it's Donn'Elvira!
You don't want her to find you.

DON GIOVANNI
(*aside, to Leporello*)

I'll hide myself behind you;
My plans are going fine.

(*stands behind Leporello*)

Elvira, hear your lover,

(*making appropriate gestures with
Leporello's arms*)

Your poor repentant lover . . .

DONNA ELVIRA
How dare you so address me?

DON GIOVANNI
Forgive the heart I offer,
One weakness, only one!

DONNA ELVIRA (*aside*)
Why should his voice yet stir me?
Am I, then, doomed forever?

LEPORELLO (*aside*)
She's quite as mad as ever!

(*crossly, to Don Giovanni*)

(If I had known your plans!)

DON GIOVANNI
(*poking Leporello in the ribs, and
making more animated gestures*)

O star, be not disdainful, be not
disdainful,
Repentant love is painful:
Your faithfulness and beauty
Have made me at heart contrite.

DONNA ELVIRA
No, I cannot believe in you,
No, I cannot!

DON GIOVANNI
You must believe,
Lest you kill me!
I've repented. Please have pity!

LEPORELLO
(*softly, to Don Giovanni*)

I'll die if I don't laugh soon.
Unholy titters fill me.
She isn't very witty.

DON GIOVANNI
Come to my arms tonight!

DONNA ELVIRA
Shall his avowal sway me?
He makes my heart betray me.
O God, may he be truthful,
I want so to believe, want to believe.
Should his avowal sway me
And make my heart betray me?
O God, may he be truthful!
I want so to believe, I want to believe.

(*disappears from the window*)

DON GIOVANNI
Nimbly events obey me,
No human force can stay me,
The fates were sweet to give me
Such talent to deceive.
No human force can stay me,
Nor doubts delay me.
What circumstance can stay me?
What art is mine when I deceive!

LEPORELLO
If he can still persuade her,
No human force can aid her.
May God look after this woman,
Incredibly naive, much too naive.
What circumstance can aid her?
May God protect this woman,
Incredibly naive, much too naive:
Her heart and mind are too naive!

Recitative

DON GIOVANNI
I think the game is mine!

LEPORELLO
You know what I think? — I think the
game is heartless!

DON GIOVANNI
Hear! Hear! Another sermon! You'll
still use my rules and obey my instructions. (*pointing at the window*)
When she comes down, remember
you're to run and embrace her, aping
my voice and gestures. From then on,
play your own game just so you go
and take her with you.

LEPORELLO
I don't like it.

GIOVANNI

Non più repliche!

LEPORELLO

E se poi mi conosce?

GIOVANNI

Non ti conoscerà, se tu non vuoi.
Zitto! Ell'apre—ehi, giudizio.

E detti.

ELVIRA

Eccomi a voi!

GIOVANNI (*a parte*).

Vediamo che farà.

LEPORELLO (*a parte*).

Che bell'imbroglio!

ELVIRA

Dunque creder potrò, ch'i pianti miei
Abbian vinto quel cor! Dunque pentito
L'amato Don Giovanni al suo dovere,
E all'amor mio ritorna?

LEPORELLO

Si, carina!

ELVIRA

Crudele! Se sapeste
Quante lagrime, e quanti
Sospiri voi mi costate!

LEPORELLO

Io, vita mia!

ELVIRA

Voi.

LEPORELLO

Poverina, quanto mi dispiace!

ELVIRA

Mi fuggirete più?

LEPORELLO

No, muso bello!

ELVIRA

Sarete sempre mio?

LEPORELLO

Sempre!

ELVIRA

Carissimo!

LEPORELLO

Carissima!

(*a parte*).

La burla mi da gusto!

ELVIRA

Mio tesoro!

LEPORELLO

Mia Venere!

ELVIRA

Son per voi tutta foco!

LEPORELLO

Io tutto cenere!

GIOVANNI (*a parte*).

Il birbo si riscalda.

ELVIRA

E non m'ingannerete?

LEPORELLO

No, sicuro.

ELVIRA

Giuratelo.

LEPORELLO

Lo giuro a questa mano,
Che bacio con trasporto, e a quei bei
    lumi!

GIOVANNI

Ih, eh, ah, ih; sei morto!

ELVIRA

Oh, Numi!

(*Fuggono* ELVIRA *e* LEPORELLO).

GIOVANNI

Ih, eh, ah, ih! Par che la sorte
Mi secondi. Veggiamo;
Le finestre son queste: ora cantiamo.

DON GIOVANNI

I don't ask you to.

LEPORELLO

But suppose she discovers?

DON GIOVANNI

If you're ingenious there's no need to worry. Quiet . . . She's coming out. Don't fail me!

(*He runs off to the side leaving Leporello alone; Donna Elvira enters from the house, and advances to meet Leporello; Don Giovanni watches their movements.*)

DONNA ELVIRA (*to Leporello*)

O my beloved!

DON GIOVANNI (*aside*)

(It's much too good to miss.)

LEPORELLO (*aside*)

(It's *too* much.)

DONNA ELVIRA

Do I dare to believe my prayers were answered, that you truly repent your past behaviour, that you, dear Don Giovanni, have owned your errors and will no more be faithless?

LEPORELLO

(*imitating Don Giovanni*)

Yes, believe it.

DONNA ELVIRA

Beloved, can you realize all the agonies your sudden desertion made me suffer?

LEPORELLO

Could I have done it?

DONNA ELVIRA

But now . . .

LEPORELLO

Now, believe me, I'm another person.

DONNA ELVIRA

And you'll be always mine?

LEPORELLO

If you will have me.

DONNA ELVIRA

And you will never leave me?

LEPORELLO

Leave you?

DONNA ELVIRA

How wonderful!

LEPORELLO

A miracle! (*aside*) (This game is not at all bad!)

DONNA ELVIRA

How I waited!

LEPORELLO

Penelope!

DONNA ELVIRA (*embracing him*)

Did you know how I loved you?

LEPORELLO

I feel I couldn't have!

DON GIOVANNI (*aside*)

(He may convince himself soon.)

DONNA ELVIRA

And now you know and love me?

LEPORELLO

More each moment!

DONNA ELVIRA

You swear you do?

LEPORELLO

Upon this hand I swear it, and with a kiss confirm it; upon this forearm . . .

DON GIOVANNI

(*pretends to waylay them*)

Stand where you are! Deliver!

LEPORELLO AND DONNA ELVIRA

A bandit!

(*They escape.*)

DON GIOVANNI

And that takes care of that! I'm free for more important matters. Let's see now . . . (*taking the mandolin which Leporello left leaning against the house*) for seducing domestics, this air works wonders.

Deh, vieni alla finestra,
O mio tesoro;
Deh, vieni a consolar,
Il pianto mio.
Se neghi a me di dar qualche ristoro;
Davanti agli occhi tuoi, morir vogl'io.
Tu ch'hai la bocca dolce,
Più del miele.
Tu che lo zucchero posti in mezzo al
    core;
Non esser gioia mia con me crudele,
Lasciati almen veder mio bell'amore!

Don GIOVANNI; MASETTO

(*con seguito di Contadini armati.*)

GIOVANNI

V'è gente alla finestra;
Forse è dessa. Ps! ps!

MASETTO

Non ci stanchiamo;—il cor mi dice
Che trovarlo dobbiamo.

GIOVANNI (*a parte*)

Qualcuno parla.

MASETTO

Fermatevi—mi pare
Ch'alcuno qui si mova.

GIOVANNI (*a parte*).

Se non fallo, è Masetto.

MASETTO

Chi va là? Non risponde?
Animo, schioppo al muso:
Chi va là?

GIOVANNI (*a parte*).

Non è solo,
Ci vuol giudizio. (*Forte.*) Amici.

    (*a parte*).

Non mi voglio scoprir. Sei tu, Masetto?

MASETTO

Appunto quello. E tu?

GIOVANNI

Non mi conosci? Il servo
Son io di Don Giovanni—

MASETTO

Leporello!
Servo di quell'indegno cavaliere?

GIOVANNI

Certo, di quel briccone.

MASETTO

Di quell'uom senz'onore, ah, dimmi un
    poco,
Dove possiam trovarlo;
Lo cerco con costor per trucidarlo.

GIOVANNI (*a parte*).

Bagatelle! (*Forte.*) Bravissimo Masetto.
Anch'io con voi m'unisco
Per fargliela a quel birbo di padrone;
Ma udite un pò qual è la mia inten-
    zione.
Metà di voi quà vadano
E gli altri vadan là,
E pian pianin lo cerchino
Lontan non sia di quà, no
Lontan non sia di quà.
Se un uom e una ragazza
Passeggian per la piazza,
Se sotto a una finestra.
Fare all'amor sentite,
Ferite pur, ferite,
Il mio padron sarà.

Canzonetta

DON GIOVANNI

O star, why keep thy beauty so cruelly
hidden?
Thy sable realm begem, bright Queen
of Love, shine!
This dark I bid thee rule, serves thee
unbidden;
And love that serves by night has made
my heart thine.

Be not of adoration distantly scornful;
Grant thy suffering subject once more
to view thee.
Despondent of thy grace, all now is
mournful,
All upon thy glance would Paradise be!

Recitative

DON GIOVANNI

She's coming to the window ... as they
all do. What's that? (*Enter Masetto,
armed with gun and pistol, followed
by some armed peasants.*)

MASETTO

Keep up your courage, for something
tells me that he's not far away.

DON GIOVANNI (*aside*)

(Now who could that be?)

MASETTO

Be vigilant! I think I hear somebody
moving.

DON GIOVANNI

(*folding his cloak closer, and pulling
his hat over his eyes*)

(If it isn't Masetto!)

MASETTO (*aloud*)

Who goes there? (*to the peasants*)
Keep together! Have your stout weapons ready! (*louder*) Who goes
there?

DON GIOVANNI (*aside*)

(This is awkward and calls for cunning.) (*imitating Leporello*) Masetto! (Let us hope that it works!)
Is that Masetto?

MASETTO (*astonished*)

Yes, I'm Masetto. And you?

DON GIOVANNI

Surely you know me. You've often seen
me with Don Giovanni.

MASETTO

Leporello! You are the man who serves
that wicked devil.

DON GIOVANNI

Too true! That shameless scoundrel!

MASETTO

Good! Then, maybe, you can help us.
Perhaps you know the place he would
choose to hide in. For we have sworn
to rout him out and kill him.

DON GIOVANNI

(Oh, is *that* all!) Most excellent Masetto, of course I'll try to help you.
I, too, have many things against my
master. We'll catch him yet. So follow my instructions.

Aria

DON GIOVANNI (*to the peasants*)

Be quick! This way with some of you,
The rest of you go there.
Look here, look there, look everywhere.
He won't be far away. No. Look sharp.
He won't be far away.

(*going from one to another*)

Perhaps you'll find him kissing
Your sweetheart in a corner
Or softly serenading
Your pretty little daughter.
Lay hold of him and bash him.
Then knock him down and thrash him.
He won't be hard to find.
You'll know him by his swagger,
His velvet cloak and feather:
Perhaps I ought to warn you
He also wears a sword,

(*trying to send the peasants off; but
they act as if they had not understood him*)

A sharp and shining sword.

(*repeating his directions*)

So when you've found him kissing
Your sweetheart in a corner,
Or softly serenading
Your pretty little daughter,
Arrest him, arrest him.
Lay hold of him and bash him,

In testa egli ha un cappello
Con candidi pennacchi,
Addosso un gran mantello,
E spada al fianco egli ha,
Andate, fate presto,
(*a Masetto*)
Tu sol verrai con me,
Noi far dobbiam il resto,
E già vedrai cos'è.

    Il Don GIOVANNI; MASETTO

GIOVANNI

Zitto! Lascia ch'io senta. Ottimamente!
Dunque dobbiamo ucciderlo?

MASETTO

Sicuro.

GIOVANNI

E non ti basteria rompergli l'ossa
Fracassargli le spalle?

MASETTO

No, no! Voglio ammazzarlo!
Vo' farlo in cento brani.

GIOVANNI

Hai buone armi?

MASETTO

Cospetto!
Ho pria questo moschetto;

    (*dandola a* GIOVANNI).

E poi questa pistola.

      (*dandola*).

GIOVANNI

E poi?

MASETTO

Non basta?

GIOVANNI

Eh, basta certo. Or prendi
Questa per la pistola,

    (*Battendolo*).

Questa per il moschetto.

MASETTO

Ahi! ahi! La testa mia—

GIOVANNI

Taci, o t'uccido.

    (*Battendolo ancora*).

Questa per l'ammazzarlo,
Questa per farlo in brani;—
Villano, mascalzon, ceffo da cani!

    (*Parte*).

MASETTO; *indi* ZERLINA

MASETTO (*Gridando forte*).

Ahi, ahi! La testa mia!
Ahi, ahi, le spalle! E il petto!

ZERLINA

M'è parso di sentire
La voce di Masetto.

MASETTO

Oh, Dio! Zerlina!
Zerlina mia, soccorso!

ZERLINA

Cos'è stato?

MASETTO

L'iniquo, lo scellerato
Mi ruppe l'ossa, e i nervi

ZERLINA

O poveretta me! Chi?

MASETTO

Leporello.
O qualche diavol che somiglia a lui.

ZERLINA

Crudel! Non tel diss'io,
Che con questa tua pazza gelosia
Ti ridurresti a qualche brutto passo.
Dove ti duole?

MASETTO

Qui.

Then knock him down and thrash him,
and bash him.
Be quick! This way with some of you,
The rest of you go there.
Look here, look there, look everywhere.
He can't be far away. No. Look sharp.
He can't be far away.

(*pushing the peasants off to either side*)

Don't lose another moment, be off this
very moment,
Helter-skelter, helter-skelter, helter-
skelter.

      (*Exeunt peasants.*)

(*to Masetto*)

But you shall come with me,
And I will go with you.

(*putting his arm familiarly around
Masetto*)

Who'll be the first to spy him?
Perhaps it will be me. Who knows?
Who knows?
Perhaps it will be you. Who knows?
Who knows?

(*promenading to and fro with Masetto*)

Perhaps it will be me,
Perhaps it will be you.

(*goes off holding Masetto*)

Recitative

(*Don Giovanni returns, leading
Masetto by the hand.*)

DON GIOVANNI

Quiet! Halt for a moment! Tell me,
Masetto; what do you mean to do to
him?

MASETTO

To kill him!

DON GIOVANNI

Suppose he got a sound hiding to remember, wouldn't that be sufficient?

MASETTO

No. No. I want to flay him, to chop
him up in pieces!

DON GIOVANNI

With what weapon?

MASETTO

I'll show you. (*hands musket and pistol
to Don Giovanni*) You see I've got
this musket, and then I've got a
pistol.

DON GIOVANNI

No others?

MASETTO

What others?

DON GIOVANNI

Here is your answer. (*beats him with
the flat of his sword*) Take that now,
that for your pretty pistol, that for
your lovely musket!

MASETTO (*crying out and falling*)

Oh! Oh! My head! I'm dying.

DON GIOVANNI

Quiet! Or you *will* die. That for your
thoughts of flaying, that for those
little pieces! You misbegotten swine,
scum of the ditches! (*throws weapons down before Masetto and exits
hastily behind tavern*)

MASETTO

Oh! Oh! My back is broken! Oh God,
what bruises! I'm dying!

      (*Zerlina enters with a lantern.*)

ZERLINA

Where on earth did that come from?
It sounded like Masetto.

MASETTO

Oh God! Zerlina! Zerlina! Hurry! I'm
dying!

ZERLINA

What has happened?

MASETTO

That scoundrel! That lying robber!
He's crippled me forever!

ZERLINA

Oh dear, Oh dear, Oh dear! Who?

MASETTO

Leporello — or else some fiend that
looked exactly like him!

ZERLINA (*helping him to rise*)

You see! Admit I told you what would
happen if you were always jealous;
and now at last it has happened as I
told you! Where did he hurt you?

MASETTO

Here.

ZERLINA

E poi?

MASETTO

Qui, e ancora qui.

ZERLINA

E poi non ti duol altro?

MASETTO

Duolmi un poco
Questo piè, questo braccio, e questa
    mano.

ZERLINA

Via, via, non è gran mal, s'il resto è
    sano.
Vientene meco a casa.
Purchè tu mi prometta
D'essere men geloso,
Io, io ti guarirò, caro il mio sposo.
Vedrai carino,
Se sei buonino,
Che bel rimedio,
Ti voglio dar.
É naturale,
Non da disgusto,
E lo speziale,
Non lo sa far, no.
É un certo balsamo,
Che porto addosso,
Dare tel posso,
S'il vuoi provar!
Saper vorresti?
Dove mi stà?
Sentilo battere
Toccami quà!

SCENA II

Cortile interno della casa di ELVIRA
LEPORELLO, *Donna* ELVIRA.

LEPORELLO

Di molte faci il lume
S'avvicina, o mio ben; stiamo qui un
    poco
Finchè da noi si scosta.

ELVIRA

Ma che temi,
Adorato mio sposo?

LEPORELLO

Nulla, nulla.
Certi riguardi—Io vo' veder, s'il lume
É già lontano. (*a parte.*) Ah, come
Da costei liberarmi?

(*forte*).

Rimanti, anima bella!

ELVIRA

Ah, non lasciarmi!

SESTETTO
ELVIRA

Sola, sola, in buio loco,
Palpitar il cor mi sento!
E m'assale un tal spavento,
Che mi sembra di morir.

LEPORELLO

Più che cerco men ritrovo
Questa porta sciagurata.
Piano, piano—l'ho trovata,
Ecco il tempo di fuggir.

(*Si nasconde*).

Don OTTAVIO*; Donna* ANNA. *E detti.*

OTTAVIO

Tergi il ciglio, o vita mia!
E da calma al tuo dolore!
L'ombra omai del genitore
Pena avrà de' tuoi martir.

ANNA

Lascia almen alla mia pena
Questo piccolo ristoro,
Sol la morte, o mio tesoro—
Il mio pianto può finir!

ZERLINA

Is that all?

MASETTO

No . . . it's here and . . . here.

ZERLINA

No other places hurt you?

MASETTO

Well, this foot's a little sore, and this arm aches, and these two fingers . . .

ZERLINA

Oh well, there's still a lot of you that's healthy. Nestle a little closer, and swear to me that you will never more be suspicious, and I'll apply a salve you'll think delicious.

Aria

ZERLINA

Nestling serenely,
Warm in my sympathy,
No aching memory
Need you endure.
Near lies your healing:
No unappealing,
Unnatural remedy
Have I in mind. No.
Herbs of some kind? No.
Mine is the cure.
It is a humanly
Virtuous property
Heaven confides in me,
Wanting it pure.
Now shall we prove it?
Where can it be?
Will you love it,
Can I be sure?

(*lays Masetto's hand on her heart*)

Here it beats lovingly.
Touch it and see!
Is it not all I swore?
Softly it beats, beats, beats.
Each throb repeats to you:
I am your comfort,
And so much more.

(*Exits with Masetto.*)

SCENE II

(*A dark courtyard, with three doors, before the house of Donna Anna. Leporello with Donna Elvira on his arm. He is wearing Don Giovanni's hat and cloak.*)

Recitative

LEPORELLO

Dear, I hear people coming. Let us move for a while into the shadow till they have all gone by us.

DONNA ELVIRA

But, my dearest, what should *we* be afraid of?

LEPORELLO

Nothing, darling. I was just thinking . . . perhaps I should . . . find out what they are doing. (*aside*) (I cannot keep this up for much longer.) I'll only be a moment.

(*Leporello goes further away.*)

DONNA ELVIRA

Ah, do not leave me!

Sextet

DONNA ELVIRA

Left alone, alone in darkness, all alone,
I feel upon me an oppression,
A chill so deadly
Fraught with fear and dark with doom
As if wafted from the tomb.

LEPORELLO (*groping his way*)

It's so dark here, I can't find it.
Little door, my pretty door, where are you hiding?

(*finds the door*)

Here it is, now. No, it isn't. (*misses again*) Ah, I've found it.
Now is the time to disappear,
Just the moment, just the time to disappear.

(*Enter Don Ottavio and Donna Anna in mourning.*)

DON OTTAVIO

Weep no longer, calm your sorrow,
What is done cannot be altered,
Anguish and sighs and tears can never
Call the dead to life again, to life again.

DONNA ANNA

Leave me, leave me to my sorrow,
Nothing here on earth can please me,
Death alone can ease me,
Death can please me,
Wipe away the guilty stain,
Dry my tears and ease my pain.

ELVIRA

Ah, dov'è lo sposo mio?

LEPORELLO (*a parte*).

Se mi trova, son perduto.

ELVIRA E LEPORELLO

Una porta là vegg'io
Cheta cheta io vo' partir.

ZERLINA; MASETTO, *con lume. E detti.*
MASETTO E ZERLINA
(*vedendo* LEPORELLO).

Ferma briccone! Dove ten vai?

ANNA E OTTAVIO

Ecco il fellone! Com'era quà?

A 4

ANNA, OTTAVIO, ZERLINA E MASETTO

Ah! mora il perfido,
Che m'ha tradito!

ELVIRA

É mio marito!
Pietà! pietà!

A 4

ANNA, OTTAVIO, ZERLINA E MASETTO

Donna Elvira
Quello ch'io vedo?
Appena il credo?
No; morrà!

LEPORELLO

Perdon, perdono!
Signori miei;
Quell'io non sono,
Sbaglia costei.
Viver lasciatemi
Per carità!

ANNA, OTTAVIO, ZERLINA E MASETTO

É Leporello!
Che inganno è questo!
Stupida resto.
Che mai sarà.

LEPORELLO

Mille torbidi pensieri
Mi s'aggiran per la testa;
Se mi salvo in tal tempesta,
É un prodigio in verità!

ANNA, OTTAVIO, ZERLINA E MASETTO

Mille torbidi pensieri
Mi s'aggiran per la testa;
Che giornata, o stelle, è questa—
Che impensata novità!

ZERLINA

Dunque quello sei tu che il mio Masetto poco fa crudelmente maltra-
tasti!

ELVIRA

Dunque tu m'ingannasti o scellerato,
spacciandoti con me da Don Giovanni!

OTTAVIO

Dunque tu in questi panni venisti qui
per qualche tradimento!

ELVIRA

A me tocca punirlo.

ZERLINA

Anzi a me.

OTTAVIO

No, no, a me.

MASETTO

Accoppatelo meco tutti tre.

LEPORELLO

Ah, pietà! Signori miei!
Ah, pietà di me!
Do ragione a voi, a lei,
Ma, ma il delitto mio non è
Il padron con prepotenza
L'innocenza mi rubò.

DONNA ELVIRA
(*unseen by the others*)

Husband, dearest, speak. Where are you?

LEPORELLO
(*by the door, unseen by the others*)

If I tell her, there'll be trouble.

DONNA ELVIRA
(*approaching the door*)

Look, a door already open.
He perhaps has gone that way.

LEPORELLO
(*Trying to escape, he is suddenly confronted by Zerlina and Masetto.*)

Look, a door already open:
Here's my chance to get away.

ZERLINA AND MASETTO

Halt! Who are you there? Where are you off to?
Ah, now we've got you, brought you to bay.

(*Leporello, forced into center, kneels and hides his face in Don Giovanni's cloak.*)

DONNA ANNA, DON OTTAVIO, ZERLINA
AND MASETTO

He is the murderer!
Bring him to judgment!
We will have vengeance!

DONNA ELVIRA
(*discovering herself and unveiling*)

O spare my husband! Forbear.

DONNA ANNA, DON OTTAVIO, ZERLINA
AND MASETTO

It's Donn'Elvira.
Would she have pardoned a sinner so hardened?
No, no, no. He dies.

(*They seize him. Leporello reveals himself and kneels down.*)

DONNA ELVIRA

Have mercy. Forbear.

LEPORELLO

No, no, don't hurt me.
You are mistaken.
I have done nothing,
I'm not the culprit.
Surely, you wouldn't kill poor little me.
(*He throws back the cloak. General astonishment; Donna Elvira flies to Donna Anna.*)

DONNA ANNA, DONNA ELVIRA,
DON OTTAVIO, ZERLINA AND MASETTO

What! Leporello! I must be dreaming,
Who would believe it? Can this be true?
Doubt, amazement, fear, foreboding
Leave me shaken and bewildered.
Day of wonder!
Some revelation is yet to follow.
What will follow none can tell.

LEPORELLO

Fear and terrible foreboding
Leave me shaken and bewildered.
Will they hang poor Leporello
Who did nothing and meant (so) well?

(*Exit Donna Anna.*)

Recitative

ZERLINA (*to Leporello*)

It was you, it was you, you savage brute, who with your blows very nearly killed Masetto.

DONNA ELVIRA (*to Leporello*)

It was you, vulgar scoundrel, who deceived me, behaving as if you were Don Giovanni.

DON OTTAVIO (*to Leporello*)

Dressed to look like his master. That clearly speaks of some nefarious purpose.

DONNA ELVIRA

Let me do the chastising.

ZERLINA

No, let me.

DON OTTAVIO

No, no, let me.

MASETTO

Let us all in a body deal with him.

Aria

LEPORELLO

Ah don't kill me on the spot.
Spare my life and I will tell you what was what, what's what.
I'll explain to you and you and you and you,
But . . . but . . . but the sinner . . .
But the guilty one I'm not.
I am not.
If you only knew my master,

Don' El.ira! Compatite!
Voi capite come andò!
Di Masetto non sò nulla
Vel' dirà questa fanciulla.
È un oretta, circumcirca,
Che con lei girando vo.
Ah voi, Signore! Non dico niente,
Certo timore, certo accidente
Di fuori chiaro,
Di dentro oscuro
Non c'è riparo
La porta, il muro, io me ne vo
Da quel lato,
Poi qui celato,
L'affar si sa,
Ma s'io sapeva, fuggia per quà!

(DONNA ANNA E LEPORELLO
partono).

ELVIRA

Ferma, perfido, ferma!

MASETTO

Il birbo ha l'ali ai piedi.

ZERLINA

Con qual arte
Si sottrasse l'iniquo!

OTTAVIO

Amici miei.
Dopo eccessi sì enormi,
Dubitar non possiam, che Don Giovan-
ni
Non sia l'empio uccisore
Del padre di Donn'Anna. In questa ca-
sa
Per poche ore fermatevi: un ricorso
Vò far a chi si deve; e in pochi istanti

Vendicarvi prometto.
Così vuole dover, pietade, affetto.
Il mio tesoro in tanto
Andate, andate a consolar!
E del bel ciglio il pianto
Cercate di asciugar.
Ditele che i suoi torti
A vendicar io vado.
Che sol di stragi e morti
Nunzio vogl'io tornar.

SCENA III

*Recinto murato, in mezzo al quale si
vede la Statua del Commendatore.*

Don GIOVANNI, *salendo il muro; indi*
LEPORELLO.

GIOVANNI

Ah! ah! ah! Questa è buona!
Or lasciala cercar. Che bella notte!
É più chiara del giorno; sembra fatta
Per gir a zonzo, a caccia di ragazze.
Vediam s'è tardi? Ah, no!
Ancor non son le due di notte. Avrei
Voglia un pò di saper com'è finito
L'affar tra Leporello e Donna Elvira;
S'egli ha avuto giudizio.

LEPORELLO

(*Senz'alito, dietro il muro*)

Alfin vuole ch'io faccia un precipizio!

GIOVANNI

É desso! Oh, Leporello!

You would pity me a lot.

(*to Donna Elvira*)

Donn'Elvira! You can help me. Won't
   you help me?
You know what he made me do.
Please forgive me, please forgive me
For the things he made me do.

(*to Masetto*)

Of Masetto I know nothing.

(*motioning to Donna Elvira*)

O most noble gracious lady, tell them
   this story.
For the past hour, perhaps longer,
Where was I? I was with you.

(*with embarrassment to Don Ottavio*)

To you, your lordship, how shall I put
   it?
I saw a sort of . . .
A sort of wall, you see,
A sort of door, you see,
And then I thought, you see,
It must lead somewhere,
Well, somehow . . . well, somehow . . .
At first (*pointing to the door*) I was
   on the outside . . .
Then on the inside . . . The rest you
   know.

(*slyly edging towards the door*)

Now you know.
Were I a liar . . . You see, I'd go.

(*making for the door*)

You'd see me go.

(*He runs out.*)

Recitative

DONNA ELVIRA

Catch him! After him! Stop him!

MASETTO

No hare could fly much faster.

ZERLINA

O how slyly he allayed our suspicions!

DON OTTAVIO

From all we've witnessed and from
what he has told us, it is only too
clear who did the murder. It was
Don Giovanni who killed Donn'

Anna's father. So I will ask you all to
stay and look after her while I lay
all the facts before the judges. Then,
very shortly, retribution shall follow.
Let our strength be in love and
friendship and honor! (*Exeunt
Donna Elvira, Zerlina and Masetto.*)

Aria

DON OTTAVIO

Fly, gentle notes, to aid her,
Sweet music, as my herald, swiftly fly!
Go to my love, persuade her
Those flowing tears to dry.
Sweet music, attend her
Of whom your grace is born:
Console her, fly, O fly!

Say she is not forsaken,
Ever shall I defend her,
Even till death defend her,
My solemn vow is taken,
Never to be forsworn:
Soon shall her wronger die.

(*Exit.*)

SCENE III

(*An enclosed churchyard, several eques-
trian statues; statue of the Commendatore, with inscription in gold let-
tering.*)

Recitative

DON GIOVANNI

(*leaps over the wall, laughing, still
wearing Leporello's hat and cloak*)

Ha-ha, ha-ha, that was lucky! I've
thrown them off the scent. How
bright the moon is! It could almost
be daylight. Just the night to be on
the prowl and go stalking after
Beauty! (*looks at his watch*) There's
time yet. It's only half-past one in
the morning. I'm dying to know how
that tale finally ended, how Leporello handled Donn'Elvira. Let us
hope he enjoyed it!

LEPORELLO (*behind the wall*)

(He likes to see me swing on the
gallows.)

DON GIOVANNI

The rascal! Leporello!

LEPORELLO

Chi mi chiama?

GIOVANNI

Non conosci il padrone!

LEPORELLO

Così nol conoscessi!

GIOVANNI

Come? Birbo!

LEPORELLO

Ah, siete voi? Scusate!

GIOVANNI

Cos'è stato?

LEPORELLO

Per cagion vostra io fui quasi accop-
pato.

GIOVANNI

Ebben, non era questo
Un onore per te?

LEPORELLO

Signor, vel dono!

GIOVANNI

Via, via, vien qua:
Che belle cose ti deggio dir!

LEPORELLO

Ma cosa fate qui?

GIOVANNI

Vien dentro, e lo saprai.
Diverse istorielle,
Che accadute mi son dacchè partisti,
Ti dirò un'altra volta; or la più bella
Ti vò solo narrar.

LEPORELLO

Donnesca, al certo.

GIOVANNI

C'è dubbio! Una fanciulla,
Bella, giovin, galante,
Per la strada incontrai; le vado ap-
presso,
La prendo per la man—fuggir mi
vuole;
Dico poche parole, ella mi piglia
Sai per chi?

LEPORELLO

Non lo so.

GIOVANNI

Per Leporello!

LEPORELLO

Per me!

GIOVANNI

Per te!

LEPORELLO

Va bene!

GIOVANNI

Per la mano
Essa allora mi prende.

LEPORELLO

Ancora meglio!

GIOVANNI

M'accarezza, m'abbraccia—
'Caro il mio Leporello!
Leporello, mio caro!' Allor m'accorsi
Ch'era qualche tua bella.

LEPORELLO (a parte).

Oh, maledetto!

GIOVANNI

Dell'inganno approfitto; non so come
Mi riconosce, grida, sento gente,—
A fuggire mi metto; e pronto pronto
Per quel muretto in questo loco io mon-
to.

LEPORELLO

E mi dite la cosa
Con tal indifferenza—

GIOVANNI

Perchè no?

LEPORELLO

Ma se fosse costei stata mia moglie?

GIOVANNI

(Ridendo molto forte).

Meglio ancora!

(Parla la Statua).

COMMENDATORE

Di rider finirai
Pria dell'aurora!

GIOVANNI

Chi ha parlato?

LEPORELLO

Ah, qualch'anima
Sarà dall'altro mondo,
Che vi conosce a fondo.

LEPORELLO (*from the wall*)
Who are you, please?

DON GIOVANNI
You know well who I am.

LEPORELLO
I don't and I don't want to!

DON GIOVANNI
No more fooling!

LEPORELLO
Oh, so it's you. I'm sorry.

DON GIOVANNI
Well, what happened?

LEPORELLO
On your behalf I came near being butchered.

DON GIOVANNI
But think what a great honor such a fate would have been!

LEPORELLO
The thought . . . consoles me.

DON GIOVANNI
Now, now, come on, come on! You look so funny with a solemn face.

LEPORELLO
What *are* you doing *here?*

DON GIOVANNI
Come in and I will tell you. (*Leporello climbs over the wall and exchanges hat and cloak with Don Giovanni.*) A lot of the adventures that have happened to me since last I saw you, I must leave for the moment. But there is one that will amuse you, I know.

LEPORELLO
A new young lady?

DON GIOVANNI
Exactly! Such a nice morsel! She was walking along all by herself when I saw her. I turned and followed. I tried to take her hand. She started running. When I spoke, though, she halted, mistaking me for . . . Can you guess?

LEPORELLO
No, I can't!

DON GIOVANNI
For Leporello!

LEPORELLO
For me?

DON GIOVANNI
For you.

LEPORELLO
How funny!

DON GIOVANNI
With a cry of delight she took *my* hand.

LEPORELLO
I'll die of laughing.

DON GIOVANNI
She embraced me. She kissed me. "O dearest Leporello, Leporello, my lover!" Of course, I knew then she was one of your dainties.

LEPORELLO
No, this is too much.

DON GIOVANNI
Things were going so nicely but then, somehow, she recognized me and screamed. People heard her. It was time to be moving so, quick as lightning, I jumped a wall and landed in this graveyard.

LEPORELLO
And you tell me this story as if it were amusing?

DON GIOVANNI
And why not?

LEPORELLO
But she might be the girl I mean to marry.

(*The moon breaks through the clouds and floods the statue of the Commendatore with ghostly light.*)

DON GIOVANNI
So she might be!
(*laughs loudly*)

STATUE
Your laughter will not last, even till morning.

DON GIOVANNI
Who could that be?

LEPORELLO
Ah, some spirit from the world of the departed, where they know all about you.

GIOVANNI

Taci, sciocco! Chi va la?

COMMENDATORE

Ribaldo, audace!
Lascia ai morti la pace.

LEPORELLO

Ve l'ho detto.

GIOVANNI

Sarà qualcun di fuori,
Che si burla di noi.

(Con indifferenza e sprezzo).

Ehi! Del Commendatore
Non e questa la statua? Leggi un poco
Quell'iscrizion.

LEPORELLO

Scusate:
Non ho imparato a leggere
A raggi della luce.

GIOVANNI

Leggi, dico!

LEPORELLO (legge).

'Dell'empio, che mi trasse al passo
    estremo,
'Qui attendo la vendetta.'
Udiste! Io tremo!

GIOVANNI

O' vecchio buffonissimo
Digli che questa sera
L'attendo a cena meco.

LEPORELLO

Che pazzia!
Vi par! Oh, Dei! mirate
Che terribil occhiate
Egli ci da! Par vivo—par che senta—
E che voglia parlar.

GIOVANNI

Orsù va là
O qui t'ammazzo! E poi ti seppellisco!

LEPORELLO

Piano, piano, signore—ora ubbidisco.

DUETTO

LEPORELLO

O, statua gentilissima
Del gran Commendatore—
Padron, mi trema il core;
Non posso terminar.

GIOVANNI

Finiscila, o nel petto
Ti metto questo acciar.

LEPORELLO (a parte).

Che impiccio! Che capriccio!
Io sentomi gelar!

GIOVANNI (a parte).

Che gusto, che spassetto!
Lo voglio far tremar.

LEPORELLO

O, statua gentilissima,
Benchè di marmo siate—
Ah, padron mio! mirate
Che seguita a guardar.

GIOVANNI

Mori, mori!

LEPORELLO

No, attendete!

(alla Statua)

Signore, il padron mio—
Badate ben, non io—
Ah! ah! che scena è questa!
Oh, Ciel! chinò la testa!

GIOVANNI

Va là che sei un buffone—

LEPORELLO

Guardate ancor, padrone.

DON GIOVANNI

Stop it, idiot! Who goes there? Who goes there?

(*puts his hand to his sword, looks about among the tombs and strikes at some of the statues*)

STATUE

Remember, remember, that the dead still remember.

LEPORELLO

Who's the idiot?

DON GIOVANNI

It's only someone outside who is trying to fool us. (*with indifference and disdain*) Well, the Commendatore makes a beautiful statue. Can you read the words on the base?

LEPORELLO

Excuse me! I haven't got the spectacles I wear for moonlight reading.

DON GIOVANNI (*touching his sword*)

Go on! Read them!

LEPORELLO

(*reading the shining inscription*)

Struck down by an assassin . . . I lie, believing . . . that Heaven will avenge me. (*recoils terror-stricken*) You hear that? I'm frightened!

DON GIOVANNI

An admirable sentiment. Ask the Commendatore if he can come to supper.

LEPORELLO

I will *not*. (*The inscription grows dim.*) Are you mad? O God, he's watching. Look how stern and angrily he glares. He follows what we're saying. Suppose he were to speak!

DON GIOVANNI

(*with hand on sword*)

How would you like . . . to lose your head or be chopped in little pieces?

LEPORELLO

While I live, I will do as Master pleases.

Duet

LEPORELLO (*to the Commendatore*)

O most illustrious monumento our Commendatore . . . (*to Don Giovanni*) I daren't. It makes me shudder . . . I can't and I won't, I won't go on.

DON GIOVANNI

O yes, you will. Would you rather . . . I prodded you with this?

LEPORELLO (*aside*)

He's mad and getting madder. I'm frozen stiff with fright.

DON GIOVANNI (*aside*)

He quivers like a jelly. I shan't forget this night.

LEPORELLO (*to the statue*)

O statue most illustrious of marble veneràble
(*starting back*) O dear God! Heaven save us! O master, look, master! The eyes begin to glow with an unearthly light.

DON GIOVANNI

(*advances menacingly*)

Shall I prod you?

LEPORELLO

No, please . . . please wait a moment. I'll continue.
(*going back*) My Lord . . . my master bids you
(My master bids, not I, sir,)
to sup with him tonight.
(*The Statue nods its head.*)
Ah! I swear he nodded. As if . . . he had accepted.

DON GIOVANNI

(*not looking at him*)

Oh, pull yourself together. Stop being so ridiculous, You're talking silly nonsense.

LEPORELLO

But watch it. Look, master, and you will see what I saw.

GIOVANNI

E che deggio guardar?

LEPORELLO

Colla marmorea testa
Ei fa così così.

GIOVANNI

Parlate, se potete,
Verrete a cena?

COMMENDATORE

Sì!

LEPORELLO

Mover mi posso appena!
Mi manca, oh Dei, la lena!
Per carità partiamo:
Andiamo via di quà!

GIOVANNI

Bizzarra è inver la scena—

GIOVANNI

Verrà il buon vecchio a cena
A prepararla andiamo,
Partiamo via di quà.

(Partono).

SCENA IV

Camera

Donna ANNA; Don OTTAVIO

OTTAVIO

Calmatevi, idol mio, di quel ribaldo
Vedrem puniti in breve i gravi eccessi,
Vendicati sarem.

ANNA

Ma il padre, oh Dio!

OTTAVIO

Convien chinar il ciglio
Al volere del Ciel. Respira, o cara,
Di tua perdita amara
Fia domani, se vuoi, dolce compenso,
Questo cor, questa mano,
Ch'il mio tenero amor!

ANNA

Oh, Dei! che dite,
In sì tristi momenti?

OTTAVIO

E che vorresti
Con indugi novelli
Accrescer le mie pene?
Crudel!

ANNA

Crudele! Ah no!
Mio ben, troppo mi spiace
Allontanarti un ben che lungamente
La nostr'alma desia. Ma il mondo! Oh
    Dio!
Non sedur la costanza
Del sensibil mio core
Abbastanza per te mi parla amore

ARIA

Non mi dir bell'idol mio,
Che son io crudel con te;
Tu ben sai quant'io t'amai,
Tu conosci la mia fè.
Calma, calma il tuo tormento!
Se di duol non vuoi ch'io mora
Forse un giorno il Cielo ancora
Sentirà pietà di me.

(Parte).

OTTAVIO

Ah, si segua il suo passo,
Io vo con lei dividere i martiri:
Saran meco men gravi i suoi sospiri.

(Parte).

DON GIOVANNI

To see cold marble move is not a sight
that I would miss.

DON GIOVANNI AND LEPORELLO

Marble or not, it nodded. It moved . . .
(*Leporello imitates the Statue. The
Statue bends its head. Don Giovanni
sees the Statue move.*) like this . . .
like this.

DON GIOVANNI (*to the Statue*)

Speak up, sir! I can't hear you. Have
you accepted my invitation?

STATUE (*inclining its head*)

Yes!

DON GIOVANNI

Was ever such a meeting.
Who saw a statue of marble eating?

LEPORELLO

Oh how my heart is beating.
Prevent, O God, this meeting! What
shall I do?

DON GIOVANNI

Come, we must go this moment
And hurry to make ready to greet our
worthy guest.
Prepare, get ready to greet our worthy
guest.

LEPORELLO

Then tell me. I hope that you can tell
me.
What *am* I to make ready, what am *I*
to serve your guest?

(*Exeunt.*)

SCENE IV

(*A room. The moon is shining through
the casement.*)

DON OTTAVIO

Be comforted, my dearest, for very soon
the long arm of Justice will reach
out to take him and your wrong be
avenged.

DONNA ANNA

But father! Poor father!

DON OTTAVIO

Whatever be our portion, we must bow
to God's will. O hear me, beloved,
and deny me no longer. Will you be
my own wife, wed me tomorrow, for
I love, I adore you with my body
and soul.

DONNA ANNA

For shame! Profane not a time sacred
to sorrow.

DON OTTAVIO

For shame! How long will you continue
to mock me? How long will you
abuse me, disdain me?

Recitative and Aria

DONNA ANNA

Disdain you? Hear me, my dearest!
None can foretell what the rising sun
may bring, a day of sorrow or a day
of rejoicing. But hear me! Remember, when the jealous misgivings of
a lover beset you, all the stars shall
fall down ere I forget you.

Let yonder moon, chaste eye of Heaven,
Cool desire and calm your soul;
May the bright stars their patience
lend you,
As their constellations roll,
Turn, turn, turn about the Pole.
Far, too far they seem from our dying,
Cold, we call them, to our sighing;
We, too proud, too evil-minded,
By sin are blinded.

See how bright the moon shines
yonder,
Silent witness to all our wrong:
Ah! but hearken! O blessed wonder!
Out of silence comes a music,
And I can hear her song.

*God will surely, surely wipe away thy
tears, my daughter;
On thy dark, His light shall break.
God is watching thee, hath not
forgotten thee,
On thy dark His light shall break.*

On my dark, His light shall break,
God will heed me, sustain me, console
me.
On my dark His light shall break.

(*Exit.*)

Recitative

DON OTTAVIO

Ah! The heavens have spoken!
That sacred harmony seemed to me a
token,
A sweet promise of marriage, not to be
broken.

(*Exit.*)

SCENA V

*Gran Sala, illuminata, con Tavola
imbandita.*

Don GIOVANNI, LEPORELLO

FINALE

GIOVANNI

Già la mensa è preparata—
Voi suonate, amici cari;
Già che spendo i miei danari,
Io mi voglio divertir
Leporello, presto in tavola.

LEPORELLO

Son prontissimo a servir.

GIOVANNI

Che ti par del bel concerto?

LEPORELLO

É conforme al vostro merto.

GIOVANNI

Ah che piatto saporito!

LEPORELLO

Ah che barbaro appetito!
Che bocconi di gigante.
Mi par proprio di svenir.

GIOVANNI

Nel veder i miei bocconi
Gli par proprio di svenir
Piatto!

LEPORELLO

Servo,
'Fra i due Litiganti!'

GIOVANNI

Versa il vino.

(*Beve*).

Eccellente marsimino!

LEPORELLO (*a parte*).

Questo pezzo di fagiano,
Piano piano vò inghiottir.

GIOVANNI

Sta mangiando quel marrano!
Fingerò di non capir.

LEPORELLO

(*udendo ancora la musica*).

Questa poi la conosco pur troppo!.

GIOVANNI

Leporello!

LEPORELLO

Padron mio!

GIOVANNI

Parla schietto, mascalzone—

LEPORELLO

Non mi lascia una flussione
Le parole preferir.

GIOVANNI

Mentre io mangio, fischia un poco.

LEPORELLO

Non so far.

GIOVANNI

Cos'è?

LEPORELLO

Scusate!
Sì eccellente è il vostro cuoco,
Che lo volli anch'io provar—

GIOVANNI

Si eccellente è il cuoco mio,
Che lo volle anch'ei provar.

SCENE V

(*A lighted hall. The table is prepared for a banquet.*)

Finale

DON GIOVANNI (*to the musicians of his private band*)

Come, my friends, strike up a measure!
Who would count the cost of pleasure?
We have all the night before us:
Let us hear how you can play.

(*to Leporello*)

Leporello! serve immediately.

LEPORELLO

Coming, sir, without delay.

(*The musicians begin the first piece, a melody from* Martin's Una Cosa rara.)

LEPORELLO

Martin . . . *Cosa rara*

DON GIOVANNI
(*eating; to Leporello*)

Don't you think these fellows play well?

LEPORELLO

So they should; they know you pay well.

DON GIOVANNI

Ah, how perfectly delicious!

LEPORELLO (*aside*)

All his appetites are vicious.
I can hardly bear to watch him,
Watch him guzzling in that way.

DON GIOVANNI (*aside*)

How he watches every mouthful.
He would like some, I dare say.
Serve me!

(*The musicians begin the second piece, from* Sarti's Fra i due litiganti il terzo gode.)

LEPORELLO

Here, sir.
From Sarti's *I Litiganti*.

DON GIOVANNI

Pour the claret.
Wine and women both are pleasant.

(*Leporello changes Don Giovanni's plate.*)

LEPORELLO (*aside*)

Why should he have all this pheasant?
Just one tiny tiny tiny tiny bit for me!

DON GIOVANNI (*aside*)

Stealing tidbits like a peasant.
Thinking that I cannot see.

(*The musicians begin to play a melody from* Mozart's Figaro.)

LEPORELLO

Figaro, that is *so* over-rated!

DON GIOVANNI
(*without looking at him*)

Leporello!

LEPORELLO (*with his mouth full*)

At your service.

DON GIOVANNI

Speak more clearly,
I can't hear you.

LEPORELLO (*clearing his throat*)

I have caught a cold, I think, sir.
For I'm hoarse, as hoarse can be.

DON GIOVANNI

While I'm eating, whistle something!

LEPORELLO

But I can't.

DON GIOVANNI
(*looking towards him*)

You can't?

LEPORELLO

(*aside*) He's caught me!
(*to Don Giovanni*) Now look, sir.
You have often praised your cook, sir,
So I wanted to sample his cooking,
And I took the liberty.

DON GIOVANNI

You believed that I wasn't looking
So you took the liberty.

Donna ELVIRA. *E detti.*
ELVIRA (*a Don* GIOVANNI).

L'ultima prova
Dell'amor mio
Ancor vogl'io
Fare con te:

(*s'inginocchia*).

Più non rammento
Gl'inganni tuoi,
Pietate io sento—

GIOVANNI E LEPORELLO (*a parte*).

Cos'è? cos'è?

ELVIRA

Da te non chiede
Quest'alma oppressa
Della sua fede
Qualche mercè.

GIOVANNI

Mi maraviglio?
Cosa volete.
Se non sorgete—
Non resto in piè.

ELVIRA

Ah, non deridere
Gli affanni miei!

GIOVANNI

Io ti derido!
Cielo! Perchè?

LEPORELLO

Quasi da piangere
Mi fa costei!

GIOVANNI

Che vuoi, mio bene?

ELVIRA

Che vita cangi!

GIOVANNI

Brava!

ELVIRA

Cor perfido!

GIOVANNI

Lascia ch'io mangi;
E se ti piace,
Mangia con me.

ELVIRA

Rimanti, barbaro,
Nel lezzo immondo,
Esempio orribile
D'iniquità.

LEPORELLO (*a parte*).

Sen non si muove
Al suo dolore,
Di sasso ha il core—
O cor non ha.

GIOVANNI

Vivan le femmine!
Viva il buon vino!
Sostegno e gloria
D'umanità.

ELVIRA (*partendo*).
Ah!
(*Parte*).

LEPORELLO

Were you looking?
Yes, I took the liberty.

(*The musicians finish the music. Exeunt
all servants but Leporello.*)

DONNA ELVIRA
(*rushes in distractedly*)

Dreams of disaster,
Visions of horror,
Drive me to seek you,
Lover untrue:
Not to reproach you,
Not for my own sake
Am I come hither,
I've come to warn you . . .

DON GIOVANNI (*rising and dismissing
the players with a sign*)

To warn? Of what?

LEPORELLO

To warn? Of what?

DONNA ELVIRA (*kneeling*)

Hear, I implore you,
One who adored you,
For your immortal
Soul I sue.

(*The distant thunder of an approaching storm is heard.*)

DON GIOVANNI (*trying to raise her*)

Why this recumbent,
Pious position?
Is it becoming?
If you prefer it,
I will kneel too.

(*He kneels.*)

DONNA ELVIRA

Ah, do not mock at my
Dread premonition!
Ah, do not mock at me!

(*He gets up and raises her.*)

DON GIOVANNI

Why should I mock at you?
(*with affected tenderness*)

Dear, it's not true.

LEPORELLO

My eyes are watering
For this poor lady!

DON GIOVANNI

My love, what is it?

DONNA ELVIRA

Beware God's anger!

DON GIOVANNI

Bravo!

DONNA ELVIRA

Beware of it!

LEPORELLO

Beware of it!

DON GIOVANNI
(*turning towards the table*)

After the brandy,
Not while I'm eating:

(*seats himself at the table again, and
begins to eat*)

If you feel hungry,
Then come and eat too.

DONNA ELVIRA (*with disdain*)

Lost, then eternally,
Wallow in lewdness,
Flaunt your iniquity,
Roll in your sty!

DON GIOVANNI
(*recklessly, raising his glass*)

Honour and glory to
Song, Wine and Women!
May I enjoy them all
Until I die.
Long may I honor them,
Song, Wine and Women.

LEPORELLO

Cold must that man be,
Heartless as marble,
Who without pity
Mocks her cry.
How cold he must be,
So heartlessly to mock her cry.

DONNA ELVIRA (*going out the middle
door she recoils, terrified*)

Ah!

DON GIOVANNI AND LEPORELLO

That cry was not in anger.
What scared her so, I wonder?

GIOVANNI

Che grido è questo mai?
Va a veder che cos'è stato.

LEPORELLO

Ah!
(*Sorte* LEPORELLO, *e ritorna
spaventato*).

GIOVANNI

Che grido indiavolato?
Leporello, che cos'è?

LEPORELLO

Ah, signor, per carità,
Non andate fuor di quà!
L'uom di sasso, l'uomo bianco—
Ah, padrone, io gelo, io manco!
Se vedeste che figura.
Se sentiste come fa—
Ta, ta, ta, ta!

GIOVANNI

Non capisco niente affatto.

LEPORELLO

Ta, ta, ta, ta!

GIOVANNI

Tu sei matto in verità.

LEPORELLO

Ah, sentite!

GIOVANNI

Qualcun batte:
Apri!

LEPORELLO

Io tremo!

GIOVANNI

Apri, dico!

LEPORELLO

Ah, Ah!

GIOVANNI

Apri!

LEPORELLO

Ah, Ah!

GIOVANNI

Matto!
Per togliermi d'intrico
Ad aprir io stesso andrò!

(*Parte*).

LEPORELLO

Non vò più veder l'amico,
Pian pianin m'asconderò.—

(*Si nasconde sotto la tavola*).
Il COMMENDATORE. *E detti.*

COMMENDATORE

Don Giovanni, a cenar teco
M'invitasti—e son venuto!

GIOVANNI

Non l'avrei giammai creduto;
Ma farò quel che potrò.
Leporello, un'altra cena
Fa che subito si porti.

LEPORELLO

Ah, padron, siam tutti morti!

COMMENDATORE

Ferma un pò!
Non si pasce di cibo mortale
Chi si pasce di cibo celeste;
Altre cure più gravi di queste—
Altra brama quaggiù mi guidò!

LEPORELLO

La terzana d'avere mi sembra,
E le membra fermar più non so!

GIOVANNI

Parla dunque—che chiedi? Che vuoi?

COMMENDATORE

Parlo, ascolta! Più tempo non ho!

GIOVANNI

Parla, parla! Ascoltandoti sto.

DON GIOVANNI (*to Leporello*)

Run and see, run and see what is the
   matter.

(*Leporello goes, and when off the stage
   cries out.*)

LEPORELLO

Ah!

DON GIOVANNI

What *can* be going on there?
Leporello, are you mad?
Why that look? Why that yell?

(*Leporello returns dismayed and shuts
   the door.*)

LEPORELLO

Ah . . . O God . . . Keep him away . . .
Don't go near that door I say . . .
Slowly, surely, he draws nearer
He . . . the statue . . . of marble . . .
   who nodded.
I could see him in the moonlight . . .
I could hear each marble shoe.
Ta. Ta. Ta. Ta.

DON GIOVANNI

Never have I heard such nonsense!

LEPORELLO

Ta. Ta. Ta. Ta.

DON GIOVANNI

I shall soon go crazy too.
(*Knocking is heard at the door.*)

LEPORELLO

There, now. Listen!

DON GIOVANNI

Someone's knocking. Answer.

LEPORELLO (*trembling*)

O master!

DON GIOVANNI

Did you hear me?

LEPORELLO (*kneeling*)

No!

DON GIOVANNI

Answer!

LEPORELLO

No!

DON GIOVANNI

Idiot! Come, pull yourself together,
While I see myself who's there, who's
   standing there.
(*takes a light and goes to open the
   door*)

LEPORELLO

(*trembling, aside*)

When I've pulled myself together
I shall crawl over there.

(*Don Giovanni opens the door. Leporello hides under the table. The ghost
   of the Commendatore appears as a
   marble statue.*)

STATUE

Don Giovanni, I gave my promise
When invited, to share your table.

DON GIOVANNI

(*striving to collect himself*)

Who would ever have believed it!
I must do the best I can.
Leporello, look alive, man.
Set a second cover quickly!

LEPORELLO (*puts his head
   from under the table*)

O I daren't. I know he'll kill us.

DON GIOVANNI

Did you hear me?

(*Leporello rises as if to obey.*)

STATUE

Stay where you are!

(*Don Giovanni starts; Leporello re-
   treats to back.*)

Those who take of the bread
   everlasting
Need no temporal substance to feed
   them.
Not for feasting have I now descended,
Graver reasons have called me to earth.

DON GIOVANNI

Well, what are they? Your reasons?
Continue.

LEPORELLO

Like a man who is sick of a fever,
All my limbs do is tremble and shake.

STATUE

Mark well my message for short is your
   time.

DON GIOVANNI

Speak your message for short is my
   time.

COMMENDATORE

Tu m'invitasti a cena,
Il tuo dover or sai!
Rispondimi: verrai
Tu a cenar meco!

LEPORELLO

Oibò! oibò! tempo non ha—scusate.

GIOVANNI

A torto di viltate
Tacciato mai sarò.

COMMENDATORE

Risolvi!

GIOVANNI

Ho già risolto.

COMMENDATORE

Verrai?

LEPORELLO

Dite di no!

GIOVANNI

Ho fermo il core in petto;
Non ho timor: verrò!

COMMENDATORE

Dammi la mano in pegno!

GIOVANNI

Eccola. Ohimè,
Che gelo è questo mai!

COMMENDATORE

Pentiti, cangia vita.
É l'ultimo momento!

GIOVANNI

No, no—ch'io non mi pento,
Vanne lontan da me!

COMMENDATORE

Pentiti! Scellerato!

GIOVANNI

No, vecchio infatuato!

COMMENDATORE

Ah, tempo più non v'è:

(Parte).

GIOVANNI (disperato).

Da qual tremore insolito
Sento assalir gli spiriti
Dond'escono que vortici
Di foco pien d'orror?

CORO

Tutto a tue colpe è poco,
Vieni, c'è un mal peggior!

GIOVANNI

Chi l'anima mi lacera,—
Chi m'agita le viscere!
Che strazio ohimè! Che smania
Che inferno! Che terror!

LEPORELLO

Che ceffo disperato!
Che gesti di dannato!
Che gridi! che lamenti
Come mi fa terror!

CORO

Tutto a tue colpe è poco,
Vieni, v'è mal peggior!

Ultima Scena

ELVIRA, ZERLINA, OTTAVIO, MASETTO

Ah, dov'è il perfido?
Dov'è l'indegno?
Tutto il mio sdegno sfogar io vo!

STATUE

He whom you have invited
Brings you this invitation.
So answer me!
Will you sit down at his table?

LEPORELLO
(standing far off, trembling)
No, don't; tell him you have no time
now.

DON GIOVANNI
(calmly and coldly)
No man has called me coward
And shall not while I live.

STATUE

Decide, then!

DON GIOVANNI *(impatiently)*
I have decided.

STATUE

You'll come, then?

LEPORELLO
Tell him you won't!

DON GIOVANNI
No man shall call me coward.
I feel no fear. I will.

STATUE
(offering his left hand)
Give me your hand and swear it.

DON GIOVANNI
(gives his right hand)
Certainly . . . *(with a cry of horror)*
let go!

STATUE
Afraid?

DON GIOVANNI
I feel a deadly cold.

STATUE
Kneel and pray God for pardon.
His mercy still can save you.

DON GIOVANNI
(vainly tries to free himself)
Let dotards talk of kneeling.
God is a fairy tale.

STATUE
Kneel, pray to God for pardon!

DON GIOVANNI
I scorn him, I defy Him!

STATUE

Pray to Him!

DON GIOVANNI
No!

STATUE
Pray!

DON GIOVANNI
No!

STATUE
Pray! Pray!

DON GIOVANNI
No! No! *(wresting his hand away with
a terrible cry)*

STATUE

Your hour of doom is come. *(Exit.)*

*(Flames appear in all directions. The
earth trembles.)*

DON GIOVANNI *(in desperation)*

Fingers of terror clutch at me,
Horrible faces grin at me,
A chasm yawns to swallow me,
A gulf of blazing fire.
Despair commands me utterly,
My bowels melt in agony,
Undying pains await me,
In darkness, ice and fire.
Ah, the darkness! ah the fire!
Ah!

LEPORELLO

Too late, in desperation
He sees his own damnation,
The house of lamentation,
Darkness and lakes of fire, red lakes of
fire.
Ah!

CHORUS *(from below)*

Worse pains than these await thee;
Enter th'undying fire.
Enter! Enter!

*(The flames increase and engulf Don
Giovanni.)*

DONNA ELVIRA, ZERLINA, DON OTTAVIO
AND MASETTO

*(All enter, accompanied by ministers
of justice.)*

Where is the wicked one?
Where is he hiding?
We come for vengeance,
Now he shall pay,
At last shall pay.

DONNA ANNA

Solo mirandolo stretto in catene
Alle mie pene calma darò.

LEPORELLO

Più non sperate di ritrovarlo,
Più non cercate, lontano andò.

I DETTI

Cos'è? Favella!
Via presto, sbrigati!

LEPORELLO

Venne un colosso,
Ma se non posso—

I DETTI

Presto favella, sbrigati!

LEPORELLO

Tra fumo e fuoco—
Badate un poco—
L'uomo di sasso—
Fermate il passo—
Giusto là sotto—
Diede il gran botto—
Giusto là il diavolo
Se'l tranguigiò.

I DETTI

Stelle! Che sento!

LEPORELLO

Vero è l'evento!

I DETTI

Ah, certo è l'ombra
Che l'incontrò.

DON OCTAVIO

Or che tutti, o mio tesoro,
Vendicati siam dal cielo,
Porgi a me un ristoro,
Non mi far languire ancor.

DONNA ANNA

Lascia o caro, un anno ancora
Allo sfogo del mio cor.

OCTAVIO E ANNA

Al desio di chi m'adora (t'adora)
Ceder deve un fido amor.

DONNA ELVIRA

Io men vado in un ritiro,
A finir la vita mia!

ZERLIA, MASETTO

Noi, Masetto a casa andiamo
A cenar in compagnia.

LEPORELLO

Ed io vado all' osteria
A trovar padron miglior.

ZERLINA, MASETTO, LEPORELLO

Resti dunque quel birbon
Con Prosperpina e Pluton!

DONNA ANNA

O for the sight of him
Locked in a dungeon!
That would my sorrow
Somewhat allay.

LEPORELLO

(*appears pale and trembling*)

Seek him no longer,
You will not find him,
It is too late now,
He's far away,
Yes, far away.

**DONNA ANNA, DONNA ELVIRA, ZERLINA,
DON OTTAVIO AND MASETTO**

We come for vengeance.
Where is he hidden?
Come, tell us, out with it!

LEPORELLO

There came a giant . . .
All made of marble.
Yes, made of marble.
See how I shudder.
As I was saying
Came through that doorway,
Seized on my master,
Seized him and held him.
Fire and smoke came
Out of the ground and . . .
Down went my master and vanished
  below.

**DONNA ANNA, DONNA ELVIRA,
DON OTTAVIO AND MASETTO**

Ah! That explains it!

LEPORELLO

That is what happened.

DONNA ANNA

Ah! 'twas the ghost who sent him
  below.
I saw it,
I saw the ghost who sent him below.

DONNA ELVIRA

I saw the ghost who sent him below
Ah, 'twas the ghost who sent him
  below.
I saw it!

ZERLINA

I saw it also.
Ah! 'twas the ghost who sent him
  below.
I saw it!
I saw the ghost who sent him below.

DON OTTAVIO

I saw it also.
Ah! 'twas the ghost who sent him
  below.
I saw it!
It sent him below.

MASETTO

Ah, 'twas the ghost. Ah, the ghost who
  sent him below.
I saw it.
I saw the ghost who sent him below.

DON OTTAVIO (*to Donna Anna*)

Now that Heaven has taken vengeance,
Turn to gladness, leave your sorrow,
O remember the one who loves you,
Dearest heart, be not unkind.

DONNA ANNA

Let me, dearest, for one year longer
Keep my father's death in mind,
Then, but then, I'll prove, I swear it,
(*giving Don Ottavio her hand*)
Ever faithful, ever kind.

DON OTTAVIO

Then, but then, you'll prove, O swear
  it,
Ever faithful, ever kind.

DONNA ELVIRA

(*to Donna Anna and Don Ottavio*)
I will hide me in a cloister,
There to fast and pray and ponder.

ZERLINA AND MASETTO

Happy, hand in hand, Masetto,
(Zerlina,)
Home together let us wander.

LEPORELLO

May I presently in yonder
Inn a better master find.

ZERLINA, MASETTO AND LEPORELLO

Leave the rascal lying, then,
Safely shut in Pluto's den.

E noi tutti o buona gente
Ripetiam allegramente
L'antichissima canzon:

TUTTI

Questo è il fin di chi fa mal.
E de' perfidi la morte
Alla vita è sempre ugual.

And, to banish melancholy,
Sing, good people, all be jolly,
Sing the old, old song again.

DONNA ANNA, DONNA ELVIRA,
ZERLINA, DON OTTAVIO, MASETTO
AND LEPORELLO

So do all deceivers end, deceivers end,
So they end, all deceivers end.

So do all wrong-doers end,
Wrong-doers end, wrong-doers end.
Rakes, betrayers, all take warning
While there's time (while there's
    time) still your ways to mend,
Your ways to mend.
Mend your ways.

Così fan Tutte

(1790)

OPERA IN TWO ACTS

Libretto by LORENZO DA PONTE

English Version by RUTH AND THOMAS MARTIN

THIS ENGLISH VERSION WAS FIRST PERFORMED BY THE METRO-
POLITAN OPERA COMPANY IN NEW YORK ON DECEMBER 28, 1951.

INTRODUCTION

Towards the end of 1789 — two years before his death — Mozart was, as usual during this period of his career, in dire financial straits. On December 29 he wrote to his friend and fellow-Mason, Michael Puchberg, "According to the present arrangement I am to receive from the management next month 200 ducats for my opera. If you can and will lend me 400 gulden until then, you will be rescuing your friend from the greatest embarrassment . . . I invite you, you alone, to come on Thursday at 10 o'clock in the morning to hear a short rehearsal of my opera. I am only inviting Haydn and yourself." The obliging Puchberg, who had already answered several appeals of this sort from his friend, sent 300 gulden.[1] (A gulden was worth about 45 cents and a ducat about two dollars; Mozart was therefore to be paid approximately $400 for his work.)

The opera in question was *Così fan tutte, osia la scuola degli amanti (Women Are Like That, or The School for Lovers)*. Mozart had been since 1787 official composer to the Imperial Court at Vienna, at a salary of 800 gulden a year, but had been given little to do besides writing dances. A successful revival of *The Marriage of Figaro* in Vienna in 1789 (it was given twelve times from August to November), however, had impressed the music-loving Emperor Joseph II, and Mozart was commissioned to write a new opera. He set to work immediately and completed the music in January 1790.

While the libretto for *Figaro* was derived from a play by Beaumarchais and that for *Don Giovanni* from an opera by Bertati and Gazzaniga and other sources, the plot of *Così fan tutte* seems to have been invented by da Ponte. The statement, found in many books on Mozart, that this plot was built, at the request of the Emperor, around an actual occurrence is based on nothing more than a rumor reported many years after the première.

Così fan tutte was performed for the first time on January 26, 1790, at the Burgtheater in Vienna with the following cast:

Fiordiligi	Adriana Ferraresi del Bene
Dorabella	Louise Villeneuve
Guglielmo	Francesco Benucci
Ferrando	Vincenzo Calvesi
Despina	Mme. Bussani
Don Alfonso	Francesco Bussani

As usual, Mozart was thoroughly familiar with the capabilities of the singers for whom he wrote. He had no high opinion of Mme. Ferraresi's powers, but she was the current mistress of da Ponte, and Mozart, probably to oblige his friend, had composed two concert arias for her (K. 577, 579). For Louise

[1] Emily Anderson, *Letters of Mozart and His Family*, London, 1938, III, 1391.

Villeneuve, Mme. Ferraresi's sister in real life as well as in the opera, Mozart had written three concert arias (K. 578, 582, 583). Calvesi had sung the tenor part of a vocal quartet (K. 479) and trio (K. 480) composed by Mozart in 1785. Benucci had created the role of Figaro and Bussani those of Bartolo and Antonio; and both men had also sung in the first Vienna performance of *Don Giovanni* (Leporello and Commendatore-Masetto, respectively). Mme. Bussani had been the first Cherubino.

The opera seems to have been fairly successful at first. Even Count von Zinzendorf, who had found *Figaro* a bore, thought "Mozart's music charming and the subject very amusing." After five performances the theater was closed for two months because of the death of Joseph II (February 20). When it was reopened, *Così fan tutte* was given five times more and then was dropped. But the following year it was performed in German at Frankfurt and Mainz and in Italian at Prague, Leipzig, and Dresden; and after Mozart's death it spread beyond Central Europe. Strangely enough, the first New York performance does not seem to have taken place until 1922.

For some peculiar reason, many 19th-century critics who did not balk at the most far-fetched coincidences in opera librettos, at the most absurd and obscure plot-convolutions, at singing dragons and informative birds, found da Ponte's plot unrealistic. What bothered these writers in the age of Romanticism even more was what they considered a flippant attitude towards love in his libretto. Many attempts to "improve" it were made, and Mozart's music was mauled and distorted to fit more edifying tales. The work was performed with an entirely new libretto at Copenhagen in 1826; two years later Mozart's opera was given in London as *Tit for Tat or The Tables Turned,* with the music "arranged" by one W. Hawes; in Paris in 1863 it turned up as *Peines d'Amour perdues,* with a text based on Shakespeare's *Love's Labour's Lost;* and as late as 1909 it appeared in Dresden as *Die Dame Kobold,* with a libretto taken from a comedy by Calderon.

The charges of incredibility and an irreverent attitude towards love are of course wholly beside the point. Mozart and da Ponte were not dealing here with recognizable human figures, as in *Figaro,* or with the creation of flesh-and-blood characters out of universal types, as in *Don Giovanni.* They were engaged in telling an amusing tale, for which a small group of stock characters was perfectly adequate. And even some of these come alive. Don Alfonso and Despina are as "real" as any characters in opera, and Fiordiligi is far from a puppet. The truth, as it seems to us, about the matter was seen as early as 1805 by a writer in a Berlin musical periodical.

> The theme of this opera [he wrote] was a satire on the highly praised fidelity of the female sex and an innocent playing with the sanctity of love. That this evidence of the infidelity of all women was regarded merely as a jest is precisely the delicate charm of the whole opera, and that this infidelity, on the other hand, is let off so easily is proof of the playful sense of beauty on the part of the composer. Everything is only masquerade, playfulness, jest, dallying, and irony . . . Mozart was not at all serious about the serious moments that crop up now and then; they served him merely as a means of

shaping the form and, one might say, of darkening, of shading the prank; even though one cannot deny that he let himself go too much in such passages, as if they had, in the process of working on them, grown in spite of himself. They should have been there merely as contrasts, to be treated, like some of the asides, not without irony. [2]

Certain it is that Mozart lavished on this work some of his most delightful music, his most exquisite craftsmanship. If some of the arias are not perhaps as telling as the best in his other mature operas, they are outnumbered by the ensembles, which are wonderfully varied in style and construction. The orchestration is Mozart at his most sparkling — in other words, the finest to be found in 18th-century music. Occasionally a mock-serious piece, aping the style of the lamenting or heroic aria of the *opera seria,* underscores the gentle irony of the work. The sly humor extends even into the Overture, which unlike that to *Figaro,* employs several themes from the opera. A subtle touch is the appearance here, as a tailpiece to one of the themes, of a jolly figure sung by Basilio in *Figaro* (Act I, No. 7) to the words "così fan tutte le belle." It is difficult to see why *Così fan tutte* has not always been accepted, and especially in our times, for what it is — a musical lark that is one of the gems of *opera buffa.*

[2] Quoted in Otto Jahn, *W. A. Mozart,* Leipzig, IV, 1859, 497.

CAST OF CHARACTERS

FIORDILIGI . . . . *Soprano*

DORABELLA . . . . *Mezzo-Soprano*

GUGLIELMO, officer, betrothed to Fiordiligi . . . . *Tenor*

FERRANDO, officer, betrothed to Dorabella . . . . *Baritone*

DESPINA, chambermaid to Fiordiligi and Dorabella . . . . . . *Soprano*

DON ALFONSO, an old philosopher . . . . *Bass-Baritone*

Soldiers, Servants, Sailors, Wedding-Guests, Townspeople.

PLACE: Naples.

THE PLOT

ACT I.

Don Alfonso, a cynical old philosopher, declares to his young friends Ferrando and Guglielmo that no women can be trusted, including their respective fiancées, the sisters Dorabella and Fiordiligi. Enraged at this slur, they accept his offer to wager 100 sovereigns that he can prove his point in twenty-four hours if they will agree to follow his instructions unquestioningly. Don Alfonso then announces to the two sisters that their sweethearts have been ordered off to the wars. There is a touching scene of farewell and the two officers ostensibly sail off, to the cheers of the villagers. Despina, maid to the sisters, finds them prostrated by their loss and pooh-poohs their lamentations, saying that one man is pretty much like another. To further his scheme Don Alfonso enlists Despina's aid and introduces to her two young and wealthy "Albanians" who are enamored of her mistresses. She does not recognize Ferrando and Guglielmo in their disguise and supports their suit. Fiordiligi and Dorabella are outraged at this intrusion upon their sorrow and angrily order the two foreigners to leave. When the young men pretend to take poison in their despair, the sisters relent somewhat. Despina appears in the disguise of a doctor and revives the "Albanians" by means of a huge magnet. They renew their ardent attack on the young ladies' affections but are again repulsed.

ACT II.

After Despina derides their constancy, the sisters, especially Dorabella, weaken and decide a flirtation will do no harm. Dorabella choose Guglielmo and Fiordiligi Ferrando. As the couples stroll in the garden Guglielmo wins Dorabella's love and gives her a golden locket in return for a picture of Ferrando. Fiordiligi, however, refuses to yield to Ferrando and decides to disguise herself as a man and join her betrothed at the front. But when Ferrando threatens to slay himself, she too gives in. Both Guglielmo and Ferrando are now utterly cast down by the clear evidence of their sweetheart's fickleness; but the triumphant Don Alfonso promises them that he will fix everything. He arranges a ceremony in which Ferrando is to marry Fiordiligi and her sister Guglielmo. In the midst of the ceremony, which is conducted by Despina in the guise of a notary, the military music to which the two officers marched off to war is heard again and it is announced that they have returned. In the confusion Ferando and Guglielmo leave the stage and come back without their disguises, explaining that they had received royal permission to return to the arms of their loved ones. The officers pretend to fly into a rage when they find the marriage contract, the sisters blame Don Alfonso and Despina for leading them astray, their lovers reveal that they were the "Albanians," Guglielmo returns Ferrando's picture to Dorabella and gets his locket back, the sisters are properly chastened, and all ends happily.

COSÌ FAN TUTTE

ATTO PRIMO

SCENA I

No. 1. TERZETTO

FERRANDO

La mia Dorabella
capace non è,
fedel quanto bella
il cielo la fè,

GUGLIELMO

La mia Fiordiligi
tradirmi non sa,
uguale in lei credo
costanza e beltà,

DON ALFONSO

Ho i crini già grigi,
ex cathedra parlo,
ma tali litigi
finiscano quà.

FERRANDO, GUGLIELMO

No, detto ci avete
che infide esser ponno,
provar cel' dovete,
se avete onestà.

DON ALFONSO

Tai prove lasciamo.

FERRANDO, GUGLIELMO

No, no le vogliamo:
o fuori la spada,
rompiam l'amistà.

DON ALFONSO

O pazzo desire!
cercar de scoprire
quel mal che trovato
meschini ci fa.

FERRANDO, GUGLIELMO

Sul vivo mi tocca,
chi lascia di bocca
sortire un accento
che torto le fa.

RECITATIVO

GUGLIELMO

Fuor la spada! sciegliete qual di noi
più vi piace.

DON ALFONSO

Io son uomo di pace, e duelli non fo,
se non a mensa.

FERRANDO

O battervi, o dir subito, perchè d'infedeltà le nostre amanti sospettate
capaci.

DON ALFONSO

Cara semplicità, quanto mi piaci!

FERRANDO

Cessate di scherzar, o giuro al cielo—

DON ALFONSO

Ed io, giuro alla terra, non scherzo,
amici miei: solo saper vorrei che
razza d'animali son queste vostre
belle, se han come tutti noi carne,
ossa, e pelle, se mangian come noi,
se veston gonne, alfin, se dee, se
donne son.

FERRANDO, GUGLIELMO

Son donne: ma son tali, son tali—

DON ALFONSO

E in donne pretendete di trovar fedeltà? Quanto mi piaci mai, semplicità!

No. 2 TERZETTO

DON ALFONSO

È la fede delle femmine
come l'araba Fenice,
che vi sia, ciascun lo dice,
dove sia,
nessun lo sa.

FERRANDO

La fenice è Dorabella.

GUGLIELMO

La fenice è Fiordiligi.

COSÌ FAN TUTTE

ACT ONE

SCENE I

No. 1. Terzet

FERRANDO

To doubt Dorabella is simply absurd,
Completely absurd!
She'll always be faithful and true to
her word!

GUGLIELMO

To doubt Fiordiligi would no more be
right,
Would no more be right,
Than trying to tell you the sun shines
at night!

DON ALFONSO

I'm well over sixty, I speak from experience,
But since you won't heed the advice of
a friend,
At least let us bring this dispute to an
end.

FERRANDO, GUGLIELMO

With no shred of proof you declared
them unfaithful.
An insult like that we could never
ignore.

DON ALFONSO

Don't ask me to prove it.

FERRANDO, GUGLIELMO
(putting their hands on their swords)
That's just what we ask you,
We want satisfaction,
Or else choose your weapon to settle
the score.

DON ALFONSO

You both must be crazy!
I only was trying to save you some
trouble,
And warn you of what is in store.

FERRANDO, GUGLIELMO

I can't take it lightly!
You slander unrightly
The highminded woman I worship,
Admire, and adore.
My honor is slighted,
Our friendship is blighted,
You wounded my pride to the core!

RECITATIVE

GUGLIELMO

Choose your weapon! You'll render us
complete satisfaction.

DON ALFONSO
(calmly)
I'm a peace-loving bachelor, and get
my satisfaction when I'm dining.

FERRANDO

Either fight with me or apologize for
casting all those slurs upon our
sweethearts and their good reputation.

DON ALFONSO

How can you be so blind! You make
me laugh!

FERRANDO

This joke has gone too far! I will not
stand for it!

DON ALFONSO

My friends, I can assure you, I spoke
in bitter earnest. May I ask one
question: what strange, uncommon
species do your lady-loves belong to?
Would you say they are goddesses,
boneless and bloodless, or do they eat
and drink like us poor mortals? Are
they angels or are they women?

FERRANDO, GUGLIELMO

They're women—but what women!

DON ALFONSO

They're women, and faithful? That you
really believe?
Are you so inexperienced, or just naive?

No. 2. Terzet

DON ALFONSO

Woman's famous faith and constancy
Is a myth and fabrication,
Though it makes good conversation,
Who can prove it?
Name me one name!

FERRANDO

I have proof in Dorabella!

GUGLIELMO

I have proof in Fiordiligi!

FERRANDO
Dorabella,

GUGLIELMO
Fiordiligi,

FERRANDO
la fenice è Dorabella.

GUGLIELMO
la fenice è Fiordiligi.

DON ALFONSO
Non è questa, non è quella,
non fu mai, non vi sarà.
E la fede delle femmine
come l'araba fenice!

FERRANDO, GUGLIELMO
La fenice è {Dorabella, Dorabella}
            {Fiordiligi, Fiordiligi}
è la fenice.

DON ALFONSO
Che vi sia, ciascun lo dice.

FERRANDO
Dorabella,

GUGLIELMO
Fiordiligi,

DON ALFONSO
Dove sia,

GUGLIELMO
Fiordiligi,

DON ALFONSO
Dove sia,

FERRANDO
Dorabella,

DON ALFONSO
Nessun lo sa,

FERRANDO
Dorabella,

GUGLIELMO
Fiordiligi.

DON ALFONSO
Nessun lo sa.

RECITATIVO

FERRANDO
Scioccherie di Poeti!

GUGLIELMO
Scempiaggini di vecchi!

DON ALFONSO
Or bene; udite, ma senza andar in
  collera: qual prova avete voi, che
  ognor costanti vi sien le vostre amanti; chi vi fè sicurtà, che invariabili
  sono i lor cori?

FERRANDO
Lunga esperienza—

GUGLIELMO
Nobil educazion—

FERRANDO
Pensar sublime—

GUGLIELMO
Analogia d'umor—

FERRANDO
Disinteresse—

GUGLIELMO
Immutabil carattere—

FERRANDO
Promesse—

GUGLIELMO
Proteste—

FERRANDO
Giuramenti—

DON ALFONSO
Pianti, sospir, carezze, svenimenti.
  Lasciatemi un po' ridere——

FERRANDO
Cospetto! finite di deriderci?

DON ALFONSO
Pian piano: e se toccar can mano oggi
  vi fo che come l'altre sono?

GUGLIELMO
Non si può dar!

FERRANDO
Dorabella!

GUGLIELMO
Fiordiligi!

FERRANDO, GUGLIELMO
No one else but {Dorabella!
{Fiordiligi!

DON ALFONSO
Fiddle-faddle, fiddle-faddle,
You are wrong, they're all the same,
They're all the same.
I repeat that woman's constancy
Is the purest sort of fiction.

FERRANDO, GUGLIELMO
I believe in { Dorabella, } you can't
{ Fiordiligi }
weaken my conviction!

DON ALFONSO
Is that all you have to offer?

FERRANDO
Dorabella!

GUGLIELMO
Fiordiligi!

DON ALFONSO
Are you serious?

GUGLIELMO
Fiordiligi!

DON ALFONSO
Can you prove it?

FERRANDO
Dorabella!

DON ALFONSO
No, no, you can't!

FERRANDO
Dorabella!

GUGLIELMO
Fiordiligi!

DON ALFONSO
I say you can't!

RECITATIVE

FERRANDO
Theoretical bombast!

GUGLIELMO
The talk of senile cynics!

DON ALFONSO
I'm flattered! However, you say that
they are virtuous. Today that may
be true, but will it be tomorrow?
How can you be so certain? Have
you any guarantee that the love they
profess is eternal?

FERRANDO
Impeccable morals.

GUGLIELMO
Old-fashioned principles.

FERRANDO
Lofty ideals.

GUGLIELMO
Highminded way of life.

FERRANDO
Utter unselfishness.

GUGLIELMO
The firmest of characters!

FERRANDO
Her promise!

GUGLIELMO
Her honor!

FERRANDO
Her devotion!

DON ALFONSO
Kisses and tears, caresses, fits of swoon-
ing! What could be more ridiculous!

FERRANDO
Damnation! When will there be an end
to this?

DON ALFONSO
Be patient! What if I could convince
you this very day that they're like
all the others?

GUGLIELMO
That is a lie!

FERRANDO
Non è.

DON ALFONSO
Giochiam.

FERRANDO
Giochiamo.

DON ALFONSO
Cento zecchini.

GUGLIELMO
E mille, se volete.

DON ALFONSO
Parola.

FERRANDO
Parolissima.

DON ALFONSO
E un cenno, un motto, un gesto, giurate, di non far di tutto questo alle vostre Penelopi.

FERRANDO
Giuriamo.

DON ALFONSO
Da soldati d'onore.

GUGLIELMO
Da soldati d'onore.

DON ALFONSO
E tutto quel farete ch'io vi dirò di far.

FERRANDO
Tutto!

GUGLIELMO
Tuttissimo!

DON ALFONSO
Bravissimi!

FERRANDO, GUGLIELMO
Bravissimo! Signor Don Alfonsetto! A spese vostre or ci divertiremo. E de' cento zecchini, che faremo?

No. 3. TERZETTO

FERRANDO
Una bella serenata
far io voglio alla mia dea.

GUGLIELMO
In onor di Citerea
un convito io voglio far.

DON ALFONSO
Sarò anch'io de' convitati?

FERRANDO, GUGLIELMO
Ci sarete, si, Signor!

FERRANDO, DON ALFONSO, GUGLIELMO
E che brindis replicati
far vogliamo al Dio d'amor.

SCENE II

No. 4. DUETTO

FIORDILIGI
Ah guarda, sorella,
ah guarda, sorella,
se bocca più bella
se aspetto più nobile può ritrovar.

DORABELLA
Osserva tu un poco,
osserva che foco ha ne' sguardi,
se fiamma, se dardi sembran non scoccar.

FIORDILIGI
Si vede un sembiante
guerriero ed amante.

DORABELLA
Si vede una faccia,
che alletta, che alletta,
e minaccia.

FERRANDO

Of course!

DON ALFONSO

Will you bet?

FERRANDO

I'm willing.

DON ALFONSO

One hundred sovereigns!

GUGLIELMO

A thousand, if you wish!

DON ALFONSO

Agreed?

FERRANDO

On my honor!

DON ALFONSO

But promise: no inkling, no mention,
not even a suggestion of our wager
to your glorious paragons.

FERRANDO

We promise.

DON ALFONSO

On your honor as soldiers?

GUGLIELMO

On our honor as soldiers!

DON ALFONSO

And till tomorrow evening you will do
what I say?

FERRANDO

Gladly!

GUGLIELMO

Most willingly!

DON ALFONSO

Your hand on it!

FERRANDO, GUGLIELMO

My hand on it! You connoisseur of
women—

FERRANDO

To see you beaten will be extremely
funny!

GUGLIELMO
(to Ferrando)

Let us plan how to spend all that
money!

No. 3. TERZET

FERRANDO

I shall serenade my goddess,
With a dozen fine musicians,
Sing her praises
In the honored old traditions.

GUGLIELMO

As the sure and happy winner
Of the bet we made before,
I shall give a gala dinner
For the sweetheart that I adore.

DON ALFONSO

May I also join the party?

FERRANDO, GUGLIELMO

Why of course, that's only fair!
Don Alfonso, you'll be there.

ALL THREE

While the sound of clinking glasses
Echoes gaily through the air,
We shall sing the endless praises
Of true women everywhere.

(*Exeunt*)

SCENE II

(*A garden at the seashore. Fiordiligi
and Dorabella, gazing at the portraits
of their lovers in the little lockets
they each wear.*)

No. 4. DUET

FIORDILIGI

See here, Dorabella,
Guglielmo, my lover!
Tell me, sister,
Where could you discover
So great a nobility
As shows in his face?

DORABELLA

This one of Ferrando,
I love it!
What light in his glances!
It sparkles, and dances
And lends him such grace!

FIORDILIGI

The face of a hero,
Audacious, yet disarming!

DORABELLA

His face is expressive,
So gracious, so kindly and charming.
Yet he's manly and possessive, so
possessive!

FIORDILIGI
Felice son io!

DORABELLA
Io sono felice!

FIORDILIGI
Se questo mio core
mai cangia desio,
Amore mi faccia
vivendo penar.

DORABELLA
Se questo mi core
mai cangia desio,
Amore mi faccia
vivendo penar.

RECITATIVO

FIORDILIGI
Mi par, che stamattina volontieri
farei la pazzarella! ho un certo foco,
un certo pizzicor entro le vene —
quando Guglielmo viene — se sa-
pessi, che burla gli vo far.

DORABELLA
Per dirti il vero, qualche cosa di nuovo
anch' io nell' alma provo: io giurerei,
che lontane non siam da gli Imenei.

FIORDILIGI
Dammi la mano: io voglio astro-
logarti: uh, che bell' Emme! e
questo è un Pì: va bene: Matrimonio Presto.

DORABELLA
Affè, che ci avrei gusto.

FIORDILIGI
Ed io non ci avrei rabbia.

DORABELLA
Ma che diavol vuol dir che i nostri
sposi ritardano a venir? son già le
sei—

FIORDILIGI
Eccoli.

DORABELLA
Non son essi: è Don Alfonso, l'amico
lor.

SCENA III

FIORDILIGI
Ben venga il Signor Don Alfonso!

DON ALFONSO
Riverisco.

DORABELLA
Cos' è? perchè qui solo? voi piangete?
parlate per pietà! che cosa è nato?
d'amante—

FIORDILIGI
L'idol mio—

DON ALFONSO
Barbaro fato!

No. 5 ARIA
DON ALFONSO
Vorrei dir, e cor non ho, e cor non ho—
balbettando il labbro va—
fuor la voce uscir non può—
ma mi resta mezza quà.
Che farete?
Che farò?
oh che gran fatalità!
dar di peggio non si può, ah non si può,
ho di voi, di lor pietà.

RECITATIVO
FIORDILIGI

DON ALFONSO
Stelle! per carità, Signor Alfonso, non
ci fate morir.
Convien armarvi, figlie mie, di costanza.

BOTH

I'm ever so happy, contented and
    happy!
If this love of mine ever fails in affec-
    tion,
Or turns in another direction,
My darling, my darling,
May Fate take revenge on my heart!

DORABELLA

Beloved, may Fate take revenge on
    my heart.

FIORDILIGI

If ever my feelings should waver or
    alter,
If ever a discord should tear us apart,

BOTH

My darling, may Fate take revenge
    on my heart.

FIORDILIGI

Beloved, may Fate take revenge on
    my heart.

DORABELLA

If ever my candor should weaken or
    falter,
If ever my fervor should fail or depart,

BOTH

My darling, may Fate take revenge
    on my heart!

RECITATIVE

FIORDILIGI

Oh, such a lovely morning I can't help
    feeling just a little roguish. I can't
    explain it, but somehow I could do
    some harmless mischief. When my
    Guglielmo gets here, how I'd love
    to tease him just a bit!

DORABELLA

To be quite honest, I myself have a
    feeling that something's bound to
    happen. I almost think we are soon
    to be married to our sweethearts.

FIORDILIGI

Give me your hand, dear, I want to
    read your future. Look at that M
    there! And here a P! That's easy:
    Matrimony Pending!

DORABELLA

That's one thing I would welcome!

FIORDILIGI

I would not mind it either.

DORABELLA

But where in the world are our two
    sweethearts? What's keeping them
    so long? It's getting late.
    (*enter Don Alfonso*)

FIORDILIGI

There they are!

DORABELLA

You're mistaken, it's Don Alfonso,
    our mutual friend.

SCENE III

FIORDILIGI

Good morning to you, Don Alfonso.

DON ALFONSO

G-good morning!

DORABELLA

Dear me! you're out of breath and
    excited. For Heaven's sake, what's
    wrong? Can't you speak faster?
    Ferrando—?

FIORDILIGI

Guglielmo—?

DON ALFONSO

What a disaster!

No. 5 ARIA

How I hate to break the news!
It's so awful my lips refuse.
I must talk, I have no choice,
But it seems I've lost my voice.
How explain it? What to say?
Oh accursed, tragic day!
When you know, you will agree,
Nothing worse could ever be!
All your joys are done and past.
Poor dear boys, the die is cast.

RECITATIVE

FIORDILIGI

Goodness! What can it be, dear Don
    Alfonso? Do not keep us in suspense.

DON ALFONSO

You must have courage, be prepared
    for a shock.

DORABELLA

Oh Dei! qual male è addivenuto mai,
qual caso rio? forse è morto il mio
bene?

FIORDILIGI

È morto il mio?

DON ALFONSO

Morti non son, ma poco men che
morti.

DORABELLA

Feriti?

DON ALFONSO

No.

FIORDILIGI

Ammalati?

DON ALFONSO

Neppur.

FIORDILIGI

Che cosa dunque?

DON ALFONSO

Al marzial campo ordin regio li chiama.

FIORDILIGI, DORABELLA

Ohimè! che sento!

FIORDILIGI

E partiran?

DON ALFONSO

Sul fatto.

DORABELLA

E non v'è modo d'impedirlo?

DON ALFONSO

Non v'è.

FIORDILIGI

Ne un solo addio?

DON ALFONSO

Gli infelici non hanno coraggio di
vedervi; ma se voi lo bramate, son
pronti—

DORABELLA

Dove son?

DON ALFONSO

Amici, entrate!

No. 6 QUINTETTO

GUGLIELMO

Sento, o Dio!
che questo piede
è restio nel girle avante.

FERRANDO

Il mio labbro palpitante
non può detto pronunziar.

DON ALFONSO

Nei momenti i più terribili
sua virtù l'eroe palesa.

FIORDILIGI, DORABELLA

Or ch'abbbiam la nuova intesa,
a voi resta a fare il meno;
fate core, fate core,
a entrambe in seno
immergeteci l'acciar.

FERRANDO, GUGLIELMO

Idol mio! la sorte incolpa
se ti deggio abbandonar!

DORABELLA

Ah no, no, non partirai!

FIORDILIGI

No crudel, non tene andrai,

DORABELLA

Voglio pria cavarmi il core.

FIORDILIGI

Pria ti vo morire ai piedi.

FERRANDO

(Cosa dici?)

GUGLIELMO

(Te n'avveddi?)

DON ALFONSO

(Saldo amico, saldo amico,
finem lauda, finem lauda!)

FIORDILIGI, DORABELLA, FERRANDO,
DON ALFONSO, GUGLIELMO

Il destin così defrauda,
le speranze de' mortali.
Ah chi mai fra tanti mali,
chi mai può la vita amar?

DORABELLA

Good Heavens! What happened to our fiancés? Are they in trouble? Is my Ferrando dead?

FIORDILIGI

Or my Guglielmo?

DON ALFONSO

Dead—they are not, but not much less than that.

DORABELLA

In prison?

DON ALFONSO

No.

FIORDILIGI

Are they ill?

DON ALFONSO

No, no.

FIORDILIGI

What could it be then?

DON ALFONSO

By royal order they must leave for the front.

FIORDILIGI, DORABELLA

Oh dear! How dreadful!

FIORDILIGI

When do they leave?

DON ALFONSO

At once!

DORABELLA

And is there no way to exempt them?

DON ALFONSO

No way.

FIORDILIGI

And no good-byes?

DON ALFONSO

Wretched fellows, they don't have the courage to face you. But if you can both bear it, I'll call them.

DORABELLA

Oh, please do!

DON ALFONSO

Come in now, my heroes!

(*enter Ferrando and Guglielmo in traveling clothes*)

No. 6. QUINTET

GUGLIELMO

All is over, the blow has fallen,
All my hopes destroyed and shattered.

FERRANDO

I am speechless, shocked and battered!
You behold a broken man!

DON ALFONSO

In the face of this catastrophe,
Steel your heart and be courageous!

FIORDILIGI, DORABELLA

Now that all has been decided,
You must do me one last favor:
Be a stoic, be heroic,
Without a waver
Plunge your sword right through my heart.

FERRANDO, GUGLIELMO

Dearest angel! The worst has happened!
Fate decrees that we must part.

DORABELLA

No, no, no, I cannot bear it!

FIORDILIGI

I will die of grief, I swear it!

DORABELLA

Let me perish, I implore you!

FIORDILIGI

Let me die right before you!

FERRANDO

(Are we winning?)

GUGLIELMO

(Are we losing?)

DON ALFONSO

(The beginning is amusing,
But tomorrow comes the sorrow!)

FIORDILIGI, DORABELLA

So does Fate take away the joy of living,
End forever all the hopes and dreams we cherished.

FERRANDO, DON ALFONSO, GUGLIELMO

So the sudden hand of Fate
Will take away the joy of living,
All the hopes and dreams we cherished.

ALL

Bowed by grief, all alone in sorrow,
Who would care to live at all?

RECITATIVO

GUGLIELMO

Non piangere, idol mio!

FERRANDO

Non disperarti, adorata mia sposa!

DON ALFONSO

Lasciate lor tal sfogo: è troppo giusta
la cagion di quel pianto.

FIORDILIGI

Chi sa s'io più ti veggio?

DORABELLA

Chi sa se più ritorni?

FIORDILIGI

Lasciami questo ferro: ei mi dia morte,
se mai barbara sorte in quel seno a
me caro—

DORABELLA

Morrei di duol, d'uopo non ho d'acciaro.

FERRANDO, GUGLIELMO

Non farmi, anima mia, quest'infausti
presagi! proteggeran gli Dei la pace
del tuo cor ne'giorni miei.

No. 7. DUETTINO

FERRANDO, GUGLIELMO

Al fato dan legge
quegli occhi vezzosi;
Amor li protegge
nè i loro riposi
le barbare stelle ardiscon turbar.
Il ciglio sereno,
mio bene, a me gira;
felice al tuo seno
io spero tornar.

RECITATIVO

DON ALFONSO

(La comedia è graziosa, e tutti due
fan ben la loro parte.)

FERRANDO

O cielo! questo è il tamburo funesto,
che a divider mi vien dal mio tesoro.

DON ALFONSO

Ecco amici, la barca.

FIORDILIGI

Io manco.

DORABELLA

Io moro.

SCENA V

No. 8. CORO

Bella vita militar!
Ogni dì si cangia loco,
oggi molto, doman poco,
ora in terra ed or sul mar.
Il fragor di trombe e pifferi,
la sparar di schioppi, e bombe,
forza accresce al braccio, e all' anima
vaga sol di trionfar.
Bella vita militar!

RECITATIVO

DON ALFONSO

Non v'è più tempo, amici, andar conviene, ove il destino, anzi il dover
v'invita.

FIORDILIGI

Mio cor—

DORABELLA

Idolo mio—

FERRANDO

Mio ben—

GUGLIELMO

Mia vita—

FIORDILIGI

Ah per un sol momento—

DON ALFONSO

Del vostro reggimento già è partita la
barca, raggiungerla convien coi poc-
chi amici che su legno più lieve attendendo vi stanno.

FERRANDO, GUGLIELMO

Abbracciami, idol mio!

FIORDILIGI, DORABELLA

Muojo d'affanno.

RECITATIVE

GUGLIELMO

Take courage, my beloved!

FERRANDO

My little sweetheart, do not yield to despair.

DON ALFONSO

My friends, you must be patient, do not console them, let them have a good cry.

FIORDILIGI

Perhaps we part forever!

DORABELLA

How can I live without you!
(*they embrace tenderly*)

FIORDILIGI

Lend me your sword, I beg you, to end my torture. Since fortune is so cruel, only death can console me!

DORABELLA

I'll die of grief, I shall not need a weapon.

FERRANDO, GUGLIELMO

Forget these ominous fancies, and remember, I love you! Trust to the gods above you, to cheer your grieving heart, and guide me safely.

No. 7. DUETTINO

FERRANDO, GUGLIELMO

Your love is a power,
An ally beside us;
A beacon, a tower,
A star that will guide us;
The barbarous fates too must bow to its reign.
So wait and be patient;
No space can divide us.
We'll soon be united and happy again.

RECITATIVE

DON ALFONSO

(The performance is charming! The way they're acting exceeds my expectations!)
(*a drum is heard*)

FERRANDO

Oh Heavens! That is the ominous signal, which will tear me away from my beloved.

DON ALFONSO

And the boat is arriving.

FIORDILIGI

Guglielmo!

DORABELLA

Ferrando!

SCENE V

(*Enter soldies, village men and women. The military march is heard in the distance. A boat arrives at the landing.*)

No. 8. CHORUS

On to glory, on to war!
We are free of care and sorrow,
Here today and there tomorrow!
Over land and over sea!
We are marching on to victory
With the flags and banners flying
For our country's honor,
While trumpets are sounding
And our spirits soar.
On to glory, on to war!

RECITATIVE

DON ALFONSO

My friends, it's time you started. You must be going, duty is calling, destiny has decided.

FIORDILIGI

My love—

DORABELLA

My dear beloved—

FERRANDO

My life—

GUGLIELMO

My treasure—

FIORDILIGI

Stay just a moment longer!

DON ALFONSO

The first one of the barges has already departed. Hurry to meet the soldiers who are waiting to escort you on board. They are getting impatient.

FERRANDO, GUGLIELMO

Just one last kiss, my darling!

FIORDILIGI, DORABELLA

I cannot bear it!

No. 9. Quintetto

FIORDILIGI

Di scrivermi ogni giorno!
giurami, vita mia!

DORABELLA

Due volte ancora tu
scrivimi, se puoi.

FERRANDO

Sii certa, sii certa,
o cara!

GUGLIELMO

Non dubitar,
non dubitar, mio bene!

DON ALFONSO

Io crepo se non rido.

FIORDILIGI

Sii costante a me sol!

DORABELLA

Serbati fido!

FERRANDO

Addio!

GUGLIELMO

Addio!

FIORDILIGI, DORABELLA

Addio!

FIORDILIGI, DORABELLA, FERRANDO,
GUGLIELMO

Mi si divide il cor,
bell' idol mio!
Addio!

CORO

Bella vita militar, ecc.

SCENA VI

RECITATIVO

DORABELLA

Dove son?

DON ALFONSO

Son partiti.

FIORDILIGI

Oh dipartenza crudelissima amara!

DON ALFONSO

Fate core, carissime figliuole; guardate,
da lontano vi fan cenno con mano i
cari sposi.

FIORDILIGI

Buon viaggio. Mia vita!

DORABELLA

Buon viaggio!

FIORDILIGI

Oh Dei! come veloce se ne va quella
barca! già sparisce! già non si vede
più. Deh faccia il cielo ch'abbia
prospero corso.

DORABELLA

Faccia che al campo giunga con fortu-
nati auspici.

DON ALFONSO

E a voi salvi gli amanti, e a me gli
amici.

No. 10. Terzettino

FIORDILIGI, DORABELLA, DON ALFONSO

Soave sia il vento,
tranquilla sia l'onda,
ed ogni elemento
benigno risponda
ai nostri desir!

SCENA VII

RECITATIVO

DON ALFONSO

Non son cattivo comico! va bene; al
concertato loco i due campioni di
Ciprigna, e di Marte mi staranno attendendo; or senza indugio, raggiun-
gerli conviene. Quante smorfie, quante buffonerie! Tanta meglio per me,
cadran più facilmente: questa razza
di gente è la più presto a cangiarsi
d'umore. Oh poverini! per femmina
giocar cento zecchini?

No. 9. QUINTET

FIORDILIGI
(*weeping*)
Be sure to write me daily,
Ev'ry day, will you promise?
Swear you'll always be true!

DORABELLA
(*weeping*)
You write me twice a day.
Twice daily, please, will you?

FERRANDO
Of course, dear, I promise, dear angel.

GUGLIELMO
Of course I will.
I promise, my dear angel.

DON ALFONSO
(*aside*)
This really is too silly!

FIORDILIGI
Swear you'll always be true!

DORABELLA
Think of me always!

FERRANDO
I promise!

GUGLIELMO
I promise!

FIORDILIGI, DORABELLA
Farewell, then!

FIORDILIGI, DORABELLA, FERRANDO,
GUGLIELMO
How I shall grieve and mourn
When we are parted!
I love you,
Forever, forever!
(*Ferrando and Guglielmo board the
boat. The two women stand at the
landing, motionless. The boat gradu-
ally recedes in the distance, to the
sound of drums.*)

CHORUS
On to glory, on to war! etc.
(*exit chorus*)

SCENE VI

RECITATIVE

DORABELLA
(*as if awakening from a trance*)
Are they gone?

DON ALFONSO
They are gone.

FIORDILIGI
This separation is a terrible blow!

DON ALFONSO
Be courageous, it's not as bad as that.
Look there, now; in the distance, on
the ship you can see your sweethearts
waving.

FIORDILIGI
God keep you, my treasure.

DORABELLA
Safe journey!

FIORDILIGI
How rapidly the vessel disappears in
the distance! In one moment they
will be out of sight. Heaven protect
them on their perilous journey!

DORABELLA
How I will miss my darling, away in
foreign lands!

DON ALFONSO
I will miss them no less my two best
friends.

No. 10. TERZETTINO

FIORDILIGI, DORABELLA, DON ALFONSO
May breezes blow lightly,
May fair winds betide you,
May stars shimmer brightly
And faithfully guide you,
Beloved so dear.
May Fortune direct you
And journey beside you,
Watch over and protect you,
Benign and responsive
To love so sincere.
(*exeunt Fiordiligi and Dorabella*)

SCENE VII

RECITATIVE

DON ALFONSO
I have a flair for comedy! My acting,
to judge from my success, has been
convincing. But Fernando and Guglielmo, can they equal my performance? I'll go and meet them to
coach them for their roles. And the
ladies! Much ado about nothing.
That means only one thing: they'll
weaken so much sooner. They're the
kind of women who are quickest to
reverse their affection. Oh you poor
fellows! You risk a hundred sov'-
reigns on two women!

Nel mare solca,
e nell' arena semina,
e il vago vento
spera in rete accogliere
chi fonda sue speranze
in cor di femmina.

SCENA VIII

RECITATIVO

DESPINA

Che vita maledetta è il far la cameriera! dal mattino alla sera si fa, si
suda, si lavora, e poi di tanto, che
si fa, nulla è per noi. E mezza ora,
che sbatto, il cioccolatte è fatto,
ed a me tocca restar ad odorarlo a
secca bocca? non è forse la mia
come la vostra? o garbate Signore,
che a voi dessi l'essenza e a me
l'odore? per Bacco, vo assagiarlo:
com' è buono! Vien gente! oh ciel!
son le padrone.

SCENA IX

DESPINA

Madame, ecco la vostra collazione.
Diamine! cosa fate?

FIORDILIGI

Ah!

DORABELLA

Ah!

DESPINA

Che cosa è nato?

FIORDILIGI

Ov' è un acciaro?

DORABELLA

un veleno, dov è?

DESPINA

Padrone, dico!

No. 11. RECITATIVO ED ARIA

DORABELLA

Ah scostati! paventa il tristo effetto
d'un disperato affetto. Chiudi quelle
finestre—odio la luce, odio l'aria, che
spiro—odio me stessa! Chi schernisce
il mio duol? chi mi consola? Deh
fuggi, per pietà! fuggi, lasciami sola.

ARIA

Smanie implacabili,
che m'agitate,
entro quest' anima
più non cessate,
finchè l'angoscia
mi fa morir.

Esempio misero
d'amor funesto,
darò all' Eumenidi,
se viva resto
col suono orribile
de' miei sospir,
col suono orribile
de' miei sospir.

RECITATIVO

DESPINA

Signora Dorabella, Signora Fiordiligi,
ditemi, che cosa è stato?

DORABELLA

Oh terribil disgrazia!

DESPINA

Sbrigatevi in buon' ora.

FIORDILIGI

Da Napoli partiti sono gli amanti
nostri.

DESPINA

Non c'è altro? ritorneran.

A man in danger,
Lost in the jungle's wilderness
Or in a shipwreck,
Is safer than the simpleton
Who founds his hopes on woman
And her fidelity.

(*Curtain*)

SCENE VIII

(*A pretty room, with several chairs, a little table, three doors. Despina alone.*)

RECITATIVE

DESPINA

There's nothing quite so thankless as being a perfect maid. From morning till midnight you work, you slave, do your best, and when you're finished, you have nothing to show for it. For example, I have to serve my mistresses' breakfast and all I get is the wonderful aroma of fresh coffee. Do they want me to live on mere aroma? Just where is it written that they should have the egg and I the shell? For once I think, I'll try some. How delicious.
(*she wipes her mouth*)
The ladies! That was a narrow escape!

SCENE IX

(*enter Fiordiligi and Dorabella, distraught*)

My ladies, I've already brought your breakfast. Bless my soul! What has happened?

FIORDILIGI
Ah!

DORABELLA
Ah!

DESPINA
What's the matter?

FIORDILIGI
Find me a dagger!

DORABELLA
And some poison for me!

DESPINA
My ladies, easy!

No. 11. RECITATIVE AND ARIA

DORABELLA

Away from here! For in my state of frenzy I might do something desp'-rate. You must draw all the curtains —I hate the sunlight, hate the air I am breathing, even myself! Who would mock my despair? Who dares console me? Away from me at once! Hurry, hurry! Far from where I am! Leave me alone here!

Come, endless agony,
Come and possess me,
Enter this heart of mine,
Burn and obsess me,
Torment and goad me
Until I die.

My love is tragedy
With none to share it.
Should cruel destiny
Force me to bear it,
Till death releases me,
I'll mourn and sigh.
Come, hopeless misery,
Deride and taunt me,
Enter this soul of mine,
Pursue and haunt me,
Pierce and corrode me
Until I die.
My love is martyrdom,
A storm that rages.
Should Fate prolong my life
Through countless ages,
I'll grieve the years away
Until I die.

(*both women collapse in their chairs, in utter despair*)

RECITATIVE

DESPINA
Dear mistress Dorabella, dear mistress Fiordiligi, tell me, what has happened?

DORABELLA
A terrible disaster!

DESPINA
Please tell me about it.

FIORDILIGI
Our fiancés left Naples and we are both deserted!

DESPINA
Oh, is that all? They will be back.

DORABELLA

Chi sa!

DESPINA

Come, chi sa? dove son iti?

DORABELLA

Al campo di battaglia.

DESPINA

Tanto meglio per loro: li vedrete
tornar carchi d'alloro.

FIORDILIGI

Ma ponno anche perir.

DESPINA

Allora poi tanto meglio per voi.

FIORDILIGI

Sciocca, che dici?

DESPINA

La pura verità: due ne perdete, vi
restan tutti gli altri.

FIORDILIGI

Ah, perdendo Guglielmo, mi pare
ch'io morrei!

DORABELLA

Ah, Ferrando perdendo, mi par, che
viva a sepellirmi andrei.

DESPINA

Brave, vi par, ma non è ver: ancora
non vi fu donna, ch'è d'amor sia
morta. Per un uomo morir! altri, ve
n'hanno, che compensano il danno.

DORABELLA

E credi che potria altro uom amar,
chi s'ebbe per amante un Guglielmo,
un Ferrando?

DESPINA

Han gli altri ancora tutto quello ch'han
essi, un uom adesso amate, un altro
n'amerete, uno val l'altro, perchè
nessun val nulla; ma non parliam
di ciò, sono ancor vivi, e vivi torneran; ma son lontani, e più tosto
che in vani pianti perdere il tempo,
pensate a divertivi.

FIORDILIGI

Divertirci?

DESPINA

Sicuro! e quel ch'è meglio far all' amor
come assassine, e come faranno al
campo i vostri cari amanti.

DORABELLA

Non offender così quelle alme belle,
di fedeltà, d'intatto amore esempi.

DESPINA

Via, via, passaro i tempi di spacciar
queste favole ai bambini.

No. 12.   ARIA

DESPINA

In uomini
In soldati
sperare fedeltà?
In uomini
sperare fedeltà?
In soldati
sperare fedeltà?
Non vi fate sentir per carità!
Non vi fate sentir per carità!

Di pasta simile son tutti quanti,
son tutti quanti.
han più degli uomini stabilità.

Mentite lagrime,
fallaci sguardi,
voci ingannevoli,
vezzi bugiardi,
son le primarie
lor qualità.
In noi non amano che il cor diletto,
poi ci dispregiano, neganci affetto,
nè val da' barbari chieder pietà.

Paghiam, a femmine, d'ugual moneta
questa malefica razza indiscreta;
amiam per comodo, per vanità.

DORABELLA

Who knows?

DESPINA

Why do you say that? Where have they gone?

DORABELLA

They have both gone to war.

DESPINA

So much the better! In that case they'll return covered with laurels.

FIORDILIGI

But if they should die?

DESPINA

Well, what about it? All the better for you!

FIORDILIGI
(rises in rage)

How dare you say that!

DESPINA

I merely tell the truth. What if you lose them? There still are all the others.

FIORDILIGI

Ah, without my Guglielmo I could not go on living!

DORABELLA

Ah, if I would lose Ferrando, then for me also death would be more than welcome.

DESPINA

Well spoken indeed, but you are wrong. I've never heard of a woman dying of love. To die for a man, when a thousand others can be had for the asking!

DORABELLA

You really mean to tell me that there are men comparing even vaguely with a Guglielmo, a Ferrando?

DESPINA

They are no better, nor are they worse than the others. Today you're loving one man, tomorrow another. One's worth the others, because they are all worthless! Why waste your time on tears? They're still alive, and will be for some time. But they're away and rather than lament in sackcloth and ashes, forget them and be gay.

FIORDILIGI
(furiously)

Forget them?

DESPINA

Exactly! By far the best cure for lonely hearts is a new romance. What else do you think your sweethearts are doing while they're away?

DORABELLA

You dare to offend those noble spirits, models of faith and paragons of virtue?

DESPINA

You think that men are stable? That's no more than an old woman's fable!

No. 12. ARIA

DESPINA

Stability in a soldier
And virtue in a man?
Who ever saw it since the world began?
Give me one good example if you can
If you can!

(laughing)

Who'd believe such a sentimental tale
Of the perfect and ever-loving male!
Dealing with woman kind, all men are
    brothers—
One like the others!
Don't be a featherbrain
Ever to trust them.
Even a weather-vane changes much
    less.
All men's duplicity
Passes believing.
Feigning simplicity,
Lying, deceiving,
And when they fool you, oh what
    finesse!
Let him be glamorous,
Clever and handsome,
Gallant and amorous,
Stronger than Samson!
Do not be gullible,
Trusting his lies!
He wants to pull the wool
Over your eyes,
Your trusting eyes!
Pay them in kind when they flirt and
    philander.
Sauce for the goose is the same for the
    gander!
Even the best of them,

SCENA X

RECITATIVO

DON ALFONSO

Che silenzio! che aspetto di tristezza
spirano queste stanze! Poverette! non
han già tutto il torto: bisogna consolarle; infin che vanno i due creduli
sposi, com' io loro commisi, a mas-
cherasi, pensiam cosa può farsi —
temo un po' per Despina,—quella
furba potrebbe riconoscerli; potrebbe
rovesciarmi le macchine, vedremo—
se mai farà bisogno un regaletto a
tempo, un zechinetto per una cameriere è un gran scongiuro. Ma per
esser sicuro, sì potria metterla in
parte a parte del secreto. Excellente
è il progetto—la sua camera è questa
—Despinetta!

DESPINA

Chi batte?

DON ALFONSO

Oh!

DESPINA

Ih!

DON ALFONSO

Despina mia, di te bisogno avrei.

DESPINA

Ed io niente di voi.

DON ALFONSO

Ti vo fare del ben.

DESPINA

A una fanciulla un vecchio come lei
non può far nulla.

DON ALFONSO

Parla piano ed osserva.

DESPINA

Me lo dona?

DON ALFONSO

Sì, se meco sei buona.

DESPINA

E che vorebbe? è loro il mio giulebbe.

DON ALFONSO

Ed oro avrai; ma ci vuol fedeltà.

DESPINA

Non c'è altro? son quà.

DON ALFONSO

Prendi ed ascolta. Sai, che le tue
padrone han perduti gli amanti.

DESPINA

Lo so.

DON ALFONSO

Tutti i lor pianti, tutti deliri loro
ancor tu sai.

DESPINA

So tutto.

DON ALFONSO

Or ben; se mai per consolarle un poco,
e trar, come diciam, chiodo per
chiodo, tu ritrovassi il modo, da
metter in lor grazia due soggetti di
garbo che vorrieno provar, già mi
capisci. C'è una mancia per te di
venti scudi, se li fai riuscir.

DESPINA

Non mi dispiace questa proposizione.
Ma con quelle buffone . . . basta,
udite: son giovani? son belli? e sopra
tutto hanno una buona borsa i vostri
concorrenti?

DON ALFONSO

Han tutto quello che piacer può alle
donne di giudizio. Li vuoi veder?

DESPINA

E dove son?

'Neath his veneer
Is like the rest of them,
Never you fear!
Perish the thought of a man who is
    true,
Do unto them as they do unto you!
    (*exeunt. Enter Don Alfonso*)

SCENE X

RECITATIVE

DON ALFONSO

Not a sound! This atmosphere of sadness! Graver than a grave-yard. Poor girls! They must be very downcast! I cannot really blame them. Meanwhile, I'll go and meet my two friends. In their present disguise I'm optimistic my strategy is foolproof! But that rascal Despina! She is clever —she might see through the masquerade. She even might upset the whole applecart! However . . . I know just how to handle a girl like Despina. A little money always goes a long way in such a case. But to further my purpose, I could even ask her to be a partner in my project. Without losing a minute I will knock at her door.
        (*knocks*)
Despinetta!

DESPINA

Who's knocking?

DON ALFONSO

I!

DESPINA
    (*entering*)
Oh!

DON ALFONSO

My dear Despina, I want to ask a favor.

DESPINA

I don't give any favors!

DON ALFONSO

Won't you listen to my offer?

DESPINA

To girls of my age, a man of your vintage offers very little.

DON ALFONSO
    (*shows her a gold piece*)
This might change your opinion.

DESPINA

A gold piece?

DON ALFONSO

Yes. It's yours for the asking.

DESPINA

What are you asking? For gold I might do it.

DON ALFONSO

The merest trifle—your good-will and your help.

DESPINA

Is that all? Go on.

DON ALFONSO

Well, then, here's my problem. Doubtlessly you have heard what has happened to your ladies?

DESPINA

I have.

DON ALFONSO

Then you have noticed that they are overcome by desperation.

DESPINA

What about it?

DON ALFONSO

Now then: suppose, in order to distract them, or, as the saying goes, make the best of a bad bargain, you help me to persuade them to meet two nice young men with romantic intentions, who are from abroad. You understand me, if you make them successful, I shall give you a most generous reward.

DESPINA

That sounds appealing. It's an attractive proposition. But those two silly females! — Tell me — your visitors, these foreigners, are they handsome? And, more important, have they well-lined pockets—these two prospective lovers?

DON ALFONSO

They are the most eligible young men any women could dream of! Is that enough?

DESPINA

Where are they now?

DON ALFONSO

Son lì: li posso far entrar?

DESPINA

Direi di si.

SCENE XI

No. 13. Sestetto

DON ALFONSO

Alla bella Despinetta
vi presento, amici miei;
non dipende che da lei,
consolar il vostro cor.

FERRANDO, GUGLIELMO

Per la man,
che lieto io bacio,
per quei rai di grazia pieni,
fa che volga a me sereni
i begli occhi il mio tesor.

DESPINA

Che sembianze!
che vestiti!
che figure!
che mustacchi!
Io non so,
se son Vallacchi?
o se Turchi
son costor?
Vallacchi?
Turchi?
Turchi?
Vallacchi?

DON ALFONSO

Che ti par di quell' aspetto?

DESPINA

Per parlarvi schietto, schietto,
hanno un muso fuor dell'uso,
vero antidoto d'amor.
Che figure, che mustacchi!
Io non so, se son Vallacchi?
O se Turchi
son costor?

FERRANDO, DON ALFONSO, GUGLIELMO

Or la cosa è appien decisa,
se costei non ci ravvisa,
non c'è più nessun timor.

FIORDILIGI, DORABELLA

Ehi, Despina! olà Despina!

DESPINA

Le padrone.

DON ALFONSO

Ecco l'istante!
fa con arte:
io quì m'ascondo.

FIORDILIGI, DORABELLA

Ragazzaccia tracotante!
che fai lì con simil gente,
con simil gente?
falli uscire immantinente,
o ti so pentir con lor.

DESPINA, FERRANDO, GUGLIELMO

Ah, madame, perdonate!
al bel piè languir mirate
due meschin, di vostro merto,
spasimanti adorator.

FIORDILIGI, DORABELLA

Giusti numi! cosa sento?
dell' enorme tradimento,
chi fu mai l'indegno autor?

DESPINA, FERRANDO, GUGLIELMO

Deh calmate,
deh calmate,
quello sdegno.

FIORDILIGI, DORABELLA

Ah, che più non ho ritegno!
tutta piena ho l'alma in petto
di dispetto e di terror!

DON ALFONSO

Right here. May I ask them in?

DESPINA

A good idea!

(*Don Alfonso opens the door and the
disguised lovers step in*)

SCENE XI

No. 13. SEXTET

DON ALFONSO

I present Miss Despinetta,
A discreet and charming person.
There is no one who knows better
How to help you reach your goal.

FERRANDO, GUGLIELMO

I am pleased and deeply honored
At the compliment you paid me,
Being kind enough to aid me
Win the goddess of my soul.

DESPINA

(*laughing to herself*)

Goodness gracious!
How loquacious!
That regalia! Those mustaches!
Did they come here from Patagonia
Or perhaps from Timbuctoo?
The Congo? China? Turkey? Malaya?

DON ALFONSO

(*softly to Despina*)

Don't you think they have some
virtue?

DESPINA

Though I do not like to hurt you,
They're fantastic,
Far too drastic,
And as lovers, they won't do!
Too outlandish, too exotic,
Positively Don Quixotic.
I am quite surprised at you.
Don Alfonso, just between us,
Did you find them on the moon
Or perhaps on Mars or Venus,
Did they land in a balloon?

FERRANDO, DON ALFONSO, GUGLIELMO

She is fooled by our (their) disguises!
Barring unforeseen surprises,
There is nothing more to fear.

FIORDILIGI, DORABELLA

(*from within*)

Eh, Despina! Come here, Despina!

DESPINA

I am coming!

DON ALFONSO

(*to Despina*)

Now, you take over, and remember,
I'll join you later.
(*He retires. Enter Fiordiligi and Dora-
bella.*)

FIORDILIGI, DORABELLA

I must say this is the limit!
You're forgetting your position.
Who has given you permission
To indulge in silly babble
With total strangers and common
rabble?
Put the creatures out the door,
Nothing less and nothing more!

DESPINA, FERRANDO, GUGLIELMO

(*All three kneel down.*)

Ah, dear ladies, how unfeeling!
Here before your feet are kneeling
Two poor slaves, begging your mercy,
That is all we're asking for.

FIORDILIGI, DORABELLA

What an outrage. What pretensions!
Who would force unwished attentions
On us now, amid our woe?
Who would dare descend so low?

DESPINA, FERRANDO, GUGLIELMO

Dearest ladies, they (we) are gentle,
Sentimental!

FIORDILIGI, DORABELLA

Now I'm thoroughly disgusted,
You are brazen and revolting!
Stop molesting us and go!

DESPINA, DON ALFONSO

(*the latter from the doorway*)

I've a certain strong suspicion
That their fury is all for show.

FERRANDO, GUGLIELMO

I am certain their opposition
And their fury is not for show.

FIORDILIGI, DORABELLA

Ah, dear love, the pangs I suffer
You will never, never know.
You are brazen and revolting
With the insults you propose.

DESPINA

Mi da un poco
di sospetto,
quella rabbia
e quel furor!

DON ALFONSO

Mi da un poco
di sospetto,
quella rabbia
e quel furor!

FERRANDO

Qual diletto
è a questo petto,
quella rabbia
e quel furor!

GUGLIELMO

Qual diletto
è a questo petto,
quella rabbia
e quel furor!

FIORDILIGI

Ah, perdon
mio bel diletto,
innocente
è questo cor.

DORABELLA

Ah, perdon
mio bel diletto,
innocente
è questo cor.

RECITATIVO

DON ALFONSO

Che susurro! che strepito, che scompiglio è mai questo! siete pazze, care
le mie ragazze? volete sollevar il
vicinato? cosa avete? ch' è nato?

DORABELLA

Oh ciel! mirate uomini in casa nostra?

DON ALFONSO

Che'male c'è?

FIORDILIGI

Che male? in questo giorno?
dopo il caso funesto?

DON ALFONSO

Stelle! sogno, o son desto? amici miei,
miei dolcissimi amici! Voi qui?
come? perchè? quando! in qual modo! Numi! quanto ne godo! (Secon-
datemi.)

FERRANDO

Amico Don Alfonso!

GUGLIELMO

Amico caro!

DON ALFONSO

Oh, bella improvisata!

DESPINA

Li conoscete voi?

DON ALFONSO

Se li conosco! questi sono i più dolci
amici, ch'io m'abbia in questo mondo, e vostri ancor saranno.

FIORDILIGI

E in casa mia che fanno?

GUGLIELMO

Ai vostri piedi due rei, due delinquen-
ti, ecco Madame! Amor—

FIORDILIGI

Numi! che sento?

FERRANDO

Amor, il nume, sì possente per voi, qui
ci conduce.

GUGLIELMO

Vista appena la luce di vostre fulgi-
dissime pupille—

FERRANDO

che alle vive faville—

DESPINA, DON ALFONSO

I am sure they won't stay faithful
And their fury is a pose.

FERRANDO, GUGLIELMO

I am certain they are faithful
And their fury is no pose.

FIORDILIGI, DORABELLA

We are thoroughly disgusted.

DESPINA, DON ALFONSO, FERRANDO,
GUGLIELMO

Their resentment can't (can) be
trusted
And this fury is a (no) pose.

FIORDILIGI, DORABELLA

I refuse to stay and listen
To the insults you propose.

DESPINA, DON ALFONSO

I've a certain strong suspicion
That this fury is all a pose.

FERRANDO, GUGLIELMO

How I relish the opposition
That this fury so clearly shows.

FIORDILIGI, DORABELLA

What a shameless imposition!
Your offensive proposition
Only adds to all our woes.

FERRANDO, GUGLIELMO

Their behavior is an admission
They are faithful as we suppose.

DESPINA, DON ALFONSO

I am nursing a suspicion
They're pretending as we suppose.

FIORDILIGI, DORABELLA

Stop molesting us and go,
We will spite you until you go.

DON ALFONSO, DESPINA

They will spite you until you go.

FERRANDO, GUGLIELMO

They will spite us until we go.

ALL

And the answer will be No!

RECITATIVE

DON ALFONSO
(entering)

What commotion! What excitement!
And why all this confusion? My
dear ladies, have you lost your
minds? You're liable to rouse all
the neighbors! What has happened,
I ask you?

DORABELLA
(furiously)

Good Lord! An outrage! Men in a
house like ours!

DON ALFONSO

Is that so bad?

FIORDILIGI
(enraged)

So bad? It is unheard of—on this
tragic occasion!

DON ALFONSO

Bless me! It can't be. Am I dreaming?
I can't believe it! My two very best
friends! You here? Really? How so?
You here! Of all people! Tell me,
when did you get here? (Play along
with me!)
(they rapturously embrace each other)

FERRANDO

I'm overjoyed to see you!

GUGLIELMO

My benefactor!

DON ALFONSO

What a very small world!

DESPINA

You've seen these men before?

DON ALFONSO

Oh, have I seen them! I have known
them since they were babies! I love
them like a father, and you will love
them also.

FIORDILIGI

What do they want in my house?

GUGLIELMO

Two humble creatures, two slaves, two
wretched wretches, lie at your feet
here, and love—

FIORDILIGI

Heavens! How dare you!
(the women draw back, weakly, followed by the persistent lovers.)

FERRANDO

And Love, our idol, leads us onward
to you, into your power.

GUGLIELMO

Overcome by your beauty, the devas-
tating splendor of your eyes—

FERRANDO

Like two fluttering butterflies—

GUGLIELMO
farfallette amorose e agonizzanti—

FERRANDO
vi voliamo davanti—

GUGLIELMO
ed ai lati ed a retro—

FERRANDO, GUGLIELMO
per implorar pietade in flebil metro!

FIORDILIGI
Stelle! che ardir!

DORABELLA
Sorella! che facciamo?

No. 14. RECITATIVO ED ARIA

FIORDILIGI
Temerari, sortite fuori di questo loco!
e non profani l'alito infausto degli
infami detti nostro cor, nostro
orecchio, e nostri affetti! Invan per
voi, per gli altri invan si cerca le
nostre alme sedur: l'intatta fede che
per noi già si diede ai cari amanti
saprem loro serbar infino a morte, a
dispetto del mondo e della sorte.

ARIA

Come scoglio immoto resta
contra i venti e la tempesta,
così ognor quest' alma è forte
nella fede e nell' amor.

Con noi nacque quella face,
che ci piace, e ci consola;
e potrà la morte sola,
far che cangi affetto il cor.
Come soglio immoto resta
contra i venti e la tempesta
così ognor quest'alma è forte
nella fede e nell' amor.

Rispettate, anime ingrate,
questo esempio di costanza,
e una barbara speranza
non vi renda audaci ancor.

RECITATIVO

FERRANDO
Ah, non partite!

GUGLIELMO
Ah, barbara restate! (Che vi pare?)

DON ALFONSO
(Aspettate!) Per carità ragazze, non
mi fate più far trista figura.

DORABELLA
E che pretendereste?

DON ALFONSO
Eh nulla; ma mi pare che un pocchin
di dolcezza — alfin son galantuomini
e sono amici miei.

FIORDILIGI
Come! e udire dovrei?

GUGLIELMO
Le nostre pene e sentirne pietà! La
celeste beltà degli occhi vostri la
piaga aprì nei nostri cui rimediar può
solo il balsamo d'amore: un solo
istante il core aprite o bella a sue
dolci facelle, a voi davanti spirar
vedrete i più fedeli amanti.

No. 15. ARIA

GUGLIELMO
Non siate ritrosi
occhietti vezzosi,
due lampi amorosi
vibrate un po' quà.
Felici rendeteci
amate con noi,
e noi felicissimi
faremo anche voi.

Guardate, toccate,
Il tutto osservate:
siam forti e ben fatti,
e come ognun vede,
sia merito, sia caso.
abbiamo bel piede,
bell' occhio, bel naso,
guardate bel piede,
osservate bell'occhio,

GUGLIELMO

Irresistibly drawn into your orbit—

FERRANDO

Like two bees by two rosebuds—

GUGLIELMO

There we hover, adoring,

BOTH

And humbly ask for mercy and consolation!

FIORDILIGI

That is enough!

DORABELLA

O sister, what to do now?

No. 14. RECITATIVE AND ARIA

FIORDILIGI

Bold intruders, leave this house this
very instant.

(*Despina becomes alarmed*)

We will not let you profane our ears,
our spirits' inmost reaches, with
your vile, sacrilegious, disgusting
speeches! Do not attempt to win
our love or ever find the way to
our hearts. Our faith is lasting and
belongs now and always to our be-
loveds, till the day of our death,
pure and unfailing, in the face of
misfortune ever prevailing.

Strongly founded, a marble tower,
Safely guarded from ev'ry foe
and hostile power,
So my heart, forever faithful,
Bears an armor no force can rend.

It is love, complete, unfailing
Bringing joy and sweetest comfort,
Over evil force prevailing,
Forever prevailing,
Love that only death can end.
Strongly founded, a marble tower,
etc.

You will never win our favor.
Bear the truth with resignation.
We are proof against temptation,
We are deaf when you implore.
Cast your idle hopes away.
There is nothing more to say.
We are faithful evermore,
For evermore!

(*the women start to leave. Ferrando
and Guglielmo try to detain them.*)

RECITATIVE

FERRANDO

Please do not leave us!

GUGLIELMO

(*to Dorabella*)
How can you be so cruel!
(*to Alfonso*)
(See, I told you!)

DON ALFONSO

(Wait till later.) Dear ladies, I implore you, your outbursts embarass
me severely.

DORABELLA

(*angrily*)
Just what are you suggesting?

DON ALFONSO

Quite simply: there's no reason to become so offensive. They are not only
gentlemen, but also friends of mine.

FIORDILIGI

Really! And why should we listen?

GUGLIELMO

Because we're suffering and deserve
to be heard. The heavenly radiance
of your beauty has thrown us into
misery for which there is no remedy
except the balm of love. Just for
one moment bestow on us the favor
of your merciful pity! You see us
lying abjectly before you. Our passion is undying!

No. 15. ARIA

GUGLIELMO

How can you refuse us
The light of your gazes,
The glow that suffuses
And dazes our hearts?
We promise you happiness
Untroubled by sadness,
A life that is paradise,
All sunshine and gladness!
Have patience, consider our
qualifications:
We're strong and athletic,
Romantic, poetic,
We're just over twenty,
With money a-plenty,
And so sympathetic,
Good-natured and healthy,
Well-balanced and wealthy,

toccate bel naso,
il tutto osservate:
e questi mustacchi
chiamare si possono
trionfi degli uomini,
penacchi d'amor,
trionfi,
penacchi, mustacchi!

SCENA XII

No. 16. TERZETTO

DON ALFONSO
E voi ridete?

FERRANDO, GUGLIELMO
Certo, ridiamo.

DON ALFONSO
Ma cosa avete?

FERRANDO, GUGLIELMO
Già lo sappiamo.

DON ALFONSO
Ridete piano.

FERRANDO, GUGLIELMO
Parlate invano.

DON ALFONSO
Ridete piano,
piano,
piano,
piano.

FERRANDO, GUGLIELMO
Parlate invano,
Parlate invano.

DON ALFONSO
Se vi sentissero,
se vi scoprissero,
si guasterebbe
tutto l'affar,
si guasterebbe
tutto l'affar.

FERRANDO, GUGLIELMO
Ah che dal ridere,

DON ALFONSO
Mi fa da ridere

FERRANDO, GUGLIELMO
l'alma dividere,
ah, ah, ah, ah, ah, ah, ah, ah,

DON ALFONSO
questo lor ridere,
ma so che in piangere
dee terminar.

FERRANDO, GUGLIELMO
Ah, che dal ridere
l'alma dividere,
Ah, ah, ah, ah!
Ah, che le viscere
sento scoppiar.

DON ALFONSO
Mi da da ridere
questo lor ridere
ma so che in piangere
dee terminar,
dee terminar,
dee terminar!

RECITATIVO

DON ALFONSO
Si può sapere un poco la cagion di quel
riso?

GUGLIELMO
Oh cospettaccio, non vi pare che abbiam giusta ragione, il mio caro
padrone?

FERRANDO
Quanto pagar volete, e a monte è la
scommessa?

GUGLIELMO
Pagate la metà.

FERRANDO
Pagate solo venti quattro zecchini.

And before you forego us—
We want you to know us—
Two models of manhood!
And then these mustaches,
So rightly notorious,
What could be more glorious
A symbol of love?
> (*the women leave*)

They make us victorious
And peerless in love!
> (*laughing*)

What glorious, victorious mustaches!

SCENE XII

No. 16. TERZET

DON ALFONSO

What is so funny?

FERRANDO, GUGLIELMO
(*trying to suppress their laughter*)
We won your money!

DON ALFONSO

You are conceited!

FERRANDO, GUGLIELMO

You are defeated!

DON ALFONSO

Can't you be quiet?

FERRANDO, GUGLIELMO

You can't deny it!

DON ALFONSO

Will you be quiet, quiet, quiet, quiet!

FERRANDO, GUGLIELMO

You can't deny it, you can't deny it!

DON ALFONSO

How inconsiderate!
Why not cooperate,
Try to be patient another day.

FERRANDO, GUGLIELMO

This is hilarious!

DON ALFONSO

It's too precarious!

FERRANDO, GUGLIELMO

I can't be serious!

DON ALFONSO

You are delirious!

FERRANDO, GUGLIELMO

Ha, ha, ha, ha, ha, ha.
What a comedy,
What a display!

DON ALFONSO

There'll be a tragedy,
Sorry to say.
Control yourself,
Don't be so gay!

FERRANDO, GUGLIELMO

It is ridiculous!

DON ALFONSO

You're too meticulous!

FERRANDO, GUGLIELMO

This is too much for me,
Past my capacity,
Of all the laughs I had
This is the best.

DON ALFONSO

Laugh in your innocence,
Happy in ignorance,
But he who laughs last
Still laughs the best.

RECITATIVE

DON ALFONSO

May I ask in all politeness, what's so
terribly funny?

GUGLIELMO

How can you ask us? I should think
we have more than ample reason,
most reverend benefactor.

FERRANDO
(*jokingly*)
Pay us each fifty sov'reigns and admit
that you are beaten!

GUGLIELMO

Or pay us at least one half!

FERRANDO

I'll even settle for a mere twenty
sov'reigns.

DON ALFONSO

Poveri innocentini! venite quà, vi
voglio porre il ditino in bocca.

GUGLIELMO

E avete ancora coraggio di fiatar?

DON ALFONSO

Avanti sera ci parlerem.

FERRANDO

Quando volete.

DON ALFONSO

Intanto silenzio e ubbidienza fino a
doman mattina.

GUGLIELMO

Siamo soldati, e amiam la disciplina.

DON ALFONSO

Or bene: andate un poco ad attend-
ermi entrambi in giardinetto, colà vi
manderò gli ordini miei.

GUGLIELMO

Ed oggi non si mangia?

FERRANDO

Cosa serve: a battaglia finita fia la cena
per noi più saporita.

No. 17. ARIA

FERRANDO

Un' aura amorosa
del nostro tesoro
un dolce ristoro
al cor porgerà.

Al cor che nudrito
da speme d'amore,
d'un esca migliore
bisogna non ha.

SCENA XIII

RECITATIVO

DON ALFONSO

Oh la saria da ridere: sì poche son le
donne costante in questo mondo e

quì vene son due! non sarà nulla —
vieni, vieni, fanciulla, e dimmi un
poco dove sono e che fan le tue
padrone?

DESPINA

Le povere buffone stanno nel giardinetto a lagnarsi coll' aria e colle
mosche d'aver perso gli amanti.

DON ALFONSO

E come credi che l'affar finirà? vogliam
sperare che faranno giudizio?

DESPINA

Io lo farei; e dove piangon esse io
riderei, disperarsi, strozzarsi perchè
parte un amante: guardate che pazzia. Se ne pigliano due, s'uno va via.

DON ALFONSO

Brava! questa è prudenza. (Bisogna
impuntigliarla.)

DESPINA

E legge di natura, e non prudenza sola:
amor cos' è? piacer, comodo, gusto,
gioja, divertimento, passatempo, allegria: non è più amore se incomodo
diventa, se invece di piacer nuoce e
tormenta.

DON ALFONSO

Ma intanto queste pazze.

DESPINA

Quelle pazze? faranno a modo nostro.
E buon che sappiano d'esser amate
da color.

DON ALFONSO

Lo sanno.

DESPINA

Dunque riameranno. Diglielo si suol
dire e lascia fare il diavolo.

DON ALFONSO

E come far vuoi perchè ritornino or
che partiti sono, e che li sentano e
tentare si lasciano queste tue bestio-
line?

DON ALFONSO

Poor, inexperienced children. Just wait a bit and I will make you eat your words!

GUGLIELMO

You want to tell us you still will not give up?

DON ALFONSO

Tomorrow morning we'll talk again.

FERRANDO

I'll be delighted.

DON ALFONSO

But meanwhile, our bet is still valid up to tomorrow morning.

GUGLIELMO

We are soldiers and gave our word of honor.

DON ALFONSO

All right! I'll go ahead then and await you behind the little garden, and there you shall receive my further orders.

GUGLIELMO

And what about our dinner?

FERRANDO

What's the diff'rence? once the battle is over, it will taste that much better to the winner!

No. 17. Aria

FERRANDO

My love is a flower,
All fragrant before me,
To soothe and restore me
With wonderful art.
Its charm and its power,
So sweet and alluring
And always enduring,
Will grow in my heart.

A spirit I nourish
With tender devotion
Forever will flourish
In glory apart.

(*exeunt Ferrando and Guglielmo*)

SCENE XIII

Recitative

DON ALFONSO

That would be too ridiculous! I've never found a woman who's faithful in this world and now I should find two! That is impossible.

(*enter Despina*)

There you are, my Despina. Your precious ladies, where are they? Are we making any progress?

DESPINA

Those simple-minded creatures, they're in the little garden and are telling the birds and bees of the loss of their lovers.

DON ALFONSO

What's your opinion on just how this will end? What can we do to achieve our objective?

DESPINA

Don't you worry! The more they will lament, the more I'll cheer them. All this ranting and raving for their former two lovers—I call that downright foolish. For each man who is gone, two more are waiting.

DON ALFONSO

Splendid! You are a wizzard! (It never hurts to flatter.)

DESPINA

It doesn't take much wisdom, its female intuition. For what is love? It's fun, pleasantry, gaiety, laughter, entertainment, merely pastime or a whim: once it gets serious, it is no longer love, because it is a burden and a nuisance.

DON ALFONSO

Let's think about our ladies.

DESPINA

That is simple. They'll do what we tell them. But do they realize how much they mean to our friends?

DON ALFONSO

They do.

DESPINA

Then let's prepare the groundwork. Expose them to temptation and leave the rest to nature.

DON ALFONSO

And tell me, your two indignant mistresses, now that they are so angry, how will you manage to calm them sufficiently, make them reconsider?

DESPINA

A me lasciate la briga di condur tutta
la macchina. Quando Despina macchina uno cosa, non può mancar
d'effetto: ho già menati mill' uomini
pel naso, saprò menar due femmine.
Son ricchi i due monsieurs mustacchi?

DON ALFONSO

Son richissimi.

DESPINA

Dove son?

DON ALFONSO

Sulla strada attendendomi stanno.

DESPINA

Ite, e sul fatto per la picciola porta a
me riconduceteli: v'aspetto, nella
camera mia. Purchè tutto facciate
quel ch'io v'ordinerò pria di domani
i vostri amici canteran vittoria; ed
essi avranno il gusto ed io la gloria.

SCENA XIV

No. 18. FINALE

FIORDILIGI, DORABELLA

Ah! che tutta in un momento
si cangiò la sorte mia,
ah, che un mar pien di tormento,
è la vita omai per me.

Finchè meco il caro bene
mi lasciar le ingrate stelle,
non sapea cos' eran pene,
non sapea languir cos' è.

SCENA XV

FERRANDO, GUGLIELMO

Si mora, sì, si mora,
onde appagar le ingrate.

DON ALFONSO

C'è una speranza ancora,
non fate, oh dei, non fate!

FIORDILIGI, DORABELLA

Stelle, che grida orribili!

FERRANDO, GUGLIELMO

Lasciatemi!

DON ALFONSO

Aspettate!

FERRANDO, GUGLIELMO

L'arsenico mi liberi
di tanta crudeltà.

FIORDILIGI, DORABELLA

Stelle, un velen fu quello?

DON ALFONSO

Veleno buono e bello,
che ad essi in pochi istanti
la vita toglierà.

FIORDILIGI, DORABELLA

Il tragico spettacolo
gelare il cor mi fa!

FERRANDO, GUGLIELMO

Barbare, avvicinatevi:
d'un disperato affetto
mirate il tristo effetto
e abbiate almen pietà.

FIORDILIGI, DORABELLA, FERRANDO,
DON ALFONSO, GUGLIELMO

Ah! che del sole il raggio
fosco per me diventa.
Tremo, le fibre e l'anima
par che mancar si senta,
nè può la lingua o il labbro
accenti articolar.

DON ALFONSO

Giacchè a morir vicini
sono quei meschinelli
pietade almeno a quelli
cercate di mostrar.

FIORDILIGI, DORABELLA

Gente, accorrete, gente!
Nessuno, o dio, ci sente!
Despina! Despina!

DESPINA

Leave it to me. In such matters, there is no one who can equal me. When Despina manages a romance, she does not miss a chance. I have succeeded in fooling a thousand men—I can fool two women. You said your friends are very wealthy?

DON ALFONSO

Lots of money!

DESPINA

Where are they?

DON ALFONSO

They are waiting to receive further orders.

DESPINA

Splendid! Then I ask you to lead them to my room through the little garden door. I'll be ready. And I know my course of action. If both of them are willing to follow my advice, then by tomorrow your two friends will lap milk and honey, and you will win your wager, and I your money.

(*exeunt. Curtain*)

SCENE XIV

(*A flower garden. Two grassy seats on either side. Fiordiligi and Dorabella*)

No. 18. FINALE

FIORDILIGI, DORABELLA

Ah, how sad and unrelenting
Is the fate that I must suffer,
Endless grief, cruelly tormenting,
Makes my life too hard to bear.
All was happiness and gladness
Till the moment we were parted.
Not a thought of grief or sadness,
Not a trouble, not a care,
Life was sweet and life was fair, ah—
Now the lovely dream is ended
And my joy destroyed forever.
All alone and unbefriended,
I shall die of dark despair.

SCENE XV

FERRANDO, GUGLIELMO
(*backstage*)

A double dose of poison,
That is the one solution!

DON ALFONSO

I beg you reconsider
So grim a resolution.

FIORDILIGI, DORABELLA

Heavens, that noise is horrible!

FERRANDO, GUGLIELMO

Don't hinder me!

DON ALFONSO

Not so hasty!
(*Ferrando and Guglielmo enter, each carrying a little flask, followed by Don Alfonso.*)

FERRANDO, GUGLIELMO

With arsenic upon our lips
We leave the world behind.
(*They drink, then throw their flasks to the ground; turning, they see the two women.*)

FIORDILIGI, DORABELLA

Goodness, they've taken poison?

DON ALFONSO

The strongest kind of poison,
Some arsenic and henbane
And strychnine all combined.

FIORDILIGI, DORABELLA

O tragic, woeful spectacle,
It makes my blood run cold!

FERRANDO, GUGLIELMO

Heartless, unfeeling womankind,
Our will to live is undermined.
You have disdained our wooing,
Brought on our sad undoing,
We cannot be consoled!

FIORDILIGI, DORABELLA

I'm terrified by suicide,
It frightens me to death!

ALL FIVE

All I can see is blackness,
Horror has stunned my feeling!
Trembling and shaking and shivering,
Giddy and faint and reeling,
I cannot utter a whisper,
I cannot draw a breath.
(*Ferrando and Guglielmo fall down on the grass.*)

DON ALFONSO

Frozen in rigor mortis
See how their muscles tighten!
Their handsome faces whiten
Upon the brink of death.

FIORDILIGI, DORABELLA

Help us, somebody come and help us!
We're powerless to save them!
Despina, Despina!

DESPINA
Chi mi chiama?

FIORDILIGI, DORABELLA
Despina! Despina!

DESPINA
Cosa vedo!
morti i meschini io credo,
o prossimi a spirar.

DON ALFONSO
Ah che pur troppo è vero:
furenti, disperati
si sono avvelenati,
oh amore singolar!

DESPINA
Abbandonar i miseri
saria per voi vergogna,
soccorrerli bisogna.

FIORDILIGI, DORABELLA, DON ALFONSO
Cosa possiam mai far?

DESPINA
Soccorrerli bisogna.

FIORDILIGI, DORABELLA, DON ALFONSO
Cosa possiam mai far?

DESPINA
Di vita ancor dan segno,
colle pietose mani
fate un po lor sostegno.
E voi con me correte:
un medico un antidoto
voliamo a ricercar.

FIORDILIGI, DORABELLA
Dei! che cimento è questo!
Evento più funesto
non si potea trovar!

FERRANDO, GUGLIELMO
Più bella comediola
non si potea trovar!

FERRANDO, GUGLIELMO
Ah!

FIORDILIGI, DORABELLA
Sospiran gl'infelici!

FIORDILIGI
Che facciamo?

DORABELLA
Tu che dici?

FIORDILIGI
In momenti si dolenti
chi potria li abbandonar?

DORABELLA
Che figure interessanti!

FIORDILIGI
Possiam farci un poco avanti.

DORABELLA
Ha fredissima la testa.

FIORDILIGI
Fredda, fredda è ancora questa.

DORABELLA
Ed il polso?

FIORDILIGI
Io non gliel' sento.

DORABELLA
Questo batte lento, lento.

FIORDILIGI, DORABELLA
Ah se tarda ancor l'aita,
speme più non v'è di vita.

FERRANDO, GUGLIELMO
Più domestiche e trattabili
sono entrambe diventate:

FIORDILIGI, DORABELLA
Poverini, poverini!
la lor morte
mi farebbe lagrimar.

FERRANDO, GUGLIELMO
Sta a veder
che lor pietade
va in amore a terminar.

DESPINA
(backstage)
Did you call me?

FIORDILIGI, DORABELLA
Despina, Despina!

DESPINA
(entering)
What has happened?
How did they come to lie here
In such a helpless state?

DON ALFONSO
Driven by hopeless passion,
Despondent and melancholic,
They swallowed pure carbolic!
All help might come too late.

DESPINA
How can you see them lying there,
With no attention paid them?
We all must try to aid them.

FIORDILIGI, DORABELLA, DON ALFONSO
Tell us what you suggest!

DESPINA
We all must try to aid them!

FIORDILIGI, DORABELLA, DON ALFONSO
Tell us what you suggest!

DESPINA
There still are signs of life left.
Raise their heads just slightly,
Stroke their foreheads lightly,
(to Don Alfonso)
Let's run and get a doctor.
I know of one who's marvelous
With people who are ill.
He's nkown for working miracles
Without a knife or pill.
He's famous for his skill.
Perhaps he'll save them still.
(Exeunt Despina and Don Alfonso.)

FIORDILIGI, DORABELLA
What can we do, I wonder?
We made a fatal blunder
And brought about their death!

FERRANDO, GUGLIELMO
(aside)
This is so very funny,
I'll laugh myself to death!
(aloud)
Ah!

FIORDILIGI, DORABELLA
Poor fellows, they are sighing!

FIORDILIGI
(standing at quite a distance from the
two lovers)
Are they suff'ring?

DORABELLA
What do you think?

FIORDILIGI
Hear them moaning,
Loudly groaning!
Who could disregard such pain?

DORABELLA
(coming a little closer)
They have quite distinguished faces.

FIORDILIGI
(coming a little closer)
Let's advance a few more paces.

DORABELLA
This one's head is simply rigid.

FIORDILIGI
This one's arms are very rigid.

DORABELLA
Is he breathing?

FIORDILIGI
He is, but rarely.

DORABELLA
This one's pulse is beating barely.

FIORDILIGI
Help must come this very minute!

FIORDILIGI, DORABELLA
Their endurance reached the limit!

FERRANDO, GUGLIELMO
(softly)
They have lost their proud relentless-
ness,
Getting tamer by the minute.

FIORDILIGI, DORABELLA
O so helpless, so pathetic!
If they die now,
I am sure that I will cry.

FERRANDO, GUGLIELMO
I'm afraid that they may weaken,
That's a thought I can't deny,
A dreadful thought I can't deny.
(Enter Despina, disguised as a doctor.)

SCENA XVI

DON ALFONSO

Eccovi il medico,
signore belle.

FERRANDO, GUGLIELMO

Despina in maschera, che trista pelle!

DESPINA

Salvete amabiles
bones puelles.

FIORDILIOI, DORABELLA

Parla un linguaggio che non sappiamo.

DESPINA

Come comandano dunque parliamo,
So il greco e l'arabo, so il turco e il
     vandalo,
lo svevo e il tartaro so ancor parlar.

DON ALFONSO

Tanti linguaggi per se conservi:
quei miserabili per ora osservi:
Preso hanno il tossico; che si può far?

FIORDILIGI, DORABELLA

Signor Dottore, che si può far?

DESPINA

Saper bisognami
pria la cagione,
E quinci l'indole
della pozione,
se calda, o frigida,
se poca, o molta,
se in una volta,
ovvero in più.

FIORDILIGI, DORABELLA, DON ALFONSO

Preso han l'arsenico,
Signor Dottore,
Qui dentro il bebbero.
La causa è amore
Ed in un sorso
sel mandar giù.

DESPINA

Non vi affannate,
non vi turbate,
Ecco una prova
di mia virtù.

FIORDILIGI, DORABELLA, DON ALFONSO

Egli ha di un ferro
la man fornita.

DESPINA

Questo è quel pezzo
di calamita
pietra Mesmerica,
ch' ebbe l'origine
nell' Alemagna,
che poi sì celebre
là in Francia fù.

FIORDILIGI, DORABELLA, DON ALFONSO

Come si muovono,
torcono, scuotono,
in terra il cranio
presto percuotono.

DESPINA

Ah lor la fronte
tenete sù.

FIORDILIGI, DORABELLA

Eccoci pronte.

DESPINA

Tenete forte,
coraggio!
or liberi
siete da morte.

FIORDILIGI, DORABELLA, DON ALFONSO

Attorno guardano:
forze riprendono:
ah questo medico vale un Perù.

FERRANDO, GUGLIELMO

Dove son!
che loco è questo?
Chi è colui? color chi sono?
son di Giove innanzi al trono?
Sei tu Palla, o Citerea?
No, tu sei l'alma mia dea;
ti ravviso al dolce viso:
e alla man ch'or ben conosco
e che sola è il mio tesor.

DESPINA, DON ALFONSO

Son effetti ancor del tosco.
Non abbiate alcun timor.

SCENE XVI

DON ALFONSO

May I present to you Doctor Fatalis?

FERRANDO, GUGLIELMO
(to themselves)

That is Despina, just as we have
planned it!

DESPINA

Salve ad libitum cum grano salis.

FIORDILIGI, DORABELLA

That may be so, but we don't understand it.

DESPINA

If you insist on it, I will translate it,
But the vernacular
Sounds less spectacular,
Completely flavorless, not recherché

DON ALFONSO

Who cares for flavor? Do us a favor,
Make a suggestion.
These frantic gentlemen have taken
poison,
They swallowed arsenic
What do you say?

FIORDILIGI, DORABELLA

What are their chances?
What do you say?

DESPINA
(Feels their pulses and puts her hand
to their foreheads.)

That will necessitate
Knowing the hist'ry,
I must investigate,
Study this myst'ry.
For instance, this suicide,
What caused it? The potion,
Have you a notion
If it was brown?

FIORDILIGI, DORABELLA, DON ALFONSO

They both took arsenic,
A double potion.
Love caused their suicide.
They had a bottle and with a swallow
They gulped it down.

DESPINA

I am delighted!
Don't get excited!
I'll make them well again,
As good as new.
Just let me show you
What I can do.

FIORDILIGI, DORABELLA, DON ALFONSO

He is producing a giant magnet!

DESPINA

(Touches the foreheads of the two im-
aginary invalids with the magnet,
then gently strokes the whole length
of their bodies.)

Old Doctor Besmer
Was my professor
Over in Germany.
Using his principles
Based on magnetics,
I now will demonstrate
My art to you.

FIORDILIGI, DORABELLA, DON ALFONSO

See them gesticulate,
Oscillate, palpitate,
And their convulsions are really
desperate!

DESPINA

Help me support them.
They are still weak.

FIORDILIGI, DORABELLA
(putting their hands to the foreheads
of the two lovers)

We'll do it gladly.

DESPINA

You're doing nicely.
That's it precisely!
They soon will be fully recovered.

FIORDILIGI, DORABELLA, DON ALFONSO

See them revive again
Fully alive again,
Thanks to the doctor's amazing
technique!

FERRANDO, GUGLIELMO
(slowly raising themselves)

Am I dead? Or am I dreaming?
Is this Eden or Valhalla?
Or the garden realm of Allah?
Are you Venus?
Or Cleopatra?
No, you are my dear beloved!
Even death can't come between us.
Here's the hand I love so dearly
And would kiss with all respect.
(They embrace the women tenderly and
kiss their hands.)

DESPINA, DON ALFONSO

It they talk a little queerly,
It's the magnet's strong effect.

FIORDILIGI, DORABELLA
Sarà ver, ma tante smorfie
fanno torto al nostro onor.

FERRANDO, GUGLIELMO
(Dalla voglia ch' ho di ridere,
    il polmon mi scoppia oror.)
Per pietà, bell' idol mio!
volgi a me le luci liete!

FIORDILIGI, DORABELLA
Più resister non poss' io!

DESPINA, DON ALFONSO
In porch' ore lo vedrete
per virtù del magnetismo
finire quel parossismo,
torneranno al primo umor.

FERRANDO, GUGLIELMO
Dammi un bacio, o mio tesoro,
Un sol bacio, o qui mi moro!

FIORDILIGI, DORABELLA
Stelle, un bacio?

DESPINA, DON ALFONSO
Secondate
per effetto di bontate.

FIORDILIGI, DORABELLA
Ah, che troppo si richiede
da una fida onesta amante
oltraggiata è la mia fede,
oltraggiato è questo cor.

DESPINA, FERRANDO, DON ALFONSO,
GUGLIELMO
Un quadretto più giocondo
non si vide in tutto il mondo,
quel che più mi fa da ridere
è quell' ira e quel furor.

FIORDILIGI, DORABELLA
Disperati, attossicati,
ite al diavol quanti siete;
tardi in ver vi pentirete
se più cresce il mio furor.

FERRANDO, GUGLIELMO
Dammi un bacio,
o mio tesoro,
un sol bacio,
o qui mi moro!

FIORDILIGI, DORABELLA
Disperati,
attossicati
ite al diavol
quanto siete
tardi inver
vi pentirete
se più cresce
il mio furor.

FERRANDO, GUGLIELMO
Un sol bacio!

FIORDILIGI, DORABELLA
Stelle, un bacio?

DESPINA, DON ALFONSO
Ch'io ben so che tanto foco
cangerassi in quel' d'amor.

FERRANDO, GUGLIELMO
Ne vorrei che tanto foco
terminassi in quel' d'amor.

ATTO SECONDO

SCENA I

RECITATIVO

DESPINA
Andate là, che siete due bizarre
    ragazze!

FIORDILIGI
Oh cospettaccio! cosa pretenderesti?

DESPINA
Per me nulla.

FIORDILIGI
Per chi dunque?

FIORDILIGI, DORABELLA

That may be, but such effusions
Mar the honor of my name.
Make them see that these delusions
Are a scandal and a shame.

DESPINA, DON ALFONSO

Please forgive them for their effusions,
Their condition is to blame.

FERRANDO, GUGLIELMO
(softly)
Though it's really too ridiculous,
I enjoy it just the same.
(aloud)
Take my heart and my devotion!
Do not spurn my burning ardor!

FIORDILIGI, DORABELLA

Who could hear without emotion?

DESPINA, DON ALFONSO

We are certain they'll recover.
Only wait a little longer,
Till they feel a trifle stronger.
It is too much to expect.

FERRANDO, GUGLIELMO

Kiss me, darling, I implore you,
Or I'll die right here before you!

FIORDILIGI, DORABELLA

Kiss you? Good Heavens!

DESPINA, DON ALFONSO

Better do it out of kindness!
Nothing to it.

FIORDILIGI, DORABELLA

What a shameless imposition
On good faith and true devotion,
Forcing us to give permission
For an outrage we abhor!

DESPINA, DON ALFONSO, FERRANDO,
GUGLIELMO

Since the dawning of creation
Was there ever a like flirtation?
This has been the gayest comedy
(frolic)
I have ever seen before.

FIORDILIGI, DORABELLA

Go away, you wicked madmen,
With your kisses and embraces!
Shameless, evil-minded badmen,
Never dare to show your faces
anymore!
There is the door!

FERRANDO, GUGLIELMO

Kiss me, darling, I implore you,
Or I'll die right here before you!

FIORDILIGI, DORABELLA

Go away, you wicked madmen,
With your kisses and embraces,
We don't want to see your faces
For a single minute more!

FERRANDO, GUGLIELMO

Darling, kiss me!

FIORDILIGI, DORABELLA

Never! How dare you!

DESPINA, DON ALFONSO

Better do it
Out of kindness.
Nothing to it.

FIORDILIGI, DORABELLA

Ah, how dare you stand and face us,
After such a bold proposal?
Are you trying to disgrace us?
Never dare to show your face!
Don't come back here any more!
Do not make our anger greater,
We disdain and spurn your love!

DESPINA, DON ALFONSO

I'm convinced that soon or later
Their disdain will turn to love.

FERRANDO, GUGLIELMO

I'm afraid that soon or later
Their disdain may turn to love.

(Curtain)

ACT TWO

SCENE I

(A room in the sister's home. Fiordiligi,
Dorabella, and Despina.)

DESPINA

For Heaven's sake, how can you be
so unrealistic?

FIORDILIGI

You little devil! What is it you want?

DESPINA

Nothing for me.

FIORDILIGI

For whom then?

DESPINA

Per voi.

DORABELLA

Per noi?

DESPINA

Per voi. Siete voi donne, o no?

FIORDILIGI

E per questo?

DESPINA

E per questo dovete far da donne.

DORABELLA

Cio è?

DESPINA

Trattar l'amore en bagatelle. Le occa-
sioni belle non negliger giammai!
cangiar a tempo, a tempo esser costanti, coquettizar con grazia, pre-
venir la disgrazia sì comune a chi si
fida in uomo, mangiar il fico, e non
gittare il pomo.

FIORDILIGI

(Che diavolo!) tai cose falle tu, se n'hai
voglia.

DESPINA

Io già faccio. Ma vorrei che anche voi
per gloria del bel sesso faceste un po'
lo stesso; per esempio: i vostri
Ganimedi son andati alla guerra;
infin che tornano fate alla militare:
reclutate.

DORABELLA

Il cielo ce ne guardi.

DESPINA

Eh! che noi siamo in terra, e non in
cielo! Fidatevi al mio zelo. Giacchè
questi forestieri v'adorano lasciatevi
adorar. Son ricchi, belli, nobili, gen-
erosi come fede fece a voi Don Alfonso; avean corraggio di morire per
voi; questi son merti che sprezzar non
si denno da giovani qual voi belle e
galanti, che pon star senza amor, non
senza amanti. (Par che ci trovin
gusto!)

FIORDILIGI

Per Bacco ci faresti far delle belle cose;
credi tu che vogliamo favola diven-
tar degli oziosi? ai nostri cari sposi
credi tu che vogliam dar tal tormento?

DESPINA

E chi dice, che abbiate a far loro alcun
torto?

DORABELLA

Non ti pare, che sia torto bastante, se
noto si facesse, che trattiamo costor?

DESPINA

Anche per questo c'è un mezzo sicuris-
simo, io voglio sparger fama, che
vengono da me.

DORABELLA

Chi vuol che il creda?

DESPINA

Oh bella! non ha forse merto una
cameriera d'aver due cicisbei? di me
fidatevi.

FIORDILIGI

No, no, son troppo audaci questi tuoi
forestieri, non ebber la baldanza fin
di chieder dei baci.

DESPINA

(Che disgrazia!) io posso assicurarvi
che le cose che han fatto furo effetti
del tossico, che han preso, convul-
sioni, deliri, follie, vaneggiamenti; ma
or vedrete, come son discreti, mani-
erosi, modesti, e mansueti, lasciateli
venir.

DORABELLA

E poi?

DESPINA

E poi: caspita! fate voi. (L'ho detto
che cadrebbero.)

FIORDILIGI

Cosa dobbiamo far?

DESPINA

Quel che volete. Siete d'ossa, e di carne,
o cosa siete?

DESPINA

For you.

DORABELLA

For us?

DESPINA

That's right. Are you both women or not?

FIORDILIGI

Can you doubt it?

DESPINA

Yes, I doubt it; you act like little schoolgirls.

DORABELLA

How so?

DESPINA

Because you think that love is serious. You must be ready when opportunity knocks. You must be equal to every new occasion, be frank or coquettish, all depending upon the man in question. That way you're always winner, and have your bread buttered on both sides.

FIORDILIGI

(What deviltry!) You may do things like that, if you want to.

DESPINA

I've always done them. But I wish that you both, for the sake of all womanhood, would follow my example. Let me tell you, now that your two Romeos have become valiant warriors, do as they did, seek your own adventures, and do it quickly.

DORABELLA

May Heaven preserve me!

DESPINA

Eh, be glad we are not yet in Heaven, but very much on earth. You have met two nice young suitors. They worship you! Then why not let them do so? They're wealthy, handsome, generous, well bred. Don Alfonso told you everything about them. They had the courage to die for your sake —is that not proof that they mean what they're saying? And aren't you both young, lovable women who deserve to be loved and adored? (Seems I am making headway!)

FIORDILIGI

I am inclined to think you want to lead us into mischief. Are you really proposing that we become the topic for gossip? And what about our lovers—do you think we would ever betray them?

DESPINA

And who said that you should. Where would be the betrayal?

DORABELLA

In my opinion, it would be bad enough if anybody heard that we met other men.

DESPINA

That is no problem. Let me take care of that for you. I'll simply spread a rumor they came to visit me.

DORABELLA

Who would believe it?

DESPINA

Why not? Any average ladies-maid has a lover—why couldn't I have two? Don't let that worry you!

FIORDILIGI

No, no! I could not do it? Those two men are so reckless! They even had the daring to beg us for kisses.

DESPINA

(Isn't that awful!) I give you my assurance that your suitors' behavior was due to the influence of poison —all their tantrums, their ravings, their fits, and all their antics. Get to know them as they really are. They are modest and decent, very polished. You'll see it for yourselves.

DORABELLA

And then?

DESPINA

And then: ask yourself! That's your business! (I knew that I could handle them.)

FIORDILIGI

What do you suggest?

DESPINA

Follow your heart. Are you made of flesh and blood, or just what are you?

No. 19. ARIA

DESPINA

Una donna
a quindici anni
dee saper
ogni gran moda,
dove il diavolo
ha la coda
cosa è beneme nal cos'è,
dee saper
la maliziette,
che innamorano
gli amanti,
finger riso,
finger pianti,
inventar i bei perché.

Dee in un momento
dar retta a cento,
colle pupille
parlar con mille,
dar speme a tutti,
sien belli o brutti,
saper nascondersi,
senza confondersi,
senza arrossire
saper mentire,
e qual regina
dall' alto soglio
col posso e voglio
farsi ubbidir.

Par ch' abbian gusto
di tal dottrina,
viva Despina
che sa servir,
che sa servir,
che sa servir!

SCENA II

RECITATIVO

FIORDILIGI

Sorella, cosa dici?

DORABELLA

Io son stordita dallo spirto infernal di
tal ragazza.

FIORDILIGI

Ma credimi è una pazza. Ti par che
siamo in caso di seguir suoi consigli?

DORABELLA

Oh certo se tu pigli pel rovescio il
negozio.

FIORDILIGI

Anzi io lo piglio per il suo vero dritto:
non credi tu delitto per due giovani
omai promesse spose il far di queste
cose?

DORABELLA

Ella non dice che facciamo alcun mal.

FIORDILIGI

E mal che basta il far parlar di noi.

DORABELLA

Quando si dice che vengon per
Despina!

FIORDILIGI

Oh, tu sei troppo larga di coscienza!
e che diranno gli sposi nostri?

DORABELLA

Nulla: o non sapran l'affare ed è tutto
finito: o sapran qualche cosa e allor
diremo che vennero per lei.

FIORDILIGI

Ma i nostri cori?

DORABELLA

Restano quel che sono; per divertirsi
un poco, e non morire della malin-
conia non si manca di fè, sorella
mia.

FIORDILIGI

Questo è ver.

DORABELLA

Dunque?

FIORDILIGI

Dunque fa un po tu: ma non voglio
aver colpa, se poi nasce un imbroglio.

No. 19. Aria

DESPINA

Any girl fifteen or over
Must pursue a woman's mission,
And with feminine intuition
Be an expert managing men.
She must know a thousand ruses
To attract the man she chooses.
Laugh or chatter,
Weep or flatter,
Know the moment where and when.
When to amuse them,
When to confuse them,
When she should tease them,
When she should please them.
She must act slyly,
Clever and wily,
In all the ritual,
New or habitual,
Never revealing
Her inner feeling.

Love is her kingdom
She rules in splendor.
Men must surrender,
Serve her and bow.
Life can be keener,
Love can be greener,
Come to Despina,
She'll tell you how!
She'll answer questions,
Give you suggestions,
How you can handle
Gossip or scandal.
She can direct you,
She can perfect you
In all formalities
And technicalities,
Never revealing
Her inner feeling.
Love is the kingdom
She rules in splendor.
Men must surrender,
Serve her and bow!

(exit Despina)

SCENE II

RECITATIVE

FIORDILIGI

I never heard such nonsense!

DORABELLA

I am speechless at the girl's unbeliev-
able badness!

FIORDILIGI

Her theories are sheerest madness! For
self-respecting women they are quite
out of question!

DORABELLA

Not quite so out of question if we
treat it as a joke.

FIORDILIGI

In my opinion, such a joke could be
dangerous. Or do you think it proper
for two ladies engaged to be married
to harbor such ideas?

DORABELLA

But she assured us we'd be doing no
harm.

FIORDILIGI

If people gossip, that would be harm
enough.

DORABELLA

But she has offered to claim them as
her suitors!

FIORDILIGI

My, what a nice, convenient type of
conscience! Think of our lovers!
What would they say?

DORABELLA

Nothing! Either they will not know
it—in that case it is simple. Or if by
chance they should hear it, then we
will tell them they are Despina's
friends.

FIORDILIGI

And our engagements?

DORABELLA

They will remain unbroken. An innocent diversion to pass away the te-
dious time of waiting can't be called
a breech of faith—don't you think
so?

FIORDILIGI

That is true.

DORABELLA

Well then?

FIORDILIGI

Do as you please. But remember I
warned you, if something should go
wrong.

DORABELLA

Che imbroglio nascer deve con tanta
precauzion, per altro ascolta, per in-
tenderci bene, qual vuoi scieglier per
te de' due Narcisi.

FIORDILIGI

Decidi tu, sorella.

DORABELLA

Io già decisi.

No. 20. DUETTO

DORABELLA

Prenderò quel brunettino,
che più lepido mi par.

FIORDILIGI

Ed intanto io col biondino
vo un po ridere e burlar.

DORABELLA

Scherzosetta ai dolci detti
io di quel risponderò.

FIORDILIGI

Sospirando i sospiretti
io dell' altro imiterò.

DORABELLA

Mi dirá, ben mio, mi moro.

FIORDILIGI

Mi dirá, mio bel tesoro!

DORABELLA

Ed intanto che diletto,

FIORDILIGI

Ed intanto che diletto,

FIORDILIGI, DORABELLA

Che spassetto io proverò!

SCENA III

RECITATIVO

DON ALFONSO

Ah, correte al giardino le mie care
ragazze! che allegria! che musica!
che canto, che brillante spettacolo!
che incanto! Fate presto, correte!

DORABELLA

Che diamine esser può?

DON ALFONSO

Tosto vedrete.

SCENA IV

No. 21. DUETTO CON CORO

FERRANDO, GUGLIELMO

Secondate, aurette amiche,
Secondate i miei desiri,
E portate i miei sospiri
Alla dea di questo cor.

Voi, che udiste mille volte
Il tenor delle mie pene;
Ripetete al caro bene,
tutto quel che udiste allor.

CORO

Secondate, aurette amiche,
il desir di sì bei cor,
il desir di sì bei cor.

RECITATIVO

DON ALFONSO

Il tutto deponete sopra quei tavolini,
e nella barca ritiratevi, amici.

FIORDILIGI, DORABELLA

Cos' è tal mascherata?

DESPINA

Animo, via, coraggio: avete perso l'uso
della favella?

FERRANDO

Io tremo, e palpito dalla testa alle
piante.

GUGLIELMO

Amor lega le membra a vero amante.

DON ALFONSO

Da brave incorraggiateli.

DORABELLA

And what could possibly happen if we do not go too far? Just one more thing: let me ask you one question. Which of them is your choice for your admirer?

FIORDILIGI

No, you decide, dear sister.

DORABELLA

I have decided!

No. 20. DUET

DORABELLA

I will choose the handsome dark one
If it's all the same to you.

FIORDILIGI

I myself prefer the blond one.
He is gay and winning too!

DORABELLA

I'll delight in his lovelorn phrases
With a most engaging smile.

FIORDILIGI

If he sighs and moons and gazes,
I will echo him in style.

DORABELLA

Mine will say, "My soul is burning!"

FIORDILIGI

Mine will say, "My heart is yearning!"

FIORDILIGI, DORABELLA

How romantic, how enchanting!
How amusing it will be! Ah!

DORABELLA

Mine will say, "I love you only!"

FIORDILIGI

Mine will say, "My heart is lonely!"

BOTH

How romantic, how enchanting!
It may be a little naughty,
But at least it will be fun,
A lot of fun!

(*They start to leave, and run into Don Alfonso.*)

SCENE III

RECITATIVE

DON ALFONSO

Ah, I'm glad that I found you! You must come into the garden! Such a frolic, with music and singing! You'll enjoy it enormously. Don't miss it! It is simply delightful!

DORABELLA

I can hardly wait to see!

DON ALFONSO

Then come with me!
(*Exeunt. Curtain.*)

SCENE IV

(*A garden at the seashore, with grass seats and two little stone tables. A boat decorated with flowers, and a band of musicians. Servants in elaborate costumes. Despina, Ferrando, and Guglielmo on-stage. Then Don Alfonso, Fiordiligi, and Dorabella.*)

No. 21. DUET AND CHORUS

FERRANDO, GUGLIELMO

Friendly breezes, bear my message
To the one I love so dearly!
Ask her favor, beg her to hear me,
Lovely goddess that I adore!
Go and tell her, friendly breezes,
How my lonely heart is breaking,
Ever longing, ever aching!
Say I love her more and more!

CHORUS

(*During this chorus, Ferrando and Guglielmo, decked with chains of flowers, rise. Don Alfonso and Despina lead them to the two women, who look at them astonished and speechless.*)
Friendly breezes, bear their message
To the dear ones they adore.

RECITATIVE

DON ALFONSO

(*To the servants who are bringing vases with flowers.*)
Just leave all the flowers over there on the tables, and then go back to your boat, my good friends.

FIORDILIGI, DORABELLA

Why all the decorations?

DESPINA

(*to Guglielmo and Ferrando*)
Here is your chance, Don't miss it! Can't you speak up—or has the cat got your tongue?

FERRANDO

I'm willing, but somehow I'm a victim of stage-fright.

GUGLIELMO

It seems I have forgotten all my lines.

DON ALFONSO

Dear ladies, please encourage them.

FIORDILIGI
Parlate!

DORABELLA
Liberi dite pur quel che bramate!

FERRANDO
Madama . . .

GUGLIELMO
Anzi madame . . .

FERRANDO
Parla pur tu.

GUGLIELMO
No. no, parla pur tu.

DON ALFONSO
Oh! cospetto del diavolo! lasciate tali
smorfie del secolo passato: Despinetta, terminiam questa festa, fa tu
con lei, quel ch'io farò con questa.

No. 22. QUARTETTO

DON ALFONSO
La mano a me date,
movetevi un pò!
Se voi non parlate,
per voi parlerò.
Perdono vi chiede
un schiavo tremante,
v'offese, lo vede,
ma solo un istante;
or pena, ma tace . . .

FERRANDO, GUGLIELMO
Tace . . .

DON ALFONSO
Or lasciavi in pace . . .

FERRANDO, GUGLIELMO
In pace . . .

DON ALFONSO
Non può quel che vuole,
vorrà. quel che può.

FERRANDO, GUGLIELMO
Non può quel che vuole,
vorrà quel che può.

DON ALFONSO
Su! via! rispondete!
guardate, e ridete?

DESPINA
Per voi la risposta
a loro darò,
per voi la risposta
a loro darò.

Quello ch'è stato, è stato,
scordiamci del passato.
Rompasi omai quel laccio,
segno di servitù;
A me porgete il braccio:
nè sospirate più.

DESPINA, DON ALFONSO
Per carità partiamo,
quel che san far veggiamo,
le stimo più
del diavolo,
s'ora non cascan giù,
le stimo più
del diavolo,
s'ora non cascan giù!

SCENA V

RECITATIVO

FIORDILIGI
Oh che bella giornata!

FERRANDO
Caldetta anzi che no.

DORABELLA
Che vezzosi arboscelli!

GUGLIELMO
Certo, certo: son belli: han più foglie
che frutti.

FIORDILIGI
Quei viali come sono leggiadri; volete
passeggiar?

FERRANDO
Son pronto, o cara, ad ogni vostro
cenno.

FIORDILIGI
Troppa grazia!

FERRANDO
(Eccoci alla gran crisi.)

FIORDILIGI
(to the lovers)

We're list'ning!

DORABELLA

Don't be afraid to say what's on your mind!

FERRANDO

My lady—

GUGLIELMO

Say "Fairest ladies."

FERRANDO

You make the speech.

GUGLIELMO

No, you, you're so much better!

DON ALFONSO

Why, this is too ridiculous! The way you are behaving is hopelessly old-fashioned. Despinetta, if they can't talk themselves, I'll do it for them. You do it for the ladies.

No. 22. QUARTET

DON ALFONSO
(Takes Dorabella by the hand.)

Step forward a little and do as I do.
(Despina takes Fiordiligi's hand.)
If you are too timid,
I will speak for you.
"If we have displeased you,
We truly lament it.
If we have disturbed you,
We deeply repent it.
Two slaves who adore you"

FERRANDO, GUGLIELMO

—dore you,

DON ALFONSO

"Have come to implore you"

FERRANDO, GUGLIELMO

Implore you,

DON ALFONSO

"Whatever you ask us, we gladly will do."

FERRANDO, GUGLIELMO
(in one big breath)

Whatever you ask us, we gladly will do.

DON ALFONSO

And now you must answer, my ladies!
You are silent? You are laughing?

DESPINA
(Stands in front of the two women.)

Since they are so bashful,
So modest and shy,
I'll venture to give you my ladies' reply.
"Let us forget what happened
And think about the future.
(Despina takes Dorabella's hand, Don Alfonso Fiordiligi's; the two ladies break the flower-chain around the two lovers.)
All former ties are broken.
Now we shall be good friends.
Let's join our hands in token
That all your suff'ring ends."

DESPINA, DON ALFONSO
(aside)

And now that we have spoken,
Let's watch it from a distance.
I think the ice is broken.
They need no more assistance.
I'm absolutely positive
The battle has been won,
Completely won!
The comedy is on!
(Exeunt Despina and Don Alfonso. Guglielmo are in arm with Dorabella. Ferrando and Fiordiligi more distant to each other. A short pantomimed scene, in which the four look at each other, sigh, giggle in embarrassment.)

SCENE V

RECITATIVE

FIORDILIGI

What a beautiful morning!

FERRANDO

I think it's a trifle too warm.

DORABELLA

Oh, what beautiful flowers!

GUGLIELMO

That's what I say. However they could smell a little stronger.

FIORDILIGI

In the garden there are nice shady alleys. Do you wish to promenade?

FERRANDO

With greatest pleasure! It's good for your health.

FIORDILIGI

I agree with you.

FERRANDO
(passing by Guglielmo)
(Now we are at the crossroads.)

DORABELLA
Cosa gli avete detto?

FERRANDO
Eh gli raccomandai di divertirla bene.

DORABELLA
Passeggiamo anche noi.

GUGLIELMO
Come vi piace. Ahimè!

DORABELLA
Che cosa avete?

GUGLIELMO
Io mi sento sì male, sì male, anima
mia, che mi par di morire.

DORABELLA
(Non otterà nientissimo.) Saranno i
rimasugli del velen che beveste.

GUGLIELMO
Ah che un veleno assai più forte io
bevo in que' crudi e focosi mongi-
belli amorosi!

DORABELLA
Sarà veleno calido; fatevi un poco
fresco.

GUGLIELMO
Ingrata, voi burlate, ed intanto io mi
moro! (Son spariti: dove diamin son
iti?)

DORABELLA
Eh via non fate.

GUGLIELMO
Io mi moro, crudele, e voi burlate?

DORABELLA
Io burlo? io burlo?

GUGLIELMO
Dunque datemi qualche segno, anima
bella, della vostra pietà.

DORABELLA
Due, se volete; dite quel che far deggio,
e lo vedrete.

GUGLIELMO
(Scherza, o dice davvero?) Questa picciola offerta d'accettare degnatevi.

DORABELLA
Un core?

GUGLIELMO
Un core: è simbolo di quello ch'arde,
languisce e spasima per voi.

DORABELLA
(Che dono prezioso!)

GUGLIELMO
L'accettate?

DORABELLA
Crudele, di sedur non tentate un cor
fedele.

GUGLIELMO
(La montagna vacilla: mi spiace ma
impegnato è l'onor di soldato.)
V'adoro!

DORABELLA
Per pietà!

GUGLIELMO
Son tutto vostro!

DORABELLA
Oh Dei!

GUGLIELMO
Cedete, o cara!

DORABELLA
Mi farete morir.

GUGLIELMO
Morremo insieme, amorosa mia speme.
L'accettate?

DORABELLA
L'accetto.

GUGLIELMO
(Infelice Ferrando!) Oh che diletto!

No. 23. DUETTO

GUGLIELMO
Il core vi dono,
bell' idolo mio;
ma il vostro vo' anch'io,
via datelo a me.

FIORDILIGI

What was it that you told him?

FERRANDO

Oh, I was only saying there's moss on the road.

DORABELLA

Shall we too take a walk?

GUGLIELMO

I am all for it!
    (*They walk.*)
Good Lord!

DORABELLA

Is something wrong?

GUGLIELMO

All at once I feel dreadful—perhaps it's some kind of fever—I may even be dying.

DORABELLA

(I don't believe a word of it.) You still are feeling effects from the poison you've taken.

GUGLIELMO

There is a far more deadly poison, a far more fatal danger, in the flame of your two glorious eyes.
(*Fiordiligi strolls off with Ferrando.*)

DORABELLA

A flattering comparison! You ought to write a poem!

GUGLIELMO

You really should not tease me, when you know how I'm suff'ring. (I can't see them. Are they hiding on purpose?)

DORABELLA

Don't be so silly!

GUGLIELMO

You are heartless and cruel to go on joking!

DORABELLA

I'm joking? You think so?

GUGLIELMO

Won't you show me a sign of pity, fairest of ladies, to uphold my morale?

DORABELLA

Only too gladly. Merely say what you wish and you shall have it!

GUGLIELMO

(She's fooling, or could she have meant it?) Will you do me one favor. Let me give you this locket.

DORABELLA

A heart?

GUGLIELMO

Yes, darling! A most appropriate symbol to reassure you of my everlasting love.

DORABELLA

(Oh, dear, it is charming!)

GUGLIELMO

You accept it?

DORABELLA

I'd like to, but my heart is not free, as you well know.

GUGLIELMO

(The iceberg is melting. I'm sorry, but my soldierly word can't be broken.) I love you!

DORABELLA

Please don't!

GUGLIELMO

I love you madly!

DORABELLA

Don't say it!

GUGLIELMO

Do not reject me!

DORABELLA

I insist that you go!

GUGLIELMO

If you reject me I'm determined to perish! You'll accept it?

DORABELLA

(*after a short hesitation, with a sigh*)
I will then!

GUGLIELMO

(What a blow for Ferrando!) I am delirious!

No. 23. DUET

GUGLIELMO

This heart is for you, dear,
My only beloved!
Give me yours to treasure
As long as I live!

DORABELLA

Mel date, lo prendo,
ma il mio non vi rendo,
invan me'l chiedete,
più meco ei non è.

GUGLIELMO

Se teco non l'hai,
perchè batte quì?

DORABELLA

Se a me tu lo dai,
che mai balza lì?

GUGLIELMO

Perchè batte, batte, batte qui?

DORABELLA

Che mai balza, balza, balza lì?

DORABELLA, GUGLIELMO

Perchè batte, batte, batte quì?
È il mio coricino,
che più non è meco,
ei venne a star teco,
ei batte così.

GUGLIELMO

Quì lascia ch' il metta.

DORABELLA

Ei quì non può star.

GUGLIELMO

T'intendo furbetta,
t'intendo furbetta.

DORABELLA

Che fai?

GUGLIELMO

Non guardar.

DORABELLA

Nel petto un Vesuvio
d'avere mi par.

GUGLIELMO

(Ferrando meschino!
possibil non par.)

GUGLIELMO

L'occhietta a me gira.

DORABELLA

Che brami?

GUGLIELMO

Rimira, rimira,
se meglio può andar.

DORABELLA, GUGLIELMO

Oh cambio felice,
di cori e d'affetti!
che nuovi diletti,
che dolce penar!

SCENA VI

RECITATIVO

FERRANDO

Barbara! perchè fuggi?

FIORDILIGI

Ho visto un aspide, un' idra, un basilisco!

FERRANDO

Ah! crudel, ti capisco! L'aspide, l'idra,
il basilisco, e quanto i Libici deserti
han di più fiero, in me solo tu vedi.

FIORDILIGI

E vero, è vero. Tu vuoi tormi la pace.

FERRANDO

Ma per farti felice.

FIORDILIGI

Cessa di molestarmi!

FERRANDO

No ti chiedo ch'un guardo.

FIORDILIGI

Partiti!

FERRANDO

Non sperarlo, se pria gli occhi men fieri
a me non giri! O ciel! ma tu mi
guardi e poi sospiri?

DORABELLA

I take it with pleasure,
But one thing I'll tell you:
The heart that you ask for
Is not there to give.

GUGLIELMO

Whose heart do I hear then,
If your heart is gone?

DORABELLA

Whose heart is so near then,
If I have your own?

GUGLIELMO

What is beating, beating loud and
clear?

DORABELLA

What is throbbing, throbbing in my
ear?

BOTH

What is beating, beating loud and
clear?
It must be my own heart,
My loving and lone heart,
A heart which is yours now
For ever and ever!
A heart true as gold,
To have and to hold!

GUGLIELMO

(Wants to put the heart where she
keeps the portrait of her lover.)
And now you must wear it!

DORABELLA

I really don't dare.

GUGLIELMO

You rascal, I know you!
Just wait till I show you!

DORABELLA

What is it?
(He gently turns her face the other way,
then takes away the portrait and puts
the heart in its place.)
Don't look yet.

DORABELLA
(to herself)

I feel so excited,
Aglow and on fire,
So strangely delighted
And filled with desire.

GUGLIELMO
(to himself)

Ferrando, poor fellow!
His future looks dire.

(aloud)

And now you may see it.

DORABELLA

Oh, may I?

GUGLIELMO

Look here, dear,
Now what do you say?

BOTH

How joyful a union
Of hearts and affection,
The noblest perfection
That love can attain!
How joyful a union
Of thought and of feeling,
So sweetly revealing
The wonder of love!
(They leave, arm in arm.)

SCENE VI
(Enter Ferrando and Fiordiligi.)

RECITATIVE

FERRANDO

You torture me! Why do you leave me?

FIORDILIGI

I've seen monstrosities, a hydra, a
writhing serpent!

FERRANDO

Now I grasp the allusion! All of them,
the hydra, the writhing serpent, and
all the horrifying monsters you could
imagine you have seen in my person.

FIORDILIGI

It's true, I admit it. You have caused
me such anguish.

FERRANDO

For your happiness only.

FIORDILIGI

If you would only leave me!

FERRANDO

All I ask is one glance.

FIORDILIGI

Never!

FERRANDO

You dismiss me, abandon me to grief
and desperation! Dear God! Is there
no hope, no consolation?

No. 24. ARIA

FERRANDO

Ah! io veggio quell' anima bella
al mio pianto resister non sà:
non è fatta per esser rubella
agli affetti di amica pietà.
In quel guardo, in quei cari sospiri,
dolce raggio lampeggia al mio cor:
già rispondi a miei caldi desiri,
già tu cedi al più tenero amor.

Ma tu fuggi,
spietata tu taci,
ed invano mi senti languir?
Ah, cessate speranze fallaci,
la crudel mi condanna a morir.

SCENA VII

RECITATIVO

FIORDILIGI

Ei parte ... senti ... Ah no! partir si
lasci, si tolga ai sguardi miei l'infausto oggetto della mia debolezza.
A qual cimento il barbaro mi pose!
un premio è questo ben dovuto a
mie colpe! In tale istante dovea di
nuovo amante, i sospiri ascoltar?
l'altrui querele dovea volger in
gioco? Ah, questo core a ragione
condanni, o giusto amore! Io ardo
e l'ardor mio non è più effetto d'un
amor virtuoso: è smania, affanno,
rimorso, pentimento, leggerezza, perfidia, è tradimento!

No. 25. RONDO

FIORDILIGI

Per pietà, ben mio, perdona
all' error d'un alma amante
fra quest' ombre, e queste piante
sempre ascoso, oh Dio, sarà!

Svenerà quest' empia voglia

l'ardir mio, la mia costanza,
perderà la rimembranza,
che vergogna e orror mi fà.

A chi mai mancò di fede
questo vano ingrato cor?
si dovea miglior mercede,
caro bene, al tuo candor,
caro bene, al tuo candor.

SCENA VIII

RECITATIVO

FERRANDO

Amico, abbiamo vinto!

GUGLIELMO

Un ambo, o un terno?

FERRANDO

Una cinquina, amico;
Fiordiligi è la modesta in carne.

GUGLIELMO

Niente meno?

FERRANDO

Nientissimo; sta atteno e ascolta come
fù.

GUGLIELMO

T'ascolto; di pur sù.

FERRANDO

Pel giardinetto come eravam d'accordo, a passeggiar mi metto; le do il
braccio; si parla di mille cose in-
differenti; alfine viensi all'amor.

GUGLIELMO

Avanti.

FERRANDO

Fingo labbra tremanti,
fingo di pianger, fingo di morir al
suo piè.

GUGLIELMO

Brava assai per mia fè! Ed ella?

FERRANDO

Ella da prima ride, scherza, mi burla—

No. 24. ARIA

FERRANDO

(*happily*)

Though you try to be deaf to my
  pleading,
I am sure you will yield in the end.
You're not meant to be cold and
  unheeding
To the love of so faithful a friend.
All your glances, so demure and
  appealing,
Make my heart glow with soft, radiant
  light.
You will yield to the force of my
  feeling,
To its boundless endurance and might.
You'll surrender to its endless delight!
But you spurn me, disdainful, uncaring,
Coldly leave me to languish and sigh!
Ah, I'm hopeless, abandoned,
  despairing,
For you cruelly condemn me to die!
  (*Exit.*)

SCENE VII

RECITATIVE

FIORDILIGI

I hurt him! Should I . . . ? ah, no!
It's better this way. At least I
will not see him, the wretched person who has caused me to weaken.
What grievous anguish the cruel man
has brought me! But I deserve it
for my shameless behavior! At such
a moment how could I ever listen to
a new lover's plea? Should I have
treated his proposal more lightly?
Yes, I am guilty. I am punished quite
justly. O dear Guglielmo! This stranger, he has aroused my heart to
passion, not to love, true and perfect.
This passion is restless, disturbing,
and deceitful, superficial! It's wicked,
faithless betrayal!

No. 25. RONDO

FIORDILIGI

Dearest love, I beg your pardon
For the faith that I have broken.
May my error remain unspoken,
Stay forgotten, unknown and past.
May my honest, true devotion,

Glowing love, and deep repentance
Purge my heart of all remembrance,
Make me worthy of you at last.

Why did I embrace temptation,
Break the tender vows I swore,
When it was my aspiration
To be faithful evermore?

Heaven grant me one kind favor,
Let my secret remain unknown.
With unfailing endeavor
For my fault I shall atone.
  (*exit*)

SCENE VIII

(*enter Ferrando and Guglielmo*)

RECITATIVE

FERRANDO

(*deliriously happy*)

Guglielmo, it can't go better!

GUGLIELMO

I knew it, I knew it!

FERRANDO

Yes, you have your wager. Fiordiligi
is the rock of Gibraltar!

GUGLIELMO

Nothing less?

FERRANDO

No, nothing! Now listen: I'll tell you
how it went.

GUGLIELMO

I'm listening. Go ahead.

FERRANDO

As we agreed, both of us went strolling
together in the garden, arm in arm,
just chatting. At first we talked about
the weather and then we talked
about love.

GUGLIELMO

Go on, friend.

FERRANDO

I said all I could hink of, swore that
I loved her, threatened to die at
her feet.

GUGLIELMO

My dear boy, you did well! And she?

FERRANDO

At the beginning she was laughing and
joking.

GUGLIELMO
E poi?

FERRANDO
E poi finge d'impieto sirsi—

GUGLIELMO
Oh cospettaccio!

FERRANDO
Alfin scoppia la bomba: "pura come
colomba al suo caro Guglielmo ella
si serba" mi discaccia superba, mi
maltratta, mi fugge, testimonio ren-
dendomi e messaggio, che una femmina ell' è senza paraggio.

GUGLIELMO
Bravo tu! bravo io! brava la mia
Penelope! lascia un po ch'io ti ab-
bracci per sì felice augurio, o mio
fido Mercurio!

FERRANDO
E la mia Dorabella? come s'è dipor-
tata? Oh non ci ho neppur dubbio!
assai conosco quella sensibil alma.

GUGLIELMO
Eppur un dubbio, parlando di quattr'
occhi, non saria mal, se tu l'avessi!

FERRANDO
Come?

GUGLIELMO
Dico così per dir! (avrei piacere
d'indorargli la pillola.)

FERRANDO
Stelle! cesse ella forse alle lusinghe tue?
ah, s'io potessi sospettarlo soltanto!

GUGLIELMO
E sempre bene il sospettare un poco
in questo mondo.

FERRANDO
Eterni Dei! favella: a foco lento non
mi far qui morir; ma no, tu vuoi
prenderti meco spasso: ella non ama,
non adora che me.

GUGLIELMO
Certo! anzi in prova di suo amor, di
sua fede questo bel ritrattino ella
mi diede.

FERRANDO
Il mio ritrato! Ah perfida!

GUGLIELMO
Ove vai?

FERRANDO
A trarle il cor dal scellerato petto,
e a vendicar il mio tradito affetto.

GUGLIELMO
Fermati!

FERRANDO
No, mi lascia!

GUGLIELMO
Sei tu pazzo? vuoi tu precipitarti per
una donna, che non val due soldi?
(Non vorrei, che facesse qualche cor-
belleria!)

FERRANDO
Numi! tante promesse e lagrime, e
sospiri, e giuramenti in sì pochi
momenti come l'empia obliò!

GUGLIELMO
Per Bacco io non lo so!

FERRANDO
Che fare or deggio! a qual partito, a
qual idea mi appiglio? Abbi di me
pietà, dammi consiglio!

GUGLIELMO
Amico, non saprei qual consiglia a te
dar!

FERRANDO
Barbara! ingrata! in un giorno! in
poch'ore!

GUGLIELMO
Certo un caso quest'è da far stupore.

GUGLIELMO

And then?

FERRANDO

For a moment I thought she wavered.

GUGLIELMO

That little vixen!

FERRANDO

But then, bang! went the bombshell. "Dare you question my virtue? I will always be faithful to my Guglielmo." She began to abuse me, called me names, and left me. So you see from her attitude there's no doubt. Fiordiligi is one woman in a million.

GUGLIELMO

Good for you, good for me, good for my faithful sweetheart! You're a friend in a million, bringer of happy tidings. I'm deliriously happy!

(they embrace)

FERRANDO

And my dear Dorabella? How did you fare with her? Why do I even ask you!

(enthusiastically)

I know your answer! How could I even doubt it?

GUGLIELMO

A little doubting, my dear undoubting Thomas, might be advisable at times.

FERRANDO

How so?

GUGLIELMO

O, it was just a thought. (I wish I knew how to sweeten his cup of bitterness!)

FERRANDO

Braggart! Are you implying she yielded to your advances? No, it can't be! I will never suspect her!

GUGLIELMO

You would be wiser to leave a little room for some suspicion.

FERRANDO

What do you mean? Speak up! If you must poison me, must it be drop by drop? But no. It can't be! Tell me that you are joking! I am her love and she loves only me.

GUGLIELMO

Surely! And to prove the fact beyond any question, she gave me this delightful little portrait.

FERRANDO

(raging)

Gave you my portrait! Ah, shame on her.

(starts to leave)

GUGLIELMO

Are you raving?

FERRANDO

(furiously)

No, I am not, but she will pay me dearly for her misdeed. How could she dare betray me?

GUGLIELMO

Calm yourself!

FERRANDO

(determined)

No, I cannot!

GUGLIELMO

This is madness! Why do you want to wreck yourself for a women so completely worthless? (If I could just prevent his from doing something foolish.)

FERRANDO

Think of it! Her deep devotion, her promises, her affection and protestations — all forgotten entirely in the wink of an eye!

GUGLIELMO

That seems to be the case.

FERRANDO

My life is ruined! What shall I do now? What use is there in living? I'm in a dreadful state! Help me, I beg you!

GUGLIELMO

I wish I could advise you, but I really don't know.
Horrible! My future! All in shambles! Torn assunder!

GUGLIELMO

This is really a case that makes you wonder!

No. 26.　ARIA

GUGLIELMO

Donne mie, la fate a tanti! a
tanti, a tanti, a tanti, a tanti!
che, se il ver vi deggio dir,
se si lagnano gli amanti,
li commincio a compatir.
Io vo bene al sesso vostro,
lo sapete, ognun lo sà,
ogni giorno ve lo mostro,
vi do segno d'amistà.

Ma quel farla a tanti e tanti, a
tanti e tanti,
m'avvilisce in verità.
Mille volte il brando presi,
per salvar il vostro onor,
mille volte, mille volte,
mille volte vi difesi
colla bocca, e più col cor.

Ma quel farla a tanti e tanti, a
tanti e tanti,
à eun vizietto seccator.
Siete vaghe, siete amabili,
più tesori il ciel vi diè;
e le grazie vi circondano,
dalla testa sino ai piè.
Ma, ma, ma la fate a tanti e tanti, a
tanti e tanti,
che credibile non è.

Ma la fate a tanti e tanti,
a tanti e tanti, a tanti,
la fate a tanti e tanti, a tanti e tanti,
che se gridano gli amanti,
hanno certo un gran perchè.

SCENA IX

RECITATIVO

FERRANDO

In qual fiero contrasto, in qual disordine di pensieri e di affetti io mi
ritrovo? Tanto insolito e novo è il
caso mio, che non altri, non io basto
per consigliarmi . . . Alfonso! Alfonso! quanto rider vorrai della mia
stupidezza! Ma, mi vendicherò! saprò

dal seno cancellar quell' iniqua . . .
saprò cancellarla—cancellarla? Troppo, o Dio, questo cor per lei mi parla.

No. 27.　CAVATINA

FERRANDO

Tradito, schernito,
dal perfido cor,
io sento,
che ancora
quest' alma
l'adora.
Io sento
per essa
le voci
d'amor.

RECITATIVO

DON ALFONSO

Bravo! questa è costanza.

FERRANDO

Andate, o barbaro, per voi misero sono.

DON ALFONSO

Via se sarete buono vi tornerò l'antica
calma. Udite: Fiordiligi a Guglielmo
si conserva fedel, e Dorabella infedel
a voi fù.

FERRANDO

Per mia vergogna.

GUGLIELMO

Caro amico, bisogna far delle differenze in ogni cosa. Ti pare che una
sposa mancar possa a un Guglielmo?
un picciol calcolo, non parlo per
lodarmi; se facciamo tra noi . . . tu
vedi, amico, che un poco di può
merto.

DON ALFONSO

Eh anch'io lo dico!

GUGLIELMO

Intanto mi darete cinquanta zecchin-
etti.

No. 26. ARIA

GUGLIELMO

I would like a word with all you lovely,
Lovely, lovely women.
I have something on my mind.
It's a basic human problem
And it touches all mankind.
Like my fellowmen and brothers,
I have worshipped before your shrine.
Like a million others,
I believed you were divine.
I've respected
And protected
Your good name in ev'ry way,
Yes, in each and ev'ry way.
But, you thankless, lovely, lovely,
  lovely women
Fill my soul with deep dismay.
With my sword I saved your virtue,
I have fought a fearless fight.
I've discovered
And uncovered
Ev'ry plot designed to hurt you.
I have been your peerless knight.
But, you wicked, lovely, lovely, lovely
  women
Put my chivalry to flight.
You're delightful, you're adorable,
You are precious, you are sweet,
You are gracious, fair, and lovable,
And we men are at your feet.
But, but, but,
You thankless, lovely, lovely, lovely
  women
Shock my heart with your deceit.
In the most poetic phrases
I have sung your sex's praises,
I have lauded
And applauded
And extolled you to the sky.
But, but, but, you wicked, lovely
  women,
When I see how you mistreat us
I begin to wonder why.
          (exit)

SCENE IX

RECITATIVE

FERRANDO

I can scarcely imagine that I myself
have become the prey of a woman's
ruthless deception! I'm so stunned
by misfortune, so disillusioned, I
feel helpless, defeated, totally dazed
and hopeless! Alfonso, Alfonso! You
were right after all! Now you will be

triumphant! But I shall be avenged!
I'll tear her image from my heart
and my mem'ry, and shall not regret
her! Not regret her? No, dear God,
I cannot! I can't forget her!

No. 27. CAVATINA

FERRANDO

Defeated, mistreated,
Despairing, forlorn!
I'll never forget her,
I'll always adore her
And ever regret her,
The love that I mourn.
Rejected, neglected,
My heart grieved and sore!
(Don Alfonso enters with Guglielmo.
They stay in the background, listen-
ing to Ferrando.)
I still love her dearly,
Forever sincerely.
My love is as great
And as strong as before.
(Don Alfonso and Guglielmo step for-
ward.)

RECITATIVE

DON ALFONSO

Bravo. That's how it should be.

FERRANDO

Stay away from me! You have caused
all my misery!

DON ALFONSO

Learn how to bear it calmly, and you
will be so much the wiser. The fact
is, Fiordiligi was faithful, at least up
to now, but Dorabella was too weak
to resist.

FERRANDO

Yes, to my shame.

GUGLIELMO

Dear Ferrando, you must be able to
see a thing in its true aspect. Where
would you find a woman who would
fail a Guglielmo? If you compare us
—I say it in all modesty—you will
have to admit, if you are honest, I
have a slight advantage.

DON ALFONSO

He's got a point there.

GUGLIELMO

And now, suppose you pay me half of
the wager.

DON ALFONSO

Volontieri: pria però di pagar vo che
facciamo qualche altra esperienza.

GUGLIELMO

Come?

DON ALFONSO

Abbiate pazienza: Infin domani siete
entrambi miei schiavi: a me voi deste
parola da soldati, di for quel ch'io
dirò. Venite; io spero mostrarvi ben
che folle è quel cervello, che sulla
frasca ancor vende l'uccello.

SCENA X

RECITATIVO

DESPINA

Ora vedo che siete una donna di garbo.

DORABELLA

Invan, Despina, di resister tentai: quel
demonietto ha un artifizio, un elo-
quenza, un tratto, che ti fà cader
giù se sei di sasso.

DESPINA

Corpo di satanasso, questo vuol dir
saper, tanto di raro noi povere
ragazze abbiamo un po di bene, che
bisogna pigliarlo allor ch'ei viene. Ma
ecco la sorella, che ceffo!

FIORDILIGI

Sciagurate! ecco per colpa vostra in
che stato mi trovo!

DESPINA

Cosa è nato, cara Madamigella?

DORABELLA

Hai qualche mal, sorella?

FIORDILIGI

Ho il diavolo, che porti me, te, lei,
Don Alfonso, i forestieri e quanti
passi ha il mondo.

DORABELLA

Hai perduto il giudizio?

FIORDILIGI

Peggio, peggio, inorridisci: io amo! e
l'amor mio non è sol per Guglielmo.

DESPINA

Meglio, meglio!

DORABELLA

E che si, che anche tu se' innamorata
del galante biondino?

FIORDILIGI

Ah, pur troppo per noi.

DESPINA

Ma brava!

DORABELLA

Tieni, settanta mille baci: tu il biondino, io'l brunetto, eccoi entrambe
spose!

FIORDILIGI

Cosa dici? non pensi agli infelici, che
stamane partir? ai loro pianti, alla
lor fedeltà tu più non pensi? Così
barbari sensi, dove, dove apprend-
esti? sì diversa da te come ti festi?

DORABELLA

Odimi: sei tu certa, che non muojano
in guerra i nostri vecchi amanti?
e allora? entrambe resterem colle
man piene di mosche: tra un bon
certo e un incerto c'è sempre un
gran divario.

FIORDILIGI

E se poi torneranno?

DORABELLA

Se torneran lor danno! noi saremo
allor mogli, noi saremo lontane mille
miglia.

FIORDILIGI

Ma non so, come mai si può cangiar
in un sol giorno un core.

DORABELLA

Che domanda ridicola! siam donne!
e poi tu com' hai fatto!

DON ALFONSO

I'll be glad to, but before I shall do it, permit me to try one more test.

GUGLIELMO

You mean?

DON ALFONSO

I'm not yet defeated. Until tomorrow you are bound to our wager, and just remember, you gave your word of honor to obey my command. Till then, I will not give up the ship, and I am still competing, for the proof of the pudding is in the eating!
(*exeunt. Curtain*)

SCENE X

(*A room with several doors, a mirror, and a little table. Dorabella and Despina on-stage.*)

RECITATIVE

DESPINA

Now at last you are acting like a woman of the world.

DORABELLA

I was not able to resist the temptation. That charming devil is so persuasive, he is so clever, so gentle, he would even succeed in melting millstones.

DESPINA

Now you are talking logic and really showing sense! Only too seldom are we poor girls permitted to snatch a bit of pleasure, so it is up to us to make hay while the sun shines! Who's coming? It's your sister. She's raving!

FIORDILIGI

How disgraceful! It's on account of you that I am in this dilemma.

DESPINA

What has happened? Why are you so excited?

DORABELLA

Is something wrong, dear sister?

FIORDILIGI

I hope the devil takes you all, you, and her, Don Alfonso, those two intruders! And all the fools in this world!

DORABELLA

Are you out of your mind?

FIORDILIGI

Worse than that! Dare I admit it? I love him! And worst of all is, I do not mean Guglielmo!

DESPINA

Sounds exciting.

DORABELLA

Do you mean that you've also started yielding, and you love your new suitor?

FIORDILIGI

(*sighing*)

Ah, yes, only too much!

DESPINA

Delightful!

DORABELLA

Sister, I simply have to kiss you. Then we both will be married! What could be more romantic!

FIORDILIGI

But how can we? Just think of our poor soldiers who have gone to the wars! Have you no feeling for those two faithful men, the grief we'd cause them? How could we deceive them? What has come over you, that you want to commit such a betrayal?

DORABELLA

Wait a bit! How do we know that the worst might not happen? Suppose they fell in battle? In that case, what would become of us? Wouldn't we be the losers? You know the saying: A bird in the hand is worth two in the bush!

FIORDILIGI

But if they should return?

DORABELLA

In that event, it's their loss! By that time we'll be married, and what's more, we'll be living abroad.

FIORDILIGI

I am still at loss to understand this sudden change of heart.

DORABELLA

That is downright ridiculous! We're women! After all, what did you do?

FIORDILIGI

Io saprò vincermi.

DESPINA

Voi non saprete nulla.

FIORDILIGI

Farò, che tu lo veda.

DORABELLA

Credi sorella, è meglio che tu ceda.

No. 28. ARIA

DORABELLA

E amore un ladroncello,
un serpentello è amor,
ei toglie e dà la pace,
come gli piace ai cor.

Per gli occhi al seno appena
un varco aprir si fa,
che l'anima in catena,
e toglie libertà.

E amore un ladroncello,
un serpentello è amor,
ei toglie e dà la pace,
come gli piace ai cor.

Porta dolcezza,
dolcezza e gusto,
se tu lo lasci far,
ma t'empie di disgusto,
se tenti ti pugnar.

E amore un ladroncello,
un serpentello è amor.
ei toglie e dà la pace,
come gli piace ai cor.

Se nel tuo petto ei siede,
s'egli ti becca quì,
fa tutto quel ch'ei chiede,
che anch'io farò così.

SCENA XI

RECITATIVE

FIORDILIGI

Come tutto conguira a sedurre il mio
cor! ma no! si mora, e non si ceda!
errai quando alla suora io mi
scopersi ed alla serva mia. Esse a
lui diran tutto, ed ei più audace,
fia di tutto capace, agle occhi mai
più non comparisca! a tutti i servi
minacierò il congedo, se lo lascian
passar, veder nol voglio quel seduttor.

GUGLIELMO

(Bravissima! la mia casta Artemisia!
la sentite?)

FIORDILIGI

Ma potria Dorabella senza saputa
mia — piano! un pensiero per la
mente mi passa: in casa mia restar
molte uniformi di Guglielmo e di
Ferrando, ardir! Despina! Despina!

DESPINA

Cosa c'è!

FIORDILIGI

Tieni un po questa chiave e senza
replica, senza replica alcuna, prendi
nel guardaroba, e quì mi porta due
spade, due cappelli, e due vestiti
de' nostri sposi.

DESPINA

E che volete fare?

FIORDILIGI

Vanne, non replicare.

DESPINA

(Comanda in abregè donna Arro-
ganza.)

FIORDILIGI

Non c'è altro; ho speranza che Dorabella stessa seguirà il bell' esempio:
al campo, al campo, altra strada
non resta per serbaci innocenti.

FIORDILIGI

But I'm not surrendering!

DESPINA

There you are quite mistaken!

FIORDILIGI

I won't! I'll never do it!

DORABELLA

Come, dearest sister, you must, or you will rue it.

No. 28. ARIA

DORABELLA

I know a naughty fellow,
A wily thief called Love.
He slyly steals your calmness,
Sweet as a turtle-dove.
The moment he has found you,
He wounds you with his dart—
He ties his chains around you
And rules your helpless heart,
I know a naughty fellow,
A wily rogue called Love,
He slyly steals your calmness,
Sweet as a turtle-dove.
He can be charming, divine, delightful,
If he's allowed his way,
But also cruel and spiteful,
Malevolent and spiteful,
If you should disobey.
I know a naughty fellow,
A wily thief called Love.
He slyly steals your calmness,
Sweet as a turtle-dove.
Each time his fire brands you,
Raging inside your breast,
Do all that he commands you
And better not protest.
If he should come and seize you,
Pulling your heart-strings tight,
Just let the rascal tease you
And do not try to fight.
Just let him seize you,
And tickle and tease you!
Just let the rascal seize you and
  tease you,
As I intend to do,
I too,
As I intend to do.
(Despina leaves with Dorabella.)

SCENE XI

RECITATIVE

FIORDILIGI

How they're plotting together to make me break my word! But no! I will not! I'd rather die. I never should have talked to Dorabella, or even to Despina. They might tell him my secret, and thus encouraged, I could never control him. I must avoid him, not even let him see me. I will give orders that any of my servants will be dismissed on the spot if they should dare to let him come near me.

GUGLIELMO

(listening at the door, unseen by Fiordiligi)

(By Jupiter! What a model of virtue! Let's hear more!)

FIORDILIGI

I'm afraid Dorabella cannot be persuaded. Wait! An idea! Now I know what to do! By some good fortune Guglielmo and Ferrando left some uniforms behind. That's lucky. Despina, Despina!

DESPINA

(enters)

My lady called?

FIORDILIGI

Go up to the attic, and without questioning and without contradiction, open your masters' trunks and bring me two helmets, two sabers, and two complete uniforms they left there.

DESPINA

What for, if I may ask you?

FIORDILIGI

Go, do as I told you!

DESPINA

(What a high and mighty tone! It is disgusting.)
(leaves)

FIORDILIGI

I am determined. Now my problem is getting Dorabella to consent to go with me. The sooner, the better. It's the only solution to preserve our integrity.

DON ALFONSO

(Ho capito abbastanza: vanne pur non temer.)

DESPINA

Eccomi.

FIORDILIGI

Vanne: sei cavalli di posta, voli .un servo ordinar, di a Dorabella che parlarle vorrei.

DESPINA

Sarà servita (Questa donna mi par di senno uscita.)

FIORDILIGI

L'abito di Ferrando sarà buono per me; può Dorabella prender quel di Guglielmo; in questi arnesi raggiungerem gli sposi nostri, a loro fianco pugnar potremo e morir se fa d'uopo: ite in malora, ornamenti fatali, io vi detesto.

GUGLIELMO

(Si può dar un amor simile a questo?)

FIORDILIGI

Di tornar non sperate alla mia fronte pria ch'io qui torni col mio ben; in vostro loco porrò questo cappello; oh come ei mi trasforma le sembianze e il viso! come appena io medesma or mi ravviso!

No. 29. DUETTO

FIORDILIGI

Fra gli amplessi, in pochi istanti,
giungerò del fido sposo,
sconosciuta a lui davanti
in quest' abito verrò.

Oh che gioja il suo bel core
proverà nel ravvisarmi!

FERRANDO

Ed intanto di dolore
meschinello, io mi morrò!

FIORDILIGI

Cosa veggio!
son tradita!
Deh, partite!

FERRANDO

Ah, no mia vita:
con quel ferro di tua mano
questo cor tu ferirai,
e se forza oh Dio non hai,
io la man ti reggerò.

FIORDILIGI

Taci, ahimè! son abbastanza
tormentata ed infelice!

FERRANDO

Ah che omai la sua costanza,

FIORDILIGI

Ah, che omai la mia costanza,

FIORDILIGI, FERRANDO

A quei sguardi, a quel che dice,
Incomincia a vacillar.

FIORDILIGI

Sorgi, sorgi—

FERRANDO

Invan lo credi.

FIORDILIGI

Per pietà, da me che chiedi?

FERRANDO

Il tuo cor, o la mia morte.

FIORDILIGI

Ah non son, non son più forte!

FERRANDO

Cedi cara—

FIORDILIGI

Dei, consiglio!

FERRANDO

Volgi a me pietoso il ciglio,
in me sol trovar tu puoi
sposo, amante, e più, se vuoi,
idol mio, più non tardar.

DON ALFONSO

(*at the door to Despina, who returns*)
(I see what she's up to. Better do
what she says.)

DESPINA

There you are.

FIORDILIGI

Thank you. Now order us horses and
a man we can trust. Tell Dorabella
that I want her at once.

DESPINA

I'm at your service. (This to-do and
commotion is beyond me!)
(*Exit.*)

FIORDILIGI

This uniform of Ferrando should be
just about my size, and Dorabella
can wear one of Guglielmo's. Disguised as soldiers, we two can go
and find our sweethearts. If it must
be, we shall fight beside them. Even
death shall not part us!
(*Throws off her headdress.*)
Off with this head-gear, this insane
decoration. Oh, how I hate it!

GUGLIELMO

Her devotion and courage are astound-
ing!

FIORDILIGI

Not until I return with my beloved
shall it adorn my head again! And,
in its stead, this helmet will disguise me! Now off to war and adventure! I'll be lucky, I'm certain!
Not a soul will suspect that I'm a
woman!

No. 29.   DUET

FIORDILIGI

By tomorrow we'll be united!
I will join you, dear Guglielmo!
Unexpected, your Fiordiligi
Will appear in her disguise.
What a wonderful surprise!
You'll be joyful and so delighted
When you see your faithful sweet-
heart!
(*stepping forward*)

FERRANDO

And I'll die here, unrequited,
Right before your very eyes!

FIORDILIGI

Why are you here? Oh, how dreadful!
Spare my feelings?

FERRANDO

Before you leave me,
(*Takes his sword from the table, and
draws it from its sheath.*)
Take this sword and plunge it through
me,
Through this loving heart you
wounded!
Take this sword and pierce my heart!

FIORDILIGI

Never! Please go! I have endured too
much unhappiness already!

FERRANDO

Her resistance starts to weaken.

FIORDILIGI

My resistance starts to weaken.

BOTH

Now my (her) courage is less steady,
And my (her) will is failing fast.

FIORDILIGI

Do not tempt me!

FERRANDO

I beg you, hear me!

FIORDILIGI

Why on earth must you pursue me?

FERRANDO

Take my life or say you love me!
(*He takes her hand and covers it with
kisses.*)

FIORDILIGI

He is strong and so appealing!
I will yield, I have a feeling.

FERRANDO

Dearest angel, say you love me!
Don't resist me any longer!

FIORDILIGI

God above me!

FERRANDO

(*with great tenderness*)
Always obey your heart's true feeling,
Yield to love sincere and tender.
Dearest, I beg you, you must
surrender!
Do not let me plead in vain!

FIORDILIGI

Giusto ciel!
crudel! hai vinto
Fa di me quel che ti par!

FIORDILIGI, FERRANDO

Abbracciamci, o caro bene,
e un conforto a tante pene
sia languir di dolce affetto,
di diletto sospirar.

SCENA XIII

RECITATIVO

GUGLIELMO

Oh poveretto me! cosa ho veduto!
cosa ho sentito mai!

DON ALFONSO

Per carità! silenzio!

GUGLIELMO

Mi pelerei la barba! mi graffierei la
pelle! e darei colle corna entro le
stelle, fu quella Fiordiligi? la Penelope, l'Artemisia del secolo! briccona, assassina furfante, ladra, cagna!

DON ALFONSO

Lasciamolo sfogar—

FERRANDO

Ebben!

GUGLIELMO

Dov' è!

FERRANDO

Chi? la tua Fiordiligi?

GUGLIELMO

La mia Fior, Fior di diavolo, che
strozzi lei prima e dopo me!

FERRANDO

Tu vedi bene, v'han delle differenze
in ogni cosa, un poco di più merto—

GUGLIELMO

Ah cessa! cessa di tormentarmi, ed una
via piuttosto studiam di castigarle
sonoramente.

DON ALFONSO

Io so, qual è: sposarle.

GUGLIELMO

Vorrei sposar piuttosto la barca di
Caronte.

FERRANDO

La grotta di Vulcano.

GUGLIELMO

La porta dell' Inferno.

DON ALFONSO

Dunque restate celibi in eterno.

FERRANDO, GUGLIELMO

Mancheran forse donne ad uomin
come noi?

DON ALFONSO

Non c'è abbondanza d'altro. Ma l'altre,
che faran, se ciò fer queste? In fondo
voi le amate queste vostre cornacchie
spennacchiate.

FERRANDO, GUGLIELMO

Ah pur troppo! Pur troppo!

DON ALFONSO

Ebben pigliatele com' elle son, natura
non potea fare l'eccezzione, il privi-
legio, di creare due donne d'altra
pasta, per i vostri bei musi; in ogni
cosa, ci vuol filosofia. Venite meco;
di combinar le cose, studierem la
maniera vo che ancor questa sera
doppie nozze si facciano. Frattanto
un' ottava ascoltate: felicissimi voi,
se la imparate.

No. 30

DON ALFONSO

Tutti accusan le donne,
ed io le scuso,
se mille volte al dì cangiano amore,

FIORDILIGI
(*trembling*)

Gracious Lord! Gracious Lord!
I am frail! I fail!
Have pity! I have fought my love
    in vain!

(*Guglielmo wants to rush in, but Don
    Alfonso holds him back.*)

BOTH

I'm so happy, it's past believing!
All our tortured hours of grieving
Are forgotten now forever!
We shall never part again!
Dearest heart,
We shall never part again!

(*Exeunt Fiordiligi and Ferrando.*)

SCENE XIII

RECITATIVE

GUGLIELMO

This should happen to me! To a
Guglielmo! Victimized by a woman!

DON ALFONSO

Compose yourself, I beg you!

GUGLIELMO

The devil with composing! I'm madder
than a hornet! I feel like flying
through the ceiling! So that is Fiordiligi! Model of virtue! My rock of
Gibraltar! That vixen, that hyena,
that serpent, tigress, viper!

DON ALFONSO
(*unruffled*)

Let him get it off his mind.

FERRANDO
(*entering*)

What now?

GUGLIELMO

Where is she?

FERRANDO

Who? Your good Fiordiligi?

GUGLIELMO

My good Fior—good for nothing! The
devil may take her, and me with her.

FERRANDO

Do you remember? I say it without
the least bit of conceit, "I have a
slight advantage!"

GUGLIELMO

Keep quiet! This is no time for joking.
We'd better think of some way to
punish those two hussies most
severely.

DON ALFONSO

I'll tell you how. Marry them!

GUGLIELMO

I'd much rather marry the devil's
grandmother!

FERRANDO

And I an ugly ogress!

GUGLIELMO

Or any female dragon!

DON ALFONSO

Then you will end your days as lonely
bachelors.

FERRANDO

For men of our kind there are women
a-plenty!

DON ALFONSO

I do not deny that. However, do you
think they would be diff'rent? You
might as well admit it, you love
your unfaithful little sweethearts.

DON ALFONSO

Yes, we love them!

FERRANDO

We love them!

DON ALFONSO

Why don't you marry them just as
they are? What gives you the right
to demand of nature to make exceptions and create two super-
human women, just because you
would like it? We cannot alter what
has already happened. There's only
one way to make your future happy.
I will make the arrangements, and
before it is evening you shall both
wear a wedding ring. And now let
me tell you an adage. If you take it
to heart, it's to your advantage.

No. 30

DON ALFONSO

Women cannot be faithful,
But I don't mind it,
For I can see the principle behind it.

altri un vizio lo chiama,
ed altri un uso,
ed a me par necessità del core.
L'amante che si trova al fin deluso,
non condanni l'altrui, ma il proprio
    errore:
giacchè giovani, vecchie, e belle e
    brutte,
ripetete con me:
Così fan tutte!

FERRANDO, DON ALFONSO, GUGLIELMO
Così fan tutte.

SCENA XIV

RECITATIVO

DESPINA

Vittoria padroncini! a sposarvi dis-
poste son le care madame: a nome
vostro loro io promisi, che in tre
giorni circa partiranno con voi:
l'ordin mi diero, di trovar un notajo,
che stipuli il contratto: alla lor
camera attendendo vi stanno. Siete
così contenti?

FERRANDO, GUGLIELMO, DON ALFONSO
Contentissimi.

DESPINA
Non è mai senza effetto, quand' entra
la Despina in un progetto.

SCENA XV

No. 31. FINALE

DESPINA
Fate presto, o cari amici,
alle faci il foco date,
e la mensa preparate
con ricchezza e nobiltà!
Delle mostre padroncine
gl'imenei son pià disposti:
e voi gite ai vostri posti
finchè i sposi vengon quà.

CORO
Facciam presto, o cari amici,
Alle faci il foco diamo,
e la mensa preparate
con ricchezza e nobiltà.

DON ALFONSO
Bravi, bravi!
ottimamente!
che abbondanza, che eleganza!
una mancia conveniente
l'un el l'altro a voi darà.
Le due coppie omai si avvanzano,
fate plauso al loro arrivo,
lieto canto e suon giulivo
empia il ciel d'ilarità.

DESPINA, DON ALFONSO
La più bella comediola

SCENA XVI

CORO
Benedetti
i doppi conjugi,
e le amabili
sponsine:
splenda lor
il ciel benefico,
ed a guisa
di galline
sien di figli
ognor prolifiche
che le agguaglino
in beltà.

FIORDILIGI, DORABELLA, FERRANDO,
GUGLIELMO
Come par che qui prometta
tutto gioja e tutto amore!
Della cara Despinetta
certo il merito sarà.

Radoppiate il lieto suono,
replicate il dolce canto,
e noi qui seggiamo intanto
in maggior giovialità.

You are wrong to upbraid them.
You have to take them as they are,
As Mother Nature made them.
You lovers, don't complain of
   disillusion.
What you need is to reach the wise
   conclusion:
All your ancestors, fathers, and
   brothers went through it.
Since they learned it from Eve:
Women always betray,
That's how they do it.

ALL THREE

"Così fan tutte!"

SCENE XIV
(Enter Despina.)

RECITATIVE

DESPINA

Hurrah for our two winners! The ladies
have decided to consent to the wedding, and shortly after, according to
your wishes, they will be prepared
to depart from the city. They gave
me orders to arrange all the details.
The notary is ready. So are the wit-
nesses. You may go now to see them.
Well, are you pleased and happy?

FERRANDO, GUGLIELMO, DON ALFONSO
Overwhelmingly!

DESPINA

In affairs of this kind depend upon
Despina's master-mind!
   (Curtain.)

SCENE XV
(A hall, richly decorated and illuminated. An orchestra at the back. Table
set for four people, with silver can-
dlesticks. Four servants in rich costumes. Despina, the Servants and
Musicians.)

No. 31. FINALE

DESPINA

Go ahead and light the candles
And complete the decorations.
Make the final preparations.
Soon the couples will be here!
We must do our ladies honor
At their wedding celebration.
      (to the musicians)
Let us plan a great ovation
When the brides and grooms appear.

SERVANTS, MUSICIANS

Go ahead and light the candles
And complete the decorations.
Make the final preparations.
Soon the couples will be here.

DON ALFONSO

(While he sings, the musicians tune
their instruments.)
This is perfect! I am delighted!
This is splendid, simply splendid!
I shall see that you're commended
In a most substantial way.
When the couples make their
   entrances,
At my signal gather near them.
Wish them luck and loudly cheer them.
Clap your hands and shout hurray.

DESPINA, DON ALFONSO

I am absolutely certain
That the ev'ning will be gay!
Very soon we'll raise the curtain
On the play within the play.
(Exeunt Despina and Don Alfonso
through different doors.)

SCENE XVI
(As the two sets of lovers enter, the
Chorus sings and the orchestra be-
gins a march.)

CHORUS

Heaven bless you with prosperity
And success in each endeavor.
With our heartfelt, true sincerity
May we wish you joy forever.
May you live in perfect harmony,
Carefree, peaceful, and untroubled,
And attain redoubled happiness
With your children at your side.
Hail the bridegroom and the bride!

FIORDILIGI, DORABELLA, FERRANDO,
GUGLIELMO

Fortune showers us with favor!
Life can hold no greater promise!

FIORDILDIGI, DORABELLA

Thank you, dearest Despinetta,

FERRANDO, GUGLIELMO

For our happiness tonight!

ALL FOUR

Dearest friends, continue singing
In your bright and merry chorus!
Sing to happy days before us
And a life of new delight!
(The betrothed couples eat.)

CORO

Benedetti i doppi conjugi ecc.

FERRANDO, GUGLIELMO

Tutto, tutto, o vita mia,
al mio foco, or ben risponde!

FIORDILIGI, DORABELLA

Pel mio sangue l'allegria
cresce, cresce e sì diffonde!

FERRANDO, GUGLIELMO

Sei pur bella!

FIORDILIGI, DORABELLA

Sei pur vago!

FERRANDO, GUGLIELMO

Che bei rai!

FIORDILIGI, DORABELLA

Che bella bocca!

FERRANDO, GUGLIELMO

Tocca e bevi,

FIORDILIGI, DORABELLA

Bevi e tocca,

FERRANDO, GUGLIELMO

Tocca, bevi,

FIORDILIGI, DORABELLA, FERRANDO,

Tocca, tocca, bevi, bevi, tocca!
E nel tuo, nel mio bicchiero
si sommerga ogni pensiero,
E non resti più memoria
del passato ai nostri cor.

GUGLIELMO

(Ah, bevessero del tossico,
Queste volpi senza onor.)

SCENA XVII

DON ALFONSO

Miei Signori, tutto à fatto;
col còntratto nuziale
il notajo è sulle scale
e ipso facto qui verrà.

FIORDILIGI, DORABELLA, FERRANDO,
GUGLIELMO

Bravo, bravo! passi subito.

DON ALFONSO

Vò a chiamarlo:
eccolo quà.

DESPINA

Augurandovi ogni bene,
il notajo Beccavivi
coll' usata a voi sen viene
notariale dignità!
È il contratto stipulato
colle regole ordinarie,
nelle forme giudiziarie,
pria tossendo, poi sedendo
clara voce leggerà.

FIORDILIGI, DORABELLA, FERRANDO,
GUGLIELMO

Bravo, bravo, in verità!

DESPINA

Per contratto da me fatto
si congiunge in matrimonio
Fiordiligi con Sempronio,
e con Tizio Dorabella,
sua legitima sorella,
quelle dame ferraresi,
questi nobili albanesi,
e per dote e contradote . . .

FIORDILIGI, DORABELLA, FERRANDO,
GUGLIELMO

Cose note, cose note!
vi crediamo,
ci fidiamo, soscriviam,
date pur quà!

DESPINA, DON ALFONSO

Bravi, bravi, in verità!

CORO

Bella vita militar,
ogni dì si cangia loco,
oggi molto e noman poco,
ora in terra ed or sul mar.

FIORDILIGI, DORABELLA, DESPINA,
FERRANDO, GUGLIELMO

Che rumor! che canto è questo!

DON ALFONSO

State cheti; io vò guardar.
Misericordia!
Numi del cielo!
Che caso orribile!
io tremo! io gelo!
gli sposi vostri—

FIORDILIGI, DORABELLA

Lo sposo mio!

CHORUS

Heaven bless you with prosperity, etc.

FERRANDO, GUGLIELMO

Happy, happy end of sorrow,
Bright new promise of joy hereafter!

FIORDILIGI, DORABELLA

Glowing hope for life tomorrow,
Filled with tender love and laughter!

FERRANDO, GUGLIELMO

You're my angel!

FIORDILIGI, DORABELLA

You're my hero!

FERRANDO, GUGLIELMO

Say you love me!

FIORDILIGI, DORABELLA

I'll always love you!

FERRANDO, GUGLIELMO

Here's to gladness!

FIORDILIGI, DORABELLA

Let's be happy!
Drink a toast to happy days together!
(*They clink their glasses.*)

FERRANDO, GUGLIELMO

Drink to happiness together!

FIORDILIGI, DORABELLA, FERRANDO

May the glow of wine's contentment
Heal our woe and drown all
  resentment.
May our sorrow and our sadness
Swiftly vanish from our mem'ry
  forevermore.

GUGLIELMO

Ah, just to think of their dishonesty
Makes me wish there had been poison
  in their wine.
(*enter Don Alfonso*)

SCENE XVII

DON ALFONSO

Now it's time that we proceeded
With the signing of the contract.
We have ev'rything that's needed,
And the couples both are here.

BOTH COUPLES

We are ready, call the notary!

DON ALFONSO ..

Honored Counselor Illegalis,
Kindly come in.
(*Enter Despina, disguised as a notary.*)

DESPINA

"Cornucopia verborum,"
As we always say in Latin.
Since we have a legal quorum,
I suggest that we proceed.
Here's the bona fide agreement
With the statement of the causes
And the modifying clauses.
With decorum,
Harum, horum,
I shall now begin to read.

THE COUPLES

Very well, proceed, proceed!

DESPINA
(*with a nasal tone*)

Marriage is the sworn intention
Of the parties I now mention.
Fiordiligi and Sempronio,
Dorabella and Antonio,
Ladies hereby called "the sisters",
To the designated misters,
Latter nobles of Albania,
Dowry, gifts, and miscellanea . . .

THE COUPLES

Never mind it, never mind it,
We will read it when we've signed it
Later on! Hand us a pen!
(*Only the two women sign the
  contract.*)

DESPINA, DON ALFONSO

Happy ladies, lucky men!
(*Don Alfonso takes the contract. The
  sound of drums and singing is heard.*)

CHORUS
(*off-stage*)

On to glory, on to war!
We are free of care and sorrow,
Here today and there tomorrow
Over land and over sea!

COUPLES, DESPINA

Hear that song! It sounds familiar!

DON ALFONSO

Wait a moment, let me look!
(*He goes to the window.*)
O boundless misery! Heaven preserve
  us!
What a catastrophe! How awful!
  How dreadful!
Your former sweethearts!

FIORDILIGI, DORABELLA

Our former sweethearts!

DON ALFONSO

in questo istante
tornaro, o Dio, ed alla riva
sbarcano già!

FIORDILIGI, DORABELLA, FERRANDO,
GUGLIELMO

Cosa mai sento!
Barbare stelle! in tal momento,
che si farà?

FIORDILIGI, DORABELLA

Presto partite!
Presto fuggite!

DESPINA, FERRANDO, DON ALFONSO,
GUGLIELMO

Ma se li (ci) veggono?
Ma se li (ci) incontrano?

FIORDILIGI, DORABELLA

Là, là, celatevi, per carità!
Numi! soccorso!
Numi, consiglio!
Chi dal periglio ci salverà?
chi?

DON ALFONSO

Rasserenatevi,
Ritranquillatevi!
In me fidatevi,
ben tutto andrà.

FIORDILIGI, DORABELLA

Mille barbari pensieri
tormentando il cor mi vanno,
se discoprono l'inganno,
ah, di noi che mai sarà!

SCENA ULTIMA

FERRANDO, GUGLIELMO

Sani e salvi agli amplessi amorosi,
delle nostre fidissime amanti,
ritorniamo di gioja esultanti,
per dar premio alla lor fedeltà.

DON ALFONSO

Giusti Numi! Guglielmo! Ferrando!
o che giubilo! qui,
come,
e quando?

FERRANDO, GUGLIELMO

Richiamati da regio contrordine,
pieni il cor di contento e di gaudio,
ritorniamo alle spose adorabili,
ritorniamo alla vostro amistà.

GUGLIELMO

Ma cos' è quel pallor, quel silenzio?

FERRANDO

L'idol mio, perchè mesto si stà?

DON ALFONSO

Dal diletto confuse ed attonite,
Mute, mute si restano là.

FIORDILIGI, DORABELLA

Ah, che al labbro le voci mi mancano.
Se non moro, un prodigio sarà.

GUGLIELMO

Permettete che sia posto
quel baul in quella stanza.
Dei! che veggio! un uom nascosto?
un notajo? qui che fa?

DESPINA

Non Signor non è un notajo,
è Despina mascherata,
che dal ballo or è tornata,
e a spogliarsi, venne quà.

FIORDILIGI, DORABELLA

La Despina, la Despina!
Non capisco come cà.

FERRANDO, GUGLIELMO

Una furba uguale a questa.
dove mai si troverà?

DON ALFONSO

I see them landing down at the
mooring.
I hate to say so, but it is true!

COUPLES

O this is shocking! How can we stay
them?
At least delay them,
What can we do?
(*The servants take the table away, and
the musicians hurry off.*)

FIORDILIGI, DORABELLA
(*to Ferrando and Guglielmo*)

You cannot stay here!
Either you hide yourselves or run away!

THE OTHER FOUR

If they discover you, what will they
do to you (us)?
(*Fiordiligi and Dorabella hide their
lovers in one room. Don Alfonso leads
Despina to another room.*)

FIORDILIGI, DORABELLA
(*frantically*)

Heaven protect us! Heaven preserve
us!
Who will advise us in our dismay?

DON ALFONSO

Just put your trust in me!
I'll save the day!

FIORDILIGI, DORABELLA

I have never been so frightened,
So upset and so bewildered.
If they learn how we deceived them,
Heaven knows what we can say!

LAST SCENE

(*Fiordiligi and Dorabella on-stage. Ferrando and Guglielmo enter, in their
soldier uniforms and hats.*)

FERRANDO, GUGLIELMO

We are home, safe and sound from
our journey,
Our perilous journey!
How we've longed for a glimpse of
your faces!
How we've yearned for your tender
embraces,
For your love so sincere to the end!

DON ALFONSO

Well, I never! Guglielmo! Ferrando!
This is marvelous!
You! Back here? So quickly!

FERRANDO, GUGLIELMO

Our commander has altered his
strategy.
To our joy we were called back to
Naples.
With our hearts full of wonderful
happiness
We return to our sweethearts and
friend.

GUGLIELMO
(*to Fiordiligi*)

Dearest love, why so pale and so silent?

FERRANDO
(*to Dorabella*)

Dearest heart, why this sorrowful air?

DON ALFONSO

They are totally speechless from
happiness.
You took them unaware,
That should show you how deeply
they care!

FIORDILIGI, DORABELLA
(*aside*)

I am speechless with terror and
misery!
I am ready to die of despair!

GUGLIELMO

If you ladies will permit us,
We will put away our baggage.
What does this mean? Is someone
hiding?
An attorney? Who is this?

DESPINA
(*Enters, without wearing her notary's
hat.*)

I am neither man nor lawyer
But Despina pure and simple.
I was trying on my costume
For tomorrow's masquerade.

FIORDILIGI, DORABELLA

How she fooled us so completely
Is a mystery to me.
It's Despina! How on earth could it
be she?

FERRANDO, GUGLIELMO

There is no one like Despina.
That is plain enough to see!
(*Don Alfonso discreetly lets the contract signed by the ladies fall to the
floor.*)

DESPINA

Una furba che m'agguagli
dove mai si troverà!

DON ALFONSO

Già cader lasciai le carte,
raccoglietele con arte.

FERRANDO

Ma che carte sono queste?

GUGLIELMO

Un contratto nuziale?

FERRANDO, GUGLIELMO

Giusto ciel! voi quì scriveste,
contradirci omai non vale,
tradimento, tradimento,
ah si faccia il scoprimento;
e a torrenti, a fiumi, a mari
indi il sangue scorrerà!

FIORDILIGI, DORABELLA

Ah! Signor son rea di morte
e la morte io sol vi chiedo,
il mio fallo tardi vedo,
con quel ferro un sen ferite
che non merita pietà!

FERRANDO, GUGLIELMO

Cosa fù?

FIORDILIGI, DORABELLA

Per noi favelli
il crudel, la seduttrice.

DON ALFONSO

Troppo vero è quel che dice,
e la prova è chiuso lì!

FIORDILIGI, DORABELLA

Dal timor io gelo, io palpito:
perchè mai li discoprì!

FERRANDO

A voi s'inchina
bella damina!
il Cavaliere dell' Albania.

GUGLIELMO

Il ritrattino
pel coricino,
ecco io le rendo
Signora mia.

FERRANDO, GUGLIELMO

Ed al magnetico
Signor Dottore
rendo l'onore
che meritò.

FIORDILIGI, DORABELLA, DESPINA

Stelle! che veggo!
Al duol non reggo!

FERRANDO, DON ALFONSO, GUGLIELMO

Son stupefatte!
Son mezze matte!

FIORDILIGI, DORABELLA

Ecco là il barbaro che c'ingannò.

DON ALFONSO

V'ingannai, ma fu l'inganno
disinganno ai vostri amanti,
che più saggi omai saranno
che faran quel ch'io vorrò.
Quà le destre, siete sposi,
abbracciatevi e tacete.
Tutti quattro ora ridete,
Ch'io già risi e riderò.

DESPINA

There is no one like Despina,
There is no one else like me.

DON ALFONSO
(*softly to the lovers*)

Here's the evidence you needed!
Take this document and read it.

FERRANDO

May I ask what's in this paper?

GUGLIELMO

Are you willing to explain it?
Can it be a marriage contract?

FERRANDO, GUGLIELMO

What a crime! And you have signed it!
To deny your guilt is useless!
To my horror I discover
You betrayed your faithful lover!
You will not escape my vengeance!
Streams of guilty blood will flow!
(*They try to go into the other room,
but the ladies hold them back.*)

FIORDILIGI, DORABELLA

Ah, I beg of you to kill me.
I am guilty, as you declare me.
Show no pity, do not spare me!
Take your saber and do your duty.
I will welcome it, for I deserve it so!

FERRANDO, GUGLIELMO

Tell the truth!

FIORDILIGI, DORABELLA
(*Point to Despina and Don Alfonso.*)

These are the traitors!
All we did was their suggestion.

DON ALFONSO

That is true without a question.
I can prove it very well.
(*Shows them the room where the lovers
had gone to hide. Ferrando and Guglielmo go into the room for a moment, then come out, without the
hats, coats, and beards, but with the
outer clothing of their former disguise, in the comic manner they had
formerly affected.*)

FIORDILIGI, DORABELLA

What a dreadful trick to play on us!
Oh, why did he have to tell?

FERRANDO

You are my goddess! I kneel before
you!
I am your hero who wants to adore
you!

GUGLIELMO
(*to Dorabella*)

Here is a portrait I know you treasure.
Give me my heart now, measure for
measure.

FERRANDO, GUGLIELMO
(*to Despina*)

Let us congratulate Doctor Fatalis,
Master of Magnets, the paragon!

FIORDILIGI, DORABELLA, DESPINA

Gracious! amazing!
Stunning and dazing!

FERRANDO, DON ALFONSO, GUGLIELMO

They're struck by thunder!
Speechless with wonder!

FIORDILIGI, DORABELLA
(*pointing to Don Alfonso*)

Here is the guilty one
Who led us on!

DON ALFONSO

Yes, I did, but my deception
Was to undeceive your lovers
And to prove there's no exception
To a rule that's always true.
Learn your lesson, heed the moral!
Let's be friends again! End your
quarrel!
Laugh about what's past and over
And I'll laugh along with you.

FIORDILIGI, DORABELLA

Idol mio, se questo è vero,
colla fede e coll' amore
compensar saprò il tuo core,
adorarti ognor saprò!

FERRANDO, GUGLIELMO

Te lo credo, gioja bella,
ma la prova io far non vò.

DESPINA

Io non so se questo è sogno,
mi confondo, mi vergogno:
manco mal se a me l'han fatta,
che a molt' altri
anch'io la fò.

FIORDILIGI, DORABELLA, DESPINA
FERRANDO, DON ALFONSO, GUGLIELMO

Fortunato l'uom, che prende
ogni cosa pel buon verso,
e tra i casi, e le vicende
da ragion guidar si fà.

Quel che suole altrui far piangere
fia per lui cagion di riso,
e del mondo in mezzo i turbini,
bella calma troverà.

FIORDILIGI, DORABELLA

Dear beloved, please forgive me!
Oh, my sweetheart, I hope to show
    you
All the loving faith I owe you!
I will prove my worth to you.
(*The lovers join hand and embrace
each other.*)

FERRANDO, GUGLIELMO

You don't have to, my beloved,
I shall ask no proof from you.

DESPINA

I who was the master schemer
Find myself a baffled dreamer.
I have learned a useful lesson,
Something that I never knew.
Tricks you play on other people,
Other people play on you!

ALL

Happy is the man of reason
Who can face the world in season.
Firm and steadfast
And uncomplaining,
He will go his cheerful way.
Things that make his brothers
    sorrowful,
He will answer with knowing laughter.
He has learned that life's adversities
Turn to joy another day.

The Magic Flute

(1791)

OPERA IN TWO ACTS

Libretto by EMANUEL SCHIKANEDER

English Version by RUTH AND THOMAS MARTIN

THIS ENGLISH VERSION WAS FIRST PERFORMED BY THE METRO-
POLITAN OPERA COMPANY IN NEW YORK ON DECEMBER 11, 1941.

INTRODUCTION

For many years it was believed that *The Magic Flute* was written under the following circumstances: Emanuel Schikaneder, a thoroughly disreputable character who had pursued a life of theatrical vagabondage, was director of a bedraggled troupe of players in a theater that was "little more than a wooden barn" in a suburb of Vienna. There he put on shows catering to the lowest tastes of the Viennese public, often playing the part of the clown in them himself. Early in 1791, in desperate financial straits, he came to Mozart, a friend and fellow Mason, with a plea that Mozart do an opera with him to help him stave off the ruin that was facing him. Mozart, always ready to help a friend, reluctantly agreed, and set to music a libretto prepared by the almost illiterate Schikaneder with the assistance of various others.

This, very briefly, is the tale as told by Otto Jahn in his biography of Mozart, and so great was the authority of that monumental work that it was accepted without question and widely repeated; it still turns up occasionally in discussions of the opera. In recent years, however, intensive research has uncovered facts that throw a different light on Schikaneder and on the circumstances leading to the creation of *The Magic Flute*.[1]

Schikaneder, who was five years older than Mozart, began his mature life as a violinist. He became a member of a theatrical company in 1773, first as a musician, then as actor, singer, stage director, and poet. This allegedly illiterate clown wrote both words and music of *Singspiele* and operettas, and played all sorts of parts, from Hamlet down. In 1778 he became director of his own company, in which he and his wife played principal roles. From September 1780 to February 1781 the company was in Salzburg, where it performed not only *Singspiele* but dramas by Shakespeare, Goethe, and Beaumarchais (*The Barber of Seville*). There Schikaneder met the Mozarts; he became so friendly with them that he gave them a free pass for three (Leopold, Wolfgang, and his sister Nannerl) to all his performances. Wolfgang wrote a German aria (now lost) to be interpolated in a comedy produced by Schikaneder. In 1784 Schikaneder arrived in Vienna, at the invitation of the Emperor, and played at the Kärntnertortheater (his first production there was Mozart's *Abduction from the Seraglio*). Soon, however, internal wranglings complicated by Schikaneder's amorous relations with the actresses in his company broke up the troupe. His wife and others formed a new group and left Vienna. He stayed on. He wrote a version of *The Marriage of Figaro;* it was rehearsed but its performance was forbidden by the Emperor at the last moment. (Perhaps it was through this version that Mozart became acquainted with Beaumarchais' play.) After working as actor and singer in the National Theater Schikaneder organized a new company and went on tour, in 1786 settling in Regensburg,

[1] See especially Otto Erich Deutsch, *Das Freihaus-Theater auf der Wieden,* Vienna, 1937; and Egon Komorzynski, *Der Vater der Zauberflöte: Emanuel Schikaneder,* Vienna, 1948.

where he had spent his childhood. After three successful years there he was once more in hot water, this time because of troubles caused by two actresses who had high-placed "protectors." At this moment he was invited by his estranged wife to come to Vienna and set up a new company in the Theater auf der Wieden, which she had inherited from a partner who had just died.

The Theater auf der Wieden was part of the "Freihaus," a tax-exempt complex of buildings belonging to Prince Starhemberg. It was far from a "wooden barn." It was a stone building, had two tiers of boxes and two galleries, and accommodated an audience of almost a thousand. Schikaneder used an orchestra of thirty-five men and a chorus of thirty. Since he had to compete with another popular theater in the Vienna suburbs, he stressed comedy and spectacle, with elaborate stage machinery, fireworks, and animals. He seems to have done fairly well, despite the competition, and there is no basis for the statement that he was in desperate need when he approached Mozart with the suggestion that they write an opera together.

The general plan of *The Magic Flute* follows that of many spectacle-comedies of the time.

> In the Viennese *Maschinenkomödien* of the period, the element of magic played a leading part; a favorite device was to let Hanswurst (in Vienna, Kasperl — a clown, or Merry Andrew), as the companion of some hero, encounter the most fearsome adventures among savages or in the realm of a magician. The hero, invariably accompanied by the buffoon, would rescue his beloved from the magician's toils with the aid of mighty spirits, all the arts of the scene-shifter and the wiles of enchantment being invoked the while. Kasperl, as the personification of the drastic humor of the Vienna populace, meets during the progress of the action a Columbine-like consort. [2]

One of the first works Schikaneder produced in the Theater auf der Wieden was a fairy opera called *Oberon*. Its text was written by one Gieseke, at that time (1789) an actor in Schikaneder's troupe who also did some writing for him. Gieseke "borrowed" generously from a libretto of the same title by Sophie Friederike Seyler, published in 1788. This "new" work, with music by Paul Wranitzky, was very successful. Schikaneder used some ideas from it in *The Magic Flute*. (Many years later Gieseke claimed that he was the real author of the libretto of *The Magic Flute,* but there is little evidence to support this belated claim.) Other sources for the libretto of our opera include a three-volume collection of fairy tales by Christoph Martin Wieland and others called *Dschinnistan*; Tobias von Gebler's play *King Thamos,* for which Mozart had written incidental music in 1773 and 1779 (K. 345); and *Sethos,* a novel about ancient Egypt by Abbé Jean Terrasson, published in 1731, translated into several languages, and much used by Masonic writers.

Borrowing ideas, scenes, characters, and various details of the plot from these and perhaps other sources, Schikaneder put together the libretto of *The Magic Flute*. Mozart worked on the music in the spring and summer of 1791. (During part of this time he was also composing the Requiem.) In August he

[2] Edgar Istel, *Mozart's "Magic Flute" and Freemasonry,* in *The Musical Quarterly,* XIII (1927), 512.

had to drop everything to write *La Clemenza di Tito,* produced in Prague on September 6th as part of the festivities celebrating the coronation of Leopold II, successor to Joseph II, as King of Bohemia. Back in Vienna by mid-September, he finished *The Magic Flute,* writing the March of the Priests and the Overture on the 28th. The first performance took place on the 30th, with the principal roles cast as follows:

Sarastro	Franz Xaver Gerl
Tamino	Benedikt Schack
Queen of the Night . .	Josefa Hofer
Pamina	Anna Gottlieb
Papageno	Emanuel Schikaneder
Monostatos	Johann Joseph Nouseul

Gerl had been educated as a boy in Salzburg, and had sung alto in the choir there. He was now a composer as well as a singer. In March 1791 Mozart had written for him an aria with orchestra and obbligato double bass, *Per questa bella mano,* K. 612. Gerl's wife sang Papagena at the première. Schack was an excellent tenor; as severe a judge as Leopold Mozart had written about him, in 1786: "He sings extremely well, has a lovely voice, ease and fluency, and a good method . . . This man really sings very beautifully." He was also a competent composer and a skilled flutist. This last fact may have determined the choice of the principal magic instrument in the opera—in the Gieseke-Wranitzky *Oberon,* from which the idea was borrowed, it was a horn that had magic properties. Schack wrote *Singspiele* and other light works. A song from one of these furnished Mozart with the theme for his Piano Variations on *Ein Weib ist das herrlichste Ding,* K. 613 (March 1791). Josefa Hofer was Constanze Mozart's older sister. While she never achieved much fame, her voice had a remarkable range and extraordinary agility, as is shown not only by her two arias in *The Magic Flute* but also by the aria *Schon lacht der holde Frühling,* K. 580, which was intended as an interpolation in a German version of Paisiello's *Barber of Seville* and written for her when Schikaneder planned a performance of that work in 1789. Anna Gottlieb had been the first Barbarina in *The Marriage of Figaro* at the age of twelve and was now seventeen. Nouseul was a valued member of the troupe as both actor and singer.

The allegedly impecunious Schikaneder had spared no effort or expense in preparing the production. Twelve new sets were built; the stage machinery included a traveling platform, covered with flowers, for the three Spirits; special lighting effects were used for the fire and water scenes and for the transformation in the finale from darkness into a stage drenched with sunlight. A contemporary journalist declares that all this cost Schikaneder 5000 florins.

The first two performances were conducted by Mozart himself, "because of high esteem for a gracious public worthy of respect, and out of friendship for the author of the work," as the original program put it. The opera got off to a slow start but soon began to make its effect. A week after the première Mozart wrote to his wife, who was ill and taking the waters at Baden, near Vienna: "I have this moment returned from the opera, which was as full as ever. As usual the duet 'Mann und Weib' and Papageno's glockenspiel in Act I had to be repeated and also the trio of the Spirits in Act II. But what always gives me most pleasure is the *silent approval*. You can see how this opera is becoming more and more popular."[3] Shortly afterwards he reported to her how he had had some fun with Schikaneder by taking over the offstage glockenspiel himself and playing it at the wrong times. On another night he invited to the opera Antonio Salieri, the Court musical director, and Caterina Cavalieri, who had created the role of Constanza in *The Abduction from the Seraglio* and had sung Donna Anna.

> You can hardly imagine how charming they were and how much they liked not only my music, but the libretto and everything. They both said that it was an *operone* [grand opera], worthy to be performed for the grandest festival and before the greatest monarch, and that they would often go to see it, as they had never seen a more beautiful or delightful show. Salieri listened and watched most attentively and from the overture to the last chorus there was not a single number that did not call forth from him a bravo! or bello! It seemed as if they could not thank me enough for my kindness.

The Magic Flute soon became a great success. A contemporary reports that although the performances started at seven o'clock, for the first two weeks people came at five, because hundreds were turned away. During the decade of Schikaneder's stewardship at the Theater auf der Wieden it was given there 223 times. A critic wrote, apparently still in the 1790s, that piano-vocal scores were being issued in Mainz, Mannheim, Offenbach, Leipzig, Berlin, and Brunswick: "therefore six times in one and the same year, a phenomenon hitherto unexampled in the history of musical literature."

Meanwhile the opera was quickly taken up by other German theaters. By 1800 it had been presented in sixty-five towns. It reached Moscow and Paris in 1801 (the French production was a brutally mutilated version, called *Les Mystères d'Isis*), London in 1811, Stockholm in 1812, Copenhagen and Milan in 1816, Brussels in 1829, and New York in 1833. What Schikaneder paid Mozart for the work is not known. And while the producer lived to grow wealthy from its success, the composer was buried in a pauper's grave nine weeks after the première.

*   *

*

Like many other artists and intellectuals of his time, Mozart was attracted by the humanitarian and democratic ideals of the Masonic order. This order, sternly opposed by Empress Maria Theresa but tolerated by her son Joseph II, achieved special prominence in Vienna in the 1770s and '80s. Mozart joined it in 1784 (so did Haydn, a few weeks later) and wrote several works especially for his lodge. Schikaneder became a member in 1788, and it has been suggested that financial support from fellow Masons helped to pay for the elaborate

[3] Anderson, III, 1436 f.

stage settings of *The Magic Flute*. In any case the opera is full of Masonic symbols and references to procedures peculiar to the order. To mention only one of the symbols, the mystic number three is stressed in many ways: the opera begins and ends in E-flat major (three flats), there are three Ladies, three Spirits, three portentous chords in the Overture, three doors on which Tamino knocks—even the serpent is cut into three pieces. The Egyptian setting is another obvious reference to Masonry, and Masonic devices are openly printed on the title page of the first edition of the libretto.

What is less apparent is the reason for the strange shift that seems to take place in the course of the plot towards the end of the first act. This change, by which the roles of the Queen of the Night as representative of the forces of Good and Sarastro as an evil magician are suddenly reversed, has given rise to much speculation and controversy. One of the earliest explanations offered was that while Schikaneder and Mozart were completing the first act, word came that a new opera being rehearsed at the competing suburban theater, *Kaspar, der Fagottist, oder die Zauberzither* (Kaspar the Bassoonist, or The Magic Zither), was based on the same subject and treated it very similarly, whereupon the authors of *The Magic Flute* decided then and there to proceed differently and avoid competition. They had already gone too far with the first act, however, to change that. This story, though frequently repeated, is not now given much credence. As has been pointed out by several writers, it was quite common in those days for the same plot to be used many times (even for the same libretto to be set by different composers). Moreover, Mozart went to hear *Kaspar* in June and thought it worthless. Another view has it that there is no shift at all in the plot: what happens in the first part of the opera is seen through the mind of Tamino, and when his eyes are opened to the true state of affairs, so are ours. Still another suggestion is that Mozart, harassed by illness and debts, grew impatient with the primitive type of entertainment Schikaneder had mapped out and insisted on a change that would introduce nobler and deeper ideas, particularly the triumph of good over evil and the Masonic belief in the brotherhood of man. According to this view, Schikaneder readily agreed, because he felt that its novelty would appeal to the public and its ideas would please the influential Masons. Neither author was disturbed about any resulting inconsistency, since they were presenting after all a fairy tale, in which a logical story-line is not required.

It may be that too much has been made of the reversal—if there is one—in the plot. Whatever else Schikaneder may have been, he was a man who lived and breathed theater. He knew precisely what was effective on the stage and what was not. And he poured all of his knowledge and experience into the libretto for *The Magic Flute*. It has action, suspense, and spectacle, low comedy and lofty idealism. Villains are thwarted, hero and heroine come triumphantly through severe trials, a prince gains his princess and a bird-catcher his bird-catcheress. There is not a dead spot in the happenings on the stage.

Nor is there one in the music. *Singspiele* had never had the stylistic consistency of the *opera seria* or the *opera buffa,* but Mozart's setting of Schikaneder's libretto is a conglomeration of styles extraordinary even for a *Singspiel*. There are simple little ditties of a folklike nature, brilliant arias of enormous technical difficulty, *buffo* pieces, exquisite trios, a solemn march that would suit a *tragédie lyrique,* a Protestant chorale treated in the strictest Baroque contrapuntal fashion, and, for the first time in a Mozart opera since the *Idomeneo* of a decade before, grand and powerful choruses. All these heterogeneous elements are fused together in the crucible of Mozart's genius. The historian can point to the Italian origin of this type of number, the French origin of that, the German origin of the other, but the astonishingly unified result can only be described as Mozartean.

Yet it is Mozartean with a new cast. For the first time in his operas the characters are not individuals or types but symbols. *The Magic Flute* is an allegory, its subject is an idea: the triumph of light over darkness, of good over evil, the victory of virtue and brotherhood. The scenes with Sarastro and the priests in the second act introduce a religious tone that is entirely new in Mozart's stage works. The use of a chorale in the theater seems to be unprecedented. In the extended scene in the first finale during which Tamino seeks Sarastro, Mozart establishes a manner of dealing with German accompanied recitative that was to have important consequences. And finally the "inwardness" of much of Mozart's music here—the combination of seriousness with a *Lied*-like directness of expression—is a new element in German opera.

All sorts of meanings were read into the allegory. In the Rhineland during the 1790s some interpreted the work in the light of the then raging French Revolution. The Queen of the Night stood for the despotic Louis XVI, Tamino for the people, Pamina for freedom, the daughter of despotism, and so on down to the smallest details: Papageno, for example, represented the wealthy class (!), "his fine feathers vanity, the panpipe rudeness, the glockenspiel gold, to whose tune everything dances."[4] From this point of view Schikaneder and Mozart were either fighters for freedom or dangerous demagogues, depending upon whether the interpreter's politics were liberal or conservative. In reactionary Austria, on the other hand, some took the Queen of the Night to represent Jacobin philosophy, whose daughter, the Republic, is rescued by the royal prince and restored to legitimacy. A later interpretation saw *The Magic Flute* as an allegorical account of the vicissitudes of Masonry in Mozart's time, with the Queen of the Night representing Maria Theresa, Monostatos the Jesuits, Tamino Joseph II, Pamina the people of Austria, and Sarastro Ignaz von Born, a celebrated scientist and highly respected leader of the Viennese Masons. There is nothing in what is known of either Schikaneder or Mozart to support any of these views.

Because of its moral and esthetic qualities, *The Magic Flute* had a profound effect on German writers and musicians. Its extolling of love and universal friendship was a theme to which German art was especially sensitive at the time. (Beethoven's Ninth Symphony was a later manifestation of this sensitive-

---

[4] E. K. Blümml, *Ausdeutungen der "Zauberflöte,"* in *Mozart-Jahrbuch,* I (1923), 113.

ness.) Goethe was so impressed that he wrote a libretto for a *Magic Flute, Part II,* which, however, remained a fragment. The special character of the music influenced Beethoven's *Fidelio* and the operas of the early German Romantic composers. As Wagner pointed out, *The Magic Flute* was the first great German opera. It is still one of the greatest.

CAST OF CHARACTERS

TAMINO, a prince . . . . *Tenor*

THREE LADIES, attendants of the Queen of the Night . . . . . *Sopranos*

PAPAGENO, a bird-catcher . . . . *Baritone*

THE QUEEN OF THE NIGHT . . . . *Soprano*

MONOSTATOS, a Moor, servant of Sarastro . . . . *Tenor*

PAMINA, daughter of the Queen of the Night . . . . *Soprano*

THREE SPIRITS . . . . *Sopranos*

TWO PRIESTS of the temple . . . . *Tenor, Bass*

SARASTRO, High Priest of Isis and Osiris . . . . *Bass*

THE SPEAKER . . . . *Bass*

PAPAGENA . . . . *Soprano*

TWO MEN IN ARMOR . . . . *Tenor, Bass*

Priests, Slaves, People.

THE PLOT

ACT I

Tamino, a Prince, roaming in strange, deserted country, is pursued by a dangerous serpent and narrowly escapes death because he is saved at the last moment by the effective arrows of the three Ladies of the Queen of the Night. The Queen, impressed by the handsome youth, sends him the portrait of her daughter, Pamina, who had been forcibly taken from her by Sarastro, high priest of the temples of Isis and Osiris. The Queen herself appears and promises Tamino her daughter's hand as reward for rescuing her. Tamino, enchanted by the portrait, at once resolves to save Pamina at any cost. Papageno, a light-hearted bird-catcher, is chosen as his companion. The Queen sends a magic flute to Tamino and a set of magic bells to Papageno to shield them from danger. Three genii are to lead them and guide them on their journey.

Tamino arrives at the temples in the realm of Sarastro. From a priest who appears at the gate of the Temple of Wisdom, Tamino learns that Pamina is alive, but that a vow of silence prohibits any further word at the time. Meanwhile, Papageno has found Pamina, who had been kept prisoner by Monostatos, a Moor in the service of Sarastro. Papageno tells Pamina about Tamino, and the two try to flee and join him, but Monostatos recaptures them and has them brought before Sarastro. Sarastro, whose life is dedicated to furthering the Brotherhood of Man, has been aware of all that has happened. Wise and all-knowing, he had torn Pamina from her mother to save her from the Queen's evil influence. He orders Tamino and Papageno to be led into the court of the temple to be prepared for the trials of purification.

ACT II

The priests assemble and Sarastro informs them of the will of the gods, who have destined Tamino for initiation into the holy brotherhood, and Pamina for his wife, if he can prove his worthiness by successfully undergoing the necessary trials.

In their wanderings through the temple vaults, exposed to various temptations, Tamino proves himself worthy. Papageno, a simple man, content to enjoy life's worldly pleasures, fails. The gods, however, are merciful, and while he is unable to attain the joy of wisdom shared by the ordained, he is given Papagena, a pretty young girl, as his life companion.

Pamina and Tamino, protected by the tones of the Magic Flute, transcend Fire and Water as the final acts of purification, and are ordained in the glories of Isis and Osiris.

DIE ZAUBERFLOETE

TAMINO

(*kommt in einem prächtigen japonischen Jagdkleide von einem Felsen herunter, mit einem Bogen, aber ohne Pfeil: eine Schlange verfolgt ihn*): Zu Hilfe! zu Hilfe! Sonst bin ich verloren, Der listigen Schlange zum Opfer erkoren!
Barmherzige Götter! Schon nahet sie sich! (*Eine grosse Schlange, Tamino verfolgend, wird sichtbar.*)
Ach, rettet mich! Ach, schützet mich!
(*Er fällt in Ohnmacht; sogleich öffnet sich die Pforte des Tempels; drei verschleierte Damen kommen herein, jede mit einem silbernen Wurfspiess.*)

3 DAMEN

Stirb, Ungeheu'r, durch uns're Macht!
(*Sie stossen die Schlange zu drei Stücken entzwei.*)
Triumph! Triumph! Sie ist vollbracht,
Die Heldentat! Er ist befreit
Durch unsres Armes Tapferkeit.
(*ihn betrachtend*): Ein holder Jüngling, sanft und schön!
So schön als ich noch nie gesehn!
Ja, ja, gewiss zum malen schön!
Würd' ich mein Herz der Liebe weihn,
So müsst' es dieser Jüngling sein.
Lasst uns zu unsrer Fürstin eilen,
Ihr diese Nachricht zu erteilen.
Vielleicht dass dieser schöne Mann
Die vor'ge Ruh ihr geben kann.

1. DAME

So geht und sagt es ihr,
Ich bleib indessen hier.

2. DAME

Nein, nein, geht ihr nur hin,
Ich wache hier für ihn.

3. DAME

Nein, nein, das kann nicht sein;
Ich schütze ihn allein.

1. DAME

Ich bleib indessen hier!

2. DAME

Ich wache hier für ihn!

3. DAME

Ich schütze ihn allein!

1. DAME

Ich bleibe!

2. DAME

Ich wache!

3. DAME

Ich schütze!

ALLE 3

Ich! Ich! Ich!
(*Jede für sich*) Ich sollte fort? Ei, ei!
Wie fein!
Sie wären gern bei ihm allein.
Nein, nein, das kann nicht sein.
(*Eine nach der andern und dann alle drei zugleich.*)
Was wollte ich darum nicht geben,
Könnt' ich mit diesem Jüngling leben!
Hätt ich ihn doch so ganz allein!
Doch keine geht, es kann nicht sein.
Am besten ist es nun ich geh'—
Du Jüngling, schön und liebevoll,
Du trauter Jüngling, lebe wohl,
Bis ich dich wieder seh'. (*Sie gehen alle drei zur Pforte des Tempels ab, die sich selbst öffnet und schliesst.*)

TAMINO

(*erwacht, sieht furchtsam umher*):
Wo bin ich? Ist's Phantasie, dass ich noch lebe, oder hat eine höhere Macht mich gerettet? (*Steht auf und sieht umher.*) Wie?—Die bösartige Schlange liegt tot zu meinen Füssen?
—(*Man hört von hinten ein Waldflötchen.*)

PAPAGANO

(*kommt während des Vorspiels einen Fussteig herunter, hat auf dem Rücken eine grosse Vogelsteige, die hoch über den Kopf geht, worin verschiedene Vögel sind; auch hält er mit beiden Händen ein Faunen-Flötchen, pfeift und singt*):
Der Vogelfänger bin ich ja,
Stets lustig, heisa, hopsasa!
Ich Vogelfänger bin bekannt
Bei Alt und Jung im ganzen Land.
Weiss mit dem Locken umzugehn
Und mich aufs Pfeifen zu versteh'n.
Drum kann ich froh und lustig sein,
Denn alle Vögel sind ja mein.

THE MAGIC FLUTE

ACT I

(Rough, rocky landscape. Tamino runs in, pursued by a serpent.)

TAMINO

O help me, protect me, my powers forsake me!
The treacherous serpent will soon overtake me.
Ah, Heavens, have mercy! I see it draw near!
(The serpent becomes visible.)
O rescue me, protect me, save me, rescue me!
(He sinks, unconscious, to the ground.)
(Three Ladies hurry in, with silver javelins.)

THREE LADIES

Die, vicious snake, before our might!
(They kill the serpent.) Rejoice! Rejoice!
The deed is done and won the fight!
We saved this youth from certain death!

FIRST LADY *(watching Tamino)*
What beauty in this gentle face!

SECOND LADY
I never saw more lovely grace!

THIRD LADY
Yes, yes, indeed, for art to trace!

THREE LADIES
If I should yield to love's sweet voice
This youth indeed would be my choice.
But now I think we ought to hurry.
To tell the Queen this startling story.
Perhaps this youth will help restore
The peace she felt in days of yore.

FIRST LADY
You both go on your way,
And I would like to stay.

SECOND LADY
No, no, you go ahead,
And let me stay instead!

THIRD LADY
No, that would never do.
I'll guard him here for you!

FIRST LADY
I'll watch him here alone!

SECOND LADY
I want to stay with him!

THIRD LADY
I'll guard him quite alone!

FIRST LADY
I'll watch him!

SECOND LADY
I'll stay here!

THIRD LADY
I'll guard him!

THREE LADIES
I! I! I!
(aside) I am to go? Well, well, how sly!
Each one would stay with him alone.
No, no! no, no! it can't be done!
With glowing love my heart is burning,
And stronger grows this ardent yearning.
O could I only call him mine!
But duty calls! We cannot stay
Together we must go away!
Fair youth, in peaceful slumber dwell
We leave you here and say farewell
Until we meet again!   *(Exeunt.)*

TAMINO
(regains consciousness, looks around, frightened)
Where am I? Is it fantasy that I am
still alive? Or did some higher power
save me? *(Rises and looks around.)*
That awful snake dead at my feet?
(The sound of a panpipe is heard.)
What do I hear? Where am I? What
a strange place! I see a queer figure
approaching. *(Withdraws, observing.
Papageno, dressed in a suit of feathers, hurries by, carrying a large birdcage on his back and a panpipe in his
hands.)*

PAPAGENO
I am a man of wide-spread fame,
And Papageno is my name.
To tell you all in simple words:
I make my living catching birds.
The moment they attract my eye
I spread my net and in they fly.
I whistle on my pipe of Pan,
In short I am a happy man.

Der Vogelfänger bin ich ja,
Stets lustig, heisa, hopsasa!
Ich Vogelfänger bin bekannt
Bei Alt und Jung im ganzen Land.
Ein Netz für Mädchen möchte ich,
Ich fing sie dutzendweis für mich;
Dann sperrte ich sie bei mir ein,
Und alle Mädchen wären mein.

Wenn alle Mädchen wären mein,
So tauschte ich brav Zucker ein,
Die, welche mir am liebsten wär',
Der gäb ich gleich den Zucker her.
Und küsste sie mich zärtlich dann,
Wär' sie mein Weib und ich ihr Mann.
Sie schlief an meiner Seite ein,
Ich wiegte wie ein Kind sie ein.

(*Pfeift, will nach der Arie nach der
Pforte gehen.*)

TAMINO (*tritt ihm entgegen*)
Heda!

PAPAGENO
Was da?

TAMINO
Sag mir, du lustger Freund, wer du
bist.

PAPAGENO
Wer ich bin? (*Für sich:*) Dumme
Frage! (*laut:*) Ein Mensch, wie du.
Wenn ich dich nun fragte, wer du
bist?

TAMINO
So würde ich dir antworten, dass ich
aus fürstlichem Geblüt bin.

PAPAGENO
Das ist mir zu hoch.—Musst dich
deutlicher erklären, wenn ich dich
verstehen soll!

TAMINO
Mein Vater ist Fürst, der über viele
Länder und Menschen herrscht;
darum nennt man mich Prinz.

PAPAGENO
Länder?—Menschen?—Prinz?—Sag du
mir zuvor: gibt's ausser diesen Ber-
gen auch noch Länder und Menschen?

TAMINO
Viele Tausende!

PAPAGENO
Da liess' sich eine Spekulation mit
meinen Vögeln machen.

TAMINO
Wie nennt man eigentlich diese Gegend? Wer beherrscht sie?

PAPAGENO
Das kann ich dir ebensowenig beant-
worten, als ich weiss, wie ich auf die
Welt gekommen bin.

TAMINO (*lacht*)
Wie? Du wüsstest nicht, wo du geboren,
oder wer deine Eltern waren?

PAPAGENO
Kein Wort!—Ich weiss nur so viel,
dass nicht weit von hier meine
Strohhütte steht, die mich vor Regen
und Kälte schützt.

TAMINO
Aber wie lebst du?

PAPAGENO
Von Essen und Trinken, wie alle
Menschen.

TAMINO
Wodurch erhältst du das?

PAPAGENO
Durch Tausch. — Ich fange für die
sternflammende Königin und ihre
Jungfrauen verschiedene Vögel; da-
für erhalt ich täglich Speise und
Trank von ihr.

TAMINO
(*für sich*): Sternflammende Königin?
—(*Laut:*) Sag mir, guter Freund,
warst du schon so glücklich, diese
Göttin der Nacht zu sehen?

PAPAGENO
Sehen?—Die sternflammende Königin
sehen? — Welcher Sterbliche kann
sich rühmen, sie je gesehn zu haben?
(*für sich:*) Wie er mich so starr
anblickt! Bald fang ich an, mich vor
ihm zu fürchten. (*Laut:*) Warum
siehst du so verdächtig und schel-
misch nach mir?

TAMINO
Weil — weil ich zweifle, ob du ein
Mensch bist.—

PAPAGENO
Wie war das?

TAMINO
Nach deinen Federn, die dich bedecken,
halt ich dich—(*geht auf ihn zu.*)

PAPAGENO
Doch für keinen Vogel?—Bleib zurück,
sag ich, und traue mir nicht; denn
ich habe Riesenkraft. (*Für sich.*)
Wenn er sich nicht bald von mir
schrecken lässt, so lauf ich davon.

Although I am a happy man,
I also have a future plan.
I dearly love my feathered friends,
But that's not where my int'rest ends.
To tell the truth I'd like to find
A pretty girl of my own kind.
In fact, I'd like to fill my net
With all the pretty girls I met.

Once all the girls were in my net,
I'd keep the fairest for my pet,
My sweetheart and my bride-to-be,
To love and cherish tenderly.
I'd bring her cake and sugar-plums,
And be content to eat the crumbs.
She'd share my little nest with me,
A happier pair could never be.
(*He whistles and turns to leave.*)

TAMINO (*steps in his way*)
Hey, there!

PAPAGENO
Who's there?

TAMINO
Tell me who you are, my jolly friend.

PAPAGENO
Who I am? (*To himself:*) Silly question! (*To Tamino:*) A man, like you. Suppose I asked you who you were?

TAMINO
Then I would tell you that I am of noble blood.

PAPAGENO
That's above me. You must explain yourself more clearly if you want me to understand you.

TAMINO
My father is a king, who rules over many lands and people. That is why they call me "Prince".

PAPAGENO
Lands? Peoples? Prince? Tell me, are there any lands and peoples beyond these mountains?

TAMINO
Thousands and thousands!

PAPAGENO
Perhaps I could do a little speculating there with my birds.

TAMINO
What is this land called? Who rules it?

PAPAGENO
I can't answer you that any more than I can tell you how I happened to come into this world.

TAMINO (*laughing*)
What? Do you mean to tell me that you do not know where you were born, or who your parents were?

PAPAGENO
Not a word! I only know that not far from here is my straw hut, which protects me from the cold and rain.

TAMINO
But by what do you live?

PAPAGENO
By eating and drinking, just as everyone else does.

TAMINO
How do you get it?

PAPAGENO
By exchange. I catch all kinds of birds for the star-flaming Queen and her ladies. In return, I receive food and drink every day from them.

TAMINO
(*To himself:*) Star-flaming Queen?
(*To Papageno:*) Tell me, good friend, were you ever fortunate enough to see this Goddess of the Night?

PAPAGENO
See her? See the star-flaming Queen? What mortal can boast of ever having seen her? (*To himself:*) The way he stares at me! Pretty soon I shall begin to be afraid of him. (*To Tamino:*) Why do you look at me with such a suspicious stare?

TAMINO
Well, I—I was wondering whether you are a human being or not.

PAPAGENO
What was that?

TAMINO
Considering those feathers covering you, you look rather—(*approaches him*)

PAPAGENO
Not like a bird, by any means? Stay away from me, I tell you, and don't trust me, because I have the strength of a giant. (*To himself:*) If he doesn't begin to be afraid of me soon, I shall have to run for it.

TAMINO

Riesenkraft? (*Er sieht auf die Schlange.*) Also warst du wohl gar mein Erretter, der diese giftige Schlange bekämpfte?

PAPAGENO

Schlange! (*Sieht sich um, weicht zitternd einige Schritte zurück.*) Ist sie tot oder lebendig?

TAMINO

Freund, wie hast du dieses Ungeheuer bekämpft?— Du bist ohne Waffen.

PAPAGENO

(*hat sich wieder gefasst*): Brauch keine!—Bei mir ist ein starker Druck mit der Hand mehr als Waffen.

TAMINO

Du hast sie also erdrosselt?

PAPAGENO

Erdrosselt! (*Für sich:*) Bin in meinem Leben nicht so stark gewesen, als heute.

DIE DREI DAMEN

(*erscheinen verschleiert. Sie drohen und rufen zugleich*): Papageno!

PAPAGENO

Aha, das geht mich an!—(*zu Tamino:*) Sieh dich um, Freund!

TAMINO

Wer sind diese Damen?

PAPAGENO

Wer sie eigentlich sind, weiss ich selbst nicht. Ich weiss nur soviel, dass sie mir täglich meine Vögel abnehmen, und mir dafür Wein, Zuckerbrot und süsse Feigen bringen.

TAMINO

Sie sind vermutlich sehr schön?

PAPAGENO

Ich denke nicht!—Denn wenn sie schön wären, würden sie ihre Gesichter nicht bedecken.

DIE DREI DAMEN

(*näher tretend, drohend*): Papageno!

PAPAGENO

(*beiseite, zu Tamino*): Sei still! Sie drohen mir schon. — (*Laut*) Du fragst, ob sie schön sind, und ich kann dir darauf nichts antworten, als dass ich in meinem Leben nichts Reizenderes sah.—(*Für sich:*) Jetzt werden sie bald wieder gut werden.—

DIE DREI DAMEN

(*noch näher tretend, drohender*): Papageno!

PAPAGENO

(*beiseite*): Was muss ich denn heute verbrochen haben, dass sie so aufgebracht wider mich sind?—(*Er überreicht den Vogelbauer. Laut:*) Hier, meine Schönen, übergeb ich meine Vögel.

1. DAME

(*reicht ihm ein Gefäss mit Wasser*): Dafür schickt dir unsere Fürstin heute zum ersten Mal statt Wein, reines, klares Wasser.

2. DAME

Und mir befahl sie, dass ich, statt Zuckerbrot, diesen Stein dir überbringen soll. (*Sie überreicht Papageno den Stein.*) Ich wünsche, dass er dir wohlbekommen möge.

PAPAGENO

Was? Steine soll ich fressen?

3. DAME

Und statt der süssen Feigen, hab ich die Ehre, dir dies goldne Schloss vor den Mund zu schlagen. (*Sie hängt ihm das Schloss vor den Mund. Papageno zeigt seinen Schmerz durch Gebärden.*)

1. DAME

Du willst vermutlich wissen, warum die Fürstin dich heute so wunderbar bestraft? (*Papageno bejaht es durch Nicken mit dem Kopf.*)

2. DAME

Damit du künftig nie mehr Fremde belügst.

3. DAME

Und dass du nie dich der Heldentaten rühmest, die andre vollzogen.

1. DAME

Sag an, hast du diese Schlange bekämpft? (*Papageno verneint es durch Schütteln mit dem Kopf.*)

2. DAME

Wer denn also? (*Papageno deutet an, dass er es nicht weiss.*)

3. DAME

Wir waren's, Jüngling, die dich befreiten.—Hier, dies Gemälde schickt dir die grosse Fürstin: es ist das Bildnis ihrer Tochter. (*Sie überreicht es.*) Findest du, sagte sie, dass diese Züge dir nicht gleichgültig sind, dann ist Glück, Ehr und Ruhm dein Los!—Auf Wiedersehen. (*Geht ab.*)

TAMINO

Strength of a giant? (*Looks at the serpent.*) Then perhaps it was you who saved me, and fought this poisonous snake?

PAPAGENO

Snake? (*Trembling, draws back a few steps.*) Is it dead or alive?

TAMINO

But, tell me, friend, how in the world did you ever fight this monster? You have no weapons!

PAPAGENO

(*has mastered himself again*)

I don't need weapons. With me, a good squeeze of the hand is more than weapons.

TAMINO

Then you choked it?

PAPAGENO

Choked it. (*To himself:*) Never in my life was I so strong as I am today. (*Enter the Three Ladies, veiled.*)

THREE LADIES

(*in a menacing tone*)

Papageno!

PAPAGENO

Ah, that's for me! (*To Tamino:*) Turn around, friend!

TAMINO

Who are these ladies?

PAPAGENO

Who they actually are, I do not know myself. I only know this much: each day they take in my birds, and give me wine, sugar-bread, and sweet figs in return.

TAMINO

I suppose they are very beautiful?

PAPAGENO

I don't think so, for if they were, they would not have to cover up their faces.

THREE LADIES

(*coming nearer, menacingly*)

Papageno!

PAPAGENO

(*Aside, to Tamino:*) Wait a minute. Now they are after me. (*Aloud:*) You asked me whether these ladies are beautiful, and I can only say that never in my life have I seen anyone more charming. (*Aside:*) Now I guess that will put them in a good humor again.

THREE LADIES

(*still nearer, and more menacingly*)

Pa-pa-ge-no!!!

PAPAGENO

(*Aside:*) Heavens, what can I have done today to have made them so angry?

(*He hands them the cage. Aloud:*) Here, lovely ladies, I have brought you my birds.

FIRST LADY

(*gives him a jug of water*)

This time, in return, the Queen sends you, instead of wine, pure, clear water.

SECOND LADY

And she ordered me, instead of sugar-bread, to give you this stone. (*Gives him the stone.*) Here's good health to you!

PAPAGENO

What, I shall eat stones?

THIRD LADY

And instead of sweet figs, I have the honor of locking up your mouth with this golden padlock. (*Does so. Papageno shows his pain through gestures.*)

FIRST LADY

I imagine you would like to know why the Queen punishes you in such a strange way? (*Papageno nods yes.*)

SECOND LADY

So that in the future you will never again tell lies to strangers!

THIRD LADY

And that you will never boast of heroic deeds achieved by others.

FIRST LADY

Tell us, did *you* kill this serpent? (*Papageno shakes his head.*)

SECOND LADY

Who did, then? (*Papageno shrugs his shoulders.*)

THIRD LADY

Prince, it was we who saved you. The great Queen sends you this portrait of her daughter. (*Hands it to him.*) If you find that these features are not indifferent to you, she says, then happiness, honor, and glory will be your destiny. Farewell. (*Exit.*)

2. DAME
Adieu, Monsieur Papageno! (*Geht ab.*)

1. DAME
Fein nicht zu hastig getrunken! (*Geht lachend ab. Papageno eilt in stummer Verlegenheit ab.*)

TAMINO
(*Ist gleich beim Empfange des Bildes aufmerksam geworden; seine Liebe nimmt zu, ob er gleich für alle diese Reden taub schien.*)
Dies Bildnis ist bezaubernd schön,
Wie noch kein Auge je gesehn!
Ich fühl' es, wie dies Götterbild
Mein Herz mit neuer Regung füllt.
Dies Etwas kann ich zwar nicht nennen
Doch fühl' ich's hier wie Feuer brennen.
Soll die Empfindung Liebe sein?
Ja, ja, die Liebe ist's allein.
O wenn ich sie nur finden könnte!
O wenn sie doch schon vor mir stände!
Ich würde, würde, warm und rein,
Was würde ich? Ich würde sie voll Entzücken
An diesen heissen Busen drücken
Und ewig wäre sie dann mein.
(*Will abgehen. Die drei Damen erscheinen.*)

1. DAME
Rüste dich mit Mut und Standhaftigkeit, schöner Jüngling! — Die Fürstin—

2. DAME
hat mir aufgetragen, dir zu sagen—

3. DAME
dass der Weg zu deinem künftigen Glücke nunmehr gebahnt sei.

1. DAME
Sie hat jedes deiner Worte gehört;— sie hat—

2. DAME
jeden Zug in deinem Gesichte gelesen,—

3. DAME
hat beschlossen, dich ganz glücklich zu machen.— Hat dieser Jüngling, sprach sie, auch so viel Mut und Tapferkeit, als er zärtlich ist, o, so ist meine Tochter ganz gewiss gerettet.

TAMINO
Kommt, Mädchen, führt mich!—Sie

sei gerettet!— Das schwöre ich bei meiner Liebe, bei meinem Herzen! (*Kurzer starker Donner.*) Ihr Götter, was ist das? (*Es wird dunkel.*)

DIE DREI DAMEN
Fasse dich!

1. DAME
Es verkündet die Ankunft unserer Königin. (*Donner.*)

DIE DREI DAMEN
Sie kommt!—(*Donner.*) Sie kommt!— (*Donner.*) Sie kommt! — (*Donner. Die Berge teilen sich, man erblickt einen Sternenhimmel und den Thron der Königin der Nacht.*)

KÖNIGIN DER NACHT
O zitt're nicht, mein lieber Sohn!
Du bist unschuldig, weise, fromm.
Ein Jüngling, so wie du, vermag am besten,
Dies tiefbetrübte Mutterherz zu trösten.
Zum Leiden bin ich auserkoren,
Denn meine Tochter fehlet mir;
Durch sie ging all mein Glück verloren,
Ein Bösewicht entfloh mit ihr.
Noch seh' ich ihr Zittern
Mit bangem Erschüttern,
Ihr ängstliches Beben,
Ihr schüchternes Streben.
Ich musste sie mir rauben sehen;
"Ach helft!" war alles, was sie sprach.
Allein vergebens war ihr Flehen,
Denn meine Hilfe war zu schwach.
Du wirst sie zu befreien gehen,
Du wirst der Tochter Retter sein;
Und werd' ich dich als Sieger sehen,
So sei sie dann auf ewig dein.
(*Mit den drei Damen ab. Das Theater verwandelt sich wieder so, wie es vorher war.*)

TAMINO
(*nach einer Pause*): Ist's denn auch Wirklichkeit, was ich sah?—O ihr guten Götter, täuscht mich nicht. (*Er will sich entfernen, Papageno tritt ihm in den Weg.*)

PAPAGENO
(*deutet traurig auf sein Schloss am Munde*). Hm hm hm hm hm hm hm hm!

TAMINO
Der Arme kann von Strafe sagen,
Denn seine Sprache ist dahin.

SECOND LADY

Adieu, Monsieur Papageno! (*Exit.*)

FIRST LADY

Don't drink too fast! (*Exit laughing. Exit Papageno, who has continued to pantomime. Tamino has not taken his eyes off the picture since he received it.*)

TAMINO

O image angel-like and fair!
No mortal can with thee compare!
I feel it, how this godly sight
Pervades my heart with new delight.
I cannot name this strange desire
Which burns my heart with glowing fire.
Can this emotion love reveal?
Ah yes! 'Tis love alone I feel.
'Tis love, 'tis love.
Love alone!
Oh, how to see her I am yearning!
Oh, how to free her I am burning!
I would then, would then, fond and true —
What would I do?
Upon this heart would I press her,
Within these loving arms caress her.
Forever then she would be mine!
(*He starts to leave. The Three Ladies approach him.*)

FIRST LADY

Prepare yourself with courage and steadfastness, noble Prince, for the Queen—

SECOND LADY

bade me to tell you—

THIRD LADY

that the path to your future happiness now lies open to you.

FIRST LADY

She has heard every word you said. She has—

SECOND LADY

read every expression of your features,—

THIRD LADY

decided to make you completely happy. "Oh, if this youth", said she, "is as zealous and brave as he is kind-hearted, then my daughter will certainly be saved!"

TAMINO

Come, maidens, lead me. She shall be saved! I swear it by my love and by my heart. (*Short, loud thunder.*) Ye Gods! What is that? (*It becomes dark.*)

THREE LADIES

Take heart!

FIRST LADY

That betokens the arrival of our Queen. (*Thunder.*)

THREE LADIES

She comes! (*Thunder.*) She comes! (*Thunder.*) She comes! (*Thunder.*) *The mountains part; against a starry heaven the Queen of the Night's throne is revealed.*)

QUEEN OF THE NIGHT
(*steps forward with Tamino*)

Oh, tremble not, my son, arise,
For you are guiltless, noble, wise.
A gentle youth like you could, like no other,
Console the deepest sorrow of a mother.
In lonely grief I am forsaken,
For my poor child no more I see.
With her my happiness was taken;
An evil fiend tore her from me.
How helpless she cowered,
Her strength overpowered!
What sad consternation!
What vain desperation!
With nameless woe my heart was bleeding.
"Ah help, ah help!" was all I heard her speak.
However, futile was her pleading.
For all my effort was too weak.
You, you, you. Shall free her from bonds of slavery!
You shall release this child of mine!
And to reward thee for thy bravery,
Forever then she shall be thine!
(*She steps back. Thunder. The mountains close; it becomes light. Rocky landscape as before.*)

TAMINO (*after a pause*)

Was it reality I saw? O good Gods, do not deceive me! (*He starts to leave, but Papageno steps in his path.*)

PAPAGENO
(*points sadly to the padlock on his mouth*)

Hm! hm! hm! hm! hm! hm! hm! hm!

TAMINO

The poor young lad must surely suffer,
He tries to talk, but all in vain!

PAPAGENO
Hm hm hm hm hm hm hm hm!

TAMINO
Ich kann nichts tun, als dich beklagen,
Weil ich zu schwach zu helfen bin.

PAPAGENO
Hm hm hm hm hm hm hm hm!
(*Die drei Damen erscheinen, und
treten zwischen Tamino und Papageno.*)

1. DAME
Die Königin begnadigt dich,
Erlässt die Strafe dir durch mich.
(*Sie nimmt ihm das Schloss vom
Munde.*)

PAPAGENO
Nun plaudert Papageno wieder.

2. DAME
Ja, plaud're. Lüge nur nicht wieder.

PAPAGENO
Ich lüge nimmer mehr, nein, nein!

DIE DREI DAMEN
Dies Schloss soll deine Warnung sein.

PAPAGENO
Dies Schloss soll meine Warnung sein.

ALLE
Bekämen doch die Lügner alle
Ein solches Schloss vor ihren Mund:
Statt Hass, Verleumdung, schwarzer
    Galle,
Bestünde Lieb' und Bruderbund.

1. DAME
(*gibt Tamino eine goldene Flöte*)
O Prinz, nimm dies Geschenk von mir!
Dies sendet uns're Fürstin dir.
Die Zauberflöte wird dich schützen,
Im grössten Unglück unterstützen.

DIE DREI DAMEN
Hiermit kannst du allmächtig handeln,
Der Menschen Leidenschaft verwandeln:
Der Traurige wird freudig sein,
Den Hagestolz nimmt Liebe ein.

ALLE
O so eine Flöte ist mehr als Gold und
    Kronen wert,
Denn durch sie wird Menschenglück
und Zufriedenheit vermehrt.

PAPAGENO
Nun, ihr schönen Frauenzimmer,
Darf ich so empfehl ich mich.

DIE DREI DAMEN
Dich empfehlen kannst du immer,
Doch bestimmt die Fürstin dich,
Mit dem Prinzen ohn' Verweilen
Nach Sarastros Burg zu eilen.

PAPAGENO
Nein, dafür bedank ich mich!
Von euch selbsten hörte ich,
Dass er wie ein Tigertier.
Sicher liess' ohn' alle Gnaden
Mich Sarastro rupfen, braten,
Setzte mich den Hunden für.

DIE DREI DAMEN
Dich schützt der Prinz, trau ihm allein.
Dafür sollst du sein Diener sein.

PAPAGENO
(*für sich*) Dass doch der Prinz beim
    Teufel wäre!
Mein Leben ist mir lieb;
Am Ende schleicht, bei meiner Ehre,
Er von mir wie ein Dieb.

1. DAME
(*gibt Papageno ein Glockenspiel*)
Hier, nimm dies Kleinod, es ist dein.

PAPAGENO
Ei, ei! Was mag darinnen sein?

DIE DREI DAMEN
Darinnen hörst du Glöckchen tönen.

PAPAGENO
Werd ich sie auch wohl spielen können?

DIE DREI DAMEN
O ganz gewiss, ja, ja, gewiss!

DIE DREI DAMEN
(*dann alle fünf zugleich*)
Silberglöckchen, Zauberflöten
Sind zu eurem Schutz vonnöten
Lebt wohl! Wir wollen geh'n.
Lebet wohl, auf Wiederseh'n!
(*Alle wollen gehen.*)

TAMINO (*zurückkommend*)
Doch, schöne Damen, saget an—

PAPAGENO
Wie man die Burg wohl finden kann?

BEIDE
Wie man die Burg wohl finden kann?

DIE DREI DAMEN
(*zurückkommend*)
Drei Knäbchen, jung, schön, hold und
    weise,
Umschweben euch auf eurer Reise:
Sie werden eure Führer sein,
Folgt ihrem Rate ganz allein.

PAPAGENO

Hm! hm! hm! hm! hm! hm! hm! hm!

TAMINO

I can no help or comfort offer.
I wish I could relieve your pain.
(*Enter the Three Ladies.*)

FIRST LADY

The Queen forgives you graciously.
(*removes his padlock*)
From punishment you shall be free.

PAPAGENO

Oh, what a joy again to chatter!

SECOND LADY

Be truthful, and you will fare better!

PAPAGENO

No lie shall ever come from me.

THREE LADIES

This padlock shall your warning be!
If one could seal the lips of liars
With such a padlock fast and tight.
Then hatred, slander's poisoned briars,
Would yield to brotherhood and right.

FIRST LADY

(*gives Tamino a golden flute*)
O Prince, upon our Queen's command,
We lay this treasure in your hand.
This magic flute will power lend you.
Its tones in danger will defend you.

THREE LADIES

Whene'er this power is asserted,
All human passions are converted;
The saddest man, to smile will learn;
The coldest heart, with love will burn.
More than gold and treasures
A magic flute like this is worth;
By its spell would human woe
Change to happiness and mirth.

PAPAGENO

To withdraw now, fairest beauties,
May I take the liberty?

THREE LADIES

No, to new and urgent duties
Our Queen has ordered you:
To Sarastro's temple yonder
With the Prince you are to wander.

PAPAGENO

No, my ladies, thank you, no!
You yourselves have told me so:
That he's savage as a boar,
Surely would Sarastro roast me,
Fry and toast me, fry and toast me,
Nothing less and nothing more!

THREE LADIES

The Prince will shield you, have no
    fear;
You will be safe while he is near.

PAPAGENO (*aside*)

Oh, would the devil only get him!
My life I rate too high.
He'll steal away, upon my honor,
Like a thief on the sly!

FIRST LADY

(*hands Papageno a little box con-
    taining bells*)
This precious case is meant for you.

PAPAGENO

Well! well! And may I see it too?

THREE LADIES

Herein are bells of silver swaying.

PAPAGENO

But shall I learn to set them playing?

THREE LADIES

O yes indeed, O yes indeed!

ALL

Flute and bell-tones' magic power
Shall be yours (ours) in danger's hour.
Fare ye well, we'll meet again.
(*The Three Ladies turn to go.*)

TAMINO

But, fairest ladies, tell us pray:

PAPAGENO AND TAMINO

Who will as guide show us the way?
(*The Three Ladies return.*)

THREE LADIES

Three spirits young and wise will guide
    you,
And on your journey stay beside you.
Rely on them where they may lead.
Only their counsel shall you heed.

TAMINO UND PAPAGENO
Drei Knäbchen, jung, schön, hold
und weise,
Umschweben uns auf unsrer Reise.

ALLE
So lebet wohl, wir wollen geh'n.
Lebt wohl, lebt wohl, auf Wiederseh'n!
(*Alle ab*).
(*Verwandlung. Ein prächtiges ägyptisches Zimmer. Zwei Sklaven tragen schöne Polster nebst einem prächtigen, türkischen Tisch heraus, breiten Teppiche auf; sodann kommt der dritte Sklave.*)

3. SKLAVE
Hahaha!

1. SKLAVE
Pst! Pst!

2. SKLAVE
Was soll denn das Lachen?

3. SKLAVE
Unser Peiniger, der alles belauschende
Mohr wird morgen sicherlich gehangen oder gespiesst.—Pamina!—
Hahaha!

1. SKLAVE
Nun?

3. SKLAVE
Das reizende Mädchen!—Hahaha!

2. SKLAVE
Nun?

3. SKLAVE
Ist entsprungen.

1. UND 2. SKLAVE
Entsprungen?

1. SKLAVE
Und sie entkam?

3. SKLAVE
Unfehlbar! — Wenigstens ist's mein
wahrer Wunsch.

1. SKLAVE
O, Dank euch, ihr guten Götter! Ihr
habt meine Bitte erhört.

3. SKLAVE
Sagt' ich euch nicht immer, es wird
doch ein Tag für uns scheinen, wo
wir gerochen, und der schwarze
Monostatos bestraft werden wird?

2. SKLAVE
Was spricht nun der Mohr zu der
Geschichte?

1. SKLAVE
Er weiss doch davon?

3. SKLAVE
Natürlich! Sie entlief vor seinen Augen.
—Wie mir einige Brüder erzählten,
die im Garten arbeiteten und von
weitem sahen und hörten, so ist der
Mohr nicht mehr zu retten; auch
wenn Pamina von Sarastros Gefolge
wieder eingebracht würde.

1. UND 2. SKLAVE
Wieso?

3. SKLAVE
Du kennst ja den üppigen Wanst und
seine Weise; das Mädchen aber war
klüger, als ich dachte. — In dem
Augenblicke, als er zu siegen glaubte,
rief sie Sarastros Namen: das erschütterte den Mohren; er blieb
stumm und unbeweglich stehen.—
Indes lief Pamina nach dem Kanal
und schiffte von selbst in einer Gondel dem Palmenwäldchen zu.

1. SKLAVE
O, wie wird das schüchterne Reh mit
Todesangst dem Palast ihrer zärtlichen Mutter zueilen!

MONOSTATOS (*von innen*)
He, Sklaven!

1. SKLAVE
Monostatos' Stimme!

MONOSTATOS
He Sklaven! Schafft Fesseln herbei!

DIE DREI SKLAVEN
Fesseln??

1. SKLAVE (*läuft zur Seitentür*)
Doch nicht für Pamina? O ihr Götter!
Da seht, Brüder, das Mädchen ist
gefangen.

2. UND 3. SKLAVEN
Pamina?—Schrecklicher Anblick!

1. SKLAVE
Seht, wie der unbarmherzige Teufel sie
bei ihren zarten Händchen fasst—
das halt ich nicht aus. (*Geht auf die
andere Seite ab.*)

TAMINO AND PAPAGENO

Three spirits young and wise will guide us,
And on our journey stay beside us.

THREE LADIES

Rely on them where they may lead.
Only their counsel shall you heed.

ALL

So fare you well, we go our way,
May fortune be with us (you) to-day
So fare ye well!   (*Exeunt.*)
(*Change of Scene. Elaborate Egyptian room. Two Slaves bring embroidered pillows and a beautiful Turkish table; they spread out rugs; then the Third Slave appears.*)

THIRD SLAVE

Ha! ha! ha!

FIRST SLAVE

Sh! sh!

SECOND SLAVE

What is the meaning of that laughter?

THIRD SLAVE

Our torturer, the ever-spying Moor, will surely be hung or put on the rack tomorrow.—Pamina! Ha! ha!

FIRST SLAVE

Well?

THIRD SLAVE

The beautiful maiden—ha! ha! ha!

SECOND SLAVE

Well?

THIRD SLAVE

has run away.

FIRST AND SECOND SLAVES

Run away?

FIRST SLAVE

And she escaped?

THIRD SLAVE

Without doubt! At least it is my sincere wish.

FIRST SLAVE

Oh, thank you, good Gods! You have heard my plea!

THIRD SLAVE

Did I not always tell you that there would come a day for us when we will be avenged, and the black Monostatos will be punished?

SECOND SLAVE

What does the Moor say to all this?

FIRST SLAVE

He knows about it, does he not?

THIRD SLAVE

Naturally! She escaped before his very eyes! As some brothers told me, who were working in the garden and who listened and watched from the distance, the Moor no longer can be saved, even if Pamina should be brought back again by Sarastro's suite.

FIRST AND SECOND SLAVES

How so?

THIRD SLAVE

You know the old thick-paunch and his ways. The maiden was more clever, however, than I thought. At the moment when be believed he had won, she called Sarastro's name. That terrified the Moor. He stood silent and motionless. Meanwhile Pamina ran to the canal and floated, driven by the stream, in a gondola towards the palm grove.

FIRST SLAVE

Oh, how the shy deer will hurry, frightened to death, to the palace of her mother!

MONOSTATOS (*off-stage*)

Ho, Slaves!

FIRST SLAVE

Monostatos's voice!

MONOSTATOS

Ho, Slaves! Bring chains!

THREE SLAVES

Chains?

FIRST SLAVE

(*runs to the side door*)
Not for Pamina! Oh, Heavens! Look there, brothers! The maiden has been caught!

SECOND AND THIRD SLAVES

Pamina?— Horrible sight!

FIRST SLAVE

See how the relentless devil grasps her by her tender hands—I cannot bear it!
(*Exit, at the other side.*)

2. SKLAVE

Ich noch weniger.—(*Auch dort ab.*)

3. SKLAVE

So was sehen zu müssen ist Höllen-
marter! (*Ab.*)

MONOSTATOS

(*sehr schnell*) Du feines Täubchen.
nur herein!

PAMINA

(*die von Sklaven hereingeführt wird*).
O welche Marter, welche Pein!

MONOSTATOS

Verloren ist dein Leben!

PAMINA

Der Tod macht mich nicht beben,
Nur meine Mutter dauert mich;
Sie stirbt vor Gram ganz sicherlich.

MONOSTATOS

He, Sklaven, legt ihr Fesseln an! (*Sie
legen ihr Fesseln an*).
Mein Hass soll dich verderben.

PAMINA

Lass mich lieber sterben
Weil nichts, du Barbar, dich rühren kann.
(*Sie sinkt ohnmächtig auf ein
Sopha*).

MONOSTATOS

Nun fort! Lass mich bei ihr allein.
(*Die Sklaven gehen ab.*)

PAPAGENO

(*von aussen am Fenster, ohne gleich
gesehen zu werden*).
Wo bin ich wohl? Wo mag ich sein?
Aha! da find ich Leute.
Gewagt, ich geh hinein. (*Geht herein.*)
Schön Mädchen, jung und fein,
Viel weisser noch als Kreide. (*Mono-
statos und Papageno besehen sich;
erschrecken einer über den andern.*)

BEIDE

Hu! das ist der Teufel sicherlich;
Hab' Mitleid! Verschone mich! Hu,
hu, hu! (*Laufen beide ab.*)

PAMINA

(*spricht wie im Traum:*) Mutter—
Mutter—Mutter! (*Sie erholt sich,
sieht sich um.*) Wie?—Noch schlägt
dies Herz?—Zu neuen Qualen erwacht?—O, das ist hart, sehr hart!—
Mir bitterer, als der Tod. (*Papageno
tritt ein.*)

PAPAGENO

Bin ich nicht ein Narr, dass ich mich
schrecken liess?—Es gibt ja schwarze
Vögel in der Welt, warum denn nicht
auch schwarze Menschen?—(*Er erblickt Pamina.*) Ah, sieh da! Hier
ist das schöne Mädchen noch.—Du
Tochter der nächtlichen Königin—

PAMINA

(*erhebt sich:*) Nächtliche Königin?—
Wer bist du?

PAPAGENO

Ein Abgesandter der sternflammenden
Königin.

PAMINA

(*freudig:*) Meiner Mutter? — O
Wonne!—Dein Name?

PAPAGENO

Papageno.

PAMINA

Papageno? — Papageno — ich erinnere
mich, den Namen oft gehört zu
haben, dich selbst aber sah ich nie.

PAPAGENO

Ich dich ebensowenig.

PAMINA

Du kennst also meine gute, zärtliche
Mutter?

PAPAGENO

Wenn du die Tochter der nächtlichen
Königin bist—ja!

PAMINA

O, ich bin es.

PAPAGENO

Das will ich gleich erkennen. (*Er sieht
das Portrait an, welches der Prinz
zuvor empfangen, und das Papageno
nun an einem Band am Halse trägt.*)
Die Augen schwarz—richtig, schwarz.
—Die Lippen rot—richtig, rot.—
Blonde Haare—blonde Haare.—Alles
trifft ein, bis auf Hände und Füsse.
Nach dem Gemälde zu schliessen,
sollst du weder Hände noch Füsse
haben; denn hier sind keine ange-
zeigt.

PAMINA

Erlaube mir—Ja, ich bin's!—Wie kam
es in deine Hände?

SECOND SLAVE

Even less can I. (*Exit by the same way.*)

THIRD SLAVE

To have to see such a thing is the torture of hell! (*Exit.*)

MONOSTATOS

My dainty lambkin, please enter!

PAMINA

O will my tortures never cease?

MONOSTATOS

Your life is at my mercy!

PAMINA

But Death cannot dismay me.
Yet for my mother's grief I mourn.
Her heart will break, by anguish torn.

MONOSTATOS
(*to the Slaves standing in the background, who approach quickly*)
Bring chains, ye slaves, and fetter her!
I'll force you to obey me.

PAMINA

I beg you rather slay me,
If naught can stir your evil heart!
(*She sinks unconscious on a sofa.*)

MONOSTATOS

Get out, get out! Leave me alone with her! (*Exeunt Slaves.*)

PAPAGENO
(*outside, at the window*)
Where am I now?
(*Monostatos does not notice him.*)
I'll have a glance.
Aha! there are some people.
All right, I'll take a chance. (*Enter.*)
Dear maiden, young and fair,
Much whiter than a pigeon—
(*Papageno sees Monostatos; Monostatos sees Papageno.*)

PAPAGENO AND MONOSTATOS

Hoo, that is the devil certainly!
Have pity! Be merciful! Hoo! Hoo!
Hoo! Hoo! (*Exeunt.*)

PAMINA

(*Speaks as in a dream:*) Mother!
Mother! Mother! (*She recovers, looks around.*) What, my heart still beats? Am I still alive? Do I wake

to new troubles? Oh, that is hard, very hard! This is more bitter to me than death! (*Papageno enters again.*)

PAPAGENO

Wasn't I a fool to be frightened? There are black birds in the world, so why not black people? Ah, see there! Here is the lovely maiden. You, daughter of the Queen of the Night—

PAMINA (*rises*)
Queen of the Night? Who are you?

PAPAGENO

A messenger of the star-flaming Queen.

PAMINA (*joyfully*)
My mother? Oh Joy! Your name?

PAPAGENO

Papageno.

PAMINA

Papageno? Papageno — I remember having heard your name often, but you yourself I never saw.

PAPAGENO

Nor I you.

PAMINA

Then you know my good, loving mother?

PAPAGENO

If you are the daughter of the Queen of the Night,—yes.

PAMINA

Yes, I am.

PAPAGENO

I'll soon find out. (*He looks at the portrait which previously had been given to the Prince and which Papageno now wears around his neck on a ribbon.*) Eyes black — right — black. Lips red—right—red. Blond hair— blond hair. Everything is correct, except the hands and feet because judging from this picture, you haven't any hands and feet, for none are painted here.

PAMINA

Let me see. Yes, it is my portrait, but how did it come into your hands?

PAPAGENO

Ich muss dir das umständlicher erzäh-
len.—Ich kam heute früh, wie ge-
wöhnlich, zu deiner Mutter Palast
mit meiner Lieferung—

PAMINA

Lieferung?

PAPAGENO

Ja, ich liefere deiner Mutter und ihren
Jungfrauen schon seit vielen Jahren
alle die schönen Vögel in den Palast.
—Eben als ich im Begriff war, meine
Vögel abzugeben, sah ich einen Menschen vor mir, der sich Prinz nennen
lässt.—Dieser Prinz hat deine Mutter
so eingenommen, dass sie ihm dein
Bildnis schenkte und ihm befahl,
dich zu befreien.—Sein Entschluss
war so schnell, als seine Liebe zu dir.

PAMINA

Liebe? (Freudig.) Er liebt mich also?
O, sage mir das noch einmal, ich
höre das Wort Liebe gar zu gern.

PAPAGENO

Das glaube ich dir, du bist ja ein
Mädchen.—Wo blieb ich denn?

PAMINA

Bei der Liebe.

PAPAGENO

Richtig, bei der Liebe! Das nenn ich
ein Gedächtnis haben! Komm, du
wirst Augen machen, wenn du den
schönen Jüngling erblickst.

PAMINA

Wohl denn, es sei gewagt! (Sie gehen,
Pamina kehrt um.) Aber wenn dies
ein Fallstrick wäre—wenn dieser nun
ein böser Geist von Sarastros Gefolge
wäre?— (Sieht ihn bedenklich an.)

PAPAGENO

Ich ein böser Geist?—Wo denkst du
hin.—Ich bin der beste Geist von
der Welt.

PAMINA

Vergib, vergib, wenn ich dich belei-
digte! Du hast ein gefühlvolles Herz.

PAPAGENO

Ach, freilich habe ich ein gefühlvolles
Herz! Aber was nützt mir das alles?
—Ich möchte mir oft alle meine
Federn ausrupfen, wenn ich bedenke,
dass Papageno noch keine Papagena
hat.

PAMINA

Armer Mann! Du hast also noch kein
Weib?

PAPAGENO

Noch nicht einmal ein Mädchen, viel
weniger ein Weib!—Und unsereiner
hat doch auch bisweilen seine lusti-
gen Stunden, wo man gern gesell-
schaftliche Unterhaltung h a b e n
möchte.—

PAMINA

Geduld, Freund! Der Himmel wird
auch für dich sorgen; er wird dir
eine Freundin schicken, ehe du dir's
vermutest.

PAPAGENO

Wenn er sie nur bald schickte!

PAMINA

Bei Männern, welche Liebe fühlen,
Fehlt auch ein gutes Herze nicht.

PAPAGENO

Die süssen Triebe mitzufühlen,
Ist dann der Weiber erste Pflicht.

BEIDE

Wir wollen uns der Liebe freu'n,
Wir leben durch die Lieb' allein.

PAMINA

Die Lieb' versüsset jede Plage,
Ihr opfert jede Kreatur.

PAPAGENO

Sie würzet uns're Lebenstage.
Sie wirkt im Kreise der Natur.

BEIDE

Ihr hoher Zweck zeigt deutlich an,
Nichts edlers sei, als Weib und Mann.
Mann und Weib, und Weib und Mann
Reichen an die Gottheit an. (Beide
ab.)

3 KNABEN

(führen Tamino herein, jeder hat einen
silbernen Palmenzweig in der Hand)
Zum Ziele führt dich diese Bahn,
Doch musst du, Jüngling, männlich
siegen.
Drum höre uns're Lehre an:
Sei standhaft, duldsam und verschwie-
gen.

TAMINO

Ihr holden Kleinen, sagt mir an,
Ob ich Pamina retten kann?

PAPAGENO

To tell you that will be a longer story. I went, early this morning, as usual, to your mother's palace to make my delivery.

PAMINA

Delivery?

PAPAGENO

Yes, for years I have delivered all the finest birds I could catch to your mother and her ladies, at the palace. Just as I was about to hand over the birds, I saw someone standing in front of me who called himself "Prince". This prince so impressed your mother that she gave him your portrait, and ordered him to set you free. His decision was just as quick as his love for you.

PAMINA (joyfully)

Love? He loves me, then? Oh, say that again! It feels so good to hear the word "love"!

PAPAGENO

That I believe, for you are a girl. But where was I then?

PAMINA

You said "love".

PAPAGENO

Right, love. That's what I call memory! Come, your eyes will be bright when you see the handsome youth.

PAMINA

Well then, let us go. (They start to go; Pamina turns around.) But suppose this is only a trap? Suppose you are but an evil genius of Sarastro? (She looks at him doubtfully.)

PAPAGENO

I? An evil genius? What are you thinking of? I am no genius at all.

PAMINA

Friend, forgive me if I have offended you. You have a tender heart.

PAPAGENO

Ah, certainly I have a tender heart! But what good does it do me? Sometimes I feel like ripping out all my feathers when I think that Papageno hasn't found a Papagena yet.

PAMINA

Poor man! Then you have no wife?

PAPAGENO

Not even a girl, let alone a wife! And people like us have their gay hours, too, when they would like to have some fun.

PAMINA

Have patience, friend. The Gods will take care of you. They will send you a wife, before you even think.

PAPAGENO

If they would only send her soon!

PAMINA

The man who feels sweet love's emotion Will always have a kindly heart.

PAPAGENO

Each maid must share his deep devotion, And from this duty never part.

PAMINA AND PAPAGENO

Let joyous love for grief atone; We live by love, by love alone.

PAMINA

To love's sweet might yields every creature. It offers everlasting joy.

PAPAGENO

Its blessings are the gift of nature, Which no one ever can destroy.

PAMINA AND PAPAGENO

Its noble aim shows clear in life: No greater good than man and wife. Wife and man, and man and wife, Reach the height of godly life.
(Exeunt.)
(Change of Scene. A grove, in the middle of which stand three temples. Three Spirits lead Tamino in.)

THREE SPIRITS

Your journey's end you soon will reach; Yet win you must by manly daring; But harken to these words we teach: Be silent, steadfast, and forbearing.

TAMINO

(has hung his flute around his neck)
Ye kindly spirits, tell me, please, May I Pamina soon release?

3 KNABEN

Dies kund zu tun, steht uns nicht an;
Sei standhaft, duldsam und verschwie-
gen.
Bedenke dies; kurz, sei ein Mann,
Dann, Jüngling, wirst du männlich
siegen. (*gehen ab.*)

TAMINO

Die Weisheitslehre dieser Knaben
Sei ewig mir ins Herz gegraben.
Wo bin ich nun? Was wird mit mir?
Ist dies der Sitz der Götter hier?
Es zeigen die Pforten, es zeigen die
Säulen,
Dass Klugheit und Arbeit und Künste
hier weilen;
Wo Tätigkeit thronet und Müssiggang
weicht,
Erhält seine Herrschaft das Laster
nicht leicht.
Ich wage mich mutig zur Pforte hinein,
Die Absicht ist edel und lauter und
rein.
Erzitt're, feiger Bösewicht!
Pamina retten ist mir Pflicht. (*Er geht
an die Pforte zur rechten Seite,
macht sie auf, und als er hinein will,
hört man von fern eine Stimme.*)

PRIESTER

Zurück!

TAMINO

Zurück! So wag ich hier mein Glück.
(*Er geht zur linken Pforte; eine
Stimme von innen.*)

PRIESTER

Zurück!

TAMINO

Auch hier ruft man zurück. (*Sieht
sich um.*)
Da seh' ich noch eine Tür!
Vielleicht find ich den Eingang hier.
(*Er klopft, ein alter Priester er-
scheint.*)

PRIESTER

Wo willst du, kühner Fremdling hin?
Was suchst du hier im Heiligtum?

TAMINO

Der Lieb' und Tugend Eigentum.

PRIESTER

Die Worte sind von hohem Sinn!
Allein wie willst du diese finden?
Dich leitet Lieb' und Tugend nicht,
Weil Tod und Rache dich entzünden.

TAMINO

Nur Rache für den Bösewicht.

PRIESTER

Den wirst du wohl bei uns nicht finden.

TAMINO

(*schnell*) Sarastro herrscht in diesen
Gründen?

PRIESTER

Ja, ja! Sarastro herrschet hier.

TAMINO

(*schnell*) Doch in dem Weisheitstempel
nicht?

PRIESTER

(*langsam*) Er herrscht im Weisheitstempel hier.

TAMINO

So ist denn alles Heuchelei! (*Will
gehen.*)

PRIESTER

Willst du schon wieder geh'n?

TAMINO

Ja, ich will geh'n, froh und frei,
Nie euren Tempel seh'n.

PRIESTER

Erklär dich näher mir,
Dich täuschet ein Betrug.

TAMINO

Sarastro wohnet hier,
Das ist mir schon genug.

PRIESTER

Wenn du dein Leben liebst,
So rede, bleibe da!
Sarastro hassest du?

TAMINO

Ich hass ihn ewig, ja!

PRIESTER

Nun gib mir deine Gründe an.

TAMINO

Er ist ein Unmensch, ein Tyrann!

PRIESTER

Ist das, was du gesagt, erwiesen?

TAMINO

Durch ein unglücklich Weib bewiesen,
Das Gram und Jammer niederdrückt.

PRIESTER

Ein Weib hat also dich berückt?
Ein Weib tut wenig, plaudert viel.
Du, Jüngling, glaubst dem Zungenspiel?
O legte doch Sarastro dir
Die Absicht seiner Handlung für!

THREE SPIRITS

To answer this is not allowed;
Be silent, steadfast, and forbearing!
Have courage, Prince, brave be and
proud.
Then you will win by manly daring.
(*Exeunt.*)

TAMINO

These words of wisdom truly spoken
Be in my heart engraved as token.
Where am I now? What will betide?
Do here the mighty gods abide?
These arches and portals, mysterious
dwelling,
Of reason, and labor, and arts are fore-
telling;
Where man is achieving and idleness
banned.
There vice and dishonesty never may
stand.
I enter the gate and all peril defy!
My purpose is blameless and noble and
high.
You, mean offender, fear my scorn!
Pamina's rescue have I sworn! (*goes
to the portal R.*)

A VOICE (*from within*)

Go back!

TAMINO

Go back! Go back!
Then I try here my luck. (*goes to the
portal L.*)

A VOICE (*from within*)

Go back!

TAMINO

Again the call "go back"? (*goes to the
portal C.*)
Another door there is near.
Perhaps I'll gain an entrance here.
(*While he is approaching the center
portal, it opens and an old Priest appears.*)

PRIEST

Who nears this holy temple door?
What are you, stranger, seeking for?

TAMINO

'Tis love and virtue that I seek.

PRIEST

These words a lofty mind bespeak.
How do you hope to earn them?
Not love nor virtue do you heed;
With death and vengeance you are
burning.

TAMINO

Yes, vengeance for a villain's deed!

PRIEST

My son, you are ensnared in error.

TAMINO (*quickly*)

Is this Sarastro's realm of terror?

PRIEST

'Tis true! Sarastro is our Lord.

TAMINO (*quickly*)

But not in wisdom's temple, too?

PRIEST (*slowly*)

He rules in wisdom's temple, too.

TAMINO

Then all is false as false can be! (*wishes
to go*)

PRIEST

You mean to leave us then?

TAMINO

Yes, I will leave, glad and free,
Never return again.

PRIEST

Do not act hastily.
You have been told a lie.

TAMINO

Sarastro dwelleth here,
And that will do for me!

PRIEST

If you don't want to die, give answer;
do not go!
You hate Sarastro so?

TAMINO

Now and forevermore!

PRIEST

So let me know the reason then.

TAMINO

He is a tyrant, foe of men!

PRIEST

Have you for such a charge foundation?

TAMINO

A woman, bowed by tribulation,
Who suffers anguished pain and grief.

PRIEST

A woman do you grant belief?,
Few deeds, much chatter, artless youth,
Is this not woman's way forsooth?
O may you hear Sarastro say
What purpose in his action lay!

TAMINO
Die Absicht ist nur allzu klar!
Riss nicht der Räuber ohn' Erbarmen
Paminen aus der Mutter Armen?

PRIESTER
Ja, Jüngling, was du sagst, ist wahr.

TAMINO
Wo ist sie, die er uns geraubt?
Man opferte vielleicht sie schon?

PRIESTER
Dir dies zu sagen, teurer Sohn,
Ist jetzt und mir noch nicht erlaubt.

TAMINO
Erklär dies Rätsel, täusch mich nicht!

PRIESTER
Die Zunge bindet Eid und Pflicht.

TAMINO
Wann also wird die Decke schwinden?

PRIESTER
Sobald dich führt der Freundschaft
Hand
Ins Heiligtum zum ew'gen Band. (*Geht
ab.*)

TAMINO
(*allein*) O ew'ge Nacht! Wann wirst
du Schwinden?
Wann wird das Licht mein Auge find-
en?

CHORUS
(*von innen*) Bald, Jüngling, oder nie!

TAMINO
Bald, sagt ihr, oder nie?
Ihr Unsichtbaren, saget mir,
Lebt denn Pamina noch?

CHORUS
Pamina lebet noch.

TAMINO
(*freudig*) Sie lebt? Ich danke euch
dafür (*er nimmt seine Flöte heraus.*)
O wenn ich doch im Stande wäre,
Allmächtige, zu eurer Ehre.
Mit jedem Tone meinen Dank
Zu schildern, wie er hier, (*aufs Herz
deutend*) entsprang.
(*Er spielt, sogleich kommen Tiere von
allen Arten hervor, ihm zuzuhören.
Er .hört auf und sie fliehen. Die
Vögel pfeifen dazu.*)
Wie stark ist nicht dein Zauberton,
Weil, holde Flöte, durch dein Spielen

Selbst wilde Tiere Freude **fühlen**
(*spielt*)
Doch nur Pamina bleibt davon (*spielt.*)
Pamina, höre, höre mich! (*spielt.*)
Umsonst! (*spielt*) Wo? (*spielt*) **Ach,**
wo find' ich dich?
(*Spielt: Papageno antwortet von innen
mit seinem Flötchen.*)
Ha, das ist Papagenos Ton! (*Spielt,
antwortet.*)
Vielleicht sah er Pamina schon,
Vielleicht eilt sie mit ihm zu mir!
Vielleicht führt mich der Ton zu
ihr. (*Er eilt ab. Papageno und Pa-
mina, ohne Fesseln, eilen herbei.*)

BEIDE
Schnelle Füsse, rascher Mut
Schützt vor Feindes List und Wut.
Fänden wir Tamino doch,
Sonst erwischen sie uns noch!

PAMINA
Holder Jüngling!

PAPAGENO
Stille, stille, ich kann's besser! (*pfeift.*)
*Tamino antwortet von innen auf
seiner Flöte.*)

BEIDE
Welche Freude ist wohl grösser?
Freund Tamino hört uns schon!
Hieher kam der Flötenton.
Welch ein Glück, wenn ich ihn finde!
Nur geschwinde, nur geschwinde!
(*Sie wollen hineingehen; Monostatos
tritt ihnen von dort her entgegen.*)

MONOSTATOS
(*ihrer spottend.*)
Nur geschwinde, nur geschwinde!
Ha, hab' ich euch noch erwischt!
Nur herbei mit Stahl und Eisen!
Wart, ich will euch Mores weisen.
Den Monostatos berücken!
Nur herbei mit Band und Stricken.
He, ihr Sklaven, kommt herbei! (*Sklaven
kommen mit Fesseln.*)

PAMINA UND PAPAGENO
Ach, nun ist's mit uns vorbei!

PAPAGENO
Wer viel wagt, gewinnt oft viel!
Komm, du schönes Glockenspiel,
Lass die Glöckchen klingen, klingen,
Dass die Ohren ihnen singen! (*Er spielt
auf seinem Glockenspiel. Sogleich
tanzen und singen Monostatos und
die Sklaven und gehen unter dem
Gesange marschmässig ab.*)

TAMINO

His purpose I can clearly read!
Was it not he, and no one other,
Who tore Pamina from her mother?

PRIEST

What you have said is true indeed.

TAMINO

Where is she whom he stole away?
Has she to death already gone?

PRIEST

No further word, beloved son,
Am I as yet allowed to say.

TAMINO

To solve this riddle, help me now!

PRIEST

My lips are sealed by solemn vow.

TAMINO

When will this veil of dark be lifted?

PRIEST

As soon as friendship's guiding hand
Will lead you to the holy band. (*Exit.*)

TAMINO

When, endless night, will you be
    riven?
When will the light to me be given?

CHORUS (*from within*)

Soon, soon, stranger, or no more.

TAMINO

Soon, soon, soon, stranger, or no more?
Mysterious voices, answer me:
Does then Pamina live?

CHORUS (*from within*)

Pamina, Pamina, yes, she lives.

TAMINO (*joyfully*)

She lives? she lives? My thanks, ye
    words of cheer!
Oh, could I show you my emotion,
My gratitude and my devotion!
With every tone let your praise be
    singing,
As from here, (*pointing to his heart*)
    here it springs! (*Plays the flute.*)
How strong your tone with magic spell,
Dear flute, is binding.
By your tone, dear flute, each being
But happiness and joy is finding.
    (*plays*)
But Pamina does not come. (*plays*)

Pamina, (*plays*) Pamina hear me, **hear**
me, pray! (*plays*)
In vain! in vain! (*plays*) Where?
    (*plays*) where? where shall I dis-
    cover you? (*plays*) (*Papageno re-
    plies.*)
Ah, that is Papageno's sound. (*plays*)
    (*Papageno replies.*)
Oh, might he have Pamina found,
Oh, might she come with him to me!
Oh, might the tone bring her to me!
    (*Exit.*)
(*Papageno and Pamina hurry in.*)

PAPAGENO AND PAMINA

Nothing ventured, nothing won!
To escape them let us run.
Let us to Tamino speed,
Or they will catch us soon indeed.

PAMINA (*calls upstage*)

O Tamino!

PAPAGENO

Quiet, quiet, let me show you how **to**
    call him.
    (*He whistles. Tamino replies.*)

PAPAGENO AND PAMINO

Then no harm did yet befall him!
What a joy to hear his tone;
(*pointing off L.*) It was he, yes **he**
    alone!
Now no more we have to worry!
Let us hurry, scurry, hurry!
(*They try to hurry away. Monostatos
    steps in their path, mocking them.*)

MONOSTATOS

Let us hurry, scurry, hurry!
Ha! just in the nick of time!
I will cast you both in irons!
I shall throw you to the lions!
So you thought that you could fool me!
(*calling upstage*) Without mercy **shall**
    my rule be!
Ho, ye slaves, bring chains and rope!

PAPAGENO AND PAMINA

Now there is no more to hope!

PAPAGENO

Now it's time to work the spell.
Come, my lovely magic-bell,
Let your melody be ringing.
Save us by your magic singing!
(*Papageno plays on his bells. **The
    Slaves** dance.*)

MONOSTATOS UND SKLAVEN
Das klinget so herrlich, das klinget so
schön!
Larala la la larala la la larala!
Nie hab' ich so etwas gehört und
geseh'n!
Larala la la larala la la larala!

PAMINA UND PAPAGENO
Könnte jeder brave Mann
Solche Glöckchen finden!
Seine Feinde würden dann
Ohne Mühe schwinden,
Und er lebte ohne sie
In der besten Harmonie.
Nur der Freundschaft Harmonie
Mildert die Beschwerden;
Ohne diese Sympathie
Ist kein Glück auf Erden. (*Ein starker
Marsch mit Trompeten und Pauken
fällt ein.*)

CHORUS
(*von innen*) Es lebe Sarastro! Sarastro
lebe!

PAPAGENO
Was soll das bedeuten? Ich zittre, ich
bebe!

PAMINA
O Freund, nun ist's um uns getan,
Dies kündigt den Sarastro an!

PAPAGENO
O wär ich eine Maus,
Wie wollt' ich mich verstecken!
Wär' ich so klein wie Schnecken,
So kröch ich in mein Haus!
Mein Kind, was werden wir nun
sprechen?

PAMINA
Die Wahrheit, wär sie auch Verbrech-
en. (*Ein Zug von Gefolge; zuletzt
fährt Sarastro auf einem Triumpf-
wagen heraus, der von sechs Löwen
gezogen wird.*)

CHORUS
Es lebe Sarastro! Sarastro soll leben!
Er ist es, dem wir uns mit Freuden
ergeben!
Stets mög' er des Lebens als Weiser
sich freun,
Er ist unser Abgott, dem alle sich
weihn. (*Dieser Chor wird gesungen,
bis Sarastro aus dem Wagen ist.*)

PAMINA
(*kniet*)
Herr, ich bin zwar Verbrecherin,
Ich wollte deiner Macht entfliehn!
Allein, die Schuld ist nicht an mir;
Der böse Mohr verlangte Liebe;
Darum, o Herr, entfloh ich dir.

SARASTRO
Steh auf, erheitre dich, o Liebe!
Denn ohne erst in dich zu dringen,
Weiss ich von deinem Herzen mehr:
Du liebest einen Andern sehr.
Zur Liebe will ich dich nicht zwingen,
Doch geb ich dir die Freiheit nicht.

PAMINA
Mich rufet ja die Kindespflicht,
Denn meine Mutter—

SARASTRO
Steht in meiner Macht.
Du würdest um dein Glück gebracht,
Wenn ich dich ihren Händen liesse.

PAMINA
Mir klingt der Muttername süsse!
Sie ist es—

SARASTRO
Und ein stolzes Weib.
Ein Mann muss eure Herzen leiten,
Denn ohne ihn pflegt jedes Weib
Aus ihrem Wirkungskreis zu schreiten.

MONOSTATOS
(*führt den Tamino herein.*)
Nun stolzer Jüngling, nur hieher!
Hier ist Sarastro, unser Herr.

PAMINA
Er ist's!

TAMINO
Sie ist's!

PAMINA
Ich glaub es kaum!

TAMINO
Sie ist's!

PAMINA
Er ist's!

TAMINO
Es ist kein Traum!

PAMINA UND TAMINO
Es schling mein Arm sich um ihn
(sie) her
Und wenn es auch mein Ende wär!
(*Sie umarmen sich.*)

CHORUS
Was soll das heissen?

MONOSTATOS AND SLAVES

This jingles so softly, this jingles so
    clear!
La la ra, la la la la ra, la la la ra.
How gently it touches my heart and my
    ear,
La la ra, la la la la ra, la la la la ra.

PAPAGENO AND PAMINA

If to every honest man
Bells like these were given,
All his foes would swiftly then
Far away be driven;
He would live contentedly,
In the sweetest harmony.
Only friendship's harmony
Lessens pain and grieving;
Without friendly sympathy,
Joy this earth is leaving.

CHORUS (from within)

We praise thee, Sarastro, the King of
wisdom!

PAPAGENO

What noise are they making?
I'm trembling, I'm shaking.

PAMINA

O friend we both are lost, I fear;
This sound means that Sarastro's near!

PAPAGENO

I wish I were a mouse,
To hiding I would hurtle!
Or could I, like a turtle,
Creep in my little house!
But say, what answer shall we give
    him?

PAMINA

Be truthful, we shall not deceive him!
(Sarastro and his suite appear.)

CHORUS

We praise thee, Sarastro, with great
    exultation!
We hail thee, Sarastro, in deep admira-
    tion!
Forever thy wisdom may govern our
    mind!
Then lead us, Sarastro, perfection to
    find!

PAMINA (kneels)

Sire! My offense is all to plain
I tried escape from your domain.
Alas! the guilt falls not on me.
The cruel Moor urged me to love him;
Therefore, my Lord, I tried to flee.

SARASTRO

Arise, console thyself, Pamina!
The name of your devoted lover
I need not ask you to impart,
I read the secret of your heart.
Through me you will not have to suffer,
But yet I will not set you free.

PAMINA

Not for myself I make this plea,
But my poor mother—

SARASTRO

                    stands within my might;
What would become of truth and right
If I had left you with your mother?

PAMINA

So sweet a name there is no other,
For she is . . . for she is . . .

SARASTRO

She is all too proud!
By man your course must be decided,
For by herself a woman
Steps beyond her sphere and is mis-
    guided.
(Enter Monostatos and Tamino.)

MONOSTATOS

My proud young friend, come here
right now!
Before Sarastro you will bow.

PAMINO

'Tis he!

TAMINO

'Tis she!

PAMINO AND TAMINO

It is no dream!
My arms will hold him (her) tight em-
    braced
Although with death I may be faced.
    (They embrace.)

MONOSTATOS

Welch eine Dreistigkeit!
Gleich auseinander! Das geht zu weit!
(*Er trennt sie. Er kniet vor Sarastro.*)
Dein Sklave liegt zu deinen Füssen:
Lass den verwegnen Frevler büssen!
Bedenk, wie frech der Knabe ist!
Durch dieses seltnen Vogels List (*auf
Papageno zeigend*)
Wollt' er Pamina dir entführen.
Allein ich wusst ihn auszuspüren.
Du kennst mich! Meine Wachsamkeit—

SARASTRO

Verdient, dass man ihr Lorbeer streut!
He, gebt dem Ehrenmann sogleich—

MONOSTATOS

Schon deine Gnade macht mich reich.

SARASTRO

Nur sieben und siebenzig Sohlenstreich!

MONOSTATOS

Ach Herr, den Lohn verhofft ich nicht!

SARASTRO

Nicht Dank, es ist ja meine Pflicht!
(*Monostatos wird abgeführt.*)

CHORUS

Es lebe Sarastro, der göttliche Weise!
Er lohnet und strafet in ähnlichem
Kreise.

SARASTRO

Führt diese beiden Fremdlinge
In unsern Prüfungstempel ein;
Bedecket ihre Häupter dann,
Sie müssen erst gereinigt sein, (*Zwei
bringen eine Art Sack, und bedecken
die Häupter der beiden Fremden.*)

CHORUS

Wenn Tugend und Gerechtigkeit
Der Grossen Pfad mit Ruhm bestreut,
Dann ist die Erd' ein Himmelreich,
Und Sterbliche den Göttern gleich.

ENDE DES ERSTEN AKTS

MONOSTATOS

Ha! what impertinence!
Asunder, wretches! What new offence!
(*He separates them and kneels be-
fore Sarastro.*)
Your slave lies here in supplication:
This traitor must make expiation!
Can you imagine what he dared?
(*pointing to Papageno*) With this rare
  bird he was prepared
To snatch Pamina from your power,
But I appeared in time to cow her.
You know me, and my eagle eye—

SARASTRO

Deserves reward, I can't deny!
As your reward you shall receive

MONOSTATOS

Your grace already makes me rich.

SARASTRO

Just seventy-seven blows with the
  switch!

MONOSTATOS (*kneels*)

Ah, Sire! That's how you thank your
  faithful Moor!
(*Is led away by the Slaves.*)

SARASTRO

My friend you're welcome, I am sure!

CHORUS

May long live Sarastro, his wisdom prevailing!
He praises and chastens in justice unfailing.

SARASTRO

To enter in our temple doors, these
  strangers may not be denied.
So let heir heads be covered then; they
  must at first be purified.
(*Two Priests bring veils and cover the
heads of Tamino and Papageno.*)

CHORUS

Let virtue and integrity
Throughout our life the mentors be.
Then doomed are evil, sin and vice,
And earth becomes a paradise.
(*Sarastro gives Pamina his hand and
goes with her to the center portal.
Tamino and Papageno, guided by
the Two Priests, turn to the exit.*)

Curtain

2. AKT

SARASTRO

Ihr, in dem Weisheitstempel eingeweihten Diener der grossen Götter Osiris
und Isis!—Mit reiner Seele erklär ich
euch, dass unsere heutige Versamm-
lung eine der wichtigsten unserer
Zeit ist.—Tamino, ein Königssohn,
wandelt an der nördlichen Pforte unseres Tempels, und seufzt mit tugend-
vollem Herzen nach einem Gegen-
stand, den wir alle mit Mühe und
Fleiss erringen müssen. — Diesen
Tugendhaften zu bewachen, ihm
freundschaftlich die Hand zu bieten,
sei heute eine unserer wichtigsten
Pflichten.

ERSTER PRIESTER

Er besitzt Tugend?

SARASTRO

Tugend!

ZWEITER PRIESTER

Auch Verschwiegenheit?

SARASTRO

Verschwiegenheit!

DRITTER PRIESTER

Ist wohltätig?

SARASTRO

Wohltätig!—Haltet ihr ihn für würdig,
so folgt meinem Beispiele. (*Sie blasen
dreimal in die Hörner.*) Gerührt über
die Einigkeit eurer Herzen, dankt
Sarastro euch im Namen der Men-
schheit.—Pamina, das sanfte, tugen-
hafte Mädchen, haben die Götter dem
holden Jünglinge bestimmt; dies ist
der Grund, warum ich sie der stolzen
Mutter entriss. — Das Weib dünkt
sich gross su sein, hofft durch Blend-
werk und Aberglauben das Volk zu
berücken und unsern festen Tempel-
bau zu zerstören. Allein, das soll sie
nicht! Tamino, der holde Jüngling
selbst, soll ihn mit uns befestigen und
als Eingeweihter der Tugend Lohn,
dem Laster aber Strafe sein. (*Der
dreimalige Akkord mit den Hörnern
wird wiederholt.*)

SPRECHER

Grosser Sarastro, deine weisheitsvollen
Reden erkennen und bewundern wir;
allein, wird Tamino auch die harten
Prüfungen, so seiner warten, bekämp-
fen?—Er ist Prinz.

SARASTRO

Noch mehr—er ist Mensch!

SPRECHER

Wenn er nun aber in seiner frühen
Jugend leblos erblasste?

SARASTRO

Dann ist er Osiris und Isis gegeben,
und wird der Götter Freuden früher
fühlen, als wir. (*Der dreimalige Akkord wird wiederholt.*) Man führe
Tamino mit seinem Reisegefährten
in den Vorhof des Tempels ein.
(*Zum Sprecher, der vor ihm nieder-
kniet.*) Und du, Freund, vollziehé
dein heiliges Amt und lehre sie die
Macht der Götter erkennen! (*Sprecher geht mit dem zweiten Priester ab.*)
O Isis und Osiris, schenket
Der Weisheit Geist dem neuen Paar!
Die ihr der Wand'rer Schritte lenket.
Stärkt mit Geduld sie in Gefahr.

CHORUS

Stärkt mit Geduld sie in Gefahr.

SARASTRO

Lasst sie der Prüfung Früchte sehen;
Doch sollten sie zu Grabe gehen,
So lohnt der Tugend kühnen Lauf,
Nehmt sie in euren Wohnsitz auf.

CHORUS

Nehmt sie in euren Wohnsitz auf.
(*Sarastro geht voraus, dann alle ihm
nach, ab.*)
(*Verwandlung. Kurzer Vorhof des
Tempels. Es ist Nacht. Tamino und
Papageno werden vom Sprecher und
dem zweiten Priester hereingeführt.
Die Priester lösen ihnen den Schleier
ab und entfernen sich damit.*)

TAMINO

Eine schreckliche Nacht! — Papageno,
bist du noch bei mir?

ACT II

(*Forest of palm trees. The Priests circle the stage in a festive procession, and take their places. At the end, Sarastro appears, advancing to a position in their midst. Three blasts on the horns are sounded by the Priests.*)

SARASTRO

Consecrated servants of the great gods Osiris and Isis in the Temple of Wisdom, with pure heart I declare that today's assembly is one of the most important of our time. Tamino, a prince, waits at the northern portal of our temple, longing with a virtuous soul for the enlightenment towards which all of us have been striving with energy and zeal. To watch over this high-minded youth, and to extend to him the hand of friendship, will be one of our foremost duties this day.

FIRST PRIEST

He is virtuous?

SARASTRO

Virtuous.

SECOND PRIEST

Can he keep silent?

SARASTRO

He can.

THIRD PRIEST

Is he benevolent?

SARASTRO

Benevolent. If you consider him worthy, follow my example. (*They blow three times on their horns.*) Moved by the unanimity of your hearts, Sarastro thanks you in the name of all mankind. Pamina, the gentle, virtuous maiden, has been designated by the gods for this noble youth; therefore I have torn her from the side of her proud mother. This woman considers herself great, and hopes through delusion and superstition to beguile the populace and to destroy the firm foundations of our temples. However, in that she shall not succeed. Tamino himself shall become one of us, and aid us to strengthen the power of virtue and wisdom. (*The three blasts on the horns are repeated.*)

SPEAKER

Great Sarastro, we admire your wise discourse. However, will Tamino be able to contend against the hard ordeals that await him? He is a prince.

SARASTRO

More than that,—he is a man.

SPEAKER

What if now, in his early youth, he pales in death?

SARASTRO

Then he would experience the celestial joys of Osiris and Isis sooner than we. (*The three blasts on the horns are repeated.*) Let Tamino and his companion be led into the court of the temple (*to the Speaker, who kneels before him:*) and you, friend, fulfil your holy office and teach to both what duty to humanity is; teach them to perceive the might of the gods. (*Exeunt Speaker and Second Priest.*)

O Isis and Osiris, favor
This noble pair with wisdom's light!
Grant them your aid in their endeavor,
Lead them to find the path of right!

SARASTRO

Let them be strong against temptation;
But if they fail in their probation,
Do not their virtue meed deny.
Take them to your abode on high.

CHORUS

Take them to your abode on high.

(*Change of Scene. Court of the temple. It is night. Tamino and Papageno are led in by the Speaker and the Second Priest. The Priests remove their veils, and depart with them.*)

TAMINO

What a horrible night! Papageno, are you still with me?

PAPAGENO
Ei, freilich!

TAMINO
Wo denkst du, dass wir uns nun befinden?

PAPAGENO
Wo? Ja, wenn's nicht finster wäre, wollt ich dir's schon sagen—aber so— (*Donnerschlag.*) O weh!—

TAMINO
Was ist's?

PAPAGENO
Mir wird nicht wohl bei der Sache!

TAMINO
Du hast Furcht, wie ich höre.

PAPAGENO
Furcht eben nicht, nur eiskalt läuft's mir über den Rücken. (*Starker Donnerschlag.*) O weh!

TAMINO
Was soll's?

PAPAGENO
Ich glaube, ich bekomme ein kleines Fieber.

TAMINO
Pfui, Papageno! Sei ein Mann!

PAPAGENO
Ich wollt, ich wär ein Mädchen! (*Ein sehr starker Donnerschlag.*) O! o! o! Das ist mein letzter Augenblick! (*Sprecher und der zweite Priester erscheinen mit Fackeln.*)

SPRECHER
Ihr Fremdlinge, was sucht oder fordert ihr von uns? Was treibt euch an, in unsere Mauern zu dringen?

TAMINO
Freundschaft und Liebe.

SPRECHER
Bist du bereit, es mit deinem Leben zu erkämpfen?

TAMINO
Ja!

SPRECHER
Auch wenn Tod dein Los wäre?

TAMINO
Ja!

SPRECHER
Prinz, noch ist's Zeit zu weichen—einen Schritt weiter, und es ist zu spät.

TAMINO
Weisheitslehre sei mein Sieg; Pamina, das holde Mädchen, mein Lohn.

SPRECHER
Du unterziehst dich jeder Prüfung?

TAMINO
Jeder!

SPRECHER
Reiche mir deine Hand!—(*Sie reichen sich die Hände.*) So! (*zu Papageno:*) Willst auch du dir Weisheitsliebe erkämpfen?

PAPAGENO
Kämpfen ist meine Sache nicht.—Ich verlange auch im Grunde gar keine Weisheit. Ich bin so ein Naturmensch, der sich mit Schlaf, Speise und Trank begnügt;—und wenn es ja sein könnte, dass ich mir einmal ein schönes Weibchen fange—

2. PRIESTER
Die wirst du nie erhalten, wenn du dich nicht unseren Prüfungen unterziehst.

PAPAGENO
Worin besteht diese Prüfung?

2. PRIESTER
Dich allen unseren Gesetzen zu unterwerfen, selbst den Tod nicht zu scheuen.

PAPAGENO
Ich bleibe ledig!

2. PRIESTER
Wenn nun aber Sarastro dir ein Mädchen aufbewahrt hätte, das an Farbe und Kleidung dir ganz gleich wäre?

PAPAGENO
Mir gleich? Ist sie jung?

2. PRIESTER
Jung und schön!

PAPAGENO
Und heisst?

2. PRIESTER
Papagena.

PAPAGENO
Wie? Pa—?

PAPAGENO

Most certainly I am!

TAMINO

Where do you think we are now?

PAPAGENO

Where we are? Well, if it were not so dark, I might be able to tell you; but this way— (*Thunder.*) Help! Help!

TAMINO

What is wrong?

PAPAGENO

I don't feel quite at ease in this affair.

TAMINO

You are afraid, I can see.

PAPAGENO

Not afraid, really,—I just have ice-cold shivers up and down my spine. (*Loud thunder.*) Oh, heavens!

TAMINO

What is it?

PAPAGENO

I think I am getting a slight fever.

TAMINO

Shame on you, Papageno, be a man!

PAPAPGENO

I wish I were a girl! (*Very loud thunder.*) Oh! Oh! My hour has come! (*Speaker and Second Priest appear with torches.*)

SPEAKER

Strangers, what do you seek from us? What prompts you to intrude upon our sanctuary?

TAMINO

Friendship and love.

SPEAKER

Are you prepared to fight for these virtues at risk of your very life?

TAMINO

I am.

SPEAKER

Even if death were your lot?

TAMINO

Yes.

SPEAKER

Prince, there is still time to turn back. One step more and it will be too late!

TAMINO

Wisdom will gain my victory; Pamina, the lovely maiden, will be my reward!

SPEAKER

Are you willing to undergo every one of the trials?

TAMINO

Every one.

SPEAKER

Give me your hand. (*They clasp hands.*)

SECOND PRIEST (*to Papageno*)

Will you, too, fight for the love of wisdom?

PAPAGENO

Fighting is not exactly in my line. To be truthful, I don't demand any wisdom, either. I'm just a child of nature, who is satisfied with sleep, food, and drink. And if I once could catch a pretty little wife—

SECOND PRIEST

That you shall never do unless you undergo our trials.

PAPAGENO

Of what do these trials consist?

SECOND PRIEST

You must subject yourself to all our laws, and not even fear death.

PAPAGENO

I'll remain single.

SECOND PRIEST

But if Sarastro has already chosen a bride for you who resembles you in color and dress perfectly?

PAPAGENO

Resembles me? Is she young?

SECOND PRIEST

Young and beautiful!

PAPAGENO

And her name is?

SECOND PRIEST

Papagena.

PAPAGENO

Pa—pa—?

2. PRIESTER
Papagena!

PAPAGENO
Papagena?—Die möcht ich aus blosser
Neugierde sehen.

2. PRIESTER
Sehen kannst du sie!—

PAPAGENO
Aber wenn ich sie gesehen habe, her-
nach muss ich sterben? (Zweiter
Priester macht eine zweifelnde Pan-
tomine.) Ja? Ich bleibe ledig!

2. PRIESTER
Sehen kannst du sie, aber bis zur ver-
laufnen Zeit kein Wort mit ihr
sprechen. Wird dein Geist so viel
Standhaftigkeit besitzen, deine Zunge
in Schranken zu halten?

PAPAGENO
O ja!

2. PRIESTER
Deine Hand! Du sollst sie sehen. (Sie
reichen sich die Hände.)

SPRECHER
(zu Tamino:) Auch dir, Prinz, legen
die Götter ein heilsames Stillschwei-
gen auf; ohne dieses seid ihr beide
verloren.—Du wirst Pamina sehen,
aber nicht sie sprechen dürfen; dies
ist der Anfang eurer Prüfungszeit.

SPRECHER UND PRIESTER
Bewahret euch vor Weibertücken:
Dies ist des Bundes erste Pflicht.
Manch weiser Mann liess sich berücken,
Er fehlte und versah sich's nicht.
Verlassen sah er sich am Ende,
Vergolten seine Treu mit Hohn.
Vergebens rang er seine Hände,
Tod und Verzweiflung war sein Lohn.
(Beide Priester ab.)

PAPAGENO
He, Lichter her! Lichter her!—Das ist
doch wunderlich, so oft einen die
Herren verlassen, sieht man mit off-
enen Augen nichts.

TAMINO
Ertrag es mit Geduld, und denke, es ist
der Götter Wille. (Die drei Damen
erscheinen mit Fackeln.)

DIE DREI DAMEN
(aus der Versenkung)
Wie, wie, wie?
Ihr an diesem Schreckensort?
Nie, nie, nie
Kommt ihr glücklich wieder fort!
Tamino, dir ist Tod geschworen!
Du, Papageno, bist verloren!

PAPAGENO
Nein, nein, das wär zu viel!

TAMINO
Papageno, schweige still!
Willst du dein Gelübde brechen.
Nichts mit Weibern hier du sprechen?

PAPAGENO
Du hörst ja wir sind beide hin.

TAMINO
Stille, sag ich, schweige still!

PAPAGENO
Immer still und immer still!

DIE DREI DAMEN
Ganz nah' ist euch die Königin.
Sie drang im Tempel heimlich ein.

PAPAGENO
Wie? Was? Sie soll im Tempel sein?

TAMINO
Stille, sag ich, schweige still!
Wirst du immer so vermessen
Deiner Eidespflicht vergessen?

DIE DREI DAMEN
Tamino, hör, du bist verloren!
Gedenke an die Königin.
Man zischelt viel sich in die Ohren
Von dieser Priester falschem Sinn.

TAMINO
(für sich) Ein Weiser prüft und achtet
nicht.
Was der gemeine Pöbel spricht.

DIE DREI DAMEN
Man sagt, wer ihrem Bunde schwört,
Der fährt zu Höll mit Haut und Haar.

PAPAGENO
Das wär' beim Teufel unerhört!
Sag an, Tamino, ist das wahr?

TAMINO
Geschwätz von Weibern nachgesagt,
Von Heuchlern aber ausgedacht.

PAPAGENO
Doch sagt es auch die Königin.

SECOND PRIEST

Papagena!

PAPAGENO

Papagena! I really would like to see her out of sheer curiosity.

SECOND PRIEST

See her you may—

PAPAGENO

But after I see her, then will I have to die? (*Second Priest shrugs his shoulders.*) Yes? I'll remain single.

SECOND PRIEST

You may see her, but as yet you must not speak a single word to her. Will your mind have sufficient strength to control your tongue?

PAPAGENO

Oh, yes!

SECOND PRIEST

Your hand! You shall see her! (*They clasp hands.*)

SPEAKER (*to Tamino*)

On you, too, Prince, the gods impose a reverent silence. If you fail in this, you both are lost. You will see Pamina, but you must not speak to her. This is the beginning of your probation time.

TWO PRIESTS

Beware of woman's crafty scheming:
This is the Order's first command!
Many a man, of wiles not dreaming,
Was tempted and could not withstand.
But then he saw he was mistaken,
The truth he came to know too late.
At last he found himself forsaken.
Death and damnation were his fate.
(*Exeunt both Priests. It becomes dark.*)

PAPAGENO

Hey! Lights! Lights! It is really strange: each time these gentlemen leave us, you cannot see your hand in front of your face!

TAMINO

Bear it with patience,—remember, it is the will of the gods! (*Enter the Three Ladies, with torches.*)

THREE LADIES

You? in this place of night and gloom?
Flee! or you meet a certain doom!
Tamino, sworn is your damnation!
For Papageno, no salvation!

PAPAGENO

This is more than I can bear!

TAMINO

Papageno, have a care!
You are bound in your probation
To be brave against temptation!

PAPAGENO

You heard yourself—this is our end!

TAMINO

Keep your promise and be still!

PAPAGENO

Always still, and always still!

THREE LADIES

The Queen has secretly come here.
In yonder temple she is near.

PAPAGENO

What's that? The Queen herself is here?

TAMINO

Quiet, quiet! hush, be still!
Thus your solemn oath forswearing
Is indeed a foolish daring.

THREE LADIES

Tamino, gone are love and glory
If so the Queen you will betray!
From lip to lip there goes a story
That you will die this very day.

TAMINO (*aside*)

A wise man hears but does not mind
The common talk of lower kind.

THREE LADIES

Who joins their order, we have heard,
Will be condemned to go to hell!

PAPAGENO

This is outrageous, on my word!
Tell me, Tamino, is it so?

TAMINO

Such gossip women oft repeat.
'Tis but a hypocrite's deceit.

PAPAGENO

But did the Queen not say it, too?

TAMINO

Sie ist ein Weib, hat Weibersinn.
Sei still, mein Wort sei dir genug:
Denk deiner Pflicht und handle klug.

DIE DREI DAMEN

(*zu Tamino*) Warum bist du mit uns
so spröde?
(*Tamino deutet bescheiden, dass er
nicht sprechen darf*) Auch Papageno
schweigt, so rede!

PAPAGENO

(*heimlich zu den Damen*) Ich möchte
gerne—woll—

TAMINO

Still!

PAPAGENO

Ihr seht, dass ich nicht soll—

TAMINO

Still!

TAMINO UND PAPAGENO

Dass du (ich) nicht kannst (kann) das
    Plaudern lassen
    Ist wahrlich eine Schand für dich!
    (mich!)

ALLE

Wir (Sie) müssen sie (uns) mit
    Scham verlassen:
Es plaudert keiner sicherlich.
Von festem Geiste ist ein Mann,
Er denket, was er sprechen kann.

PRIESTER

(*von innen; Chorus.*) Entweiht ist die
    heilige Schwelle,
Hinab mit den Weibern zu Hölle!
(*Ein schrecklicher Akkord mit allen
Instrumenten; Donner, Blitz und
Schlag; zugleich zwei starke Don-
ner.*)

DIE DREI DAMEN

O weh, o weh! (*Sie stürzen in die
Versenkung.*)

PAPAGENO

O weh, o weh, o weh! (*Er fällt zu
Boden. Dann fängt der dreimalige
Akkord an. Sprecher und zweiter
Priester mit Fackeln treten ein.*)

SPRECHER

Heil dir, Jüngling! Dein standhaft
männliches Betragen hat gesiegt. Wir
wollen also mit reinem Herzen unsere Wanderschaft weiter fortsetzen.
(*Er gibt ihm den Schleier um.*) So!
Nun komm! (*Er geht mit Tamino
ab.*)

2. PRIESTER

Was seh ich! Freund, stehe auf! Wie
ist dir?

PAPAGENO

Ich lieg in einer Ohnmacht!

2. PRIESTER

Auf! Sammle dich und sei ein Mann!

PAPAGENO

(*Steht auf:*) Aber sagt mir nur, meine
Herren, warum muss ich denn alle
diese Qualen und Schrecken empfinden?—Wenn mir ja die Götter
eine Papagena bestimmten, warum
denn mit so viel Gefahren sie erringen?

2. PRIESTER

Diese neugierige Frage mag deine Ver-
nunft dir beantworten. Komm!
Meine Pflicht heischt, dich weiter-
zuführen. (*Er gibt ihm den Schleier
um.*)

PAPAGENO

Bei so einer ewigen Wanderschaft
möcht einem wohl die Liebe auf
immer vergehen. (*Zweiter Priester
geht mit ihm ab.*)
(*Verwandlung. Garten. Pamina schla-
fend auf dem Sitz unter den Rosen.*)

MONOSTATOS

Ha, da find ich ja die spröde Schöne!
Welcher Mensch würde bei so einem
Anblick kalt und unempfindlich blei-
ben? Das Feuer, das in mir glimmt,
wird mich noch verzehren! (*Er sieht
sich um.*) Wenn ich wüsste—dass ich
so ganz allein und unbelauscht wäre
—Ein Küsschen, dächte ich, liesse
sich entschuldigen.
Alles fühlt der Liebe Freuden,
Schnäbelt, tändelt, herzt und küsst;
Und ich sollt die Liebe meiden,
Weil ein Schwarzer hässlich ist!
Ist mir denn kein Herz gegeben?
Bin ich nicht von Fleisch und Blut?
Immer ohne Weibchen leben
Wäre wahrlich Höllenglut!
Drum so will ich, weil ich lebe,
Schnäbeln, küssen, zärtlich sein!
Lieber guter Mond vergebe:
Eine Weisse nahm mich ein.
Weiss ist schön, ich muss sie küssen!
Mond, verstecke dich dazu!
Sollt' es dich zu sehr verdriessen,
O so mach' die Augen zu!
(*Er schleicht langsam und leise
hin. Die Königin kommt unter Don-
ner aus der mittleren Versenkung,
und so, dass sie gerade vor Pamina
zu stehen kommt.*)

TAMINO

She talks just as all women do.
Believe my word and hold your tongue.
Act like a man! Be brave and strong!

THREE LADIES

Tamino, why do you repel us?
(*Tamino indicates by gestures that he dares not speak.*)
And Papageno too? Pray, tell us.

PAPAGENO
(*aside to the Ladies*)

I would with pleasure, but . . .

TAMINO

Hush!

PAPAGENO

You see, my mouth is shut!

TAMINO

Hush!

PAPAGENO AND TAMINO

That I (you) cannot resist temptation
Is really a disgrace to see.

THREE LADIES

We must withdraw in resignation;
No one will talk, I clearly see.

THREE LADIES, PAPAGENO AND TAMINO

We (they) must withdraw in resignation;
No one will talk, I clearly see.
A man is firm and strong of will;
He stands aloof, reserved, and still.

CHORUS (*from within*)

These women profane our station.
Condemn them to death and damnation!
(*The stage darkens. Thunder and lightning.*)

THREE LADIES

Alas! alas! (*They rush out, horrified. Papageno falls to the ground.*)

PAPAGENO

Alas! alas! alas!
(*Speaker and Priest enter, carrying veils and torches.*)

SPEAKER

Hail to thee, Prince! Thy steadfast, manly bearing has gained a victory! Thus we wish, with purest heart, to continue our travels. (*Covers Tamino's head with a veil.*) Come, then! Exeunt Speaker and Tamino.)

SECOND PRIEST

What do I see? Friend, arise! What has befallen you?

PAPAGENO

I am lying in a faint!

SECOND PRIEST

Arise! Collect yourself, and be a man!

PAPAGENO (*rises*)

But tell me, Sir, why must I become acquainted with all these torments and horrors? If the gods really have selected a Papagena for me, why do I have to exert myself so hard to win her?

SECOND PRIEST

Let your reason answer that inquisitive question. Come, my duty demands that I lead you onwards. (*Covers Papageno's head with a veil.*)

PAPAGENO

With such eternal wandering, one really feels like giving up love forever. (*Exeunt Second Priest and Papageno.*)
(*Change of Scene. Garden. Pamina asleep under the rosebushes.*)

MONOSTATOS

Ha, here I find the prudish beauty! What man could remain cold and unmoved before such a vision! The fire which burns within me will surely consume me. (*He looks around.*) If I knew—that I was all alone and unobserved—One little kiss, I should think, could be excused.
All the world is full of lovers,
Man and maiden, bird and bee.
Why am I not like the others?
No one ever looks at me!
Why should I not be a match for
Some delightful demoiselle?
If I have to die a batchelor,
I prefer to live in hell!
This is just the right occasion,
It's too good a chance to miss!
I don't need to use persuasion,
All I do is steal a kiss!
I'm alone,—well then, so be it!
Just one tender warm embrace!
Moon, if you don't want to see it,
Turn away your jealous face.
(*Creeps softly up to Pamina. The Queen appears suddenly, with thunder and lightning.*)

KÖNIGIN
(*zu Monostatos:*) Zurück!

PAMINA
(*erwacht:*) Ihr Götter!

MONOSTATOS
(*prallt zurück:*) O weh!—Die Göttin
der Nacht.

PAMINA
Mutter! Mutter! meine Mutter! (*Sie
fällt ihr in die Arme.*)

MONOSTATOS
Mutter? Hm, das muss man von weitem
belauschen. (*Schleicht ab.*)

KÖNIGIN
Verdank es der Gewalt, mit der man
dich mir entriss, dass ich noch deine
Mutter mich nenne.— Siehst du hier
diesen Stahl?—Er ist für Sarastro
geschliffen.—Du wirst ihn töten. (*Sie
dringt ihr den Dolch auf.*)

PAMINA
Aber, liebste Mutter!—

KÖNIGIN
Kein Wort!
Der Hölle Rache kocht in meinem
   Herzen,
Tod und Verzweiflung flammet um
   mich her!
Fühlt nicht durch dich Sarastro Todes-
   schmerzen,
So bist du meine Tochter nimmermehr!
Verstossen sei auf ewig,
Verlassen sei auf ewig,
Zertrümmert sei auf ewig
Alle Bande der Natur,
Wenn nicht durch dich Sarastro wird
   erblassen!
Hört, Rachegötter, hört der Mutter
   Schwur!
(*Sie versinkt.*)

PAMINA
(*den Dolch in der Hand:*) Morden
soll ich?—Götter, das kann ich nicht!
(*Steht in Gedanken. Monostatos
kommt schnell, heimlich und freudig.*) Götter, was soll ich tun?

MONOSTATOS
Dich mir anvertrauen. (*Nimmt ihr
den Dolch.*)

PAMINA (*erschrickt*)
Ha!

MONOSTATOS
Warum zitterst du? Vor meiner schwar-
zen Farbe, oder vor dem ausgedach-
ten Mord?

PAMINA (*schüchtern*)
Du weisst also?—

MONOSTATOS
Alles.—Du hast also nur einen Weg,
dich und deine Mutter zu retten.

PAMINA
Der wäre?

MONOSTATOS
Mich zu lieben.

PAMINA (*zitternd, für sich*)
Götter!

MONOSTATOS
Nun, Mädchen! Ja oder nein!

PAMINA (*entschlossen*)
Nein!

MONOSTATOS (*voll Zorn*)
Nein? (*Sarastro tritt hinzu. Monostatos
erhebt den Dolch.*) So fahre denn
hin! (*Sarastro schleudert Monostatos
zurück.*) Herr, ich bin unschuldig.
(*Auf die Kniee fallend*)

SARASTRO
Ich weiss, dass deine Seele ebenso
schwarz als dein Gesicht ist.—Geh!

MONOSTATOS (*im Abgehen*)
Jetzt such ich die Mutter auf, weil die
Tochter mir nicht beschieden ist.
(*Ab.*)

PAMINA
Herr, strafe meine Mutter nicht! Der
Schmerz über meine Abwesenheit—

SARASTRO
Ich weiss alles. Du sollst sehen, wie ich
mich an deiner Mutter räche.
In diesen heil'gen Hallen
Kennt man die Rache nicht,
Und ist ein Mensch gefallen,
Führt Liebe ihn zur Pflicht.
Dann wandelt er an Freundes Hand
Vergnügt und froh in's bessre Land.
In diesen heil'gen Mauern,
Wo Mensch den Menschen liebt,
Kann kein Verräter lauern,
Weil man dem Feind vergibt.
Wen solche Lehren nicht erfreun
Verdienet nicht ein Mensch zu sein.
(*Gehen Beide ab.*)
(*Verwandlung. Eine kurze Halle. Ta-
mino und Papageno werden ohne
Schleier von den zwei Priestern
hereingeführt.*)

QUEEN (*to Monostratos*)
Away with you!

PAMINA (*awakens*)
O Gods!

MONOSTATOS
(*startled, jumps back*)
What's this?—The Queen of the Night!

PAMINA
Mother! Mother! My mother! (*Falls into her arms.*)

MONOSTATAS (*aside*)
Mother! Hm! I'll have to watch this from the distance.

QUEEN
You may thank the power by which you were torn from me, that I still call myself your mother. Do you see this dagger? It has been sharpened for Sarastro. You will kill him—

PAMINA
But dearest Mother—

QUEEN
Not a word!
The wrath of hell within my breast I cherish;
Death, desperation prompt the oath I swore.
If by your hand Sarastro does not perish,
Then as my child I shall know you nevermore.
Abandoned be forever,
Forsaken be forever,
And shattered be forever
All the force of nature's tie
If not through you Sarastro's life be taken!
Hark! Gods of vengeance, hear a mother's cry! (*Exit. Thunder.*)

PAMINA (*dagger in hand*)
I shall murder? Gods! I cannot, I cannot do that! What shall I do? (*Monostatos comes to her side quickly steathily, and with joy.*)

MONOSTATOS
Confide yourself to me. (*Takes the dagger away from her.*)

PAMINA (*frightened*)
Ah!

MONOSTATOS
Why do you tremble? Because I am black, or because of the murder that is planned?

PAMINA (*timidly*)
You know, then?

MONOSTATOS
Everything. There is only one way for you to save yourself and your mother.

PAMINA
And that is?

MONOSTATOS
To love me!

PAMINA (*trembling, aside*)
O Gods!

MONOSTATOS
Well, maiden, yes or no?

PAMINA (*firmly*)
No!

MONOSTATOS (*angrily*)
No? (*Sarastro comes up to them. Monostatos raises the dagger.*) Then die! (*Sarastro holds Monostatos back.*) Lord, I am innocent! (*Falls upon his knees.*)

SARASTRO
I know that your soul is just as black as your face. Go!

MONOSTATOS (*while leaving*)
Now I shall look up the mother, because the daughter is not meant for me. (*Exit.*)

PAMINA
Sire, do not punish my mother. The sorrow over having lost me—

SARASTRO
I know everything. However, you shall see how I take revenge upon your mother.
Within these holy portals,
Revenge remains unknown,
And to all erring mortals,
Their way by love is shown.
And guided forth by friendship's hand,
They journey to a better land.
Within this holy dwelling,
In brother-love one lives.
Of hatred is no telling,
For man his foe forgives.
Who by this law is led aright,
Will ever share the gods' delight.
(*Exeunt.*)
(*Change of Scene. A short hallway. Tamino and Papageno, without the veils, are led in by the two Priests.*)

SPRECHER

Hier seid ihr euch beide allein über-
lassen. — Sobald die Posaune tönt,
dann nehmt ihr euren Weg (*nach
rechts zeigend*) dahin. — Prinz, lebt
wohl! Noch einmal, vergesst das
Wort nicht: Schweigen. (*Ab.*)

ZWEITER PRIESTER

Papageno, wer an diesem Ort sein Still-
schweigen bricht, den strafen die
Götter durch Donner und Blitz. Leb
wohl! (*Ab. Tamino setzt sich auf
eine Bank.*)

PAPAGENO (*Nach einer Pause*)

Tamino!

TAMINO

St!

PAPAGENO

Das ist ein lustiges Leben!—Wär ich
lieber in meiner Strohhütte, oder im
Wald, so hört ich doch manchmal
einen Vogel pfeifen.

TAMINO (*verweisend*)

St!

PAPAGENO

Mit mir selbst werd ich wohl sprechen
dürfen; und auch wir zwei können
zusammen sprechen, wir sind ja
Männer.

TAMINO (*verweisend*)

St!

PAPAGENO (*singt*)

La la la—la la la!—Nicht einmal
einen Tropfen Wasser bekommt man
bei diesen Leuten, viel weniger sonst
was. (*Ein altes hässliches Weib
kommt mit einem grossen Becher
mit Wasser. Papageno sieht sie lange
an.*) Ist das für mich?

WEIB

Ja, mein Engel!

PAPAGENO

(*sieht sie wieder an, trinkt*)

Nicht mehr und nicht weniger als
Wasser.—Sag du mir, du unbekannte
Schöne, werden alle fremden Gäste
auf diese Art bewirtet?

WEIB

Freilich, mein Engel!

PAPAGENO

So, so!—Auf diese Art werden die
Fremden auch nicht gar zu häufig
kommen.—

WEIB

Sehr wenig.

PAPAGENO

Kann mir's denken.—Geh, Alte, setze
dich her zu mir, mir ist die Zeit
verdammt lange.—(*Weib setzt sich
zu ihm.*) Sag mir, wie alt bist du
denn?

WEIB

Wie alt?

PAPAGENO

Ja!

WEIB

Achtzehn Jahr und zwei Minuten.

PAPAGENO

Achtzig Jahr und zwei Minuten?

WEIB

Achtzehn Jahr und zwei Minuten.

PAPAGENO

Ha ha ha!—Ei, du junger Engel! Hast
du auch einen Geliebten?

WEIB

Ei, freilich!

PAPAGENO

Ist er auch so jung wie du?

WEIB

Nicht ganz, er ist um zehn Jahre älter.

PAPAGENO

Um zehn Jahre ist er älter als du?—Das
muss eine Liebe sein!—Wie nennt
sich denn dein Liebhaber?

WEIB

Papageno!

PAPAGENO (*erschrickt, Pause*)

Papageno? — Wo ist er denn, dieser
Papageno?

WEIB

Da sitzt er, mein Engel!

PAPAGENO

Ich wär dein Geliebter?

WEIB

Ja, mein Engel!

SPEAKER

Once more you are both left by yourselves. As soon as you hear the trumpet call, start on your way in this direction. (*Points to the right.*) Prince, farewell. Once more, do not forget the word: silence. (*Exit.*)

SECOND PRIEST

Papageno, anyone who breaks his silence in this place in punished by the gods with thunder and lightning. Farewell. (*Exit. Tamino sits on a bench.*)

PAPAGENO (*after a pause*)

Tamino!

TAMINO

Sh!

PAPAGENO

This is a jolly life! If only I were in my straw hut or in the woods, at least I would hear a bird sing once in a while.

TAMINO (*reprimanding*)

Sh!

PAPAGENO

Well, I should think that at least I am allowed to talk to myself! And also, we two can talk to each other, because we are men.

TAMINO (*reprimanding*)

Sh!

PAPAGENO (*sings*)

La la la—la la la. Not even a single drop of water does one get from these people, let alone anything else. (*An old, ugly Woman appears, a big cup in her hands. Papageno looks at her for a long time.*) Is that for me?

WOMAN

Yes, my angel!

PAPAGENO

(*looks at her again, drinks*)

No more, no less than water. Tell me, you unknown beauty, are all foreign guests treated in this fashion?

WOMAN

Surely, my angel.

PAPAGENO

Is that so? In that case, the foreigners don't come too frequently, I guess.

WOMAN

Very seldom.

PAPAGENO

That's what I thought. Come, Grandma, sit down here with me. I feel frightfully bored here. (*The Woman sits down at his side.*) You tell me, how old are you?

WOMAN

How old?

PAPAGENO

Yes.

WOMAN

Eighteen years and two minutes.

PAPAGENO

Eighty years and two minutes?

WOMAN

Eighteen years and two minutes.

PAPAGENO

Ha ha ha! Well, you young angel! Tell me, do you have a sweetheart?

WOMAN

Naturally.

PAPAGENO

And is he as young as you are?

WOMAN

Not quite, he is ten years older.

PAPAGENO

Ten years older than you? That must be quite a fiery love! What is the name of your sweetheart?

WOMAN

Papageno.

PAPAGENO

(*falls from his seat*)

Papageno? Where is he then, this Papageno?

WOMAN

He is sitting right here, my angel.

PAPAGENO

(*Extempore:*) There he *was* sitting. So I am your sweetheart?

WOMAN

Yes, my angel.

PAPAGENO
Sag mir, wie heisst du denn?

WEIB
Ich heisse—(*Starker Donner, die Alte
hinkt schnell ab.*)

PAPAGENO
O weh! (*Tamino steht auf, droht mit
dem Finger.*) Nun sprech ich kein
Wort mehr! (*Die drei Knaben bring-
en Flöte und Glockenspiel.*)

3 KNABEN
Seid uns zum zweiten Mal willkommen,
Ihr Männer, in Sarastros Reich.
Er schickt, was man euch abgenommen,
Die Flöte und die Glöckchen euch.
Wollt ihr die Speisen nicht ver-
    schmähen,
So esset, trinket froh davon.
Wenn wir zum dritten Mal uns sehen,
Ist Freude eures Mutes Lohn.
Tamino, Mut! Nah ist das Ziel.
Du, Papageno, schweige still!
(*Unter dem Terzett setzen sie den
Tisch in die Mitte und fliegen auf.*)

PAPAGENO
Tamino, wollen wir nicht speisen? (*Tamino bläst auf seiner Flöte. Papageno isst.*) Blase du nur fort auf
deiner Flöte, ich will meine Brocken
blasen. — Herr Sarastro führt eine
gute Küche. — Auf die Art, ja, da,
will ich schon schweigen, wenn ich
immer solche gute Bissen bekomme.
—Nun, ich will sehen, ob auch der
Keller so gut bestellt ist (*Er trinkt.*)
Ha! das its Götterwein! (*Die Flöte
schweigt.*)

PAMINA (*freudig eintretend*)
Du hier?—Gütige Götter! Dank euch!
Ich hörte deine Flöte—und so lief
ich pfeilschnell dem Tone nach.—
Aber du bist traurig?—Sprichst nicht
eine Silbe mit deiner Pamina? Liebst
du mich nicht mehr? (*Tamino seufzt
und winkt ihr fort.*) Papageno, sage
du mir, sag, was ist meinem Freund?
(*Papageno hat einen Brocken in dem
Munde, winkt ihr fortzugehen.*) Wie?
Auch du? O, das ist mehr als Tod!
(*Pause.*) Liebster, einziger Tamino!
Ach, ich fühl's, es ist verschwunden,
Ewig hin der Liebe Glück!
Nimmer kommt ihr, Wonnestunden,
Meinem Herzen mehr zurück.
Sieh, Tamino, diese Tränen,

Fliessen, Trauter, dir allein!
Fühlst du nicht der Liebe Sehnen,
So wird Ruhe im Tode sein (*Ab*).

PAPAGENO (*isst hastig*)
Nicht wahr, Tamino, ich kann auch
schweigen, wenn's sein muss.—(*Er
trinkt.*) Der Herr Koch und der Herr
Kellermeister sollen leben! (*Dreimaliger Posaunenton. Tamino winkt
Papageno, dass er mit ihm gehen
soll.*) Geh du nur voraus, ich komm
schon nach. (*Tamino will ihn mit
Gewalt fortführen.*) Der Stärkere
bleibt da! (*Tamino geht ab.*) Jetzt
will ich mir's erst recht wohl sein
lassen. Ich ging jetzt nicht fort, und
wenn Herr Sarastro seine sechs Löwen an mich spannte. (*Die Löwen
erscheinen.*) O Barmherzigkeit, ihr
gütigen Götter! Tamino rette mich!
Die Herren Löwen machen eine
Mahlzeit aus mir. (*Tamino kommt
zurück, bläst seine Flöte, die Löwen
verschwinden.*) Ich gehe schon!
Heiss du mich einen Schelmen, wenn
ich dir nicht in allem folge. (*Dreimaliger Posaunenton.*) Das geht uns
an.—Wir kommen schon.—Aber hör
einmal, Tamino, was wird denn noch
alles mit uns werden? (*Tamino deutet gen Himmel.*) Die Götter soll ich
fragen? (*Tamino deutet Ja.*) Ja, die
könnten uns freilich mehr sagen, als
wir wissen! (*Dreimaliger Posaunenton. Tamino reisst ihn mit Gewalt
fort.*) Eile nur nicht so, wir kommen
noch immer zeitig genug, um uns
braten zu lassen. (*Beide ab. Verwandlung. Das Innere einer Pyra-
mide.*)

CHORUS
O Isis und Osiris, welche Wonne!
Die düst're Nacht verscheucht der
    Glanz der Sonne.
Bald fühlt der edle Jüngling neues
    Leben,
Bald ist er unserm Dienste ganz erge-
    ben.
Sein Geist ist kühn, sein Herz ist rein,
Bald wird er unser würdig sein.
(*Tamino wird hereingeführt.*)

SARASTRO
Prinz, dein Betragen war bis hieher
männlich und gelassen; nun hast du
noch zwei gefährliche Wege zu wandern. Schlägt dein Herz noch ebenso

PAPAGENO

Tell me, what is your name?

WOMAN

My name is— (*Loud thunder. Woman quickly hobbles away.*)

PAPAGENO

Oh, oh! (*Tamino rises, shakes a warning finger at him.*) From now on I won't speak another word! (*The Three Spirits bring flute and bells.*)

THREE SPIRITS

Here in Sarastro's hallowed border
We bid you welcome once again,
And by Sarastro's will and order
You may your flute and bells regain.
(*A table, with food and drink, rises from out of the ground.*)
No more shall we privation suffer;
May what we bring for all amend.
When for the third time aid we proffer,
Hardship and trouble are at end.
Tamino, hear: triumph you will.
You, Papageno, pray be still!
(*They hand Tamino the flute and Papageno the glockenspiel, and withdraw.*)

PAPAGENO

Tamino, shall we not have something to eat? (*Tamino plays on his flute. Papageno eats.*) You just keep on playing your flute, and I will play a game for myself! Mr. Sarastro certainly has a good cook. This way I would not mind keeping quiet, if I am always treated to such good food. Now I will see if his cellar is a good as his kitchen. (*Drinks.*) Ha, this is wine fit for the gods! (*The flute is silent.*)

PAMINA (*entering joyfully*)

You here? Kindly Gods! I thank you. I heard the sound of your flute and I followed the tone swift as an arrow. But you are sad? You speak no word to your Pamina? (*Tamino sighs and motions her away.*) Do you love me no more? (*Tamino sighs again.*) Papageno, you tell me what troubles my friend? (*Papageno has his mouth full and motions her away*: Hm, hm, hm!) You, too? Oh, this is worse than death! (*Pause.*) My dearest Tamino!

Ah, I feel, to grief and sadness,
Ever turned is love's deilght.
Gone forever joy and gladness,
In my heart reigns mournful night.
See, Tamino, see my anguish,
See my tears for you, my own.
If for love you do not languish,
Peace I find then in death alone. (*Exit slowly.*)

PAPAGENO (*eats eagerly*)

Isn't it true, Tamino, that I, too, can keep silent if need be? (*Drinks.*) Long live the chef and the wine steward! (*Three blasts of the trumpet. Tamino motions Papageno to go with him.*) You just go ahead, I'll come right after you. (*Tamino tries to lead him away by force.*) The strongest one stays here. (*Exit Tamino.*) Now I'll begin to have a good time. I would not leave now, even if Mr. Sarastro sent his six lions after me. (*The Lions appear.*) Have mercy! Ye good Gods! Tamino, save me! These lions will make a meal of me! (*Tamino returns, blows his flute, and the lions retire.*) I'm coming, I'm coming. Call me a rascal if I don't do everything you tell me. (*Three blasts of the trumpet.*) That is for us. We are coming! But hear, Tamino, whatever will become of us? (*Tamino points skyward.*) I should ask the gods? (*Tamino nods.*) Yes, they really could tell us more than we know. (*Three trumpet blasts. Tamino drags Papageno away by force.*) Don't hurry so much, we shall be there in time to be roasted! (*Exeunt both. Change of Scene. The interior of a pyramid. The Priests enter, led by Sarastro.*)

CHORUS OF PRIESTS

O Isis and Osiris! Sacred wonder!
The gloomy night by light is rent asunder.
The noble youth, through suffering recreated,
Shall be to holy office consecrated.
His heart is bold, and pure his mind;
Soon will the gods be satisfied.
(*Tamino is led in.*)

SARASTRO

Prince, thus far your actions have been manly and patient. Now you have still two dangerous trials to undertake. If your heart still beats as

warm für Pamina, und wünschest du einst als ein weiser Fürst zu regieren, so mögen die Götter dich ferner begleiten. — Deine Hand. — Man bringe Pamina! (*Zwei Priester bringen Pamina, welche mit einem Schleier bedeck ist.*)

PAMINA

Wo bin ich?—Saget, wo ist mein Jüngling?

SARASTRO

Er wartet deiner, um dir das letzte Lebewohl zu sagen.

PAMINA

Das letzte Lebewohl?—

SARASTRO

Hier!

PAMINA (*entrückt*)

Tamino!

TAMINO
(*sie von sich weisend*)

Zurück!

PAMINA

Soll ich dich, Teurer, nicht mehr sehn?

SARASTRO

Ihr werdet froh euch wiedersehn.

PAMINA

Dein warten tödliche Gefahren.

TAMINO

Die Götter mögen mich bewahren.

PAMINA

Dein warten tödliche Gefahren.

TAMINO UND SARASTRO

Die Götter mögen mich (ihn) bewahren.

PAMINA

Du wirst dem Tode nicht entgehen,

TAMINO UND SARASTRO

Der Götter Wille mag geschehen,
Ihr Wink soll mir (ihm)·Gesetze sein.

PAMINA

O liebest du, wie ich dich liebe,
Du würdest nicht so ruhig sein.

TAMINO UND SARASTRO

Glaub mir, ich fühle (er fühlet) gleiche Triebe,
Werd (Wird) ewig dein Getreuer sein.

SARASTRO

Die Stunde schlägt, nun müsst ihr scheiden.

PAMINA UND TAMINO

Wie bitter sind der Trennung Leiden!

SARASTRO

Tamino muss nun wieder fort.

TAMINO

Pamina, ich muss wirklich fort.

PAMINA

Tamino muss nun wirklich fort.

SARASTRO

Nun muss er fort.

TAMINO

Nun muss ich fort.

PAMINA

So musst du fort.

TAMINO

Pamina, lebe wohl!

PAMINA

Tamino, lebe wohl!

SARASTRO

Nun eile fort.
Dich ruft dein Wort.
Die Stunde schlägt, wir seh'n uns wieder.

PAMINA UND TAMINO

Ach, gold'ne Ruhe, kehre wieder! (*Entfernen sich.*)
(*Es wird dunkel.*)

PAPAGENO (*von aussen:*)

Tamino! Tamino! Willst du mich denn gänzlich verlassen? (*kommt tappend herein.*) Wenn ich nur wenigstens wüsste, wo ich wäre. — Tamino! Tamino!—So lang ich lebe, bleib ich nicht mehr von dir!— Nur diesmal verlass mich armen Reisegefährten nicht! (*Er kommt an die Tür links vorn.*)

EINE STIMME (*ruft*)

Zurück! (*Donnerschlag; das Feuer schlägt zur Tür heraus.*)

PAPAGENO

Barmherzige Götter! — Wo wend ich mich hin? Wenn ich nur wüsste, wo ich hereinkam! (*Er kommt an die Türe, wo er hereinkam.*)

DIE STIMME

Zurück! (*Donner und Feuer wie oben.*)

PAPAGENO

Nun kann ich weder vorwärts noch zurück! (*Weint.*) Muss vielleicht am Ende gar verhungern!—Schon recht! —Warum bin ich mitgereist.

warmly for Pamina, and if in time to come you wish to rule as a wise monarch, then may the gods lead you further. Your hand. Have Pamina brought here. (*Two Priests bring her in, veiled.*)

PAMINA
Where am I? Where is Tamino?

SARASTRO
He awaits you, to bid you a last farewell.

PAMINA
A last farewell?

SARASTRO
Here.

PAMINA, (*joyfully*)
Tamino!

TAMINO
(*motions her to stay away*)
Away!

PAMINA
Must I from thee forever part?

SARASTRO
To meet again with joyous heart.

PAMINA
Your path is dark with death and terror.

TAMINO
The gods preserve my steps from error.

PAMINA
Within my soul a voice is sighing:
A certain death awaits you here.

TAMINO AND SARASTRO
To heaven's will is no denying
What fate decrees, we all must bear.

PAMINA
If you did love as I do love you,
Your grief were equal to my own,
You would not have so stern a tone.

TAMINO AND SARASTRO
This (his) heart does warmly glow, believe me,
My (his) faithful heart is yours alone.

SARASTRO
The hour has come, the time of parting!

PAMINA AND TAMINO
Oh, bitter, bitter pain of parting.

SARASTRO
Tamino now must go away.

TAMINO
Pamina.

PAMINA
Tamino.

PAMINA AND TAMINO
Fare you well!

SARASTRO
Now hasten forth,
To prove your worth.

PAMINA AND TAMINO
Oh, golden calmness, end this grieving.

SARASTRO
The time has come, you must be gone!
But not forever, but not forever!

PAMINA AND TAMINO
Fare you well! Fare you well!
(*Pamina is led away by two Priests. Sarastro withdraws with Tamino; the Priests follow. It becomes dark.*)

PAPAGENO (*offstage*)
Tamino! Tamino! Are you leaving me all alone? (*Enters, feeling his way.*) If I only knew where I was! Tamino! Tamino! As long as I live I shall never leave your side again. Just this once don't desert your poor fellow traveller! (*He comes to the door through which Tamino has left.*)

A VOICE (*from outside*)
Halt! (*Thunder; flames burst from the door.*)

PAPAGENO
Merciful Gods, where shall I turn? If I only knew where I came in! (*Comes to the door where he had entered.*)

VOICE (*from outside*)
Halt! (*Thunder; flames burst from the door.*)

PAPAGENO
Now I can go neither forward nor backward. (*Cries.*) Perhaps I will have to starve here! Serves me right! Why did I come with him?

SPRECHER (*mit einer Fackel*)
Mensch! Du hättest verdient, auf immer in finsteren Klüften der Erde zu wandern—die gütigen Götter aber entlassen dich der Strafe. — Dafür aber wirst du das himmlische Vergnügen der Eingeweihten nie fühlen.

PAPAGENO
Je nun, es gibt noch mehr Leute meinesgleichen!—Mir wäre jetzt ein gutes Glas Wein das grösste Vergnügen.

SPRECHER
Sonst hast du keinen Wunsch in dieser Welt?

PAPAGENO
Bis jetzt nicht.

SPRECHER
Man wird dich damit bedienen!—(*Ab. Sogleich kommt ein grosser Becher, mit rotem Wein angefüllt, aus der Erde.*)

PAPAGENO
Juchhe! da ist er schon!—(*Trinkt.*) Herrlich!—Himmlisch!—Göttlich!— Ha! ich bin jetzt so vergnügt, dass ich bis zur Sonne fliegen wollte, wenn ich Flügel hätte!—Ha!—Mir wird ganz wunderlich ums Herz! — Ich wünschte—ja, was denn?
Ein Mädchen oder Weibchen
Wünscht Papageno sich!
O so ein sanftes Täubchen
Wär Seligkeit für mich.
Dann schmeckte mir Trinken und Essen,
Dann könnt' ich mit Fürsten mich messen,
Des Lebens als Weiser mich freun
Und wie im Elysium sein.
Ein Mädchen oder Weibchen
Wünscht Papageno sich!
O so ein sanftes Täubchen
Wär Seligkeit für mich.
Ach kann ich denn keiner von allen
Den reizenden Mädchen gefallen?
Helf eine mir nur aus der Not,
Sonst gräm ich mich wahrlich zu Tod.
Ein Mädchen oder Weibchen
Wünscht Papageno sich!
O so ein sanftes Täubchen
Wär Seligkeit für mich.
Wird keine mir Liebe gewähren,
So muss mich die Flamme verzehren;
Doch küsst mich ein weiblicher Mund,
So bin ich schon wieder gesund.

(*Das alte Weib, tanzend, und auf ihren Stock dabei sich stützend, kommt herein.*)

WEIB
Da bin ich schon, mein Engel!

PAPAGENO
Du hast dich meiner erbarmt?

WEIB
Ja, mein Engel!

PAPAGENO
Das ist ein Glück!

WEIB
Und wenn du mir versprichst, mir ewig treu zu bleiben, dann sollst du sehen, wie zärtlich dein Weibchen dich lieben wird.

PAPAGENO
Ei, du zärtliches Närrchen!

WEIB
O, wie will ich dich umarmen, dich liebkosen, dich an mein Herz drücken!

PAPAGENO
Auch ans Herz drücken?

WEIB
Komm, reich mir zum Pfand unseres Bundes deine Hand!

PAPAGENO
Nur nicht so hastig, lieber Engel! So ein Bündnis braucht doch auch seine Überlegung.

WEIB
Papageno, ich rate dir, zaudre nicht!— Deine Hand, oder du bist auf immer hier eingekerkert.

PAPAGENO
Eingekerkert?

WEIB
Wasser und Brot wird deine tägliche Kost sein. — Ohne Freund, ohne Freundin musst du leben, und der Welt auf immer entsagen.

PAPAGENO
Wasser trinken?—der Welt entsagen? Nein, da will ich doch lieber eine Alte nehmen, als gar keine.—Nun, da hast du meine Hand mit der Versicherung, dass ich dir immer getreu bleibe, (*für sich*) so lang' ich keine Schönere sehe.

SPEAKER (*with a torch*)

Miserable! You deserve to wander forever in the dark abysses of the earth! But the clement gods exempt you from this punishment. However, you shall never experience the heavenly pleasures of the ordained.

PAPAGENO

I don't care a fig about the ordained. Anyway, there are more people like me in the world. At the moment, to me the greatest pleasure would be a glass of wine.

SPEAKER

Other than this you have no further wish in the world?

PAPAGENO

Not so far.

SPEAKER

You shall be served with it. (*Exit. A big cup filled with wine appears at once.*)

PAPAGENO

Hurrah! There it is already! (*Drinks.*) Marvellous! Heavenly! Divine! Ha! I am so delighted now that I should like to fly to the sun, if I had wings. Ha! Something strange is happening in my heart! I want—I wish—but what? (*Plays the glockenspiel.*)

I'd give my finest feather
To find a pretty wife,
Two turtle-doves together,
We'd share a happy life.
And happily then ever after
We'd frolic in gladness and laughter!
And all of my dreams would come true!
Our life would be heaven for two!
I'd give my finest feather, etc. . . .
I'm sure there are girls all around me
But none of them seems to have found me.
With no one to love me or care,
I'll certainly die of despair.
I'd give my finest feather, etc. . . .
With no one to give me affection,
I'm buried in hopeless dejection!
But all that I need is a kiss
To put me in heavenly bliss.
(*The old Woman enters, hobbling and supporting herself on her stick.*)

WOMAN

Here I am, my angel!

PAPAGENO

So you took pity on me, then?

WOMAN

Yes, my angel.

PAPAGENO

What wonderful luck I have!

WOMAN

And if you promise to be true to me forever, then you will see how tenderly your little wife will love you.

PAPAGENO

Oh, what a tender goose you are!

WOMAN

Oh, how I shall embrace you, caress you, press you to my heart!

PAPAGENO

Even press me to your heart?

WOMAN

Come, give me your hand as a pledge of our union.

PAPAGENO

Not so fast, dear angel! Such a marriage needs some consideration, after all.

WOMAN

Papageno, I advise you, don't hesitate! Your hand, or you shall be imprisoned here forever.

PAPAGENO

Imprisoned?

WOMAN

Bread and water shall be your daily diet. You must live without friends or sweetheart and renounce the world forever.

PAPAGENO

Renounce the world forever? Drink water? No! In that case I'll take an old one rather than none at all. Well, here you have my hand with the assurance that I shall always be true to you (*aside*) until I find someone prettier.

WEIB

Das schwörst du?

PAPAGENO

Ja, das schwör ich! (*Weib verwandelt sich in ein junges Mädchen, welches ebenso gekleidet ist wie Papageno.*) Pa-Pa-Papagena!—(*Er will sie umarmen.*)

SPRECHER

(*kommt und nimmt sie bei der Hand:*) Fort mit dir, junges Weib! Er ist deiner noch nicht würdig! (*Er drängt sie hinaus, Papageno will nach.*) Zurück! sag ich.

PAPAGENO

Eh ich mich zurückziehe, soll die Erde mich verschlingen. (*Er sinkt hinab.*) O ihr Götter! (*Er springt wieder heraus und läuft ab. Verwandlung. Kurzer Palmengarten.*)

3 KNABEN

Bald prangt, den Morgen zu verkünden,
Die Sonn' auf goldner Bahn.
Bald soll der Aberglaube schwinden,
Bald siegt der weise Mann.
O holde Ruhe, steig hernieder,
Kehr in der Menschen Herzen wieder;
Dann ist die Erd' ein Himmelreich,
Und Sterbliche den Göttern gleich.

1. KNABE

Doch seht, Verzweiflung quält Paminen!

2. UND 3. KNABE

Wo ist sie denn?

1. KNABE

Sie ist von Sinnen!

3 KNABEN

Sie quält verschmähter Liebe Leiden.
Lasst uns der Armen Trost bereiten.
Fürwahr, ihr Schicksal geht uns nah.
O wäre nur ihr Jüngling da!
Sie kommt, lasst uns bei Seite gehn,
Damit wir, was sie mache, sehn. (*Sie gehen bei Seite.*)

PAMINA

(*Halb wahnwitzig, mit einem Dolch in der Hand*)
Du also bist mein Bräutigam!
Durch dich vollend ich meinen Gram!

3 KNABEN

Welch dunkle Worte sprach sie da?
Die Arme ist dem Wahnsinn nah.

PAMINA

Geduld, mein Trauter, ich bin dein!
Bald werden wir vermählet sein!

3 KNABEN

Wahnsinn tobt ihr im Gehirne,
Selbstmord steht auf ihrer Stirne. (*zu Pamina*) Holdes Mädchen, sieh uns an!

PAMINA

Sterben will ich, weil der Mann
Den ich nimmermehr kann hassen,
Sein Traute kann verlassen.
(*Auf den Dolch zeigend*)
Dies gab meine Mutter mir.

3 KNABEN

Selbstmord strafet Gott an dir!

PAMINA

Lieber durch dies Eisen sterben,
Als durch Liebesgram verderben.
Mutter, durch dich leide ich,
Und dein Fluch verfolget mich.

3 KNABEN

Mädchen, willst du mit uns gehn?

PAMINA

Ha, des Jammers Mass ist voll!
Falscher Jüngling, lebe wohl!
Sieh, Pamina stirbt durch dich,
Dieses Eisen töte mich! (*will sich erstechen.*)

3 KNABEN

Ha! Unglückliche, halt ein!
Sollte dies dein Jüngling sehen,
Würde er vor Gram vergehen;
Denn er liebet dich allein.

PAMINA (*erholt sich*)
Was? Er fühlte Gegenliebe,
Und verbarg mir seine Triebe,
Wandte sein Gesicht von mir?
Warum sprach er nicht mit mir?

3 KNABEN

Dieses müssen wir verschweigen,
Doch wir wollen dir ihn zeigen,
Und du wirst mit Staunen sehen,
Dass er dir sein Herz geweiht,
Und den Tod für dich nicht scheut.
Komm, wir wollen zu ihm gehn.

WOMAN

You swear that?

PAPAGENO

Yes, I swear it. (*Woman changes into a maiden, dressed alike Papageno.*) Pa-Pa- Papagena! (*He wishes to embrace her.*)

SPEAKER

(*enters and takes her by the hand*) Begone, young woman! He is not yet worthy of you. (*He drags her out. Papageno wants to follow.*) Back, I say, or woe unto you!

PAPAGENO

Before I withdraw, the earth shall swallow me up! (*He sinks into the earth.*) Oh, Gods above! (*Jumps out of the trap. Extempore:*) Sir, how dare you meddle in my family affairs? (*Change of Scene. Palm garden.*)

THREE SPIRITS

Soon speeds the morning light proclaiming
The sunshine's golden way.
This youth, the pow'rs of dark defaming,
Shall see the light of day.
O calmness from above descending,
Reprieve all men from grief unending.
Then doomed are evil, sin, and vice,
And earth becomes a paradise.

FIRST SPIRIT

But see, Pamina's torn by sadness!

SECOND AND THIRD SPIRITS

Where is she then?

FIRST SPIRIT

She strays in madness,

THREE SPIRITS

Condemned by love to desperation;
Let us to her bring consolation.
In truth, her life to us is dear!
Oh, were her lover only here!
She comes, let's stand aside and wait.
We must prevent her tragic fate.
(*They withdraw upstage. Pamina rushes in with a dagger in her hand.*)

PAMINA (*to the dagger*)

So only you remain to me?
My heart from pain through you I free.

THREE SPIRITS (*aside*)

What darksome words we overhear?
Poor maiden, she is mad, I fear.

PAMINA

O death, receive me as your bride,
With you I will in peace abide.

THREE SPIRITS

Madness at her heart is tearing.
Thus to death she goes despairing.
(*to Pamina*) Lovely maiden, hear us now.

PAMINA

End my being,—'tis the vow
That despairing I have taken;
By my love I am forsaken!
(*pointing to the dagger*) This my mother gave to me!

THREE SPIRITS

Heaven's law will chasten thee!

PAMINA

Rather by this blade I perish,
Than a loveless life to cherish.
Mother, Mother. Your curse is my bane
And through you I suffer pain.

THREE SPIRITS

Maiden, will you come with us?

PAMINA

No! I drain the cup of woe!
Faithless lover, I must go!
See, Pamina dies through thee! (*tries to stab herself*)
Deadly weapon, set me free!
(*The Three Spirits snatch the dagger from her.*)

THREE SPIRITS

Ah, unhappy maid, have done!
Of your prince let me remind you;
He would die should thus he find you.
For 'tis you he loves alone.

PAMINA

Oh, he was not then unfeeling,
But his love within concealing,
As he turned his face away?
Why in silence did he stay?

THREE SPIRITS

This to tell thee is forbidden,
But no longer be it hidden
That his heart is thine alone.
He is faithful, he is wise,
Even death for thee defies.
Come, Tamino waits for thee!

PAMINA
Führt mich hin, ich möcht' ihn sehn.

ALLE 4
Zwei Herzen, die vor Liebe brennen,
Kann Menschenohnmacht niemals
trennen.
Verloren ist der Feinde Müh,
Die Götter selbsten schützen sie. (Geh-
en alle ab.)

2 GEHARNISCHTE MÄNNER
Der, welcher wandert diese Strasse voll
Beschwerden,
Wird rein durch Feuer, Wasser, Luft
und Erden:
Wenn er des Todes Schrecken über-
winden kann,
Schwingt er sich aus der Erde himmel
an:
Erleuchtet wird er dann im Stande
sein,
Sich den Mysterien der Isis ganz zu
weih'n.

TAMINO
Mich schreckt kein Tod als Mann
zu handeln,
Den Weg der Tugend fortzuwandeln.
Schliesst mir die Schreckenspforten auf!
Ich wage froh den kühnen Lauf. (will
gehen.)

PAMINA
(von innen) Tamino, halt! Ich muss
dich sehn!

TAMINO
Was hör ich? Paminens Stimme?

2 GEHARN MÄNNER
Ja, ja, das ist Paminens Stimme.

TAMINO UND 2 GEHARN MÄNNER
Wohl mir (dir), nun kann sie mit
mir (dir) geh'n,
Nun trennet uns (euch) kein Schicksal
mehr,
Wenn auch der Tod beschieden wär!

TAMINO
Ist mir erlaubt, mit ihr zu sprechen?

2 GEHARN MÄNNER
Dir ist erlaubt, mit ihr zu sprechen.

TAMINO UND 2 GEHARN MÄNNER
Welch Glück, wenn wir uns (euch)
wiederseh'n,
Froh Hand in Hand in Tempel geh'n!
Ein Weib, das Nacht und Tod nicht
scheut,

Ist würdig und wird eingeweiht. (Die
Türe wird aufgemacht; Tamino und
Pamina umarmen sich.)

PAMINA
Tamino mein! O welch ein Glück!

TAMINO
Pamina mein! O welch ein Glück!—
Hier sind die Schreckenspforten,
Die Not und Tod mir dräu'n.

PAMINA
Ich werde aller Orten
An deiner Seite sein;
Ich Selbsten führe dich,
Die Liebe leitet mich (nimmt ihn bei
der Hand.)
Sie mag den Weg mit Rosen streu'n
Weil Rosen stets bei Dornen sein.
Spiel du die Zauberflöte an;
Sie schütze uns auf unsrer Bahn.
Es schnitt in einer Zauberstunde
Mein Vater sie aus tiefstem Grunde
Der tausendjähr'gen Eiche aus,
Bei Blitz und Donner, Sturm und Braus.
Nun komm und spiel die Flöte an,
Sie leite uns auf grauser Bahn.

ALLE 4
Wir wandeln (Ihr wandelt) durch des
Todes Macht
Froh durch des Todes düstre Nacht.
(Die Türen werden nach ihnen zu-
geschlagen; man sieht Tamino und
Pamina wandern; man hört Feuer-
geprassel und Windgeheul, manchmal auch den Ton dumpfen Donners, und Wassergeräusch.
Tamino bläst seine Flöte; gedämpfte
Pauken akkompagnieren manchmal
darunter. Sobald sie vom Feuer her-
auskommen, unmarmen sie sich und
bleiben in der Mitte.)

PAMINA UND TAMINO
Wir wandelten durch Feuergluten,
Bekämpften mutig die Gefahr.
Dein Ton sei Schutz in Wasserfluten,
So wie er es im Feuer war.
(Tamino bläst; man sieht sie hinunter
steigen und nach einiger Zeit wieder
heraufkommen; sogleich öffnet sich
eine Türe; man sieht einen Eingang
in einen Tempel, welcher hell be-
leuchtet ist. Eine feierliche Stille.)

PAMINA UND TAMINO
Ihr Götter, welch ein Augenblick!
Gewähret ist uns Isis Glück!

PAMINA
Guide me on, my love to see!

THREE SPIRITS AND PAMINA
Two hearts which love has bound to-
gether
The storms of life will firmly weather.
No foe will threaten them with wrath;
The gods will smile upon their path.
(*Exeunt.*)
(*Change of Scene. Rocky caves. At left,
glowing fire; at right, a waterfall.
Twilight.*)

TWO MEN IN ARMOR
Man, wandering on his road must bear
the tribulation
Of fire and water, earth and air's pro-
bation.
If he prevails against the lures of evil's
might,
He soon will know the joys of heaven's
light.
Enlightened, he will now himself pre-
pare,
The holy mysteries of Isis all to share.
(*Tamino is led in by the Two Priests.*)

TAMINO
By fear of death I am not shaken.
The path of virtue I have taken.
Unlock the fatal doors to me;
My course will firm and gallant be.

PAMINA (*offstage*)
Tamino, wait! Ah, wait for me!

TAMINO
What is this? Pamina calling.

MEN IN ARMOR
Ah yes, that is Pamina calling.

TAMINO AND MEN IN ARMOR
Rejoice! Together we (you) may fare.
No force on earth our (your) lives
shall rend,
Even though death may be our (your)
end.

TAMINO
Am I allowed to break my silence?

MEN IN ARMOR
You are allowed to break your silence.
(*Exeunt the Two Priests.*)

TAMINO AND MEN IN ARMOR
What joy when next we meet again,
And hand in hand the temple gain!
A woman who has death disdained
Is worthy and will be ordained.
(*The Two Priests enter with Pamina.*)

PAMINA (*embracing Tamino*)
Tamino mine! Oh, happy fate!

TAMINO
Pamina mine! Oh, happy fate! (*points
towards the rocky caves*)
Beyond those gates unfolding
Both death and menace hide.

PAMINA
Your every act upholding,
I shall not leave your side.
In me your trust confide,
For Love my way will guide.
(*She takes him by the hand.*)
Our path with roses it adorns,
For roses always grow with thorns.
Take now the magic flute and play;
Its golden tones protect our way.
'Twas shaped at midnight's witching
hour
By my father, with his magic power,
From branch of oak-tree, strong and
old,
While storming thunder wildly rolled.
Now take the magic flute and play;
Its tones will guide our fearsome way.

PAMINA, TAMINO, AND
TWO MEN IN ARMOR
We (you) wander by sweet music's
might
With gladness through the vale of
night.
(*March. Tamino and Pamina pass
through the fiery cave, she with her
hand on Tamino's shoulder, while he
plays his flute.*)

PAMINA AND TAMINO (*embracing*)
The fire's flames we have transcended,
The danger we have firm withstood;
And still by magic tones defended,
We penetrate the water's flood. (*They
turn to the water cave.*)
(*Change of Scene without Curtain.
Temple, brightly illuminated.*)

PAMINA AND TAMINO
O Gods, what ecstasy divine!
On us the smiles of Isis shine!

CHORUS (*von innen*)
Triumph, Triumph, du edles Paar!
Besieget hast du die Gefahr;
Der Isis Weihe ist nun dein.
Kommt, tretet in den Tempel ein!
(*Verwandlung. Das Theater verwandelt sich wieder in den vorigen Garten.*)

PAPAGENO
(*ruft mit seinem Pfeifchen*)
Papagena! Papagena! Papagena!
(*pfeift*)
Weibchen! Täubchen! meine Schöne!
Vergebens! Ach, sie ist verloren,
Ich bin zum Unglück schon geboren.
Ich plauderte, und das war schlecht,
Und drum geschieht es mir schon recht.
Seit ich gekostet diesen Wein,
Seit ich das schöne Weibchen sah,
So brennt's im Herzenskämmerlein,
So zwickt es hier, so zwickt es da.
Papagena, Herzensweibchen!
Papagena, liebes Täubchen!
's ist umsonst, es ist vergebens!
Müde bin ich meines Lebens!
Sterben macht der Lieb ein End,
Wenn's im Herzen noch so brennt.
(*Nimmt einen Strick von seiner Mitte.*)
Diesen Baum da will ich zieren,
Mir an ihm den Hals zuschnüren,
Weil das Leben mir missfällt;
Gute Nacht, du schwarze Welt!
Weil du böse an mir handelst,
Mir kein schönes Kind zubandelst,
So ist's aus, so sterbe ich;
Schöne Mädchen, denkt an mich!
Will sich eine um mich Armen,
Eh' ich hänge, noch erbarmen,
Wohl, so lass ich's diesmal sein.
Rufet nur; ja oder nein!
Keine hört mich; alles stille.
(*Sieht sich um.*)
Also ist es euer Wille?
Papageno, frisch hinauf!
Ende deinen Lebenslauf! (*Sieht sich um.*)
Nun, ich warte noch, es sei,
Bis man zählet eins, zwei, drei (*pfeift.*)
Eins! (*sieht sich um und pfeift*) Zwei!
(*pfeift, sieht sich um*) Drei!
Nun wohlan, es bleibt dabei,
Weil mich nichts zurücke hält,
Gute Nacht, du falsche Welt! (*Will sich hängen. Die drei Knaben fahren herunter.*)

3 KNABEN
Halt ein, o Papageno! und sei klug,

Man lebt nur einmal, dies sei dir genug!

PAPAGENO
Ihr habt gut reden, habt gut scherzen;
Doch brennt es euch wie mich im Herzen,
Ihr würdet auch nach Mädchen gehn.

3 KNABEN
So lasse deine Glöckchen klingen;
Dies wird dein Weibchen zu dir bringen.

PAPAGENO
Ich Narr vergass der Zauberdinge.
(*Nimmt sein Instrument heraus.*)
Erklinge, Glockenspiel, erklinge!
Ich muss mein liebes Mädchen seh'n!
(*Unter diesem Schlagen laufen die drei Knaben zu ihrem Flugwerk und bringen das Weib heraus.*)
Klinget, Glöckchen, klinget!
Schafft mein Mädchen her!
Klinget, Glöckchen, klinget!
Bringt mein Weibchen her.

3 KNABEN
(*im auffahren*)
Nun, Papageno, sieh dich um.
(*Papageno sieht sich um; beide haben unter dem Ritornell komisches Spiel.*)

PAPAGENO
Pa—pa—pa—pa—pa—pa—Papagena!

PAPAGENA
Pa—pa—pa—pa—pa—pa—Papageno!

PAPAGENO
Bist du mir nun ganz gegeben?

PAPAGENA
Nun, bin ich dir ganz gegeben.

PAPAGENO
Nun, so sei mein liebes Weibchen!

PAPAGENA
Nun, so sei mein Herzenstäubchen!

BEIDE
Welche Freude wird das sein,
Wenn die Götter uns bedenken,
Unsrer Liebe Kinder schenken,
So liebe, kleine Kinderlein!

PAPAGENO
Erst einen kleinen Papageno.

PAPAGENA
Dann eine kleine Papagena.

CHORUS (*offstage*)
Rejoice! The victory is gained!
The journey's end you have attained!
On you the smiles of Isis shine!
Come enter in the temple's shrine!
(*Sarastro leads Tamino and Pamina
into the temple. Change of Scene.
Garden. Enter Papageno, girded with
a rope. He whistles twice.*)

PAPAGENO
Papagena, Papagena, Papagena!
(*whistles*) Dearest! Sweetest! Papagena!
'Tis hopeless! Ah! How she has failed
me!
Since I was born bad luck has trailed
me!
By chattering I lost my maid,
And for this crime I am repaid.
Since I have tasted of that wine,
Since I have seen my lovely bride,
All I can do is fume and fret!
I am upset, I can't forget.
Papagena! Pretty darling!
Papagena, lovely starling!
No more hope, there's no forgiving!
Sick and tired am I of living.
Since my love was all in vain,
I shall die to end my pain. (*takes the
rope in his hands*)
Yonder tree shall be my gallows.
There I'll hang to end my sorrows.
Thus to life I make rebuff.
World, good-night, I have enough!
For I was too harshly treated,
All my hopes have been defeated.
Very soon I'll cease to be.
Lovely maidens, think of me!
Will not someone show compassion
Ere I hang in such a fashion?
Well, this once I let it go.
Just reply: say yes or no. (*looks
around*)
No one answers, all is quiet, here I
stand deserted!
Then my end can't be averted.
Papageno, go ahead,
Tie the noose and you are dead! (*looks
around*)
Well, once more I'll try, let's see,
Till I count from one to three.
(*whistles and speaks*) One, two, two
and a half, two and three quarters,
three.
(*sings:*) No one came, my lot is cast;
So this moment is my last.
Not a hand will mine restrain.
Fare thee well, thou world of pain!
(*starts to hang himself*)

(*The Three Spirits enter switftly.*)

THREE SPIRITS
Hold back!
Papageno, hear our plea:
You live but once, and that enough
should be.

PAPAGENO
My little friends, you are mistaken;
For if like me you were forsaken,
You, too, your luck with girls would
try.

THREE SPIRITS
Then take your magic bells and play
them.
Your little sweetheart will obey them.

PAPAGENO
How very foolishly I acted,
I truly must have been distracted.
Play out, my silver bells, keep ringing,
And bring my maiden to my side.
(*plays the glockenspiel*)
Silver bells, keep ringing, bring my
maiden here,
(*The Three Spirits bring Papagena.*)

THREE SPIRITS
Now, Papageno, turn around.
(*Exeunt.*)

PAPAGENO AND PAPAGENA
Pa-pa-pa-pa-pa-pa-pa-ge-na(o)!

PAPAGENO
Now you will be mine forever.

PAPAGENA
Now I will be thine forever.

PAPAGENO
Come and be my little starling.

PAPAGENA
I will be your heart's own darling!

PAPAGENO AND PAPAGENA
What a joy for us is near
When the gods, their bounty showing,
And their grace on us bestowing,
Will send us tiny children dear.

PAPAGENO
First we will have a Papageno.

PAPAGENA
Then we will have a Papagena.

PAPAGENO

Dann wieder einen Papageno.

PAPAGENA

Dann wieder eine Papagena.

BEIDE

Es ist das höchste der Gefühle,
Wenn viele, viele, viele, viele
Papageno, Papagena
Der Eltern Segen werden sein.
(*beide ab.*)
(*Der Mohr, die Königin mit allen ih-
ren Damen, kommen von beiden
Versenkungen; sie tragen schwarze
Fackeln in der Hand.*)

MONOSTATOS

Nur stille, stille, stille, stille!
Bald dringen wir im Tempel ein.

KÖNIGIN UND DAMEN

Nur stille, stille, stille, stille!
Bald dringen wir im Tempel ein.

MONOSTATOS

Doch, Fürstin, halte Wort! Erfülle—
Dein Kind muss meine Gattin sein.

KÖNIGIN

Ich halte Wort; es ist mein Wille,
Mein Kind soll deine Gattin sein.

3 DAMEN

Ihr Kind soll deine Gattin sein.

MONOSTATOS

Doch still, ich höre schrecklich rauschen
Wie Donnerton und Wasserfall.

KÖNIGIN UND DAMEN

Ja, fürchterlich ist dieses Rauschen,
Wie fernen Donners Widerhall.

MONOSTATOS

Nun sind sie in des Tempels Hallen.

ALLE 5

Dort wollen wir sie überfallen,
Die Frömmler tilgen von der Erd
Mit Feuersglut und mächt'gem
Schwert.

MONOSTATOS UND DAMEN

Dir, grosse Königin der Nacht,
Sei uns'rer Rache Opfer gebracht.
(*Man hört Donner, Blitz, Sturm. Sog-
leich verwandelt sich das ganze
Theater in eine Sonne. Sarastro steht
erhöht; Tamino, Pamina, beide in
priesterlicher Kleidung. Neben ihnen
die ägyptischen Priester auf beiden
Seiten. Die drei Knaben halten
Blumen.*)

**KÖNIGIN DER NACHT, MONOSTATOS
UND 3 DAMEN**

Zerschmettert, zernichtet ist unsere
Macht,
Wir alle gestürzet in ewige Nacht!

SARASTRO

Die Strahlen der Sonne vertreiben die
Nacht,
Vernichten der Heuchler erschlichene
Macht.

CHORUS

Heil sei euch Geweihten! Ihr dranget
durch Nacht.
Dank sei dir, Osiris, dank dir, Isis,
gebracht!
Es siegte die Stärke, und krönet zum
Lohn
Die Schönheit und Weisheit mit ewiger
Kron.

PAPAGENO AND PAPAGENA

Then comes another Papageno(a),
Papageno(a), Papageno(a)!
It is the greatest joy of any
When many, many
Pa-pa-pa-pa-pa-pa-pa-page-no(a)s
    upon their parents blessing bring.
                        (*Exeunt.*)
(*Change of Scene. Rocky landscape.
Night. Enter Monostatos, the Queen,
and the Three Ladies, with burning
torches.*)

MONOSTATOS, QUEEN, AND
THREE LADIES

Now stilly, stilly, stilly, stilly,
As we approach the temple door.

MONOSTATOS

My lady, keep thy word, fulfil it:
Thy child must wed the faithful Moor.

QUEEN

I keep my word, I firmly wish it!
My child shall wed the faithful Moor.

THREE LADIES

Her child shall wed the faithful Moor.
(*Thunder and sound of water.*)

MONOSTATOS

Be still, I hear a fearful roaring,
Like thunder's rage and waterfall.

QUEEN AND THREE LADIES

Yes, dreadfully resounds the roaring,
Like distant thunder's sullen call.

MONOSTATOS

Within these halls they now assemble.
QUEEN, THREE LADIES, AND

MONOSTATOS

We will assail them in their temple.
We shall destroy this canting horde
By savage blow and flaming sword.

THREE LADIES AND MONOSTATOS
                        (*kneeling*)

Thou great and mighty Queen of
    Night,
Their lives are thine by law and right.
(*Thunder, lightning, storm.*)

QUEEN, THREE LADIES, AND
MONOSTATOS

Demolished, extinguished, defeated our
    might,
We plunge to destruction and infinite
    night. (*They sink into the earth.*)
(*Change of Scene without Curtain.
Temple of the Sun. Sarastro stands
on an eminence. Before him stand
Tamino and Pamina.*)

SARASTRO

The sun's radiant glory has vanquished
    the night,
The powers of darkness have yielded to
    light.

CHORUS

Hail to thee, great Isis!
Hail to thee, Osiris!
You guided their ways.
Praise, praise, praise to thee, Osiris!
Thanks, thanks to Isis we raise!
Thus courage has triumphed, and vir-
    tue will rise,
The laurels of wisdom receiving as
    prize.

NORTON PAPERBACKS ON MUSIC